Fodor's '07

W9-CIM-255

WASHINGTON, D.C.

Where to Stay and Eat
for All Budgets

Must-See Sights
and Local Secrets

Ratings You Can Trust

Fodor's Travel Publications   New York, Toronto, London, Sydney, Auckland
www.fodors.com

FODOR'S WASHINGTON, D.C. 2007

Editors: Amy B Wang, Mary Beth Bohman, Denise Leto, Rachel Klein Lisberg

Editorial Production: Bethany Cassin Beckerlegge, Eric B. Wechter

Editorial Contributors: Shane Christensen, Matthew Cordell, Coral Davenport, Cynthia Hacinli, John A. Kelly, Erin Renner, Sylvia Renner, Mitchell Tropin, CiCi Williamson

Maps: David Lindroth, *cartographer;* Robert Blake and Rebecca Baer, *map editors;* Additional cartography provided by Henry Colomb, Mark Stroud, and Ali Baird, Moon Street Cartography

Design: Fabrizio La Rocca, *creative director;* Moon Sun Kim, *cover design;* Guido Caroti, *art director;* Melanie Marin, *senior picture editor*

Cover Photo (Lincoln Memorial): John Hicks/eStock Photo

Production/Manufacturing: Angela L. McLean

COPYRIGHT

ISBN-10: 1–4000–1719–X

ISBN-13: 978–1–4000–1719–5

ISSN: 0743–9741

SPECIAL SALES

This book is available for special discounts for bulk purchases for sales promotions or premiums. Special editions, including personalized covers, excerpts of existing books, and corporate imprints, can be created in large quantities for special needs. For more information, write to Special Markets/Premium Sales, 1745 Broadway, MD 6-2, New York, New York 10019, or e-mail specialmarkets@randomhouse.com.

AN IMPORTANT TIP & AN INVITATION

Although all prices, opening times, and other details in this book are based on information supplied to us at press time, changes occur all the time in the travel world, and Fodor's cannot accept responsibility for facts that become outdated or for inadvertent errors or omissions. So **always confirm information when it matters,** especially if you're making a detour to visit a specific place. Your experiences—positive and negative—matter to us. If we have missed or misstated something, **please write to us.** We follow up on all suggestions. Contact the Washington, D.C., editors at editors@fodors.com or c/o Fodor's at 1745 Broadway, New York, New York 10019.

PRINTED IN THE UNITED STATES OF AMERICA

10 9 8 7 6 5 4 3 2 1

Be a Fodor's Correspondent

Your opinion matters. It matters to us. It matters to your fellow Fodor's travelers, too. And we'd like to hear it. In fact, we *need* to hear it.

When you share your experiences and opinions, you become an active member of the Fodor's community. That means we'll not only use your feedback to make our books better, but we'll publish your names and comments whenever possible. Throughout our guides, look for "Word of Mouth," excerpts of your unvarnished feedback.

Here's how you can help improve Fodor's for all of us.

Tell us when we're right. We rely on local writers to give you an insider's perspective. But our writers and staff editors—who are the best in the business—depend on you. Your positive feedback is a vote to renew our recommendations for the next edition.

Tell us when we're wrong. We're proud that we update most of our guides every year. But we're not perfect. Things change. Hotels cut services. Museums change hours. Charming cafés lose charm. If our writer didn't quite capture the essence of a place, tell us how you'd do it differently. If any of our descriptions are inaccurate or inadequate, we'll incorporate your changes in the next edition and will correct factual errors at fodors.com *immediately.*

Tell us what to include. You probably have had fantastic travel experiences that aren't yet in Fodor's. Why not share them with a community of like-minded travelers? Maybe you chanced upon a beach or bistro or B&B that you don't want to keep to yourself. Tell us why we should include it. And share your discoveries and experiences with everyone directly at fodors.com. Your input may lead us to add a new listing or highlight a place we cover with a "Highly Recommended" star or with our highest rating, "Fodor's Choice."

Give us your opinion instantly at our feedback center at www.fodors.com/feedback. You may also e-mail editors@fodors.com with the subject line "Washington D.C. Editors." Or send your nominations, comments, and complaints by mail to Washington D.C. Editors, Fodor's, 1745 Broadway, New York, NY 10019.

You and travelers like you are the heart of the Fodor's community. Make our community richer by sharing your experiences. Be a Fodor's correspondent.

Happy traveling!

Tim Jarrell, Publisher

CONTENTS

Be a Fodor's Correspondent 3
About This Book 6
When to Go 7
What's Where 10
If You Like 16
Great Itineraries 18
On the Calendar 20
Fodor's Choice 26

1 EXPLORING WASHINGTON 29
The Mall 31
The Monuments 46
The White House Area 56
Capitol Hill 68
East End 83
Georgetown .99
Dupont Circle 108
Adams-Morgan 118
Foggy Bottom 123
Cleveland Park 130
Upper Northwest 134
Arlington 137
Alexandria 145
Around Washington 150

2 WHERE TO EAT 155

3 WHERE TO STAY 192

4 NIGHTLIFE & THE ARTS 221
The Arts 222
Nightlife 232

5 SPORTS & THE OUTDOORS 244

6 SHOPPING 254

7 SIDE TRIPS 276
C&O Canal & Great Falls Parks 278
Annapolis, Maryland 284
Frederick, Maryland 298

Mount Vernon, Woodlawn &
    Gunston Hall 301
Fredericksburg, Virginia 306
SMART TRAVEL TIPS 317
INDEX 339
ABOUT OUR WRITERS 352

MAPS

Washington, D.C., Area 8–9
Washington, D.C. 12–13
Exploring Washington 32–33
The Mall 36
The Monuments 48
The White House Area 59
The White House Floor Plan:
    Ground & First Floors 66
Capitol Hill 70
U.S. Capitol: Second-Floor Plan 72
East End 87
Georgetown 101
Dupont Circle 110
Adams-Morgan 120
Foggy Bottom 127
Cleveland Park 131
Upper Northwest 135
Arlington, Virginia 140
Old Town Alexandria, Virginia 148
Where to Eat in Adams-Morgan &
    Woodley Park 160
Where to Eat in Washington 164–165
Where to Eat in Georgetown &
    Glover Park 181
Where to Stay in Washington . .196–197
C&O Canal & Great Falls Parks 282
Annapolis, Maryland 286

Frederick, Maryland 298
Mount Vernon, Woodlawn &
   Gunston Hall 302
Fredericksburg, Virginia 307

CLOSEUPS

Recent Changes in
   Washington, D.C. 34
A City of Statues 51

L'Enfant, the City's Architect 77
U Street on the Rise 123
Lee, the Rebel General 141
Good Brews 176
Traveling with Children? 198
Lodging Alternatives 200
After-Hours Restaurants 235
Tickets & Venues 252
D.C.'s Museum Shops 262

ABOUT THIS BOOK

Our Ratings

Sometimes you find terrific travel experiences and sometimes they just find you. But usually the burden is on you to select the right combination of experiences. That's where our ratings come in.

As travelers we've all discovered a place so wonderful that its worthiness is obvious. And sometimes that place is so experiential that superlatives don't do it justice: you just have to be there to know. These sights, properties, and experiences get our highest rating, **Fodor's Choice**, indicated by orange stars throughout this book.

Black stars highlight sights and properties we deem **Highly Recommended**, places that our writers, editors, and readers praise again and again for consistency and excellence.

By default, there's another category: any place we include in this book is by definition worth your time, unless we say otherwise. And we will.

Disagree with any of our choices? Care to nominate a place or suggest that we rate one more highly? Visit our feedback center at www.fodors.com/feedback.

Budget Well

Hotel and restaurant price categories from ¢ to $$$$ are defined in the opening pages of the relevant chapters. For attractions, we always give standard adult admission fees; reductions are usually available for children, students, and senior citizens. Want to pay with plastic? **AE, D, DC, MC, V** following restaurant and hotel listings indicate if American Express, Discover, Diner's Club, MasterCard, and Visa are accepted.

Restaurants

Unless we state otherwise, restaurants are open for lunch and dinner daily. We mention dress only when there's a specific requirement and reservations only when they're essential or not accepted—it's always best to book ahead.

Hotels

Hotels have private bath, phone, TV, and air-conditioning and operate on the European Plan (aka EP, meaning without meals), unless we specify that they use the Continental Plan (CP, with a continental breakfast), Breakfast Plan (BP, with a full breakfast), or Modified American Plan (MAP, with breakfast and dinner), or are all-inclusive (AI, including all meals and most activities). We always

list facilities but not whether you'll be charged an extra fee to use them, so when pricing accommodations, find out what's included.

Many Listings

★	Fodor's Choice
★	Highly recommended
⊠	Physical address
⊹	Directions
⌂	Mailing address
☎	Telephone
📠	Fax
⊕	On the Web
✉	E-mail
🎫	Admission fee
◷	Open/closed times
☞	Start of walk/itinerary
Ⓜ	Metro stations
▭	Credit cards

Hotels & Restaurants

☷	Hotel
⇥	Number of rooms
◇	Facilities
†○†	Meal plans
✕	Restaurant
⌂	Reservations
🜹	Dress code
✎	Smoking
⬚▯	BYOB
✕☷	Hotel with restaurant that warrants a visit

Other

⚘	Family-friendly
🏛	Contact information
⇨	See also
⊠	Branch address
☞	Take note

WHEN TO GO

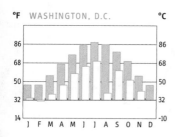

°F WASHINGTON, D.C. °C

Climate

Washington has two delightful seasons: spring and autumn. In spring, the city's ornamental fruit trees are budding, and its many gardens are in bloom. By autumn, most of the summer crowds have left and you can enjoy the sights in peace. Summers can be uncomfortably hot and humid. Winter weather is often bitter, with a handful of modest snowstorms that bring this southern city to a standstill. When lawmakers break for recess (at Thanksgiving, Christmas, Easter, July 4, the entire month of August, and other holiday periods), the city slows down a bit.

🗂 Forecasts **Weather Channel Connection** ☎ 900/932–8437 95¢ per minute from a Touch-Tone phone ⊕ www.weather.com.

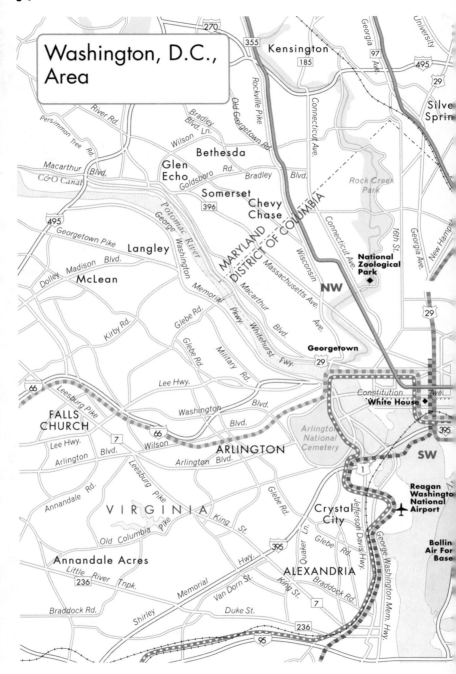

Washington, D.C., Area

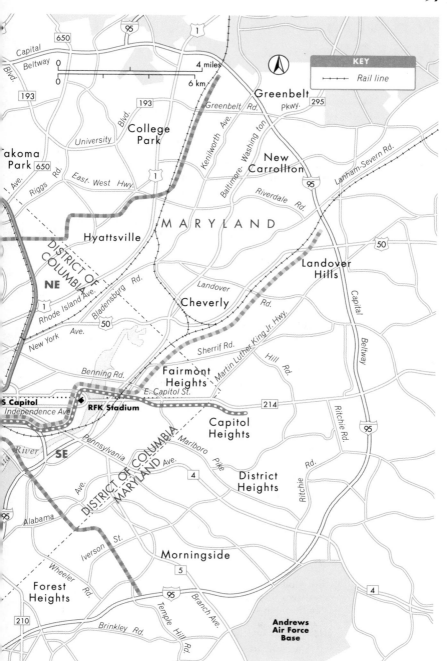

WHAT'S WHERE

It's often said that Washington doesn't have any old-fashioned neighborhoods the way, for example, nearby Baltimore does. Although it's true that Washingtonians are not given to huddling together on their front stoops, each area of the city does have a clearly defined personality, and some, such as Capitol Hill, can even feel like a small town.

THE MALL

This expanse of green, which stretches due west from the Capitol to the Washington Monument, is lined on the north and south by some of America's finest museums, almost all of which are free. Lindbergh's *Spirit of St. Louis,* some of Andy Warhol's soup cans, the Hope Diamond, Julia Child's kitchen, a tyrannosaurus rex, and myriad other modern and classical artifacts await you. Of course, the 300-foot-wide Mall is more than just a front yard for museums: it's a picnicking park and a running path, an outdoor stage for festivals and fireworks, and America's town green. During your visit here, you're equally likely to see residents playing soccer or softball, protestors wielding signs and banners, or children cavorting on the restored 1947 carousel. First one on gets to ride the dragon.

THE MONUMENTS

The Washington Monument punctuates the Mall halfway between the Capitol and the Lincoln Memorial, which features a somber statue of the seated president gazing out over the reflecting pool. Lincoln also sees the Mall's most recently added monument, the World War II Memorial, and is flanked by both the Vietnam Veterans Memorial and the Korean War Veterans Memorial. The rotunda of the Jefferson Memorial rises to the southeast beside the Tidal Basin, where you can rent paddleboats and admire more than 200 cherry trees, gifts from Japan and the focus of a festival each spring. The popular Franklin Delano Roosevelt Memorial, which covers 7 meandering acres along the Tidal Basin, provides one of the best views of the Washington skyline.

THE WHITE HOUSE AREA

In a city full of immediately recognizable images, perhaps none is more familiar than the White House. But, no matter how magnificent, it doesn't completely overshadow the neighborhood's other wonders, some of the city's oldest houses and two important art galleries: the Renwick Gallery—the Smithsonian's museum of American decorative arts—and the Corcoran Gallery of Art, known for its collections of photography, European impressionist paintings, and post–World War II American art.

CAPITOL HILL	The Capitol, where the Senate and the House have met since 1800, along with the Supreme Court and the Library of Congress, dominate this neighborhood. But the Hill is more than just the center of government. There are charming residential blocks of Victorian row houses here filled with young hill staffers, who have attracted a fine assortment of restaurants, bars, and shops. Union Station, Washington's train depot, has vaulted and gilded ceilings, arched colonnades, statues of Roman legionnaires, a shopping mall, and a movie theater multiplex. While you're in town, you may want to drop in on your state's congressional representatives.
EAST END	In what was once Downtown—the area within the diamond formed by Massachusetts, Louisiana, Pennsylvania, and New York avenues—are Chinatown, Ford's Theatre, and several important museums. Thanks to an ongoing revival, the Penn Quarter section—now somewhat vaguely called the East End—has become arguably the most interesting part of town. Galleries and restaurants are sprouting up behind the refurbished cast-iron facades that give the neighborhood its unique look.
	Within Federal Triangle, a few blocks away and bordered by Pennsylvania and Constitution avenues and 15th Street NW, you can find the National Archives, which houses the original Declaration of Independence, the Constitution, and the Bill of Rights. The National Building Museum has the largest columns in the world as well as displays devoted to architecture. Other nearby museums include the National Museum of Women in the Arts, the National Portrait Gallery, and the Smithsonian American Art Museum. The Old Post Office Pavilion is also here, as is the International Spy Museum.
GEORGETOWN	The capital's wealthiest neighborhood (and one that's attractive to architecture buffs) is always hopping, even if most of its once unique merchants have given way to stores and eateries found at malls around the country. Restaurants, bars, nightclubs, and boutiques cluster along Wisconsin and M streets. Originally used for shipping, the C&O Canal today is a part of the National Park system: walkers follow the towpath and canoeists paddle the calm waters; you can also go on a leisurely trip aboard a mule-drawn canal barge. Washington Harbour is a riverfront development of restaurants, offices, apartments, and upscale shops; Georgetown Park is a multilevel shopping extravaganza; and Georgetown University is the oldest Jesuit

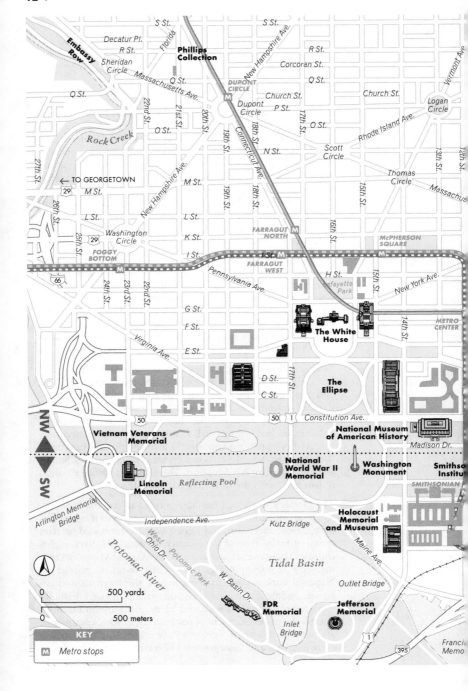

S St.

Decatur Pl.

R St.

Sheridan Circle

Embassy Row

Phillips Collection

Massachusetts Ave.

Q St.

Florida

S St.

New Hampshire Ave.

R St.

Corcoran St.

DUPONT CIRCLE

Q St.

Church St.

Dupont Circle

P St.

Church St.

Logan Circle

Vermont Ave.

Q St.

21st St.

20th St.

19th St.

18th St.

17th St.

O St.

O St.

N St.

Scott Circle

Rhode Island Ave.

13th St.

12th St.

22nd St.

Connecticut Ave.

Rock Creek

27th St.

← TO GEORGETOWN
29

M St.

New Hampshire Ave.

M St.

19th St.

18th St.

Thomas Circle

Massachus

16th St.

26th St.

L St.

29

Washington Circle

K St.

FARRAGUT NORTH M

McPHERSON SQUARE

25th St.

FOGGY BOTTOM

I St.

M

I St. M

FARRAGUT WEST

15th St.

H St.

New York Ave.

66

24th St.

23rd St.

22nd St.

Pennsylvania Ave.

Lafayette Park

14th St.

METRO CENTER

G St.

Virginia Ave.

F St.

The White House

E St.

D St.

17th St.

The Ellipse

C St.

Vietnam Veterans Memorial

50

50 1 Constitution Ave.

National Museum of American History

Madison Dr.

National World War II Memorial

Washington Monument

Smithso Institu

Lincoln Memorial

Reflecting Pool

SMITHSONIAN

Arlington Memorial Bridge

Independence Ave.

Kutz Bridge

Holocaust Memorial and Museum

Maine Ave.

Potomac River

West Potomac Park

Ohio Dr.

W. Basin Dr.

Tidal Basin

Outlet Bridge

0   500 yards

0   500 meters

FDR Memorial

Jefferson Memorial

Inlet Bridge

1

395

Franci Memo

KEY
M *Metro stops*

NW

SW

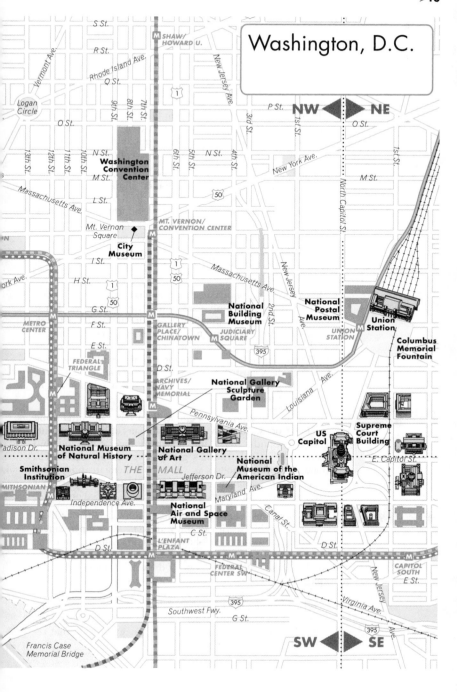

Washington, D.C.

WHAT'S WHERE

school in the country. Dumbarton Oaks's 10 acres of formal gardens provide one of the loveliest spots in Washington. With its cobblestone side streets and many nooks and crannies, this is one of D.C.'s best neighborhoods for a good stroll.

DUPONT CIRCLE

Fashionable, vibrant Dupont Circle has a cosmopolitan air owing partly to its many restaurants, shops, and specialty bookstores. It's also home to the most visible segment of Washington's gay community. This neighborhood is especially popular in the warmer months, when 17th Street becomes a scene—witnessed by drinkers and diners enjoying the strip's countless outdoor eating and drinking establishments—and the round green in the middle of Dupont teems with sunbathers, chessmasters, and musicians.

The exclusive Kalorama neighborhood is a peaceful, tree-lined enclave filled with embassies and luxurious homes. For a glimpse of that "beautiful view," look down over Rock Creek Park's 1,800 acres of green, where there's a planetarium, an 18-hole golf course, and equestrian and bicycle trails. The Phillips Collection is also in Kalorama; its best-known paintings include Auguste Renoir's *Luncheon of the Boating Party,* Edgar Degas's *Dancers at the Barre,* and a self-portrait of Paul Cézanne.

ADAMS-MORGAN

One of Washington's most ethnically diverse and interesting neighborhoods, Adams-Morgan holds many offbeat restaurants and shops, and a brash and amazingly diverse bar-and-club scene. The neighborhood's grand 19th-century apartment buildings and row houses as well as its bohemian atmosphere have attracted young urban professionals, the businesses that cater to them, and the attendant parking and crowd problems.

FOGGY BOTTOM

Foggy Bottom—a name earned years ago when smoke from factories combined with swampy air to produce a permanent fog along the waterfront—has three main claims to fame: the State Department, the Kennedy Center, and George Washington University. Watergate, one of the world's most legendary apartment-office complexes, is notorious for the events that took place here on June 17, 1972. Although the street life tapers off once you leave Pennsylvania Avenue, and many of the 19th-century architectural gems have been replaced by generic office buildings, there are pockets of Foggy Bottom that remain exquisitely charming.

CLEVELAND PARK	Tree-shaded Cleveland Park, in northwest Washington, has attractive houses and a suburban character. Arts and Crafts bungalows abound, as do Victorian mansions and large green spaces. Connecticut Avenue, the neighborhood's main artery, holds a more satisfying selection of restaurants and boutiques than some more famous areas of town.
	One neighborhood treasure is the Loews Cineplex Uptown, a marvelous 1930s art deco movie house that still has its gigantic screen and balcony seating. The National Zoological Park, one of the foremost zoos in the world, is nearby. Star denizens include Komodo dragons and two giant pandas.
UPPER NORTHWEST	This area, to the north of Georgetown and stretching up to the Maryland border, is best known for Washington National Cathedral, an eye-catching Gothic-style building completed in 1990 after more than 80 years of construction. About a mile north, just past the Tenleytown/American University Metro stop and at the highest point in the city, is Fort Reno, the site of the only Civil War battle within Washington proper.
ARLINGTON, VIRGINIA	Although separated from the District by the Potomac River, Arlington plays an important role in Washington life, not just as a commuter suburb but as the final resting place and memorial for many important Americans. In addition to the U.S. Marine Corps War Memorial, which captures in bronze the famous World War II flag raising at Iwo Jima, Arlington contains one of the most-visited spots in the world. Arlington National Cemetery is home to the graves of more than 250,000 veterans, as well as the final resting place of John Kennedy, his brother Robert, and his widow, Jacqueline Kennedy Onassis, who originally suggested the Eternal Flame as a memorial to her husband. Also poignant is the vigil soldiers keep at the Tomb of the Unknowns.
ALEXANDRIA, VIRGINIA	Alexandria's history is linked to the most significant events and people of the colonial, Revolutionary, and Civil War periods. This colorful past is still alive on the cobbled streets; on the revitalized waterfront, where clipper ships dock and craftspeople display their goods; and in restored 18th- and 19th-century homes, churches, and taverns.

IF YOU LIKE

Awe-inspiring Architecture

The mix of stately Federal buildings, outstanding museums, countless monuments, and early and influential urban planning have made Washington a wonderland for architecture buffs. The massive redbrick National Building Museum, devoted to architecture and the building arts, is a good place to start your exploration. Its exhibits outline the capital's architectural history, from its monuments to its residential neighborhoods. The museum is an architectural study in itself. The open interior, one of the city's great spaces, has been the site of inaugural balls for more than 100 years. And its eight central Corinthian columns, rising to a height of 75 feet, are the largest in the world.

After the building museum, the Mall is the easiest place to get your architecture fix. Notable works by famous architects—including Robert Mills's Washington Monument, James Renwick's French-inspired Smithsonian Castle and Renwick Gallery, and I. M. Pei's East Building of the National Gallery of Art—dot this expanse of green. No architectural tour would be complete without a visit to the Washington National Cathedral, the sixth-largest cathedral in the world. Its Gothic arches, flying buttresses, and imaginative stonework, including gargoyles that draw on pop culture as well as tradition, will impress even the most hardened cathedral viewer. (Look for the gargoyle resembling *Star Wars'* Darth Vader.) Inside, its many chapels and vaults contain stained-glass depictions of life, one commemorating the moon landing.

The soul of the nation takes tangible form in stone as you walk the streets south, east, and west of Union Station, the grand beaux arts rail terminal that even today welcomes thousands to Washington. The city's power grid is focused on the White House. The vice president's office in the Old Executive Office Building, which resembles a giant wedding cake, is across the street. A close look at the glorious Capitol, which has a grand and inspiring rotunda, is almost mandatory.

The Great Outdoors

Rock Creek Park, twice the size of New York's Central Park, meanders through Northwest D.C. from Foggy Bottom past the National Zoo into Montgomery County, Maryland. Teddy Roosevelt often spent his afternoons trekking across untamed sections of the park with diplomats and dignitaries; he made sure to return after dark so that their appearance "would scandalize no one." Today this gorgeous expanse of forest is enjoyed for its trails, playing fields, golf course, and arts venues.

C&O Canal National Historic Park roughly parallels the Potomac River from Georgetown to Cumberland, Maryland. From 1828 to 1924, mules, using the 12-foot-wide towpath that runs alongside the canal, pulled coal-bearing barges; today, canoeists paddle on the slow-moving water, while hikers and bikers use the towpath. In warmer months you can hop a mule-drawn boat for an hour-long trip.

The waters of the Potomac cascade dramatically over a steep, jagged gorge, creating the spectacle that gives the 800-acre Great Falls Park its name. You can also walk over a series of bridges to Olmsted Island in the middle of the Potomac River for a spectacular view of the falls. Hikers follow trails, climbers scale the rock faces leading down to the water, and experienced kayakers shoot the rapids.

Great Gardens

The paths of the **Constitution Gardens** wind through groves of trees, around a lake— a memorial to signers of the Declaration of Independence—and past the sobering Vietnam Veterans Memorial. The 10 acres of formal gardens on **Dumbarton Oaks,** landscaped in a variety of styles, are some of the loveliest in the city, attracting gorgeous butterflies when flowers are in bloom. Exotic water lilies, lotuses, hyacinths, and other water-loving plants thrive at the **Kenilworth Aquatic Gardens,** a sanctuary of quiet pools and marshy flats. The gardens are home to a variety of wetland animals, including turtles, frogs, muskrats, and some 40 species of birds.

Military Memorials

Washington is the final resting place of many who served and fell in defense of our country. More than 250,000 veterans are buried in **Arlington National Cemetery,** where you can trace America's history through the aftermath of its battles. The guard at the Tomb of the Unknowns is changed at least each hour with a precise ceremony. The **U.S. Marine Corps War Memorial,** built in honor of the World War II battle at Iwo Jima, is near the cemetery. The **Naval Heritage Center,** where you can look up the service records of navy veterans is next to the statue that serves as the Navy Memorial.

Other major war memorials cluster around the Lincoln Memorial, including the **National World War II Memorial** and the **Korean War Veterans Memorial.** The **Vietnam Veterans Memorial,** a shining black granite wall, half sunk into the lawn, is inscribed with more than 58,000 names of men and women who died in that conflict.

World-Class Museums

Even if D.C. were not the seat of the U.S. government, the city would remain a top tourist destination, based on the strength of its museums alone. Their names often include the word *national,* implying that the very best of America is inside. Many are part of the Smithsonian Institution. In its **National Air and Space Museum** you can touch a moon rock and see numerous spiky spacecraft. The Smithsonian's **National Museum of Natural History** houses more than 120 million specimens, plus an insect zoo. The **National Museum of American History** has George Washington's false teeth and the original Star-Spangled Banner. Elsewhere, the city's art makes the senses reel. Among the masterworks in the **National Gallery of Art** is Leonardo da Vinci's pensive *Ginevra de'Benci.* The cozier **Phillips Collection** houses Pierre Bonnard's *Open Window* and other treasures. Close by but a world away in mood is the **U.S. Holocaust Memorial Museum,** a shattering testament to man's inhumanity to man.

GREAT ITINERARIES

WASHINGTON IN 3 TO 5 DAYS

You could easily spend several weeks exploring Washington, D.C., but if you're here for just a short period, make sure to plan your time carefully. The following suggested itineraries (one set is geared specifically for those traveling with children) can help you structure your visit efficiently.

Days 1 & 2

Spend both days on the Mall checking out the museums and monuments. The National Museum of Natural History, the National Air and Space Museum (also the most crowded), the National Gallery of Art, and the U.S. Holocaust Memorial Museum are the most popular. Take time out for a walk from the Washington Monument to the Lincoln Memorial and around the Tidal Basin, where you can see the Jefferson Memorial and the FDR Memorial, and take a leisurely paddleboat ride around the cherry trees.

Day 3

Explore Capitol Hill, where you'll have the option of visiting the Capitol, the U.S. Botanic Gardens, the Library of Congress, the Supreme Court, and the Folger Shakespeare Library. Call your senators or congressional representatives in advance for tickets to see Congress in session. It's an unforgettable experience. Likewise, check the Supreme Court's Web site for weekday dates of oral arguments. Show up at 9:30 in the morning for admission either to a short (three-minute) or all-morning visit.

Day 4

Head to the National Zoo for the morning. Say hi to the pandas, then, if it's nice out, hop on the Metro to Dupont Circle for lunch. Walk west on P Street NW to Georgetown, where the options for lattes, shopping, and leisurely strolling (for architecture buffs) abound. In inclement weather take a cab from the zoo straight to Georgetown's Washington Harbour, where you can dine until the sun comes out, then explore the neighborhood.

Day 5

Split your last day between Adams-Morgan and Dupont Circle. These two neighborhoods have unusual shops, restaurants, and clubs, although each area has its own personality. Ethiopian, El Salvadoran, and Mexican cuisines abound in Adams-Morgan. Dupont Circle is a destination favored by art lovers, thanks to an assortment of art galleries as well as the Phillips Collection. It's also where you'll find the renowned bookstore Kramerbooks & Afterwords.

Washington in 1 Day

Head for the Mall. Start at either end—the Capitol or the Lincoln Memorial—and walk leisurely to the opposite end. You won't have time to see everything along the way, but you'll walk past or have in sight most of the attractions Washington is famous for: the Lincoln Memorial, the Korean War Veterans Memorial, the Vietnam Veterans Memorial, the Tidal Basin and Jefferson Memorial, the Washington Monument (and, to the north, the White House), most of the Smithsonian museums, the National Gallery of Art, and the Capitol.

WASHINGTON IN 3 TO 5 DAYS—WITH CHILDREN

Days 1 & 2

Spend both days on the Mall, checking out the museums and monuments. Even children who can't read the Gettysburg Address etched on the walls of the Lincoln Memorial can recognize the building from its picture on the back of a penny. At the Vietnam Veterans Memorial, children old enough to hold a pencil can make rubbings of the names (paper and pencils are available at the site from a Park Service ranger or a volunteer on duty). Both the National Museum of the American Indian and the National Air and Space Museum can keep kids occupied for hours. Consider investing in Tourmobile tickets for a respite from walking, particularly in hot weather. For breaks, ride the carousel on the Mall or sit by the fountain in the National Gallery of Art Sculpture Garden.

Day 3

Older children may enjoy morning tours of the Bureau of Engraving and Printing or the Capitol before heading off to the National Zoo. If you have younger children, start and end the day at the zoo. On cold or hot days, take advantage of the numerous indoor animal houses. If little ones wear out, you can rent strollers.

Days 4 & 5

Plan on a visit to either the National Museum of American History or the National Museum of Natural History, both of which have interactive children's exhibits that are open most afternoons. If you and your children still have stamina, grab a bite to eat on your way to the National Postal Museum or the U.S. Botanic Gardens. On your final day, take older children to the International Spy Museum, followed by a trip to the Washington Navy Yard or Old Town Alexandria. With younger children, see creatures of the deep at the National Aquarium, followed by a visit to the Smithsonian's National Museum of Natural History or the Hirshhorn Museum and Sculpture Garden.

Washington in 1 Day

Head right to the Washington Monument, where you have, in both directions, a breathtaking view of the Mall. From here head to the National Air and Space Museum; on the way, you can stop to ride a painted pony at the carousel near the Smithsonian castle or perhaps take a few minutes to wander through the Hirshhorn Museum and Sculpture Garden. If you still have time, visit either the National Museum of American History or the National Museum of Natural History.

ON THE
CALENDAR

	The following festivals and other events, sponsored by various organizations throughout D.C., go some way toward representing the city's local, regional, and national pride. Check out ⊕ www.washington.org, the Web site of the Washington D.C. Convention and Tourism Corporation, for more information about these and other events throughout the year.
WINTER Early December	National Cathedral Christmas Celebration and Services (☎ 202/537–6200 ⊕ www.cathedral.org/cathedral.) Seasonal carols, pageants, and choral performances take place as the days shorten. Campagna Center's Annual Scottish Christmas Walk (☎ 703/549–0111 ⊕ www.campagnacenter.org.) This popular Alexandria event salutes Scottish heritage with a parade, bagpipers, house tours, and crafts.
December	People's Christmas Tree Lighting. Military bands perform to mark the lighting of this gigantic evergreen on the west side of the Capitol in early December. The Speaker of the House presides.
	National Christmas Tree Lighting/Pageant of Peace (☎ 202/208–1631 ⊕ www.pageantofpeace.org.) Each year in early December, accompanied by music and caroling, the president lights the tree at dusk on the Ellipse, followed by more music and caroling. For the following few weeks the Ellipse grounds host choral performances, a Nativity scene, a Yule log, and a display of lighted Christmas trees representing each U.S. state and territory.
Mid-December	Historic Alexandria Candlelight Tours (☎ 703/838–4242 ⊕ oha.ci.alexandria.va.us.) Seasonal tours, featuring music and refreshments, take place at sites including Alexandria's Gadsby's Tavern Museum, Lee-Fendall House, and Carlyle House.
Mid-January	Martin Luther King Jr.'s birthday. This Monday holiday celebrates the civil rights hero who staged one of Washington's most powerful protests, culminating with his 1963 speech at the Lincoln Memorial. Local festivities include speeches, church services, and dance and choral performances.
Mid-January	Restaurant Week (☎ No phone ⊕ www.washington.org/restaurantwk.) Each year, during this promotion, more than 100 restaurants throughout D.C., including some of the city's best, offer three-course *prix-fixe* lunch and dinner menus for around $20 and $30 respectively—often a steal. Make your reservations early for the top spots, as gourmands come out of the woodwork for this week.
Late January–early February	Chinese Lunar New Year Festival. This late-winter holiday explodes on Chinatown's streets with firecrackers and a dragon-led parade.

February	Black History Month. Washington, D.C., has what may be the nation's richest range of activities celebrating African-American history. The events are often held in locations important in the lives of prominent black citizens such as Benjamin Banneker, Mary McCloud Bethune, Frederick Douglass, Thurgood Marshall, Duke Ellington, and Marvin Gaye. Exhibits, special events, and cultural programming take place all month at multiple locations, including the Smithsonian, the Martin Luther King Jr. Memorial Library, and the African-American Civil War Memorial.
Mid-February	Lincoln's birthday. Celebrate the birth of the 16th president with a wreath-laying ceremony and reading of the Gettysburg Address at the Lincoln Memorial on February 12. Frederick Douglass's birthday (☎ 202/426–5961.) The former slave who became a hero of the Abolitionist movement lived in Washington after the Civil War. His birthday, actually unknown, is marked with a wreath-laying ceremony at the Frederick Douglass National Historic Site in Anacostia each February 14. George Washington's birthday. Fans of the first president have many activities to choose from during President's Day weekend, including a parade and a reenactment of his farewell address in Old Town Alexandria, a Birthnight Banquet and Ball at Gadsby's Tavern Museum, a birthday celebration and wreath-laying ceremony at Mount Vernon, and Revolutionary War reenactments at Fort Ward Park.
Early March	Spring Antiques Show (☎ 301/933–9433, 202/547–9215 during the show ⊕ www.pappabello.com.) As many as 200 dealers convene for this event at the D.C. Armory the first weekend in March.
Mid-March	Alexandria's St. Patrick's Day parade (☎ 703/237–2199 ⊕ www.ballyshaners.com.) This Virginia celebration usually takes place the weekend before the parade in Washington. St. Patrick's Day (☎ 703/751–4956 ⊕ www.dcstpatsparade.com.) Celebrate the wearin' o' the green with a parade down Constitution Avenue at noon. The days that follow feature theater, folk music, and dance concerts, and the bars are particularly welcoming all over town. Bach Marathon (☎ 202/363–2202 ⊕ www.chevychasepc.org.) Washington honors Johann Sebastian's birthday. Ten local organists play the 2,500-pipe Rieger tracker pipe organ at Chevy Chase Presbyterian Church from 2 PM to 7 PM. A catered German dinner follows the marathon.
SPRING March or April	White House Easter Egg Roll (☎ 202/456–2200 or 202/208–1631 ⊕ www.whitehouse.gov/easter.) This unique Washington event, which some say was started by Dolley Madison, brings children ages three to six to the White House lawn on Easter Monday.

ON THE CALENDAR

Late March–early April	**Smithsonian Kite Festival** (☎ 202/357–3030 ⊕ www.kitefestival.org.) Thanks to a bizarre law still on the D.C. books, kite-flying is forbidden in Washington except on one day in the spring. Kite makers and fliers of all ages are welcome to this event on the Washington Monument grounds. **National Cherry Blossom Festival** (☎ 202/661–7584 ⊕ www.nationalcherryblossomfestival.org.) Washington's most eye-catching annual festival opens with a Japanese lantern-lighting ceremony at the Tidal Basin. Some years, the cherry trees actually cooperate with the festival's planners and bloom on schedule.
Mid-April	**Thomas Jefferson's birthday** (☎ 202/426–6841.) This architect of American democracy is commemorated on April 13 by military drills and a wreath-laying service at his memorial. **White House Spring Garden & Grounds Tour** (☎ 202/456–2200 ⊕ www.whitehouse.gov.)Visitors can take in the Jacqueline Kennedy Rose Garden and the South Lawn, while military bands perform.
Mid–late April	**Georgetown House Tour** (☎ 202/338–2287 ⊕ www.georgetownhousetour.com.) This event gives you the rare opportunity to view private homes in this exclusive neighborhood. Admission includes high tea at historic St. John's Georgetown Parish Church. **Alexandria Garden Tour** (☎ 800/644–7776 ⊕ www.vagardenweek.org.) Six private gardens and another half-dozen historical sights are open to the public, with afternoon tea at the Athenaeum.
Late April	**Smithsonian Craft Show** (☎ 888/832–9554 ⊕ www.smithsoniancraftshow.org.) This show, held at the National Building Museum, exhibits one-of-a-kind objects by 120 top U.S. artisans.
Late April–early May	**Filmfest DC** (☎ 202/628–3456 ⊕ www.filmfestdc.org.) Screenings take place at several venues around town. Each year a different region of the world is highlighted. Buy tickets ahead of time.
Early May	**National Cathedral Flower Mart** (☎ 202/537–3185 ⊕ www.cathedral.org/ahg.) Sponsored by the All Hallows Guild, which is dedicated to the care of the cathedral grounds, this colorful flower show salutes a different country each year.
	Georgetown Garden Tour (☎ 202/965–1950 ⊕ www.georgetowngardentour.com.) Visitors can take a peek inside private gardens in one of the city's lushest neighborhoods.
Mid-May	**Joint Service Open House** (☎ 301/981–4600 ⊕ www.dcmilitary.) com. Andrews Air Force Base in Maryland is the host of two days of aircraft and weapons displays, parachute jumps, and either the Navy's Blue Angels or the Army's Golden Knights taking to the skies.

SUMMER Late May	Memorial Day Concert (☎ 202/972–9556.) This annual music event, featuring the National Symphony Orchestra at 8 PM on the Capitol's West Lawn, officially welcomes summer to D.C. Memorial Day at Arlington National Cemetery (☎ 703/607–8000.) The president takes part in a wreath-laying ceremony at the Tomb of the Unknowns. The accompanying services at the Memorial Amphitheatre feature military bands. Memorial Day at the U.S. Navy Memorial (☎ 202/737–2300 Ext. 768.) The Navy Band presents an outdoor evening concert capping the wreath-laying ceremonies during the day. Memorial Day at the Vietnam Veterans Memorial (☎ 202/393–0090.) The National Symphony gives a concert after a wreath-laying ceremony at the wall. Memorial Day Jazz Festival (☎ 703/883–4686.) Lighter-hearted big-band music and hot jazz, performed by local musicians and touring names, can be found across the Potomac in Alexandria. D.C. Black Pride Festival (☎ 202/737–5767 ⊕ www.dcblackpride.org.) This four-day festival, with workshops, cultural activities, and special events, celebrates the achievements of black gay, lesbian, bisexual, and transgendered people.
Early June	Capital Pride Festival (☎ 202/797–3510 ⊕ www.capitalpride.org.) This weeklong festival, the nation's fourth-largest celebrating gay, lesbian, bisexual, and transgendered citizens, features a parade with eye-catching floats, plus street performers and community events. National Race for the Cure (☎ 703/848–8884 ⊕ www.natl-race-for-the-cure.org.) The first Saturday in June is reserved for the world's largest 5-km (3.1-mi) race, sponsored by the Susan G. Komen Breast Cancer Foundation.
June	Washington Shakespeare Theatre Free for All (☎ 202/547–1122 ⊕ www.shakespearetheatre.org.) For two weeks, the theater company mounts free nightly performances at the open-air Carter Barron Amphitheatre in Rock Creek Park. Tickets are required and can be picked up at numerous locations around town.
Early–mid-June	Capital Jazz Fest (☎ 301/218–0404 ⊕ www.capitaljazz.com.) This weekend showcase for contemporary performers, held in Columbia, MD, has included David Sanborn and Grover Washington Jr.
June–August	Military Band Summer Concert Series (☎ 202/433–2525, 703/696–3399, 202/433–4011, or 202/767–5658.) This series is held on Tuesday evenings at various locations throughout the Washington area and Friday evenings on the west steps of the Capitol at 8 PM. Every August the *1812 Overture* is performed with real cannons at the Sylvan Theater, at the base of the Washington Monument.

ON THE
CALENDAR

Late June–early July	**Smithsonian's Folklife Festival** (☎ 202/275–1150 ⊕ www.folklife.si.edu.) Created for the Bicentennial, this engrossing two-week festival is now held on the National Mall each year. It juxtaposes the rich traditions of various corners of the United States and cultures around the world, and features traditional dance and music performances, storytelling, arts-and-crafts demonstrations, and ethnic food of all sorts.
July	**National Cathedral's Summer Music Festival** (☎ 202/537–6216 ⊕ www.cathedral.org/cathedral.) Free performances under the church's gargoyles include everything from Renaissance choral music to contemporary instrumental fare.
July 4	**Independence Day Celebration** (☎ 202/619–7222.) July 4 at the nation's capital includes a grand parade past many monuments. In the evening people camp out on the Mall to hear the National Symphony Orchestra playing from the Capitol's West Lawn and watch the awe-inspiring fireworks over the Washington Monument.
Late July	**Korean War Armistice Day Ceremony** (☎ 202/619–7222.) This ceremony marks the 1953 cease-fire with a formal wreath-laying ceremony at the Korean War Veterans Memorial.
	Virginia Scottish Games (☎ 703/912–1943 ⊕ www.vascottishgames.org.) Highland dancing, bagpipes, athletic contests, fiddling competitions, animal events, and a British antique auto show are part of this event, held on the grounds of the Episcopal High School in Alexandria.
Early September	**Labor Day Weekend Concert** (☎ 202/619–7222 National Park Service, 202/467–4600 Kennedy Center.) The National Symphony Orchestra performs on the Capitol's West Lawn. **John F. Kennedy Center's Open House** (☎ 202/467–4600 ⊕ www.kennedy-center.org.) This event showcases musicians, dancers, and other performers. **National Black Family Reunion Celebration** (☎ 202/737–0120 ⊕ www.ncnw.org/blackfamily.htm.) Families from all over the United States travel to D.C. to partake in this huge event, which includes free performances by nationally renowned R&B and gospel singers, exhibits, and food on the Washington Monument grounds. **Adams Morgan Day** (☎ 202/232–1960 ⊕ www.ammainstreet.org.) Family, community diversity, and good ethnic food are all celebrated with a large neighborhood street festival.
FALL Late September	**National Cathedral Open House** (☎ 202/537–3129 ⊕ www.cathedral.org/cathedral.) Visitors can share in crafts, music, and activities on the cathedral's grounds.

October	Artomatic (☎ 202/661–7589 ⊕ www.artomatic.org.) This grass-roots event has evolved into a biannual showcase for the work of hundreds of local painters, sculptors, filmmakers, writers, dancers, poets, and musicians. For each festival, an unlikely site becomes an art gallery for a month. Reel Affirmations Film Festival (☎ 202/986–1119 ⊕ www.reelaffirmations.org.) This is D.C.'s gay and lesbian film festival, showing features, shorts, documentaries, and animated works from all over the world.
Late October	White House Fall Garden & Grounds Tour (☎ 202/456–2200 ⊕ www.whitehouse.gov.) Like a similar event in spring, this tour gives you an up-close view of places that can normally be seen only on TV or from the wrong side of a fence. Marine Corps Marathon (☎ 800/786–8762 ⊕ www.marinemarathon.com.) Thousands of runners, including international record-holders and many first-timers, assemble on the fourth Sunday in October for this race that threads through the city. Visitors who need to get to an airport or train station on the day of the race should check the race route before setting out. Theodore Roosevelt's birthday (☎ 202/619–7222.) Celebrate the legacy of this popular president with activities on Roosevelt Island, including tours of the island, exhibits, performances by Roosevelt impersonators, and family activities. Washington International Horse Show (⊕ www.wihs.org.) D.C.'s major equestrian event, held at the MCI Center, draws horse lovers from around the world.
Mid-November	Veterans Day (☎ 703/607–8000 Cemetery Visitor Center, 202/619–7222 National Park Service.) Services take place at Arlington National Cemetery, the Vietnam Veterans Memorial, and the U.S. Navy Memorial. A wreath-laying ceremony is held at 11 AM at the Tomb of the Unknowns.

FODOR'S
CHOICE

The sights, restaurants, hotels, and other travel experiences on these pages are our editors' top picks—our Fodor's Choices. They're the best of their type in the area covered by the book—not to be missed and always worth your time. In the destination chapters that follow, you will find all the details.

HISTORY

Capitol. Home of the Senate and the House of Representatives and reminiscent of the Roman Pantheon in design, the marble Capitol is an architectural marvel filled with frescoes and statues.

J. Edgar Hoover Federal Bureau of Investigation Building. Despite its rough debut (Hoover himself is said to have called it the "ugliest building I've ever seen"), the FBI tour that takes place here has become one of the most popular activities in the city.

Mount Vernon. Here you can tour the plantation workshops and reconstructed slave quarters as well as the kitchen, the carriage house, the gardens, and the tomb of George and Martha Washington. The sweeping Potomac views are a bonus.

U.S. Naval Academy. Crisply uniformed midshipmen populate the 329 scenic acres of this institution, alongside the Severn River in Annapolis, Maryland.

Washington National Cathedral. Like its 14th-century counterparts, this 20th-century cathedral has a nave, flying buttresses, transepts, and vaults that were built stone by stone.

MONUMENTS

Franklin Delano Roosevelt Memorial. With its waterfalls, wide walkways, and inspiring messages, this rambling memorial is ideal for contemplation.

Jefferson Memorial. Jefferson always admired the Pantheon in Rome, so architect John Russell Pope drew from the same source when he designed this graceful memorial facing the Tidal Basin.

Lincoln Memorial. Many consider the Lincoln Memorial the city's most inspiring monument. The somber Daniel Chester French statue of the seated president, in the center, gazes out over the Reflecting Pool.

Tomb of the Unknowns. At this moving shrine in Arlington National Cemetery, soldiers from the Army's U.S. Third Infantry keep watch around the clock.

Vietnam Veterans Memorial. Maya Lin's black-granite memorial is a stark tribute to those who died in this war.

MUSEUMS	**National Air and Space Museum.** At the most-visited museum in the world, you'll find displays of the airplanes and spacecraft that have made history. The flight-simulating IMAX movies are not to be missed.
	National Archives. Its three most famous documents—the original Declaration of Independence, Constitution, and Bill of Rights—draw millions of reverential viewers every year.
	National Gallery of Art. John Russell Pope's domed West Building and I. M. Pei's East Building house one of the world's finest collections of paintings, sculptures, and graphics.
	United States Holocaust Memorial Museum. In a clear and often graphic fashion, this moving museum tells the stories of the 11 million people killed by the Nazis.
RESTAURANTS $$$$	**Citronelle,** Georgetown. In this embodiment of California chic, the kitchen's glass front lets you watch the chefs scurrying to and fro as they prepare, say, salmon with green and white asparagus sauce.
$$$$	**Inn at Little Washington,** Washington, VA. Since 1978 Patrick O'Connell and his partner have been turning out New American food that wins raves from all and sundry.
$$$$	**Maestro,** Virginia suburbs. Both traditional Italian cooking and Chef Fabio Trabocchi's creative takes on the classics are on the menu at the Ritz-Carlton in Tysons Corner.
$$$–$$$$	**2941,** Virginia Suburbs. A lake in the woods, a koi pond, artisanal breads, and a playful menu draw diners to Falls Church.
$$–$$$$	**Jaleo,** Downtown and Bethesda, MD. At these lively Spanish bistros you can make a meal out of many hot and cold tapas (appetizer-size dishes). Entrées, including grilled fish and paella, are equally good.
$$–$$$$	**Komi,** Dupont Circle. Chef-owner Johnny Monis keeps it personal at his small Mediterranean-influenced restaurant.
$$–$$$	**Galileo,** Downtown. A spacious, popular Italian restaurant, Galileo makes everything in-house: the sausages and pasta as well as the bread sticks and mozzarella.
$$–$$$	**Palena,** Cleveland Park. Opt for a crisp puff pastry with sardines and greens in the main dining room or a cheeseburger with truffles in the equally fabulous lounge.

FODOR'S CHOICE

$$–$$$	**Vidalia,** Dupont Circle. Vidalia onions are a specialty, but only in season—only the freshest seasonal ingredients make it to the menu here.
$–$$	**Sushi-Ko,** Georgetown. Look to the daily specials when you're ordering at this top address for sushi—the dishes are always creative.
¢–$$	**Zaytinya,** Downtown. The ingredients and techniques of Turkey and Greece come through in the small dishes served at this stylish and popular downtown spot.
$	**Pizzeria Paradiso.** Both the Dupont Circle original and the larger Georgetown branch serve well-executed, delicious Italian basics, including *panini* (pressed, grilled sandwiches), salads, and gelato along with the pizza that's made them famous.
¢–$	**Ben's Chili Bowl,** U Street corridor. This longtime veteran of U Street serves some of the best chili dogs you're likely to come across. Extra-late hours make it that much easier to fit a "half-smoke" or a regular in—and maybe even some cheese fries.
LODGING $$$$	**Four Seasons Hotel,** Georgetown. Impeccable service and a wealth of amenities have long made this a favorite with celebrities, hotel connoisseurs, and families alike.
$$$$	**Ritz-Carlton Washington, D.C.,** Foggy Bottom. Marble tubs, goose down pillows, Egyptian linens, and a sprawling health club: it's nothing but luxury at the more traditional of Washington's two Ritz-Carltons.
$$$	**Hay-Adams Hotel,** Downtown. Outstanding service and some stunning White House views distinguish this elegant boutique hotel in an Italian Renaissance mansion.

Exploring
Washington

Updated by
Coral
Davenport

THE BYZANTINE WORKINGS of the federal government; the sound-bite–ready oratory of the well-groomed politician; the murky foreign policy pronouncements issued from Foggy Bottom: they all cause many Americans to cast a skeptical eye on anything that happens "inside the Beltway." Washingtonians take it all in stride, though, reminding themselves that, after all, those responsible for political hijinks don't come *from* Washington, they come *to* Washington. Besides, such ribbing is a small price to pay for living in a city whose charms extend far beyond the bureaucratic. World-class museums and art galleries (nearly all of them free), tree-shaded and flower-filled parks and gardens, bars and restaurants that benefit from a large and creative immigrant community, and nightlife that seems to get better with every passing year are as much a part of Washington as floor debates or filibusters.

The city that calls to mind politicking, back-scratching, and delicate diplomatic maneuvering is itself the result of a compromise. Tired of its nomadic existence after having set up shop in eight locations, Congress voted in 1785 to establish a permanent federal city. Northern lawmakers wanted the capital on the Delaware River, in the North; Southerners wanted it on the Potomac, in the South. A deal was struck when Virginia's Thomas Jefferson agreed to support the proposal that the federal government assume the war debts of the colonies if New York's Alexander Hamilton and other Northern legislators would agree to locate the capital on the banks of the Potomac. George Washington himself selected the site of the capital, a diamond-shape, 100-square-mi plot that encompassed the confluence of the Potomac and Anacostia rivers, not far from his estate at Mount Vernon. To give the young city a head start, Washington included the already thriving tobacco ports of Alexandria, Virginia, and Georgetown, Maryland, in the District of Columbia. In 1791, Pierre-Charles L'Enfant, a French engineer who had fought in the Revolution, created the classic plan for the city.

It took the Civil War—and every war thereafter—to energize the city, by attracting thousands of new residents and spurring building booms that extended the capital in all di-

> **CAPITAL FACTS**
>
> Residents of the capital of the free world couldn't vote in a presidential election until 1961, weren't granted limited home rule until 1973, and are now represented in Congress by a single nonvoting delegate.

rections. Streets were paved in the 1870s, and the first streetcars ran in the 1880s. Memorials to famous Americans such as Lincoln and Jefferson were built in the first decades of the 20th century, along with the massive Federal Triangle, a monument to thousands of less-famous government workers.

Despite the growth and the important role that African-Americans have played in Washington's history (black mathematician Benjamin Banneker surveyed the land with Pierre-Charles L'Enfant), this city continues to struggle for full racial and ethnic equality. Today all District license plates are imprinted with the slogan TAXATION WITHOUT REPRESENTATION, a protest against the District's lack of status in Congress. Homeless people sleep on steam grates next to multimillion-dollar government buildings. But violent crime, although it still exists, is down (as it is in many other big cities) from the drug-fueled violent days of the late 1980s and early 1990s. Although it's little consolation to those affected, most crime is restricted to neighborhoods far from the areas visited by tourists.

There's no denying that Washington, the world's first planned capital, is also one of its most beautiful. And although the federal government dominates many of the city's activities and buildings, there are always places where you can leave politics behind. Washington is a city of vistas—pleasant views that shift and change from block to block, a marriage of geometry and art. Unlike other large cities, Washington isn't dominated by skyscrapers, largely because, in 1899, Congress passed a height-restrictions act to prevent federal monuments from being overshadowed by commercial construction. Its buildings stretch out gracefully and are never far from expanses of green. Like its main industry, politics, Washington's design is a constantly changing kaleidoscope that invites inspection from all angles.

THE MALL

The Mall is the heart of almost every visitor's trip to Washington. With nearly a dozen museums ringing the expanse of green, it's the closest thing the capital has to a theme park (unless you count the federal government itself, which has uncharitably been called Disneyland on the Potomac). You may have to stand in an occasional line, but unlike the amusements at the real Disneyland, almost everything you'll see here is free. ■ TIP→ **You may, however, need free, timed-entry tickets to some sites such as the Washington Monument, the Capitol, and the Holocaust Museum.** These are usually available at the museum information desk or by phone, for a service charge, from Ticketmaster (☎ 202/432–7328).

Of course, the Mall is more than just a front yard for these museums. Bounded on the north and south by Constitution and Independence avenues and on the east and west by 3rd and 14th streets, it's a picnicking park, a jogging path, an outdoor stage for festivals and fireworks, and America's town green. Nine of the Smithsonian Institution's 14 D.C. museums lie within these boundaries.

It wasn't always this way. In the middle of the 19th century, horticulturist Andrew Jackson Downing took a stab at converting the Mall into a large, English-style garden, with carriageways curving through groves of trees and bushes. This was far from the "vast esplanade" L'Enfant had in mind, and by the dawn of the 20th century the Mall had become an eyesore. It was dotted with sheds and bisected by railroad tracks. There was even a railroad station at its eastern end.

In 1900 Senator James McMillan, chairman of the Committee on the District of Columbia, asked a distinguished group of architects and artists to come up with ways to improve Washington's park system. The McMillan Commission, which included architects Daniel Burnham and Charles McKim, landscape architect Frederick Law Olmsted, and sculptor Augustus Saint-Gaudens, didn't confine its recommendations to

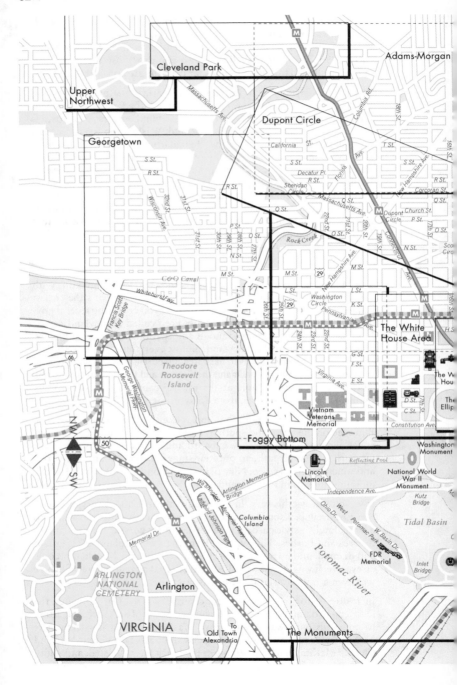

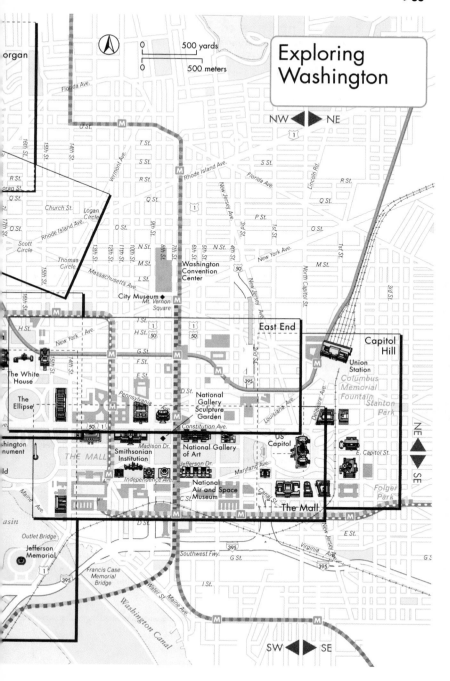

Exploring Washington

500 yards
500 meters

NW ◆ NE

SW ◆ SE

NE ▲ SE ▼

CLOSE UP

Recent Changes in Washington, D.C.

A SURGE OF NEW ADDITIONS are set for the District in 2006 and 2007. The once down-at-the-heels neighborhood of Penn Quarter is now thoroughly revitalized and continues to explode with new development. The neighborhood is home to what was the most hotly anticipated reopening of 2006, the **National Portrait Gallery** and **Smithsonian American Art Museum,** which, after having been closed to the public for six years, reopened their doors under one roof—the landmark marble **Old Patent Office,** restored to its former glory. In 2007 the same neighborhood will welcome the six-story multimedia new **Newseum,** and will welcome back the hugely popular tours of the **FBI Building,** suspended since 2001. It will also see the addition of a major new arts center from the prestigious **Shakespeare Theater.** On Capitol Hill, 2007 will see the opening of the vast new **Capitol Visitors' Center,** an underground behemoth whose expanse—and expense—continues to grow. Outside the dome, the gracious new **National Garden** is expected to open in fall 2006. Visitors looking for the popular **Capital Children's Museum** will have to wait for it to reemerge in 2008 on L'Enfant Plaza. Meanwhile, families can instead visit the National Zoo, where they'll see what many tourists and locals consider the most exciting new addition to the city: the adorable new **giant panda cub,** Tai Shan, one of only a handful of the endangered animals left in the world. Visitors hoping to see him should plan early—he is expected to be returned to China in mid-2007. Sports fans will know that Washington has gained another exciting addition that has nothing to do with politics or marble museums. D.C. once again has its own major league baseball team, and hometown pride for the **Nationals** (aka the Nats) has swept the city. **Heightened security** has been a tourist concern since the events of September 11, 2001. You will encounter metal detectors and your bags will be searched at all government buildings and museums, and you may be asked for a photo ID. For the easiest visit, carry a small bag of essentials that can be easily opened by a security guard, and expect to wait at the more popular attractions such as the Air and Space Museum and the National Gallery of Art. Government buildings such as the Capitol and the Supreme Court Building do not allow loitering, and there's a list of prohibited items on the Court's Web site (⊕ www.supremecourtus.gov). Tours of the **Pentagon, Treasury Building,** and **Eisenhower Executive Building** have been suspended indefinitely.

The good news is that **White House** tours have been reinstated, as have those at the **Bureau of Engraving and Printing** and **U.S. Naval Observatory.** Not only can school and military groups visit the president's house, but self-guided tours can be arranged for any group of 10 or more that makes a reservation in advance. For more information, call ☎ 202/456-7041.

parks; its 1902 report would shape the way the entire capital looked for decades. The Mall received much of the group's attention and is its most stunning accomplishment. L'Enfant's plan was rediscovered; the sheds, railroad tracks, and carriageways were removed; and Washington finally had the monumental core it had been denied for so long.

TIMING Don't try to see all the Mall's attractions in a day. Few people have the stamina for more than a half day of museum or gallery going at a time; children definitely don't. ■ TIP→ **To avoid mental and physical exhaustion, try to devote at least two days to the Mall.** Do the north side one day and the south the next. Or split your sightseeing on the Mall into a walking day, when you take in the scenic views and enjoy the architecture of each museum (the Mall museums are free, so a quick peek inside doesn't cost anything), and a museum day, when you go back to spend time with the exhibits that catch your interest. Afterward, plan something relaxing that doesn't require more walking—picnicking or getting a snack in one of the many museum cafeterias probably makes more sense than, say, shopping.

TOP 5: THE MALL

- **Hirshhorn Sculpture Garden:** Picnic beneath the giant Lichtenstein paint-stroke then head inside the museum to catch an avant-garde video installation.

- **Museum of American History:** Get lost in the nation's attic where you can see everything from Thomas Jefferson's desk to Judy Garland's ruby slippers.

- **Museum of Natural History:** Be dazzled by the enormous Hope Diamond—then select which rocks would suit you best from the spectacular array of precious jewels, worn by everyone from Marie Antoinette to Mae West.

- **National Air and Space Museum:** Feel like you're flying in the soaring cinema of the IMAX theater; then play pilot firsthand by strapping into one of the museum's 360-degree rotation flight simulators.

- **The National Gallery of Art:** Pay homage to *Ginevra de'Benci*, the only painting by Leonardo da Vinci on display in the Western Hemisphere.

What to See

⓮ Arthur M. Sackler Gallery. When Charles Freer endowed the gallery that bears his name, he insisted on a few conditions: objects in the collection could not be lent out, nor could objects from outside the collections be put on display. Because of the restrictions it was necessary to build a second, complementary museum to house the Asian art collection of Arthur M. Sackler, a wealthy medical researcher and publisher who began collecting Asian art as a student in the 1940s. Sackler allowed Smithsonian curators to select 1,000 items from his ample collection and pledged $4 million toward the construction of the museum. The collection includes works from China, Southeast Asia, Korea, Tibet, and Japan. Articles in the permanent collection include Chinese ritual bronzes, jade ornaments from the third millennium BC, Persian manuscripts, and Indian paintings in gold, silver, lapis lazuli, and malachite. The lower level connects to the Freer Gallery of Art. ⊠ *1050 Independence Ave. SW, The Mall* ☎ *202/633–1000, 202/357–1729 TDD* ⊕ *www.asia.si.edu* ⊠ *Free* ☉ *Daily 10–5:30* Ⓜ *Smithsonian.*

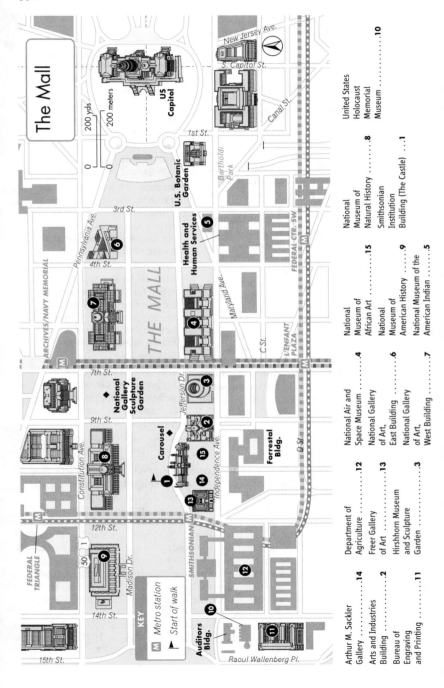

The Mall

200 yds
200 meters

US Capitol

U.S. Botanic Garden

Health and Human Services

THE MALL

National Gallery Sculpture Garden

Carousel

Forrestal Bldg.

Auditors Bldg.

KEY

Ⓜ Metro station

▲ Start of walk

Arthur M. Sackler Gallery **14**
Arts and Industries Building **2**
Bureau of Engraving and Printing **11**

Department of Agriculture **12**
Freer Gallery of Art **13**
Hirshhorn Museum and Sculpture Garden **3**

National Air and Space Museum **4**
National Gallery of Art, East Building **6**
National Gallery of Art, West Building **7**

National Museum of African Art **15**
National Museum of American History **9**
National Museum of the American Indian **5**

National Museum of Natural History **8**
Smithsonian Institution Building (The Castle) . . . **1**

United States Holocaust Memorial Museum **10**

A GOOD WALK

THE MALL
Numbers in the box correspond to numbers in the margin and on The Mall map.

Start your tour of the museums on the Mall in the **Smithsonian Institution Building** ❶ ☛ (aka the Castle), where the Smithsonian Information Center can orient you and help you plan your time. Walk east on Jefferson Drive past the beaux arts **Arts and Industries Building** ❷, toward the **Hirshhorn Museum and Sculpture Garden** ❸, which exhibits modern and contemporary art.

Cross 7th Street to reach the **National Air and Space Museum** ❹, one of the most-visited museums in the world. Continue east on Jefferson Drive to 4th Street past the construction site bounded by 3rd and 4th streets and Independence Avenue and Jefferson Drive SW, where the Smithsonian's **National Museum of the American Indian** ❺ began operations in 2004; the planned 3-acre site of the National Garden is just beyond. The conservatory of the **U.S. Botanic Garden,** renovated in 2002, is on the right at Maryland Avenue and 1st Street SW. Walk north past the Capitol Reflecting Pool and cross 3rd Street to get to the **National Gallery of Art, East Building** ❻, which generally displays 19th- and 20th-century works. Next door, the **National Gallery of Art, West Building** ❼ exhibits works from the 13th to the 20th century. If you're

visiting in winter, you can cross 7th Street and put on skates in the National Gallery Sculpture Garden Ice Rink; it's a cooling fountain in summer. Exit on Madison Drive to the **National Museum of Natural History** ❽, which has some 124 million objects in its collection, including the lifelike models of our warm-blooded cousins in Mammal Hall. The next building to the west is the **National Museum of American History** ❾, which contains everything from Thomas Jefferson's desk to Julia Child's kitchen.

Go south on 14th Street, crossing the Mall and Independence Avenue, to the **United States Holocaust Memorial Museum** ❿, a powerful reminder of humanity's capacity for evil. One block to the south is the **Bureau of Engraving and Printing** ⓫, the source of all U.S. paper money. Head back north up 14th Street, cross Independence Avenue, and turn right, passing below overpasses connecting the two buildings of the **Department of Agriculture** ⓬. Just across 12th Street is the **Freer Gallery of Art** ⓭, which holds a collection of Asian treasures. East of the Freer, off Independence Avenue, are the brick paths benches of the 4-acre Enid Haupt Memorial Garden. The garden sits on two underground museums, the **Arthur M. Sackler Gallery** ⓮, sister museum to the Freer, and the **National Museum of African Art** ⓯, with objects from hundreds of African cultures.

🏛 ❷ **Arts and Industries Building.** In 1876 Philadelphia was host of the U.S. International Exposition in honor of the nation's Centennial. After the festivities, scores of exhibitors donated their displays to the federal government. To house the objects that had suddenly come its way, the Smithsonian commissioned this redbrick-and-sandstone structure. Designed by Adolph Cluss, the building was originally called the United States National Museum, the name that's still engraved above the doorway. The second Smithsonian museum to be constructed, it was finished in 1881, just in time to hold President James Garfield's inaugural ball.

The Arts and Industries Building's artifacts were eventually moved to other museums as the Smithsonian grew. It was restored to its original appearance and reopened during the Bicentennial celebrations. Until recently the building housed changing exhibits from the Smithsonian collection, but it's now closed for renovations with no date yet set for reopening. ⊠ *900 Jefferson Dr. SW, The Mall* ☎ *202/633–1000 or 202/357–1500* ⊕ *www.si.edu* Ⓜ *Smithsonian.*

🏛 ⓫ **Bureau of Engraving and Printing.** Paper money has been printed here since 1914, when the bureau relocated from the redbrick-towered Auditors Building at the corner of 14th Street and Independence Avenue. In addition to all the paper currency in the United States, stamps, military certificates, and presidential invitations are printed here, too. You can only enter the bureau on the official tours, which last about 35 minutes. From March through September, same-day timed-entry tour passes are issued starting at 8 AM at the Raoul Wallen-

> **CAPITAL FACTS**
>
> The Bureau of Engraving and Printing turns out some $38 million worth of currency a day.

berg Place SW entrance. ⊠ *14th and C Sts. SW, The Mall* ☎ *202/874–3019 or 202/874–2330, 866/874–2330 tour information* ⊕ *www.moneyfactory. com* 🎫 *Free* ☉ *Sept.–Apr., weekdays 9–2; May–Aug., weekdays 9–2 and 5–6:30; tours every 15 min, Sept.–Apr., weekdays 9–10:45 and 12:30–2; May–Aug., weekdays 9–10:45, 12:30–2, and 5–7* Ⓜ *Smithsonian.*

⓬ **Department of Agriculture.** Although there's little of interest inside, this complex is too gargantuan to ignore. The offices of the governmental agency responsible for setting and carrying out the nation's agricultural policies are divided up between two buildings. The older white-marble building, on the north side of Independence Avenue, was begun in 1903. Its cornices on the north side depict forests as well as grains, flowers, and fruits—some of the vegetation the department keeps an eye on. The newer building, south of Independence Avenue, and built between 1930 and 1936, covers two city blocks. ⊠ *Independence Ave. between 12th and 14th Sts. SW, The Mall* ⊕ *www.usda.gov* Ⓜ *Smithsonian.*

★ ⓭ **Freer Gallery of Art.** Home to one of the world's finest collections of Asian art, the Smithsonian's Freer Gallery of Art was made possible by an endowment from Detroit industrialist Charles L. Freer, who retired in 1900 and devoted the rest of his life to collecting art. Opened in 1923, four years Freer's death, the collection includes more than 27,000 works of art from the Far and Near East. The Asian porcelains, Japanese screens,

Chinese paintings and bronzes, Korean stoneware, Islamic manuscripts, and other items date from Neolithic times to the 20th century.

Freer's friend James McNeill Whistler introduced him to Asian art, and the American painter is represented in the vast collection. On display is the Peacock Room, a blue-and-gold dining room decorated with painted leather, wood, and canvas. It was designed by Whistler for a British shipping magnate. Freer paid $30,000 for the entire room and moved it from London to the United States in 1904. The works of other American artists influenced by the Far East are also on display. A lower-level exhibition gallery connects the building to the Arthur M. Sackler Gallery. ⊠ *12th St. and Jefferson Dr. SW, The Mall* ☎ *202/633–1000, 202/357–1729 TDD* ⊕ *www.asia.si.edu* ⊠ *Free* ☉ *Daily 10–5:30* Ⓜ *Smithsonian.*

★ ❸ **Hirshhorn Museum and Sculpture Garden.** Sculpture on the National Mall runs mostly along the lines of classical marble columns and graven images of dead presidents. But in 2003, the Hirshhorn shook up that venerable lineup with a bold new addition: a 32-foot-tall sculpture of a yellow cartoon brushstroke by pop-art iconographer Roy Lichtenstein, which has since become a beloved local landmark and an apt symbol of the museum itself. Conceived as the nation's museum of modern and contemporary art, the Hirshhorn is home to more than 12,000 top-notch works by masters ranging from Pablo Picasso, Joan Miró, and Piet Mondrian to Willem de Kooning, Andy Warhol, and Edward Hopper. These are displayed in a striking round poured-concrete building, which stands out from its serious, marble neighbors. Designed by Gordon Bunshaft, it was dubbed the "Doughnut on the Mall" when it was constructed in 1974, but today it's seen as a fitting home for contemporary art.

Of especial renown is the Hirshhorn's sculpture collection, on show throughout the building and grounds. Inside, highlights include masterpieces by Henry Moore, Alberto Giacometti, Constantin Brancusi, and a roomful of giant, playful Alexander Calder mobiles, which alone merit a visit. ■ TIP→ **Outside, sculptures dot a sunken grass-and-granite garden, which makes an inspiring spot for an outdoor lunch.** In addition to the Lichtenstein, the garden boasts Henri Matisse's *Backs I–IV* and Auguste Rodin's *Burghers of Calais.*

Most of the collection was bequeathed by the museum's founder, Joseph H. Hirshhorn, a Latvian immigrant who made his fortune in this country running uranium mines. But it's also constantly being updated with the very best of contemporary art, which often includes fun, interactive installations. In 2005, the museum opened a Black Box room for video and multimedia art, along with pieces such as Danish artist Olafur Eliasson's *Round Rainbow,* a room in which a rotating round prism transforms a beam of light into undulating colors bathing the walls and visitors' faces. ⊠ *Independence Ave. and 7th St. SW, The Mall* ☎ *202/ 633–1000, 202/633–8043 TDD* ⊕ *www.hirshhorn.si.edu* ⊠ *Free* ☉ *Museum daily 10–5:30, sculpture garden 7:30–dusk* Ⓜ *Smithsonian or L'Enfant Plaza (Maryland Ave. exit).*

☙ ❹ **National Air and Space Museum.** It's believed that this is the most-visited museum in the world, attracting more than 9 million people each year. Its 23 galleries tell the story of aviation from the earliest human attempts at flight. As you walk through, look up to see the world's most famous

Fodor's Choice ★

aircraft, including the *Wright 1903 Flyer,* which Wilbur Wright piloted over the sands of Kitty Hawk, North Carolina; Charles Lindbergh's *Spirit of St. Louis*; the X-1 rocket plane in which Chuck Yeager broke the sound barrier; and an X-15, the first aircraft to exceed Mach 6.

Other highlights include a backup model of the Skylab orbital workshop that you can walk through; the *Voyager,* the airplane that Dick Rutan and Jeana Yeager flew nonstop around the world in 1986; and the Lockheed Vega that Amelia Earhart piloted in 1932: it was the first solo transatlantic flight by a woman. You can also see a piece of the moon: a 4-billion-year-old slice of rock collected by *Apollo 17* astronauts. A permanent exhibition on the history of the scientific study of the universe is on the first floor.

Don't let long lines deter you from seeing a show in the museum's Lockheed Martin IMAX Theater. Films shown on the five-story-high screen—including the now-classic *To Fly!*, *Straight Up: Helicopters in Action*, and *Space Station 3-D*, for which special viewing glasses are provided—employ swooping aerial scenes that make you feel as if you've left the ground. ■ TIP➜ Buy tickets up to two weeks in advance or as soon as you arrive (prices vary); then tour the museum. Upstairs, the Albert Einstein Planetarium's "all-dome" digital technology creates a feeling of movement through space. A shuttle bus runs from the museum entrance on the Mall to the **National Air and Space Museum Steven F. Udvar-Hazy Center,** which opened at Washington Dulles International Airport in northern Virginia in 2003 to commemorate the 100th anniversary of the Wright brothers' flight. There you can see a Concorde, the space shuttle *Enterprise,* the fabled Lockheed SR-71 Blackbird (which in 1990 flew from Los Angeles to Washington, D.C., in slightly more than an hour), and the *Enola Gay* (which in 1944 dropped on Japan the first atomic devices to be used in war). ⊠ *Independence Ave. and 6th St. SW, The Mall* ☎ *202/357–1729, 202/357–1686 movie information, 202/357–1729 TDD* ⊕ *www.nasm.si.edu* ☞ *Free, IMAX $7.50, planetarium $7.50* ☉ *Daily 10–5:30* Ⓜ *Smithsonian.*

NEED A BREAK? A fast-food–style restaurant at the eastern end of the National Air and Space Museum, the **Wright Place** (☎ 202/357–4700), is open weekdays 7:30–5 and weekends 9–5 (if the museum is not yet open for the day, enter through the glass doors at the east end of the museum). It's operated by McDonald's, and although at first glance it looks like the offerings are mostly burgers and fries, you can also find pizza from Donato's, scrambled eggs and roast chicken from Boston Market, and Caesar and green salads. Two ice-cream kiosks are set among the tables. On the second level is the upscale **Mezza Café,** serving Lavazza coffee, muffins, scones, and fruit salad as well as wine and beer. There's also a small Lavazza stand outside, on the west terrace of the museum.

Ⓒ ❻ **FodorśChoice** ★ **National Gallery of Art, East Building.** The atrium is dominated by Alexander Calder's mobile *Untitled,* and the galleries display modern and contemporary art, although you'll also find major temporary exhibitions that span many years and artistic styles. Permanent works include Pablo Picasso's *The Lovers* and *Family of Saltimbanques,* four of Matisse's cutouts, Miró's *The Farm,* and Jackson Pollock's *Lavender Mist.*

The East Building opened in 1978 in response to the changing needs of the National Gallery. The trapezoidal shape of the site prompted architect I. M. Pei's dramatic approach: two interlocking spaces shaped like triangles provide room for galleries, auditoriums, and administrative offices. Although the building's triangles contrast sharply with the symmetrical classical facade and gentle dome of the West Building, both structures are constructed of pink marble from the same Tennessee quarries. Despite its severe angularity, Pei's building is inviting. The ax-blade-like southwest corner has been darkened and polished smooth by thousands of hands irresistibly drawn to it.

To reach the East Building from the West Building, you can take the underground concourse, lined with gift shops, a café, and a cafeteria. ■ TIP➡ **But to best appreciate the angularity of the East Building, enter it from outside rather than from underground.** Exit the West Building through its eastern doors, and cross 4th Street. (As you cross, look to the north: seeming to float above the Doric columns and pediment of the D.C. Superior Court are the green roof and redbrick pediment of the National Building Museum, four blocks away.) ⊠ *Constitution Ave. between 3rd and 4th Sts. NW, The Mall* ☎ *202/737–4215, 202/842–6176 TDD* ⊕ *www.nga.gov* ▭ *Free* ☉ *Mon.–Sat. 10–5, Sun. 11–6* Ⓜ *Archives/Navy Memorial.*

❼ National Gallery of Art, West Building. The two buildings of the National Gallery hold one of the world's foremost collections of paintings, sculptures, and graphics. ■ TIP➡ **If you want to view the museum's holdings in (more or less) chronological order, it's best to start your exploration in the West Building.** The rotunda, with 24 marble columns surrounding a fountain topped with a statue of Mercury, sets the stage for the masterpieces on display in more than 100 galleries. A recorded tour of the building's better-known holdings is available for a $5 rental fee on the main floor adjacent to the rotunda. If you'd rather explore on your own, get a map at one of the two art information desks; one is just inside the Mall entrance (off Madison Drive), and the other is near the Constitution Avenue entrance on the ground floor. The Micro Gallery near the rotunda maintains computerized information on more than 1,700 works of art from the permanent collection. Touch-screen monitors provide access to color images, text, animation, and sounds to help you better understand—and appreciate—the works on display.

Fodor'sChoice
★

The National Gallery's permanent collection includes works from the 13th to the 20th centuries. A comprehensive survey of Italian paintings and sculpture includes *The Adoration of the Magi,* by Fra Angelico and Filippo Lippi, and *Ginevra de'Benci,* the only painting by Leonardo da Vinci on display in the Western Hemisphere. Flemish and Dutch works, displayed in paneled rooms, include *Daniel in the Lions' Den,* by Peter Paul Rubens, and a self-portrait by Rembrandt. In the Chester Dale Collection are works by impressionists such as Edgar Degas, Claude Monet, Auguste Renoir, and Mary Cassatt. Salvador Dalí's *Last Supper* is also in this building.

The **National Gallery of Art Sculpture Garden** is between 7th and 9th streets along the Mall. Granite walkways take you through the garden, which is planted with shade trees, flowering trees, and perennials. Sculptures on display from the museum's permanent collection include Roy Lichtenstein's playful *House I;* Alexander Archipenko's *Woman Combing Her Hair;* Miró's *Personnage Gothique, Oiseau-Eclair;* and Isamu Noguchi's *Great Rock of Inner Seeking.* The huge central fountain becomes a skating rink during the winter.

Opened in 1941, the domed West Building was a gift to the nation from Andrew Mellon. (The dome was one of architect John Russell Pope's favorite devices. He also designed the Jefferson Memorial and the National Archives, which has a half-dome rotunda.) A wealthy financier and industrialist, Mellon served as secretary of the treasury under three presidents and as ambassador to the United Kingdom. He first came to D.C. in 1921 and lived for many years near Dupont Circle, in a building that today houses the National Trust for Historic Preservation. Mellon had long collected great works of art, acquiring some on his frequent trips to Europe. In 1930 and 1931, when the Soviet government was short on cash and selling off many of its art treasures, Mellon bought more than $6 million worth of old masters, including Raphael's *The Alba Madonna* and Sandro Botticelli's *Adoration of the Magi.* Mellon promised his collection to America in 1936, the year before his death. He also donated the funds for the gallery's construction and resisted suggestions that it be named after him. ⊠ *Constitution Ave. between 4th and 7th Sts. NW, The Mall* ☎ *202/737–4215, 202/842–6176 TDD* ⊕ *www.nga.gov* 🎫 *Free* ⊙ *Mon.–Sat. 10–5, Sun. 11–6* Ⓜ *Archives/Navy Memorial.*

NEED A BREAK?

For a quick, casual meal, try the **Cascade Café**, in the concourse between the East and West buildings of the National Gallery of Art. Open 10–3 Monday to Saturday and 11:30–4 Sunday, it carries sandwiches and salads, as well as espresso and gelato that's made in-house. The **Garden Café** (☎ 202/215–5966), on the ground floor of the National Gallery's West Building, gracefully combines food and art by presenting dishes related to current exhibitions, as well as traditional American fare. It's open 11–3 Monday to Saturday and noon–6:30 Sunday. The **Pavilion Café** has indoor and outdoor seating and a panoramic view of landscaping in the National Gallery of Art Sculpture Garden. On offer are specialty pizzas and sandwiches. From September through May it's open 10–5 Monday to Saturday and 11–6 Sunday; from June through August it's open 10–6 Monday to Thursday and Saturday, 10–8 Friday, and 11–6 Sunday.

★ ☾ ⓯ **National Museum of African Art.** Opened in 1987, this unique underground building houses galleries, a library, photographic archives, and educational facilities. Its rotating exhibits present African visual arts, including sculpture, textiles, photography, archaeology, and modern art. Long-term installations explore the sculpture of sub-Saharan Africa, the art of Benin, the pottery of Central Africa, the archaeology of the ancient Nubian city of Kerma, and the artistry of everyday objects. The museum's educational programs include films with contemporary perspectives on African life, storytelling programs, festivals, and hands-on workshops for families, all of which bring Africa's oral traditions, literature, and art to life. Workshops and demonstrations by African and African-American artists offer a chance to meet and talk to practicing artists.■ **TIP→** **If you're traveling with children, look for the museum's free guide to the permanent Images of Power and Identity exhibition.** ✉ *950 Independence Ave. SW, The Mall* ☎ *202/633–1000, 202/357–1729 TDD* ⊕ *www.nmafa.si.edu* ✉ *Free* ⊗ *Daily 10–5:30* Ⓜ *Smithsonian.*

★ ☺ ❾ **National Museum of American History.** Opened in 1964 as the National Museum of History and Technology and renamed in 1980, the museum explores America's cultural, political, technical, and scientific past. The incredible diversity of artifacts helps the Smithsonian live up to its nickname, "the nation's attic." This is the museum that displays Muhammad Ali's boxing gloves, Judy Garland's ruby slippers from *The Wizard of Oz,* and the Bunkers' living room furniture from *All in the Family.*

You can wander for hours on the museum's three floors. Exhibits on the first floor emphasize the history of science and technology and include farm machines, automobiles, and a 280-ton steam locomotive. The permanent Science in American Life exhibit shows how science has shaped American life with breakthroughs such as the mass production of penicillin, the development of plastics, and the birth of the environmental movement. Another permanent exhibit looks at 19th-century life in three communities: industrial-age Bridgeport, Connecticut; the Jewish immigrant community in Cincinnati, Ohio; and African-Americans living in Charleston, South Carolina. Also here are Lewis and Clark's compass and a life mask of Abraham Lincoln. The second floor is devoted to U.S. social and political history and has an exhibit on everyday American life just after the Revolution. A permanent exhibit, First Ladies: Political Role and Public Image, displays gowns worn by presidential wives, but it goes beyond fashion to explore the women behind the satin, lace, and brocade. The third floor has installations on money, musical instruments, and photography.

Be sure to check out Horatio Greenough's statue of the first president (near the west-wing escalators on the second floor). Commissioned by Congress in 1832, it was intended to grace the Capitol Rotunda. It was there for only a short while, however, because the toga-clad likeness proved distasteful to some legislators, who grumbled that it looked as if the father of our country had just emerged from a bath. For a more interactive visit, check out the Hands on History Room, where you can try some 30 activities, such as pedaling a high-wheeler bike or plucking an old stringed instrument. In the Hands on Science Room you can conduct one of 25 experiments, including testing a water sample and exploring DNA fingerprinting. ✉ *Constitution Ave. and 14th St. NW, The Mall* ☎ *202/633–1000, 202/357–1729 TDD* ⊕ *www.americanhistory.si. edu* ✉ *Free* ⊗ *Daily 10–5:30; call for hrs of Hands on History and Hands on Science rooms* Ⓜ *Smithsonian or Federal Triangle.*

NEED A BREAK? The **Palm Court** (☎ 202/633–1000), on the first floor of the National Museum of American History, is designed like an old-fashioned ice-cream parlor. A good place for lunch, the restaurant is open 10–5:30 daily. The National Museum is also the perfect place for souvenirs. In the four stores in the building, you can purchase presidential souvenirs, reproductions of newspapers with notable headlines, and even personalized dog tags.

🐾 ❺ **National Museum of the American Indian.** The Smithsonian's newest museum, which opened in 2004, covers 10,000 years of the history of the native groups living in the Western Hemisphere. The exterior, clad in limestone from Minnesota, has been treated to give it a weathered appearance. The result is one of the loveliest buildings on the Mall. Inside, on three floors that open up on one side to a view of the Potomac Theater on the ground floor, are wood and stone carvings, clothing and headgear, baskets and pottery, and nearly a million other crafts and works of art from the Americas. *1,000 Roads,* a film about the lives of contemporary Native Americans, is shown hourly in the museum's Lelawi Theater. The ground-level café serves dishes inspired by native cultures, ranging from plaintain chips and *pupusas* (thick corn pancakes usually stuffed with cheese) to maple-roasted turkey, salmon, and other regional specialties. ■ TIP→ **Free timed-entrance passes, required for entry, are distributed beginning at 10 AM from the museum's east entrance, but by midday, especially during winter months, you may find that you don't actually need one.** You can also buy the passes in advance online for a fee. ✉ *4th St. and Independence Ave. SW* ☎ *202/633–1000* ⊕ *www.americanindian. si.edu* ✆ *Free* ☉ *Daily 10–5:30* Ⓜ *L'Enfant Plaza.*

★ 🐾 ❽ **National Museum of Natural History.** This is one of the great natural history museums in the world, filled with bones, fossils, and other natural delights—124 million specimens in all. It was constructed in 1910, and two wings were added in the 1960s.

The first-floor rotunda is dominated by a stuffed, 8-ton, 13-foot-tall African bull elephant, one of the largest ever found. (The tusks are fiberglass; the original ivory ones were far too heavy for the stuffed elephant to support.) Off to the right is the popular **Dinosaur Hall.** Fossilized skeletons here range from a 90-foot-long diplodocus to a tiny *Thescelosaurus neglectus* (a small dinosaur so named because its disconnected bones sat for years in a college drawer before being reassembled).

Beyond the Dinosaur Hall is one of two new permanent exhibitions, **African Voices.** It depicts the people and culture of Africa with refreshingly up-to-date displays, including a Somali camel herder's portable house, re-creations of markets in Ghana (housewares, cola nuts, and yams are for sale), a Tunisian wedding tunic, and artifacts showing the Yoruba influence on Afro-Brazilian culture.

The west wing houses displays of birds, mammals, and sea life. The latest addition, **Mammal Hall** not only explains mammals' role in the food chain, their evolution, and diversity, but does so with close to 300 fossil specimens and lifelike models. Watch out for the cheetah above you on the tree branch. Hands-on exhibits allow you to handle elephant tusks, petrified wood, seashells, rocks, feathers, and other items from nature.

The highlight of the second floor is the **Janet Annenberg Hooker Hall of Geology, Gems, and Minerals.** Objects on display include a pair of

Marie Antoinette's earrings, the Rosser Reeves ruby, spectacular crystals and minerals, and, of course, the Hope Diamond, a blue gem found in India and reputed to carry a curse (Smithsonian guides are quick to dismiss this notion).

Also on the second floor is the **O. Orkin Insect Zoo,** named for the pest-control magnate who donated the money to modernize the exhibits. Here you can view at least 60 species of live insects, and there are tarantula feedings Tuesday through Friday at 10:30, 11:30, and 1:30.

The second IMAX theater on the Mall—the other is in the National Air and Space Museum—is the Samuel C. Johnson IMAX theater, which shows two- and three-dimensional natural-history films, including the 3-D movie *T-REX.* The theater is also open Friday evenings from 6 for the "IMAX and Jazz Café," an evening of live entertainment, food, and special IMAX films not shown during the day. Tickets for the theater can be purchased at the museum box office. ⊠ *Constitution Ave. and 10th St. NW, The Mall* ☎ *202/633–1000, 202/357–1729 TDD* ⊕ *www. mnh.si.edu* ⟟ *Free, IMAX $8* ⊙ *Museum daily 10–5:30; Discovery Room Tues.–Fri. noon–2:30, weekends 10:30–3:30; free passes for Discovery Room distributed during regular museum hours near Discovery Room door* Ⓜ *Smithsonian or Federal Triangle.*

▶ ❶ **Smithsonian Institution Building.** The first Smithsonian museum constructed, this red sandstone, Norman-style building is better known as the Castle. It was designed by James Renwick, the architect of St. Patrick's Cathedral in New York City. Although British scientist and founder James Smithson had never visited America, his will stipulated that should his nephew, Henry James Hungerford, die without an heir, Smithson's entire fortune would go to the United States, "to found at Washington, under the name of the Smithsonian Institution, an establishment for the increase and diffusion of knowledge." The museums on the Mall are the Smithsonian's most visible example of this ideal, but the organization also sponsors traveling exhibitions and maintains research posts in outside-the-Beltway locales such as the Chesapeake Bay and the tropics of Panama.

Smithson died in 1829, Hungerford in 1835, and in 1838 the United States received gold sovereigns worth $515,169. After eight years of congressional debate over the propriety of accepting a foreign citizen's funds, the Smithsonian Institution was finally established on August 10, 1846. The Castle building was completed in 1855 and originally housed all of the Smithsonian's operations, including the science and art collections, research laboratories, and living quarters for the institution's secretary and his family. The statue in front of the Castle's entrance is not of Smithson but of Joseph Henry, the scientist who served as the institution's first secretary. Smithson's body was brought to America in 1904 and is entombed in a small room to the left of the Castle's Mall entrance.

■ TIP➔ **Today the Castle houses Smithsonian administrative offices as well as the Smithsonian Information Center, which can help you get your bearings and decide which attractions to visit.** A 24-minute video gives an overview of the Smithsonian museums and the National Zoo, and monitors display information on the day's events. Interactive touch-screens provide more detailed information on the museums as well as other attractions in the capital. The center opens at 9 AM, an hour before the other museums, so you can plan your day without wasting sightseeing time. ⊠ *1000 Jefferson Dr. SW, The Mall* ☎ *202/633–1000, 202/357–1729 TDD* ⊕ *www.si.edu* ☜ *Free* ⊙ *Daily 9–5:30* Ⓜ *Smithsonian.*

❿ **United States Holocaust Memorial Museum.** Museums usually celebrate the best that humanity can achieve, but this museum instead documents the worst. A permanent exhibition tells the stories of the millions of Jews, Gypsies, Jehovah's Witnesses, homosexuals, political prisoners, the mentally ill, and others killed by the Nazis between 1933 and 1945. Striving to give a you-are-there experience, the graphic presentation is as extraordinary as the subject matter: upon arrival, you are issued an "identity card" containing biographical information on a real person from the Holocaust. As you move through the museum, you read sequential updates on your card. The museum recounts the Holocaust through documentary films, video- and audiotaped oral histories, and a collection that includes items such as a freight car like those used to transport Jews from Warsaw to the Treblinka death camp, and the Star of David patches that Jews were made to wear. Like the history it covers, the museum can be profoundly disturbing; it's not recommended for children under 11, although Daniel's Story, in a ground-floor exhibit not requiring tickets, is designed for children ages 8 and up. Plan to spend two to three hours here. After this powerful experience, the adjacent Hall of Remembrance provides a space for quiet reflection. In addition to the permanent exhibition, the museum also has a multimedia learning center, a resource center for students and teachers, a registry of Holocaust survivors, and occasional special exhibitions. Timed-entry passes (distributed on a first-come, first-served basis at the 14th Street entrance starting at 10 AM or available in advance through tickets.com) are necessary for the permanent exhibition. ■ TIP→ **Allow extra time to enter the building in spring and summer, when long lines can form.** ⊠ *100 Raoul Wallenberg Pl. SW, enter from Raoul Wallenberg Pl. or 14th St. SW, The Mall* ☎ *202/488–0400, 800/400–9373 tickets.com* ⊕ *www.ushmm. org* ☜ *Free* ⊙ *Daily 10–5:30* Ⓜ *Smithsonian.*

Fodor'sChoice ★ (margin note)

THE MONUMENTS

Washington is a city of monuments. In the middle of traffic circles, on tiny slivers of park, and at street corners and intersections, statues, plaques, and simple blocks of marble honor the generals, politicians, poets, and statesmen who helped shape the nation. The monuments dedicated to the most famous Americans are west of the Mall on ground reclaimed from the marshy flats of the Potomac. This is also the location of Washington's greatest single display of cherry trees, gifts from Japan.

TIMING Allow four or five hours to tour the monuments. This includes time to relax on a park bench and to grab a snack from a vendor or one of the snack bars east of the Washington Monument and near the Lincoln Memorial. If you're visiting during the first two weeks in April, take extra time around the Tidal Basin and the Washington Monument to marvel at the cherry blossoms. From mid-April through November, you might want to spend an hour taking a paddleboat ride in the Tidal Basin. In summer, if it's hot, you may want to hop a Tourmobile bus and travel between the monuments in air-conditioned comfort.

What to See

THE AWAKENING. – J. Seward Johnson Jr.'s colossal aluminum sculpture of a bearded giant with head and limbs breaking through the ground is great fun—especially for kids. The 70-foot-tall work was installed at the southern tip of East Potomac Park for a sculpture exhibition in 1980. ✉ *Hains Pt., E. Potomac Park, Southwest.*

OFF THE BEATEN PATH

⑩ **Constitution Gardens.** Many ideas were proposed to develop this 50-acre site. It once held "temporary" buildings erected by the navy before World War I and not removed until after World War II. President Nixon is said to have favored something resembling Copenhagen's Tivoli Gardens. The final design was plainer, with paths winding through groves of trees and, on the lake, a tiny island paying tribute to the signers of the Declaration of Independence, their signatures carved into a low stone wall. In 1986 President Reagan proclaimed the gardens a living legacy to the Constitution; in that spirit, a naturalization ceremony for new citizens now takes place here each year. ✉ *Constitution Ave. between 17th and 23rd Sts. NW* ⊕ *www.nps.gov/coga* Ⓜ *Foggy Bottom.*

TOP 5: THE MONUMENTS **1**

- **Franklin Delano Roosevelt Memorial:** Get to know the inimitable FDR with a stroll through his life and presidential terms, depicted in the four outdoor rooms, surrounded by waterfalls and cherry trees.

- **The Jefferson Memorial:** Read the immortal words of the Declaration of Independence and see the statue of its author, then admire the monument's Pantheon-style dome (along with Washington's famous cherry trees) from a paddleboat on the tranquil Tidal Basin.

- **The Lincoln Memorial:** Imagine the immortal words of the Gettysburg Address while gazing on the craggy marble lines of the 16th president's face, a dramatic experience, especially at dusk.

- **Vietnam Memorial:** Spend time in silent contemplation, seeing your own face reflected through the names on the black marble.

- **The Washington Monument:** Take in all the District and miles of Maryland and Virginia from the top of this Washington icon.

NEED A BREAK?

At the circular **snack bar** just west of the Constitution Gardens lake you can get hot dogs, potato chips, candy bars, soft drinks, and beer at prices lower than those charged by most street vendors.

East Potomac Park. This 328-acre finger of land extends from the Tidal Basin between the Washington Channel to the east and the Potomac River to the west. There are playgrounds, picnic tables, tennis courts, swimming pools, a driving range, two 9-hole golf courses, miniature golf, and an 18-hole golf course. Double-blossoming cherry trees line Ohio Drive

Constitution Gardens **10**

Franklin Delano Roosevelt Memorial **5**

Jefferson Memorial **4**

Korean War Veterans Memorial **6**

Lincoln Memorial **7**

Lockkeeper's House **11**

National World War II Memorial **2**

Tidal Basin **3**

Vietnam Veterans Memorial **8**

Vietnam Women's Memorial **9**

Washington Monument **1**

The Monuments

KEY

Ⓜ Metro station

▶ Start of walk

and bloom about two weeks after the single-blossoming variety that attracts throngs to the Tidal Basin each spring. *The Awakening* sculpture is on Hains Point, at the tip of the park, where the Anacostia River merges with the Potomac. ✉ *Maine Ave. SW heading west, or Ohio Dr. heading south, follow signs carefully; Ohio Dr. closed to traffic on summer weekends and holidays 3 PM–6 AM* ☎ *202/619–7222* Ⓜ *Smithsonian.*

🐾 ❺ **Franklin Delano Roosevelt Memorial.** This monument, designed by Lawrence
FodorsChoice Halprin, was unveiled in 1997. The 7½-acre memorial to the 32nd
★ president employs waterfalls and reflection pools, four outdoor gallery rooms—one for each of Roosevelt's terms as president—and 10 bronze sculptures. The granite megaliths that connect the galleries are engraved with some of Roosevelt's most famous quotes, including, "The only thing we have to fear is fear itself." Although today the memorial is one of the most popular in the District, a delight to toddlers as well as to those who remember FDR firsthand, it's had its share of controversy. When unveiled, the monument did not depict Roosevelt with a wheelchair, which he used for

> **CAPITAL FACTS**
>
> In 2001, after much protest by disability advocate groups, Congress approved adding a bronze statue to the FDR memorial showing the president in his wheelchair. When it was added to the entrance of the memorial in 2001, it became the first statue to show a world leader in a wheelchair.

the last 24 years of his life, including those in which he led the nation through World War II. However, this was the first D.C. memorial purposely designed to be wheelchair accessible, and the first to honor a First Lady. A bronze statue of Eleanor Roosevelt stands in front of the United Nations symbol. ✉ *West side of Tidal Basin, The Mall* ☎ *202/426–6841* ⊕ *www.nps.gov/fdrm* 🎟 *Free* ⊙ *24 hrs; staffed daily 8 AM–midnight* Ⓜ *Smithsonian.*

❹ **Jefferson Memorial.** The monument honoring the third president of the
FodorsChoice United States incorporates his own architectural taste in its design. Jef-
★ ferson had always admired the Pantheon in Rome—the rotundas he designed for the University of Virginia were inspired by its dome—so the memorial's architect, John Russell Pope, drew from the same source. In the 1930s Congress decided that Jefferson deserved a monument positioned as prominently as those in honor of Washington and Lincoln, so workers scooped and moved tons of river bottom to create dry land on this spot directly south of

> **CAPITAL FACTS**
>
> The Jefferson Memorial was dubbed "Jefferson's muffin"; critics lambasted the design as outdated and too similar to that of the Lincoln Memorial.

the White House. Dedicated in 1943, it houses a statue of Jefferson, and its walls are lined with inscriptions based on the Declaration of Independence and his other writings. ■ TIP➡ **One of the best views of the White House can be seen from its top steps.** ✉ *Tidal Basin, south bank, The Mall*

A GOOD WALK

THE MONUMENTS

Numbers in the box correspond to numbers in the margin and on The Monuments map.

Start with the tallest of them all, the 555-foot **Washington Monument** ❶ ▶, at the Mall's western end. Then walk southwest past the **National World War II Memorial** ❷, dedicated in 2004, and cross Independence Avenue to the **Tidal Basin** ❸. The path that skirts the basin leads to the Outlet Bridge and the **Jefferson Memorial** ❹. Continue along the sidewalk that hugs the Tidal Basin. Cross Inlet Bridge, bear right, and enter the **Franklin Delano Roosevelt Memorial** ❺; you'll be going through in reverse, but this won't spoil enjoyment of the memorial's drama. Exit the memorial through its entrance and bear right on West Basin Drive. At the next traffic light, cross Independence Avenue and walk left toward the **Korean War Veterans Memorial** ❻, in a grove of trees called Ash Woods.

Your next stop is the **Lincoln Memorial** ❼. After visiting, walk down its steps and to the left to the **Vietnam Veterans Memorial** ❽. From there take the path that passes the **Vietnam Women's Memorial** ❾ on your way to the **Constitution Gardens** ❿. Walk north to Constitution Avenue and head east to the stone **Lockkeeper's House** ⓫ at the corner of Constitution Avenue and 17th Street, an artifact from a failed waterway.

☎ *202/426–6821* ⊕ *www.nps.gov/thje* ✉ *Free* ☉ *Daily 8 AM–midnight* Ⓜ *Smithsonian.*

❻ **Korean War Veterans Memorial.** Dedicated in 1995, this memorial to the 1.5 million United States men and women who served in the Korean War highlights the high cost of freedom. The statue group in the triangular Field of Service depicts 19 soldiers of many races on patrol in rugged Korean terrain. They're heading toward an American flag. To the south of the soldiers stands a 164-foot-long granite wall etched with the faces of 2,400 unnamed servicemen and servicewomen with a silver inlay reading FREEDOM IS NOT FREE. The adjacent Pool of Remembrance honors all who were killed, captured, wounded, or missing in action; it's a quiet spot for contemplation. ⊠ *West end of Mall at Daniel French Dr. and Independence Ave., The Mall* ☎ *202/426–6841* ⊕ *www.nps.gov/kwvm* ✉ *Free* ☉ *24 hrs; staffed daily 8 AM–midnight* Ⓜ *Foggy Bottom.*

❼ **Lincoln Memorial.** Nowadays many people consider the Lincoln Memorial the most inspiring monument in the city. This was not always the case. Although today it would be hard to imagine D.C. without the Lincoln and Jefferson memorials, both were criticized when first built. Some complained that the Jefferson Memorial blocked the view of the Potomac from the White House. Detractors of the Lincoln Memorial thought it inappropriate that the humble president be honored with what amounts to a modified but grandiose Greek temple. The white Colorado-marble memorial was designed by Henry Bacon and completed in 1922.

FodorśChoice
★

A City of Statues

WITH MORE EQUESTRIAN STATUES than any other city in the nation, green-streaked stone-and-metal men atop steeds are everywhere, watching the city from traffic circles, squares, and parks. The statues proliferated in the 19th century; Civil War generals who went into politics seemed virtually assured of this legacy—regardless of their success in either endeavor. Some of the statues reveal more than stories of men in battle.

Henry James wrote of America's first equestrian statue, "the most prodigious of all Presidential effigies, Andrew Jackson, as archaic as a Ninevite king, prancing and rocking through the ages." Standing in Lafayette Square across from the White House, the statue of Jackson is by sculptor Clark Mills, who had never seen an equestrian statue, much less created one. To get the proportions of the rearing horse correct, Mills had a horse trained to remain in an upright position so he could study the anatomy of its muscles.

Directly up 16th Street from Lafayette Square at Massachusetts and Rhode Island avenues is a statue of Lt. Gen. Winfield Scott (1786–1866), in the circle bearing his name. "Old Fuss and Feathers" was to be shown atop his favorite mount, a lightweight mare. However, right before the statue was cast, some of Scott's descendants decided that a stallion would be a more appropriate horse to ride into battle (regardless of historical accuracy). The sculptor, H. K. Brown, was forced to give the horse a last-minute sex change.

Farther up Massachusetts Avenue, at 23rd Street, is a statue of Civil War Gen.

Philip Henry Sheridan, also in a circle bearing his name. The piece is by Gutzon Borglum, who completed more than 170 public statues, including the head of Abraham Lincoln in the Capitol Rotunda, and whose final work was Mount Rushmore's presidential faces. The statue of the leader riding Rienzi (who was later renamed Winchester for Sheridan's victory there) stands in the type of circle Pierre-Charles L'Enfant envisioned in his plan for Washington—a small, formal park where avenues come together surrounded by isolated houses and buildings.

The statue of Gen. William Tecumseh Sherman at 15th Street and Treasury Place is often overlooked—in summer, the general's head is obscured by trees, and all year long he presents his back and his mount's hindquarters to pedestrians. He's positioned where he is thought to have stood while reviewing the Union troops on their victorious return from Georgia. The bar at the Hotel Washington, which affords some of the best views of the city, is also the place for a good look at Sherman.

A long-held theory says that the number of raised legs on the mount of an equestrian statue reveals how the rider died: one leg raised means the rider died of wounds sustained in battle, two legs raised means the rider died in battle, and four feet on the ground means the rider died of natural causes. Actually, though, it isn't true. Of the more than 30 equestrian statues in Washington, only about a third (including Scott, Sheridan, and Sherman, but not Jackson) are true to the "code."

—Lisa Greaves

The 36 Doric columns represent the 36 states in the Union at the time of Lincoln's death; their names appear on the frieze above the columns. Above the frieze the 48 states in the Union when the memorial was dedicated are named. (Alaska and Hawaii are represented with an inscription on the terrace that leads up to the memorial.)

Daniel Chester French's somber statue of the seated president, in the center of the memorial, gazes out over the Reflecting Pool. Although the 19-foot-high sculpture looks as if it were cut from one huge block of stone, it's actually composed of 28 interlocking pieces of Georgia marble. (The memorial's original design called for a 10-foot-high sculpture, but experiments with models revealed that a statue that size would be lost in the cavernous space.) Inscribed on the south wall is the Gettysburg Address, and on the north wall is Lincoln's second inaugural address. Above each inscription is a mural painted by Jules Guerin: on the south wall is an angel of truth freeing a slave; the unity of North and South are depicted opposite. The memorial served as a fitting backdrop for Martin Luther King Jr.'s "I Have a Dream" speech in 1963.

Many visitors look only at the front and inside of the Lincoln Memorial, but there is much more to explore. On the lower level is the Lincoln Museum, a small exhibit financed with pennies collected by schoolchildren. There's also a set of windows that overlook the huge structure's foundation. Stalactites (hanging from above) and stalagmites (rising from below) have formed underneath the marble tribute to Lincoln. ■ TIP→ Although visiting the area around the Lincoln Memorial during the day allows you to take in an impressive view of the Mall to the east, the best time to see the memorial itself is at night. Spotlights illuminate the outside, and inside light and shadows play across Lincoln's face. ⊠ *West end of Mall, The Mall* ☎ *202/426–6895* ⊕ *www.nps.gov/linc* ➢ *Free* ☉ *24 hrs; staffed daily 8 AM–midnight* Ⓜ *Foggy Bottom.*

❶ **Lockkeeper's House.** The stone Lockkeeper's House is the only remaining monument to Washington's unsuccessful experiment with a canal. The waterway's lockkeeper lived here until the 1870s, when the waterway was covered over with B Street (renamed Constitution Avenue in 1932). The house is not open to visitors. ⊠ *Constitution Ave. and 17th St., The Mall* Ⓜ *Federal Triangle.*

❷ **National World War II Memorial.** More than a decade passed between the time this memorial was authorized by Congress and its construction and 2004 dedication. During that time, the placement of the monument, which recognizes the sacrifices of men and women in combat overseas and on the home front during World War II, provoked a fair amount of controversy. Some believe the placement of the memorial interrupts the vista between the Washington Memorial and the Lincoln Memorial and heralds a future in which the Mall is cluttered with monuments. Others find the site highly appropriate.

Like that of the Vietnam Veterans Memorial before it, the design, by Frederick St. Florian, was also controversial. But unlike "the Wall," this memorial's formal, old-fashioned layout won't please those looking for new forms of architectural expression. An imposing circle of 56 granite pillars, each bearing a bronze wreath, represents the U.S. states and territories of 1941–45. Also part of the monument are four bronze eagles, a bronze garland, and two 43-foot-tall arches that surround the large circular plaza. Inside, the Field of Gold Stars commemorates the more than 400,000 Americans who lost their lives in the war. At the monument's center is the Rainbow Pool, here since the 1960s but newly renovated for the memorial. Also in the plaza are two fountains and two waterfalls. ⊠ *17th St., east of Washington Monument, The Mall* ⊕ *www.wwiimemorial.com* ☎ *Free* ⊘ *24 hrs* Ⓜ *Smithsonian.*

❄ ❸ **Tidal Basin.** This placid pond was part of the Potomac until 1882, when portions of the river were filled in to improve navigation and create additional parkland. At the **boathouse** (☎ 202/479–2426), on the northeast bank of the Tidal Basin, you can rent paddleboats during the warmer months. Rental cost is $8 per hour for a two-person boat, $16 per hour for a four-person boat. The boathouse is open from mid-March through October from 10 to 6.

Two grotesque sculpted heads on the sides of the Inlet Bridge can be seen as you walk along the sidewalk that hugs the basin. The inside walls of the bridge also sport two other interesting sculptures: bronze, human-headed fish that spout water from their mouths. The bridge was refurbished in the 1980s at the same time the chief of the park, Jack Fish, was retiring. Sculptor Constantine Sephralis played a little joke: these fish heads are actually Fish's head.

Once you cross the bridge, continue along the Tidal Basin to the right. This route is especially scenic when the cherry trees are in bloom. The first batch of these trees arrived from Japan in 1909. The trees were infected with insects and fungus, however, and the Department of Agriculture ordered them destroyed. A diplomatic crisis was averted when the United States politely asked the Japanese for another batch, and in 1912 First Lady Helen Taft planted the first tree. The second was planted by the wife of the Japanese ambassador, Viscountess Chinda. About 200 of the original trees still grow near the Tidal Basin. (These cherry trees are the single-flowering Akebeno and Yoshino variety. Double-blossom Fugenzo and Kwanzan trees grow in East Potomac Park and flower about two weeks after their more famous cousins.)

The trees are now the centerpiece of Washington's two-week Cherry Blossom Festival, held each spring since 1935. The festivities are kicked off by the lighting of a ceremonial Japanese lantern that rests on the north shore of the Tidal Basin, not far from where the first tree was planted. The once-simple celebration has grown over the years to include concerts, martial-arts demonstrations, and a parade. Park-service experts try their best to predict exactly when the buds will pop. The trees are usually in bloom for about 10–12 days in late March or early April. When winter refuses to release its grip, the parade and festival are held anyway, without the presence of blossoms, no matter how inclement the weather. And when the weather complies and the blossoms are at their peak at the time of the festivities, Washington rejoices. ⊠ *Bordered by Independence and Maine Aves., The Mall* Ⓜ *Smithsonian.*

NEED A BREAK? If you've worked up an appetite at the Tidal Basin, head four blocks down Maine Avenue to the **Maine Avenue Seafood Market,** where vendors sell fresh fish and shellfish. Seven restaurants stretch along the avenue, including local seafood powerhouse Phillips Flagship. All have terraces overlooking the Washington Channel and the motorboats, houseboats, and sailboats moored here.

8 Vietnam Veterans Memorial. Renowned for its power to evoke reflection, the Vietnam Veterans Memorial was conceived by Jan Scruggs, a former infantry corporal who had served in Vietnam. The stark design by Maya Lin, a 21-year-old architecture student at Yale, was selected in a 1981 competition. Upon its completion in 1982, the memorial was decried by some veterans as a "black gash of shame." With the addition of Frederick Hart's realistic statue of three soldiers and a flagpole south of the wall, most critics were won over.

Fodor'sChoice ★

The wall is one of the most-visited sites in Washington, its black granite panels reflecting the sky, the trees, and the faces of those looking for the names of friends or relatives who died in the war. The names of more than 58,000 Americans are etched on the face of the memorial in the order of their deaths. Consult the directories at the entrance and exit to the wall for an alphabetical listing of the names. For help in finding a name, ask a ranger at the blue-and-white hut near the entrance. Many of those visiting bring paper and crayons or charcoal to make rubbings of the names; you can also get paper and pencil from a park ranger (ask at the same blue-and-white booth). Thousands of offerings are left at the wall each year: letters, flowers, medals, uniforms, snapshots. The National Park Service collects these and stores them in a warehouse in Maryland. Some of the items are also on display at the National Museum of American History. Tents are often set up near the wall by veterans' groups; some provide information on soldiers who remain missing in action, and others are on call to help fellow vets and relatives deal with the sometimes overwhelming emotions that grip them when visiting the wall for the first time. ⊠ *Constitution Gardens, 23rd St. and Constitution Ave. NW, The Mall* ☎ *202/634-1568* ⊕ *www.nps.gov/vive* ▦ *Free* ☾ *24 hrs; staffed daily 8 AM–midnight* Ⓜ *Foggy Bottom.*

9 Vietnam Women's Memorial. After years of debate over its design and necessity, the Vietnam Women's Memorial, honoring the women who served in that conflict, was finally dedicated on Veterans Day 1993. Sculptor Glenna Goodacre's stirring bronze group depicts two uniformed women caring for a wounded male soldier while a third woman kneels nearby. The eight trees around the plaza commemorate each of the women in the military who died in Vietnam. ⊠ *Constitution Gardens, southeast of Vietnam Veterans Memorial, The Mall* ⊕ *www.nps.gov/vive/memorial/women.htm* ▦ *Free* ☾ *24 hrs; staffed daily 8 AM–midnight* Ⓜ *Foggy Bottom.*

★ ☺ ⌐ **1 Washington Monument.** At the western end of the Mall, the 555-foot, 5-inch Washington Monument punctuates the capital like a huge exclamation point. Visible from nearly everywhere in the city, it's truly a landmark.

In 1833, after years of quibbling in Congress, a private National Monument Society was formed to select a designer and to search for funds

1

to construct this monument. Robert Mills's winning design called for a 600-foot-tall decorated obelisk rising from a circular colonnaded building. The building at the base was to be an American pantheon, adorned with statues of national heroes and a massive statue of Washington riding in a chariot pulled by snorting horses.

Because of the marshy conditions of L'Enfant's original site, the position of the monument was shifted to firmer ground 100 yards southeast. (If you walk a few steps north of the monument, you can see the stone marker that denotes L'Enfant's original axis.) The cornerstone was laid in 1848 with the same Masonic trowel Washington himself had used to lay the Capitol's cornerstone 55 years earlier. The National Monument Society continued to raise funds after construction was begun, soliciting subscriptions of $1 from citizens across America. It also urged states, organizations, and foreign governments to contribute memorial stones for the construction. Problems arose in 1854, when members of the anti-Catholic Know-Nothing party stole a block donated by Pope Pius IX, smashed it, and dumped its shards into the Potomac. This action, combined with a lack of funds and the onset of the Civil War, kept the monument at a fraction of its final height, open at the top, and vulnerable to the rain. A clearly visible ring about a third of the way up the obelisk testifies to this unfortunate stage of the monument's history: although all of the marble in the obelisk came from the same Maryland quarry, the stone used for the second phase of construction came from a different stratum and is of a slightly different shade.

In 1876 Congress finally appropriated $200,000 to finish the monument, and the Army Corps of Engineers took over construction, simplifying Mills's original design. Work was finally completed in December 1884, when the monument was topped with a 7½-pound piece of aluminum, at that time one of the most expensive metals in the world. Four years later the monument was opened to visitors, who rode to the top in a steam-operated elevator. (Only men were allowed to take the 20-minute ride; it was thought too dangerous for women, who, as a result, had to walk up the stairs if they wanted to see the view.)

The view from the top takes in most of the District and parts of Maryland and Virginia. You are no longer permitted to climb the more than 800 steps leading to the top. (Incidents of vandalism and a number of heart attacks on the steps convinced the park service that letting people walk up on their own wasn't a good idea.)

■ TIP➔ **The Washington Monument uses a free timed-ticket system. A limited number of tickets are available each day at the kiosk on 15th Street, beginning a half hour before the monument opens, though in spring and summer lines are likely to start well before then.** Tickets are good during a specified half-hour period. ⊠ *Constitution Ave. and 15th St. NW, The Mall* ☎ *202/ 426–6841, 800/967–2283 for up to 6 advance tickets* ⊕ *www.nps.gov/ wamo* ▨ *Free, advance tickets require a $2 service-and-handling fee per ticket* ☉ *Daily 9–5* Ⓜ *Smithsonian.*

West Potomac Park. Between the Potomac and the Tidal Basin, West Potomac Park is best known for its flowering cherry trees, which bloom for two weeks in late March or early April. During the rest of the year, West Potomac Park is just a nice place to relax, play ball, or admire the views at the Tidal Basin.

THE WHITE HOUSE AREA

In a world full of recognizable images, few are better known than the whitewashed, 132-room mansion at 1600 Pennsylvania Avenue. The residence of perhaps the single most powerful person on the planet, the White House has an awesome majesty, having been the home of every U.S. president but George Washington. This is where the buck stops in America and where the nation turns in times of crisis. After having a look at the White House, strike out into the surrounding streets to explore the president's neighborhood, which includes some of the city's oldest houses.

TIMING Touring the area around the White House could easily take a day, depending on how long you visit each of the museums along the way. The walk itself might take half a day or longer. If you enjoy history, you may be most interested in Decatur House, the DAR Museum, and the Octagon Museum. If it's art you want, devote the hours to the Corcoran and Renwick galleries instead.

What to See

American Red Cross. The national headquarters for the American Red Cross is composed of three buildings. The primary one, a neoclassical structure of blinding-white marble built in 1917, commemorates the service and devotion of the women who cared for the wounded on both sides during the Civil War. Its Georgian-style board-of-governors hall has three stained-glass windows designed by Louis Comfort Tiffany. The building at 1730 E Street NW, dedicated to the women of World War I, houses the American Red Cross Visitor Center and has six galleries that ex-

---

TOP 5

■ **Corcoran Gallery of Art:** The great 19th-century American painters were inspired by the sublime majesty of the American West. See the most definitive works—Albert Bierstadt's *Mount Corcoran* and Frederick Church's *Niagara.*

■ **Hotel Washington's Rooftop Terrace:** The only better view in town is from the Washington Monument, but here there's a fully stocked bar. A must-do at sunset.

■ **Pershing Park:** It may not be New York's Central Park, but this charming ice rink may be Washington's best-kept secret.

■ **The Renwick Gallery:** If the White House tour doesn't satisfy your inner decorating diva, perhaps the Tiffany *objets d'art*, intricately carved antique tables and opulent Victorian Grand Salon here will do the trick.

■ **The White House:** Though you're only allowed into eight of the 132 rooms, there's no denying the thrill of touring 1600 Pennsylvania Avenue—especially around Christmas, when you'll see the already lavish rooms gilded with fabulous decorations, enormous trees, and even a miniature marzipan White House.

plain the organization's work, from what happens to the blood you donate to how the Red Cross assists the military and provides disaster relief both at home and abroad. ✉ *430 17th St. NW, White House area* ☎ *202/737–8300* ⊗ *Weekdays 8:30–4* Ⓜ *Farragut W.*

🔞 **Art Museum of the Americas.** Changing exhibits highlight 20th-century Latin American artists in this small gallery, part of the Organization of American States. There are also documentaries on South and Central American art. A public garden connects the Art Museum and the OAS building. ✉ *201 18th St. NW, White House area* ☎ *202/458–6016* ⊕ *www.museum.oas.org* ▩ *Free* ⊗ *Tues.–Sun. 10–5* Ⓜ *Farragut W.*

Blair House. A green canopy marks the entrance to Blair House, the residence used by heads of state visiting Washington. Harry S. Truman lived here from 1948 to 1952 while the White House was undergoing much-needed renovations. A plaque on the fence honors White House policeman Leslie Coffelt, who died in 1950 when Puerto Rican separatists attempted to assassinate President Truman here. The house is closed to the public. ✉ *1651 Pennsylvania Ave., White House area* Ⓜ *McPherson Sq.*

Boy Scouts Memorial. Near the Ellipse stands this statue of a uniformed Boy Scout flanked by a male figure representing Patriotism and a female figure holding the light of faith. ✉ *East of Ellipse, near 15th St. NW, White House area* Ⓜ *McPherson Sq.*

❽ **Corcoran Gallery of Art.** The beaux arts building, its copper roof green with age, was designed by Ernest Flagg and completed in 1897. (The museum's first home was in what is now the Renwick Gallery.) The gallery's permanent collection of 14,000 works includes paintings by the greatest of the early American portraitists: John Copley, Gilbert Stuart, and Rembrandt Peale. The Hudson River School is represented by works such as *Mount Corcoran* by Albert Bierstadt and Frederic Church's *Niagara.* There are also portraits by John Singer Sargent, Thomas Eakins, and Mary Cassatt. The Walker Collection shows late-19th- and early-20th-century European paintings, including works by Gustave Courbet, Claude Monet, Camille Pissarro, and Pierre-Auguste Renoir. Dutch, Flemish, and

> **CAPITAL FACTS**
>
> The Corcoran is Washington's largest nonfederal art museum, as well as its first art museum.

French Romantic paintings are on display at the Clark Collection, as is the restored 18th-century Salon Doré that was once part of the Hotel de Clermont in Paris. Be sure to see Samuel Morse's *Old House of Representatives* and Hiram Powers's *Greek Slave,* which scandalized some parts of Victorian society but was seen by thousands. (The statue, of a nude woman with her wrists chained, was considered so shocking that separate viewing hours were established for men and women; children under 16 weren't allowed to see it at all.) Photography and works by contemporary American artists are also among the Corcoran's strengths. The Corcoran College of Art and Design, housed in the museum, is the

A GOOD WALK

THE WHITE HOUSE AREA

Numbers in the box correspond to numbers in the margin and on the White House Area map.

Your first stop should be the **White House Visitor Center** ❶ ⌖ at 14th and E streets. Walk north four blocks on 15th Street, and then turn left to the **White House** ❷. Across Pennsylvania Avenue is **Lafayette Square** ❸, full of statues, trees, and flowers. Beyond the park, on H Street, is the golden-dome **St. John's Episcopal Church** ❹, the so-called Church of the Presidents. Head west on H Street to Jackson Place and the Federal-style **Decatur House** ❺, designed by Benjamin Latrobe and built in 1818 for pirate fighter Stephen Decatur. Walk down Jackson Place to Pennsylvania Avenue and turn right to the **Renwick Gallery** ❻, another member of the Smithsonian family of museums, and its neighbor Blair House, used as a residence by visiting heads of state. Go south on 17th Street past the **Eisenhower Executive Office Building** ❼, which once held the State, War, and Navy departments. At the corner of 17th Street and New York Avenue is the **Corcoran Gallery of Art** ❽, one of the few large, non-Smithsonian museums in Washington. Proceed one block west on New York Avenue to the unusually shaped **Octagon Museum** ❾, with exhibits on the architecture and history of

Washington. A block south on 18th Street is the **Department of the Interior** ❿, decorated with 1930s murals illustrating the department's work as overseer of most of the country's federally owned land and natural resources.

Walk back east on E Street to 17th Street and the three buildings of the American Red Cross, one of which has three Tiffany stained-glass windows. A block south is Memorial Continental Hall, headquarters of the Daughters of the American Revolution and the location of the **DAR Museum** ⓫, which has 33 rooms decorated in period styles. Just across C Street (to the south of Continental Hall) is the headquarters of the **Organization of American States** ⓬, in the House of the Americas. Behind the House of the Americas is the **Art Museum of the Americas** ⓭, a small gallery with works by 20th-century Latin American artists. Head east on Constitution Avenue and take the first left after 17th Street, following the curving drive that encircles the **Ellipse.** Take E Street east to 15th Street; then turn left and pass between the mammoth **William Tecumseh Sherman Monument** ⓮ on the left and **Pershing Park** ⓯ on the right. Continue north up 15th Street to the impressive **Treasury Building** ⓰.

only four-year art college in the Washington area. The **Winder Building** (✉ 604 17th St., White House area), one block north, was erected in 1848 as one of the first office blocks in the capital. It served as the headquarters of the Union Army during the Civil War. ✉ *500 17th St. NW, White House area* ☎ *202/639–1700* ⊕ *www.corcoran.org* 🎫 *$8, free Thurs. after 5* ☾ *Wed. and Fri.–Sun. 10–5, Thurs. 10–9* ☾ *Closed Mon. and Tues., except for holiday Mon.* Ⓜ *Farragut West or Farragut North.*

Art Museum of the
Americas **13**

Corcoran
Gallery of Art **8**

DAR Museum ..**11**

Decatur
House **5**

Department of
the Interior **10**

Eisenhower
Executive Office
Building **7**

Lafayette Square. .**3**

Octagon
Museum **9**

Organization
of American
States **12**

Pershing Park ...**15**

Renwick
Gallery **6**

St. John's Episcopal
Church **4**

Treasury
Building **16**

White House **2**

White House
Visitor Center **1**

William Tecumseh
Sherman
Monument **14**

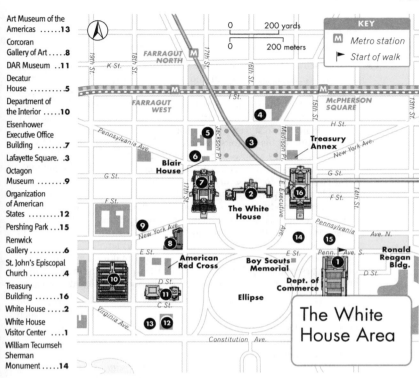

The White
House Area

**NEED A
BREAK?**

The Corcoran Gallery's **Café des Artistes** (☎ 202/639–1700) has a lunch menu of salads, light entrées, desserts, and an assortment of fruit and vegetable shakes. The café also serves continental breakfast and an English tea with scones and clotted cream and light fare on Thursday, when the museum is open late. Sunday brunch, when gospel singers perform, is very popular. The café is closed Monday and Tuesday.

🖐 ⑪ **DAR Museum.** The headquarters of the Daughters of the American Revolution, the beaux arts Memorial Continental Hall was the site of the DAR's annual congress until the larger Constitution Hall was built around the corner. An entrance on D Street leads to the museum. Its 33,000-item collection includes fine examples of colonial and Federal furniture, textiles, quilts, silver, china, porcelain, stoneware, earthenware, and glass. Thirty-three period rooms are decorated in styles representative of various U.S. states, ranging from an 1850 California adobe parlor to a New Hampshire attic filled with 18th- and 19th-century toys. Two galleries—one of them permanent—hold decorative arts. Tours are available weekdays 10–2:30 and all day on Saturday. During the "Colonial Adventure" tours, held the first and third Sunday of the month at 1:30 and 3 from September through May, costumed docents use the objects on display to teach children ages five to seven about day-to-day life in colonial America. Make reservations at least 10 days in advance. ✉ *1776 D St. NW, White House area* ☎ *202/628–1776* ⊕ *www.dar. org* 🖭 *Free* ⊗ *Weekdays 9:30–4, Sat. 9–5* Ⓜ *Farragut W.*

❺ **Decatur House.** Designed by Benjamin Latrobe, Decatur House was built for naval hero Stephen Decatur and his wife, Susan, in 1819. A redbrick Federal-style building on the corner of H Street and Jackson Place, it was the first private residence on Lafayette Square. Decatur had earned the affection of the nation in battles against the British and the Barbary pirates. Planning to start a political career, he used the money Congress awarded him for his exploits to build this home near the White House. Tragically, only 14 months after he moved in, Decatur was killed in a duel with James Barron, a disgruntled former navy officer who held Decatur responsible for his court-martial. Later occupants of the house included Henry Clay, Martin Van Buren, and the Beales, a prominent western family whose modifications of the building include a parquet floor with the state seal of California. The house, now operated by the National Trust for Historic Preservation, has a first floor furnished as it was in Decatur's time. The second floor is done in the Victorian style favored by the Beales, who owned it until 1956 (thus making Decatur House both the first and last private residence on the square). The museum shop around the corner (entrance on H Street) sells books, postcards, and gifts.

Many of the row houses along Jackson Place date from the pre–Civil War or Victorian period; even the more modern additions, though—such as those at 718 and 726—are designed to blend with their more historic neighbors. Count Rochambeau, aide to General Lafayette, is honored with a statue at Lafayette Square's southwest corner. ✉ *748 Jackson Pl. NW, White House area* ☎ *202/842–0920* ⊕ *www.decaturhouse.org* 🖭 *Free* ⊗ *Tues.–Sat. 10–5, Sun. noon–4; tours every hr at quarter past the hr* Ⓜ *Farragut W.*

❿ **Department of the Interior.** The outside of the building is somewhat plain, but inside there's art that reflects the department's work. Along the hallways are heroic oil paintings of dam construction, gold panning, and cattle drives. A guided tour takes you past more of the three-dozen murals throughout the building. ■ TIP→ **Reservations for the tour are required at least two weeks in advance.** The **Department of the Interior Museum** (☎ 202/208–4743), on the first floor, displays more art. You can enter the building at its E Street or C Street doors; adults must show photo ID. The small museum tells the story of the Department of the Interior, a huge agency dubbed "the Mother of Departments" because from it grew the departments of Agriculture, Labor, Education, and Energy. Soon after it opened in 1938, the museum became one of the most popular attractions in

> **CAPITAL FACTS**
>
> Designed by Waddy B. Wood and built in 1937, the Department of the Interior was the first large federal building with escalators and central air-conditioning.

Washington; evening hours were maintained even during World War II. The museum is open weekdays from 8:30 to 4:30; admission is free.

Today the Department of the Interior oversees most federally owned land and natural resources. Exhibits in the museum outline the work of the Bureau of Land Management, the U.S. Geological Survey, the Bureau of Indian Affairs, the National Park Service, and other department branches. The museum retains a New-Deal-era flavor that carries through to its meticulously created dioramas of historic events and American locales. Depending on your tastes, this makes the place either quaint or outdated. The Indian Craft Shop across the hall from the museum sells Native American pottery, dolls, carvings, jewelry, baskets, and books. ⊠ *C and E Sts. between 18th and 19th Sts. NW, White House area* ⊕ *www.doi.gov* ✑ *Free* Ⓜ *Farragut W.*

❼ Eisenhower Executive Office Building. Once one of the most detested buildings in the city, the Eisenhower Executive Office Building (still called the Old Executive Office Building by locals) is now one of the most beloved. It was built between 1871 and 1888 as the State, War, and Navy Building, headquarters of those three executive-branch offices. Its architect, Alfred B. Mullett, styled it after the Louvre, but detractors quickly criticized the busy French Empire design—with a mansard roof, tall chimneys, and 900 freestanding columns—as an inappropriate counterpoint to the Greek Revival Treasury Building that sits on the other side of the White House. A 1930 plan was approved by Congress to replace the exterior in a Greek Revival style, but was shelved in 1933 because of the depressed economy. The granite edifice may look like a wedding cake, but its high ceilings and spacious offices make it popular with occupants, who include members of the executive branch. Nine presidents, including both Roosevelts, Richard Nixon, and George H. W. Bush, have had offices here during their careers. The former office of the secretary of the navy is done in the opulent style of the turn of the 20th century; it has been an office for every vice president (except Hubert Humphrey) since Lyndon B. Johnson. The building has played host to numerous historic events: it was here that Secretary of State Cordell Hull met with Japanese diplomats after the bombing of Pearl Harbor, and it was the site of both the first presidential press conference in 1950 and the first televised press conference five years later. Tours here have been suspended indefinitely, and visitors are not allowed inside. ⊠ *East side of 17th St., west of White House, White House area* ☎ *202/395– 5895* Ⓜ *Farragut W.*

Ellipse. From this expanse of lawn you can see the Washington Monument and the Jefferson Memorial to the south and the red-tile roof of the Department of Commerce to the east, with the tower of the Old Post Office sticking up above it. To the north you have a good view of the rear of the White House (the Ellipse was once part of its backyard); the rounded portico and Harry Truman's second-story porch are clearly visible. The White House's south lawn, also visible, is a heliport for *Marine One,* the president's helicopter. It's on the northern edge of the Ellipse that the National Christmas Tree is put up each year. In early December the president lights it during a festive ceremony that marks the official beginning of the holiday season. On spring and summer Wednesday evenings at 7, the U.S. Army holds a Twilight Tattoo of musical marching and gun salutes here.

The Ellipse's weather-beaten **gatehouse** (at the corner of Constitution Avenue and 17th Street) once stood on Capitol Hill. It was designed in 1828 by Charles Bulfinch, the first native-born American to serve as architect of the Capitol, and was moved here in 1874 after Frederick Law Olmsted redesigned the Capitol grounds. A twin of the gatehouse stands at Constitution Avenue and 15th Street. The **Boy Scouts Memorial** is nearby. ⊠ *Bounded by Constitution Ave. and E, 15th, and 17th Sts., White House area* Ⓜ *Farragut W or McPherson Sq.*

❸ **Lafayette Square.** With such an important resident across the street, the National Capital Region's National Park Service gardeners lavish extra attention on this square's trees and flower beds. It's an intimate oasis amid downtown Washington.

When Pierre-Charles L'Enfant proposed the location for the Executive Mansion, the only building north of what is today Pennsylvania Avenue was the Pierce family farmhouse, which stood at the northeast corner of the present square. An apple orchard and a family burial ground were there as well. During the construction of the White House, workers' huts and a brick kiln were set up, and soon residences began popping up around the square (though sheep would continue to graze on it for years). Soldiers camped in the square during the War of 1812 and the Civil War, turning it both times into a muddy pit. Today, protesters set their placards up in Lafayette Square, jockeying for positions that face the White House. Although the National Park Service can't restrict the protesters' freedom of speech, it does try to limit the size of their signs.

In the center of the park is a large **statue of Andrew Jackson.** Erected in 1853 and cast from bronze cannons that Jackson captured during the War of 1812, this was the second equestrian statue made in America. (The first one, of King George III, was in New York City. Colonists melted it down for bullets during the Revolutionary War.)

Jackson's is the only statue of an American in the park. The other statues are of foreign-born soldiers who helped in America's fight for independence. In the southeast corner is the park's namesake, the **Marquis de Lafayette,** the young French nobleman who came to America to fight in the Revolution. When Lafayette returned to the United States in 1824, he was given a rousing welcome, wined and dined in the finest homes and showered with gifts of cash and land.

The colonnaded building across Madison Place at the corner of Pennsylvania Avenue is an annex to the Treasury Department. The modern redbrick building farther on, at 717 Madison Place, houses judicial offices. Its design, with squared-off bay windows, is echoed in the taller building that rises behind it and in the **New Executive Office Building** on the other side of Lafayette Square. Planners in the 1920s recommended that the private houses on Lafayette Square, many built in the Federal style, be torn down and replaced with a collection of uniform neoclassical-style government buildings. A lack of funds kept the neighborhood intact, and demolition was not even scheduled until 1957. In the early '60s Jacqueline Kennedy intervened and asked that the historic town houses and residential character be saved. A new plan devised by John Carl Warnecke set the large office buildings behind the historic row houses.

The next house down, yellow with a second-story ironwork balcony, was built in 1828 by Benjamin Ogle Tayloe. During the McKinley administration, Ohio senator Marcus Hanna lived here, and the president's frequent visits earned it the nickname the "Little White House." Dolley Madison lived in the Cutts-Madison House, next door, after her husband died. Both the Tayloe and Madison houses are now part of the U.S. Court of Claims complex.

A bit farther north on Madison Place is a statue of **Thaddeus Kosciuszko**, the Polish general who fought alongside American colonists against the British. ⊠ *Bounded by Pennsylvania Ave., Madison Pl., H St., and Jackson Pl., White House area* Ⓜ *McPherson Sq.*

NEED A BREAK?

Bernard Baruch, adviser to Woodrow Wilson and other presidents, used to eat his lunch in Lafayette Park; you can, too. Nearby, **Loeb's Restaurant** (⊠ 15th and I Sts. NW, White House area ☎ 202/371-1150) is a New York–style deli that serves salads and sandwiches to eat there or to go.

❾ **Octagon Museum.** Why this six-sided building is named the Octagon remains a subject of debate. Some say it's because the main room is a circle, and was built by rounding out the angles of an eight-sided room; others say it's for the eight angles formed by the odd shape of the six walls—an old definition of an octagon. Designed by Dr. William Thornton (the Capitol's architect), it was built for John Tayloe III, a wealthy Virginia plantation owner, and was completed in 1801. Thornton chose the unusual shape to conform to the acute angle formed by L'Enfant's intersection of New York Avenue and 18th Street.

After the White House was burned in 1814, the Tayloes invited James and Dolley Madison to stay in the Octagon. It was in a second-floor study that the Treaty of Ghent, which ended the War of 1812, was ratified. By the late 1800s the building was used as a rooming house. In the 20th century the house served as the headquarters of the American Institute of Architects before the construction of the AIA's rather unexceptional building behind it. It's now the Museum of the American Architectural Foundation.

A renovation in the 1960s revealed the intricate plaster molding and the original 1799 Coade stone mantels (named for the woman who invented a now-lost method of casting crushed stone). A far more thorough restoration, completed in 1996, returned the Octagon to its 1815 appearance, topped off by a historically accurate, cypress-shingle roof with balustrade. The galleries have changing exhibits on architecture, city planning, and Washington history and design. ⊠ *1799 New York Ave. NW, White House area* ☎ *202/638–3105* ⊕ *www.archfoundation. org* ⊠ *$5* ☉ *Tues.–Sun. 10–4* Ⓜ *Farragut W or Farragut N.*

⑫ **Organization of American States.** The headquarters of the Organization of American States, which is made up of nations from North, South, and Central America, contains a patio adorned with a pre-Columbian–style fountain and lush tropical plants. ■ TIP→ **This tiny rain forest is a good place to rest when Washington's summer heat is at its most oppressive.** The upstairs Hall of the Americas contains busts of generals and statesmen from the 34 OAS member nations, as well as each country's flag. The OAS runs the Art Museum of the Americas. ⊠ *17th St. and Constitution Ave. NW, White House area* ☎ *202/458–3000* ⊕ *www.oas.org* ⌘ *Free* ☉ *Weekdays 9–5:30* Ⓜ *Farragut W.*

⓯ Pershing Park. A quiet, sunken garden honors General John J. "Black Jack" Pershing, the first to hold the title General of the Armies, a rank Congress created in 1919 to recognize his military achievements. Engravings on the stone walls recount pivotal campaigns from World War I, where Pershing commanded the American expeditionary force and conducted other military exploits. Ice-skaters glide on the square pool here in winter. ⊠ *15th St. and Pennsylvania Ave., White House area* Ⓜ *McPherson Sq.*

NEED A BREAK? One block north of Pershing Park is the venerable **Hotel Washington** (⊠ 515 15th St. NW, White House area ☎ 202/638–5900 ⊕ www.hotelwashington.com), where the view from the Rooftop Terrace is one of the best in the city. From May to October, you can sit outside. (During cooler months, an extension shields you from the elements.) Drinks, coffee, and a light menu are available.

❻ Renwick Gallery. The Renwick Gallery of the Smithsonian American Art Museum has exquisitely made utilitarian items, as well as crafts made from traditional materials such as fiber and glass. The words DEDICATED TO ART are engraved above the entrance to the French Second Empire–style building, designed by architect James Renwick in 1859 to house the art collection of Washington merchant and banker William Wilson Corcoran. Corcoran was a Southern sympathizer who spent the duration of the Civil War in Europe. While he was away, the government used his unfinished building as a quartermaster general's post.

In 1871 the Corcoran, as it was then called, opened as the first private art museum in the city. Corcoran's collection quickly outgrew the building, and in 1897 it was moved to what's now the Corcoran Gallery of Art. After a stint as the U.S. Court of Claims, the building Renwick designed was restored, renamed after its architect, and opened in 1972 as the Smithsonian's Museum of American Crafts. Although crafts such as handwoven rugs and delicately carved tables were once considered less "artistic" than, say, oil paintings and sculptures, they have come into their own. Not everything in the museum is Shaker furniture and enamel jewelry, though. The second-floor Grand Salon is still furnished in the opulent Victorian style Corcoran favored when his collection adorned its walls. ⊠ *Pennsylvania Ave. at 17th St. NW, White House area* ☎ *202/633–2850, 202/357–1729 TDD* ⊕ *www.americanart.si.edu* ⌘ *Free* ☉ *Daily 10–5:30* Ⓜ *Farragut W.*

❹ St. John's Episcopal Church. The golden-dome so-called Church of the Presidents sits across Lafayette Park from the White House. Every president since Madison has visited the church, and many have worshipped here regularly. Built in 1816, the church was the second building on the square.

Benjamin Latrobe, who worked on both the Capitol and the White House, designed it in the form of a Greek cross, with a flat dome and a lantern cupola. The church has been altered somewhat since then; additions include the Doric portico and the cupola tower. You can best sense the intent of Latrobe's design while standing under the saucer-shape dome of the original building. Not far from the center of the church is Pew 54, where visiting presidents are seated. The kneeling benches of many pews are embroidered with the presidential seal and the names of several chief executives. Brochures are available inside for self-guided tours. ⊠ *16th and H Sts. NW, White House area* ☎ *202/347–8766* 🖃 *Free* ⊙ *Weekdays 9–3, guided tours by appointment* Ⓜ *McPherson Sq.*

⓰ **Treasury Building.** Once used to store currency, this is the largest Greek Revival edifice in Washington. Robert Mills, the architect responsible for the Washington Monument and the Patent Office (now the Smithsonian American Art Museum), designed the grand colonnade that stretches down 15th Street. Construction of the Treasury Building started in 1836 and, after several additions, was finally completed in 1869. Its southern facade has a **statue of Alexander Hamilton,** the department's first secretary. After the death of President Lincoln, the Andrew Johnson Suite was used as the executive office by the new president while Mrs. Lincoln moved out of the White House. Other vestiges of its earlier days are the two-story marble Cash Room and a 19th-century burglarproof vault lining. Tours have been suspended indefinitely; call ahead if you're planning a visit. ⊠ *15th St. and Pennsylvania Ave. NW, White House area* ☎ *202/622–0896, 202/622–0692 TDD* Ⓜ *McPherson Sq. or Metro Center.*

NEED A BREAK? The **Benkay** (⊠ 727 15th St. NW, lower level, White House area ☎ 202/737–1515) restaurant has a budget-price lunchtime sushi buffet and an after-dinner karaoke scene. The luxurious **Old Ebbitt Grill** (⊠ 675 15th St. NW, White House area ☎ 202/347–4800), a longtime Washington institution, is still a popular watering hole for journalists and TV news correspondents. About a block from the Treasury Building is a popular urban mall, the **Shops** (⊠ National Press Bldg., F and G Sts. between 13th and 14th Sts. NW, White House area), which has 10 full-service restaurants in its food court.

★ ☾ ➋ **White House.** This is surely the best-known address in the United States: 1600 Pennsylvania Avenue. Pierre-Charles L'Enfant called it the President's House; it was known formally as the Executive Mansion; and in 1902 Congress officially proclaimed it the White House after long-standing common usage of that name. Irishman James Hoban's plan, based on the Georgian design of Leinster Hall in Dublin and of other Irish country houses, was selected in a 1792 contest. The building has undergone many structural changes since then. Andrew Jackson installed running water. James Garfield put in the first elevator. Between 1948 and 1952, Harry Truman had the entire structure gutted and restored, adding a second-story porch to the south portico. Each family that has called the White House home has left its imprint on the 132-room mansion.

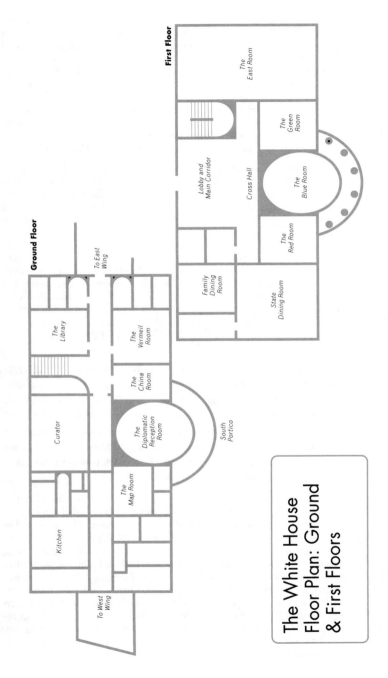

Ground Floor

To East Wing

The Library

Curator

Kitchen

The Map Room

The China Room

The Vermeil Room

The Diplomatic Reception Room

South Portico

To West Wing

First Floor

The East Room

Lobby and Main Corridor

Cross Hall

The Green Room

The Blue Room

The Red Room

Family Dining Room

State Dining Room

The White House
Floor Plan: Ground
& First Floors

1

■ TIP→ **The White House is open to visitors, but you'll need to do some serious advance planning: visitors wishing to tour the White House must make arrangements at least three months in advance through the office of their member of Congress. Non-U.S. citizens must make arrangements through their embassy.** The self-guided tour includes several rooms on the ground floor and, on the State Floor, the large white-and-gold **East Room,** the site of presidential social events. In 1814 Dolley Madison saved the room's full-length portrait of George Washington from torch-carrying British soldiers by cutting it from its frame, rolling it up, and spiriting it out of the White House. (Dolley also rescued her own portrait.) One of Abraham Lincoln's sons once harnessed a pet goat to a chair and went for a ride through the East Room during a reception.

The Federal-style **Green Room,** named for the moss-green watered silk that covers its walls, is used for informal receptions and "photo opportunities" with foreign heads of state. Notable furnishings here include a New England sofa that once belonged to Daniel Webster and portraits of Benjamin Franklin, John Quincy Adams, and Abigail Adams. The president and his guests are often shown on TV sitting in front of the Green Room's English Empire mantel, engaging in what are generally described as "frank and cordial" discussions.

The elliptical **Blue Room,** the most formal space in the White House, is furnished with a gilded Empire-style settee and chairs that were ordered by James Monroe. (Monroe asked for plain wooden chairs, but the furniture manufacturer thought such unadorned furnishings too simple for the White House and took it upon himself to supply chairs more in keeping with their surroundings.) The White House Christmas tree is placed in this room each year. (Another well-known elliptical room, the president's **Oval Office,** is in the West Wing of the White House, along with other executive offices.)

The **Red Room** is decorated in early 19th century American Empire style, with furniture by the New York cabinetmaker Charles-Honoré Lannuier. The mantel is the twin of the one in the Green Room.

The **State Dining Room,** second in size only to the East Room, can seat 140 people. It's dominated by G. P. A. Healy's portrait of Abraham Lincoln, painted after the president's death. The mantel is inscribed with a quote from one of John Adams's letters: "I pray heaven to bestow the best of blessings on this house and all that shall hereafter inhabit it. May none but honest and wise men ever rule under

> **CAPITAL FACTS**
>
> The White House wasn't ready for its first occupant, John Adams, the second U.S. president, until 1800: George Washington, who seems to have slept everywhere else, never stayed here.

this roof." In Teddy Roosevelt's day a stuffed moose head hung over the mantel. ⊠ *1600 Pennsylvania Ave. NW, Downtown* ☎ *202/208–1631, 202/456–7041 24-hr information line* ⊕ *www.whitehouse.gov* Ⓜ *Federal Triangle.*

▶ **❶** **White House Visitor Center.** Since White House tours are self-guided, it's a good idea to come here before doing the tour, so you can first get some context by looking at the display of photographs, artifacts, and videos that relate to the White House's construction, decor, and residents. ✉ *Entrance: Department of Commerce's Baldrige Hall, E St. between 14th and 15th Sts., White House area* ☍ *1450 Pennsylvania Ave. NW* ☏ *202/208–1631, 202/456–7041 24-hr information line* ⊕ *www.nps. gov/whho/WHVC* ☜ *Free* ☾ *Daily 7:30–4* Ⓜ *Federal Triangle.*

⓮ **William Tecumseh Sherman Monument.** Sherman, whose Atlanta Campaign in 1864 cut a bloody swath of destruction through the Confederacy, was said to be the greatest Civil War general, as the sheer size of this massive monument would seem to attest. Mounted on his steed, the general is surrounded by four sentries who keep watch, seemingly over the adjacent Treasury Department building. The names of landmark battles on his famous march to the sea are inscribed around the sides of the monument base. ✉ *Bounded by E and 15th Sts., East Executive Ave., and Alexander Hamilton Pl., White House area* Ⓜ *Federal Triangle.*

CAPITOL HILL

The people who live and work on "the Hill" do so in the shadow of the edifice that lends the neighborhood its name: the gleaming white Capitol. More than just the center of government, however, the Hill also includes charming residential blocks lined with Victorian row houses and a fine assortment of restaurants, bars, and shops.

Capitol Hill's exact boundaries are disputed: however, most say it's bordered to the west, north, and south by the Capitol, H Street NE, and I Street SE, respectively. Some argue that Capitol Hill extends east to the Anacostia River; others say that it ends at 14th Street near Lincoln Park. The neighborhood does, in fact, seem to be extending its boundaries as urban pioneers and members of Capitol Hill's active historic-preservation movement restore more and more 19th-century houses.

The Capitol serves as the point from which the city is divided into quadrants: northwest, southwest, northeast, and southeast. North Capitol Street, which runs north from the Capitol, separates northeast from northwest; East Capitol Street separates northeast and southeast; South Capitol Street separates southwest and southeast; and the Mall (Independence Avenue on the south and Constitution Avenue on the north) separates northwest from southwest.

TIMING Touring Capitol Hill should take you about four hours, allowing for about an hour each at the Capitol, the Botanic Garden, and the Library of Congress. ■ TIP→ **If you want to see Congress in action, bear in mind that the House and Senate are usually not in session during August.** Supreme Court cases are usually heard October through April, Monday through Wednesday of two weeks in each month. The side trip to the two sites near Catholic University, the Pope John Paul II Cultural Center and the National Shrine of the Immaculate Conception, will take about half a day. The side trip to the navy and marine sites also takes about four hours.

What to See

🔟 **Bartholdi Fountain.** Frédéric-Auguste Bartholdi, sculptor of the Statue of Liberty, created this delightful fountain, some 30 feet tall, for the Philadelphia International Exposition of 1876. The aquatic monsters, sea nymphs, tritons, and lighted globes all represent the elements of water and light. The U.S. government bought the fountain after the exposition and placed it on the grounds of the old Botanic Garden on the Mall. It was moved to its present location in 1932 and was restored in 1986. The surrounding Bartholdi Park, which has benches and dense plantings, fills with brown-baggers at lunchtime. ⊠ *1st St. and Independence Ave. SW, The Mall* Ⓜ *Federal Center.*

☁️ 5️⃣ **Capitol.** Before heading to the Capitol, pay a little attention to the grounds, landscaped in the late 19th century by Frederick Law Olmsted, a cocreator of New York City's Central Park. On these 68 acres are both the city's tamest squirrels and the highest concentration of TV news correspondents, jockeying for a good position in front of the Capitol for their "stand-ups." A few hundred feet northeast of the Capitol are two cast-iron car shelters, left from the days when horse-drawn trolleys served the Hill. Olmsted's six pinkish, bronze-top lamps directly east from the Capitol are worth a look, too.

Fodor'sChoice ★

TOP 5: CAPITOL HILL

■ **The Capitol:** See democracy in action. Watch congressmen and women debate, insult, and wrangle their way through the job of making laws in the Capitol's House and Senate chambers.

■ **Folger Shakespeare Library:** You'd think it was in London or Stratford-on-Avon, but the world's foremost Shakespeare collection is right here on Capitol Hill. Pay homage to the treasured First Folio of the Bard's plays, along with other world-class exhibits.

■ **The Hawk and Dove:** Listen in on power players' partisan arguments and locals' debates on the Redskins (and the other way around), over pints at this quintessential DC bar and Capitol Hill institution.

■ **The Library of Congress:** Take a break from debate to gaze at the Gutenberg Bible, the lavishly sculpted Great Hall, and the oft-featured-on-film splendor of the gilded Main Reading Room.

■ **Supreme Court Building:** Round out your firsthand look at the three branches of government by watching the Supreme Court justices hear precedent-setting arguments at the highest court in the land.

The design of the building itself was the result of a competition held in 1792; the winner was William Thornton, a physician and amateur architect from the West Indies. With its central rotunda and dome, Thornton's Capitol is reminiscent of Rome's Pantheon. This similarity must have delighted the nation's founders, who sought inspiration from the principles of the Republic of Rome.

The cornerstone was laid by George Washington in a Masonic ceremony on September 18, 1793, and in November 1800, both the Senate and the House of Representatives moved down from Philadelphia to occupy

Bartholdi
Fountain **10**

Capitol **5**

Folger
Shakespeare
Library **16**

Frederick
Douglass
Townhouse . . .**14**

Grant
Memorial **7**

James Garfield
Memorial **8**

Library of
Congress
Jefferson
Building **11**

National Postal
Museum **2**

Peace
Monument **6**

Robert A. Taft
Memorial **4**

Sewall-
Belmont
House **13**

South Side of
East Capitol
Street **15**

Supreme
Court
Building **12**

Thurgood
Marshall
Federal
Judiciary
Building **3**

Union
Station **1**

United States
Botanic
Garden **9**

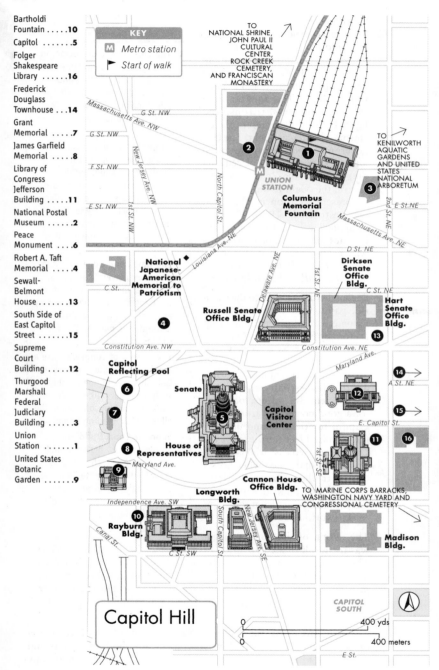

Capitol Hill

A GOOD WALK

CAPITOL HILL
Numbers in the box correspond to numbers in the margin and on the Capitol Hill map.

Start your exploration of the Hill at the beautifully restored **Union Station ①** ⌐. You can take a side trip to the Pope John Paul II Cultural Center and the National Shrine of the Immaculate Conception by taking the Metro from Union Station to Brookland–Catholic University. If you're not making the diversion, head to the **National Postal Museum ②**, across the street from the arcade to the right of the main Union Station exit. Just east of the station is the **Thurgood Marshall Federal Judiciary Building ③**, with a spectacular atrium. Follow Delaware Avenue from the Columbus fountain directly in front of Union Station. On the left you pass the Russell Senate Office Building (1st Street and Constitution Avenue NE). To the right, a block west on Constitution Avenue, is the **Robert A. Taft Memorial ④**. Behind it, on the triangle formed by New Jersey and Louisiana avenues and D Street NW, is the **National Japanese American Memorial to Patriotism**; it honors the Japanese-American soldiers who fought in World War II and also list the 10 internment camps where 120,000 Japanese-Americans were held from 1942 to 1945. Heading southward again, cross Constitution Avenue to the **Capitol ⑤**. Walk down Capitol Hill and out the westernmost exit to the white-marble **Peace Monument ⑥**. Walking south on 1st Street NW, you pass the Capitol Reflecting Pool, the **Grant Memorial ⑦**, and the **James Garfield Memorial ⑧**. Across

Maryland Avenue is the **United States Botanic Garden ⑨**, an indoor museum of orchids, cacti, and other flora. The ornate **Bartholdi Fountain ⑩** is in a park across Independence Avenue. Continue east on Independence Avenue, walking back up Capitol Hill past the Rayburn, Longworth, and Cannon House office buildings, to the Jefferson Building of the **Library of Congress ⑪**.

Continue on 1st Street NE to the **Supreme Court Building ⑫**, near East Capitol Street. One block north, at the corner of Constitution Avenue and 2nd Street, is the redbrick **Sewall-Belmont House ⑬**, dating from 1800. For a taste of the residential side of the Hill, follow Maryland Avenue to Stanton Park; then walk two blocks south on 4th Street NE to A Street NE. The **Frederick Douglass Townhouse ⑭** is between 3rd and 4th streets. The houses on the **south side of East Capitol Street ⑮** are a sampling of the different architectural styles on the Hill. At the corner of 3rd and East Capitol streets stands the **Folger Shakespeare Library ⑯**, the world's foremost collection of works by and about the playwright.

If you'd like to make a side trip to visit the Navy and Marine Corps sites on Capitol Hill, head east on East Capitol Street to 8th Street SE and take the bus south to I Street SE, in front of the **Marine Corps Barracks.** Walk under the highway overpass to the **Washington Navy Yard** complex, enter from the gate at 9th and M streets SE, and follow signs for the Navy Art Museum, Navy Art Gallery, Marine Corps Historical Center, and the USS *Barry.*

Ceremonial
Office of
the Vice
President 3

Congresswomen's
Suite 13

Democratic
Cloakrooms 6

House
Chamber 17

House
Document
Room 14

House
Reception
Room 16

Marble Room
(Senators'
Retiring
Room) 2

Old Senate
Chamber 9

Prayer Room .. 11

President's
Room 1

Representatives'
Retiring
Rooms 18

Republican
Cloakrooms 7

Rotunda 10

Senate
Chamber 5

Senators'
Conference
Room 8

Senators'
Reception
Room 4

Statuary Hall .15

West Front ... 12

United States Capitol: Second-Floor Plan

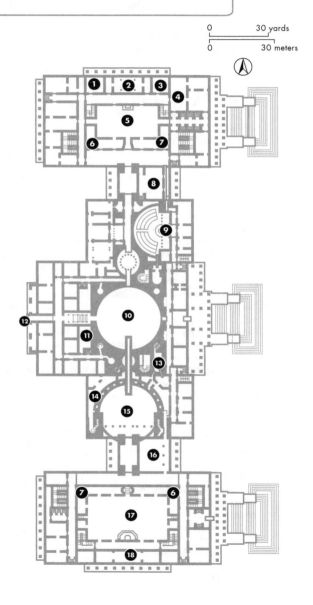

0   30 yards

0   30 meters

the first completed section: the boxlike portion between the central rotunda and today's north wing. (Subsequent efforts to find the cornerstone Washington laid have been unsuccessful, though when the east front was extended in the 1950s, workers found a knee joint thought to be from a 500-pound ox that was roasted at the 1793 celebration.) By 1807 the House wing had been completed, just to the south of what's now the domed center, and a covered wooden walkway joined the two wings.

The "Congress House" grew slowly and suffered a grave setback on August 24, 1814, when British troops led by Sir George Cockburn marched on Washington and set fire to the Capitol, the White House, and numerous other government buildings. (Cockburn reportedly stood on the House Speaker's chair and asked his men, "Shall this harbor of Yankee democracy be burned?" The question was rhetorical; the building was torched.) The wooden walkway was destroyed and the two wings gutted, but the walls were left standing after a violent rainstorm doused the flames. Fearful that Congress might leave Washington, residents raised money for a hastily built "Brick Capitol" that stood where the Supreme Court is today. Architect Benjamin Henry Latrobe supervised the rebuilding, adding American touches such as the corncob-and-tobacco-leaf capitals to columns in the east entrance of the Senate wing. He was followed by Boston-born Charles Bulfinch, and in 1826 the Capitol, its low wooden dome sheathed in copper, was finished.

North and south wings were added in the 1850s and 1860s to accommodate a growing government trying to keep pace with a growing country. The elongated edifice extended farther north and south than Thornton had planned, and in 1855, to keep the scale correct, work began on a taller, cast-iron dome. President Lincoln was criticized for continuing this expensive project while the country was in the throes of the Civil War, but he called the construction "a sign we intend the Union shall go on." This twin-shell dome, a marvel of 19th-century engineering, rises 285 feet above the ground and weighs 4,500 tons. It expands and contracts up to 4 inches a day, depending on the outside temperature. The allegorical figure atop the dome, often mistaken for Pocahontas, is called *Freedom*. Sculptor Thomas Crawford had first planned for the 19½-foot-tall bronze statue to wear the cloth liberty cap of a freed Roman slave, but Southern lawmakers, led by Jefferson Davis, objected. An "American" headdress composed of a star-encircled helmet surmounted with an eagle's head and feathers was substituted. A light just below the statue burns whenever Congress is in session.

The Capitol has continued to grow. In 1962 the east front was extended 33½ feet, creating 100 additional offices. Preservationists have fought to keep the west front from being extended, because it's the last remaining section of the Capitol's original facade. A compromise was reached in 1983, when it was agreed that the facade's crumbling sandstone blocks would simply be replaced with stronger limestone.

Tours start under the center of the **Rotunda's** dome. At the dome's center is Constantino Brumidi's 1865 fresco, *Apotheosis of Washington*. The figures in the inner circle represent the 13 original states; those in the outer ring symbolize arts, sciences, and industry. The flat, sculpture-style frieze around the Rotunda's rim depicts 400 years of American history and was started by Brumidi in 1877. While painting Penn's treaty with the Indians, the 74-year-old artist slipped on the 58-foot-high scaffold and almost fell off. Brumidi managed to hang on until help arrived, but he died a few months later from the shock of the incident. The work was continued by another Italian, Filippo Costaggini, but the frieze wasn't finished until American Allyn Cox added the final touches in 1953.

The Rotunda's eight immense oil paintings are of scenes from American history. The four scenes from the Revolutionary War are by John Trumbull, who served alongside George Washington and painted the first president from life. Thirty people have lain in state or in honor in the Rotunda, including ten presidents, from Abraham Lincoln to Ronald Reagan. The most recently honored was Civil Rights activist Rosa Parks, who in 2005 became the first woman to lie in honor.

South of the Rotunda is **Statuary Hall,** once the legislative chamber of the House of Representatives. The room has an architectural quirk that maddened early legislators: a slight whisper uttered on one side of the hall can be heard on the other. (This parlor trick doesn't always work; sometimes the hall is just too noisy.) When the House moved out, Congress invited each state to send statues of two great deceased residents for placement in the former chamber. Because the weight of the accumulated statues threatened to make the floor cave in, some of the sculptures were dispersed to other spots in the Capitol.

To the north, on the Senate side, is the chamber once used by the Supreme Court and, above it, the splendid Old Senate Chamber (closed until further notice), both of which have been restored. In the Brumidi Corridor (also closed until further notice), on the ground floor of the Senate wing, frescoes and oil paintings of birds, plants, and American inventions adorn the walls and ceilings. Intricate, Brumidi-designed bronze stairways lead to the second floor. The Italian artist also memorialized several American heroes, painting them inside trompe l'oeil frames. Some frames were left blank. The most recent one to be filled, in 1987, honors the crew of the space shuttle *Challenger.*

The **Capitol Visitor Center,** a $550-million subterranean education and information area beneath the east side of the building, is tentatively scheduled to open in mid-2007. However, visitors should be advised that the football stadium-size project has been plagued by delays and has already pushed forward its opening three times. When it does finally open, plans call for an expansive dining area, gift shops, two movie theaters, an interactive museum, and several new high-end facilities for members of Congress. Tours will run from this site Monday through Saturday from 9:30 AM to 4:30 PM. Until then, free, timed-entry tickets will continue to be distributed, one per person, on a first-come, first-served basis, at the Capitol Guide Service kiosk located along the curving sidewalk southwest of the Capitol (near the intersection of 1st Street, SW, and Independence Avenue). Tickets are distributed starting at 9 AM. Free gallery passes to watch the House or Senate in session can be obtained only from your senator's or representative's office; both chambers are closed to the public when Congress is not in session. ■ TIP➔ Note that there's a strict limit on the baggage and possessions that can be brought into the building: there are no facilities for checking personal belongings. If you're planning a visit, call ahead to check the status of tours and access; security measures may change. ✉ *East end of Mall, Capitol Hill* ☎ *202/224–3121 Capitol switchboard, 202/225–6827 guide service* ⊕ *www.aoc. gov* ⊠ *Free* Ⓜ *Capitol S or Union Station.*

Congressional Cemetery. Established in 1807 "for all denomination of people," this cemetery was the first national cemetery created by the government. Notables buried here include U.S. Capitol architect William Thornton, Marine Corps march composer John Philip Sousa, Civil War photographer Mathew Brady, and FBI director J. Edgar Hoover. There are also 76 members of Congress, many of them beneath ponderous markers. A brochure for a self-guided walking tour is available at the office and in a mailbox near the main gate. ✉ *1801 E St. SE, Capitol Hill* ☎ *202/543–0539* ⊕ *www.congressionalcemetery.org* ☾ *Daily dawn–dusk; office Mon.–Wed. and Fri.* Ⓜ *Stadium Armory or Potomac Ave.*

★ ⑯ **Folger Shakespeare Library.** The Folger Library's collection of works by and about Shakespeare and his times is second to none. The white-marble art deco building, designed by architect Paul Philippe Cret and dedicated in 1932, is decorated with scenes from the Bard's plays. Inside is a reproduction of a 16th-century inn-yard theater—the site for performances of chamber music, baroque opera, and Shakespearean plays—and a gallery, designed in the manner of an Elizabethan Great Hall, which holds rotating exhibits from the library's collection. Henry Clay Folger, the library's founder, was Standard Oil's president and chairman of the board. ✉ *201 E. Capitol St. SE, Capitol Hill* ☎ *202/544–4600* ⊕ *www. folger.edu* ⊠ *Free* ☾ *Mon.–Sat. 10–4* Ⓜ *Capitol S.*

OFF THE BEATEN PATH

FRANCISCAN MONASTERY AND GARDENS – Not far from the National Shrine of the Immaculate Conception, this Byzantine-style Franciscan monastery contains facsimiles of Holy Land shrines such as the Grotto of Bethlehem and the Holy Sepulchre. Underground are reproductions of the catacombs of Rome. The rose gardens are especially beautiful. Take the Metro here from Union Station. The monastery and shrine are about the same distance from the Metro, but in opposite directions. ✉ *14th and Quincy Sts. NE, Catholic University* ☎ *202/526–6800* ⊕ *www.myfranciscan.org* ⊠ *Free* ☾ *Daily 9–5, catacombs tours on the hr, except noon; Mon.–Sat. 9–4, Sun. 1–4; last tour at 3* Ⓜ *Brookland/ Catholic University.*

⓮ **Frederick Douglass Townhouse.** In the first Washington home of the fiery abolitionist and writer are two restored rooms with Douglass memorabilia. The rest of the house is the Caring Institute, a nonprofit service organization inspired by the life and works of Mother Teresa. ✉ *316–320 A St. NE, Capitol Hill* ☎ *202/547–4273* ⊠ *Free* ☾ *By appointment only.*

❼ **Grant Memorial.** The 252-foot-long memorial to the 18th American president and commander in chief of the Union forces during the Civil War is one of the largest sculpture groups in the city. The pedestal statue of Ulysses S. Grant on horseback displays his composure in the face of chaos. The soldiers and horses are notable for their realism; sculptor Henry Shrady spent 20 years researching and completing the memorial. ☒ *Near 1st St. and Maryland Ave. SW, Capitol Hill* Ⓜ *Federal Center.*

❽ James Garfield Memorial. Near the United States Botanic Garden is a memorial to the 20th president of the United States. James Garfield was assassinated in 1881 after only a few months in office. His bronze statue stands on a pedestal with three other bronze figures seated around it; one bears a tablet inscribed with the words LAW, JUSTICE, AND PROSPERITY. ☒ *1st St. and Maryland Ave. SW, Capitol Hill* Ⓜ *Federal Center.*

OFF THE
BEATEN
PATH

KENILWORTH AQUATIC GARDENS – Exotic water lilies, lotuses, hyacinths, and other water-loving plants thrive in this 14-acre sanctuary of quiet ponds and marshy flats. The gardens' wetland animals include turtles, frogs, beavers, spring azure butterflies, and some 40 species of birds. ■ TIP➔ **In July nearly everything blossoms; early morning is the best time to visit, when day-bloomers are just opening and night-bloomers have yet to close.** The nearest Metro stop is a 15-minute walk away. ☒ *Anacostia Ave. and Douglas St. NE, Anacostia* ☎ *202/426–6905* ⊕ *www.nps.gov/nace/keaq* ⊠ *Free* ⊙ *Gardens and visitor center, daily 7–4; garden tours daily at 9, 10, and 11* Ⓜ *Deanwood.*

★ ⓫ Library of Congress. The largest library in the world has more than 130 million items on approximately 530 mi of bookshelves. Only 29 million of its holdings are books—the library also has 2.7 million recordings, 12 million photographs, 4.8 million maps, and 58 million manuscripts. Also here is the Congressional Research Service, which, as the name implies, works on special projects for senators and representatives.

Built in 1897, the copper-dome Thomas Jefferson Building is the oldest of the three buildings that make up the library. Like many other structures in Washington, the library was criticized when it was completed. Detractors thought its design, based on the Paris Opera House, was too florid. Congressmen were even heard to grumble that its dome—topped with the gilt "Flame of Knowledge"—competed with that of their Capitol. It's certainly decorative, with busts of Dante, Goethe, Nathaniel Hawthorne, and other great writers perched above its entryway. The *Court of Neptune,* Roland Hinton Perry's fountain at the base of the front steps, rivals some of Rome's best fountains.

Provisions for a library to serve members of Congress were originally made in 1800, when the government set aside $5,000 to purchase books that legislators might need to consult. This small collection was housed in the Capitol but was destroyed in 1814, when the British burned the

L'Enfant, the City's Architect

1

THE LIFE OF Pierre-Charles L'Enfant, architect of the city of Washington, has all the elements of a television miniseries: handsome, idealistic, 22-year-old Parisian volunteer in the American war for independence rises to rank of major of engineers; becomes popular with fellow officers (and their wives); becomes toast-of-the-town architect in New York City; is selected by President George Washington to plan the new Federal City; gets fired amid controversy; dies bitter and broke; is vindicated posthumously.

L'Enfant was educated as an architect and engineer in France. At least two of his teachers profoundly influenced his career and, ultimately, his plan for Washington. He learned painting from his father, who was a battle-scene and landscape painter, and he studied landscape architecture with André LeNotre, who designed the gardens at Versailles. After Congress voted in 1785 to create a permanent Federal City, L'Enfant enthusiastically wrote to George Washington in 1789 with an offer to create a capital "magnificent enough to grace a great nation." He got the job, and arrived in Washington in 1791 to survey the land with black mathematician Benjamin Banneker.

L'Enfant's 1791 plan borrowed much from Versailles, with ceremonial circles and squares, a grid pattern of streets, and broad, diagonal avenues. He described Jenkins Hill, the gentle rise on which he intended to erect the "Congress House," as "a pedestal waiting for a monument." He envisioned the area west of the Congress House as a "Grand Avenue, 400 feet in breadth, and about a mile in length, bordered with gardens, ending in a slope from the houses on each side." (This is the area we now know as the Mall.)

Pennsylvania Avenue was to be a broad, grand, uninterrupted straight line running from the Capitol to the site chosen for the Executive Mansion. (The construction of the Treasury Building in 1836 ruined this straight sight line.) The area just north of the White House was to be part of "President's Park" (it was basically the president's front yard). But in yet another change to L'Enfant's plans, Thomas Jefferson, concerned that large, landscaped White House grounds weren't befitting a democratic country, ordered that the area be turned into a public park (now Lafayette Park).

Though skillful at city planning, the headstrong L'Enfant had trouble with the game of politics. Things went slightly awry early on when L'Enfant had difficulty with the engravers of the city plan, they got worse when he expressed his resentment at dealing with Secretary of State Thomas Jefferson rather than the president, and they hit rock bottom when he enraged the city commissioners by tearing down a manor house being constructed where he had planned a street. The house belonged to Daniel Carroll—one of the commissioners. Only 11 months after his hire, L'Enfant was let go by Jefferson. L'Enfant continued to work as an architect, but when he died in 1825, he felt he hadn't been recognized for his genius. His contributions to the city were finally recognized when, in 1909, amid much ceremony, his body was moved from his original burial site in Maryland to Arlington Cemetery at the request of the Washington, D.C., board of commissioners.

city. Thomas Jefferson, then in retirement at Monticello, offered his personal library as a replacement, noting that "there is, in fact, no subject to which a Member of Congress may not have occasion to refer." Jefferson's collection of 6,487 books, for which Congress eventually paid him $23,950, laid the foundation for the great national library. (Sadly, another fire in 1851 destroyed two-thirds of Jefferson's books.) By the late 1800s it was clear that the Capitol could no longer contain the growing library, and the Jefferson Building was constructed. The **Adams Building,** on 2nd Street behind the Jefferson, was added in 1939. A third structure, the **James Madison Building,** opened in 1980; it's just south of the Jefferson Building, between Independence Avenue and C Street. Less architecturally interesting than the Jefferson Building, the Adams does attract visitors for evening literary readings and small exhibitions, which are open from 8:30 AM to 6 PM. The U.S. Copyright Office, in Room 401, is where all copyright registrations are issued.

The Jefferson Building opens into the Great Hall, richly adorned with mosaics, paintings, and curving marble stairways. The grand, octagonal Main Reading Room, its central desk surrounded by mahogany readers' tables under a 160-foot-high domed ceiling, may inspire some researchers and overwhelm others. Computer terminals have replaced card catalogs, but books are still retrieved and dispersed the same way: readers (18 years or older) hand request slips to librarians and wait patiently for their materials to be delivered. Researchers aren't allowed in the stacks, and only members of Congress and other special borrowers can check books out. Items from the library's collection—which includes one of only three perfect Gutenberg Bibles in the world—are on display in the Jefferson Building's second-floor Southwest Gallery and Pavilion. Information about current and upcoming exhibitions, which can include oral history projects, presidential papers, photographs, and the like, is available by phone or on the Library's Web site. ■ TIP→ **To even begin to come to grips with the magnitude of scope and grandeur of the library, taking one of the free hourly tours is strongly recommended.** Well-informed docents are a font of fascinating information about the library's history and holdings; they can decode the dozens of quirky allegorical sculptures and paintings throughout the building, and can bring you into spaces—such as the glassed-in observation deck over the Main Reading Room—that are closed to solo visitors. ✉ *Jefferson Bldg., 1st St. and Independence Ave. SE, Capitol Hill* ☎ *202/707–4604, 202/707–5000, or 202/707–6400* ⊕ *www.loc.gov* ⊠ *Free* ☉ *Mon.–Sat. 10–5:30; reading room hrs may extend later. Free tours Mon.–Sat. at 10:30, 11:30, 1:30, and 2:30, and weekdays at 3:30* Ⓜ *Capitol S.*

NEED A BREAK?

It's easy to grab a bite near the Library of Congress. The sixth-floor dining halls of the library's **Madison Building** offer great views and inexpensive fare to the public weekdays from 9 to 10:30 and from 12:30 to 3. Or head for the south side of Pennsylvania Avenue SE, between 2nd and 4th streets, which is lined with restaurants and bars frequented by those who live and work on the Hill. **Le Bon Café** (✉ 210 2nd St. SE, Capitol Hill ☎ 202/547-7200) is a cozy French bistro that serves excellent coffees, pastries, and light lunches. **Bullfeathers** (✉ 410

1

1st St. SE, Capitol Hill ☎ 202/543–5005), which has a 40-foot-long bar, has been serving beer and burgers to members of the House since 1980.

True to its name, **The Hawk 'n' Dove** (✉ 329 Pennsylvania Ave. SE, Capitol Hill ☎ 202/543–3300) may well be the best place in town to overhear aides talk partisan politics over pints. The menu is long on the likes of pastrami sandwiches and old-fashioned chipped beef on toast.

Marine Corps Barracks and Commandant's House. The Marine Corps Barracks, the nation's oldest continuously active marine installation, is the home of the U.S. Marine Band. On Friday evenings from May to August, you can attend the hour-long ceremony given on the parade deck by the Marine Band (the "President's Own") and the Drum and Bugle Corps (the "Commandant's Own"). Entry to the grounds at other times is by tour only. ✉ *8th and I Sts. SE, Capitol Hill* ☎ *202/433–4173* ⊕ *www.mbw.usmc.mil* ✉ *Free* ☉ *Public concerts May–Aug., 9 PM; general admission ticket line begins at 7 PM, or reserve tickets by phone or online. Tours Mon.–Thurs. at 10 AM and 1 PM by advance phone reservation only* Ⓜ *Eastern Market.*

☕ ❷ **National Postal Museum.** The Smithsonian's stamp collection, housed here, consists of a whopping 11 million stamps. Exhibits, underscoring the important part the mail has played in America's development, include horse-drawn mail coaches, railway mail cars, airmail planes, and a collection of philatelic rarities. The National Museum of Natural History has the Hope Diamond, but the National Postal Museum has the container used to mail the gem to the Smithsonian. The family-oriented museum has more than 40 interactive and touch-screen exhibits. The museum takes up only a portion of what is the old Washington City Post Office, designed by Daniel Burnham and completed in 1914. Nostalgic odes to the noble mail carrier are inscribed on the exterior of the marble building; one of them, "The Letter," eulogizes the "Messenger of sympathy and love / Servant of parted friends / Consoler of the lonely / Bond of the scattered family / Enlarger of the common life." ✉ *2 Massachusetts Ave. NE, Capitol Hill* ☎ *202/633–5555, 202/633–9849 TDD* ⊕ *www.postalmuseum.si.edu* ✉ *Free* ☉ *Daily 10–5:30* Ⓜ *Union Station.*

OFF THE
BEATEN
PATH

NATIONAL SHRINE OF THE IMMACULATE CONCEPTION – The largest Catholic church in the United States, the National Shrine of the Immaculate Conception was begun in 1920, built with funds from every parish in the country. Dedicated in 1959, the shrine is a blend of Romanesque and Byzantine styles, with a bell tower that recalls that of St. Mark's in Venice. Take the Metro here from Union Station; the shrine is about a half mile from the station, halfway to the Pope John Paul II Cultural Center. ✉ *400 Michigan Ave. NE, Catholic University* ☎ *202/526–8300* ⊕ *www.nationalshrine.com* ✉ *Free* ☉ *Apr.–Oct., daily 7–7; Nov.–Mar., daily 7–6; Sat. vigil mass at 5:15; Sun. mass at 7:30, 9, 10:30, noon, 1:30 (in Latin), and 4:30* Ⓜ *Brookland/Catholic University.*

❻ **Peace Monument.** A white-marble memorial of a woman symbolizing America, grief-stricken over sailors lost at sea during the Civil War, is weeping on the shoulder of a second female figure representing History. The plaque inscription refers movingly to navy personnel who "fell in defence of the union and liberty of their country 1861–1865." ✉ *Traffic circle at 1st St. and Pennsylvania Ave. NW, The Mall* Ⓜ *Union Station.*

Pope John Paul II Cultural Center. Part museum, part place of pilgrimage, the Pope John Paul II Cultural Center is a spectacular architectural embodiment of the Roman Catholic church's desire to celebrate its charismatic leader and its rich artistic tradition. Themes covered include church and papal history, representations of the Virgin Mary, Polish heritage, and the Catholic tradition of community activism. These are explored through traditional displays of art and artifacts as well as with audiovisual presentations and interactive computer stations. The center is about a mile from the Metro and can easily be combined with a visit to the National Shrine of the Immaculate Conception. ✉ *3900 Harewood Rd. NE, Catholic University* ☎ *202/635–5400* ⊕ *www.jp2cc.org* 🎫 *$5* ⊙ *Tues.–Sat. 10–5, Sun. noon–5* Ⓜ *Brookland/Catholic University.*

❹ **Robert A. Taft Memorial.** In the triangle formed by Louisiana, New Jersey, and Constitution avenues, a monolithic carillon pays tribute to the longtime Republican senator and son of the 27th president. ✉ *Constitution and New Jersey Aves. NW, Capitol Hill* Ⓜ *Union Station.*

⓭ **Sewall-Belmont House.** Built in 1800 by Robert Sewall, this is one of the oldest homes on Capitol Hill. Today it's the headquarters of the National Woman's Party. A museum inside chronicles the early days of the women's movement and the history of the house; there's also a library open to researchers by appointment. From 1801 to 1813 Secretary of the Treasury Albert Gallatin lived here; he finalized the details of the Louisiana Purchase in his front-parlor office. This building was the only private house in Washington that the British set on fire during their invasion of 1814. They did so after a resident fired on advancing British troops from an upper-story window (a fact later documented by the offending British general's sworn testimony, 30 years later, on behalf of the Sewalls in their attempt to secure war reparations from the U.S. government). This shot was, in fact, the only armed resistance the British met that day. The house is filled with period furniture and portraits and busts of suffragists such as Lucretia Mott, Elizabeth Cady Stanton, and longtime resident Alice Paul, who drafted the first version of the Equal Rights Amendment in 1923. ✉ *144 Constitution Ave. NE, Capitol Hill* ☎ *202/546–1210* ⊕ *www.sewallbelmont.org* 🎫 *Suggested donation $5* ⊙ *Tours on the hr Tues.–Fri. 11–3, Sat. noon–4* Ⓜ *Union Station.*

⓯ **South Side of East Capitol Street.** Walk along East Capitol Street, the border between the northeast and southeast quadrants of the city, for a sample of the residential area of the Hill. The house on the corner of East Capitol Street, No. 329, has a striking tower with a bay window and stained glass. Next door are two Victorian houses with iron trim below the second floor. No. 317, an antebellum Greek Revival frame house, sits behind a tidy garden. ✉ *Between 3rd and 4th Sts. SE, Capitol Hill* Ⓜ *Capitol S or Union Station.*

⓬ **Supreme Court Building.** It wasn't until 1935 that the Supreme Court got its own building: a white-marble temple with twin rows of Corinthian columns designed by Cass Gilbert. In 1800 the justices arrived in Washington along with the rest of the government but were for years shunted around various rooms in the Capitol; for a while they even met in a tavern. William Howard Taft, the only man to serve as both president and chief justice, was instrumental in getting the court a home of its own, though he died before it was completed.

The Supreme Court convenes on the first Monday in October and remains in session until it has heard all of its cases and handed down all of its decisions (usually the end of June). On Monday through Wednesday of two weeks in each month, the justices hear oral arguments in the velvet-swathed court chamber. The main hall of the Supreme Court is lined with busts of former chief justices; the courtroom itself is decorated with allegorical friezes. Visitors who want to listen can choose to wait in either of two lines. One, the "three- to five-minute" line, shuttles you through, giving you a quick impression of the court at work. If you choose the other, and you'd like to stay for the whole show, it's best to be in line by 8:30 AM. ■ TIP→ **The *Washington Post* carries a daily listing of what cases the court will hear.** ✉ *1 1st St. NE, Capitol Hill* ☎ *202/ 479–3000* ⊕ *www.supremecourtus.gov* ⊠ *Free* ☉ *Weekdays 9–4:30* Ⓜ *Union Station or Capitol S.*

❸ **Thurgood Marshall Federal Judiciary Building.** If you're in the Union Station neighborhood, it's worth taking a moment to peer inside the signature work of architect Edward Larabee Barnes. The atrium encloses a garden of bamboo five stories tall. ✉ *1 Columbus Circle NE, Capitol Hill* Ⓜ *Union Station.*

▶ ❶ **Union Station.** With a 96-foot-high coffered ceiling gilded with 8 pounds of gold leaf, the city's train station is one of the capital's great spaces. Back in 1902 the McMillan Commission—charged with suggesting ways to improve the city's appearance—recommended that the many train lines that sliced through the capital share one depot. Union Station, opened in 1908, was the first building completed under the commission's plan. Chicago architect and commission member Daniel H. Burnham patterned it after the Roman Baths of Diocletian (AD 305).

For many coming to Washington, the capital city is first seen framed through the grand station's arched doorways. In its heyday, during World War II, more than 200,000 people passed through the building daily. By the 1960s, however, the decline in train travel had turned the station into an expensive white-marble elephant. It was briefly, and unsuccessfully, transformed into a visitor center for the Bicentennial, but by 1981 rain was pouring in through its neglected roof, and passengers boarded trains at a ramshackle depot behind the station.

The Union Station you see today is the result of a restoration, completed in 1988, intended to begin a revival of Washington's east end. Between train travelers and visitors to the shops, restaurants, and a nine-screen movie theater, 70,000 people a day pass through the beaux arts building. The jewel of the structure is its main waiting room. Forty-six statues of Roman legionnaires, one for each state in the Union when the station was completed, ring the grand room. The statues were the subject of controversy when the building was first opened. Pennsylvania Railroad president Alexander Cassatt (brother of artist Mary) ordered sculptor Louis Saint-Gaudens (brother of sculptor Augustus) to alter the statues, convinced that the legionnaires' skimpy outfits would upset female passengers. The sculptor obligingly added a shield to each figure, obscuring any offending body parts.

The east hall, now filled with vendors, is decorated with Pompeiian-style tracery and plaster walls and columns painted to look like marble. The station also has a secure presidential waiting room, now restored. This room was by no means frivolous: 20 years before Union Station was built, President Garfield was assassinated in the public waiting room of the old Baltimore and Potomac terminal on 6th Street.

The **Columbus Memorial Fountain,** designed by Lorado Taft, sits in the station's front plaza. A steely eyed Christopher Columbus stares into the distance, flanked by a hoary, bearded figure (the Old World) and a Native American brave (the New). ☒ *50 Massachusetts Ave. NE, Capitol Hill* ☏ *202/289–1908* ⊕ *www.unionstationdc.com* Ⓜ *Union Station.*

NEED A BREAK?

On Union Station's lower level are more than 20 food stalls with everything from pizza to sushi. There are several restaurants throughout the station, the largest of which is **America** (☏ 202/682–9555), with a menu of regional foods that lives up to its expansive name. The two-level **Center Cafe,** in the main hall of Union Station, is a perfect spot for people-watching.

🄲 ❾ **United States Botanic Garden.** This glistening, plant-filled oasis, established by Congress in 1820, is the oldest botanic garden in North America. The Palm House conservatory is the center of attention. Now called the Jungle, it houses rain-forest plants and includes walkways 24 feet aboveground. With equal attention paid to science and aesthetics, the Botanic Garden contains plants from all around the world, with an emphasis on tropical and economically useful plants, desert plants, and orchids. On a 3-acre plot immediately to the west, the new **National Garden** is being constructed. It's scheduled to open in September 2006. ☒ *1st St. and Maryland Ave. SW, Capitol Hill* ☏ *202/225–8333* ⊕ *www.usbg. gov* ⊠ *Free* ☉ *Daily 10–5* Ⓜ *Federal Center SW.*

OFF THE BEATEN PATH

UNITED STATES NATIONAL ARBORETUM – During azalea season (mid-April through May), this 446-acre oasis is a blaze of color. In early summer, clematis, peonies, rhododendrons, and roses bloom. At any time of year, the 22 original Corinthian columns from the U.S. Capitol, reerected here in 1990, are striking; construction on a wheelchair-accessible path to the columns began in 2005, and the path will eventually link to other arboretum sites, including the National Bonsai and Penjing Museum, the National Herb Garden, and the azalea collections. The arboretum is ideal for a relaxing stroll, picnic, or scenic drive. On weekends, a tram tours the Arboretum's curving roadways at 10:30, 11:30, 1, 2, 3, and 4; tickets are $3. The **National Herb Garden** and the **National Bonsai Collection** are also here. ☒ *3501 New York Ave. NE, Northeast* ☏ *202/245–2726* ⊕ *www.usna.usda.gov* ⊠ *Free* ☉ *Arboretum and herb garden daily 8–5, bonsai collection daily 10–3:30* Ⓜ *Weekends only, Union*

Station, then X6 bus (runs every 40 min); weekdays, Stadium/Armory, then B2 bus to Bladensburg Rd. and R St.

Washington Navy Yard. A 115-acre historic district with its own street system, the Washington Navy Yard is the navy's oldest outpost on shore. Established in 1799 as a shipbuilding facility, it was burned during the War of 1812. Rebuilt and converted to weapons production by the mid-19th century, it gradually fell into disuse until the 1960s, when it was revived as an administrative center.

The **Navy Museum** (☎ 202/433–4882 Navy Museum, 202/433–4882 USS Barry ⊕ www.history.navy.mil), in Building 76, chronicles the history of the U.S. Navy from the Revolution to the present. Exhibits range from the fully rigged foremast of the USS *Constitution* (better known as Old Ironsides) to a U.S. Navy Corsair fighter plane dangling from the ceiling. All around are models of fighting ships, working periscopes, displays on battles, and portraits of the sailors who fought them. The decommissioned U.S. Navy destroyer *Barry,* open weekdays 10–4, floats a few hundred yards away in the Anacostia River. In front of the museum is a collection of guns, cannons, and missiles. Call ahead to schedule a free weekday highlights tour—and to double-check visiting hours and access policy, especially during periods of heightened security. Hours for the Navy Museum are generally weekdays 9–4, and appointments are necessary for those without Department of Defense or military ID. On weekdays, civilian visitors should enter at 9th Street and M Street. Visitors can enter at 6th Street and M Street on weekends. Note that weekend visitors should make reservations a week in advance.

The **Navy Art Gallery** (☎ 202/433–3815 ⊕ www.history.navy.mil), in Building 67, exhibits navy-related paintings, sketches, and drawings, many created during combat by navy artists. The bulk of the collection illustrates World War II. Hours for the Navy Art Gallery are Wednesday through Friday 9–4, Saturday 10–4, and Sunday noon–4. ⊠ *O and 11th Sts. SE, Capitol Hill* ☎ *Free; park free with advance reservation* Ⓜ *Eastern Market.*

EAST END

Just because Washington is a planned city doesn't mean the plan was executed flawlessly. Pierre-Charles L'Enfant's design has been alternately shelved and rediscovered several times in the past 200 years. Nowhere have the city's imperfections been more visible than on L'Enfant's grand thoroughfare, Pennsylvania Avenue. By the early 1960s it had become a national disgrace; the dilapidated buildings that lined it were pawn shops and cheap souvenir stores. Washington's downtown—once within the diamond formed by Massachusetts, Louisiana, Pennsylvania, and New York avenues—had its problems, too, many the result of riots that rocked the capital in 1968 after the assassination of Martin Luther King Jr. In their wake, many businesses left the area and moved north of the White House.

But in recent years, developers have rediscovered the "East End," and buildings are now being torn down, built up, and remodeled at an amazing pace. ■ TIP→ **Penn Quarter, the neighborhood immediately surrounding the once down-at-the-heels stretch of Pennsylvania Avenue, has blossomed into one of the hottest addresses in town for nightlife and culture.** With its proximity to the venerable Ford's Theater and the National Theater, a newly opened theater by the acclaimed progressive Woolly Mammoth company, and a major new expansion and arts center from the prestigious Shakespeare Theater due to open in 2007, the neighborhood can rightfully claim to be Washington's own theater district. Meanwhile, new galleries, restaurants, and other cultural hotspots are constantly appearing. The mother of all these will be the big-screen, multimedia Newseum, also set to open in 2007. In the meantime, the city's high-end late-night crowds flock to the neighborhood's new clubs and lounges, like G Street's sleek, Franco-Indian cocktail IndeBleu, a red-hot contender for the trendiest spot in town.

The walk explores the newly revitalized neighborhood that was once the city's downtrodden downtown, then swings around to check progress on the monumental street that links the Capitol with the President's house. Annual openings of new sights and museums mean the East End is now densely packed with major attractions—far too many to see at once. Exploring all of them (with the exception of the small Marian Koshland) can take more than an hour, so pick the two that appeal most. Though the walk passes by all the main draws, those intrigued by intrigue might want to limit themselves to touring the J. Edgar Hoover FBI Building and the International Spy Museum; art lovers might focus on the National Portrait Gallery and Smithsonian American Art Museum; history buffs on the National Archives and touring the National Building Museum; media junkies

> **CAPITAL FACTS**
>
> While riding through a dilapidated East End in his inaugural parade, a disgusted John F. Kennedy is said to have turned to an aide and said, "Fix it!"

will want to visit the Newseum and the Marian Koshland Science Museum, which looks at the science behind media headlines. (Note: where E Street meets Pennsylvania Avenue, the intersection creates an odd one-block stretch that looks like Pennsylvania Avenue but is technically E Street; Buildings usually choose to associate themselves with the more prestigious-sounding Pennsylvania Avenue.)

TIMING   Although many of the walk's attractions are places you only look at, it's still an all-day affair. You may or may not think the best time to visit the National Aquarium is for the shark feedings (Monday, Wednesday, and Saturday at 2), piranha feedings (Tuesday, Thursday, and Sunday at 2), or alligator feedings (Friday at 2), when the frenzy of the crowds jockeying to see the action often rivals that inside the tanks.

What to See

OFF THE BEATEN PATH

ANACOSTIA MUSEUM AND CENTER FOR AFRICAN AMERICAN HISTORY AND CULTURE – The richness of African-American culture is on display in this Smithsonian museum and research facility in southeast Washington's Anacostia neighborhood. The museum's facade uses traditional African design elements: brickwork patterns evoke West African kente cloth, and the concrete cylinders reference the stone towers of Zimbabwe and are ornamented with diamond patterns like those found on the adobe houses of Mali. Special exhibitions showcase fine art—photography, painting, sculpture—as well as crafts, social history, and popular culture. ⊠ *1901 Fort Pl. SE, Anacostia* ☎ *202/287–3306* ⊕ *www.si.edu/anacostia* ⊠ *Free* ☾ *Daily 10–5* Ⓜ *Anacostia, then W2/W3 bus.*

⑳ Apex Building. The triangular Apex Building, completed in 1938, is the home of the Federal Trade Commission. Relief decorations over the doorways on the Constitution Avenue side depict agriculture (the harvesting of grain, by Concetta Scaravaglione) and trade (two men bartering over an ivory tusk, by Carl Schmitz). Michael Lantz's two heroic statues, flanking the rounded eastern portico, depict a muscular, shirtless workman wrestling with a wild horse and represent man controlling trade. Just across 6th Street is a three-tier fountain decorated with the signs of the zodiac; it's a memorial to Andrew Mellon. As secretary of the treasury, Mellon constructed the $125 million Federal Triangle. (A deep-pocketed philanthropist, Mellon was the driving force behind the National Gallery of Art, just across Constitution Avenue.) ⊠ *7th St. and Pennsylvania Ave. NW, The Mall* Ⓜ *Archives/Navy Memorial.*

㉒ Canadian Embassy. A spectacular edifice constructed of stone and glass, the Canadian Embassy was designed by Arthur Erickson and completed in 1988. The columns of the rotunda represent Canada's 12 provinces and territories. Inside, a gallery periodically displays exhibits on Canadian culture and history. ⊠ *501 Pennsylvania Ave. NW, The Mall* ☎ *202/682–1740* ⊕ *www.canadianembassy.org* ⊠ *Free* ☾ *Weekdays 9–5 during exhibitions only* Ⓜ *Archives/Navy Memorial.*

TOP 5: EAST END

■ **J. Edgar Hoover Federal Bureau of Investigations Building:** See the FBI from the inside, and learn how the Feds investigate the nation's most wanted.

■ **International Spy Museum:** Indulge your inner James Bond with a look at 007's silver Aston Martin from *Goldfinger*–along with plenty of more serious toys used by the CIA, FBI, and KGB.

■ **The National Archives:** After genuflecting before the Declaration of Independence, Constitution, and Bill of Rights, lose yourself in the depths of the National Archives' Public Vault, where you might see anything from the Emancipation Proclamation to *Mad Magazine*.

■ **National Building Museum:** Imagine tuxedoed campaign contributors twirling sequin-encrusted socialites around the colossal columns of the Great Hall, site of the Presidential Inaugural Ball; then check out the permanent exhibitions to learn about the nation's capital.

■ **Old Patent Office Building:** Enjoy the newly displayed treasures of Washington's most celebrated renovation now that the Patent Building has reopened. It will house the Smithsonian American Art Museum and the National Portrait Gallery, where you can see iconic images of everyone from George Washington to Marilyn Monroe.

A GOOD WALK

EAST END

Numbers in the box correspond to numbers in the margin and on the East End map.

Start at the beaux arts landmark of the **City Museum** ❶ ▶. Walk southwest on New York Avenue to the **National Museum of Women in the Arts** ❷.

Across the street is the **Inter-American Development Bank Cultural Center.** Walking south, you'll reach the city's largest public library, the **Martin Luther King Jr. Memorial Library** ❸, at 9th and G streets. Walk over to 6th Street and up to H Street to and up to H Street to Washington's tiny **Chinatown** ❹. Close by is the site of the **Surratt Boarding House** ❺, where Lincoln's assassins plotted. Walk to 6th and F streets and walk left on F Street to get to the **National Building Museum** ❻, the site of inaugural balls for more than 100 years. Across F Street from the National Building Museum is Judiciary Square, where city and federal courthouses, as well as the **National Law Enforcement Officers Memorial** ❼, are located.

Just across F Street and to the left is the Hotel Monaco, which is housed in the former **Tariff Commission Building.** Walk west on F Street, then head a block south on 6th street to the new **Marian Koshland Science Museum** ❽. Going back up to F Street and continuing west, you'll reach the newly restored **Old Patent Office Building,** housing two of the Smithsonian's recently renovated non-Mall museums. On the south side is the **National Portrait Gallery** ❾. On the north is the **Smithsonian American Art Museum** ❿. Across the street at 800 F Street is the **International Spy Museum** ⓫.

Turn left off F Street onto 10th Street to **Ford's Theatre** ⓬, where Abraham Lincoln was shot. The place where he died, the **Petersen House** ⓭, is across the street. Follow Pennsylvania Avenue three blocks west to **Freedom Plaza** ⓮. Across E Street from the plaza is the **National Theatre.**

The cluster of limestone buildings south of Freedom Plaza between 15th Street, Pennsylvania Avenue, and Constitution Avenue is **Federal Triangle.** The triangle includes, from west to east, the Department of Commerce Building, home of the **National Aquarium** ⓯; the **John A. Wilson Building;** the **Ronald Reagan Building and International Trade Center** ⓰; the **Old Post Office** ⓱; the Internal Revenue Service Building; the Department of Justice (the **J. Edgar Hoover Federal Bureau of Investigation Building** ⓲ is across Pennsylvania Avenue and not actually part of the Federal Triangle); the **National Archives** ⓳; and the **Apex Building** ⓴, home of the Federal Trade Commission. Due to open in 2007 is the giant glass-fronted new **Newseum** ㉑. The white-stone-and-glass building across Pennsylvania Avenue is the **Canadian Embassy** ㉒. Across 7th Street, near the General Winfield Scott Hancock Memorial, is the **Navy Memorial** ㉓, consisting of the *Lone Sailor* and a huge map carved into the plaza.

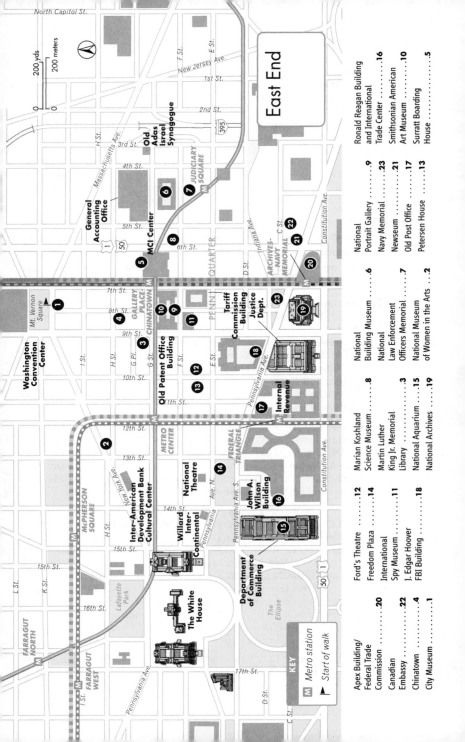

North Capitol St.

F St.

E St.

New Jersey Ave.

1st St.

2nd St.

395

East End

200 yds

200 meters

Mt. Vernon Square

Old Adas Israel Synagogue

Massachusetts Ave.

H St.

3rd St.

4th St.

General Accounting Office

5th St.

6

JUDICIARY SQUARE

M

MCI Center

1
50

8

6th St.

5

7th St.

8th St.

GALLERY PLACE

CHINATOWN

M

10

9

I St.

G Pl.

H St.

G St.

Washington Convention Center

4

3

Old Patent Office Building

9th St.

11

PENN

Tariff Commission Building

Justice Dept.

F St.

12

10th St.

13

11th St.

Pennsylvania Ave.

18

E St.

17

Internal Revenue

12th St.

2

METRO CENTER

M

FEDERAL TRIANGLE

14

13th St.

Inter-American Development Bank Cultural Center

National Theatre

Ave. N.

14th St.

Willard Inter-Continental

Pennsylvania

John A. Wilson Building

Pennsylvania Ave. S.

16

15

Department of Commerce Building

New York Ave.

H St.

McPHERSON SQUARE

M

15th St.

L St.

K St.

FARRAGUT NORTH

M

FARRAGUT WEST

M

Lafayette Park

The White House

16th St.

15th St.

The Ellipse

50
1

17th St.

D St.

C St.

Constitution Ave.

Indiana Ave.

D St.

C St.

ARCHIVES-NAVY MEMORIAL

M

22

21

20

QUARTER

Constitution Ave.

PENN QUARTER

19

23

KEY

M Metro station

▲ Start of walk

Apex Building/
Federal Trade
Commission **20**
Canadian
Embassy **22**
Chinatown **4**
City Museum **1**

Ford's Theatre **12**
Freedom Plaza **14**
International
Spy Museum **11**
J. Edgar Hoover
FBI Building **18**

Marian Koshland
Science Museum **8**
Martin Luther
King Jr. Memorial
Library **3**
National Aquarium ...**15**
National Archives **19**

National
Building Museum **6**
National
Law Enforcement
Officers Memorial **7**
National Museum
of Women in the Arts ..**2**

National
Portrait Gallery **9**
Navy Memorial **23**
Newseum **21**
Old Post Office **17**
Petersen House **13**

Ronald Reagan Building
and International
Trade Center **16**
Smithsonian American
Art Museum **10**
Surratt Boarding
House **5**

4 Chinatown. If you don't notice you're entering Washington's compact Chinatown by the Chinese characters on the street signs, the ornate, 75-foot-wide **Friendship Arch** spanning H Street might clue you in. Though Chinatown's main cross streets may appear somewhat down-at-the-heels, this area borders many blocks undergoing revitalization, and it's still the place to go for Chinese food in the District. Cantonese, Szechuan, Hunan, and Mongolian are among the regional styles you'll find here. Nearly every restaurant has a roast duck hanging in the window, and the shops here sell Chinese food, arts and crafts, and newspapers. Most interesting are traditional pharmacies purveying folk medicines such as dried eels, powdered bones, and unusual herbs for teas and broths believed to promote health, longevity, and sexual potency. ⊠ *Bounded by G, H, 5th, and 8th Sts., East End* Ⓜ *Gallery Pl./Chinatown.*

NEED A BREAK?

If the smells of Chinese cooking have activated your taste buds, try **Full Kee** (⊠ **740 6th St. NW, Downtown),** popular with Chinatown residents, government bureaucrats, and tourists. Adventurous diners should ask for items off the Chinese menu. For everyone else, the English menu includes noodle dishes, congee (a savory porridge), hot pots, dumplings, and other Cantonese specialties.

▶ **1 City Museum.** This beautiful beaux arts Carnegie Library building, once the city's Central Public Library, was renovated in 2003 and had a short life as the only museum devoted to the nation's capital. Although its exhibits are no longer open to the public, visitors can use the Kiplinger Research Library, which contains artifacts, papers, maps, photographs, and other resources relating to Washington's neighborhoods, ethnic groups, and history. ⊠ *801 K St. NW, East End* ☎ *202/383–1850* ⊕ *www.citymuseumdc.org* ⊡ *Free* ☉ *Tues.–Thurs. 10–5* Ⓜ *Gallery Pl./Chinatown or Mt. Vernon Sq./UDC.*

Federal Triangle. To the south of Freedom Plaza, this mass of government buildings was constructed between 1929 and 1938. Notable are the Department of Commerce, which holds the National Aquarium; the John A. Wilson Building; the Old Post Office; the Internal Revenue Service Building; the Department of Justice; the National Archives; and the Apex Building, which houses the Federal Trade Commission.

Before Federal Triangle was developed, government workers were scattered throughout the city, largely in rented offices. Looking for a place to consolidate this workforce, city planners hit on the area south of Pennsylvania Avenue, which was known as Murder Bay for its notorious collection of rooming houses, taverns, tattoo parlors, and brothels. A uniform classical architectural style, with Italianate red-tile roofs and interior plazas reminiscent of the Louvre, was chosen for the building project. Federal Triangle's planners envisioned interior courts filled with plazas and parks, but the needs of the motorcar foiled any such grand plans. ⊠ *15th St. and Pennsylvania and Constitution Aves., The Mall* Ⓜ *Federal Triangle.*

🐾 **12 Ford's Theatre.** In 1859 Baltimore theater impresario John T. Ford leased the First Baptist Church building that stood on this site and turned it into a successful music hall. The building burned down late in 1863, but Ford built a new structure on the same spot. The events that occurred less than two years later would shock the nation and close the theater. On the night of April 14, 1865, during a performance of *Our American Cousin,* John Wilkes Booth entered the state box and shot Abraham Lincoln in the back of the head. The stricken president was carried across the street to the

> **CAPITAL FACTS**
>
> The federal government bought Ford's Theatre in 1866 for $100,000 and converted it into office space. It was remodeled as a Lincoln museum in 1932 and was restored to its 1865 appearance in 1968.

house of tailor William Petersen. Charles Augustus Leale, a 23-year-old surgeon, was the first man to attend to the president. To let Lincoln know that someone was nearby, Leale held his hand throughout the night. Lincoln died the next morning.

The basement museum contains artifacts such as Booth's pistol and the clothes Lincoln was wearing when he was shot. The theater itself presents a complete schedule of plays; *A Christmas Carol* is an annual holiday favorite. ☒ *511 10th St. NW, East End* ☎ *202/426–6924* ⊕ *www. nps.gov/foth* ☐ *Free* ☉ *Daily 9–5; theater closed to visitors during rehearsals and matinees, generally Thurs. and weekends; Lincoln museum in basement remains open at these times* Ⓜ *Metro Center or Gallery Pl.*

OFF THE BEATEN PATH

FREDERICK DOUGLASS NATIONAL HISTORIC SITE – Cedar Hill, the Anacostia home of abolitionist Frederick Douglass, was the first Black National Historic Site that Congress designated. Douglass, a former slave who delivered rousing abolitionist speeches at home and abroad, resided here from 1877 until his death in 1895. The house has a wonderful view of Washington across the Anacostia River and contains many of Douglass's personal belongings. A major restoration of the house, planned for 2006, is intended to restore it to look as it did when Douglass lived here. A short film on his life is shown at a nearby visitor center. Reservations are required for tours. To get here, take the B2 bus from the Anacostia Metro stop. ☒ *1411 W St. SE, Anacostia* ☎ *202/426–5961, 800/967–2283 tour reservations* ⊕ *www.nps.gov/frdo* ☐ *Free* ☉ *Mid-Oct.–mid-Apr., daily 9–4; mid-Apr.–mid-Oct., daily 9–5; call ahead for tour times* Ⓜ *Anacostia.*

⓮ **Freedom Plaza.** In 1988 Western Plaza was renamed Freedom Plaza in honor of Martin Luther King Jr. The east end is dominated by a statue of General Casimir Pulaski, a Polish nobleman who led an American cavalry corps during the Revolutionary War and was mortally wounded in 1779 at the Siege of Savannah. He gazes over a plaza inlaid with a detail from L'Enfant's original 1791 plan for the Federal City. The "President's Palace" and the "Congress House" are outlined in bronze, and the Mall is represented by a green lawn. Cut into the edges are quotations about the capital city, not all of them complimentary. ■ TIP→ **To compare L'Enfant's vision with today's reality, stand in the middle of the map's Pennsylvania Avenue and look west.** L'Enfant had planned an unbroken vista from the Capitol to the White House, but the Treasury Building, begun in 1836, ruined the view. Turning to the east, you'll see the U.S. Capitol sitting on the former Jenkins Hill.

There's a lot to see and explore in the blocks near Freedom Plaza. The beaux arts Willard Inter-Continental is on the corner of 14th Street and Pennsylvania Avenue NW. Just north of Freedom Plaza, on F Street between 13th and 14th streets, are the Shops, a collection of stores in the **National Press Building,** itself the address for dozens of media organizations. The Shops' upstairs Food Hall has sit-down restaurants and fast-food places. Washington's oldest stage, the National Theatre, also overlooks the plaza. ⊠ *Bounded by 13th, 14th, and E Sts. and Pennsylvania Ave., East End* Ⓜ *Federal Triangle.*

Inter-American Development Bank Cultural Center. Founded in 1959, the IADB finances economic and social development in Latin America and the Caribbean. Its small cultural center holds changing exhibits of paintings, sculptures, and artifacts from member countries. It's across the street from the National Museum of Women in the Arts. ⊠ *1300 New York Ave. NW, East End* ☎ *202/623–1000 or 202/623–3774* ⊕ *www.iadb. org* 🎫 *Free* ☉ *Weekdays 11–6* Ⓜ *Metro Center.*

🅱 ⑪ **International Spy Museum.** Cryptologists, masters of disguise, and former officials of the CIA, FBI, and KGB are among the advisers of this museum, which displays the largest collection of spy artifacts anywhere in the world. Fittingly, it's just a block away from FBI headquarters. Fans of novelist John Le Carré will revel in exhibits such as the School for Spies, which describes what makes a good spy and how they are trained; the Secret History of History, about spying from biblical times to the early 20th century; Spies Among Us, about spying in the world wars; War of the Spies, devoted to sophisticated Cold War spy techniques; and 21st-Century Spying, in which espionage experts analyze the latest spy trends. Five buildings, some dating from the 19th century, were combined to create the museum complex; one, the Warder-Atlas building, held Washington's Communist party in the 1940s. Same-day tickets are available for specific touring times. ■ TIP→ **Advance tickets are recommended, particularly in spring and summer.** A large gift shop, a café, and the restaurant Zola are here as well. ⊠ *800 F St. NW, East End* ☎ *202/393–7798* ⊕ *www.spymuseum.org* 🎫 *$15, children $12* ☉ *Apr.–Oct., daily 9–8; Nov.–Mar., daily 10–6; hrs subject to change; check Web site before visiting* Ⓜ *Gallery Pl./Chinatown.*

🅱 ⑱ **J. Edgar Hoover Federal Bureau of Investigation Building.** A brief film outlines the bureau's work, and exhibits describe famous past cases and illustrate the FBI's fight against organized crime, terrorism, bank robbery, espionage, extortion, and other criminal activities. There's everything from gangster John Dillinger's death mask to a poster display of the 10 Most Wanted criminals. (Look carefully: two bad guys were apprehended as a result of tips from tour takers!) You also might see the laboratories where the FBI painstakingly studies evidence.

Fodor'sChoice ★

> **CAPITAL FACTS**
>
> The hulking FBI building was decried from birth as hideous. Even Hoover himself is said to have called it the "ugliest building I've ever seen." But the one-hour FBI tour is one of the most popular activities in the city.

The high point of the tour comes at the end: an agent gives a live-ammo firearms demonstration in the indoor shooting range. Tours of the building's interior have been suspended for renovations until early 2007, and visitors should call ahead to confirm that they have started running again. ⊠ *10th St. and Pennsylvania Ave. NW, East End* ☎ *202/324–3447* ⊕ *www.fbi.gov* Ⓜ *Federal Triangle or Gallery Pl./Chinatown.*

John A. Wilson Building. Renamed in honor of the late city council chairman who died in 1993, this beaux arts structure, formerly known as the District Building, was built in 1908 and listed on the National Register of Historic Places in 1972. ⊠ *1350 Pennsylvania Ave. NW, East End* ⊕ *www.fbi.gov* Ⓜ *Federal Triangle.*

❽ Marian Koshland Science Museum. Sponsored by the National Academy of Sciences, this small but engaging new museum (it opened in late 2004) explores and explains the science behind current news headlines. A permanent exhibit includes animations of groundbreaking science with interactive displays showing how these discoveries make their way into the public realm. The other exhibits illustrate the research of the Academy on subjects which intersect with public policy, such as global warming and DNA sequencing. The highlight of the global warming display is Bessy, a model cow whose emissions of methane (the second greatest contributor to the greenhouse effect) are part of a wider explanation showing connections to El Niño and hurricanes. In the DNA section, the bright computer panels explore how genetic sequencing is connected to everything from finding the origin of SARS to criminal investigations. Though the interactive exhibits are fun and educational, they are aimed at ages 13 and up. ⊠ *Corner of 6th and E Sts., NW, East End* ☎ *202/334–1201* ⊠ *$5* ☉ *Sun., Mon., and Wed.–Sat. 10–6* Ⓜ *Gallery Pl./Chinatown and Judiciary Sq.*

❸ Martin Luther King Jr. Memorial Library. The only D.C. building designed by Ludwig Mies van der Rohe, one of the founders of modern architecture, this squat black building at 9th and G streets is the city's largest public library. A mural on the first floor depicts events in the life of the Nobel Prize–winning civil rights activist and reverend. Used books are almost always on sale at bargain prices in the gift shop. ⊠ *901 G St. NW, East End* ☎ *202/727–1111* ⊠ *Free* ☉ *Mon.–Thurs. 10–9, Fri. and Sat. 10–5:30, Sun. 1–5* Ⓜ *Gallery Pl./Chinatown or Metro Center.*

☺ MCI Center. The Washington Wizards, Washington Mystics, and Georgetown Hoyas play basketball here, and the Washington Capitals take the ice during hockey season. This is also the site of concerts and shows—including ice-skating extravaganzas and the circus. ⊠ *601 F St. NW, between 6th and 7th Sts., East End* ☎ *202/628–3200 MCI Center, 202/ 432–7328 Ticketmaster* Ⓜ *Gallery Pl./Chinatown or Metro Center.*

☺ ⓯ National Aquarium. The western base of Federal Triangle between 14th and 15th streets is the home of the Department of Commerce, charged with promoting U.S. economic development and technological advancement. When it opened in 1932, it was the world's largest government office building. It's a good thing there's plenty of space, because the National Aquarium is now housed inside. Established in 1873, it's the country's oldest public aquarium, with more than 1,200 fish and other creatures—such as eels, sharks, and alligators—representing 270 species of fresh- and saltwater life. The exhibits look somewhat dated, but the easy-to-view tanks, accessible touching pool (with crabs and sea urchins), low admission fee, and lack of crowds make this a good outing with children. ⊠ *14th St. and Constitution Ave. NW, East End* ☎ *202/482–2825* ⊕ *www.nationalaquarium.com* ✉ *$3.50* ☯ *Daily 9–5, last admission at 4:30; sharks fed Mon., Wed., and Sat. at 2; piranhas fed Tues., Thurs., and Sun. at 2; alligators fed Fri. at 2* Ⓜ *Federal Triangle.*

☾ ⑲ **National Archives.** The National Archives are at once monument, museum, and the nation's memory. Headquartered in a grand marble edifice on Constitution Avenue, the National Archives and Records Administration is charged with preserving and archiving the United States' most historically important government records. Its 8 billion paper records and 4 billion electronic records date back to 1775, and cover a vast array of subjects.

Fodor'sChoice
★

Its three most famous documents, which draw millions of reverential viewers every year, are the original Declaration of Independence, Constitution, and Bill of Rights. These are housed in the Archives' cathedral-like rotunda, each on a marble platform, encased in bulletproof glass, and floating in pressurized helium, which protects the irreplaceable documents. The dim lighting in the rotunda, also meant to protect the charters, adds to the sense of monumental solemnity when viewing them. There's often a long line to get into one of the capital's most compelling draws. To ease the pain of the wait, the rotunda's anteroom offers a rotating display of stellar items including the original Emancipation Proclamation and the bible on which George Washington was sworn into his first term as president.

To the right of the rotunda as you leave America's founding charters, you'll see, displayed with great majesty, the 1297 Magna Carta, the document of English common law whose language inspired the Constitution. Added to the Archives' permanent exhibit in 2005, the Magna Carta is one of only four remaining originals in the world, and the only one on permanent display in the U.S.

Though these documents are the star attractions, there's still much more to see. In 2004, the Archives opened, to great acclaim, the Public Vaults, a 10,000-square-foot permanent exhibit showcasing the fascinating history and breadth of their holdings. Here you might see anything from the treaty of the Louisiana Purchase to the first edition of *Mad Magazine* (used as evidence in Congressional hearings on juvenile delinquency). The exhibit also includes holdings from the Archives' 300,000 reels of motion picture film and 200,000 sound recordings. You could see films of flying saucers, used as evidence in Congressional UFO hearings, and listen to recordings of the Nuremberg trials, or Congress debating Prohibition. Also on display are hundreds of the Archives' fascinating objects, such as a tape recorder used in the Watergate break-in, and the rifle Lee Harvey Oswald used to assassinate John F. Kennedy.

Many of the exhibits are interactive and kid-friendly. One room of letters from children to U.S. presidents includes a letter from seventh-grader

Andy Smith, asking Ronald Regan for Federal funds to clean up a disaster area—his room.

■ TIP→ **While this section operates as a museum, the Archives are also a research resource open to anyone.** This is the place for family genealogists to find birth, death, military and census records, immigrant ships' passenger lists, letters, and maps since the beginning of the nation's history. Assistants in the Archives can help you track down ancestors' records, or anything else you might be looking for. ⊠ *Constitution Ave. between 7th and 9th Sts. NW, The Mall* ☎ *202/501–5000, 202/501–5205 tours* ⊕ *www.nara.gov* ✉ *Free* ◷ *Apr.–Labor Day, daily 10–9; Labor Day–Mar., daily 10–5:30; tours weekdays at 10:15 and 1:15* Ⓜ *Archives/ Navy Memorial.*

❂ ▶ ★ **❻ National Building Museum.** The open interior of this mammoth redbrick edifice is one of the city's great spaces and has been the site of many an inaugural ball. (The first ball was for Grover Cleveland in 1885; because the building wasn't finished at the time, a temporary wooden roof and floor were built.) The eight central Corinthian columns are among the largest in the world, rising to a height of 75 feet. Although they resemble Siena marble, each is made of 70,000 bricks that have been covered with plaster and painted. For years, the annual *Christmas in Washington* TV special has been filmed in this breathtaking hall.

Formerly known as the Pension Building, it was erected between 1882 and 1887 to house workers who processed the pension claims of veterans and their survivors, an activity that intensified after the Civil War. The office is said to be the source of the term *red tape,* a reference to the material used to tie up veterans' papers, both literally and figuratively. The architect, U.S. Army Corps of Engineers' General Montgomery C. Meigs, took as his inspiration Rome's Palazzo Farnese. The museum is devoted to architecture and the building arts: recent exhibits have covered home improvement in 20th-century America, the preservation of Mount Vernon, and tools as an art form. The hands-on displays here are great for kids.

Before entering the building, walk down its F Street side. The terra-cotta frieze by Caspar Buberl between the first and second floors depicts soldiers marching and sailing in an endless procession around the building. Architect Meigs lost his eldest son in the Civil War, and, though the frieze depicts Union troops, he intended it as a memorial to all who were killed in the bloody war. Meigs designed the Pension Building with workers' comfort in mind. Note the three "missing" bricks under each window that allowed for air to circulate and helped keep the building cool. Tours are offered at 12:30 Monday through Wednesday; 11:30, 12:30, and 1:30 Thursday through Saturday; and 12:30 and 1:30 Sunday. Family programs are available at 2:30 Saturday and Sunday. ⊠ *401 F St. NW, between 4th and 5th Sts., East End* ☎ *202/272–2448* ⊕ *www. nbm.org* ✉ *Free* ◷ *Mon.–Sat. 10–5, Sun. 11–5* Ⓜ *Judiciary Sq.*

❼ National Law Enforcement Officers Memorial. This 3-foot-high wall bears the names of more than 15,000 American police officers killed in the line of duty since 1792. On the third line of panel 13W are the names of six officers killed by William Bonney, better known as Billy the Kid. J. D. Tippit, the Dallas policeman killed by Lee Harvey Oswald, is honored on the ninth line of panel 63E. Some of the most recent additions include the names of the 71 officers who died in the terror attacks of 2001. Two blocks from the memorial is a visitor center with exhibits on its history. Computers there allow you to look up officers by name, date of death, state, and department. A small shop sells souvenirs. Call to arrange for a free tour. In 2000 President Clinton authorized a bill to allow the construction of a National Law Enforcement Museum, scheduled for completion in 2008. ⊠ *605 E St. NW, East End* ☎ *202/737–3400* ⊕ *www.nleomf.com* ⊠ *Free* ☉ *Weekdays 9–5, Sat. 10–5, Sun. noon–5* Ⓜ *Gallery Pl./Chinatown or Judiciary Sq.*

❷ National Museum of Women in the Arts. Works by female artists from the Renaissance to the present are showcased at this museum. The beautifully restored 1907 Renaissance Revival building was designed by Waddy B. Wood; it was once a Masonic temple, for men only. In addition to displaying traveling shows, the museum has a permanent collection that includes paintings, drawings, sculpture, prints, and photographs by Georgia O'Keeffe, Mary Cassatt, Élisabeth Vigée-Lebrun, Frida Kahlo, and Camille Claudel. ⊠ *1250 New York Ave. NW, East End* ☎ *202/783–5000* ⊕ *www.nmwa.org* ⊠ *$10* ☉ *Mon.–Sat. 10–5, Sun. noon–5* Ⓜ *Metro Center.*

❾ National Portrait Gallery. This museum is in the Old Patent Office Building along with the Smithsonian American Art Museum. The building, and the two museums, reopened in 2006 after a six-year renovation. The Portrait Gallery now has 30% more exhibition space devoted to the intersection of art, biography and history, with its collection of more than 19,000 images of men and women who have contributed significantly to U.S. history. Among the collection's highlights are the iconic "Lansdowne" portrait of George Washington, by Gilbert Stuart, the portrait of Benjamin Franklin by Joseph Duplessis (featured on the new $100 bill), Edgar Degas' portrait of Mary Cassatt, Jo Davidson's portrait of Gertrude Stein, and John Singleton Copley's self-portrait. The collections also include portraits of all the U.S. presidents and more than 1,600 *Time* magazine covers. ⊠ *8th and F Sts. NW, East End* ☎ *202/ 633–1000, 202/357–1729 TDD* ⊕ *www.npg.si.edu* ☉ *Closed during renovation* Ⓜ *Gallery Pl./Chinatown.*

National Theatre. Except for brief periods spent as a movie house, the National Theatre has been mounting plays in this location since 1835. ■ TIP➜ **If you plan ahead, you can take a free tour that includes the house, stage, backstage, wardrobe room, dressing rooms, the area under the stage, the Helen Hayes Lounge, and the memorabilia-filled archives.** Tours are given for a minimum of 10 people, and only when there is no show; make reservations at least two weeks in advance. ⊠ *1321 Pennsylvania Ave. NW, intersection of*

> **CAPITAL FACTS**
>
> Helen Hayes saw her first play at the National Theatre at the age of six; she then vowed to become an actress.

13th and E Sts., East End ☎ *202/628–6161* ⊕ *www.nationaltheatre. org* 🖎 *Free* Ⓜ *Metro Center.*

㉓ **Navy Memorial.** A huge outdoor plaza, this memorial includes a granite world map and a 7-foot statue, *The Lone Sailor.* In summer, military bands perform on its concert stage. Next to the memorial, in the Market Square East Building, is the Naval Heritage Center, which has a gift shop and the Navy Log Room, where you can use computers to look up the service records of navy veterans. The 242-seat, wide-screen Arleigh & Roberta Burke Theater shows a rotating series of historical sea-service movies at noon. A memorial to General Winfield Scott Hancock, whose forces repelled Pickett's Charge at Gettysburg, is in the park adjacent to the Navy Memorial. ✉ *701 Pennsylvania Ave. NW, East End* ☎ *202/737–2300* ⊕ *www.lonesailor.org* 🖎 *Films free* ☉ *Naval Heritage Center Mar.–Nov., Mon.–Sat. 9:30–5* Ⓜ *Archives/Navy Memorial.*

㉑ **Newseum.** Set to open in 2007, the vast, 600,000-square-foot new Newseum will be a far larger, snazzier, and a more central incarnation of Washington's original museum of news, journalism, and the First Amendment, which opened in Arlington in 1997 and closed in 2002. Visitors will enter into the Great Hall of news, a 90-foot-high media-saturated atrium, overlooked by a giant screen showing breaking news anda news zipper. There are galleries devoted to news history, broadcast and online news, global news, and photojournalism. After looking through exhibits displaying 500 years of the history of news, visitors can try their hand at writing on deadline or wrestling with a Teleprompter in the Interactive Newsroom. In a space removed from the newsroom-like bustle of the rest of the museum will be a Journalists' Memorial, honoring more than 1,600 reporters and editors who lost their lives while covering news. ✉ *555 Pennsylvania Ave. NW, East End* ☎ *888/639–7386* ⊕ *www. newseum.org* Ⓜ *Archives/Navy Memorial.*

Old Adas Israel Synagogue. This is the oldest synagogue in Washington. Built in 1876 at 6th and G streets NW, the redbrick Federal Revival–style building was moved to its present location in 1969 to make way for an office building. Exhibits in the Lillian and Albert Small Jewish Museum inside explore Jewish life in Washington. ✉ *701 3rd St. NW, East End* ☎ *202/789–0900* 🖎 *Suggested donation $3* ☉ *Museum Sun.–Thurs. noon–3* Ⓜ *Judiciary Sq.*

Old Patent Office Building. Considered by many to be the finest example of Greek Revival architecture in the United States, this was called "the noblest of Washington buildings" by no less an admirer than Walt Whitman. The building itself, and the two museums it houses—the National Portrait Gallery, which has presidential portraits, *Time* magazine covers, and Civil War photographs, paintings, and prints, and the National Museum of American Art, with displays on Early American and western art, are at long last open again after a six-year renovation.

Construction of the south wing, designed by Washington Monument architect Robert Mills, started in 1836. When the huge Greek Revival quadrangle was completed in 1867, it was the largest building in the country. Many of its rooms housed glass display cabinets filled with the scale models that were required to accompany patent applications.

During the Civil War, the Patent Office, like many other buildings in the city, was turned into a hospital. Among those caring for the wounded here were Clara Barton and Walt Whitman. In the 1950s the building was threatened with demolition to make way for a parking lot, but the efforts of preservationists saved it. ⊠ *G St. between 7th and 9th Sts., East End* ☎ *202/633–1000* Ⓜ *Gallery Pl./Chinatown.*

🐾 **⑰** **Old Post Office.** When it was completed in 1899, this Romanesque structure on Federal Triangle was the largest government building in the District, the first with a clock tower, and the first with an electric power plant. Despite these innovations, it earned the sobriquet *old* after only 15 years, when a new District post office was constructed near Union Station. When urban planners in the 1920s decided to impose a uniform design on Federal Triangle, the Old Post Office was slated for demolition. The fanciful granite building was saved first because of a lack of money during the Depression, then thanks to the intercession of preservationists. Major renovation was begun in 1978, and in 1983 the Old Post Office Pavilion—an assortment of shops and restaurants inside the airy central courtyard—opened.

▇ TIP→ **Park service rangers who work at the Old Post Office consider the observation deck in the clock tower one of Washington's best-kept secrets. Although not as tall as the Washington Monument, it offers nearly as impressive a view.** Even better, it's usually not as crowded, the windows are bigger, and—unlike the monument's windows—they're open, allowing cool breezes to waft through. (For self-guided tours, use the entrance at 12th Street and Pennsylvania Avenue and take the glass elevator to the 9th floor.) On the way down don't miss the Congress Bells, cast at the same British foundry as those in London's Westminster Abbey. The bells are rung to honor the opening and closing of Congress and on other important occasions, such as when the Redskins win the Super Bowl.

Cross 10th Street from the Old Post Office Pavilion. Look to your left at the delightful trompe l'oeil mural on the side of the **Lincoln Building** two blocks up. It appears as if there's a hole in the building. There's also a portrait of the building's namesake. ⊠ *12th St. and Pennsylvania Ave. NW, East End* ☎ *202/606–8691 tower, 202/289–4224 pavilion* ⊕ *www.oldpostofficedc.com* 🎫 *Free* ☉ *Tower early May–early Sept., daily 8–10:45, mid-Sept.–early May, daily 10–5:45; pavilion Apr.–Labor Day, Mon.–Sat. 10–8, Sun. noon–7, Labor Day–Apr., Mon.–Sat. 10–7, Sun. noon–6* Ⓜ *Federal Triangle.*

Pennsylvania Avenue. The capital's most historically important thoroughfare repeatedly threads through sightseeing walks. Newly inaugurated presidents travel west on Pennsylvania Avenue en route to the White House. Thomas Jefferson started the parade tradition in 1805 after taking the oath of office for his second term. He was accompanied by a few friends and a handful of congressmen. Four years later James Madison made things official by instituting a proper inaugural celebration.

1

The flag holders on the lampposts are clues that Pennsylvania Avenue remains the city's foremost parade route. With the Capitol at one end and the White House at the other, the avenue symbolizes both the separation and the ties between these two branches of government.

When Pennsylvania Avenue first opened in 1796, it was an ugly, dangerous bog. Attempts by Jefferson to beautify the road with poplar trees were only partially successful: many were chopped down by fellow residents for firewood. In the mid-19th century, crossing the rutted thoroughfare was treacherous, and rainstorms often turned the street into a river. The avenue was finally paved with wooden blocks in 1871.

At the convergence of 7th Street and Pennsylvania and Indiana avenues is a multitude of statues and monuments. The **Grand Army of the Republic** memorial pays tribute to the soldiers who won the Civil War. Less conventional is the nearby **Temperance Fountain,** which has a heron on its top. It was designed and built in the 19th century by Henry D. Cogswell, a teetotaling physician who hoped the fountain, which once dispensed ice-cold water, would help lure people from the evils of drink.

Redevelopment has rejuvenated Pennsylvania Avenue and the neighboring **Penn Quarter,** the name given to the mix of condominiums, apartments, retail spaces, and restaurants in the blocks bounded by Pennsylvania Avenue and 6th, 9th, and G streets. In addition to the Hotel Monaco, the International Spy Museum, and the Newseum, the area contains the Lansburgh complex, at the corner of 8th and E streets. Built around three existing buildings (including the defunct Lansburgh department store), the complex includes the nationally acclaimed Shakespeare Theatre, due to add a new arts center expansion in 2007. Ⓜ *Archives/Navy Memorial.*

🅭 **Petersen House.** Lincoln died in the house of William Petersen, a tailor, on the morning of April 15, 1865, after being shot at Ford's Theatre the night before. You can see the house's restored front and back parlors and the bedroom where the president died. Call in advance for tour times. ✉ *516 10th St. NW, East End* ☎ *202/426–6830* ⊕ *www.nps.gov/foth* 🎟 *Free* ☉ *Daily 9–5* Ⓜ *Metro Center or Gallery Pl./Chinatown.*

> **NEED A BREAK?**
>
> Leave the Lincoln tragedy behind and get some comfort food at the **Marvelous Market** (✉ 730 7th St. NW, East End ☎ 202/628–0824). At this informal eatery you can get fresh sandwiches, soups, chips, and other bakery fare, including what may be the best brownies in Washington.

🅰 **Ronald Reagan Building and International Trade Center.** This $818 million, 3.1-million-square-foot colossus is the largest federal building to be constructed in the Washington area since the Pentagon, and the first to be designed for use by both the government and the private sector. A blend of classical and modern architecture, the Indiana-limestone structure replaced what for 50 years had been an enormous parking lot, an eyesore that interrupted the flow of the buildings of Federal Triangle. At present, the Reagan Building houses the Environmental Protection Agency, the U.S. Customs Service, and the U.S. Agency for International Development. The **D.C. Visitor Information Center** (☎ 202/328–4748 ⊕ www.dcvisit.com), located here, is a convenient place to pick up brochures, see a free historical video, and get tickets for tours or evening performances. There's also a multilingual touch-screen computer kiosk with information about the city (the same machine lets you send a free e-mail postcard with your photo to anyone in the world). Hours for the visitor center and its gift shop are 8–6 weekdays and 8–5 Saturday. The building has a food court on the lower level, and a theatrical group, the Capitol Steps, performs works of political satire here on Friday and Saturday nights at 7:30. ⊠ *1300 Pennsylvania Ave. NW, East End* ⊠ *Free* Ⓜ *Federal Triangle.*

❿ Smithsonian American Art Museum. This museum is in the Old Patent Office Building along with the National Portrait Gallery. As the United States' first federal art collection, the Smithsonian American Art Museum is now considered to be the world's biggest and most diverse collection of American art. Its more than 41,000 holdings span three centuries, from colonial portraits to 20th-century abstractionists. Especially strong are the museum's collections of New Deal art, American impressionist paintings, photography of western expansion, African-American and Latino art, and folk art. Among the 7,000 American artists represented are John Singleton Copley, Winslow Homer, Mary Cassatt, Georgia O'-Keeffe, Edward Hopper, David Hockney and Robert Rauschenberg. ⊠ *8th and G Sts. NW, East End* ☎ *202/275–1500, 202/357–1729 TDD* ⊕ *www.americanart.si.edu* Ⓜ *Gallery Pl./Chinatown.*

❺ Surratt Boarding House. A plaque by the front door attests that John Wilkes Booth and his co-conspirators plotted Abraham Lincoln's assasination here. The current occupant of the building is a Chinese restaurant. ⊠ *604 H St. NW, East End* Ⓜ *Gallery Pl./Chinatown.*

Tariff Commission Building (Old General Post Office). The Tariff Commission Building, designed by Robert Mills and finished in 1866, is one of three historic structures to occupy the same site. When the Capitol was burned by the British in 1814, Congress met temporarily in a hotel that stood here. Another earlier building housed the nation's first public telegraph office, operated by Samuel F. B. Morse. It now houses the Hotel Monaco. ⊠ *700 F St. NW, East End* Ⓜ *Gallery Pl./Chinatown.*

Willard Inter-Continental. There was a Willard Hotel on this spot long before this ornate structure was built in 1901. The original Willard was *the* place to stay in Washington if you were rich or influential (or wanted to give that impression). Abraham Lincoln stayed there while waiting to move into the nearby White House. Julia Ward Howe stayed there during the Civil War and wrote "The Battle Hymn of the Republic" after gazing down from her window to see Union troops drilling on Pennsylvania Avenue. It's said the term *lobbyist* was coined to describe the favor seekers who would buttonhole President Ulysses S. Grant in the hotel's public rooms. The second Willard, with a mansard roof dotted with circular windows, was designed by Henry Hardenbergh, architect of New York's Plaza Hotel. Although it was just as opulent as the hotel it replaced, it fell on hard times after World War II. In 1968 it closed, standing empty until 1986, when it reopened, amid much fanfare, after an ambitious restoration. ⊠ *1401 Pennsylvania Ave. NW, East End* ☎ *202/ 628–9100 or 800/327–0200* ⊕ *www.washington.interconti.com.*

GEORGETOWN

Long before the District of Columbia was formed, Washington's oldest and wealthiest neighborhood was a separate city with a harbor full of ships and warehouses filled with tobacco. Washington has filled in around Georgetown over the years, but the former tobacco port retains an air of aloofness. Its narrow streets, which don't conform to Pierre-Charles L'Enfant's plan for the Federal City, are home to a great deal of foot traffic and an active nightlife.

The area that would come to be known as George (after George II), then George Towne, and finally Georgetown was part of Maryland when it was settled in the early 1700s by Scottish immigrants, many of whom were attracted to the region's tolerant religious climate. Georgetown's position—at the farthest point up the Potomac that's accessible by boat—made it an ideal transit and inspection point for farmers who grew tobacco in Maryland's interior. In 1789 the state granted the town a charter, but two years later Georgetown—along with Alexandria, its counterpart in Virginia—was included by George Washington in the Territory of Columbia, site of the new capital.

While Washington struggled, Georgetown thrived. Wealthy traders built their mansions on the hills overlooking the river; merchants and the working class lived in modest homes closer to the water's edge. In 1810 a third of Georgetown's population was African-American—both free people and slaves. The Mt. Zion United Methodist Church on 29th Street is the oldest organized black congregation in the city. When the church stood at 27th and P streets, it was a stop on the Underground Railroad (the original building burned down in the mid-1800s).

> **CAPITAL FACTS**
>
> The flat-front, redbrick Federal house at 3307 N Street was the home of then-Senator John F. Kennedy and his family before the White House beckoned.

Georgetown's rich history and success instilled in all its residents a feeling of pride that still lingers today. (When Georgetowners thought the dismal capital was dragging them down, they asked to be given back to Maryland, the way Alexandria was given back to Virginia in 1845.) Tobacco eventually became a less important commodity, and Georgetown became a milling center, using water power from the Potomac. When the Chesapeake & Ohio (C&O) Canal was completed in 1850, the city intensified its milling operations and became the eastern end of a waterway that stretched 184 mi to the west. The canal took up some of the slack when Georgetown's harbor began to fill with silt and the port lost business to Alexandria and Baltimore, but the canal never became the success it was meant to be.

In the years that followed, Georgetown was a far cry from the fashionable spot it is today. Clustered near the water were a foundry, a fish market, paper and cotton mills, and a power station for the city's streetcar system, all of which made Georgetown a smelly industrial district. It still had its Georgian, Federal, and Victorian homes, though, and when the New Deal and World War II brought a flood of newcomers to Washington, Georgetown's tree-shaded streets and handsome brick houses were rediscovered. Pushed out in the process were many of Georgetown's renters, which included many of its black residents.

Today some of Washington's most famous residents call Georgetown home, including former *Washington Post* executive editor Ben Bradlee, political pundit George Stephanopoulos, Senator (and 2004 presidential nominee) John Kerry, and *New York Times* op-ed doyenne Maureen Dowd. Georgetown's historic preservationists are among the most vocal in the city, and many want protection from is the crush of people who descend on their community every night. This is one of Washington's main areas for restaurants, bars, nightclubs, and boutiques. On M Street and Wisconsin Avenue, you can indulge just about any taste and take home almost any upscale souvenir. A place to park is harder to find.

TOP 5: GEORGETOWN

- **C&O Canal:** Walk or bicycle along the path here, which offers graciously bucolic scenery from Georgetown all the way to Maryland.

- **Cox's Row:** Ogle some of Washington's finest architecture—and the homes of some of its most powerful residents—with a walk through this area, circling down past the campus of Georgetown University.

- **Dumbarton Oaks:** Stroll through the 10 acres of formal gardens—possibly Washington's loveliest oasis.

- **M Street:** Indulge in some serious designer retail therapy (or just window shopping) on this fabulous street.

- **Washington Harbour:** Come on a warm night to enjoy sunset drinks while overlooking Watergate, the Kennedy Center, and the Potomac River.

Georgetown owes some of its charm and separate growth to geography. This town-unto-itself is separated from Washington to the east by Rock Creek. On the south it's bordered by the Potomac, on the west by Georgetown University. How far north does Georgetown reach? Probably not much farther than the large estates and parks above R Street, though developers and real estate agents would be happy to include all the land up to Canada if it increased property value here.

There's no Metro stop in Georgetown, so you have to take a bus or taxi or walk to this part of Washington. It's about a 15-minute walk from the Dupont Circle or Foggy Bottom Metro station. ■ TIP➔ **Perhaps the best transportation deal in Georgetown is the Georgetown Metro Connection.** These little blue buses have two routes, one along Wisconsin Avenue and K Street to the Foggy Bottom Metro and the second along M Street to the Dupont Circle and Rosslyn Metros. Buses run daily every 10 minutes. Other options include the G2 Georgetown University bus, which goes west from Dupont Circle along P Street, and the 34 and 36 Friend-

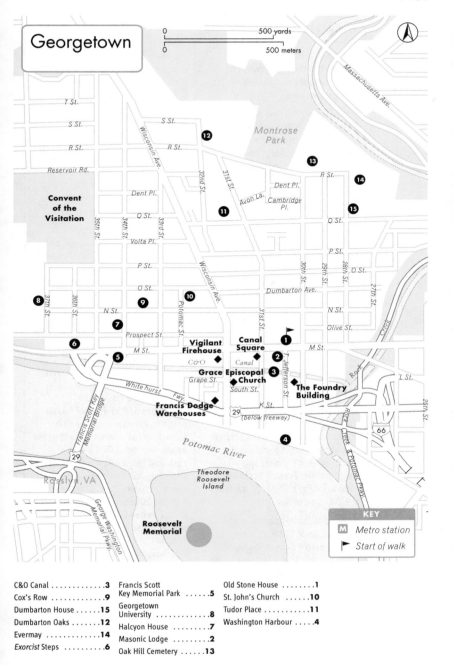

Georgetown

0 ——— 500 yards
0 ——— 500 meters

T St.
S St.
R St.
Reservoir Rd.

S St.
R St.

Montrose Park

Convent of the Visitation

Wisconsin Ave.
35th St.
34th St.
33rd St.
32nd St.
31st St.

Dent Pl.
Q St.
Volta Pl.
P St.
O St.
N St.
Prospect St.
M St.

Dent Pl.
Avon La.
Cambridge Pl.

R St.
Q St.
P St.
Dumbarton Ave.
N St.
Olive St.
M St.

30th St.
29th St.
28th St.
27th St.

Massachusetts Ave.

37th St.
36th St.

Vigilant Firehouse
C&O ◆
Canal
Grape St.

Grace Episcopal Church ◆
South St.

Canal Square ◆

Francis Dodge Warehouses ◆
29
(below freeway)

K St.

The Foundry Building ◆

Jefferson St.
31st St.

White hurst Fwy.
Francis Scott Key Memorial Bridge
29

Rosslyn, VA

George Washington Memorial Pkwy.

Potomac River

Theodore Roosevelt Island

Roosevelt Memorial

Rock Creek & Potomac Pkwy.
66
L St.
25th St.

KEY
Ⓜ Metro station
► Start of walk

8 **7** **6** **5** **9** **10** **11** **12** **13** **14** **15** **1** **2** **3** **4**

C&O Canal **3**

Cox's Row **9**

Dumbarton House **15**

Dumbarton Oaks **12**

Evermay **14**

Exorcist Steps **6**

Francis Scott
Key Memorial Park **5**

Georgetown
University **8**

Halcyon House **7**

Masonic Lodge **2**

Oak Hill Cemetery **13**

Old Stone House **1**

St. John's Church **10**

Tudor Place **11**

Washington Harbour **4**

A GOOD WALK

Numbers in the box correspond to numbers in the margin and on the Georgetown map.

Start your exploration of Georgetown at 31st and M streets, in front of the **Old Stone House** ❶ ▶, possibly Washington's only pre–Revolutionary War building. From the Old Stone House, cross over M Street to Thomas Jefferson Street (between 30th and 31st streets). The 200-year-old, two-story brick structure at No. 1058 was built as a **Masonic Lodge** ❷. Follow Thomas Jefferson Street as it passes over the **C&O Canal** ❸, whose towpath and waters are now used by runners, bikers, and canoeists. In spring and summer you can take a mule-drawn canal boat ride. Cross K Street to **Washington Harbour** ❹, a development that includes waterfront restaurants, offices, apartments, and pricey shops. Cross the canal again at Wisconsin Avenue. Both M Street and Wisconsin Avenue are lined with restaurants and boutiques selling just about anything you could want—but don't expect any bargains. The **Francis Scott Key Memorial Park** ❺ lies at the foot of the D.C. side of Key Bridge.

To head to the residential area, continue on M Street past the old brick streetcar barn at No. 3600 (now offices), turn right, and climb the 75 *Exorcist* steps ❻. If you're not up to the climb, walk up 34th Street instead. **Halcyon House** ❼ was built in 1763 by the first

secretary of the navy. The beautiful campus of **Georgetown University** ❽, the oldest Jesuit school in the country, is a few blocks to the west. **Cox's Row** ❾, a group of five Federal houses between 3339 and 3327 N Street, was built in 1817 by a former mayor of Georgetown. The redbrick house at 3307 N Street was the home of then-Senator John F. Kennedy and his family before they moved downtown to 1600 Pennsylvania Avenue.

Turn left onto Potomac Street and walk a block up to O Street, several blocks of which still have cobblestones and trolley tracks. **St. John's Church** ❿ was built in 1809. Cross Wisconsin Avenue and go up 31st Street to Q Street, where through the trees you can see **Tudor Place** ⓫, a neoclassical mansion with a dramatic domed portico. Walk up 32nd Street to **Dumbarton Oaks** ⓬, a former estate that contains two excellent art collections and 10 acres of formal gardens. Dumbarton Oaks Park sprawls to the north and west of the estate, Montrose Park lies to the east, and farther east is **Oak Hill Cemetery** ⓭, overlooking Rock Creek. Walk south on 28th Street past the 200-year-old Georgian manor house **Evermay** ⓮, now a private home with lovely grounds. Around the corner on Q Street is **Dumbarton House** ⓯, headquarters of the National Society of the Colonial Dames of America. It's filled with magnificent period antiques.

ship Heights buses, which leave from 22nd and Pennsylvania and deposit you at 31st and M.

TIMING   You can easily spend a pleasant day in Georgetown, partly because some sights (Tudor Place, Dumbarton Oaks, Oak Hill Cemetery, Evermay, and Dumbarton House) are somewhat removed from the others and partly because the street scene, with its intriguing shops and people-watching, invites you to linger. Georgetown is almost always crowded. It's not very car-friendly either, especially at night; driving and parking are usually difficult. The wise take the Metro to Foggy Bottom or Dupont Circle and then walk 15 minutes from there, or take a bus or taxi.

What to See

C&O Canal. This waterway kept Georgetown open to shipping after its harbor had filled with silt. George Washington was one of the first to advance the idea of a canal linking the Potomac with the Ohio River across the Appalachians. Work started on the C&O Canal in 1828, and when it opened in 1850, its 74 locks linked Georgetown with Cumberland, Maryland, 184 mi to the northwest (still short of its intended destination). Lumber, coal, iron, wheat, and flour moved up and down the canal, but it was never as successful as its planners had hoped it would be. Many of the bridges spanning the canal in Georgetown were too low to allow anything other than fully loaded barges to pass underneath, and competition from the Baltimore & Ohio Railroad eventually spelled an end to profitability. Today the canal is part of the National Park System; walkers follow the towpath once used by mules while canoeists paddle the canal's calm waters. Between April and November you can go on a mule-drawn trip aboard the *Georgetown* canal boat. Tickets for the rides, which last about an hour, are available across the canal, next to the Foundry Building. Barge rides are also available at Great Falls, at the end of MacArthur Boulevard, in nearby Potomac, Maryland. Barge rides are given late March through mid-June and early September through early November, Wednesday to Friday at 11 and 2:30, and on weekends at 11, 1, 2:30, and 4. From mid-June through early September, barge rides are Wednesday to Friday at 11, 1, and 2:30, and on weekends at 11, 1, 2:30, and 4; the cost is $8. ⊠ *Canal Visitor Center, 1057 Thomas Jefferson St. NW, Georgetown* ☎ *202/653–5190.*

Canal Square. This 1850s warehouse was converted into a retail and office complex in the 1970s, retaining much of the original brickwork. In the interior courtyard are retail shops and several art galleries, notably the small but innovative **Museum of Contemporary Art** (☎ 202/342–6230 ⊕ www.mocadc.org). ⊠ *1054 31st St. NW, Georgetown.*

Cox's Row. Architecture buffs, especially those interested in Federal and Victorian houses, enjoy wandering along the redbrick sidewalks of upper Georgetown. The average house here has two signs on it: a brass plaque notifying passersby of the building's historic interest and a window decal that warns potential burglars of its state-of-the-art alarm system. To get a representative taste of the houses in the area, walk along the 3300 block of N Street. The group of five Federal houses between 3339 and 3327 N Street is known collectively as Cox's Row, after

Colonel John Cox, a former mayor of Georgetown, who built them in 1817 and resided at 3339.

⑮ Dumbarton House. Its symmetry and the two curved wings on its north side make Dumbarton, built around 1800, a distinctive example of Federal architecture. The first occupant of the house, Joseph Nourse, was registrar of the U.S. Treasury. Other well-known Americans have spent time here, including Dolley Madison, who stopped here when fleeing Washington in 1814. One hundred years later, the house was saved from demolition by being moved 100 feet uphill, when Q Street was cut through to the Dumbarton Bridge. Since 1928 it has served as the headquarters of the National Society of the Colonial Dames of America.

Eight rooms inside Dumbarton House have been restored to Federal-era splendor, with period furnishings such as mahogany American Chippendale chairs, hallmark silver, Persian rugs, and a breakfront cabinet filled with rare books. Other notable items include Martha Washington's traveling cloak, a British soldier's red coat, and a 1789 Charles Willson Peale portrait of the children of Benjamin Stoddert, the first secretary of the navy (the portrait has a view of Georgetown harbor in the background). To see the house's interior, you must take the 45-minute guided tour. ✉ *2715 Q St. NW, Georgetown* ☎ *202/337–2288* ⊕ *www.dumbartonhouse.org* ✉ *Suggested donation $5* ☉ *Tues.–Sat. 10–1. Tours at 10:15, 11:15, 12:15, and 1:15.*

⑫ Dumbarton Oaks. Don't confuse Dumbarton Oaks with the nearby Dumbarton House. In 1944 one of the most important events of the 20th century took place here, when representatives of the United States, Great Britain, China, and the Soviet Union met in the music room to lay the groundwork for the United Nations.

Career diplomat Robert Woods Bliss and his wife, Mildred, bought the property in 1920 and tamed the sprawling grounds, and removed later 19th-century additions that had obscured the Federal lines of the 1801 mansion. In 1940 the Blisses gave the estate to Harvard University, which maintains world-renowned collections of Byzantine and pre-Columbian art here. Both collections are small but choice, reflecting the enormous skill and creativity going on at roughly the same time in two very different parts of the world. The Byzantine collection includes beautiful examples of both religious and secular items executed in mosaic, metal, enamel, and ivory. Pre-Columbian works—artifacts and textiles from Mexico and Central and South America by peoples such as the Aztec, Maya, and Olmec—are arranged in an enclosed glass pavilion designed by Philip Johnson. Normally on view to the public are the lavishly decorated music room and selections from Mrs. Bliss's collection of rare illustrated garden books. Because of ongoing renovations at the estate, both art collections and the music room are closed until 2007.

■ **TIP→** If you have even a mild interest in flowers, shrubs, trees, and magnificent natural beauty, visit Dumbarton Oaks's 10 acres of formal gardens, one of the loveliest spots in Washington (enter at 31st and R streets). Planned by noted landscape architect Beatrix Farrand, the gardens incorporate elements of traditional English, Italian, and French styles such as a formal rose garden, an English country garden, and an orangery (circa 1810). A full-time crew of a dozen gardeners toils to maintain the stunning collection of terraces, geometric gardens, tree-shaded brick walks, fountains, arbors, and pools. Plenty of well-positioned benches make this a good place for resting weary feet, too. ⊠ *1703 32nd St. NW, Georgetown* ☎ *202/339–6401 or 202/339–6400* ⌑ *$7* ⊙ *Gardens Apr.–Oct., daily 2–6; Nov.–Mar., daily 2–5.*

14 **Evermay.** A Georgian manor house built around 1800 by real estate speculator Samuel Davidson, Evermay is almost hidden by its black-and-gold gates and high brick wall. Davidson wanted it that way. He sometimes ran newspapers ads warning sightseers to avoid his estate "as they would a den of devils or rattlesnakes." The mansion is in private hands, but its grounds are occasionally opened for garden tours. ⊠ *1623 28th St. NW, Georgetown* ☎ *202/338–1118* ⊕ *www.evermay.org.*

6 *Exorcist* **Steps.** The heights of Georgetown to the north above N Street contrast with the busy jumble of the old waterfront. You can walk up M Street, past the old brick streetcar barn at No. 3600 (now a block of offices), turn right, and climb the 75 steps that figured prominently in the horror movie *The Exorcist*. If you prefer a less-demanding climb, walk up 34th Street instead. ⊠ *M and 36th Sts., Georgetown.*

The Foundry Building. This building gets its name from the machine shop that was here from 1856 to 1866. It housed several businesses after that, and around the turn of the 19th century it was a veterinary hospital for mules that worked on the canal. A 2003 renovation replaced the shopping mall and movie theater that stood here during the last half of the 20th century with a new office complex. ⊠ *1055 Thomas Jefferson St. NW, Georgetown.*

NEED A BREAK? If the crowds of Georgetown become overwhelming, step into **Ching Ching Cha** (⊠ 1063 Wisconsin Ave. NW, Georgetown ☎ 202/333–8288), a Chinese teahouse where tranquillity reigns supreme. In addition to tea, lunch and dinner may be ordered from a simple menu with light, healthful meals presented in lacquer bento boxes.

Francis Dodge Warehouses. The last three buildings at the foot of the west side of Wisconsin Avenue are reminders of Georgetown's mercantile past. They were built around 1830 by trader and merchant Francis Dodge. Note the heavy stone foundation of the southernmost warehouse, its star-end braces, and the broken hoist in the gable end. According to an 1838 newspaper ad, Georgetown shoppers could visit Dodge's grocery to buy items such as "Porto Rico Sugar, Marseilles soft-shelled Almonds and Havanna Segars." Although the traders of yesteryear have been replaced by small nonprofit organizations, the buildings don't look as if they house modern offices, and their facades make an interesting snapshot. ⊠ *1000–02 Wisconsin Ave. NW, Georgetown.*

5 **Francis Scott Key Memorial Park.** A small, noisy park near the Key Bridge honors the Washington attorney who "by the dawn's early light" penned the national anthem during the War of 1812. Key was inspired when he saw that Britain's night bombardment of Fort McHenry in Baltimore harbor had failed to destroy the fort's flag. A replica of the 15-star, 15-stripe flag flies over the park (the original is on display at the National Museum of American History). Here, Georgetown's quaint demeanor contrasts with the silvery skyscrapers of Rosslyn, Virginia, across the Potomac. ⊠ *M St. between 34th St. and Key Bridge, Georgetown.*

❽ Georgetown University. Founded in 1789 by John Carroll, first American bishop and first archbishop of Baltimore, Georgetown is the oldest Jesuit school in the country. About 12,000 students attend Georgetown, known now as much for its perennially successful basketball team as for its fine programs in law, medicine, foreign service, and the liberal arts. When seen from the Potomac or from Washington's high ground, the Gothic spires of Georgetown's older buildings give the university an almost medieval look. ⊠ *37th and O Sts., Georgetown* ☎ *202/687–5055* ⊕ *www.georgetown.edu.*

Grace Episcopal Church. In the mid- to late 19th century, the Gothic Revival Grace Episcopal Church served the boatmen and workers from the nearby C&O Canal. The area was then one of the poorest in Georgetown. ⊠ *1041 Wisconsin Ave. NW, Georgetown* ☎ *202/333–7100* ☉ *Services Sat. 6 PM and Sun. 8:30 and 10 AM.*

❼ Halcyon House. Built in 1783 by Benjamin Stoddert, the first secretary of the navy, Halcyon House has been the object of many subsequent additions and renovations. It's now a motley assortment of architectural styles. Prospect Street, where the house is set, gets its name from the fine views it affords of the waterfront and the river below. The house is closed to the public. ⊠ *34th and Prospect Sts., Georgetown.*

❷ Masonic Lodge. A two-story brick structure, Georgetown's Masonic Lodge, which isn't open to visitors, was built around 1810. Freemasonry, the world's largest secret society, was started by British stonemasons and cathedral builders as early as the 14th century; the fraternal order now has a much broader international membership that has included U.S. presidents—among them George Washington—as well as members of Congress. It's no accident that the Freemasons chose Georgetown to be the site of a lodge. Although Georgetown today is synonymous with wealth, for most of its history it was a working-class city, and the original names of its streets—Water Street, Canal Road, Fishing Lane—attest to the past importance of traditional trades to the region's economy. The area south of M Street (originally called Bridge Street because of the bridge that spanned Rock Creek to the east) was inhabited by tradesmen, laborers, and merchants who were good candidates for expanding the Masons' ranks. Among the lodge's interesting details are a pointed facade and recessed central arch, features that suggest the society's traditional attachment to the building arts. ⊠ *1058 Thomas Jefferson St., Georgetown.*

Montrose Park. Originally owned by 19th-century rope-making magnate Richard Parrot, this tract of land was purchased by Congress in the early 20th century "for the recreation and pleasure of the people." A popular spot for locals out with their toddlers and dogs, the park is good for

1

an outing or short break. There are tennis courts, a swing set, and picnic tables. ✉ *3001 R St. NW, Georgetown.*

13 **Oak Hill Cemetery.** The funerary obelisks, crosses, and gravestones here spread out over four landscaped terraces on a hill overlooking Rock Creek. Near the brick-and-sandstone gatehouse entrance is an 1850 Gothic-style chapel designed by Smithsonian Castle architect James Renwick. Across from the chapel is the resting place of actor, playwright, and diplomat John H. Payne, who is remembered today primarily for his song "Home Sweet Home." A few hundred feet to the north is the circular tomb of William Corcoran, founder of the Corcoran Gallery of Art, who donated the land for the cemetery. ■ TIP➜ **Cameras and backpacks are forbidden in the cemetery; they can be checked-in at the entrance.** ✉ *3001 R St. NW, Georgetown* ☎ *202/337–2835* ⬛ *Free* ☉ *Weekdays 10–4.*

▶ **1** **Old Stone House.** What was early American life like? Here's the capital's oldest window into the past. Work on this fieldstone house, thought to be Washington's oldest surviving building, was begun in 1764 by a cabinetmaker named Christopher Layman. Now a museum, it was used as both a residence and a place of business by a succession of occupants. Five of the house's rooms are furnished with the simple, sturdy artifacts—plain tables, spinning wheels, and so forth—of 18th-century middle-class life. The National Park Service maintains the house and its lovely gardens, which are planted with fruit trees and perennials. ✉ *3051 M St. NW, Georgetown* ☎ *202/426–6851* ⬛ *Free* ☉ *Wed.–Sun. 10–4.*

10 **St. John's Church.** West of Wisconsin Avenue, a several-blocks-long stretch of O Street has remnants from an earlier age: cobblestones and streetcar tracks. Residents are so proud of the cobblestones that newer concrete patches are scored so that they fit in. Prominent in this section of Georgetown is one of the oldest churches in the city, St. John's Church, built in 1796 and attributed to Dr. William Thornton, architect of the Capitol. Interior alterations reflect a Victorian, rather than Federal, style. St. John's is also noted for its stained-glass windows, including a small Tiffany. ✉ *3240 O St. NW, Georgetown* ☎ *202/338–1796* ☉ *Services Sun. at 9 and 11, Thurs. at 11:30.*

11 **Tudor Place.** Stop at Q Street between 31st and 32nd streets; look through the trees to the north, at the top of a sloping lawn, and you'll see the neoclassical Tudor Place, designed by Capitol architect Dr. William Thornton and completed in 1816. On a house tour you'll see Francis Scott Key's desk, items that belonged to George Washington, and spurs belonging to soldiers who were killed in the Civil War. The grounds contain many specimens planted in the early 19th century. The house was built for Thomas Peter, son of Georgetown's first mayor, and his wife, Martha Custis, Martha Washington's granddaughter. It was because of this connection to the president's family that Tudor Place came to house many items from Mount Vernon. The yellow stucco house is interesting for its architecture—especially the dramatic, two-story domed portico on the south side—but its familial heritage is even more remarkable: Tudor Place stayed in the same family for 178 years, until 1983, when Armistead Peter III died. Before his death, Peter established a foundation to restore the house and open it to the public. Tour reservations are advised. ✉ *1644 31st St. NW, Georgetown* ☎ *202/965–0400* ⊕ *www.tudorplace.org* 🗎 *House and garden tour, suggested donation $6* ⊙ *House tours Tues.–Fri. at 10, 11:30, 1, and 2:30; Sat. hourly 10–4; last tour at 3. Sun. at noon, 1, 2, and 3. Garden Nov.–Mar. and June–Aug., Mon.–Sat. 10–4; Apr., May, Sept., and Oct., Mon.–Sat. 10–4, Sun. noon–4.*

❹ **Washington Harbour.** Stately columns and the liberal use of glass in its construction are hallmarks of Washington Harbour, a 6-acre glittering postmodern riverfront development designed by Arthur Cotton Moore. Included are restaurants such as the two-story Sequoia, Tony & Joe's Seafood Place, and the Riverside Grille, as well as offices, apartments, and upscale shops. Highlights of the central plaza are a large fountain and a futuristic, lighthouselike structure made up of four towering white columns. Several restaurants offer outdoor dining. From the edge of Washington Harbour you can see the Watergate complex and Kennedy Center to the east; meanwhile you can hear the waters of the Potomac gently lap at the edge of the dock. Those who prefer the water to the streets often arrive by boat, docking just yards from outdoor diners. At night, the area sparkles like a Christmas scene, with hundreds of twinkling white lights. ✉ *3000 K St. NW, Georgetown.*

DUPONT CIRCLE

The main thoroughfares of Connecticut, New Hampshire, and Massachusetts avenues all intersect at Dupont Circle. With a small, handsome park and a splashing fountain in the center, Dupont Circle is more than an island around which traffic flows, making it an exception among Washington circles. The activity spills over into the surrounding streets, one of the liveliest, most vibrant neighborhoods in D.C.

Development near Dupont Circle started during the post–Civil War boom of the 1870s. As the city increased in stature, the nation's wealthy and influential citizens began building their mansions near the circle. The area underwent a different kind of transformation in the middle of the 20th century, when the middle and upper classes deserted Washington for the suburbs, and in the 1960s the circle became the starting point for politically themed marches and protests attended by students and others. Today the neighborhood is more upscale, and its many restaurants, offbeat shops, coffeehouses, art galleries, and specialty bookstores lend it a distinctive, cosmopolitan air. Stores and clubs catering to the neighborhood's large gay community are abundant.

TIMING Visiting the Dupont Circle area takes at least half a day, although you can find things to keep you busy all day. The most time-consuming sites are probably the Phillips Collection, the National Geographic Society's Explorers Hall, and Anderson House, although the Textile and the American Jewish Military History museums can be captivating as well.

What to See

❹ **Anderson House.** A palatial home that's a mystery even to many longtime Washingtonians, Anderson House isn't an embassy, though it does have a link to that world. Larz Anderson was a diplomat from 1891 to

1913 whose career included postings to Japan and Belgium. Anderson and his heiress wife, Isabel, toured the world, picking up objects that struck their fancy. They filled their residence, which was constructed for them in 1905, with the booty of their travels, including choir stalls from an Italian Renaissance church, Flemish tapestries, and a large—if spotty—collection of Asian art. All this remains in the house for you to see.

In accordance with the Andersons' wishes, the building also serves as the headquarters of a group to which Larz belonged: the Society of the Cincinnati. The oldest patriotic organization in the country, the society was formed in 1783 by a group of officers who had served with George Washington during the Revolutionary War. The group took its name from Cincinnatus, a distinguished Roman farmer who, circa 500 BC, led an army against Rome's enemies and later quelled civil disturbances in the city. After each success, rather than seek the political power that could have easily been his, he returned to simple farm life. The story impressed the American officers; they, too, would leave the battlefields to get on with the business of forging a new nation. (One such member went on to name the city in Ohio.) Today's members are direct descendants of those American revolutionaries.

TOP 5: DUPONT CIRCLE

- **Anderson House:** Glimpse into the life of a fabulously wealthy turn-of-the-19th-century U.S. diplomat, Larz Anderson, and his glamorous, art-loving wife, Isabel. This magnificent mansion is preserved as it was built it in 1905 and filled its rococo pink-and-white marble rooms with treasures from Anderson's posts from Japan to Belgium.

- **Dupont Circle:** Grab a cup of coffee and a *City Paper* and take in the scene—artists, hipsters, power-lunchers, chess players, Olympic-caliber bike messengers—around the always-buzzing fountain.

- **Gallery Hop:** On the first Friday of every month, D.C.'s best art scene is on display when most of Dupont Circle's art spaces are open late, free, and often with bars.

- **National Geographic Society:** See *National Geographic* magazine come to life at the society's Explorers Hall.

- **Phillips Collection:** Admire masterpieces such as Renoir's *Luncheon of the Boating Party* and Degas's *Dancers at the Barre* at the country's first museum of modern art—outstanding (and newly renovated).

Many of the displays in the society's museum focus on the colonial period and the Revolutionary War. One room—painted in a marvelous trompe l'oeil style that makes the walls seem as if they're covered with sculpture—is filled with military miniatures from the United States and France. (Because of the important role France played in defeating the British, French officers were invited to join the society. Pierre-Charles L'Enfant, "Artist of the Revolution" and planner of Washington, designed the society's eagle medallion.)

The house is often used by the federal government to entertain visiting dignitaries. Amid the glamour and patriotic spectacle of the mansion

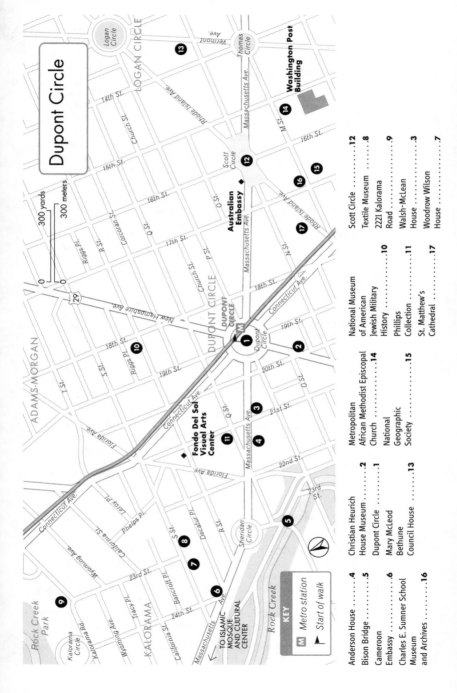

Dupont Circle

300 yards
300 meters

KEY

M Metro station
▲ Start of walk

Anderson House **4**
Bison Bridge **5**
Cameroon
Embassy **6**
Charles E. Sumner School
Museum
and Archives **16**

Christian Heurich
House Museum **2**
Dupont Circle **1**
Mary Mcleod
Bethune
Council House **13**

Metropolitan
African Methodist Episcopal
Church **14**
National
Geographic
Society **15**

National Museum
of American
Jewish Military
History **10**
Phillips
Collection **11**
St. Matthew's
Cathedral **17**

Scott Circle **12**
Textile Museum **8**
2221 Kalorama
Road **9**
Walsh-McLean
House **3**
Woodrow Wilson
House **7**

A GOOD WALK

DUPONT CIRCLE
Numbers in the box correspond to numbers in the margin and on the Dupont Circle map.

Start in **Dupont Circle** ❶ ▶ itself. Head southwest down New Hampshire Avenue to the **Christian Heurich House Museum** ❷, built by a beer magnate. Cross New Hampshire Avenue and go onto O Street. Turn right on 21st Street to admire the opulent **Walsh-McLean House** ❸, which isn't open to tours. Head west on Massachusetts Avenue to No. 2118, **Anderson House** ❹.

Head west on Q Street to the **Bison Bridge** ❺, so called because of its four bronze statues of the shaggy, horned beasts. Walk north on 23rd Street and turn left on Massachusetts Avenue and walk north one block, where the **Cameroon Embassy** ❻ is housed in a fanciful mansion. Turn right on S Street and go past the statue of Irish patriot Robert Emmet. The former home of the 28th president, the **Woodrow Wilson House** ❼, is a few hundred feet down S Street. Right next door is the **Textile Museum** ❽.

From the Textile Museum, walk north on 23rd Street until it dead-ends at the Tudor mansion at **2221 Kalorama Road** ❾. Turn right and walk up Kalorama. Turn right down Connecticut Avenue. On the left at 1919 Connecticut is the Washington Hilton & Towers, the site of John Hinckley's 1981 assassination attempt on Ronald Reagan (the shots were fired at the entrance on T Street NW). Go left on R Street for two blocks to the **National Museum of American Jewish Military History** ❿. Follow R Street back across Connecticut Avenue to the **Fondo Del Sol Visual Arts Center,** a nonprofit center featuring art, poetry, and music of the Americas. Walk south on 21st Street and discover some of the many private art galleries in the area.

One of Washington's great art museums is the **Phillips Collection** ⓫ at 21st and Q streets, filled with Impressionist and modern art masterpieces. Continue east on Q Street, and then turn right at Connecticut to the circle. Follow Massachusetts Avenue east to the corner of 16th Street is the **Australian Embassy,** which has occasional art exhibits. And now you've arrived at yet another circle—**Scott Circle** ⓬.

Take a slight detour along N Street to Vermont Avenue to visit **Mary McLeod Bethune Council House** ⓭. Follow Vermont Avenue south to Thomas Circle and turn right on M Street. After a block, the **Metropolitan African Methodist Episcopal Church** ⓮ is on your left. Continue on M Street to 17th Street, to the **National Geographic Society** ⓯, which has an interactive museum. The **Charles E. Sumner School Museum and Archives** ⓰, across M Street from the National Geographic offices, was built in 1872 as a school for black children. Head up 17th Street to Rhode Island Avenue and walk a half block west to **St. Matthew's Cathedral** ⓱.

are two idiosyncratic painted panels in the solarium that depict the Andersons' favorite motorcar sightseeing routes around Washington. ⊠ *2118 Massachusetts Ave. NW, Dupont Circle* ☎ *202/785–2040* ⊕ *www.thesocietyofthecincinnati.addr.com/anderson.htm* ⊠ *Free* ☉ *Tues.–Sat. 1–4* Ⓜ *Dupont Circle.*

Australian Embassy. Many foreign embassies in Washington are hosts to art exhibits or cultural programs open to the public. One of the best galleries is at the Australian Embassy, which periodically displays masterpieces from Down Under. If you're lucky, you might see aboriginal artifacts and dot paintings of striking originality and beauty, as well as contemporary landscapes and portraits with a uniquely Australian character. ⊠ *1601 Massachusetts Ave. NW, Dupont Circle* ☎ *202/797–3000* ⊕ *www.austemb.org* ⊠ *Free* ☉ *Weekdays 9–5 by appointment only* Ⓜ *Dupont Circle.*

❺ Bison Bridge. Tour guides at the Smithsonian's National Museum of Natural History are quick to remind you that America never had buffalo; the big, shaggy animals that roamed the plains were bison. (True buffalo are African and Asian animals of the same family.) Although it's officially the Dumbarton Bridge, locals call it the Bison Bridge because of the four bronze statues designed by A. Phimister Proctor. The sides of the structure, which stretches across Rock Creek Park into Georgetown, are decorated with busts of Native Americans, the work of architect Glenn Brown, who, along with his son Bedford, designed the bridge in 1914. The best way to see the busts is to walk the footpath along Rock Creek. ⊠ *23rd and Q Sts. NW, Georgetown and Dupont Circle* Ⓜ *Dupont Circle.*

❻ Cameroon Embassy. The westernmost of the beaux arts mansions built along Massachusetts Avenue around 1900 now houses the Cameroon Embassy. It's a fanciful castle with a conical tower, bronze weather vane, and intricate detailing around the windows and balconies. ⊠ *2349 Massachusetts Ave. NW, Dupont Circle* Ⓜ *Dupont Circle.*

⓰ Charles E. Sumner School Museum and Archives. Built in 1872 for the education of black children, the school takes its name from the Massachusetts senator who delivered a blistering attack against slavery in 1856 and was savagely caned as a result by a congressman from South Carolina. The building was designed by Adolph Cluss, who created the Arts and Industries Building on the Washington Mall. It's typical of the District's Victorian-era public schools. Beautifully restored in 1986, the school serves mainly as a conference center, though it's the site of changing art exhibits and houses a permanent collection of memorabilia relating to the city's public school system. ⊠ *1201 17th St. NW, Downtown* ☎ *202/442–6060* ⊠ *Free* ☉ *Mon.–Sat. 10–5; often closed for conferences* Ⓜ *Farragut N.*

❷ Christian Heurich House Museum. This opulent Romanesque Revival mansion, once known as the Brewmaster's Castle, was the home of Christian Heurich, a German orphan who made his fortune in the beer business. Heurich's brewery was in Foggy Bottom, where the Kennedy Center stands today. Brewing was a dangerous business in the 19th century, and fires more than once reduced Heurich's brewery to ashes. Perhaps because of this he insisted that his home, completed in 1894, be fireproof; in fact, it was the first building in Washington with residential fireproofing. Although 17 fireplaces were installed—some with onyx facings, one with the bronze image of a lion staring out from the back—not a single one ever held a fire.

Most of the furnishings in the house were owned and used by the Heurichs. The Victorian interior is an eclectic gathering of plaster detailing, carved wooden doors, and painted ceilings. The downstairs breakfast room, in which Heurich, his wife, and their three children ate most of their meals, is decorated like a rathskeller and adorned with German sayings such as "A good drink makes old people young."

Heurich must have taken proverbs seriously. He drank beer daily, had three wives (in succession), and lived to be 102. (In 1986 Heurich's grandson Gary started brewing the family beer again, now renamed Foggy Bottom Lager. Though the beer is currently from Utica, New York, Gary vows to someday build another brewery near Washington.)

After Heurich's widow died in 1955, the house was turned over to the Historical Society of Washington, D.C.; until 2003 it was used as a museum. The current owners, descendants of Christian Heurich, offer guided tours and rent the house for special events. ⊠ *1307 New Hampshire Ave. NW, Dupont Circle* ☎ *202/429–1894* ⊕ *www.heurichhouse. org* ⊡ *$5* ⊙ *Tours Wed. at 12:15 and 1:15* Ⓜ *Dupont Circle.*

⌐ ❶ **Dupont Circle.** Originally known as Pacific Circle, this hub was the westernmost circle in Pierre-Charles L'Enfant's original design for the Federal City. The name was changed in 1884, when Congress authorized construction of a bronze statue honoring Civil War hero Admiral Samuel F. Dupont. The statue fell into disrepair, and Dupont's family—who had never liked it anyway—replaced it in 1921. The marble fountain that stands in its place, with allegorical figures Sea, Stars, and Wind, was created by Daniel Chester French, the sculptor of Lincoln's statue in the Lincoln Memorial.

As you look around the circumference of the circle, you can see the peculiar constraints within which architects in Washington must work. Because a half-dozen streets converge on Dupont Circle, the buildings around it are, for the most part, wedge shaped and set on plots of land formed like massive slices of pie. Only two of the great houses that stood on the circle in the early 20th century remain today. The Renaissance-style house at **15 Dupont Circle,** next to P Street, was built in 1903 for Robert W. Patterson, publisher of the *Washington Times-Herald.* Patterson's daughter, Eleanor Medill "Cissy" Patterson, who succeeded him as publisher, was known for giving parties that attracted notables such as William Randolph Hearst, Douglas MacArthur, and J. Edgar Hoover. In 1927, while Cissy was living in New York City and the White House was being refurbished, Calvin Coolidge and his family stayed here. While they did, they received American aviator Charles Lindbergh; some of the most famous photographs of Lindy were taken as he stood on the house's balcony and smiled down at the crowds below. In 1948 Cissy willed the house to the American Red Cross, and the Washington

Club, a private club, bought it from the organization in 1951. The **Sulgrave Club,** at the corner of Massachusetts Avenue, with its rounded apex facing the circle, was also once a private home and is now a private club as well. ✉ *Intersection of Connecticut, Massachusetts, and New Hampshire Aves.* Ⓜ *Dupont Circle.*

NEED A BREAK?

Connecticut Avenue near Dupont Circle is filled with restaurants and other good places for a rest. At the independent bookstore and café **Kramerbooks & Afterwords** (✉ 1517 Connecticut Ave. NW, Dupont Circle ☎ 202/387–1400) you can relax over dinner or a drink after browsing through the many books. For lunch or a light dinner (or just a cup of tea and an oatmeal cookie), visit **Teaism** (✉ 2009 R St. NW, Dupont Circle ☎ 202/667–3827). In addition to several dozen varieties of tea, there's a selection of seafood and vegetarian entrées, many available in bento boxes and seasoned with tea.

Fondo Del Sol Visual Arts Center. A nonprofit museum devoted to the cultural heritage of Latin America and the Caribbean, the Fondo Del Sol Visual Arts Center has changing exhibitions covering contemporary, pre-Columbian, and folk art. The museum also offers a program of lectures, concerts, poetry readings, exhibit tours, and an annual summer festival with salsa and reggae music. ✉ *2112 R St., Dupont Circle* ☎ *202/483–2777* ⊕ *www.dkmuseums.com/fondo.html* ✉ *Suggested donation $3* 🕑 *Wed.–Sat. 1–6* Ⓜ *Dupont Circle.*

NEED A BREAK?

The Dupont Circle branch of **Pan Asian Noodles and Grill** (✉ 2020 P St. NW, Dupont Circle ☎ 202/872–8889) is one of two locations in Washington. Both offer reasonably priced Asian noodle dishes. The pad thai and drowned noodles are both popular, as are more obscure Filipino and Indonesian dishes.

⑬ Mary McLeod Bethune Council House. Exhibits in this museum focus on the achievements of African-American women, including Mary McLeod Bethune, who founded Florida's Bethune-Cookman College, established the National Council of Negro Women, and served as an adviser to President Franklin D. Roosevelt. ✉ *1318 Vermont Ave. NW, Dupont Circle* ☎ *202/673–2402* ✉ *Free* 🕑 *Mon.–Sat. 10–4* Ⓜ *McPherson Sq.*

⑭ Metropolitan African Methodist Episcopal Church. Completed in 1886, the Gothic-style Metropolitan African Methodist Episcopal Church has become one of the most influential African-American churches in the city. Abolitionist orator Frederick Douglass worshipped here, and Bill Clinton chose the church for both of his inaugural prayer services. ✉ *1518 M St. NW, Downtown* ☎ *202/331–1426* Ⓜ *Farragut N.*

🜚 ⑮ National Geographic Society. Founded in 1888, the society is best known for its magazine. It has sponsored numerous expeditions throughout its 100-year history, including those of admirals Robert Peary and Richard Byrd and underwater explorer Jacques Cousteau. Explorers Hall, entered from 17th Street, invites you to learn about the world in a decidedly interactive way: you can experience a mini-tornado, or use video touch screens that explain geographic concepts and then quiz you. The most dramatic events take place in Earth Station One Interactive Theatre, a 72-seat amphitheater that sends the audience on a journey around the world. The centerpiece is a hand-painted globe, 11 feet in diameter, that floats and spins on a cushion of air, showing off different features of the planet. ✉ *17th and M Sts. NW, Dupont Circle* ☎ *202/857–7588, 202/857–7689 group tours* ⊕ *www.nationalgeographic.com* 💲 *Free* ⊘ *Mon.–Sat. 9–5, Sun. 10–5* Ⓜ *Farragut N.*

⑩ National Museum of American Jewish Military History. The museum's focus is on American Jews in the military, who have served in every war the nation has fought. On display are weapons, uniforms, medals, recruitment posters, and other military memorabilia. The few religious items— a camouflage yarmulke, and rabbinical supplies fashioned from shell casings and parachute silk—underscore the sometimes strange demands placed on religion during war. ✉ *1811 R St. NW, Dupont Circle* ☎ *202/265–6280* 💲 *Free* ⊘ *Weekdays 9–5, Sun. 1–5* Ⓜ *Dupont Circle.*

★ ⑪ Phillips Collection. The first permanent museum of modern art in the country, the masterpiece-filled Phillips Collection is unique both in origin and content. In 2006, the Phillips is scheduled to unveil a major new 30,000-square-foot expansion, which will include exhibition spaces for large-scale contemporary art, a 180-seat auditorium, a sculpture garden, and a new café.

In 1918 Duncan Phillips, grandson of a founder of the Jones and Laughlin Steel Company, started to collect art for a museum that would stand as a memorial to his father and brother, who had died within 13 months of each other. Three years later what was first called the Phillips Memorial Art Gallery opened in two rooms of this Georgian Revival house near Dupont Circle.

Having no interest in a painting's market value or its faddishness, Phillips searched for pieces that impressed him as outstanding products of a particular artist's unique vision. Holdings include works by Georges Braque, Paul Cézanne, Paul Klee, Henri Matisse, and John Henry Twachtman; the museum's collection of the work of Pierre Bonnard is the largest in the country. The exhibits change regularly. The collection's best-known paintings include Renoir's *Luncheon of the Boating Party, Repentant Peter,* by both Goya and El Greco, *A Bowl of Plums* by 18th-century artist Jean-Baptiste Siméon Chardin, Degas's *Dancers at the Barre,* and Vincent van Gogh's *Entrance to the Public Garden at Arles.* A self-portrait of Cézanne was the painting Phillips said he would save first if the gallery caught fire. During the 1920s, Phillips and his wife, Marjorie, started to support American Modernists such as John Marin, Georgia O'Keeffe, and Arthur Dove.

The Phillips is a comfortable museum. Works of an artist are often grouped together in "exhibition units," and, unlike most other galleries (where uniformed guards appear uninterested in the masterpieces around them), the Phillips employs students of art, many of whom are artists themselves, to sit by the paintings and answer questions.

■ TIP➔ **On Thursday the museum stays open late for live jazz, gallery talks, and a cash bar. From September to May, the museum holds a Sunday afternoon concert series at 5 PM in the music room. It's free with museum admission.**

✉ 1600 21st St. NW, Dupont Circle ☎ 202/387–2151 ⊕ www. phillipscollection.org ⊐ Free for permanent collection on weekdays; admission varies on weekends and for special exhibitions ⊙ Oct.–May, Tues., Wed., Fri., and Sat. 10–5, Thurs. 10–8:30, Sun. noon–7; June–Sept., Tues., Wed., Fri., and Sat. 10–5, Thurs. 10–8:30, Sun. noon–5. Tours Sat. at 2 and Thurs. at 6 and 7. Gallery talk 1st and 3rd Thurs. of month at 12:30 Ⓜ Dupont Circle.

⑰ St. Matthew's Cathedral. John F. Kennedy frequently worshipped in this Renaissance-style church, the seat of Washington's Roman Catholic diocese, and in 1963 Kennedy's funeral Mass was held within its richly decorated walls. Set in the floor, directly in front of the main altar, is a memorial to the slain president: "Here rested the remains of President Kennedy at the requiem mass November 25, 1963, before their removal to Arlington where they lie in expectation of a heavenly resurrection." A memorial to nuns who served as nurses during the Civil War is across Rhode Island Avenue. *✉ 1725 Rhode Island Ave. NW, Dupont Circle ☎ 202/347–3215 ⊐ Free ⊙ Weekdays and Sun. 7–6:30, Sat. 8–6:30; tours usually Sun. at 2:30 Ⓜ Farragut N.*

⑫ Scott Circle. The equestrian statue of General Winfield Scott (1786–1866), who pioneered the use of light artillery in the Mexican War, was cast from cannons captured during that conflict. On the west side of the traffic circle is a statue of fiery orator Daniel Webster. ■ TIP→ **If you walk to the south side of the circle and look down 16th Street, you'll get a familiar view of the columns of the White House, six blocks away.** Across the circle is a memorial to S. C. F. Hahnemann, founder of homeopathy and the namesake of Hahnemann Medical School in Philadelphia. His statue sits in a recessed wall, his head surrounded by a mosaic of colorful tiles. *✉ Massachusetts and Rhode Island Aves. and 16th St., Downtown Ⓜ Archives/Navy Memorial.*

⑧ Textile Museum. In the 1890s, George Hewitt Myers, an heir to the Bristol-Myers fortune, bought his first Oriental rug for his dorm room at Yale. Later, Myers lived two houses down from Woodrow Wilson, at 2310 S Street, in a home designed by John Russell Pope, architect of the National Archives and the Jefferson Memorial. Myers bought the Waddy B. Wood–designed house next door, at No. 2320, and opened his museum to the public in 1925. Today the collection includes more than 17,000 textiles and carpets. Rotating exhibits are taken from a permanent collection of historic and ethnographic items that include Coptic and pre-Columbian textiles, Kashmir embroidery, and Turkman tribal rugs. There's at least one show of modern textiles—such as quilts or fiber art—yearly. *✉ 2320 S St. NW, Kalorama ☎ 202/667–0441 ⊕ www.textilemuseum. org ⊐ Suggested donation $5 ⊙ Mon.–Sat. 10–5, Sun. 1–5; highlight tours Sept.–May, Wed. and weekends at 1:30 Ⓜ Dupont Circle.*

⑨ 2221 Kalorama Road. S Street is an informal dividing line between the Dupont Circle area to the south and the Kalorama neighborhood to the north. The name for this peaceful, tree-filled enclave—Greek for "beautiful view"—was contributed by politician and writer Joel Barlow, who bought the large tract in 1807. Kalorama is filled with embassies and luxurious homes. The Tudor mansion at 2221 Kalorama Road, where

23rd Street runs into Kalorama Road, was built in 1911 for mining millionaire W. W. Lawrence, but since 1936 it has been the residence of the French ambassador. For a taste of the beautiful view that so captivated Barlow, walk west on Kalorama Road, and then turn right on Kalorama Circle. At the bottom of the circle you can look down over Rock Creek Park, the finger of green that pokes into northwest Washington.

❸ Walsh-McLean House. Tom McLean was an Irish prospector who made a fortune in Colorado gold and came to Washington to show it all off. The city on the Potomac was the perfect place to establish a presence for America's late-19th-century nouveau riche. It was easier to enter "society" in the nation's planned capital than in more established cities such as New York or Philadelphia, and wealthy industrialists and entrepreneurs flocked here. Walsh announced his arrival with this 60-room mansion. His daughter, Evalyn Walsh-McLean, the last private owner of the Hope Diamond (now in the National Museum of Natural History), was one of the city's leading hostesses. Today the house is used as an embassy by the Indonesian government and isn't open for tours. ✉ *2020 Massachusetts Ave. NW, Dupont Circle* Ⓜ *Dupont Circle.*

OFF THE BEATEN PATH

WASHINGTON POST BUILDING – Although the newspaper is no longer printed here, the claim to fame of the main *Washington Post* building when it opened in 1951 was that the printing plant and editorial offices were stacked so compactly in one small downtown location. You can see the newsroom that broke the Watergate story on a 45-minute guided tour of the building, which is otherwise not open to the public. In addition to the newsroom, there's a small museum dedicated to the history of the newspaper and old and new printing processes. ■ TIP➡ **For the guided tour, you must reserve a spot by phone two to six weeks in advance.** ✉ *1150 15th St. NW, Downtown* ☎ *202/334–7969* ⊕ *www.washingtonpost.com* ✉ *Free* ☉ *Tours Mon. on the hr 10–3.*

❼ Woodrow Wilson House. President Wilson and his second wife, Edith Bolling Wilson, retired in 1920 to this Georgian Revival designed by Washington architect Waddy B. Wood. (Wood also designed the Department of the Interior and the National Museum of Women in the Arts.) The house was built in 1915 for a carpet merchant.

President Wilson suffered a stroke toward the end of his second term, in 1919, and he lived out the last few years of his life on this quiet street. Edith made sure he was com-

CAPITAL FACTS

Until the Clintons bought a house here, Wilson was the only president who stayed in D.C. after leaving the White House. (He's still the only president buried in the city, inside the National Cathedral.)

fortable; she had a bed constructed that had the same dimensions as the large Lincoln bed Wilson had slept in while in the White House. She also had the house's trunk lift (a sort of dumbwaiter for trunks) converted to an Otis elevator so the partially paralyzed president could move from floor to floor. When the streetcars stopped running in 1962, the elevator stopped working; it had received its electricity directly from the streetcar line.

Wilson died in 1924. Edith survived him by 37 years. After she died in 1961, the house and its contents were bequeathed to the National Trust for Historic Preservation. On view inside are items such as a Gobelins tapestry, a baseball signed by King George V, and the shell casing from the first shot fired by U.S. forces in World War I. The house also contains memorabilia related to the history of the short-lived but influential League of Nations, including the colorful flag Wilson hoped would be adopted by that organization. ✉ *2340 S St. NW, Kalorama* ☎ *202/387–4062* 🖭 *$5* ⊙ *Tues.–Sun. 10–4* Ⓜ *Dupont Circle.*

ADAMS-MORGAN

To the young and hip, Washington has the staid reputation of a town more interested in bureaucracy than bling, with all the vitality of a seersucker suit. It may have the Hope Diamond, these detractors say, but that's about the only thing that really sparkles. What they mean, of course, is that Washington isn't New York City. And thank goodness, say Washingtonians, who wouldn't want to give up their clean subway, comfortable standard of living, or place in the political spotlight, even if it did mean being able to get a decent pastrami sandwich or a martini at three in the morning. Besides, Washington does have Adams-Morgan. It may not be the Lower East Side, but it's close enough in spirit to satisfy all but the most hardened black-clad cynics.

Adams-Morgan (roughly, the blocks north of Florida Avenue, between Connecticut Avenue and 16th Street NW) is Washington's most ethnically diverse neighborhood. And as is often the case, that means it's one of Washington's most interesting areas—a United Nations of cuisines, offbeat shops, and funky bars and clubs. The name itself, fashioned in the 1950s by neighborhood civic groups, serves as a symbol of the area's melting pot character: it's a conjunction of the names of two local schools, the predominantly white Adams School and the largely black Morgan

TOP 5: ADAMS-MORGAN

- **District of Columbia Arts Center:** Pop into here for a look at work by emerging artists showcased in one of the city's alternative hubs.

- **Eat Ethiopian food:** Savor spicy stews scooped up with sourdough bread at any one of the half-dozen Ethiopian restaurants lining 18th Street.

- **Idle Time Books:** Hang out like a local—relax in one of Tryst's overstuffed armchairs with a laptop or a copy of *The New Republic* and a coffee, or kill hours browsing the "rare and medium-rare" selections.

- **Rock Creek Park:** See a world-class Shakespeare production for free, gaze at the heavens in the planetarium, or just jog through the miles of verdant trails in this gorgeous park.

- **Stay out all night:** If you want to have fun until the sun comes up, Adams-Morgan is where to do it: don't miss live music at Madam's Organ, the friendly international crowd at Rumba, and the scensters at the Left Bank.

A GOOD WALK

ADAMS-MORGAN

Numbers in the box correspond to numbers in the margin and on the Adams-Morgan map.

Some walks are most enjoyable if followed in the suggested sequence; in this case, it's probably more fun to wander from the path to make your own discoveries. Begin by walking east on Calvert Street from the Woodley Park/Zoo Metro stop and turning left on Columbia Road. At tables stretched along the street, vendors hawk watches, leather goods, knockoff perfumes, CDs, sneakers, clothes, and handmade jewelry. The store signs—Casa Lebrato, Urgente Express (the business specializes in shipping to and from Central America)—are a testament to the area's Latin flavor; on these blocks you hear as much Spanish as you do English.

Cross Columbia Road at Ontario Road and backtrack west. On Saturday morning a market springs up on the plaza at the southwest corner of 18th and Columbia, with vendors selling fruits, vegetables, flowers, and fresh bread.

If Columbia Road east of 18th is Adams-Morgan's Latin Quarter, 18th Street south of Columbia is its restaurant corridor. Along the next few blocks are restaurants serving dishes from China, Mexico, India, El Salvador, Ethiopia, France, the Caribbean, Thailand, Argentina, Italy, South America, Vietnam, and, believe it or not, the United States.

You can also feed your hunger for the outré or offbeat with the shops on 18th Street. Here you'll find collectibles such as Mission furniture, Russel Wright crockery and Fiesta ware, aerodynamic art deco armchairs, Bakelite telephones, massive chromium toasters, kidney-shape coffee tables, skinny neckties, and oddball salt-and-pepper shakers. On the west side of 18th Street are antiques shops as well as secondhand shops set up in alleys or warehouses. Nearby is the **District of Columbia Arts Center** ➊ ▶, a combination art gallery and performance space.

On 16th Street there are several points of interest, including the **All Souls' Unitarian Church** ➋, the **Mexican Cultural Institute** ➌, the **Meridian House and the White-Meyer House** ➍, and the **House of the Temple** ➎. Hop on an S2 or S4 bus toward Silver Spring to visit the National Museum of Health and Medicine.

Of course, one measure of any neighborhood is the tone it takes when the sun goes down. In spring and summer, restaurants open their windows or set out tables on the sidewalks. Those with rooftop seating find diners lining up to eat under the stars. Washington can be notoriously hot in summer, but one of Adams-Morgan's charms has always been that its slight elevation wraps it in cooling breezes. Although the neighborhood's bar and club scene isn't as varied as its restaurant scene, catering primarily to a rowdy student crowd, there are some standouts. Remember that the last trains leave the Woodley Park Metro station around midnight. If that's too early for you, be prepared to take a cab.

All Souls'
Unitarian
Church 2

District of
Columbia
Arts Center 1

House of the
Temple 5

Meridian
House and
the White-
Meyer
House 4

Mexican Cultural
Institute 3

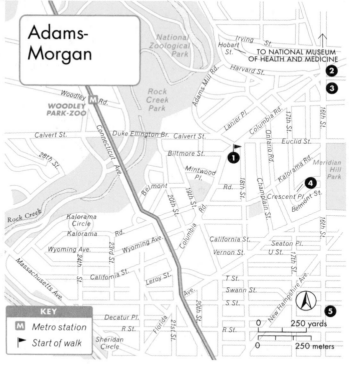

School. Today Adams-Morgan also has every shade in between, with large Latin American and West African populations.

The neighborhood's grand 19th-century apartment buildings and row houses, along with its fun character, have attracted young professionals, the businesses that cater to them, the attendant parking and crowd problems, and the rise in real estate values. All this has caused some longtime Adams-Morganites to wonder if their neighborhood is in danger of becoming another Georgetown.

Adams-Morgan already has one thing in common with Georgetown: there's no Metro stop. It's a pleasant 15-minute walk from the Woodley Park/Zoo Metro station: walk south on Connecticut, then turn left on Calvert Street, and cross over Rock Creek Park on the Duke Ellington Bridge. Or you can get off at the Dupont Circle Metro stop and walk east to (and turn left onto) 18th Street. The heart of Adams-Morgan is at the crossroads of Adams Mill Road, Columbia Road, and 18th Street.

TIMING   If you want to shop, a wander around Adams-Morgan can occupy the better part of an afternoon. And if you take advantage of the restaurants and nightlife here, there's no telling when your head will hit the pillow.

What to See

Rock Creek Cemetery. Rock Creek, the city's oldest cemetery, is administered by the city's oldest church, St. Paul's Episcopal, which erected its first building in 1712. (A single brick wall is all that remains of the original structure.) Many beautiful and imposing monuments are in the cemetery. The best known and most moving honors Marian Hooper "Clover" Adams, wife of historian Henry Adams; she committed suicide in 1885. Sculptor Augustus Saint-Gaudens created the enigmatic figure of a seated, shroud-draped woman, calling it *The Peace of God That Passeth Understanding*, though it's best known simply as "Grief." It may be the most moving sculpture in the city. ☒ *Rock Creek Church Rd. and Webster St. NW, Northwest* ☎ *202/829–0585* ☉ *Daily 7:30–dusk.*

② **All Souls' Unitarian Church.** Founded by prominent Americans such as John Quincy Adams and Charles Bulfinch, the original All Souls' congregation fostered both the early Abolitionist movement and women's suffrage. The current building, erected in 1924, mirrors the design of St. Martin-in-the-Fields in London. During the 20th century, the church was a cornerstone of the civil rights movement and community activism. Luminaries such as Ralph Waldo Emerson, Margaret Mead, and Noam Chomsky have spoken here, and the parish was home to the Reverend James Reeb, killed in Selma, Alabama, in 1965. ☒ *16th and Harvard Sts. NW, Adams-Morgan* ☎ *202/332–5266* ☉ *Tues.–Thurs. 10–6, Sun. service at 10:50 AM.*

> **CAPITAL FACTS**
>
> The tower of the All Souls' Unitarian Church contains a bell cast by Paul Revere's son.

▶ **❶** **District of Columbia Arts Center.** A combination art gallery and performance space, the DCAC exhibits the work of local artists and is the host of offbeat plays and performance art. Drop in for open-mike nights, stand-up comedians, avant-garde theater, and the like. ☒ *2438 18th St. NW, Adams-Morgan* ☎ *202/462–7833* ⊕ *www.dcartscenter.org* 🎟 *Gallery free, performance costs vary* ☉ *Wed.–Sun. 2–7, Fri. and Sat. 2–10; during performances, generally Thurs.–Sun. 7–midnight.*

❺ **House of the Temple.** An eye-catching Masonic shrine, the House of the Temple was patterned after the Mausoleum at Halicarnassus, in present-day Turkey. Tours are available on a drop-in basis. The two sphinxes at the entrance symbolize Wisdom and Power. ☒ *1733 16th St. NW, Adams-Morgan* ☎ *202/232–3579* 🎟 *Free* ☉ *Tours weekdays 8–2.*

❹ **Meridian House and the White-Meyer House.** Meridian International Center, a nonprofit promoting international understanding, owns two handsome mansions designed by John Russell Pope. The 30-room Meridian House was built in 1920 by Irwin Boyle Laughlin, scion of a Pittsburgh steel family and former ambassador to Spain. The Louis XVI–style home is furnished with parquet floors, ornamental iron grillwork, handsome moldings, period furniture, tapestries, and a garden planted with European linden trees. Next door is the Georgian-style house built for Henry White (former ambassador to France) that was later the childhood home of Katharine Graham (née Meyer), publisher of the *Washington Post*. The first floors of both houses are open to the public and hold periodic art exhibits with an international flavor. ⊠ *1630 and 1624 Crescent Pl. NW, Adams-Morgan* ☎ *202/667–6800* 🖭 *Free* ⊙ *Wed.–Sun. 2–5.*

❸ **Mexican Cultural Institute.** This glorious Italianate house, designed by Nathan Wyeth and George A. Fuller, architects of the White House's West Wing housed the Embassy of Mexico until 1989. It's now the the Mexican Cultural Institute, which promotes Mexican art, culture, and science. Exhibits have included works by 19th- and 20th-century Mexican artists such as Diego Rivera, José Clemente Orozco, David Alfaro, and Juan O'Gorman. ⊠ *2829 16th St. NW, Adams-Morgan* ☎ *202/728–1628* ⊕ *portal.sre.gob.mx/imw* 🖭 *Free* ⊙ *Tues.–Sat. 11–5:30.*

National Museum of Health and Medicine. Open since the 1860s, this medical museum illustrates medicine's fight against injury and disease. It has one of the world's largest collections of microscopes. ■ TIP➡ **Because some exhibits are fairly graphic (the wax surgical models and the preserved organs come to mind), the museum may not be suitable for young children or the squeamish.** To get here from Adams-Morgan, catch Bus S2 or S4 to Silver Spring on 16th Street. ⊠ *Walter Reed Army Medical Center, 6825 16th St. NW, Adams-Morgan* ☎ *202/782–2200* ⊕ *nmhm. washingtondc.museum* 🖭 *Free* ⊙ *Daily 10–5:30; tours 2nd and 4th Sat. of month at 1.*

🌣 **Rock Creek Park.** The 1,800 acres surrounding Rock Creek have provided a cool oasis for D.C. residents ever since Congress set them aside for recreational use in 1890. Bicycle routes and hiking and equestrian trails wind through the groves of dogwoods, beeches, oaks, and cedar, and 30 picnic areas are scattered about. Rangers at the **Nature Center and Planetarium** (⊠ South of Military Rd., 5200 Glover Rd. NW, Northwest ☎ 202/426–6829) introduce visitors to the park and keep track of daily events; guided nature walks leave from the center weekends at 2. The center and planetarium are open Wednesday through Sunday from 9 to 5. The renovated 19th-century **Klingle Mansion** (⊠ 3545 Willliamsburg La. NW, Northwest) is used as the National Park Service's Rock Creek headquarters. Also in distant areas of the park are Fort Reno, Fort Bayard, Fort Stevens, and Fort DeRussy, remnants of the original ring of forts that guarded Washington during the Civil War, and the Rock Creek Park Golf Course, an 18-hole public course. Landscape architect Horace Peaslee created oft-overlooked **Meridian Hill Park** (⊠ 16th and Euclid Sts., Adams-Morgan), a noncontiguous section of Rock Creek Park, after a 1917 study of the parks of Europe. As a result, it contains elements of parks in France (a long, straight mall bordered with plants), Italy (terraces and wall fountains), and Switzerland (a lower-level reflecting pool based on one in Zurich). It's also unofficially known as Malcolm X Park in honor of the civil rights leader. Drug activity once made it unwise to visit Meridian Hill alone; it's somewhat safer now, but avoid it after dark. ☎ *202/282–1063 park information.*

U Street on the Rise

THE REVIVAL OF U STREET NW IN THE 1990s turned the area into a provocative spot for anyone looking for cutting-edge shopping, welcoming restaurants, and live music. For Washington's African-Americans, the glory of U Street never went away.

A thriving neighborhood for two centuries, U Street was especially vibrant from the 1920s to the 1950s, when it was home to jazz genius Duke Ellington, social activist Mary McLeod Bethune, and poets Langston Hughes and Georgia Douglas Johnson. The area's nightclubs were hosts to Louis Armstrong, Cab Calloway, and Sarah Vaughn. Buildings designed by African-American architects dotted the landscape, and black-owned businesses abounded.

Although the neighborhood was nearly destroyed in the rioting that followed the 1968 assassination of Martin Luther King Jr., its historical importance was already cemented. In the 1950s, Supreme Court Justice

Thurgood Marshall organized the landmark *Brown v. Board of Education* case at the 12th Street YMCA. Nearby Howard University, a renowned black college, has been educating future professionals since 1867.

The U Street neighborhood of today may be the most integrated and diverse section of the city. Signs of its longevity include the elegant Duke Ellington mural above the 13th Street exit of the U Street Metro stop, as well as the restoration of the vaudeville-era Lincoln Theater, and an influx of new businesses. The self-guided Greater U Street Heritage Trail starts at the U Street/African-American Civil War Memorial Metro stop. It includes 14 stops marked by signposts. You can pick up a brochure of sites, with a map, from businesses on U Street or from the museum at the African-American Civil War Memorial, 1200 U Street NW. Information is also available through Cultural Tourism D.C. at www.culturaltourismdc.org.

FOGGY BOTTOM

The Foggy Bottom area of Washington—bordered roughly by the Potomac and Rock Creek to the west, 20th Street to the east, Pennsylvania Avenue to the north, and Constitution Avenue to the south— has three main claims to fame: the State Department, the Kennedy Center, and George Washington University. In 1763 a German immigrant named Jacob Funk purchased this land, and a community called Funkstown sprang up on the Potomac. This nickname is only slightly less amusing than the pres-

> **CAPITAL FACTS**
>
> The smoke-belching factories ensured work for the hundreds of German and Irish immigrants who settled in Foggy Bottom in the 19th century.

ent one, which is derived from the wharves, breweries, lime kilns, and glassworks that were near the water. Smoke from these factories combined with the swampy air of the low-lying ground to produce a permanent fog along the waterfront.

By the 1930s, however, industry was on the way out, and Foggy Bottom had become a poor part of Washington. The opening of the State Department headquarters in 1947 reawakened middle-class interest in the neighborhood's modest row houses. Many of them are now gone, and Foggy Bottom today suffers from a split personality: its tiny, one-room-wide row houses sit next to large, mixed-use developments.

Although the Foggy Bottom neighborhood has its own Metro stop, many attractions are a considerable distance away. If you don't relish long walks or time is limited, check the Foggy Bottom map to see if you need to make alternate travel arrangements to visit specific sights.

TIMING Foggy Bottom is a half-day walk. Touring the State Department and the Federal Reserve Building should take about two hours. It takes a fair amount of time to walk between sites, because this area isn't as densely packed with points of interest as most others are.

TOP 5: FOGGY BOTTOM

- **Department of State:** Tour the lavish diplomatic reception rooms, where you can see historic paintings and furniture, like the desk on which the treaty ending the Revolutionary War was signed; and imagine the international tête-à-têtes that shape foreign policy.

- **Federal Reserve Building:** Unravel the mysteries of the Fed in a tour of the palatial marble building.

- **John F. Kennedy Center for the Performing Arts:** See a free performance by anyone from Norah Jones to the National Symphony Orchestra here on the Millennium Stage.

- **Thompson's Boat Center:** Take in Washington's marble monuments, lush Roosevelt Island, and the Virginia coastline with a canoe ride down the Potomac.

- **Watergate:** Have a cocktail among the sumptuous floral arrangements, listen to the tinkling piano, and recall this hotel's most famous guests.

What to See

⑤ American Pharmaceutical Association. You might think the American Pharmaceutical Association is a rather odd sightseeing recommendation—even for a casual glance as you're passing. But the white-marble building was designed in 1934 by noted architect John Russell Pope, who also designed the Lincoln Memorial and the National Gallery of Art, the American Pharmaceutical Association is as much a symbol of modern Washington as any government edifice. It's the home of one of more than 3,000 trade and professional associations (some as obscure as the Cast Iron Soil Pipe Institute and others as well known as the AARP) that have chosen the capital for their headquarters, eager to represent their members' interests before the government. ⊠ *Constitution Ave. and 23rd St., Foggy Bottom* ☎ *202/429–7565* Ⓜ *Foggy Bottom.*

❿ Arts Club of Washington. Built in 1806 by Timothy Caldwell, this Federal-style house was once the residence of James Monroe and since

1

1916 has been the headquarters of the Arts Club, a nonprofit organization dedicated to the promotion of the arts in the nation's capital. Exhibits in the Monroe House and adjoining MacFeely House galleries represent many styles, with the work of local artists well represented. ⊠ *2017 I St. NW, Foggy Bottom* ☎ *202/331–7282* ✉ *Free* ☉ *Tues.–Fri. 10–5, Sat. 10–2* Ⓜ *Farragut W.*

⓫ **B'nai B'rith Klutznick National Jewish Museum.** This gallery, inside B'nai B'rith International's headquarters and available for viewing only by advance reservation, displays highlights of the collection upon which B'nai B'rith plans to found a National Jewish Museum in Washington. Key objects on display from the museum's permanent collection include George Washington's 1790 letter to a Rhode Island synagogue promising that the United States will give "to Bigotry No Sanction" as well as an international selection of artifacts celebrating the contributions of Jewish people. Call for information about cultural and educational programs. This exhibition space replaces the former B'nai B'rith Klutznick Museum in Dupont Circle. ⊠ *2020 K St. NW, 7th fl., Foggy Bottom* ☎ *202/857–6600* ⊕ *www.bnaibrith.org* ✉ *$5* ☉ *Mon.–Thurs. noon–3 by reservation only* Ⓜ *Foggy Bottom or Farragut W.*

❹ **Department of State.** United States foreign policy is formulated and administered by battalions of brainy analysts in the huge Department of State building (often referred to as the State Department), which also serves as United States Diplomatic Corps headquarters. All is presided over by the secretary of state, who is fourth in line for the presidency (after the vice president, Speaker of the House, and president *pro tempore* of the Senate) should the president be unable to serve. On the top floor are the opulent Diplomatic Reception Rooms, decorated like the great halls of Europe and

> **CAPITAL FACTS**
>
> The largest room in the State Department has a specially loomed carpet so heavy and large it had to be airlifted in by helicopter.

the rooms of colonial American plantations. Furnishings include a Philadelphia highboy, a Paul Revere bowl, and the desk on which the Treaty of Paris, which ended the Revolutionary War, was signed in 1783. ■ TIP→ **The rooms are used 15–20 times a week to entertain foreign diplomats and heads of state; you can see them, too, but you need to register for a tour three months in advance.** The tours are recommended for those 13 and over. ⊠ *2201 C St. NW, Foggy Bottom* ☎ *202/647–3241, 202/ 736–4474 TDD* ⊕ *www.state.gov* ✉ *Free* ☉ *Tours weekdays at 9:30, 10:30, and 2:45* Ⓜ *Foggy Bottom.*

❼ **Federal Reserve Building.** This imposing marble edifice, its bronze entryway topped by a massive eagle, was designed by Folger Library architect Paul Cret. Its appearance seems to say, "Your money's safe with us." Even so, there's no money here (the Fed sets interest rates and thereby seeks to keep the economy on track). The building's stately facade belies a friendlier interior, with a varied collection of art and four special art exhibitions every year. A 45-minute tour includes a film that explains the Fed's origins and mission. *Enter on* ⊠ *20th St. and Constitution Ave.*

A GOOD WALK

Numbers in the box correspond to numbers in the margin and on the Foggy Bottom map.

Start your exploration near the Foggy Bottom Metro station at 23rd and I streets. The sprawling campus of **George Washington University** ❶ ▶ covers much of Foggy Bottom south of Pennsylvania Avenue between 19th and 24th streets. Walk west from the Metro station on the I Street pedestrian mall, and then turn left on New Hampshire Avenue. At Virginia Avenue you run into the **Watergate** ❷ apartment-office complex, forever a part of our language for the role it played in the downfall of a president. Walk south on New Hampshire Avenue, past the Saudi Arabian Embassy, to the **John F. Kennedy Center for the Performing Arts** ❸, Washington's premier cultural center. Walk back up New Hampshire Avenue; then turn right on G Street, right on Virginia Avenue (follow the outstretched arm of the statue of Benito Juárez, the 19th-century Mexican statesman), and right on 23rd Street. The Pan American Health Organization, American headquarters of the World Health Organization, is at 23rd Street and Virginia Avenue, in the circular building that looks like a huge car air filter. Two blocks down 23rd Street is the massive **Department of State** ❹.

Follow 23rd Street to Constitution Avenue and turn left. On the south side of Constitution are the Lincoln and Vietnam Veterans memorials. The John Russell Pope–designed **American Pharmaceutical Association** ❺ building sits at the corner of Constitution Avenue and 23rd Street. One block east is the **National Academy of Sciences** ❻, which has a bust of Einstein outside. You can tour the white-marble **Federal Reserve Building** ❼ to find out exactly what it is the Fed does. Turn left on 20th Street. Crossing Virginia Avenue and continuing north on 20th Street takes you back onto the campus of George Washington University. To the right—near No. 1901—are the only two remaining 18th-century row houses that made up the **Seven Buildings** ❽. The modern glass office building at **2000 Pennsylvania Avenue NW** ❾ incorporates a row of hollowed-out and refurbished Victorian houses as part of its facade. Across Pennsylvania Avenue, on the small triangle where I Street intersects it, is the **Arts Club of Washington** ❿, a onetime home of James Monroe. Walk north on 20th Street to the **B'nai B'rith Klutznick National Jewish Museum** ⓫ at 2020 K Street NW. The museum is inside the headquarters of B'nai B'rith.

NW, Foggy Bottom ☎ 202/452–3000, 202/452–3149 *building tours,* 202/452–3686 *art tours* ⊕ *www.federalreserve.gov* ✉ *Free* ⊙ *Weekdays 11–4 during art exhibitions, tours of permanent art collection by appointment only; building tours Thurs. at 2:30* Ⓜ *Foggy Bottom.*

▶ ❶ **George Washington University.** George Washington had always hoped the capital would hold a renowned university. He even left 50 shares of stock

American
Pharmaceutical
Association **5**

Arts Club of
Washington ..**10**

B'nai B'rith
Klutznick National
Jewish
Museum **11**

Department
of State **4**

Federal
Reserve
Building **7**

George
Washington
University **1**

John F.
Kennedy
Center for the
Performing
Arts **3**

National
Academy of
Sciences **6**

Seven
Buildings **8**

2000
Pennsylvania
Avenue NW ...**9**

Watergate **2**

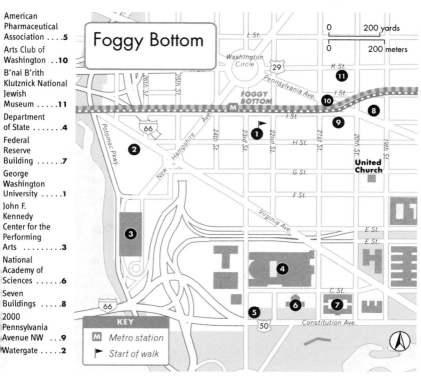

Foggy Bottom

| 0 | 200 yards |
| 0 | 200 meters |

KEY

Ⓜ *Metro station*

⚑ *Start of walk*

---

in the Patowmack Canal Co. to endow it. But congress never acted upon his wishes. It wasn't until 1822 that the university that would eventually be named after the first president began to take shape. The private Columbian College in the District of Columbia opened that year with the aim of training students for the Baptist ministry. In 1904 the university shed its Baptist connections and changed its name to George Washington University. In 1912 it moved to its present location and since that time has become the second-largest landholder in the District (after the federal government). Students have included J. Edgar Hoover and Jacqueline Bouvier (the future Jackie Kennedy). In addition to residing in modern university buildings, GWU occupies many 19th-century houses. ⊠ *South of Pennsylvania Ave. between 19th and 24th Sts., Foggy Bottom* ☎ *202/994–1000* ⊕ *www.gwu.edu* Ⓜ *Foggy Bottom.*

★ ❸ **John F. Kennedy Center for the Performing Arts.** Thanks to the Kennedy Center, Washington regularly plays host to world-class performers. Before 1971, Washington after dark was primarily known for cocktail parties, not culture. The opening of the Kennedy Center in that year instantly established the capital as a locale for the performing arts on an international scale. Concerts, ballets, opera, musicals, and drama are presented in the center's six theaters, and movies are screened periodically in the American Film Institute's theater. In 2005 the center opened a new Family Theater, which will showcase world-class performances for children and their families, as well as arts education programs.

The idea for a national cultural center had been proposed by President Eisenhower in 1955. John F. Kennedy had also strongly supported the idea, and soon after his assassination Congress decided to dedicate the center to him. Some critics have called the center's square design unimaginative—it has been dubbed the cake box that the more decorative Watergate came in—but no one can deny that the building's big. The Grand Foyer, lighted by 18 1-ton Orrefors crystal chandeliers, is 630 feet long. (Even at this size it's mobbed at intermission.) Many of the center's furnishings were donated by foreign countries: the chandeliers came from Sweden; the tapestries on the walls came from Brazil, France, and Mexico; and the 3,700 tons of white Carrara marble for the interior and exterior of the building were a gift from Italy. Flags fly in the Hall of Nations and the Hall of States, and in the center of the foyer is a 7-foot-high, bronze, oddly textured bust of Kennedy by sculptor Robert Berks.

A 10-year construction project, begun in 2003 and designed to create a plaza that will visually and physically connect the art center's somewhat isolated site to the rest of the city, is under way. Designed by architect Rafael Vinoly, and budgeted at $400 million by the Department of Transportation, the Plaza Project will allow pedestrians to walk from the Kennedy Center to the nearby monuments.

In addition to the regular performances in the six theaters, each year the Kennedy Center produces festivals that highlight different musical traditions and cultures. The hugely popular annual open house is a free, daylong extravaganza of theater, dance, and music, with nonstop entertainment both indoors and outdoors. There also are free performances every evening at 6 p.m. on the Millennium Stage.

Two restaurants on the Roof Terrace Level range from casual fare to more formal dining. It can get noisy as jets fly overhead to nearby Ronald Reagan National Airport, but you can get one of the city's better views from the terrace: to the north are Georgetown and the National Cathedral; to the west, Theodore Roosevelt Island and Rosslyn, Virginia; and to the south, the Lincoln and Jefferson memorials. ⊠ *New Hampshire Ave. and Rock Creek Pkwy. NW, Foggy Bottom* ☎ *202/467–4600* ⊕ *www.kennedy-center.org* ✉ *Free* ⊙ *Daily 10–until end of last show* Ⓜ *Foggy Bottom (free shuttle-bus service every 15 mins to and from Kennedy Center on performance days).*

❻ **National Academy of Sciences.** Inscribed in Greek under the cornice is a quotation from Aristotle on the value of science—appropriate for a building that houses the offices of the National Academy of Sciences, the National Academy of Engineering, the Institute of Medicine, and the National Research Council. There are often free art exhibits here—not all of them relating to science—and, from September to May, free Sunday afternoon concerts. In front of the academy is Robert Berks's sculp-

1

ture of Albert Einstein, done in the same mashed-potato style as the artist's bust of JFK in the Kennedy Center. ⊠ *2100 C St. NW, Foggy Bottom* ☎ *202/334–2436* ⊕ *www.nationalacademies.org* ✉ *Free* ⊙ *Weekdays 9–5* Ⓜ *Foggy Bottom.*

❽ **Seven Buildings.** Only two structures remain of the string of 18th-century row houses known as the Seven Buildings. One of the five that were demolished served as President Madison's executive mansion after the British burned the White House in 1814. The two survivors are dwarfed by the taller office block behind them and have been integrated into the Mexican Embassy, which is at 1911 Pennsylvania Avenue NW. ⊠ *Near 1901 Pennsylvania Ave., Foggy Bottom* Ⓜ *Foggy Bottom.*

❾ **2000 Pennsylvania Avenue NW.** It's a shame that so many important historical buildings fail to survive as a city matures. The row of residences on Pennsylvania Avenue between 20th and 21st streets escaped the fate of the Seven Buildings by being incorporated—literally—into the present. The Victorian houses have been hollowed out and refurbished to serve as the entryway for a modern glass office structure at 2000 Pennsylvania Avenue. The backs of the buildings are under the sloping roof of the development, preserved as if in a terrarium. Ⓜ *Foggy Bottom.*

United Church. Foggy Bottom's immigrant past is still part of the present at the United Church. Built in 1891 for blue-collar Germans in the neighborhood, the church still conducts services in German the first and third Sunday of every month at 9:30 September through May and at 8:30 June through August. ⊠ *1920 G St. NW, Foggy Bottom* ☎ *202/ 331–1495* Ⓜ *Foggy Bottom.*

❷ **Watergate.** Thanks to the events that took place on the night of June 17, 1972, the Watergate is possibly the world's most notorious apartment-office complex. As President Richard Nixon's aides E. Howard Hunt Jr. and G. Gordon Liddy sat in the Howard Johnson Motor Lodge across the street, five of their men were caught trying to bug the Democratic National Committee, headquartered on the sixth floor, in an attempt to subvert the democratic process on behalf of the then-president of the United States. A marketing company occupies the space today.

The suffix -*gate* is attached to any political scandal nowadays, but the Watergate itself was named after a monumental flight of steps that led down to the Potomac behind the Lincoln Memorial. The original Watergate was the site of band concerts until plane noise from nearby Ronald Reagan National Airport made the locale impractical.

Even before the break-in, the Watergate—which opened in 1965—was well known. Within its curving lines and fabled hallways have lived some of Washington's most famous—and infamous—residents, including Attorney General John Mitchell and presidential secretary Rose Mary Woods of Nixon White House fame, as well as D.C. insiders such as Jacob Javits, Alan Cranston, Bob and Elizabeth Dole, Monica Lewinsky, and Secretary of State Condoleezza Rice. The embassy of Yemen is also in the Watergate. ⊠ *2600 Virginia Ave. NW, Foggy Bottom* Ⓜ *Foggy Bottom.*

CLEVELAND PARK

Cleveland Park, a tree-shaded neighborhood in northwest Washington, owes its name to onetime summer resident Grover Cleveland and its development to the streetcar line that was laid along Connecticut Avenue in the 1890s. President Cleveland and his wife, Frances Folson, escaped the heat of downtown Washington in 1886 by establishing a summer White House on Newark Street between 35th and 36th streets. Many prominent Washingtonians followed suit. When the streetcar came through in 1892, construction in the area snowballed. Developer John Sherman hired local architects to design houses and provided amenities such as a fire station and a streetcar-waiting lodge to entice home buyers out of the city and into "rural" Cleveland Park. Today the neighborhood's attractive houses and suburban character are popular with Washington professionals. (Sadly, the Clevelands' retreat no longer stands.)

TIMING The amount of time you spend at the zoo depends on you. Popular visiting times are during the elephant-training session at 11 A.M. and the sea-lion training demonstration at 11:30 A.M.

What to See

▶ ❶ **Cineplex Odeon Uptown.** If you're in the mood for a movie during your stay and want to see it in a grand entertainment palace of yesteryear, the Cineplex Odeon Uptown is the place to go. Jack Valenti, until recently the president of the Motion Picture Association of America, called the huge single screen "probably the best we have in this town." Unlike most of the nation's other old theaters, which have been chopped up and transformed into multiplexes, this art deco theater, the only one of its kind left in Washington, has remained true to its origins. There's an inviting balcony with its own concession stand. ⊠ *3426 Connecticut Ave. NW, Cleveland Park* ☎ *202/ 966–5400 or 202/966–5401* Ⓜ *Cleveland Park.*

TOP 5: CLEVELAND PARK

- **Cineplex Odeon Uptown:** Finish off the day by taking in a movie at the monumental 1936 art deco theater.

- **Hillwood Museum and Gardens:** Look at the bounty Grape-Nuts can buy: enough Imperial Russian art and Fabergé eggs to stuff a stunning 40-room mansion, and 12 gorgeous acres of formal French and Japanese gardens make cereal heiress Marjorie Merriweather Post's estate well worth the trip.

- **Kreeger Museum:** Check out the Mirós, Picassos, and Kandinskys shown inside this museum's cool modernist architecture.

- **National Zoo:** Melt over the giant panda family here (this is a must for visitors in early 2007, as Tai Shan, the panda cub, is scheduled to be returned to China in mid-2007).

- **Woodley Park:** Walk through this wealthy neighborhood to admire architectural gems such as the city's finest art deco apartment, the Kennedy-Rodman.

Cineplex
Odeon
Uptown **1**

Kennedy-
Warren **2**

National
Zoological
Park **3**

Wardman
Tower **4**

Cleveland Park

HILLWOOD MUSEUM AND GARDENS – Hillwood House, cereal heiress Marjorie Merriweather Post's 40-room Georgian mansion, contains a large collection of 18th- and 19th-century French and Russian decorative art that includes gold and silver work, icons, tapestries, porcelain, and Fabergé eggs. Also on the estate are a dacha (summer cottage) filled with Russian objects and an Adirondacks-style cabin that houses Native American artifacts. The 12-acre estate grounds are composed of lawns, formal French and Japanese gardens, greenhouses, and paths that wind through plantings of azaleas, laurels, and rhododendrons. ■ TIP→ **Make reservations for the house tour well in advance, as well as for lunch in the café, where Eastern European specialties are on the menu.** Children under six are restricted to the gardens only. ⊠ *4155 Linnean Ave. NW, Northwest* ☏ *202/686–5807 or 202/686–8500* ⊕ *www.hillwoodmuseum.org* ⊠ *House and grounds $12* ⊙ *House tours, reservations required, Feb.–Dec., Tues.–Sat. 9–5* Ⓜ *Van Ness/UDC.*

❷ **Kennedy-Warren.** Lovers of art deco shouldn't miss the Kennedy-Warren. The apartment house is a superb example of the style, with period detailing such as decorative aluminum panels and a streamlined entryway, stone griffins under the pyramidal copper roof, and stylized carved eagles flanking the driveways. A second tower was added in 2003. Per-

OFF THE
BEATEN
PATH

A GOOD WALK

CLEVELAND PARK
Numbers in the box correspond to numbers in the margin and on the Cleveland Park map.

Start your exploration at the Cleveland Park Metro station at Connecticut Avenue and Ordway Street NW. The colonial-style Park and Shop on the east side of Connecticut Avenue was Washington's first shopping center with off-street parking. The art deco style is well represented by many of the buildings and apartments along some of the main thoroughfares in northwest Washington, including Connecticut Avenue. The **Cineplex Odeon Uptown** ❶ ▶, a marvelous art deco movie house from 1936. Continue south on Connecticut Avenue, where you cross a sliver of Rock Creek Park via a bridge decorated with eight art deco lights. Off to your left is the city's finest art deco apartment house, the **Kennedy-Warren** ❷, with stylized

carved eagles flanking the driveways. Follow Connecticut Avenue two more blocks to the **National Zoological Park** ❸, another member of the Smithsonian family. Tian Tian, Mei Xiang, and their cub, Tai Shan, the zoo's most famous residents, are among a handful of giant pandas in the United States.

Stately old apartment buildings line Connecticut Avenue south of the zoo. Cross Cathedral Avenue to enter Woodley Park. The cross-shape **Wardman Tower** ❹, at the corner of Connecticut Avenue and Woodley Road, was built in 1928 as a luxury apartment building. Once known for its famous residents, it's now part of the Marriott Wardman Park Hotel. Get back on the Metro and ride two stops to Van Ness to visit Hillwood Museum and Gardens, a mansion with beautiful gardens.

haps in keeping with its elegant architecture, this is one of the last apartment buildings in town still to have a doorman. ⊠ *3133 Connecticut Ave. NW, Cleveland Park* Ⓜ *Cleveland Park.*

OFF THE BEATEN PATH

KREEGER MUSEUM – You need to take a car or taxi to reach the Kreeger Museum. Its cool white domes and elegant lines stand in stark contrast to the traditional feel of the rest of the Foxhall Road neighborhood. The building, designed by Philip Johnson, was once the home of GEICO insurance executive David Lloyd Kreeger and his wife, Carmen. The collection includes works by Renoir, Degas, Cézanne, and Munch, as well as traditional African artifacts. ⊠ *2401 Foxhall Rd. NW, Foxhall* ☎ *202/337–3050* ⊕ *www.kreegermuseum.org* ⊑ *$8* ⊘ *Sat. 10–4, tours, reservations required, Tues.–Fri. at 10:30 and 1:30, Sat. at 10:30.*

☼ ❸ **National Zoo.** Part of the Smithsonian Institution, the National Zoo is one of the foremost zoos in the world. Created by an Act of Congress in 1889, the 163-acre park was designed by landscape architect Frederick Law Olmsted, who also designed the U.S. Capitol grounds. (Before the zoo opened in 1890, live animals used as taxidermists' models had been kept on the Mall.) On July 9, 2005, the zoo welcomed its most famous resident, Tai Shan, a giant panda cub born to parents Tian Tian and Mei Xiang, who had come from China in 2000. Tai Shan is the first giant panda cub to survive from birth at the National Zoo, and only the third to survive in the U.S. From the moment he arrived, Tai Shan became the hottest ticket in town, reducing hardened Washingtonians to mush at the sight of his intensely cuddly cuteness. Visitors hoping to see the cub should make plans early. ■ TIP➔ **Free timed-entry tickets to see the pandas may be reserved weeks in advance, and Tai Shan won't be around for long—he is scheduled to be returned to China in early 2007.** His parents will be around for a few more years—they are scheduled to be returned to China in 2010. Elsewhere in the zoo, innovative compounds show many animals in naturalistic settings, including the Great Flight Cage— a walk-in aviary—from May to October (they're moved indoors during the colder months). Between 10 and 2 each day, you can catch the orangutan population traveling on the "O Line," a series of cables and towers near the Great Ape House that allows the primates to swing hand over hand about 35 feet over your head. The Reptile Discovery Center, the Bird Resource Center, and an exhibition called "How Do You Zoo?" all teach children about biology. The most ambitious addition to the zoo is Amazonia, a reproduction of a South American rain-forest ecosystem. Fish swim behind glass walls, while overhead, monkeys and birds flit from tree to tree. In 2001 ring-tailed and red-fronted lemurs were installed in an exhibit called Lemur Island. The Cheetah Conservation Area is a grassy compound with a family of the world's fastest cats. The American Prairie exhibit includes some grasses that are toweringly tall and examines the resurgence of the bison, nearly killed off in the 19th century. ✉ *3001 Connecticut Ave. NW, Woodley Park* ☎ *202/673–4800 or 202/673–4717* ⊕ *www.si.edu/natzoo* ✑ *Free, parking $16* ⊙ *May–mid-Sept., daily 6 AM–8 PM; mid-Sept.–Apr., daily 6–6. Zoo buildings open at 10 and close before zoo closes* Ⓜ *Cleveland Park or Woodley Park/Zoo.*

❹ Wardman Tower. At the corner of Connecticut Avenue and Woodley Road is the cross-shape, Georgian-style tower built by developer Harry Wardman in 1928 as a luxury apartment building. Washingtonians called the project Wardman's Folly, convinced no one would want to stay in a hotel so far from the city—some 25 blocks from the White House; most upscale residential buildings, especially older ones, are within a few blocks. Contrary to predictions, however, Wardman Tower was famous for its well-known residents, who included Dwight D. Eisenhower, Herbert Hoover, Clare Booth Luce, Dean Rusk, Earl Warren, and Caspar Weinberger. It's now part of the Marriott Wardman Park Hotel. ✉ *2660 Woodley Rd. NW, Woodley Park* Ⓜ *Woodley Park/Zoo.*

Woodley Park. The stretch of Connecticut Avenue south of the National Zoo is bordered by venerable apartment buildings. Passing Cathedral Avenue (the first cross street south of the zoo entrance), you enter a part of town known as Woodley Park. Like Cleveland Park to the north, Woodley Park grew as the streetcar advanced into this part of Washington. In 1800 Philip Barton Key, uncle of Francis Scott Key, built Woodley, a

Georgian mansion on Cathedral Avenue between 29th and 31st streets. The white stucco mansion was the summer home of four presidents: Van Buren, Tyler, Buchanan, and Cleveland. It's now owned by the private Maret School. Ⓜ *Woodley Park/Zoo.*

UPPER NORTHWEST

Several good sights, including the National Cathedral, are on the portions of Massachusetts Avenue or Wisconsin Avenue to the north of Georgetown. To get here via public transportation, take the Friendship Heights bus, which travels north along Wisconsin Avenue in Georgetown. Some sights are immediately adjacent to Red Line Metro stops, but all can be easily reached by serious walkers, who will appreciate the leafy thoroughfares of these neighborhoods. For others, driving or cabbing may be the best way to visit.

What to See

Numbers in the text correspond to numbers in the margin and on the Upper Northwest map.

❼ Fort Reno Park. At 429 feet above sea level, this highest point in Washington has been used in different eras as a Civil War fort, the site of telegraph and radio towers, and a reservoir. In 1864 Abraham Lincoln watched nearby as outnumbered Union troops defended the capital from a formidable Confederate advance led by General Early, in the only battle to take place in Washington, D.C. Today it's enjoyed by soccer players, dogpark regulars, and picnickers. Most of the Civil War–era earthworks are gone, and two curious faux-medieval towers, built in 1929, mark the reservoir site, which is not accessible to the public. Nonetheless, the park has an appealing city view and plenty of room to run around. Free outdoor concerts take place each week in summer (see schedule on Web site). ✉ *Chesapeake St. NW at Nebraska Ave. NW, Upper Northwest* ☎ *202/521–1493 summer outdoor concert info only* ⊕ *www.fortreno.com* ⌨ *Free* ☉ *Daily dawn–dusk. Concerts June–Aug., Mon. and Thurs. at 7:15* Ⓜ *Tenleytown/American University.*

> ### TOP 5: UPPER NORTHWEST
>
> - **Fort Reno Park:** See a free concert–and an amazing view–from the highest point in the city.
> - **Glover-Archbold Park:** Take a hike through the verdant beeches and elms that make this park a wilderness oasis in the city.
> - **Islamic Mosque and Cultural Center:** Admire the 162-foot minaret, Iranian carpets, and carved verses of the Koran at Washington's oldest Islamic house of worship.
> - **U.S. Naval Observatory:** View the heavens through one of the world's most powerful telescopes.
> - **Washington National Cathedral:** Look for the Darth Vader gargoyle on the soaring towers of this cathedral, then relax among the rose bushes in the Bishop's garden.

Fort Reno
Park 7

Glover-
Archbold
Park 5

Howard
University
Law School 6

Islamic Mosque
and Cultural
Center 1

Kahlil Gibran
Memorial
Garden 2

St. Sophia
Cathedral 3

Washington
National
Cathedral 4

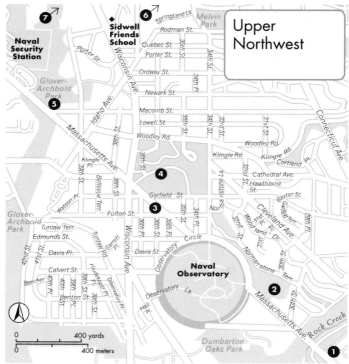

Upper
Northwest

⑤ Glover-Archbold Park. Groves of beeches, elms, and oaks flourish at this 183-acre park, part of the Rock Creek system. A 3½-mi nature trail runs the length of Glover-Archbold, a gift to the city in 1924. ⊠ *Garfield St. NW and New Mexico Ave. NW or Wisconsin Ave. at Van Ness St. NW, Upper Northwest* Ⓜ *Tenleytown/American University.*

⑥ Howard University Law School. The cradle of the modern civil rights movement, Howard has granted diplomas to generations of African-Americans, including Oliver Hill, Thurgood Marshall, and Charles Hamilton Houston, architects of the landmark 1954 Supreme Court decision *Brown v. Board of Education,* which ended legalized school segregation. Founded in 1867 as part of Howard University (which has its own campus in northwest Washington), the law school began educating students, including recently freed slaves, in 1869. ⊠ *2900 Van Ness St. NW, Upper Northwest* ☎ *202/806–8000* ⊕ *www.law.howard.edu* ☉ *Daily; guided tours by appointment.* Ⓜ *Van Ness/UDC.*

① Islamic Mosque and Cultural Center. The Muslim faithful are called to prayer five times a day from atop the 162-foot-high minaret of the Islamic Mosque and Cultural Center. Dedicated in 1957, the mosque is the oldest Islamic house of worship in D.C. and people from more than 75 countries worship here. The ornate interior is filled with deep-pile Persian rugs and covered with Islamic art. Each May the Muslim Women's Association sponsors a bazaar, with crafts, clothing, and food for sale. Visitors wearing shorts are not admitted to the mosque; women must cover their heads with scarves. ⊠ *2551 Massachusetts Ave. NW, Upper Northwest* ☎ *202/332–8343* ☉ *Center daily 10–5; mosque open for all 5 prayers, dawn–after sunset* Ⓜ *DuPont Circle.*

❷ **Kahlil Gibran Memorial Garden.** This tiny urban park combines Western and Arab symbols; it's perfect for contemplation. From the Massachusetts Avenue entrance, a stone walk bridges a grassy swale. Farther on are limestone benches, engraved with sayings from Gibran, that curve around a fountain and a bust of the Lebanese-born poet. ⊠ *3100 block of Massachusetts Ave. NW, Upper Northwest* Ⓜ *Woodley Park or Dupont Circle.*

❸ **St. Sophia Cathedral.** The Greek Orthodox St. Sophia Cathedral is noted for the handsome mosaic work on the interior of its dome. The cathedral holds a festival of Greek food and crafts each spring and fall. ⊠ *Massachusetts Ave. at 36th St. NW, Upper Northwest* ☎ *202/333–4730* ☉ *Services Sun. at 9 and 10* Ⓜ *Woodley Park.*

U.S. Naval Observatory. The grounds of the U.S. Naval Observatory, one of the oldest scientific agencies in the country (it was founded in 1830), are also home to the U.S. Vice President's residence. ■ TIP→ **Though you won't get to see the Cheneys' house up close during the tour, it does explain why visiting the observatory is such a high-security affair, with reservations required up to four weeks in advance.** Despite the security and the infrequency of tours (usually only held twice a month), the visit is well worth the wait. The observatory is internationally recognized as the world's preeminent authority on precise time and astrometry (the determination of the position of stars and celestial objects). The 90-minute tour gives you a look at the master clock, and the 2,000-pound 12-inch refracting telescope is said to offer the best heavenly views available at any publicly accessible observatory. ⊠ *3450 Massachusetts Ave. Upper Northwest* ☎ *202/762–1489* ⊕ *www.usno.navy.mil* ☒ *Free* ☉ *Tours run on alternate Mon. evenings, 8:30–10* Ⓜ *Woodley Park.*

❹ **Washington National Cathedral.**
Fodor'sChoice Construction of Washington National Cathedral—the sixth-largest
★ cathedral in the world—started in 1907; it was finished and consecrated in 1990.Like its 14th-century Gothic counterparts, the stunning National Cathedral (officially the Cathedral Church of St. Peter and St. Paul) has a nave,

CAPITAL FACTS
Skilled stone carvers have adorned the Washington National Cathedral with fanciful gargoyles, including one of Darth Vader.

flying buttresses, transepts, and vaults that were built stone by stone. The tomb of Woodrow Wilson, the only president buried in Washington, is on the nave's south side. ■ TIP→ **The expansive view of the city from the Pilgrim Gallery is exceptional.** The cathedral is Episcopalian but has held services of many denominations, as well as state events such as the funerals of presidents.

On the grounds of the cathedral is the compact, English-style **Bishop's Garden.** Boxwoods, ivy, tea roses, yew trees, and an assortment of arches, bas-reliefs, and stonework from European ruins provide a restful counterpoint to the cathedral's towers. ✉ *Wisconsin and Massachusetts Aves. NW, Upper Northwest* ☎ *202/537–6200, 202/537–6207 tour information* ⊕ *www.cathedral.org/cathedral* ✑ *Suggested tour donation $3* ☉ *Early May–early Sept., weekdays 10–5, Sat. 10–4:30, Sun. 8–5; early Sept.–early May, daily 10–5. Sun. services at 8, 9, 10, 11, and 4; evening prayer daily at 4:30; tours every 15 min Mon.–Sat. 10–11:30 and 12:45–3:15, Sun. 12:45–2:30* Ⓜ *Cleveland Park or Tenleytown.*

ARLINGTON

The Virginia suburb of Arlington County was once part of the District of Columbia. Carved out of the Old Dominion when Washington was created, it was returned to Virginia along with the rest of the land west of the Potomac in 1845. Washington hasn't held a grudge, though, and there are two attractions in Arlington—both linked to the military—that should be a part of any complete visit to the nation's capital: Arlington National Cemetery and the U.S. Marine Corps War Memorial. Both are accessible by Metro, and a trip across the Potomac to Arlington is a very worthwhile half day of sightseeing.

TIMING Visiting all the sites at Arlington National Cemetery could take half a day or longer, depending on your stamina and interest.

What to See

❸ **Arlington House.** It was in Arlington that the two most famous names in Virginia history—Washington and Lee—became intertwined. George Washington Parke Custis—raised by Martha and George Washington, his grandmother and step-grandfather—built Arlington House (also known as the Custis-Lee Mansion) between 1802 and 1817 on his 1,100-acre estate overlooking the Potomac. After his death, the property went to his daughter, Mary Anna Randolph Custis. In 1831, Mary married Robert E. Lee, a graduate of West Point. For the next 30 years they lived at Arlington House.

CAPITAL FACTS
Arlington House and the estate were confiscated in May 1864 and sold to the federal government when the Lees failed to pay $92.07 in property taxes in person.

In 1861 Lee was offered command of the Union forces. He declined, insisting that he could never take up arms against his native Virginia. The Lees left Arlington House that spring, never to return. Federal troops crossed the Potomac not long after that, fortified the estate's ridges, and turned the home into the Army of the Potomac's headquarters. (Survivors of General Lee were eventually compensated for the land.) Union

A GOOD WALK

ARLINGTON

Numbers in the box correspond to numbers in the margin and on the Arlington, VA, map.

To begin your exploration, take either a 10-minute Metro ride from downtown or walk across Memorial Bridge (southwest of the Lincoln Memorial) to **Arlington National Cemetery** ❶ ►. The visitor center has detailed maps, and the staff can help you find specific graves. Next to the visitor center is the Women in Military Service for America Memorial. West of the visitor center are the **Kennedy graves** ❷, where John F. Kennedy, two of his children who died in infancy, and his wife, Jacqueline Bouvier Kennedy Onassis, are buried. Robert E. Lee and family lived in **Arlington House** ❸. Walk south on Crook Walk following the signs to the **Tomb of the Unknowns** ❹, where the remains of unknown servicemen from Korea and both world wars are

buried. Steps from the Tomb of the Unknowns is **Section 7A** ❺, where many distinguished veterans are buried. To reach the sites at the northern end of the cemetery and to make your way into the city of Arlington, first walk north along Roosevelt Drive to Schley Drive (past the Memorial Gate); then turn right on Custis Walk to the Ord and Weitzel Gate. On your way you pass **Section 27** ❻, where 3,800 former slaves are buried. Leave the cemetery through the Ord and Weitzel Gate, cross Marshall Drive carefully, and walk to the 49-bell **Netherlands Carillon** ❼, where, even if your visit doesn't coincide with a performance, you can enjoy a good vista of Washington. To the north is the **United States Marine Corps War Memorial** ❽, better known as the Iwo Jima Memorial, which honors all marines who lost their lives while serving their country.

forces built three fortifications on the land, and 200 nearby acres were set aside as a national cemetery. Sixty-five soldiers were buried there on June 15, 1864, and by the end of the Civil War more than 16,000 headstones dotted Arlington plantation's hills. Soldiers from the Revolutionary War and the War of 1812 were reinterred at Arlington as their bodies were discovered in other resting places.

The building's heavy Doric columns and severe pediment make Arlington House one of the area's best examples of Greek Revival architecture. The plantation home was de-

CAPITAL FACTS

Long before Arlington was a cemetery, the land was part of the 1,100-acre estate of George Washington Parke Custis, a descendant of Martha and (by marriage) George Washington, whose daughter married Robert E. Lee.

signed by George Hadfield, a young English architect who, for a while, supervised construction of the Capitol. The view of Washington from the front of the house is superb. In 1955 Arlington House was designated a memorial to Robert E. Lee. It looks much as it did in the 19th century, and a quick tour takes you past objects once owned by the Custises and the Lees.

In front of Arlington House, next to a flag that flies at half staff whenever there's a funeral in the cemetery, is the **grave of Pierre-Charles L'Enfant,** designer of the Federal City. ✉ *Between Lee and Sherman Drs.* ☎ *703/557–0613* ⊕ *www.nps.gov/arho* ✆ *Free* ☉ *Daily 9:30–4:30.*

★ ⊳ ❶ **Arlington National Cemetery.** More than 250,000 American war dead, as well as many notable Americans (among them Presidents William Howard Taft and John F. Kennedy, General John Pershing, and Admiral Robert E. Peary), are interred in these 612 acres across the Potomac River from Washington, established as the nation's cemetery in 1864. While you're here, there's a good chance you might hear the clear, doleful sound of a trumpet playing taps or the sharp reports of a gun salute. There are an average of 28 funerals held daily (it's projected that the cemetery will be filled in 2020). Although not the largest cemetery in the country, Arlington is certainly the best known, a place where you can trace America's history through the aftermath of its battles.

To get here, you can take the Metro, travel on a Tourmobile bus, or walk across Arlington Memorial Bridge (southwest of the Lincoln Memorial). If you're driving, there's a large paid-parking lot at the skylighted visitor center on Memorial Drive. Stop at the center for a free brochure with a detailed map of the cemetery. If you're looking for a specific grave, the staff can consult microfilm records and give you directions to it. You should know the deceased's full name and, if possible, his or her branch of service and year of death.

Tourmobile tour buses leave every 15–20 minutes from just outside the visitor center April through September, daily 8:30–6:30, and October through March, daily 8:30–4:30. You can buy tickets here for the 40-minute tour of the cemetery, which includes stops at the Kennedy grave sites, the Tomb of the Unknowns, and Arlington House. Touring the ceme-

TOP 5: ARLINGTON

- **Arlington House:** Visit the gracious marble-columned estate that was home to Civil War über general Robert E. Lee.

- **John F. Kennedy's Grave:** See the eternal flame at the most-visited grave in the country.

- **Netherlands Carillon:** Hear the 49 bells played on a Saturday afternoon, and don't forget to catch a good look at Washington from across the Potomac River.

- **Section 27:** Walk through this part of the Arlington National Cemetery where you'll see the graves of freed slaves who worked on the Arlington House estate, many of whom also fought with distinction in the Civil War.

- **Tomb of the Unknowns:** Pay your respects to America's fallen at this moving site.

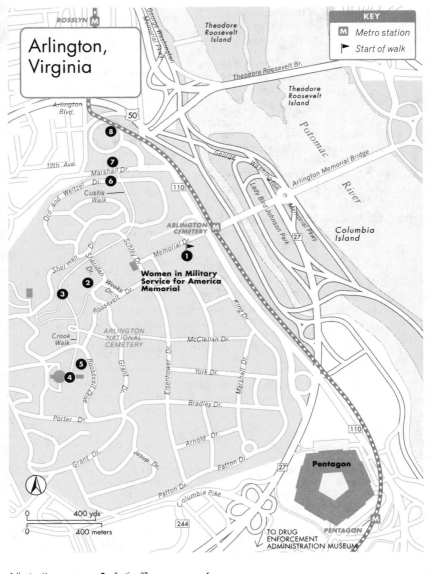

Arlington, Virginia

Arlington House **3**

Arlington National
Cemetery **1**

Kennedy graves **2**

Netherlands Carillon **7**

Section 7A **5**

Section 27 . . . .**6**

Tomb of the
Unknowns **4**

United States
Marine Corps
War Memorial **8**

Lee, the Rebel General

ROBERT E. LEE (1807–70) is a tragic figure in American history. Lee felt forced by principle and his family connections to lead a rebellion that resulted in more than half a million deaths and left the South in ruins. The only greater tragedy might have been if the Confederate States of America had won independence, which would have permitted slavery to go on and very probably would have led to even further political fractures and endless fighting among half a dozen nations across North America.

The youngest of the seven children of Revolutionary War hero Colonel Henry ("Light-Horse Harry") Lee, Robert Edward Lee was born to Ann Hill Carter at Stratford Plantation on Virginia's genteel Northern Neck. His family tree is a chart of the Old Dominion's leading families, crowned by his marriage to Martha Washington's great-granddaughter Mary Anna Randolph Custis. Light-Horse Harry's relative poverty left the boy unable to afford a private education, but Lee sought and won appointment to West Point, and there began the legend of his prowess: he rose to corps adjutant, the highest cadet rank; stood second in the class of 1829; and never received a single demerit over the course of the four years. Advancement in the peacetime army was slow, even after he transferred from the elite engineer corps to the casualty-prone cavalry, and Lee still was but a captain when the Mexican War began in 1846. There his skill at military engineering, his strength and powers of endurance, and his great personal bravery caused his commander, General Winfield Scott, to describe Lee as "the very best soldier I ever saw in the field."

When the Civil War broke out in the spring of 1861, Scott advised President Abraham Lincoln to offer Colonel Lee command of the Union Army. Lee agonized but finally concluded that "I cannot raise my hand against my native state" and resigned his federal commission. Then, although he despised slavery, the root cause of the conflict, he offered his sword to the South. Union troops quickly overtook his house, and the plantation was converted into a refuge for fleeing slaves and a graveyard that eventually became Arlington National Cemetery. Lee was appointed military adviser to President Jefferson Davis, receiving a field command only after Confederate general Joseph E. Johnston was wounded in 1862. Lee so harried Union general George McClellan in the bloody Seven Days battles that McClellan went into camp and abandoned any attempt to further menace the Confederate capital of Richmond.

Lee renamed his force the Army of Northern Virginia and launched a series of campaigns that defeated superior Union forces. Lincoln was forced to fire one commanding general after another until he found Ulysses S. Grant. Finally, in the spring of 1865, Grant smashed his way into Richmond and defeated Lee.

At the age of 58, ailing and penniless, Lee began a new career as president of Washington College (now Washington and Lee University), in Lexington, Virginia. Lee died in 1870 and was entombed in a crypt beneath the college chapel.

tery on foot means a fair bit of hiking, but it can give you a closer look at some of the thousands of graves spread over these rolling Virginia hills. If you decide to walk, head west from the visitor center on Roosevelt Drive and then turn right on Weeks Drive. ⊠ *West end of Memorial Bridge* ☎ *703/607–8000 to locate a grave* ⊕ *www.arlingtoncemetery.org* ⌂ *Cemetery free, parking $3.75 for the first 3 hrs. Tourmobile $5.25* ⊙ *Apr.–Sept., daily 8–7; Oct.–Mar., daily 8–5.*

OFF THE
BEATEN
PATH

DRUG ENFORCEMENT ADMINISTRATION MUSEUM – Just across the street from the Fashion Centre at Pentagon City—a destination in itself for shoppers—is the DEA Museum, within the U.S. Drug Enforcement Administration's headquarters. It explores the effect of drugs on American society, starting with quaint 19th-century ads for opium-laced patent medicines and "cocaine tooth drops" (opiates, cannabis, and cocaine were unregulated then). But documentation of these addictive substances' medical dangers, as well as the corrosive political effect of the opium trade, which China detested, is hard-hitting. A similar contrast is found between the period feel of artifacts from a 1970s head shop and displays on the realities of present-day drug trafficking. ⊠ *700 Army Navy Dr., at Hayes St.* ☎ *202/307–3463* ⊕ *www.deamuseum.org* ⌂ *Free* ⊙ *Tues.–Fri. 10–4* Ⓜ *Pentagon City.*

★ ❷ **Kennedy graves.** An important part of any visit to Arlington National Cemetery is a visit to the graves of John F. Kennedy and other members of his family. JFK is buried under an eternal flame near two of his children, who died in infancy, and his wife, Jacqueline Bouvier Kennedy Onassis. The graves are a short walk west of the visitor center. Across from them is a low wall engraved with quotations from Kennedy's inaugural address. The public has been able to visit JFK's grave since 1967; it's now the most-visited grave site in the country. Nearby, marked by a simple white cross, is the grave of his brother Robert Kennedy. ⊠ *Sheridan and Weeks Drs.*

❼ **Netherlands Carillon.** A visit to Arlington National Cemetery affords the opportunity for a lovely and unusual musical experience, thanks to a 49-bell carillon presented to the United States by the Dutch people in 1960 in gratitude for aid received during World War II. Guest carillon players perform on Saturday afternoon May through September and on July 4. Times vary; call for details. ■ TIP→ **For one of the most inclusive views of Washington, look to the east across the Potomac. From this vantage point, the Lincoln Memorial, the Washington Monument, and the Capitol appear in a side-by-side formation.** ⊠ *Meade and Marshall Drs.* ☎ *703/ 289–2500.*

Pentagon. This office building, the headquarters of the United States Department of Defense, is the largest in the world. The Capitol could fit into any one of its five wedge-shape sections. Approximately 23,000 military and civilian workers arrive daily. Astonishingly, this mammoth office building, completed in 1943, took less than two years to construct.

The structure was reconstructed following the September 2001 crash of hijacked American Airlines Flight 77 into the northwest side of the building. The damaged area was removed in just over a month, and re-building proceeded rapidly (in keeping with the speed of the original construction). Renovations on all areas damaged by the terrorist attack were completed by spring 2003.

Tours of the building are given on a very limited basis to educational groups by advance reservation; tours for the general public have been suspended indefinitely. ⊠ *I–395 at Columbia Pike and Rte. 27* ☏ *703/ 695–1776* ⊕ *www.defenselink.mil/pubs/pentagon.*

❺ Section 7A. Many distinguished veterans are buried in this area of Arlington National Cemetery near the **Tomb of the Unknowns,** including boxing champ Joe Louis, ABC newsman Frank Reynolds, actor Lee Marvin, and World War II fighter pilot Colonel "Pappy" Boyington. ⊠ *Crook Walk near Roosevelt Dr.*

❻ Section 27. More than 3,800 former slaves are buried in this part of Arlington National Cemetery. They're all former residents of Freedman's Village, which operated at the Custis-Lee estate for more than 30 years beginning in 1863 to provide housing, education, and employment training for ex-slaves who had traveled to the capital. In the cemetery, the headstones are marked with their names and the word *Civilian* or *Citizen.* Buried at Grave 19 in the first row of Section 27 is William Christman, a Union private who died of peritonitis in Washington on May 13, 1864. He was the first soldier interred at Arlington National Cemetery during the Civil War. ⊠ *Ord and Weitzel Dr. near Custis Walk.*

OFF THE
BEATEN
PATH

THEODORE ROOSEVELT ISLAND – The island preserve in the Potomac River has 2½ mi of nature trails through marshland, swampland, and upland forest. It's an 88-acre tribute to the conservation-minded 26th president. Cattails, arrowarum, pickerelweed, willow, ash, maple, and oak all grow on the island, which is also a habitat for frogs, raccoons, birds, lizards, and the occasional red or gray fox. The 17-foot bronze statue of Roosevelt, reachable after a long walk toward the center of the woods, was done by Paul Manship. A pedestrian bridge connects the island to a parking lot on the Virginia shore, which is accessible by car from the northbound lanes of the George Washington Memorial Parkway. ⊠ *From downtown D.C., take Constitution Ave. west across Theodore Roosevelt Bridge to George Washington Memorial Pkwy. north and follow signs or walk or bike across bridge beginning at Kennedy Center* ☏ *703/289–2500 park info* ⊒ *Free* ☉ *Island daily dawn–dusk* Ⓜ *Rosslyn.*

FodorśChoice
★

❹ Tomb of the Unknowns. Many countries established a memorial to their war dead after World War I. In the United States, the first burial at the Tomb of the Unknowns took place at Arlington National Cemetery on November 11, 1921, when the Unknown Soldier from the "Great War" was interred under the large white-marble sarcophagus. Unknown servicemen killed in World War II and Korea were buried in 1958. The unknown serviceman killed in Vietnam was laid to rest on the plaza on Memorial Day 1984 but was disinterred and identified in 1998. Officials then decided to leave the Vietnam War unknown crypt vacant. Soldiers from the Army's U.S. Third Infantry ("The Old Guard") keep watch over the tomb 24 hours a day, regardless of weather conditions. Each sentinel marches exactly 21 steps, then faces the tomb for 21 seconds, symbolizing the 21-gun salute, America's highest military honor. The guard is changed with a precise ceremony during the day—every half hour from April through September and every hour the rest of the year. At night the guard is changed every hour.

The Memorial Amphitheater west of the tomb is the scene of special ceremonies on Veterans Day, Memorial Day, and Easter. Decorations awarded to the unknowns by foreign governments and U.S. and foreign organizations are displayed in an indoor trophy room. Across from the amphitheater are memorials to the astronauts killed in the *Challenger* shuttle explosion and to the servicemen killed in 1980 while trying to rescue American hostages in Iran. Rising beyond that is the mainmast of the USS *Maine,* the American ship that was sunk in Havana Harbor in 1898, killing 299 men and sparking the Spanish-American War. ⊠ *End of Crook Walk.*

❽ United States Marine Corps War Memorial. Better known simply as the Iwo Jima, this memorial, despite its familiarity, has lost none of its power to stir the emotions. Honoring marines who have given their lives since the Corps was formed in 1775, the statue, sculpted by Felix W. de Weldon, is based on Joe Rosenthal's Pulitzer Prize–winning photograph of five marines and a navy corpsman raising a flag atop Mt. Suribachi on the Japanese island of Iwo Jima on February 19, 1945. By executive order, a real flag flies 24 hours a day from the 78-foot-high memorial. On Tuesday evening at 7 p.m. from late May to late August there's a Marine Corps sunset parade on the grounds of the memorial. On parade nights a free shuttle bus runs from the Arlington Cemetery visitors' parking lot.

North of the memorial is the Arlington neighborhood of Rosslyn. Like parts of downtown Washington and Crystal City farther to the south, Rosslyn is almost empty at night, once the thousands of people who work there have gone home. Its tall buildings provide a bit of a skyline, but this has been controversial: some say the two silvery, 31-story wing-shape towers, formerly the Gannett Buildings, are too close to the flight path followed by jets landing at Ronald Reagan National Airport.

Women in Military Service for America Memorial. What is now this memorial next to the visitor center was once the Hemicycle, a huge carved retaining wall faced with granite at the entrance to Arlington National Cemetery. Built in 1932, the wall was reworked, with stairways added leading to a rooftop terrace. Inside are 16 exhibit alcoves showing the contributions that women have made to the military—from the Revolutionary War to the present—as well as the history of the memorial itself. A 196-seat theater shows films and is used for lectures and conferences. A computer database has pictures, military histories, and stories of thousands of women veterans. A fountain and reflecting pool front the classical-style Hemicycle and entry gates.

ALEXANDRIA

1

Just a Metro ride (or bike ride) from Washington, Alexandria attracts those who seek a break from the monuments and hustle-and-bustle of the District. Here you can encounter America's colonial heritage. Founded in 1749 by Scottish merchants eager to capitalize on the booming tobacco trade, Alexandria emerged as one of the most important colonial ports. Alexandria has been associated with the most significant events and personages of the colonial, Revolutionary, and Civil War periods. In Old Town this colorful past is revived through restored 18th- and 19th-century homes, churches, and taverns; on the cobbled streets; and on the revitalized waterfront, where clipper ships dock and artisans display their wares.

One way to reach Alexandria is to take the Metro to the King Street stop (about 25 minutes from Metro Center) and walk about 10 blocks on King Street, going away from the Masonic memorial. To drive here, take either the George Washington Memorial Parkway or Jefferson Davis Highway (Route 1) south from Arlington.

TIMING The Alexandria tour should take about four hours, not counting a trip to the George Washington Masonic National Memorial. A visit to the memorial adds about another hour and a half if you walk there and take the guided tour. If you're traveling by Metro, plan to finish your visit at the memorial and then get on the Metro at the King Street station.

> ## TOP 5: ALEXANDRIA
>
> - **Alexandria Black History Resource Center:** Alexandria was once among the South's largest slave-trading ports—and this is where you can learn the darker side of the city's history.
>
> - **Old Town:** Pick up a map at Ramsay House, then set off for a self-guided ramble through this quaint area's cobblestone streets.
>
> - **Stabler-Leadbeater Apothecary:** Get lost among the 18th-century apothecary bottles and Native-American remedies used by the likes of George Washington and Robert E. Lee.
>
> - **Torpedo Factory Art Center:** Watch artists at work, buy a one-of-a-kind piece of jewelry, see archaeological artifacts extracted from beneath the city, and take a look inside a torpedo factory.
>
> - **U.S. Patent and Trademark Museum:** Check out gizmos and gadgets galore—including several from Thomas Edison.

What to See

★ ⑫ **Alexandria Black History Resource Center.** Here, at the site of the Robert H. Robinson Library, a building constructed in the wake of a landmark 1939 sit-in protesting the segregation of Alexandria libraries, the history of African-Americans in Alexandria and Virginia from 1749 to the present is recounted. The federal census of 1790 recorded 52 free blacks living in the city, and the port town was one of the largest slave exportation

Alexandria Black History Resource Center 12
Athenaeum 4
Boyhood Home of Robert E. Lee 11
Captain's Row .5
Carlyle House ..8
Christ Church .14
Friendship Fire House 16
Gadsby's Tavern Museum 9
George Washington Masonic Nat'l Memorial 17
John Q. Adams Center 6
Lee-Fendall House 10
Lloyd House ..13
Lyceum 15
Old Presbyterian Meeting House 3
Ramsay House 1
Stabler-Leadbeater Apothecary 2
Torpedo Factory Arts Center 7
U.S. Patent and Trademark Museum 18

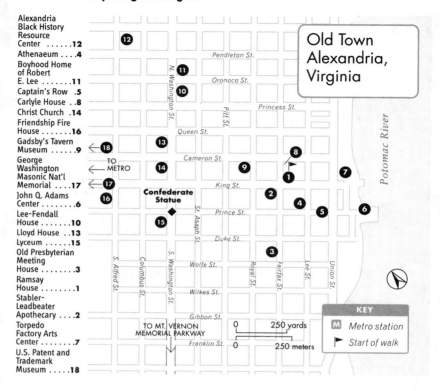

points in the South, with at least two bustling slave markets. ✉ *638 N. Alfred St., Old Town* ☎ *703/519–3391 or 703/838–4356* ⊕ *oha.ci. alexandria.va.us/bhrc* ⬛ *Free* ☯ *Tues.–Sat. 9–4; Sun. 1–5.*

🌑 **Athenaeum.** One of the most noteworthy structures in Alexandria, the Athenaeum is a striking, reddish-brown Greek Revival edifice at the corner of Prince and Lee streets. It was built as a bank in the 1850s. The building, home to the Northern Virginia Fine Arts Association, is open most Friday afternoons from noon to 3 p.m. as a volunteer-staffed gallery showing ongoing art exhibits. ✉ *201 Prince St., Old Town* ☎ *703/548–0035.*

🌑 **Boyhood Home of Robert E. Lee.** The childhood home in Alexandria of the commander in chief of the Confederate forces, Robert E. Lee, is a fine example of a 19th-century town house with Federal architecture. The house was sold in 2000 to private owners who have made it their home. It's no longer open to visitors, but some of the home's furnishings are displayed at the Lyceum. ✉ *607 Oronoco St., Old Town.*

🌑 **Captain's Row.** Many of Alexandria's sea captains once lived on this block. The cobblestones in the street were allegedly laid by Hessian mercenaries who had fought for the British during the Revolution and were held

A GOOD WALK

ALEXANDRIA

Numbers in the box correspond to numbers in the margin and on the Old Town Alexandria, VA, map.

Start your walk through Old Town at the Alexandria Convention & Visitors Association, in **Ramsay House** ❶ ▶, the oldest house in Alexandria. Across the street, near the corner of Fairfax and King streets, is the **Stabler–Leadbeater Apothecary** ❷, used by George Washington and the Lee family. Two blocks south on Fairfax Street, just beyond Duke Street, stands the **Old Presbyterian Meeting House** ❸. Walk back up Fairfax Street one block and turn right on Prince Street to Gentry Row, the block between Fairfax and Lee streets. At the corner of Prince and Lee streets is the **Athenaeum** ❹. Many of the city's sea captains built their homes on the block of Prince Street between Lee and Union, which became known as **Captain's Row** ❺. Walk a block east on Prince Street to **John Q. Adams Center for the History of Otolaryngology** ❻. Then head back to Union and walk a block north to King Street to the **Torpedo Factory Art Center** ❼. Take Cameron Street away from the river. **Carlyle House** ❽, built in 1753, is at the corner of Cameron and North Fairfax streets.

One block west along Cameron, at Royal Street, is **Gadsby's Tavern Museum** ❾. Continue west on Cameron Street for two blocks, turn right on St. Asaph Street, and walk up to Oronoco Street. Two historic Lee homes are on Oronoco between North Washington and St. Asaph streets. On the near side of Oronoco is the **Lee-Fendall House Museum** ❿; the **boyhood home of Robert E. Lee** ⓫ is across Oronoco on the St. Asaph Street corner.

Although a minority, there were 52 free blacks living in Alexandria in 1790. The **Alexandria Black History Resource Center** ⓬ is two blocks north and two blocks west of Lee's boyhood home. Head back to North Washington Street and go south to the corner of Queen Street. The **Lloyd House** ⓭, a fine example of Georgian architecture. At the corner of Cameron and North Washington streets, one block south, stands the Georgian country-style **Christ Church** ⓮. Walk south two blocks to the **Lyceum** ⓯ at the corner of South Washington and Prince streets. Two blocks to the west on South Alfred Street is the **Friendship Fire House** ⓰. It's a long walk (or a quick ride on Bus 2 or 5 west on King Street) but worth the trouble to visit the **George Washington Masonic National Memorial** ⓱ on Callahan Drive at the King Street Metro station 1 mi west of the center of the city. Across the street is the **U.S. Patent and Trademark Museum** ⓲.

---

in Alexandria as prisoners of war. ⊠ *Prince St. between Lee and Union Sts., Old Town.*

❽ **Carlyle House.** The grandest of Alexandria's older houses, Carlyle House was patterned after a Scottish country manor house. The structure was completed in 1753 by Scottish merchant John Carlyle. This was General Edward Braddock's headquarters and the place where he met with five royal governors in 1755 to plan the strategy and funding of the early campaigns of the French and Indian War. ⊠ *121 N. Fairfax St., Old Town* ☎ *703/549–2997* ☜ *$4* ☉ *Tues.–Sat. 10–4:30, Sun. noon–4:30, guided tours every ½ hr.*

⓮ Christ Church. Both Washington and Lee were pewholders in this Episcopalian church. (Washington paid £36 and 10 shillings—a lot of money in those days—for Pew 60.) Built in 1773, Christ Church is a good example of Georgian church architecture. It has a fine Palladian window, an interior balcony, and an English wrought-brass-and-crystal chandelier. Docents give tours during visiting hours. ⊠ *118 N. Washington St., Old Town* ☎ *703/549–1450* ⊕ *www.historicchristchurch.org* ☜ *Free* ☉ *Mon.–Sat. 9–5, Sun. 2–4.*

Confederate Statue. In 1861, when Alexandria was occupied by Union forces, the 800 soldiers of the city's garrison marched out of town to join the Confederate Army. In the middle of Washington and Prince street this statue marks the point at which they assembled. In 1885 Confederate veterans proposed a memorial to honor their fallen comrades. The statue, based on John A. Elder's painting *Appomattox,* is of a lone soldier glumly surveying the battlefields after General Robert E. Lee's surrender. Names of 100 Alexandria Confederate dead are carved on the base.

🐚 ⓰ Friendship Fire House. Alexandria's showcase firehouse, home to the area's first volunteer fire company beginning in 1774, is outfitted in typical 19th-century firefighting fashion. Artifacts include leather water buckets, axes, and hand-drawn fire trucks. ⊠ *107 S. Alfred St., Old Town* ☎ *703/838–3891* ☜ *Free* ☉ *Fri. and Sat. 10–4, Sun. 1–4.*

🐚 ❾ Gadsby's Tavern Museum. This museum is housed in the old City Tavern and Hotel, which was a center of political and social life in the late 18th century. A tour takes you through the taproom, dining room, assembly room, ballroom, and communal bedrooms. Friday evening tours visit the same rooms but are led by a costumed guide using a candle-lighted lantern. ⊠ *134 N. Royal St., Old Town* ☎ *703/838–4242 or 703/548–1388* ⊕ *www.*

> **CAPITAL FACTS**
>
> George Washington went to birthday celebrations in the ballroom at the Gadsby Tavern.

gadsbystavern.org ☜ *$4, $2 children 11–17, lantern tours $5* ☉ *Nov.–Mar., Tues.–Sat. 11–4, Sun. 1–4, last tour at 3:15; Apr.–Oct., Tues.–Sat. 10–5, Sun. 1–5, last tour at 4:15; tours 15 min before and after the hr. Lantern tours Mar.–Nov., Fri. 7–9:30.*

⓱ George Washington Masonic National Memorial. Alexandria, like Washington, has no tall buildings, so the spire of this memorial dominates the surroundings. The building fronts King Street, one of Alexandria's major east-west arteries; from the ninth-floor observation deck you get a spectacular view of Alexandria, with Washington in the distance. The building contains furnishings from the first Masonic lodge in Alexandria, in which George Washington was a member; he became a Mason in 1752 and was a Worshipful Master, a high rank, at the same time he served as president. ✉ *101 Callahan Dr., Old Town* ☎ *703/683–2007* ⊕ *www.gwmemorial.org* ✆ *Free* ⊙ *Daily 9–5; 50-min guided tours of building and deck daily at 9:30, 10:30, 11:30, 1, 2, 3, and 4.*

❻ John Q. Adams Center for the History of Otolaryngology. Otolaryngolophiles, aka those interested in ear, nose, and throat medicine, will naturally be in heaven here, but so will lovers of quirky medical history. This science and history museum is a treasure trove of eyebrow-raising antique surgical instruments, rare manuscripts, and oral histories relating to ear, nose, and throat treatment and surgery, as well as plenty of fun facts about the procedures through the ages. Among them: that Scribonius Largus, who practiced medicine during the time of Roman emperor Claudius (41–54), recommended the use of the electric ray fish in the treatment of facial neuralgia. ✉ *1 Prince St., Old Town* ☎ *703/836–4444* ⊕ *www.entnet.org* ✆ *Free* ⊙ *Weekdays 9–5.*

❿ Lee-Fendall House Museum. The short block of Alexandria's Oronoco Street between Washington and St. Asaph streets is the site of two Lee-owned houses. One is the Lee-Fendall House, the home of several illustrious members of the Lee family, and the other is the boyhood home of Robert E. Lee. The Lee-Fendall House is decorated with Victorian furnishings and some Lee pieces. Labor leader John Lewis lived here from 1937 to 1969. ✉ *614 Oronoco St., Old Town* ✆ *$4* ⊙ *Feb.–mid-Dec., Tues.–Sat. 10–4, Sun. 1–4; sometimes closed weekends.*

⓭ Lloyd House. A fine example of Georgian architecture, Lloyd House was built in 1797 and is owned by the city of Alexandria. The interior is no longer open to the public, so it can be admired only from outside. ✉ *220 N. Washington St., Old Town.*

⓯ Lyceum. Built in 1839, the Lyceum served as a library, a Civil War hospital, a residence, and an office building. It was restored in the 1970s and now houses two galleries with exhibits on the history of Alexandria, a third gallery with changing exhibits, and a gift shop. Some travel information for the entire state is also available here. ✉ *201 S. Washington St., Old Town* ☎ *703/838–4994* ⊕ *www.alexandriahistory.org* ✆ *Free* ⊙ *Mon.–Sat. 10–5, Sun. noon–5.*

❸ Old Presbyterian Meeting House. Built in 1774, the Old Presbyterian Meeting House was, as its name suggests, more than a church. It was Alexandria's gathering place, vital to Scottish patriots during the Revolution. Eulogies for George Washington were delivered here on December 29, 1799. In a corner of the churchyard is the Tomb of the Unknown Soldier of the American Revolution. ✉ *321 S. Fairfax St., Old Town* ☎ *703/549–6670* ⊕ *www.opmh.org* ✆ *Free* ⊙ *Sanctuary weekdays 9–3; key available at church office at 316 S. Royal St.; Sun. services 8:30 and 11.*

▶❶ Ramsay House. The best place to start a tour of Alexandria's Old Town is at the **Alexandria Convention & Visitors Association**, in Ramsay House, the home of the town's first postmaster and lord mayor, William Ramsay. The structure is believed to be the oldest house in Alexandria. Travel counselors here provide brochures and maps for self-guided walking tours and can also give you a 24-hour permit for free parking at any two-hour metered spot. Many tour companies give guided walking tours that leave from here. Ticket prices vary, though most are within the $10 range. Call ahead to get guided tour times. ⊠ *221 King St., Old Town* ☎ *703/838–4200 or 800/388–9119, 703/838–6494 TDD* ⊕ *www.funside.com* ⊗ *Daily 9–5.*

❷ Stabler-Leadbeater Apothecary. Once patronized by George Washington and the Lee family, Alexandria's Stabler-Leadbeater Apothecary is the second-oldest apothecary in the country (the oldest is reputedly in Bethlehem, Pennsylvania). Some believe that it was here, on October 17, 1859, that Lt. Col. Robert E. Lee received orders to lead marines sent from the Washington Barracks to help suppress John Brown's insurrection at Harper's Ferry (then part of Virginia). The shop now houses a small museum of 18th- and 19th-century apothecary memorabilia, including one of the finest collections of apothecary bottles in the country (some 800 bottles in all). ⊠ *105–107 S. Fairfax St., Old Town* ☎ *703/836–3713* ▦ *$2.50* ⊗ *Mon.–Sat. 10–4, Sun. 1–5.*

★ ❼ Torpedo Factory Art Center. Torpedoes were manufactured here by the U.S. Navy during World War I and World War II. Now the building houses the studios and workshops of about 160 artists and artisans and has become one of Alexandria's most popular attractions. You can view the workshops of printmakers, jewelry makers, sculptors, painters, and potters, and most of the art and the crafts are for sale. On the second Thursday of every month, the building hosts an Art Night, in which the galleries stay open until 9. The Torpedo Factory also houses the **Alexandria Archaeology Program** (☎ 703/838–4399 ⊕ www.alexandriaarchaeology.org), a city-operated research facility devoted to urban archaeology and conservation. Artifacts from excavations in Alexandria are on display here. Admission is free; hours are Tuesday through Friday 10–3, Saturday 10–5, and Sunday 1–5. ⊠ *105 N. Union St., Old Town* ☎ *703/838–4565* ⊕ *www.torpedofactory. org* ▦ *Free* ⊗ *Daily 10–5; galleries open until 9 on 2nd Thurs. of the month.*

❽ U.S. Patent and Trademark Museum. From Thomas Edison to the TiVo, this museum tells the story of how the thousands of objects (and images, such as the Nike swoosh and Coca-Cola cursive) that permeate our lives are invented and trademarked. ⊠ *600 Dulany St., Alexandria* ☎ *571/272–0095* ⊕ *www.uspto.gov/web/offices/ac/ahrpa/opa/museum* ▦ *Free* ⊗ *Weekdays 9–5, Sat. noon–5.*

AROUND WASHINGTON

The city and environs of Washington (including parts of Maryland and Virginia) are dotted with worthwhile attractions that are outside the walks in this chapter. You may find some intriguing enough to go a little out of your way to visit. The nearest Metro stop is noted only if it's within reasonable walking distance of a given sight.

Bethesda, Maryland

Bethesda was named in 1871 after the Bethesda Meeting House, which was built by the Presbyterians. Their house of worship's name alludes to the biblical pool of Bethesda, which reputedly had great healing power. Today, people seek healing in Bethesda at the U.S. Naval Regional Medical Center and the National Institutes of Health, and meet here to enjoy the burgeoning restaurant scene. Although Bethesda has changed from a small community into an urban destination, time has stood still east of Bethesda in much of Chevy Chase, a town of exclusive country clubs, elegant houses, and huge trees.

McCrillis Gardens. A favorite of picnickers, bird-watchers, and runners, particularly in the spring, the Gardens is a pleasant respite from the nearby city, with many local plants and animals making it their home. ⊠ *6910 Greentree Rd.* ☎ *301/365–1657* ⊕ *www.mc-mncppc.org/parks/ brookside/mccrilli.shtm* ⊠ *Free* ⊙ *Gardens daily 10–dusk, gallery Tues.–Sun. noon–4.*

National Institutes of Health (NIH). One of the world's foremost biomedical research centers, with a sprawling 300-acre campus, the NIH has tours for the public, including an orientation tour of some of its foremost research and clinical facilities, and a tour of the National Library of Medicine. Visitors wishing to tour the hospital facilities must reserve in advance. ■ TIP→ **With a four-to-six-week lead time, the NIH will custom-craft a tour that takes visitors through facilities of particular interest to them.** Although best known for its books and journals—there are more than 5 million—the National Library of Medicine also houses historical medical references dating from the 11th century. A library tour includes a look at historical documents, the library's databases, and their "visible human," which shows everything from how the kneecap works to how physicians use surgical simulators. The guides have useful advice on how to start medical research (to do any research, you must arrive at least 1 ½ hours before closing time). ⊠ *Visitor Information Center, 9000 Rockville Pike, Bldg. 10* ☎ *301/496–1776* ⊠ *National Library of Medicine, 8600 Rockville Pike, Bldg. 38A* ☎ *301/496– 6308* ⊕ *www.nih.gov* ⊠ *Free* ⊙ *Call for tour times, library hrs, and information on forms of ID to bring, plus other security measures* Ⓜ *Medical Center.*

★ ℭ **Strathmore.** Local and national artists exhibit in the galleries and musicians perform year-round at this mansion built around 1900. Whimsical pieces, part of the permanent collection, are on display in the sculpture garden. A $100 million renovation, completed in 2005, introduced the 1,976-seat **Music Center at Strathmore,** now home of the Baltimore Symphony Orchestra. Other programming ranges from classical performers to popular acts playing Broadway, jazz, gospel, and rock, as well as dance troupes. A free series that includes poetry, music, art talks (including some for children), and demonstrations takes place on certain Wednesday evenings (call ahead for specific dates and hours). Strathmore's Tea is served in a well-lighted wood-panel salon, Tuesday and Wednesday at 1 PM. During July and August, Backyard Theater performers entertain children. ⊠ *Tuckerman La.* ☎ *301/581–5200, 301/581–5108 Tea* ⊕ *www.strathmore.org* ⊠ *Free, Backyard Theater $6, tea $18, reservations essential* ⊘ *Mon., Tues., Thurs., and Fri. 10–4, Wed. 10–9, Sat. 10–3* Ⓜ *Grosvenor/Strathmore.*

Elsewhere in Maryland

Brookside Gardens. Fans of formal gardens, regional plants, or just fragrant blooms can find plenty to soothe the senses in this 50-acre garden within Wheaton Regional Park. Guided tours of individual gardens and conservatories are available throughout the year, and a horticultural reference library is in the airy visitor center. ⊠ *1500 Glenallan Ave., Wheaton* ☎ *301/962–1400* ⊕ *www.mc-mncppc.org/parks/brookside* ⊠ *Free* ⊘ *Gardens daily sunrise–sunset; conservatories daily 10–5; visitor center daily 9–5; horticultural reference library weekdays 10–3.*

Ⓒ **College Park Aviation Museum.** One of College Park's claims to fame is the world's oldest continuously operating airport. Opened in 1909, it has been the site of numerous aviation firsts and continues to be a working airport. Orville and Wilbur Wright tested military planes here, and their presence is evident in the artifacts of early aviation on display. The 27,000-square-foot museum affiliated with the Smithsonian has interactive exhibits and an animatronic Wilbur Wright. A full-scale reproduction of the 1911 Wright Model B Aeroplane is also here. ⊠ *1985 Corporal Frank Scott Dr., College Park* ☎ *301/864–6029* ⊕ *www.collegeparkaviationmuseum.com* ⊠ *$4 adults, $3 seniors, $2 children* ⊘ *Daily 10–5.*

★ Ⓒ **Goddard Space Flight Center.** Goddard Space Flight Center was established in 1959 as NASA's first center devoted to the exploration of space, rocketry, and robotics. Exhibits and tours highlight Robert Goddard's contributions to America's space program, as well as the development of cutting-edge technologies in space science, including the Hubble Telescope. Visitors can participate in demonstrations and talks by NASA scientists. The Main Gallery reflects the space program's legendary past and exciting future, and the Earth Science Gallery has earth science themes in a high-tech, 2,600-foot gallery. Children may bring preassembled model rockets for monthly rocket launchings the first Sunday of the month at 1p.m. ⊠ *Soil Conservation and Greenbelt Rds., Greenbelt* ☎ *301/286–8955* ⊕ *www.nasa.gov/goddard* ⊠ *Free* ⊘ *Tues.–Fri. 9–4, weekends noon–4* Ⓜ *Greenbelt, then Bus T15, T16, or T17.*

Ⓒ **National Capital Trolley Museum.** Although a fire in 2003 destroyed almost a third of the museum's collection, 11 antique trolleys and streetcars from major American and European cities are now on display. Train buffs will love the model of 1930s Washington with trolley lines intact. ⊠ *1313 Bonifant Rd., between Layhill Rd. and New Hampshire Ave., Silver Spring* ☎ *301/384–6088* ⊕ *www.dctrolley.org* ⊠ *Free, trolley ride*

$3, $2 children and seniors ◎ *Jan.–Nov., Thurs. and Fri. 10–2, week-ends year-round and some major holidays noon–5.*

ⓒ **National Cryptologic Museum.** A 30-minute drive from Washington, Maryland's National Cryptologic Museum is a surprise, telling in a public way the anything-but-public story of "signals intelligence," the government's gleaning of intelligence from radio signals, messages, radar, and the cracking of other governments' secret codes. Connected to the supersecret National Security Agency, the museum recounts the history of intelligence from 1526 to the present. Displays include rare cryptographic books from the 16th century, items used in the Civil War, World War II cipher machines, and a Cray supercomputer of the sort that does the code work today. Newer exhibits include props from the film *Windtalkers*; artifacts from intelligence programs of the Korean, Vietnam, and Cold wars; and one of the earliest intelligence satellites. ⊠ *Colony Seven Rd. near Fort Meade; Baltimore–Washington Pkwy. to 32E, exit at 32W and follow detour signs for 32E, or call for directions* ☎ *301/688–5849* ⊕ *www.nsa.gov/museum* ⊡ *Free* ◎ *Weekdays 9–4, 1st and 3rd Sat. 10–2.*

Temple of the Church of Jesus Christ of Latter-day Saints. A striking Mormon temple in suburban Maryland—one of its white towers is topped with a golden statue of the Mormon angel and prophet Moroni—the Temple of the Church of Jesus Christ of Latter-day Saints has become a Washington landmark for the way it seems to rise up from the distance, appearing like a modern-day Oz. The temple is closed to non-Mormons, but the grounds and visitor center offer a lovely view of the white-marble temple and surroundings. Tulips, dogwoods, and azaleas bloom in the 57-acre grounds each spring. In December, Washingtonians enjoy the Festival of Lights—300,000 of them—and a live Nativity scene. ⊠ *9900 Stoneybrook Dr., Kensington* ☎ *301/587–0144* ⊕ *www.washingtonlds.org* ◎ *Grounds and visitor center daily 10–9.*

Elsewhere in Virginia

ⓒ **Flying Circus Airshow.** Stunt flying and wing walking are among the attractions at the Flying Circus Airshow. Billing itself as the only remaining barnstorming show in the country, the Flying Circus operates out of a Virginia aerodrome about 90 minutes by car from Washington. Biplane rides are available before and after the show. In addition to the air show, special events—such as model rocket day, antique car day, motorcycle day, and hot rod day—are held most Sundays. Call ahead for attraction information. ⊠ *Rte. 17, between Fredericksburg and Warrenton, Bealeton* ☎ *540/439–8661* ⊕ *www.flyingcircusairshow.com* ⊡ *$10* ◎ *May–Oct., Sun. gates open at 11, show starts at 2:30.*

★ ⓒ **National Air and Space Museum Steven F. Udvar-Hazy Center.** This gargantuan Smithsonian facility displays more than 200 aircraft, 135 spacecraft, rockets, satellites, and experimental flying machines, including a Concorde, the space shuttle *Enterprise,* the fabled Lockheed SR-71 Blackbird, which in 1990 flew from Los Angeles to Washington, D.C., in slightly more than an hour, and the *Enola Gay,* which in 1944 dropped on Japan the first atomic devices to be used in war. An IMAX theater at this facility also shows films about flight and exploration. Shuttle buses that go between the center and the National Air and Space Museum on the Mall leave four times daily and cost $12. ✉ *14390 Air and Space Museum Pkwy., Chantilly* ☎ *202/633–1000* ⊕ *www.nasm.si. edu/udvarhazy* ✇ *Free, IMAX $7.50, parking $12* ☉ *Daily 10–5:30.*

Where to Eat

Updated by
Cynthia
Hacinli

WEST AFRICAN DELICACIES such as *moi-moi,* a jumble of black-eyed peas, tomatoes, and corned beef; *feijoada,* a rich Brazilian casserole of black beans, pork, and smoked meats; bouillabaisse, the fish stew from France; Italian favorites such as pasta carbonara; succulent lamb kabobs or crisp falafel (vegetable fritters) from the Middle East; crunchily addictive Vietnamese spring rolls; spicy Carolina shrimp with steaming white grits; and some of the finest marbled steaks and butter-soft prime rib this side of the Mississippi: these are just a few of the dazzling dishes you'll find in the nation's capital.

As host to visitors and transplants from around the world, Washington benefits from the constant infusion of different cultures. Despite D.C.'s lack of true ethnic neighborhoods and the kinds of restaurant districts found in many other cities, you *can* find almost any cuisine here, from Burmese to Ethiopian. Even the city's French-trained chefs, who once set the standard in fine dining, have been influenced by contemporary cooking, spicy Asian and Mexican fare, sushi, and appetizer-size Spanish tapas. High-end restaurants in town have also begun to add bar menus with smaller plates that are much less expensive than their entrées but done with the same finesse.

Wall-to-wall restaurants line 18th Street NW, which extends south from Columbia Road. In this section of Adams-Morgan, small ethnic spots open and close frequently; it's worth taking a stroll down the street to see what's new and interesting. Although the area has retained some of its Latin American identity, the newer eating establishments tend to be Asian, contemporary, Italian, and Ethiopian. Parking can be impossible on weekends. You can walk from the nearest Metro stop, Woodley Park/Zoo, in 10 to 15 minutes, but even though it's a relatively safe stretch at night, arriving by taxi may be more convenient. Woodley Park has culinary temptations of its own, with a lineup of popular ethnic restaurants near the Metro.

"Downtown" covers everything between Georgetown and Capitol Hill. The "new downtown," centered at Connecticut Avenue and K Street, has many of the city's blue-chip law firms and deluxe eateries—places that feed expense-account diners and provide the most elegance, most attentive service, and often the best food. But "old downtown," farther east, is where the action is these days. Restaurants of all stripes (usually casual and moderately priced) have sprung up to serve the crowds that attend games at the MCI Center. The entire downtown area, however, has been in a state of culinary flux, with famed restaurants closing their doors and new ones—including some upscale, trendy spots—blossoming. Stylish lounges and microbrew pubs are also part of the scene, and Chinatown has been suffering as rents go up and long-standing favorites have to close or relocate.

Chinatown itself, centered on G and H streets NW between 6th and 8th, is the city's one officially recognized ethnic enclave. Here Burmese, Thai, and other Asian cuisines add variety to the many traditional Chinese restaurants. The latter entice you with huge, brightly lighted signs and offer such staples as beef with broccoli or spicy kung pao chicken with roasted peanuts. But discriminating diners will find far better food at the smaller, less flashy restaurants.

KNOW-HOW

GETTING THERE

Most restaurants are easily accessible by Metro; some are not. Details on Metro stops are provided when this form of public transportation is realistic for the average traveler.

PRICES

Every D.C. neighborhood has places where you can eat on the cheap as well as upscale mink-and-pearls spots. The least expensive restaurants are often homegrown variations on the fast-food counter-service theme. A bit pricier but still a bargain are family-run ethnic places where a meal for two can be had for less than $50. One way to keep prices down at more upscale places is to go for pretheater menus, where choices may be limited and the tab lower. Many high-end restaurants now have separate bar menus that showcase the creativity of the chef at gentler prices. This usually means eating at the bar or at tables in the lounge area, which, depending on the restaurant, can be as appealing as the dining room. Sticking to appetizers and grazing is another cost-cutting gambit, as is going to a heavy hitter for lunch rather than dinner: this is usually at least a third cheaper (a modest dinner for two might cost $60). Finally, many restaurants have come-hither inducements early in the week. You might be able to bring your own wine on a Monday night, or maybe wines and cocktails are half price on Tuesdays. And if you're dining with a group, make sure not to overtip: review your check to see if a gratuity has been added, as many restaurants automatically tack on a 15% tip for groups of six, eight, or more.

The restaurants we list are the cream of the crop in every price range. All restaurants are open daily for lunch and dinner unless stated otherwise.

RESERVATIONS & DRESS

It's always a good idea to make reservations; we mention them only when they're essential or are not accepted. Book as far ahead as you can, and reconfirm as soon as you arrive. However, even when reservations are not accepted, large groups should call ahead. Dress is mentioned only when men are required to wear a jacket or a jacket and tie, but gentlemen may be more comfortable wearing jackets and ties in $$$ and $$$$ restaurants, even when there is no formal dress code.

THE WRITING ON THE WALL

Look for recent reviews in *Washingtonian* magazine (⊕ www.washingtonian.com), the *Washington Post* (⊕ www.washingtonpost.com), the *Washington Times* (⊕ www.washtimes.com) and www.chowhound.com. Proud restaurant owners display favorable reviews on doors or in windows.

WHAT IT COSTS					
	$$$$	$$$	$$	$	¢
AT DINNER	over $35	$26–$35	$18–$25	$10–$17	under $10

Prices are per person for a main course at dinner.

Capitol Hill has a number of bars that cater to congressional types who need to fortify themselves with food and drink after a day spent running the country. Dining options are augmented by Union Station, which houses some decent—if pricey—restaurants. There's also a large food court offering quick bites that range from barbecue to sushi.

Dupont Circle, which lies south of U Street and north of K Street, is dense with restaurants and cafés, many with outdoor seating. Chains such as Starbucks have put fancy coffee on every corner, but home-grown espresso bars, such as the 24-hour Kramerbooks & Afterwords, as well as Teaism, have more character and are more interesting for breakfast and light or late fare.

Georgetown's main drags are Wisconsin Avenue and M Street, and here white-tablecloth establishments

---

TOP 5

- **Citronelle, Georgetown:** The mischievous and witty Michel Richard really knows how to play with his food.
- **Inn at Little Washington, Virginia Suburbs:** Over-the-top Anglo-posh digs and lavish attention make all comers feel like royalty.
- **Galileo, Downtown:** It's dinner theater for the millennium.
- **Maestro, Virginia Suburbs:** Don't expect an ordinary hotel restaurant: The chef turns Italian cuisine inside out—and he wears a headset.
- **Café Atlántico's Minibar, Downtown:** It's the place to go when you're after a thrill-a-minute, literally.

---

coexist easily next to hole-in-the-wall joints. The closest Metro stop is Foggy Bottom, a 15- to 20-minute walk away; consult the Georgetown map before you set out, and consider taking a cab. Restaurants in the adjacent West End—bounded roughly by Rock Creek Park to the west, N Street to the north, 20th Street to the east, and K Street to the south—are worth checking out as well. North from Georgetown on Wisconsin Avenue, there are good restaurants in the Glover Park area, including one of the city's best sushi bars, Sushi-Ko.

In the 1930s and 1940s, the U Street corridor, which begins just down the hill from 18th Street, was the place to enjoy a late-night drink and hear jazz greats such as Duke Ellington, Billie Holiday, and Charlie Parker. After decades of neglect and devastation from riots in the 1960s, the area saw a burst of revitalization. With some of the hippest bars in the District, quirky vintage stores, small and lively nightclubs, and numerous cafés, the neighborhood draws a young crowd day and night. The area is still rough around the edges, however, so use caution. Restaurants stay open late on weekend nights and serve everything from burgers to gourmet pizza and Ethiopian dishes at low prices.

Interesting restaurant districts also thrive outside the city limits and are accessible by the Metro. Downtown Bethesda, Maryland, is luring the cognoscenti from Georgetown with Spanish, French, Italian, Vietnamese, and Thai fare. Bethesda is a 20-minute drive from Georgetown up Wisconsin Avenue; by Metro it's a 15- to 20-minute ride from Metro Center to the Bethesda Metro stop or a five-minute ride from the Foggy Bottom Metro stop.

Virginia has its own ritzy Georgetown equivalent in Old Town Alexandria, and bragging rights to some of the D.C. area's best Asian restaurants go to Arlington. There, Wilson Boulevard is lined with popular Vietnamese establishments and branches of D.C. restaurants. The Clarendon Metro station makes these Asian restaurants readily accessible, but the King Street Metro station is, unfortunately, a 15-minute walk from most Old Town Alexandria eateries.

Farther afield, the Eden Center in Falls Church, about a 15-minute drive from downtown Washington, is home to Vietnamese shops and groceries and a clutch of Vietnamese restaurants. One of the best is Huong Que, or Four Sisters, whose namesakes, along with their parents and brothers, own and run the place.

Adams-Morgan & Woodley Park

African

$ ✕ **Meskerem.** Ethiopian restaurants abound in Adams-Morgan, but Meskerem is distinctive for its bright, appealingly decorated dining room and its balcony. Entrées are served family-style on a large tray lined with *injera*, a thin sourdough bread. Scoop up mouthfuls of the hearty dishes with extra injera. Specialties include stews made with spicy *berbere* chili sauce; *kitfo*, buttery beef served very rare or raw like steak tartare; and a tangy, green-chili–vinaigrette potato salad. There's live Ethiopian music on Fridays and Saturdays. ⊠ *2434 18th St. NW, Adams-Morgan* ☎ *202/462–4100* ⌒ *Reservations essential* ⊟ *AE, DC, MC, V* Ⓜ *Woodley Park/Zoo.*

¢–$ ✕ **Bukom Café.** Sunny African pop music, palm fronds, kente cloth, and a spicy West African menu all brighten this narrow, two-story dining room. Entrées range from *egusi* (goat with melon seeds) and *kumasi* (chicken in peanut sauce) to vegetarian dishes such as *jollof* (rice with vegetables and tomato sauce). Live reggae and calypso keep this place hopping at night. ⊠ *2442 18th St. NW, Adams-Morgan* ☎ *202/265–4600* ⊟ *AE, D, MC, V* ☽ *No lunch* Ⓜ *Woodley Park/Zoo.*

Cajun/Creole

¢–$ ✕ **Bardia's New Orleans Café.** Locals swarm to this cozy café, where great food is accompanied by jazz. Seafood, whether batter fried, blackened, or sautéed, is always a winner. The house favorite is the blackened catfish. Po'boy sandwiches (subs on French bread) are reasonably priced, fresh, and huge. Breakfast items, served all day, include traditional eggs Benedict or eggs New Orleans, with fried oysters, crabmeat, and hollandaise: they're both delicious. Don't leave without trying the outstanding beignets (fried puffs of dough sprinkled with powdered sugar). ⊠ *2412 18th St. NW, Adams-Morgan* ☎ *202/234–0420* ⌒ *Reservations not accepted* ⊟ *AE, MC, V* Ⓜ *Woodley Park/Zoo.*

Bardia's
New Orleans
Café **10**

Bukom
Café **6**

Cashion's
Eat Place **9**

Grill from
Ipanema **11**

La
Fourchette **7**

Lauriol
Plaza **12**

Lebanese
Taverna **2**

Mama
Ayesha's
Restaurant **3**

Meskerem **8**

Mixtec **5**

New
Heights **1**

Pasta Mia **4**

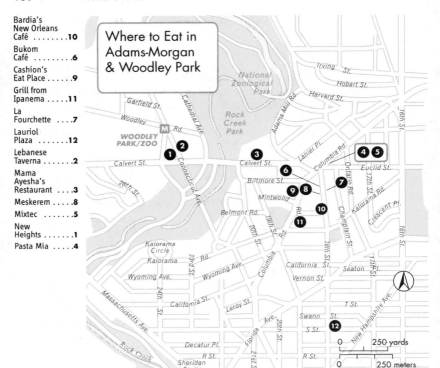

Where to Eat in
Adams-Morgan
& Woodley Park

Contemporary

$$-$$$ ✕ **New Heights.** This inviting restaurant has 11 large windows that over-look nearby Rock Creek Park. The sophisticated contemporary cook-ing blends bold world flavors into the traditional dishes of the American repertoire. Truffled potato-leek soup gets dolled up with a cheddar cheese pierogi; king salmon wrapped in *katifi* (shredded wheat) is one of the more unusual entrées. Chocophiles will appreciate the bittersweet chocolate praline crunch with malted-milk chocolate ice cream. ⊠ *2317 Calvert St. NW, Woodley Park* ☎ *202/234–4110* ▤ *AE, D, DC, MC, V* ☺ *Closed Mon. and Tues.* Ⓜ *Woodley Park/Zoo.*

★ **$-$$$** ✕ **Cashion's Eat Place.** Walls are hung with family photos, and tables are jammed with regulars feasting on up-to-date, home-style cooking in Ann Cashion's very personal restaurant. The menu changes daily, but roast chicken, steak, and seafood are frequent choices. Side dishes, such as garlicky mashed potatoes or buttery potatoes Anna, sometimes upstage the main course. If it's available, order the chocolate terrine layered with walnuts, caramel, mousse, and ganache. ▪ **TIP➜ At Sunday brunch, many entrées are a fraction of the normal price.** ⊠ *1819 Columbia Rd. NW, Adams-Morgan* ☎ *202/797–1819* ⌖ *Reservations essential* ▤ *AE, MC, V* ☺ *Closed Mon. No lunch Tues.–Sat.* Ⓜ *Woodley Park/Zoo.*

French

$-$$ ✕ **La Fourchette.** On a block in Adams-Morgan where restaurants seem to open and close weekly, La Fourchette has stayed in business for nearly a quarter of a century by offering good bistro food at reasonable prices. Most of the menu consists of daily specials such as venison with shallots and pepper sauce, chicken in beurre blanc, or sweetbreads in a mushroom-cream sauce. This place looks as a bistro should, with an exposed-brick wall, a tin ceiling, bentwood chairs, and vaguely postimpressionist murals. ⊠ *2429 18th St. NW, Adams-Morgan* ☎ *202/332–3077* ☐ *AE, DC, MC, V* Ⓜ *Woodley Park/Zoo.*

Italian

¢–$ ✕ **Pasta Mia.** Patrons don't seem to mind waiting their turn to eat in this affordable, 40-seat trattoria. Pasta Mia's southern Italian appetizers and entrées all cost around $10. Large bowls of steaming pasta are served with a generous layer of freshly grated Parmesan. Some best sellers are fusilli with broccoli and whole cloves of roasted garlic, rich spinach fettuccine, and penne *arrabbiata* (in a spicy marinara sauce with olives). Tiramisu, served in a teacup, is a civilized way to finish your meal. ⊠ *1790 Columbia Rd. NW, Adams-Morgan* ☎ *202/328–9114* ⌕ *Reservations not accepted* ☐ *MC, V* ☉ *Closed Sun. No lunch* Ⓜ *Woodley Park/Zoo.*

Latin American

$$ ✕ **The Grill from Ipanema.** Brazilian cuisine, from zesty seafood stews to grilled steak, is the focus here. Appetizers include fried yucca with spicy sausages and—for adventurous eaters—fried alligator. Former Second Lady Tipper Gore adores the *mexilhão á carioca,* garlicky mussels cooked in a clay pot. Traditional feijoada, the stew that's the national dish of Brazil, is served every day. ⊠ *1858 Columbia Rd. NW, Adams-Morgan* ☎ *202/986–0757* ⌕ *Reservations essential* ☐ *AE, D, DC, MC, V* ☉ *No lunch weekdays* Ⓜ *Woodley Park/Zoo.*

¢–$ ✕ **Lauriol Plaza.** This longtime favorite on the border of Adams-Morgan and Dupont Circle serves Latin American, Cuban, and Spanish dishes—seviche, paella, fajitas, and so on—to enthusiastic crowds. Rustic entrées such as Cuban-style pork and *lomo saltado* (Peruvian-style strip steak with onions, tomatoes, and jalapeño peppers) are specialties. The dining room can get noisy, but the roof terrace is a popular alternative in good weather. ∎ TIP➔ **The two hours of free parking for customers is especially enticing: this street may be the most difficult place to park in the city.** ⊠ *1835 18th St. NW, Adams-Morgan* ☎ *202/387–0035* ⌕ *Reservations not accepted* ☐ *AE, D, DC, MC, V* Ⓜ *Dupont Circle.*

Mexican

♻ $ ✕ **Mixtec.** Don't expect tortilla chips as a starter at this truly Mexican restaurant—it doesn't serve them. Mixtec's tacos *al carbón* lack the lettuce and cheese toppings of their fast-food counterparts: they consist simply of charcoal-grilled beef or pork encased in fresh corn tortillas and accompanied by grilled spring onions. Fajitas, enchiladas, and seafood are cooked in the regional styles of Veracruz, Mazatlán, and Acapulco. The *licuados* (fruit drinks) are refreshing complements to the sometimes spicy dishes. And the staff is very accommodating to children. ⊠ *1792 Columbia Rd. NW, Adams-Morgan* ☎ *202/332–1011* ⚏ *Reservations not accepted* ▤ *MC, V* Ⓜ *Woodley Park/Zoo.*

Middle Eastern

$ ✕ **Lebanese Taverna.** Arched ceilings, cedar panels etched with leaf patterns, woven rugs, and brass lighting fixtures give the Taverna a warm elegance. Start with an order of Arabic bread baked in a wood-burning oven. Lamb, beef, chicken, and seafood are either grilled on kabobs, slow roasted, or smothered with a garlicky yogurt sauce. A group can make a meal of the meze platters—a mix of appetizers and sliced *shawarma* (spit-roasted lamb). ⊠ *2641 Connecticut Ave. NW, Woodley Park* ☎ *202/265–8681* ▤ *AE, MC, V* Ⓜ *Woodley Park/Zoo.*

$ ✕ **Mama Ayesha's Restaurant.** Journalists and politicians frequent this family-run eatery for its reasonably priced fare. Staples such as chicken and lamb kabobs can be had for less than $12, baskets of complimentary pita bread are served hot, and the crisp falafel is among the best in town. ⊠ *1967 Calvert St. NW, Adams-Morgan* ☎ *202/232–5431* ▤ *AE, D, DC, MC, V* Ⓜ *Woodley Park/Zoo.*

Capitol Hill

American

$$–$$$$ ✕ **Charlie Palmer.** It's hard not to feel like a master of the universe when ensconced in this coolly elegant dining room with a drop-dead view of the Capitol. Oversize floral arrangements, tones of blue-gray, a dramatic glass-enclosed wine cellar, and quasi-Danish modern furniture form a backdrop to the contemporary cuisine. Dry-aged rib eye, marinated hanger steak, and filet mignon with roasted shallots are the meaty choices. But soft-shell crabs and butter-steeped lobster make a good showing, too, as do sides such as mashed Yukon Golds and goat-cheese tubetti that seems like deluxe macaroni and cheese. The lemon pound cake finishes things off nicely. ⊠ *101 Constitution Ave., Capitol Hill* ☎ *202/547–8100* ▤ *AE, D, DC, MC, V* ☉ *Closed Sun. No lunch Sat.* Ⓜ *Union Station.*

$$–$$$ ✕ **The Capital Grille.** Just a few blocks from the U.S. Capitol, this New England–tinged steak house is a favorite among Republican congressmen. Politics aside, the cuisine, wine list, and surroundings are all top-shelf. Don't let the meat hanging in the window distract you from the fact that this restaurant has a lot more to offer than fine dry-aged porterhouse cuts and delicious cream-based potatoes. For instance, don't miss the pan-fried calamari with hot cherry peppers. A second location in Tysons Corner has the same menu but a slightly different wine list. ⊠ *601 Pennsylvania Ave. NW, Capitol Hill* ☎ *202/737–6200* ⊕ *www.thecapitalgrille.com* ⚏ *Reservations essential* ▤ *AE, D, DC, MC, V* ☉ *No lunch Sun.* Ⓜ *Navy Memorial/Archives.*

$–$$ ✕ **Monocle.** The nearest restaurant to the Senate side of the Capitol, Monocle's drawing card is old-style Capitol Hill atmosphere. The regional American cuisine is reliable though rarely adventurous. The crab cakes, either as a platter or in a sandwich, are a trademark, and you might encounter specials such as pot roast or a first-rate fish dish.

■ TIP→ This is a great place to spot members of Congress at lunch and dinner. ⊠ *107 D St. NE, Capitol Hill* ☎ *202/546–4488* ⊟ *AE, DC, MC, V* ⊘ *Closed weekends* Ⓜ *Union Station.*

↻ ¢–$ ✕ **The Market Lunch.** A walk around the Capitol, a stroll through Eastern Market, and then a hefty pile of blueberry pancakes from Market Lunch make for a perfect Saturday morning or afternoon on the Hill. The casual counter service and informal seating make it ideal for kids. Locals wait in long lines to dine on ham, eggs, grits, or pancakes in the morning or crab cakes, fried shrimp, or fish for lunch. But don't be mistaken: eating here is not a leisurely experience. On Saturdays you must be in line by noon. ■ TIP→ Follow convention and order quickly, eat, and give up your seat for the next customer. ⊠ *North end of Eastern Market, 225 7th St. SE, Capitol Hill* ☎ *202/547–8444* ⊟ *No credit cards* ⊘ *Closed Mon. No dinner* Ⓜ *Eastern Market.*

↻ ¢ ✕ **Jimmy T's Place.** Five blocks from the Capitol, this D.C. institution is tucked in the first floor of an old Capitol Hill row house. The small diner is packed daily with sassy waiters, talkative regulars, and its two boisterous owners, who run the grill. Soak in the local culture or read the paper as you enjoy favorites such as grits, bacon, omelets, or the homey eggs Benedict, made with a toasted English muffin, a huge piece of ham, and lots of hollandaise sauce. The anything-goes atmosphere makes it a great place for kids. Breakfast is served all day. ⊠ *501 East Capitol St. SE, Capitol Hill* ☎ *202/546–3646* ⊟ *No credit cards* ⊘ *Closed Mon. and Tues.* Ⓜ *Eastern Market.*

Belgian

$–$$ ✕ **Belga Cafe.** You can go traditional with mussels and the crispiest of french fries or dabble in what the chef calls Euro-fusion at this sleek café done up with dark wood, exposed brick, and creamy chairs and linens. Classic dishes such as *waterzoi,* the Belgian chicken stew, and carbonnade of beef made with beer, are expertly turned out, and newer takes such as the fabulously crisp fried sweetbreads in rosemary *jus* (stock) and seared scallops with snow peas broaden the options. Belgium is a beer-drinking country, and the beer list is suitably long and well conceived. Crowds at lunch and dinner sometimes mean a short wait even with a reservation. ⊠ *514 8th St. SE, Capitol Hill* ☎ *202/544–0100* ⊟ *AE, MC, V* ⊘ *Closed Mon.*

French

$$–$$$ ✕ **Bistro Bis.** A zinc bar, spacious brown leather booths, and a glass-front display kitchen create great expectations at Bistro Bis, the second restaurant from the owner of the much-acclaimed Vidalia. The seasonal menu seamlessly merges modern American standards with French bistro classics. For a first course, be sure to try the steak tartare and a tart topped with caramelized onions, bacon, Muenster cheese, and crème fraîche. Main-course hits include duck confit and grilled salmon with porcini mushrooms, braised oxtail, celery-root puree, and bordelaise sauce. ⊠ *Hotel George, 15 E St. NW, Capitol Hill* ☎ *202/661–2700* ⚐ *Reservations essential* ⊟ *AE, D, DC, MC, V* Ⓜ *Union Station.*

$–$$ ✕ **Montmartre.** With its sidewalk café, cheerful yellow walls, fresh flowers, and lusty yet chic fare, Montmartre evokes the Left Bank of Paris.

Where to Eat in Washington

Aatish on the Hill **68**
Ardeo/Bardeo **1**
B. Smith's **66**
Belga Cafe **76**
Ben's Chili Bowl **8**
Bistro Bis **73**
Bistrot du Coin **9**
Bombay Club **35**
Bread Line **34**
Burma **62**
Butterfield 9 . . . .**45**
Cada Vez **3**
Café Atlántico **55**
Café MoZU **50**
Café Nema **7**
The Capital Grille **51**
Caucus Room **56**
Ceiba **42**
Charlie Palmer **74**
CityZen **50**
Coppi's Organic
Restaurant **5**
DC Coast **39**
Dish **28**
Equinox **36**
Firefly **21**
Full Kee **63**
Galileo **26**
Georgia Brown's **41**
Gerard's Place **40**
Horace & Dickie's **69**
Inde Bleu **61**
i Ricchi **22**
Jaleo **58**
Jimmy T's Place **70**
Johnny's Half
Shell **15**
Kaz Sushi Bistro **30**
Kinkead's **29**
Komi **17**
Kramerbooks &
Afterwords **12**
Le Paradou **54**
Marcel's **27**
The Market Lunch **71**
Marrakesh **65**
Matchbox **64**

Monocle **67**
Montmartre **72**
Morton's of
Chicago **31**
Nooshi **25**
Nora **10**
Obelisk **14**
Occidental Grill **44**
Oceanaire
Seafood Room **47**
Old Ebbitt Grill **43**
Olives **37**
Palena **2**
Palette **38**
Palm **20**
Pizzeria Paradiso **13**
Polly's Café **6**
Poste **57**
Red Sage **46**
Sala Thai **16**
Sam and Harry's **23**
701 Pennsylvania
Avenue **52**
Skewers–Café Luna . . .**18**
Tabard Inn **19**
Taberna del
Alabardero **33**
Teaism **11, 53**
Teatro Goldoni **32**
TenPenh **49**
Tortilla Cafe **75**
Tosca **48**
Utopia **4**
Vidalia **24**
Zaytinya **60**
Zola **59**

Here is an unpretentious bistro that straddles classic and modern effortlessly with dishes like cream of chestnut soup, braised rabbit with olives and shiitake mushrooms, hangar steak with caramelized shallots, and cod with homemade spaetzle. It's a politicians' hangout, but you'd never know it by the cozy, rustic feel of the place. ☒ *327 7th St., Capitol Hill* ☎ *202/544–1244* ⚄ *Reservations essential* ▭ *AE, D, MC, V* ☉ *Closed Mon.* Ⓜ *Eastern Market.*

Indian

¢–$ ✕ **Aatish on the Hill.** The Pakistani word for volcano, *Aatish* is an appropriate name for a restaurant specializing in tandoori cooking, in which meats, seafood, vegetables, and breads are prepared in the intense heat of a clay oven. What distinguishes this restaurant is the quality of its cooking: its samosas, appetizers made of flaky pastry wrapped around a spiced mixture of potatoes and peas, are models of the form. The tandoori chicken is moist and delicious. Lamb dishes are also well prepared, especially the lamb *karahi,* sautéed in a wok with ginger, garlic, tomatoes, vegetables, and spices. ☒ *609 Pennsylvania Ave. SE, Capitol Hill* ☎ *202/544–0931* ⚄ *Reservations essential* ☉ *No lunch Sun.* ▭ *AE, D, MC, V* Ⓜ *Eastern Market.*

Salvadoran

¢–$ ✕ **Tortilla Cafe.** Across from bustling Eastern Market, this small takeout restaurant, where there are just a few tables, serves the best *pupusas* (cornmeal dough rounds stuffed with meat, cheese, or corn) in town. The menu is a mix of mostly El Salvadoran and Mexican fare with favorites such as tamales, Peruvian seviche, and fried plantains served with sour cream and refried beans. If it's available, order the homey Salvadoran Stew made with large chunks of beef, celery, carrots, and potatoes. The café is open 10–7 weekdays, 7–7 Saturday, and 8–7 Sunday. ☒ *210 7th St. SE, Capitol Hill* ☎ *202/547–5700* ⚄ *Reservations not accepted* ▭ *AE, D, MC, V* Ⓜ *Eastern Market.*

Southern

$–$$$ ✕ **B. Smith's.** If you're in the mood for shrimp and grits, Southern-influenced B. Smith's is the spot for you. To start try the jambalaya, but skip the overly bready fried green tomatoes. The Swamp Thing entrée may not sound pretty, but this mix of mustard-seasoned shrimp and crawfish with collards is inspired. Seafood, as well as anything with barbecue sauce, is highly recommended, as are the red beans and rice. Desserts are comforting, slightly dressed-up classics: coconut cake, warm bread pudding, and sweet-potato–pecan pie. ☒ *Union Station, 50 Massachusetts Ave. NE, Capitol Hill* ☎ *202/289–6188* ⚄ *Reservations essential* ▭ *AE, D, DC, MC, V* Ⓜ *Union Station.*

¢ ✕ **Horace & Dickie's.** The self-proclaimed home of the jumbo fish sandwich, this small, crowded restaurant has a loyal flock of regulars willing to wait in long lines for the $4.86 sandwich that's made up of four pieces of fried fish on white bread. Make sure to pick up some of the Southern-style sides such as macaroni and cheese, or get a slice of bean pie for dessert. The restaurant, which is takeout only, is open until 2 AM Monday–Saturday and until 8 PM on Sunday. ■ TIP➔ **Use caution and** visit during daylight hours: The neighborhood can be rough. ☒ *809 12th St. NE, Capitol Hill* ☏ *202/397–6040* ▭ *No credit cards.*

Downtown

African

$$$ ✕ **Marrakesh.** In a part of the city better known for auto-supply shops, Marrakesh supplies a taste of Morocco in a fixed-price ($29 per person, not including drinks) feast shared by everyone at your table. Appetizers consist of a platter of three salads followed by *b'stella,* a traditional chicken pie made with crisp layers of phyllo dough and seasoned with cinnamon. The first main course is chicken with lemon and olive. A beef or lamb dish is next, followed by vegetable couscous, fruit, mint tea, and pastries. Belly dancers perform nightly. Lunch is available for groups of 10 or more only, by reservation. ☒ *617 New York Ave. NW, Downtown* ☏ *202/393–9393* ♣ *Reservations essential* ▭ *No credit cards* Ⓜ *Mt. Vernon/UDC.*

American

★ $$$$ ✕ **CityZen.** The Mandarin Hotel's rarefied dining room has fast become a destination for those serious about food. In a glowing space with soaring ceilings, chef Eric Zeibold, formerly of Napa Valley's famed French Laundry, creates luxe fixed-price meals from the finest ingredients. Unexpected little treasures from the kitchen, such as scrambled eggs with white truffles shaved at the table and buttery miniature Parker House rolls, abound. Main courses run to black bass over caramelized cauliflower and braised veal shank with potato gnocchi, and desserts such as Meyer lemon soufflé seem spun out of air. A three-course meal is $70, and the tasting menus run $90–$125. ☒ *Mandarin Oriental, 1330 Maryland Ave. SW, Downtown* ☏ *202/787–6868* ♣ *Reservations essential* ▭ *AE, D, DC, MC, V* ☺ *Closed Mon. No lunch.*

$$–$$$$ ✕ **Butterfield 9.** Light-color wood paneling, gleaming white linen, and stunning black-and-white photographs make Butterfield 9 one of the most handsome restaurants in town. Chef Arthur Rivaldo's contemporary style of cooking glories in complexity. The menu changes every two months and has included hits such as a foie gras with black-truffle cannoli appetizer, and main courses such as *gremolata*-crusted halibut (garnished with chopped lemon peel, garlic, and parsley) and filet mignon with Roquefort butter and veal essence. The rhubarb potpie and other seasonal desserts are well worth a taste. ☒ *600 14th St. NW, Downtown* ☏ *202/289–8810* ♣ *Reservations essential* ▭ *AE, D, DC, MC, V* ☺ *No lunch weekends* Ⓜ *Metro Center.*

$$–$$$$ ✕ **Caucus Room.** Here is the quintessential Washington political restaurant. The limited partnership that owns it includes a Democratic super-lobbyist and a former Republican National Committee chairman. The dark wood and rich leather within make it perfect for business lunches or dinners, and the many private dining rooms are popular for political fund-raising events. The menu changes about three times a year, but you can count on prime meats, and seafood dishes including sea bass and seared tuna. ☒ *401 9th St. NW, Downtown* ☏ *202/*

393–1300 ▭ *AE, D, DC, MC, V* ✆ *Closed Sun. No lunch weekends* Ⓜ *Navy Archives.*

$–$$$ ✕ **Old Ebbitt Grill.** People flock here to drink at the several bars, which seem to go on for miles, and to enjoy well-prepared buffalo wings, hamburgers, and Reuben sandwiches. The Old Ebbitt also has Washington's most popular raw bar, which serves farm-raised oysters. Pasta is homemade, and daily fresh fish or steak specials are served until 1 AM. Despite the crowds, the restaurant never feels cramped, thanks to its well-spaced, comfortable booths. ■ TIP→ **Service can be slow at lunch; if you're in a hurry, try the café-style Ebbitt Express next door.** ✉ *675 15th St. NW, Downtown* ☎ *202/347–4800* ▭ *AE, D, DC, MC, V* Ⓜ *Metro Center.*

$–$$ ✕ **Matchbox.** The miniburgers, served on toasted brioche buns with a huge mound of fried onion strings, get the most press, but the main clue on what to order at this convivial triple-decker bar-restaurant is the glowing wood-burning pizza oven. The personal pizzas are "New York–style," with a thin, crisp crust. You probably won't mistake them

> **WORD OF MOUTH**
>
> "A very 'D.C.' restaurant . . . is Old Ebbitt Grill near the White House. . . . If you eavesdrop, there's no telling what you might hear!"   –sallyjane3

for the very best of New York, but the Margherita is good nevertheless. Homey plates such as pork loin with a bourbon cream sauce and spicy pecan-crusted chicken add substance to the menu. There's a great lineup of draft beers and oddball martinis. ✉ *713 H St. NW, Downtown* ☎ *202/289–4441* ✆ *Closed Sun.* Ⓜ *Gallery Place/Chinatown.*

$–$$ ✕ **Zola.** Swanky and chic, Zola channels a 1940s vibe with its snug banquettes, oval bar carts, and dramatic red flourishes. Food is fun without being over the top, and dishes have a Southern bent. Crisp rock shrimp spill over honeyed corn bread, a veal steak sidles up to polenta fritters, and rainbow chard gets a hit of applewood-smoked bacon. Dessert follows suit with sweets such as lemon chiffon pudding and chocolate fondue with Rice Krispies treats. Cocktail names reflect the restaurant's location inside the Spy Museum; there are daily wine flights as well. The bar menu includes a burger and a (slightly glammed-up) lobster roll. ✉ *800 F St. NW, Downtown* ☎ *202/654–0999* ▭ *AE, D, DC, MC, V* ✆ *No lunch weekends* Ⓜ *Gallery Place/Chinatown.*

Asian

$–$$$ ✕ **TenPenh.** One of the closest restaurants to the White House, this hopping venue is always buzzing with socialites, political junkies, and politicians. Chef Jeff Tunks's menu draws from many Asian cuisines—Chinese, Thai, Vietnamese, and Filipino. Main courses range from the chef's distinctive Chinese smoked lobster to lamb chops with an Asian-influenced pesto crust. Banana spring rolls with ginger ice cream and mango salsa is one creation from pastry chef David Guas. ✉ *10th St. and Pennsylvania Ave. NW, Downtown* ☎ *202/393–4500* ⌂ *Reservations essential* ▭ *AE, D, DC, MC, V* ✆ *Closed Sun.* Ⓜ *Navy Archives.*

★ ¢–$$$ ✕ **Full Kee.** Many locals swear by Full Kee, which has a wide assortment of Cantonese-style roasted meats. ■ TIP→ **Order from the house special-**

ties, not the tourist menu; the meal-size soups garnished with roast meats are the best in Chinatown. Tried-and-true dishes include the steamed dumplings, crispy duck, eggplant with garlic sauce, and sautéed leek flower. ☒ *509 H St. NW, Chinatown* ☎ *202/371–2233* ▭ *No credit cards* Ⓜ *Gallery Place/Chinatown.*

$–$$ ✕ **Kaz Sushi Bistro.** Traditional Japanese cookery is combined with often inspired improvisations ("freestyle Japanese cuisine," in the words of chef-owner Kaz Okochi) at this serene location. For a first-rate experience, sit at the sushi bar and ask for whatever is freshest and best. The chef's years of experience preparing fugu—the legendarily dangerous blowfish, available only in winter—means you're in good hands, though the experience is pricey at $150 per person. It's not all sushi here: innovations include sake-poached scallops with lemon-cilantro dressing. ☒ *1915 I St. NW, Downtown* ☎ *202/530–5500* ▭ *AE, DC, MC, V* ☻ *Closed Sun. No lunch weekends* Ⓜ *Farragut West.*

¢–$ ✕ **Nooshi.** Always packed, with long lines waiting for tables and take-out, this attractive Pan-Asian noodle house has remarkably good Chinese, Japanese, Thai, Indonesian, Malaysian, and Vietnamese dishes; all are served on plates appropriate to the cuisine. Try the Thai drunken noodles, which are soused in sake; gado-gado, a "cooked" Filipino salad; or the Vietnamese rice noodles with grilled chicken. After the restaurant added its extensive sushi menu, it changed its name to Nooshi (noodles plus sushi). ☒ *1120 19th St. NW, Dupont Circle* ☎ *202/293–3138* ⌚ *Reservations essential* ▭ *AE, DC, MC, V* ☻ *No lunch Sun.* Ⓜ *Farragut North.*

¢ ✕ **Burma.** Myanmar, formerly called Burma, is bordered by India, Thailand, and China, which gives a good indication of the cuisine at this Chinatown restaurant. Curry and tamarind share pride of place with lemon, cilantro, and soy seasonings. Batter-fried eggplant and squash are paired with complex, peppery sauces. Green-tea-leaf and other salads leave the tongue with a pleasant tingle. Such entrées as mango pork and tamarind fish are equally satisfying. ☒ *740 6th St. NW, 2nd fl., Downtown* ☎ *202/638–1280* ⌚ *Reservations essential* ▭ *AE, D, DC, MC, V* ☻ *No lunch weekends* Ⓜ *Gallery Place/Chinatown.*

☺ ¢ ✕ **Teaism.** This informal teahouse stocks more than 50 teas (black, white, and green) imported from India, Japan, and Africa, but it also serves healthful and delicious Japanese, Indian, and Thai food as well as tea-friendly sweets like ginger scones, plum muffins, and salty oat cookies. You can mix small dishes—tandoori kabobs, tea-cured salmon, Indian flat breads—to create meals or snacks. There's also a juicy ostrich burger or *ochazuke,* green tea poured over seasoned rice. The smaller Connecticut Avenue branch (enter around the corner, on H Street; closed on weekends) is tucked neatly on a corner adjacent to Lafayette Park and the White House, a casual reprieve from neighboring high-priced restaurants. It's a perfect spot to grab lunch after touring the nation's power center. Breakfast is served daily. The original Teaism is on Dupont Circle. ☒ *400 8th St. NW, Downtown* ☎ *202/638–7740* ▭ *AE, MC, V* Ⓜ *Navy/Archives* ☒ *800 Connecticut Ave. NW, Downtown* ☎ *202/835–2233* Ⓜ *Farragut West.*

Contemporary

$$$$ ✕ **Equinox.** Virginia-born chef-owner Todd Gray looks to area purveyors for hard-to-find heirloom and local foodstuffs at his low-key American eatery. The furnishings and the food are simple and elegant. The fresh ingredients speak for themselves: grilled quail with a truffle reduction, rare duck breast served on a cabbage salad, crab cakes with diced mango, and barbecued salmon with a sauce of roasted peppers and corn. There are three fixed-price multicourse dinners; an à la carte menu ($$) is available at lunch. ✉ *818 Connecticut Ave. NW, Downtown* ☏ *202/ 331–8118* ⌕ *Reservations essential* ▱ *AE, DC, MC, V* ⊘ *No lunch weekends.* Ⓜ *Farragut West.*

$$$–$$$$ ✕ **Café MoZU.** Banks of windows with views of the Potomac and a spare Japanese sensibility set the tone for this airy dining room at the Mandarin Oriental. The food has a Eurasian bent, with dishes such as oysters six ways, Kobe rib-eye steak with citrus sauce, sautéed black cod with miso, and the witty black-and-white martini shake, the attention-getter on the dessert roster. The café regularly serves tea with offerings way beyond the usual Earl Grey (every evening from 6 to 10:30, though the times change often), and an à la carte sushi menu is the ticket for those on the run. Though almost every seat in the house is a good one, the banquettes are most in demand. ✉ *Mandarin Oriental, 1330 Maryland Ave. SW, Downtown* ☏ *202/787–6868* ▱ *AE, D, DC, MC, V.*

★ **$$–$$$$** ✕ **Inde Bleu.** Visual drama and culinary fun are the twin concepts at this restaurant where French technique meets American foodstuffs and Indian spices. Quaff mangotinis while lounging on orange futons in the noisy, high-energy bar, or head for one of the two stylish dining rooms upstairs. You can make a meal of starters such as the tower of crab and lobster spiked with curry oil or minidosas filled with wild mushrooms, or go the more traditional route with a main course. Sea bass with thin fried leeks and tandoori rack of lamb are hall-of-famers. Leave room for the sweet "spaghetti and meatballs," made with saffron-cardamom ice cream and warm Indian milk balls. ✉ *707 G St. NW, Downtown* ☏ *202/333–2538* ▱ *AE, D, MC, V* ⊘ *No lunch* Ⓜ *Gallery Place.*

$$–$$$$ ✕ **Red Sage.** The multimillion-dollar southwestern interior at this upscale rancher's haven near the White House has a barbwire-and-lizard theme and a pseudo-adobe warren of dining rooms. Start with the ginger-cured salmon, prepared in-house, and move on to the always-popular pecan-crusted chicken breast or pan-seared yellowfin tuna. Upstairs at the Border Café, you can order from a comparatively inexpensive Tex-Mex menu (¢–$). ✉ *605 14th St. NW, Downtown* ☏ *202/638–4444* ▱ *AE, D, DC, MC, V* ⊘ *No lunch Sun.* Ⓜ *Metro Center.*

$$–$$$ ✕ **DC Coast.** Chef Jeff Tunks's menu at this sophisticated downtown spot brings the foods of three coasts—Atlantic, Gulf, and Pacific—to Washington. Come for lunch to try his version of the mid-Atlantic's best-known seafood delicacy, crab cakes. They're among the best in town (and if you call ahead of time, you can order them for dinner). If you're homesick for New Orleans, try the gumbo; again served only at lunch. For Pacific Rim cooking, you can't beat the smoked lobster. ■ TIP➜ **The bar scene is one of the liveliest in the downtown area.** ✉ *1401 K St. NW, Downtown* ☏ *202/216–5988* ⌕ *Reservations essential* ▱ *AE, D, DC, MC, V* ⊘ *Closed Sun. No lunch Sat.* Ⓜ *McPherson Square.*

$$-$$$ ✕ **Occidental Grill.** One of the most venerable restaurants in the city covers its walls with photos of politicians and other notables who have come here for the food and the attentive service. The standbys are best—chopped salad, grilled tuna or swordfish, lamb shank, veal meat loaf. More than half of the menu is seafood. ✉ *Willard Inter-Continental, 1475 Pennsylvania Ave. NW, Downtown* ☎ *202/783–1475* ⚱ *Reservations essential* ▤ *AE, DC, MC, V* Ⓜ *Metro Center.*

$-$$$ ✕ **701 Pennsylvania Avenue.** Cuisine drawn from Italy, France, Asia, and the Americas graces the menu here, where a meal might begin with seared tuna wrapped in potato and progress to a rack of lamb with eggplant-wrapped ratatouille or linguine with rock shrimp. In the Wine Bar, sample from caviar and tapas menus and more than 20 wines by the glass. The three-course fixed-price ($25.95) pretheater dinner is popular, and convenient if you're attending a performance at the Shakespeare, National, Warner, or Ford's theater. Live jazz plays nightly. ✉ *701 Pennsylvania Ave. NW, Downtown* ☎ *202/393–0701* ⚱ *Reservations essential* ▤ *AE, D, DC, MC, V* ⊗ *No lunch weekends* Ⓜ *Archives/Navy Memorial.*

$-$$ ✕ **Poste.** Inside the trendy Hotel Monaco, Poste woos with a towering skylit space that until 1901 was the General Post Office. Homing in on modern American brasserie fare, chef Robert Weland conjures up such satisfying dishes as foie gras terrine with cognac jelly and pan-roasted sirloin with truffled frites. In season, pan-fried softshell crabs are not to be missed. For dessert, there's a dream of a bourbon pecan tart topped with caramel sauce and ice cream. In warmer months, the neoclassical courtyard is a serene spot for cocktails and light fare. Year-round, the lively bar inside attracts see-and-be-scenesters with booths on raised platforms. ✉ *Hotel Monaco, 555 8th St. NW, Downtown* ☎ *202/783–6060* ▤ *AE, D, DC, MC, V* Ⓜ *Gallery Place/Chinatown.*

🐣 ¢ ✕ **Bread Line.** Crowded, quirky, sometimes chaotic, this restaurant specializes in breads and bread-based foods and makes not only the city's best baguette but also some of its best sandwiches. Owner Mark Furstenberg makes everything on the premises, from the breakfast bagels and muffins to the ciabatta loaves for the tuna salad sandwich with preserved lemons. It's best to arrive early or late to avoid the noontime rush. Outdoor seating is available in warmer months. ✉ *1751 Pennsylvania Ave. NW, Downtown* ☎ *202/822–8900* ⚱ *Reservations not accepted* ▤ *AE, MC, V* ⊗ *Closed weekends. No dinner* Ⓜ *Farragut West.*

HOTEL HOT SPOTS

Don't overlook restaurants in the city's luxury hotels. The Occidental Grill at the Willard InterContinental, Maestro in the Ritz-Carlton at Tysons Corner, Citronelle at the Latham, Bistro Bis inside the Hotel George, and Café MoZU and CityZen at the Mandarin Oriental are noteworthy for their artfully prepared food. Also look for restaurants sprouting up in new or restored hotels, especially downtown around the MCI Center and on the West End near the Kennedy Center. Notables include Cafe 15 at the Sofitel Hotel, Poste at The Hotel Monaco, Firefly at the Hotel Madera, and Dish at the River Inn.

French

$$$-$$$$ ✕ **Gerard's Place.** Don't let the simplicity of the name lead you to underestimate this sophisticated spot owned by acclaimed French chef Gerard Pangaud. In the striking dining room you're served dishes with intriguing combinations of ingredients, including Gerard's signature poached lobster with a ginger, lime, and sauternes sauce; venison served with dried fruits and pumpkin and beet purees; or seared tuna with black olives and roasted red peppers. If your appetite and wallet are willing, try the five-course fixed-price ($85) dinner. ✉ *915 15th St. NW, Downtown* ☎ *202/737–4445* ⌕ *Reservations essential* ▤ *AE, DC, MC, V* ✆ *Closed Sun. No lunch Sat.* Ⓜ *McPherson Square.*

$$$-$$$$ ✕ **Le Paradou.** Modern elegance is the idea in this dining room of taupes and beiges, midcentury modern objects, oversized floral arrangements, and a grand crystal chandelier. The food on the changing menu is updated French—think lobster with a ginger-carrot jus, lamb chops with tomato confit and olive sauce, and Dover sole with zucchini flowers. Besides the à la carte menu, there are fixed-price menus, $110 for six courses, $145 for nine courses. The bar menu with entrées in the $24 to $27 range is an even more budget-friendly option. Wines are mostly French and tend toward the pricey, but the creative sommelier just might find you a deal. ✉ *678 Indiana Ave. NW, Downtown* ☎ *202/347–6780* 🏛 *Jacket required* ▤ *AE, D, DC, MC, V* ✆ *Closed Sun. No lunch weekends* Ⓜ *Archives/Navy Memorial.*

Indian

$-$$ ✕ **Bombay Club.** One block from the White House, the beautiful Bombay Club tries to re-create the refined aura of British private clubs in colonial India. Potted palms and a bright blue ceiling above white plaster moldings adorn the dining room. On the menu are unusual seafood specialties and a large number of vegetarian dishes, but the real standouts are the breads and the seafood appetizers. The bar, furnished with rattan chairs and dark-wood paneling, serves hot hors d'oeuvres at cocktail hour. Most men wear jackets here. ✉ *815 Connecticut Ave. NW, Downtown* ☎ *202/659–3727* ⌕ *Reservations essential* ▤ *AE, D, DC, MC, V* ✆ *No lunch Sat.* Ⓜ *Farragut West.*

Italian

$$-$$$ ✕ **Galileo.** Sophisticated Piedmont-style cooking is served at what is really three restaurants under one roof by entrepreneur-chef Roberto Donna. These days, the main dining room is eclipsed by Laboratorio, Donna's restaurant within a restaurant, where he cooks a 12-course meal in a glamorous open kitchen ($110 weekdays, $125 weekends), and the osteria in the lounge where prices are low (¢–$) and the fare rustic. ■ TIP➜ **Reservations for one of the 30 Laboratorio seats must be made several months in advance.** ✉ *1110 21st St. NW, Downtown* ☎ *202/293–7191* ⌕ *Reservations essential* ▤ *AE, D, DC, MC, V* ✆ *No lunch weekends* Ⓜ *Foggy Bottom/GWU.*

Fodor'sChoice ★

$$-$$$ ✕ **Olives.** Celebrity chef Todd English's D.C. outpost seems always to have a crowded dining room at lunch and dinner. The upstairs room, which overlooks the open kitchen, is where the action is, but the spacious downstairs dining room is more comfortable, albeit formal. Hearty

starters include English's special butternut-squash–stuffed tortelli and a goat-cheese-and-onion tart topped with a boned quail. Most plates have so much going on that there are bound to be some hits and some misses, but the spit-roasted chicken is done well, as is the salmon atop a bowl of clam chowder. ✉ *1600 K St. NW, Downtown* ☎ *202/452– 1866* ⌕ *Reservations essential* ▤ *AE, DC, MC, V* ⊙ *Closed Sun. No lunch Sat.* Ⓜ *Farragut North.*

$$–$$$ ✕ **Teatro Goldoni.** Named for an 18th-century playwright, this restaurant with a colorful Venetian-inspired interior is a showcase for chef Fabrizio Aielli's modern Italian cooking and for traditional Venetian cuisine. For a first course, try an unusual pasta dish, such as squid-ink noodles or cannelloni stuffed with shiitake mushroom puree. At the center of the menu is a selection of fresh fish, which may be grilled, roasted, or cooked in parchment paper Venetian-style. There's also a wide selection of vegetarian entrées, and more than 30 frozen vodkas at the bar. There is live jazz on Friday and Saturday. ✉ *1909 K St. NW, Downtown* ☎ *202/955–9494* ▤ *AE, D, DC, MC, V* ⊙ *Closed Sun. No lunch Sat.* Ⓜ *Farragut North.*

$–$$$ ✕ **Tosca.** Chef Cesare Lanfranconi spent several years in the kitchen at Galileo, Washington's best Italian restaurant, before starting sleek, sophisticated Tosca. The food draws heavily from Lanfranconi's native Lake Como region but isn't limited by it. Polenta topped with wild mushrooms is a great choice: the sweet corn taste is intense but tempered by the mushrooms' earthiness. Pasta dishes include a tasty ravioli stuffed with ricotta and crushed amaretto cookies. Save room for dessert, particularly the chef's version of tiramisu, served in a martini glass. ✉ *1112 F St. NW, Downtown* ☎ *202/367–1990* ⌕ *Reservations essential* ▤ *AE, D, DC, MC, V* ⊙ *No lunch weekends* Ⓜ *Metro Center.*

Latin American

$$–$$$ ✕ **Ceiba.** At this very popular Latin restaurant, you will probably want to start with a mojito or pisco sour cocktail, then nip into the smoked swordfish carpaccio or Jamaican crab fritters. This is a menu as much for grazing as it is for full-fledged dining, though the main courses satisfy: rib eye with chimichurri sauce, and feijoada made from pork shanks are examples. Also stellar are desserts such as Mexican vanilla-bean cheesecake with guava jelly and cinnamon-dusted churros to dip in Mexican hot chocolate. Islandy murals, angular cream banquettes, an open kitchen, and vaulted ceilings set the scene. ✉ *701 14th St. NW, Downtown* ☎ *202/393–3983* ▤ *AE, D, DC, MC, V* ⊙ *Closed Sun. No lunch Sat.* Ⓜ *Metro Center.*

★ $–$$ ✕ **Café Atlántico.** The menu is always exciting at this *nuevo Latino* restaurant with friendly service. Guacamole is made tableside, and scallops are served with coconut rice, ginger, squid, and squid-ink oil. On weekends, Atlántico offers "Latino dim sum," tapas-size portions of dishes such as duck confit with passion-fruit oil, pineapple shavings, and plantain powder. À la carte, the plates are $3 to $9, or for $35 you can get a deluxe tasting menu ($25 for a vegetarian tasting menu). The bar makes mean cocktails with *cachaça*, a liquor distilled from sugarcane juice. You are unlikely to find a more extensive selection of South

American wines anywhere in the city. At Minibar, a six-stool bar on the second floor, you can explore an $85 prix-fixe meal of 30 creative morsels, such as a foie gras "lollipop" coated with cotton candy, conjured up before your eyes. ■ TIP→ **Minibar is arguably the most adventurous dining experience in the city, which means you have to reserve at least a week in advance for this restaurant within a restaurant.** ⊠ *405 8th St. NW, Downtown* ☎ *202/393–0812* ⌁ *Reservations essential* 🖃 *AE, DC, MC, V* Ⓜ *Archives/Navy Memorial.*

Middle Eastern

¢–$$ ✕ **Zaytinya.** This sophisticated urban dining room with soaring ceilings
Fodor'sChoice   is a local favorite for meeting friends or dining with a group. Zaytinya,
★   which means "olive oil" in Turkish, devotes practically its entire menu to Turkish, Greek, and Lebanese small plates, known as meze. To get the full experience, make a meal of three or four of these such as the popular braised lamb with eggplant puree and cheese, or the baba ghanouj, made of mashed eggplant. ■ TIP→ **So many options make this a great choice for vegetarians and meat lovers alike.** Reservations for times after 6:30 are not accepted; come prepared to wait on Friday and Saturday nights. ⊠ *701 9th St. NW, Downtown* ☎ *202/638–0800* 🖃 *AE, DC, MC, V* Ⓜ *Gallery Place/Chinatown.*

Seafood

$$–$$$ ✕ **Kinkead's.** This multichambered restaurant has a raw bar downstairs and more formal dining rooms upstairs, both of which have been updated in the past year, but the mood of quiet elegance remains. The open kitchen upstairs allows you to watch chef Robert Kinkead and company turn out an eclectic menu of mostly seafood dishes inspired by Kinkead's New England roots and by the cooking of Asia and Latin America. Don't miss the signature dish, salmon encrusted with pumpkin seeds and served with a ragout of crab, shrimp, and corn. Save room for dessert, because the chocolate and caramel sampler, which includes a chocolate-and-caramel soufflé, is a knockout. ⊠*2000 Pennsylvania Ave. NW, Foggy Bottom* ☎ *202/296–7700* ⌁ *Reservations essential* 🖃 *AE, D, DC, MC, V* ⊙ *No lunch Sat.* Ⓜ *Foggy Bottom/GWU.*

$–$$$ ✕ **Oceanaire Seafood Room.** This link in a Minneapolis-based chain is a beautiful throwback to another era, with dark-wood paneling, semicircular red booths, white tablecloths, and a pink glow that makes everybody look great. Oceanaire distinguishes itself primarily with first-rate ingredients; you see it at its best by ordering simply, picking from the list of fresh fish that heads the menu—perhaps walleye pike or local rockfish. The portions are often big enough to feed a family of four. This place is a good time, and even better if you go with a group. ⊠ *1201 F St. NW, Downtown* ☎ *202/347–2277* ⌁ *Reservations essential* 🖃 *AE, D, DC, MC, V* ⊙ *No lunch weekends* Ⓜ *Metro Center.*

Southern

$$–$$$ ✕ **Palette.** Sophisticated southern fare is served in a slick gallerylike dining room of pale wood and frosted glass at the Madison Hotel. The chef is from South Carolina, so Low Country cooking dominates. On the changing menu, appetizer highlights have included roasted quail with

bleu cheese vinaigrette and caramelized fennel, a crab cake over silky creamed corn, and smoky chicken spread on grilled sweet potato bread. Organic lamb T-bone steaks with cashew-mint pesto and rockfish with a puree of peas and ramps are worthy examples in the main course lineup. Desserts such as the poached fig pudding cake with vanilla ice cream and bourbon caramel sauce are pure Dixie. ⊠ *Madison Hotel, 1177 15th St. NW, Downtown* ☎ *202/587–2700* ⊟ *AE, D, DC, MC, V* ⊗ *No lunch Sun.* Ⓜ *McPherson Square.*

$–$$ ✕ **Georgia Brown's.** An elegant New South eatery and a favorite hangout of local politicians, Georgia Brown's serves shrimp Carolina-style (head intact, with steaming grits on the side); thick, rich crab soup; and such specials as grilled salmon and slow-cooked green beans with bacon. Fried green tomatoes are filled with herb cream cheese, and a pecan pie is made with bourbon and imported Belgian dark chocolate. The airy, curving dining room has white honeycomb windows and an unusual ceiling ornamentation of bronze ribbons. ⊠ *950 15th St. NW, Downtown* ☎ *202/393–4499* ⊟ *AE, D, DC, MC, V* ⌕ *Reservations essential* ⊗ *No lunch Sat.* Ⓜ *McPherson Square.*

Spanish

$$–$$$$ ✕ **Jaleo.** You are encouraged to make a meal of the long list of tapas
Fodor'sChoice at this lively Spanish bistro, although entrées such as paella are just as
★ tasty. Tapas highlights include the *gambas al ajillo* (sautéed garlic shrimp), fried potatoes with spicy tomato sauce, and the grilled chorizo. Save room for the crisp apple charlotte and the chocolate hazelnut torte. Flamenco dancers heat up the restaurant on Wednesdays. ⊠ *480 7th St. NW, Downtown* ☎ *202/628–7949* ⊟ *AE, D, DC, MC, V* Ⓜ *Gallery Place/Chinatown.*

$$–$$$ ✕ **Taberna del Alabardero.** A lovely formal dining room, skillful service, and sophisticated cooking make this restaurant one of Washington's best. Start with tapas: piquillo peppers stuffed with *bacalao* (salt cod) or roasted leg of duck in a phyllo pastry pouch. Proceed to a hefty bowl of gazpacho or white garlic soup and venture on to authentic paella and fine Spanish country dishes. French-toast-like *torrijas* are a light ending to this rich fare. The plush interior and handsome bar make things romantic and help attract a well-heeled clientele. ⊠ *1776 I St. NW, at 18th St., Downtown* ☎ *202/429–2200* ⌕ *Reservations essential* ⌂ *Jacket required* ⊟ *AE, D, DC, MC, V* ⊗ *Closed Sun. No lunch Sat.* Ⓜ *Farragut West.*

Steak

$$$$ ✕ **Morton's of Chicago.** Enjoy a steak on the patio at the downtown location of this national chain, one block from The Renaissance Mayflower, a D.C. landmark hotel. In classic steak-house tradition, the emphasis is on quantity as well as quality; the New York strip and porterhouse steaks are well over a pound each. If you have an even larger appetite (or you plan to share), there's a 48-ounce porterhouse for $84. Prime rib, lamb, veal, chicken, lobster, and grilled fish are also on the menu. ⊠ *1050 Connecticut Ave. NW, Downtown* ☎ *202/955–5997* ⊟ *AE, D, DC, MC, V* Ⓜ *Farragut North.*

Good Brews

SEVERAL NOTEWORTHY MICROBREWERIES and brewpubs call the Washington area home. The Olde Heurich Brewing Company, successor to the Christian Heurich Brewing Co. (founded 1873), makes Foggy Bottom ale and lager, available at select bars, restaurants, and stores in metro D.C., but they do not currently operate a brewpub.

At the **Capitol City Brewing Company's** three locations—Capitol Hill near Union Station (2 Massachusetts Ave. NW ☎ 202/842-2337); Downtown (1100 New York Ave. NW ☎ 202/628-2222); Arlington, VA (2700 S. Quincy St. ☎ 703/578-3888)—you'll find ales, pilsners, and lagers along with beer-friendly eats such as bratwurst, burgers, fish-and-chips, and a root beer float, made with the house-brewed root beer. Kolsch, made with ale and lager yeasts, is an unusual must-try.

In Virginia, Alexandria's **Shenandoah Brewing Company** (652 S. Pickett St. ☎ 703/823-9508) is an award winner. Aficionados praise its stouts and ales, especially the Bourbon

Stoney Stout, aged in oak casks previously used to make premium bourbon. The feel in the Shenandoah brewpub is industrial and the menu limited to foods grown or made in Virginia: peanuts, potato chips, a raft of chilis, and a delicious beer-queso dip. If you have a few hours and are planning to return to the area in a month or two, you can brew a batch of your own beer.

Two national chains also have brewpubs in the D.C. area. California-based **Gordon Biersch** (900 F St. NW ☎ 202/783-5454) makes lagers such as its crisp Golden Export in a converted downtown bank building, where you can go for beer and anything from pizza to meat loaf. With brewpubs in Arlington, Virginia (4238 Wilson Blvd., #1256 ☎ 703/516-7688) and Bethesda, Maryland (7900 Norfolk Ave. ☎ 301/652-1311), Colorado-based **Rock Bottom Brewery** pours ales, lagers, and porters alongside fixings such as fried chicken, barbecued ribs, pizza, and cheesecake made with the house stout.

Dupont Circle

American

☾ $ ✕ **Kramerbooks & Afterwords.** This popular bookstore-cum-café is a favorite neighborhood breakfast spot. ■ TIP→ **It's also a late-night haunt on weekends, when it's open around the clock.** There's a simple menu with soups, salads, and sandwiches, but many people drop in just for cappuccino and dessert. The "dysfunctional family sundae"—a massive brownie soaked in amaretto with a plethora of divine toppings—is a local favorite, and especially popular with kids. Live music, from rock to blues, is performed Wednesday through Sunday 10 PM to midnight. ✉ *1517 Connecticut Ave. NW, Dupont Circle* ☎ *202/387–1462* ⚐ *Reservations not accepted* ▤ *AE, D, MC, V* Ⓜ *Dupont Circle.*

Asian

¢–$ ✕ **Sala Thai.** Who says the spice in Thai food has to be sweat-inducing? Sala Thai makes the food as spicy as you wish, but the chef is interested in flavor, not fire. Among the subtly seasoned dishes are *panang goong* (shrimp in curry-peanut sauce), chicken sautéed with ginger and pineapple, and flounder with a choice of four sauces. Mirrored walls and warm lights soften this small dining room, as do the friendly service and largely local clientele. ⊠ *2016 P St. NW, Dupont Circle* ☎ *202/872–1144* ⊟ *AE, D, DC, MC, V* Ⓜ *Dupont Circle.*

✆ ¢ ✕ **Teaism.** This novel counterpoint to the many area coffee bars carries an impressive selection of more than 50 teas, which complement the small, tasty Japanese, Indian, and Thai dishes. *Bento* boxes, which contain a salad, entrée, and rice, are full meals. Teaism is also a casual place to enjoy a hot drink with ginger scones or other sweet treats, which makes it popular with the stroller set. This is the original Teaism; there are two Downtown locations as well. ⊠ *2009 R St. NW, Dupont Circle* ☎ *202/667–3827* ⊟ *AE, MC, V* Ⓜ *Dupont Circle.*

Contemporary

$$–$$$$ ✕ **Komi.** Johnny Monis, the young, energetic chef-owner of this small, Fodor'sChoice personal restaurant, offers one of the most adventurous dining experiences in the city. Weekdays the menu's à la carte; on weekends it's prix ★ fixe, $58 for five courses. Food is contemporary with a Mediterranean influence in this yellow sponge-painted, wood-floored dining room. Star plates include fresh sardines with pickled lemons, suckling pig over apples and bacon with polenta, and mascarpone-filled dates with sea salt. ⊠ *1509 17th St., Dupont Circle* ☎ *202/332–9200* ⌣ *Reservations essential* ⊟ *AE, D, MC, V* ☉ *Closed Mon. No lunch* Ⓜ *Dupont Circle.*

$$–$$$ ✕ **Nora.** The organic food served here, like the quilt-decorated dining room, is sophisticated and attractive. Peppered beef carpaccio with manchego cheese is a good starter. Entrées such as seared rockfish with artichoke broth, grilled lamb chops with a white-bean sauce, and risotto with winter vegetables emphasize well-balanced, complex ingredients. ⊠ *2132 Florida Ave. NW, Dupont Circle* ☎ *202/462–5143* ⌣ *Reservations essential* ⊟ *AE, D, MC, V* ☉ *Closed Sun. No lunch* Ⓜ *Dupont Circle.*

> **WORD OF MOUTH**
>
> "The Tabard Inn has been in DC forever, and my dinner there the other weekend proved why. As a single diner I often feel slighted, not at the Tabard Inn. I had a lovely round table in the courtyard and a dinner that exceeded my expectations." –Rex

$$–$$$ ✕ **Tabard Inn.** Fading portraits and overstuffed furniture make the lobby lounge look like an antiques store, but this hotel restaurant's culinary sensibility is thoroughly modern. The menu, which changes daily, consistently offers interesting seafood and vegetarian options. A popular entrée is the branzino, a flaky white fish, served with artichokes, preserved lemon, and lentils in an olive sauce. A vegetarian option might be porcini risotto with kalamata olives, Roma tomatoes, and pesto.

■ TIP➜ **In good weather you can dine in the courtyard.** ⊠ *Hotel Tabard Inn, 1739 N St. NW, Dupont Circle* ☎ *202/331–8528* ⊟ *AE, DC, MC, V* Ⓜ *Dupont Circle.*

$$–$$$
Fodor'sChoice
★

× **Vidalia.** There's a lot more to chef Jeffrey Buben's distinguished restaurant than the sweet Vidalia onion, which is a specialty in season. Inspired by the cooking and the ingredients of the South and the Chesapeake Bay region, Buben's version of New American cuisine revolves around the best seasonal fruits, vegetables, and seafood he can find. Try the roasted onion soup with spoon bread, the shrimp on yellow grits, or the sensational lemon chess pie. The sleek modern surroundings, including a wine bar, are equal to the food. ⊠ *1990 M St. NW, Dupont Circle* ☎ *202/659–1990* ⊟ *AE, D, DC, MC, V* ☉ *Closed Sun. in July and Aug. No lunch weekends* Ⓜ *Dupont Circle.*

$–$$
× **Firefly.** The backlighted, amber bar and birch-log wall create a warm and natural look at this showcase for contemporary American bistro food. Start with roasted beets and goat cheese or roasted turnip soup. More standard comfort food includes a grilled pork tenderloin with Dijon mustard, and roast chicken with bacon-braised cabbage and prunes. The small wine list, made up mostly of California boutique labels, is well chosen and priced fairly. ⊠ *Hotel Madera, 1310 New Hampshire Ave. NW, Dupont Circle* ☎ *202/861–1310* ⊟ *AE, D, DC, MC, V* Ⓜ *Dupont Circle.*

French

¢–$$
× **Bistrot du Coin.** An instant hit in its Dupont Circle neighborhood, this moderately priced French bistro with a monumental zinc bar is noisy, crowded, and fun. The comforting, traditional bistro fare includes starter portions of mussels in several different preparations. Steaks, garnished with a pile of crisp fries, are the main attraction, but you might also try the duck-leg confit or tripe *à la niçoise* (a stew of tripe and fresh tomatoes). Wash it down with house Beaujolais, Côtes du Rhône, or Alsatian white. ⊠ *1738 Connecticut Ave. NW, Dupont Circle* ☎ *202/234–6969* ⊟ *AE, D, DC, MC, V* Ⓜ *Dupont Circle.*

Italian

$$$$
× **Obelisk.** Come here for eclectic Italian cuisine. The five-course fixed-price ($65) menu, your only option, changes every day, combining traditional dishes with chef Peter Pastan's innovations. Representative main courses are lamb with garlic and sage and braised grouper with artichoke and thyme. The minimally decorated dining room is tiny, with closely spaced tables. ⊠ *2029 P St. NW, Dupont Circle* ☎ *202/872–1180* ⚑ *Reservations essential* ⊟ *DC, MC, V* ☉ *Closed Sun. and Mon. No lunch* Ⓜ *Dupont Circle.*

$–$$$
× **i Ricchi.** An airy space accented with terra-cotta tiles, cream-color archways, and floral frescoes, i Ricchi remains a favorite of critics and upscale crowds for its earthy Tuscan cuisine, often prepared using the wood-burning grill or oven. Skewered shrimp and rolled pork roasted in wine and fresh herbs star on the spring–summer menu. Fall and winter bring grilled lamb chops, hearty soups, and sautéed beef fillet. ⊠ *1220 19th St. NW, Dupont Circle* ☎ *202/835–0459* ⚑ *Reservations essential* ⊟ *AE, DC, MC, V* ☉ *Closed Sun. No lunch Sat.* Ⓜ *Dupont Circle.*

2

🕙 **$** ✕ **Pizzeria Paradiso.** A trompe l'oeil ceiling adds space and light to a sim-
Fodor'sChoice ple interior at the ever-popular Pizzeria Paradiso. The restaurant sticks
★ to crowd-pleasing basics: pizzas, panini, salads, and desserts. Although
the standard pizza is satisfying, you can enliven it with fresh buffalo moz-
zarella or unusual toppings such as potatoes, capers, and mussels. Wines
are well chosen and well priced. The intensely flavored gelato is a house
specialty. A larger location is in Georgetown. ⊠ *2029 P St. NW, Dupont
Circle* 🕾 *202/223–1245* ⟋ *Reservations not accepted* ▭ *DC, MC, V*
Ⓜ *Dupont Circle.*

Middle Eastern

¢–**$$** ✕ **Skewers–Café Luna.** As the name implies, the focus at Skewers is on
kabobs, here served with almond-flaked rice or pasta. Lamb with egg-
plant and chicken with roasted peppers are the most popular variations,
but vegetable kabobs and skewers of filet mignon and seasonal seafood
are equally tasty. With nearly 20 choices, the appetizer selection is huge.
You can enjoy the cheap eats (chicken-and-avocado salad, mozzarella-
and-tomato sandwiches, vegetable lasagna, pizza) downstairs at Café
Luna or the reading room–coffeehouse upstairs at Luna Books. ⊠ *1633
P St. NW, Dupont Circle* 🕾 *202/387–7400 Skewers, 202/387–4005 Café
Luna* ▭ *AE, D, DC, MC, V* Ⓜ *Dupont Circle.*

Seafood

$$ ✕ **Johnny's Half Shell.** It's almost always crowded, but Johnny's Half
Shell is worth the wait. Owners John Fulchino and Ann Cashion (both
of Cashion's Eat Place in Woodley Park) have created a modern version of the traditional mid-Atlantic seafood house. Sit at the bar for
oysters on the half shell and a beer, or settle into one of the roomy
booths for a first course of the best fried oysters in town followed by
rockfish or wood-grilled lobster. For dessert, a favorite is the spectacular chocolate angel food cake with caramel sauce. ⊠ *2002 P St.
NW, Dupont Circle* 🕾 *202/296–2021* ▭ *AE, MC, V* ⊘ *Closed Sun.*
Ⓜ *Dupont Circle.*

Steak

$$–$$$$ ✕ **Sam and Harry's.** Cigar-friendly Sam and Harry's is understated, gen-
teel, and packed at lunch and dinner. Miniature crab cakes are a good
way to begin, but the real draws are prime meats such as porterhouse
and New York strip steak served on the bone. Seafood specials change
daily; Maine lobster is one possibility. End the meal with warm pecan
pie laced with melted chocolate or a "turtle cake" of caramel and choco-
late that is big enough for two. ⊠ *1200 19th St. NW, Dupont Circle*
🕾 *202/296–4333* ⟋ *Reservations essential* ▭ *AE, D, DC, MC, V*
⊘ *Closed Sun. No lunch Sat.* Ⓜ *Dupont Circle.*

$–$$$ ✕ **Palm.** A favorite lunchtime hangout of power brokers, the Palm has
walls papered with caricatures of the famous patrons who have dined
there. Main attractions include gargantuan steaks and Nova Scotia lob-
sters, several kinds of potatoes, and New York cheesecake. One of
Palm's best-kept secrets is that it's also a terrific old-fashioned Italian
restaurant. Try the veal marsala for lunch or, on Thursday, the tasty shrimp
in marinara sauce. ⊠ *1225 19th St. NW, Dupont Circle* 🕾 *202/293–*

9091 ☆ *Reservations essential* ▤ *AE, D, DC, MC, V* ☺ *No lunch week-ends* Ⓜ *Dupont Circle.*

Georgetown/West End/Glover Park

American

$$–$$$ ✕ **Palena.** Chef Frank Ruta and pastry chef Ann Amernick met while work-
Fodor'sChoice   ing in the White House kitchens. At their contemporary American restau-
★   rant, the French- and Italian-influenced menu changes seasonally.
Sometimes Ruta and Amernick team up, as for an appetizer of crisp puff
pastry with fresh sardines and greens. Ruta goes it alone with chervil-
and-morel soup, a veal chop with a barley-stuffed pepper, and a pork
chop with flavorful baked beans. Comforting desserts such as a sprightly
lemon-caramel tart or a chocolate torte are a perfect match for the earthy
cooking. Reservations are not accepted for the equally fabulous lounge,
where the inexpensive menu ($) includes a cheeseburger with truffles, a
hot dog made in-house, and an extravagant platter of fries, fried onion
rings, and paper-thin fried Meyer lemon slices. ⊠ *3529 Connecticut
Ave. NW, Cleveland Park* ☎ *202/537–9250* ☆ *Reservations essential for
restaurant* ▤ *AE, D, DC, MC, V* ☺ *Restaurant and lounge closed Sun.
Restaurant closed Mon. No lunch* Ⓜ *Cleveland Park.*

$–$$ ✕ **Ardeo/Bardeo.** The trendy new-
American Ardeo and its loungelike
counterpart, Bardeo, sit side by side
in the ever-popular culinary strip of
Cleveland Park. Ardeo is known
for its clean design, professional
and knowledgeable staff, and creative menu. Everything is skillfully
prepared, from pan-roasted New
Zealand rack of lamb to seared rare
sesame tuna. The pecan-crusted
soft-shell crab is a special treat.
Bardeo has similar options in
smaller portions. ⊠ *3311 Connecticut Ave. NW, Cleveland Park*
☎ *202/244–6750* ▤ *AE, D, MC,
V* Ⓜ *Cleveland Park.*

> ## WORD OF MOUTH
>
> "Palena is a very fine restaurant
> that manages to get better with
> time . . . we have had dozens of
> meals there and I can't remember
> a bad one. The front of the restau-
> rant is a special bargain. I would
> especially recommend the roast
> chicken which is unlike any other
> roast chicken in my memory."
>
> –Cheryl

$–$$ ✕ **Dish.** If the gaslighted fireplace and William Wegman's 8-foot diptych
of a reclining dog don't make you feel at home, the updated comfort
food here will probably do the trick. Potted ham with biscuits and mustard oil, pulled-duck barbecue, and cannoli with roasted figs are among
the better-than-Mom-ever-made stars on the menu. The kitchen makes
that old warhorse, spinach dip, with roasted artichokes and serves it with
pita triangles. It's no wonder this casually chic address has become a
neighborhood favorite. It's two blocks from the Kennedy Center. ⊠ *River
Inn, 924 25th St. NW, West End* ☎ *202/338–8707* ▤ *AE, MC, V*
☺ *No lunch weekends* Ⓜ *Foggy Bottom/GWU.*

 ℭ ¢   ✕ **Five Guys.** One of the quirky traditions of this homegrown fast-food
burger house is to note on the menu board where the potatoes for that
day's fries come from, be it Maine, Idaho, or elsewhere. The place gets

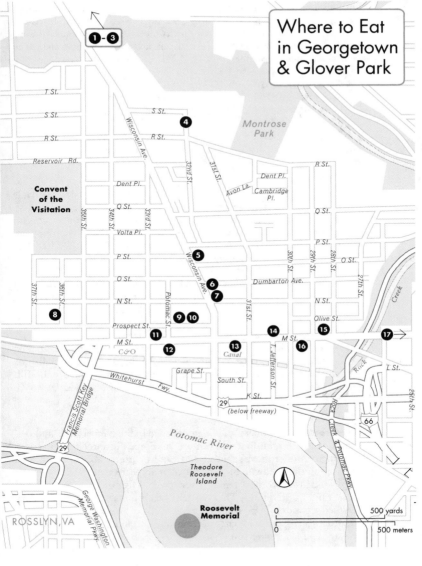

Where to Eat in Georgetown & Glover Park

Aditi **11**
Bistro Français **13**
Bistro Lepic & Wine Bar . . .**4**
Black Salt **17**
Cafe Milano **9**
Citronelle **16**
Five Guys **6**
Georgetown Café **5**
Heritage India **2**
La Chaumière **15**
Miss Saigon **14**
Morton's of Chicago **10**
Paolo's **7**
Pizzeria Paradiso **12**
1789 . . . .**8**
Sushi –Ko **1**
Two Amys **3**

just about everything else right, too, from the grilled hot dogs and hand-patted burger patties—most folks get a double—to the fresh hand-cut fries with the skins on and the high-quality toppings such as sautéed onions and mushrooms. ■ TIP→ **Add an eclectic jukebox to all of the above and you've got a great burger experience.** ⊠ *1335 Wisconsin Ave. NW, Georgetown* ☎ *202/337–0400* ▤ *MC, V.*

¢ ✕ **Georgetown Café.** With its unpretentious looks, cheap prices, and eclectic menu of classics, this café is a bit of an oddball for Georgetown. Students and other locals frequent it for the pastas, pizzas, kabobs, gyros, and home-style American favorites such as roast beef, baked chicken, and mashed potatoes. Open 24 hours daily, this is a good spot for a late-night snack. ⊠ *1623 Wisconsin Ave. NW, Georgetown* ☎ *202/333–0215* ⚭ *Reservations not accepted* ▤ *D, MC, V.*

Asian

$–$$ ✕ **Sushi-Ko.** At one of the city's best Japanese restaurants, daily specials
Fodor'sChoice are always innovative: sesame oil–seasoned trout is layered with crisp
★ wonton crackers, and a sushi special might be salmon topped with a touch of mango sauce and a sprig of dill. And you won't find ginger, mango, or green-tea ice cream at the local Baskin-Robbins. ⊠ *2309 Wisconsin Ave. NW, Georgetown* ☎ *202/333–4187* ⚭ *Reservations essential* ▤ *AE, MC, V* ⊘ *No lunch Sat.–Mon.*

¢–$ ✕ **Miss Saigon.** Shades of mauve and green, black art deco accents, and potted palms decorate this Vietnamese restaurant, where careful attention is paid to presentation as well as to seasoning. Begin with crisp egg rolls or chilled spring rolls, then proceed to exquisite salads of shredded green papaya topped with shrimp or beef. Daily specials include imaginative preparations of the freshest seafood. In addition, "caramel"-cooked and grilled meats are standouts. Prices are moderate, especially for lunch, but you may have to order several dishes to have your fill. ⊠ *3057 M St. NW, Georgetown* ☎ *202/333–5545* ▤ *AE, DC, MC, V* Ⓜ *Foggy Bottom/GWU.*

Belgian

$$–$$$$ ✕ **Marcel's.** Chef Robert Wiedmaier trained in the Netherlands and Belgium, and in this, his first solo venture, his French-inspired Belgian cooking focuses on robust seafood and poultry preparations. Start with mussels, if they're available, and move on to perfectly seared diver scallops in saffron broth or tender roasted monkfish on a ragout of potatoes, olives, and onions. The roast chicken is a marvel, white and dark cooked separately to perfect tenderness and moistness. In season, be sure to order the fig tart with citrus crème anglaise and honey-cinnamon ice cream. ⊠ *2401 Pennsylvania Ave. NW, Foggy Bottom* ☎ *202/296–1166* ⚭ *Reservations essential* ▤ *AE, DC, MC, V* Ⓜ *Foggy Bottom/GWU.*

Contemporary

$$$$ ✕ **Citronelle.** See all the action in the glass-front kitchen at chef Michel
Fodor'sChoice Richard's flagship California-French restaurant. Appetizers might include
★ foie gras with lentils prepared three ways, and main courses run to lobster medallions with lemongrass, saddle of lamb crusted with herbs, and breast of squab. Desserts are luscious: a crunchy napoleon with filament-like pastry and the very special "chocolate bar," Richard's dense, rich

2

take on a Snickers candy bar. A chef's table in the kitchen gives you a ringside seat (reserve at least a month ahead). The fixed-price menu ranges from $85 to $150; the bar menu ($–$$$) has morsels such as mushroom "cigars" and Serrano ham. ⊠ *Latham Hotel, 3000 M St. NW, Georgetown* ☎ *202/625–2150* ✍ *Reservations essential* ᠍ *Jacket required* ⊟ *AE, D, DC, MC, V* ☺ *No lunch.*

$$–$$$$ ✕ **1789.** This dining room with Early American paintings and a fireplace could easily be a room in the White House. But all the gentility of this 19th-century townhouse-restaurant is offset by the down-to-earth food on the menu, which changes daily. The soups, including the seafood stew, are flavorful. Rack of lamb and fillet of beef are specialties, and the seafood dishes are excellent. Service is fluid and attentive. Bread pudding and crème brûlée are sweet finishes. ⊠ *1226 36th St. NW, Georgetown* ☎ *202/965–1789* ✍ *Reservations essential* ᠍ *Jacket required* ⊟ *AE, D, DC, MC, V* ☺ *No lunch.*

French

$–$$$ ✕ **Bistro Français.** Washington's chefs head to Bistro Français for minute steak, sirloin with black pepper or red wine sauce, and rotisserie chicken. Daily specials may include *suprême* of salmon with broccoli mousse and beurre blanc. In the less formal café, sandwiches and omelets are available in addition to entrées. The Bistro also has fixed-price lunches ($14.95), early and late-night dinner specials ($19.95), and all-you-can-eat brunches on weekends ($18.95). ■ **TIP→ It stays open until 3 AM on weekday mornings and 4 AM on weekends.** ⊠ *3128 M St. NW, Georgetown* ☎ *202/338–3830* ⊟ *AE, DC, MC, V.*

$–$$$ ✕ **La Chaumière.** A favorite of Washingtonians seeking an escape from the hurly-burly of Georgetown, La Chaumière ("the thatched cottage") has the rustic charm of a French country inn, particularly in winter, when its central stone fireplace warms the room. Fish stew, mussels, and scallops are on the regular menu, and there are always several grilled fish specials. Venison and other hard-to-find meats round out the entrées. ■ **TIP→ Many diners plan their meals around the specials, particularly the couscous on Wednesday and the cassoulet on Thursday.** ⊠ *2813 M St. NW, Georgetown* ☎ *202/338–1784* ✍ *Reservations essential* ⊟ *AE, DC, MC, V* ☺ *Closed Sun. No lunch Sat.*

$–$$ ✕ **Bistrot Lepic.** Relaxed and upbeat, with bright yellow walls and colorful paintings, this small, crowded neighborhood bistro is French in every regard—starting with the flirty servers. Traditional bistro fare has been replaced with potato-crusted salmon served with French grapes and ouzo-grape sauce, but the standards such as veal cheeks remain. The wine is all French, with many wines available by the glass. The wine bar (¢) on the second floor has a menu of small plates such as terrine of foie gras, smoked trout salad, and onion-bacon tart; seating is first-come, first-served, but if you reserve in advance, you can order from the full menu up there. ⊠ *1736 Wisconsin Ave. NW, Glover Park* ☎ *202/333–0111* ✍ *Reservations essential* ⊟ *AE, D, DC, MC, V.*

Indian

¢–$$ ✕ **Heritage India.** You feel like a guest in a foreign land dining at this restaurant: there's incredible attention to detail in everything from the tapestried chairs to the paintings of India and the traditional tandoori and curry dishes. *Tahli* is a variety plate of six or seven curry, lamb, or chicken dishes with rice and bread, served in small bowls or compartments on a silver platter. Wine is presented in a small glass pitcher. Whatever you choose, the experience is as fascinating as the meal. ⊠ *2400 Wisconsin Ave. NW, Glover Park* ☎ *202/333–3120* ⌲ *Reservations essential* ☰ *AE, D, MC, V.*

¢–$ ✕ **Aditi.** The two-story dining room with burgundy carpets, pastel walls, and brass sconces seems too upscale for a moderately priced Indian restaurant. The first floor is small, with a dramatic staircase leading to a larger room whose windows overlook the busy street. Tandoori and curry dishes are expertly prepared and not aggressively seasoned; if you want your food spicy, request it. Rice-based *biryani* entrées make good lighter fare. ⊠ *3299 M St. NW, Georgetown* ☎ *202/625–6825* ⌲ *Reservations essential* ☰ *AE, D, DC, MC, V.*

Italian

$$–$$$$ ✕ **Cafe Milano.** By night you're likely to rub shoulders with local socialites, sports figures, visiting celebrities, and the Euro-crowd at Cafe Milano's cheek-by-jowl bar. Expect authentic, sophisticated Italian cooking and a pricey wine list. Specialties are fried stuffed olives and smelts, thin-crust pizzas, pasta dishes such as lobster with linguine and orecchiette with anchovies, air-dried ricotta, and beautifully composed and dressed salads, favored by ladies who lunch. ⊠ *3251 Prospect St. NW, Georgetown* ☎ *202/333–6183* ☰ *AE, D, DC, MC, V.*

¢–$$$ ✕ **Paolo's.** At one of Georgetown's busiest corners, this bright and airy restaurant is always buzzing with activity. It's great for people-watching from the outdoor patio or from inside, looking out the large French windows next to the brick pizza oven. The modern menu has daily specials as well as the standard fare of pizzas, salads, and homemade pastas. For a twist, try espresso-rubbed steak salad. ⊠ *1303 Wisconsin Ave. NW, Georgetown* ☎ *202/333–7353* ☰ *AE, D, DC, MC, V.*

♺ ¢–$ ✕ **Pizzeria Paradiso.** This large and spacious eatery is the second location of what might be the most popular pizzeria in town (the original
FodorśChoice   is in Dupont Circle). The thin-crust pizzas are baked in a brick oven.
★   Also on the menu are bright salads, paninis, flavorful gelatos, well-priced wines, and a full bar. The restaurant has a new rathskeller-style beer pub on its lower level called Birreria Paradiso. Foggy Bottom, the closest Metro stop, is about a 15-minute walk. ⊠ *3282 M St. NW, Georgetown* ☎ *202/337–1245* ☰ *D, DC, MC, V.*

♺ ¢–$ ✕ **Two Amys.** Judging from the long lines here, the best pizza in D.C. is uptown. Simple recipes allow the ingredients to shine through at this Neapolitan pizzeria. You may be tempted to go for the D.O.C. pizza (it has *Denominazione di Origine Controllata* approval for Neapolitan authenticity), but don't hesitate to try the daily specials. Roasted peppers with anchovies and deviled eggs with parsley-caper sauce have by now become classics. At busy times, the wait for a table can exceed an hour. ⊠ *3715 Macomb St. NW, Glover Park* ☎ *202/885–5700* ⌲ *Reservations not accepted* ☰ *MC, V* ☉ *Closed Mon.*

Seafood

$$–$$$ ✕ **Black Salt.** Just beyond Georgetown in the residential neighborhood of Palisades, Black Salt is part fish market, part gossipy neighborhood hangout, part swanky restaurant. Fish offerings dominate—there is only one beef item on the dinner menu—and are varied and pristine, balancing classics like oyster stew and fried Ipswich clams with more offbeat fixings like fluke with cider vinegar, lobster with kaffir lime, and a tiramisu martini for dessert. The place can get crowded and loud, and advance reservations are a must for weekends. Regulars consider a meal at the bar a good fallback—it's one of the friendliest spots around. ✉*4883 MacArthur Blvd., Palisades* ☎ *202/342–9101* ⌕ *Reservations essential* ▭ *AE, D, DC, MC, V* ⊘ *Closed Mon.*

Steak

$$$$ ✕ **Morton's of Chicago.** A national steak-house chain that claims to serve the country's best beef, Morton's is always jumping. Other options include lamb, veal, chicken, lobster, and grilled fish. There's also a 48-ounce porterhouse ($84) that is best shared. ✉ *3251 Prospect St., Georgetown* ☎ *202/342–6258* ⌕ *Reservations essential* ▭ *AE, D, DC, MC, V* ⊘ *No lunch.*

U Street

American

⟳ **¢–$** ✕ **Ben's Chili Bowl.** Long before U Street became hip, Ben's was serving
Fodor'sChoice chili. Chili on hot dogs, chili on "half-smoke" sausages, chili on burg-
★ ers, and just plain chili. Add cheese fries if you dare. The faux-marble bar and shiny red vinyl stools give the impression that little has changed since the 1950s, but turkey and vegetarian burgers and meatless chili are a nod to modern times. Ben's closes at 2 AM Monday through Thursday, at 4 AM on Friday and Saturday, and at 8 PM Sundays. Southern-style breakfast is served from 6 AM weekdays and from 7 AM on Saturday. ✉ *1213 U St. NW, U Street corridor* ☎ *202/667–0909* ⌕ *Reservations not accepted* ▭ *No credit cards* Ⓜ *U Street/Cardozo.*

¢–$ ✕ **Polly's Café.** Tables can be hard to come by on weekend nights at Polly's Café, a cozy oasis with a fireplace. That's when locals arrive ready to swill beer, eat better-than-average bar food and starters such as smoked mozzarella salad, and enjoy jukebox favorites from every era. Nightly specials such as trout over couscous are among more substantial plates. The hearty brunch, available every day, is one of Washington's best values. ✉ *1342 U St. NW, U Street corridor* ☎ *202/265–8385* ⌕ *Reservations not accepted* ▭ *MC, V* Ⓜ *U Street/Cardozo.*

> **BEST FOR BRUNCH**
>
> - **Bistro Français, Georgetown.** Weekends.
> - **Cashion's Eat Place, Adams-Morgan.** Sunday.
> - **Kramerbooks & Afterwords, Dupont Circle.** Daily.
> - **The Market Lunch, Capitol Hill.** Tuesdays–Sundays.
> - **Polly's Cafe, U Street.** Daily.
> - **Teaism, Dupont Circle and Downtown.** Daily.

Eclectic

¢–$$　✕ **Utopia.** Here New Orleans meets Italy and the Mediterranean. Lamb couscous, seafood bisque, and pasta dishes such as the Chef's Advice (which combines shrimp, chicken, andouille sausage, and sweet peppers) are hits. Utopia has live music nightly, with excellent jazz and Brazilian bands and a very reasonable $15-per-person minimum for table service. ⊠ *1418 U St. NW, U Street corridor* ☎ *202/483–7669* ♨ *Reservations essential* ⊟ *AE, D, DC, MC, V* Ⓜ *U Street/Cardozo.*

$　✕ **Cada Vez.** Inside what was once a post office, Cada Vez (Spanish for "every time") has a menu that combines traditional tastes in often unusual ways to produce such dishes as savory jerk-chicken egg rolls or salmon stuffed with a rich shrimp mousse. Live music, frequently jazz, is performed nearly every night in the large, open space. ⊠ *1438 U St. NW, U Street corridor* ☎ *202/667–0785* ⊟ *AE, D, DC, MC, V* ⊘ *Closed Sun. and Mon. No lunch* Ⓜ *U Street/Cardozo.*

¢–$　✕ **Café Nema.** Somali, North African, and Middle Eastern cuisines are combined to form simple but flavorful entrées at Café Nema. Grilled chicken, lamb, and beef kabobs and salmon steak are paired with fresh vegetables and an outstanding curried basmati rice pilaf that has bits of caramelized onion, cloves, and raisins. *Sambousa* (flaky fried triangles of dough filled with curried vegetables or meat) and hummus appetizers are well prepared. There's a good selection of pastas, salads, and sandwiches. Live jazz plays Thursdays. ⊠ *1334 U St. NW, U Street corridor* ☎ *202/667–3215* ⊟ *AE, D, DC, MC, V* Ⓜ *U Street/Cardozo.*

Italian

$–$$　✕ **Coppi's Organic Restaurant.** An Italian bicycling motif permeates this restaurant, from the posters, photographs, and gear hanging on the walls to the monogrammed racing shirts worn by the staff. The wood oven–baked pizzas are always good, but the frequently changing menu also includes antipasto, fresh pastas, meat, and fish—all made with organic ingredients. Look for items such as asparagus, English peas, and favas gently sautéed with butter and mint, or pastas such as gnocchi with black-truffle pesto, and *trenette* with porcini and strip steak. For dessert, there's biscotti made in the brick oven and a sweet calzone filled with Nutella. ⊠ *1414 U St. NW, U Street corridor* ☎ *202/319–7773* ⊟ *AE, D, DC, MC, V* ⊘ *No lunch* Ⓜ *U Street/Cardozo.*

Maryland Suburbs

Belgian

★ **$–$$**　✕ **Mannequin Pis.** The last thing you'd expect from Olney, a small suburb 30 minutes north of Washington, is a restaurant serving the foods of northern Belgium. Chef-owner Bernard Dehaene, a native of Brussels, takes pride in the authenticity of his 45-seater. He offers a huge selection of Belgian beer (about 50 types) and an arsenal of mussels served in more than 30 sauces. One favorite is the Mussels Brussels, served in a broth of leek, house-smoked bacon, goat cheese, and beer. As for entrées, the menu changes monthly, but the rack of lamb and the organic chicken are good bets. Make weekend reservations two weeks in advance. ✉ *18064 Georgia Ave., Olney, MD* ☎ *301/570–4800* ⌨ *Reservations essential* ▤ *MC, V.*

Contemporary

$$–$$$ ✕ **Grapeseed.** This Napa-style wine bar is an oenophile's haven—you can get scores of wines by the glass or half-pour as well as bottle. With a menu divided into beginnings, middles, and ends, Grapeseed attracts solo diners making a meal of it at the bar as well as couples and foursomes eating in the intimate dining room done in rich hues of plum and burgundy. The fare cuts a wide swath with dishes like goat cheese mousse with hazelnuts, braised veal cheeks with balsamic vinegar, fried chicken with waffles, and steamed mussels with tomatoes, garlic, and wine. In warm weather, the door-sized front window opens to the street and makes the place feel like an airy café. ✉ *4865 Cordell Ave., Bethesda, MD* ☎ *301/986–9592* ⌨ *Reservations essential* ▤ *AE, D, DC, MC, V* ⊗ *No lunch* Ⓜ *Bethesda.*

Indian

★ $–$$ ✕ **Passage to India.** In a city with dozens of Indian restaurants, Passage to India stands out. Carved wooden doors and enameled panels strike an exotic note in the serene dining room. The fare on the regional menu is at once lush and aromatic with dishes like coconut-scented calamari, butter and tandoori chicken, and lamb with apricots. Vegetables are given special attention in preparations like lotus root and peas in curry and pureed spinach with corn topping. ✉ *4931 Cordell Ave., Bethesda, MD* ☎ *301/656–3373* ▤ *AE, D, MC, V.*

Seafood

🕒 $–$$$ ✕ **Bethesda Crab House.** This modest, noisy, ultracasual restaurant is the best place in the Washington area to enjoy one of the Chesapeake Bay area's great delicacies—blue crabs steamed with Old Bay seasoning. Order as many crabs as you want; when they're ready, they'll be dumped on your paper-covered table. That's your cue to pick up a mallet and knife and attack the crustaceans. (The waiters gladly give instructions.) Then settle back with a beer for some serious crab pickin'. The price varies with the time of year. It's a good idea to call in advance to reserve your crabs—the restaurant sometimes runs out. ✉ *4958 Bethesda Ave., Bethesda, MD* ☎ *301/652–3382* ▤ *MC, V* Ⓜ *Bethesda.*

$–$$$ ✕ **Crisfield.** Because it's about as gracious as a neighborhood barbershop, Crisfield's relatively high prices might seem absurd. But you get your money's worth with an eyeful of old Maryland frozen in time and some of the best no-nonsense seafood in the area. Crab cakes don't get any more authentic, and you know they're made by hand because they don't look perfect. The creamy, chunky clam chowder is rendered with similar down-home care. The place retains an old-school charm; for maximum effect, sit at the bar and watch the waiters shuck clams. ✉ *8012 Georgia Ave., Silver Spring, MD* ☎ *301/589–1306* ⌨ *Reservations not accepted* ▤ *AE, MC, V* ⊗ *Closed Mon.* Ⓜ *Silver Spring.*

Southwestern

🕒 ¢–$$ ✕ **Rio Grande Café.** It's worth braving Rio Grande's crowds for the quail, goat, and other upscale Tex-Mex fare. Crates of Mexican beer stacked against the walls serve as decoration, as does a functioning perpetual-motion tortilla machine, an object of fascination to the many kids who frequent this family-friendly spot. ■ TIP→ **Big portions make this a good spot for families.** A young bar crowd likes to knock back the potent combination of frozen sangria and frozen margarita swirled in a frosted soda glass. A sibling location operates in Arlington, Virginia. ⊠ *4919 Fairmont Ave., Bethesda, MD* ☎ *301/656–2981* ▭ *AE, D, DC, MC, V* ⚫ *Reservations not accepted* Ⓜ *Bethesda.*

🐾 ¢ ✕ **California Tortilla.** The biggest reason to wait with the lunchtime crowds at California Tortilla is in its namesake—the massive, overstuffed specialty tortilla. The bestseller at this lively, home-grown, fastfood minichain is the blackened chicken Caesar, but there are lots of favorites. Don't miss the *queso*, a flavorful cheese dip. It's made in-house and is always served piping hot. Also make sure to test at least a few of the hot sauces—there are about 50 varieties on hand. ⊠ *4862 Cordell Ave., Bethesda, MD* ☎ *301/654–8226* ▭ *MC, V* Ⓜ *Bethesda.*

Virginia Suburbs

Afghan

$ ✕ **Panjshir.** Inside, this restaurant's Falls Church location favors plush red and dark wood, whereas the Vienna branch is more into pinks; however, both serve succulent kabobs of beef, lamb, and chicken, as well as fragrant stews (with or without meat) over rice. Entrées come with Afghan salad and bread. ⊠ *924 W. Broad St., Falls Church, VA* ☎ *703/536–4566* ▭ *AE, DC, MC, V* ☽ *Closed Sun.*

American

$$–$$$$ ✕ **The Capital Grille.** A small oasis of urban restaurants is tucked into a pocket of high-end stores in suburban Tysons Corner. Among them is this spot serving fine dry-aged beef cuts and traditional sides. It's a branch of the Capital Grille on Capitol Hill. ⊠ *1861 International Dr., McLean, VA* ☎ *703/448–3900* ▭ *AE, D, DC, MC, V* ☽ *No lunch weekends.*

$–$$$ ✕ **Ashby Inn.** If there's a recipe for a perfect country inn, John and Roma Sherman have it. Head an hour west from D.C., and your reward is extraordinary comfort food. Dishes are made with the freshest local ingredients and presented in an intimate setting. Try the arugula salad with just-picked greens from the inn's garden. The roasted chicken, the first item the Ashby ever offered, remains sublime. Sunday brunch is from 12:30 to 2. ⊠ *692 Federal St., Paris, VA* ☎ *540/592–3900* ▭ *MC, V* ☽ *No lunch Mon.–Sat. No dinner Sun.–Tues.*

$–$$ ✕ **Carlyle Grand Café.** Whether you eat at the bustling bar or in the dining room upstairs, you'll find an imaginative, generous interpretation of modern American cooking. Start with the blue crab fritter or the housemade potato chips drizzled with bleu cheese, then move on to entrées such as pecan-crusted trout, veal meat loaf, and roast pork tenderloin with a citrus glaze. The warm flourless chocolate–macadamia nut waffle with vanilla ice cream and hot fudge sauce has become a local classic. You can even buy a loaf of the bread at the restaurant's own bakery, the Best Buns Bread Company, next door. ⊠ *4000 S. 28th St., Arlington, VA* ☎ *703/931–0777* ▭ *AE, D, DC, MC, V.*

2

$-$$ ✕ **Majestic Café.** The art deco façade of this 1930s-era landmark remains; inside, the café has a modern sensibility. The cooking style moves between the latest American dishes and traditional southern fare. Some of the best plates are the sides, such as hush puppies with rémoulade (a mayo-based sauce that includes shallots, garlic, tarragon, and chives), fluffy spoon bread, and stewed tomatoes. Starters such as a gratin of oysters and ham and main courses such as balsamic-glazed salmon also satisfy. The restaurant is about eight blocks from the Metro. ⊠ *911 King St., Old Town, Alexandria, VA* ☎ *703/837–9117* ▭ *AE, D, DC, MC, V* ☉ *Closed Mon.* Ⓜ *King Street.*

Asian

¢–$ ✕ **Café Dalat.** In the heart of Arlington's "Little Saigon," you can find low-priced Vietnamese fare in far-from-fancy but clean and pleasant Café Dalat, where service is extremely speedy. The sugarcane shrimp is excellent, and *da ram gung* is a sinus-clearing dish of simmered chicken and ginger. All the appetizers are winners, in particular the crispy spring rolls and the tangy Vietnamese shrimp salad in lemon vinaigrette. ⊠ *3143 Wilson Blvd., Arlington, VA* ☎ *703/276–0935* ▭ *MC, V* Ⓜ *Clarendon.*

¢–$ ✕ **Little Viet Garden.** The patrons here swear by the spring rolls, beef-broth-and-glass-noodle soups, beef tips and potato stir-fried with onion in a smoky sauce, and crispy crêpes stuffed with chicken, shrimp, bean sprouts, and green onion. Reserve a table on the outdoor terrace bordered by a flower box–lined white fence. ⊠ *3012 Wilson Blvd., Arlington, VA* ☎ *703/522–9686* ▭ *AE, D, DC, MC, V* Ⓜ *Clarendon.*

☺ ¢ ✕ **Pho 75.** To refer to Pho 75's product as mere soup would be a disservice to the procession of flavors that comes with every mouthful—but that is what *pho* is: a Hanoi-style beef soup packed with noodles and thinly sliced pieces of meat that are cooked in seconds by the steaming broth. A plate of fresh bean sprouts, mint leaves, lemon, and green chilies comes with every order: you can spice up your feast-in-a-bowl as you wish. Pho comes in either a large ($5.45) or small ($4.75) bowl, quite a bargain either way. ⊠ *1771 Wilson Blvd., Suite B, Falls Church, VA* ☎ *703/204–1490* ▭ *No credit cards.*

Barbecue

☺ ¢–$ ✕ **Rocklands.** This homegrown barbecue stop is known for its flavorful pork ribs smoked over hickory and red oak. Sides like silky corn pudding, rich mac 'n' cheese, and crunchy slaw are as good as the meats, which cover everything from beef brisket and chopped pork barbecue to chicken and fish. Come early for dinner: they close at 8 PM daily. The D.C. outpost does mostly takeout, but the restaurants in Alexandria, Rockville, and a new location in Arlington cater to more of a sit-down, family crowd. ⊠ *25 S. Quaker La., Alexandria, VA* ☎ *703/778–9663* ⌂ *Reservations not accepted* ▭ *AE, MC, V.*

Contemporary

$$$$ ✕ **Inn at Little Washington.** A 90-minute drive from the District takes you

Fodor's Choice ★ past hills and farms to this fantasy of an English country manor, where the service matches the setting. Dinner (without wine) is $118 Sunday to Thursday, $128 Friday, and $158 Saturday. After a first course of tiny canapés such as a mini-BLT on housemade bread, soup follows—perhaps chilled fruit or creamy leek. Braised duck and seared foie gras over watercress might come next, then squab over garlic polenta. Desserts, including the "palette" of pastel-hue sorbets, are fanciful, or choose the cheese plate, delivered on a life-size, mooing faux cow. ⊠ *Middle and Main Sts., Washington, VA* ☎ *540/675–3800* ⌂ *Reservations essential* ☰ *MC, V* ⊙ *Closed Tues. in Jan., Mar., July, and Aug.*

$$$–$$$$
Fodor'sChoice
★

× **2941.** Soaring ceilings, a woodsy lakeside location, and a koi pond make this one of the most striking dining rooms in the area. Jonathan Krinn's playful cooking continually surprises with plates like roasted veal tenderloin and sweetbreads with eggplant puree, truffled free range chicken, a deconstructed "creamsicle" of orange sorbet and Tahitian vanilla ice cream, and little gifts from the kitchen like rainbow-hued housemade cotton candy. It's a family affair, too. Krinn's dad makes the artisanal breads that run from rosemary olive to cherry almond. You can order à la carte, go for the bargain pretheater menu (three courses for $45), or splurge on one of the tasting menus ranging from $75 to $110. ⊠ *2941 Fairview Park Dr., Falls Church, VA* ☎ *703/270–1500* ⌂ *Reservations essential* ☰ *AE, D, DC, MC, V* ⊙ *No lunch Sat.*

★ **$$–$$$$**

× **Colvin Run Tavern.** Urban refinement in the suburbs? Well, if anyone was to achieve it, who better than D.C. restaurateur Robert Kinkead, chef-owner of the popular downtown seafood destination named after himself. Colvin Run divides its entrées evenly among seafood, poultry, and meat. The menu changes daily, with options such as roasts (served from a tableside carving cart), breast of squab with roasted foie gras, and scallops with parsley-caper puree. The names of the four dining rooms reflect the East Coast regions that inspire this cuisine (Nantucket, Shenandoah, Charleston, and Camden). ⊠ *8045 Leesburg Pike, Vienna, VA* ☎ *703/356–9500* ⊕ *www.kinkead.com* ☰ *AE, D, DC, MC, V* ⊙ *No lunch weekends.*

$$–$$$

× **Restaurant Eve.** There are two ways to dine—in the bistro or the chef's tasting room—at this understated restaurant in charming Old Town. Comfortably contemporary in shades of pale moss and cinnamon, the bistro is known for plates such as bacon, egg, and cheese salad and pork belly confit. Glossy wood floors and buttercup-yellow couches set the scene in the more intimate, expensive tasting room, where a five-course meal is $75 and a nine-course meal $90 per person. Here, look for the distinctive lobster crème brûlée, butter-poached halibut with leek cream, and fried apple with ricotta tart. Even a Bloody Mary gets new life here, with lemongrass and chilies. ⊠ *110 S. Pitt St., Alexandria, VA* ☎ *703/706–0450* ☰ *AE, D, MC, V* ⊙ *Closed Sun. No lunch Sat.* Ⓜ *King St.*

French

★ **$$$$**

× **L'Auberge Chez François.** Tucked into the Virginia countryside, this sprawling restaurant serves the German-influenced cuisine of Alsace. The decor is both romantic and kitschy—a fireplace dominates the main dining room, German knickknacks line the walls, and red-jacketed waiters courteously guide you through the meal. Choucroute (sausage, duck, smoked pork, and foie gras served atop sauerkraut), red snapper in a pastry crust for two, and medallions of beef and veal are a few of the generously portioned, outstanding entrées. You are asked in advance whether you'd like a soufflé. Say yes, unless it's the Alsatian plum tart that's calling you instead. ✉ *332 Springvale Rd., Great Falls, VA* ☎ *703/759–3800* *Reservations essential* *Jacket required* *AE, D, DC, MC, V* *Closed Mon. No lunch.*

$$–$$$ ✕ **La Bergerie.** Authentic Provençal and Basque cooking are the high points at this elegant Old Town restaurant. Look for dishes such as goat cheese and sun-dried tomato tart, escargots with garlic butter, calves' liver with sautéed onions, sea scallops with morels, quail with truffles, and sweetbreads. Don't forget to order the Grand Marnier dessert soufflé or the apple tart in advance. ✉ *218 N. Lee St., Alexandria, VA* ☎ *703/683–1007* *Reservations essential* *Jacket and tie* *AE, D, DC, MC, V* *No lunch Sun.*

Italian

$$$$ ✕ **Maestro.** The Ritz-Carlton's dining room is one of the brightest restaurant stars in metro D.C. In the state-of-the-art open kitchen, Chef Fabio Trabocchi emphasizes both traditional Italian cooking and his creative takes on the classics. The menu changes often, but you might find potato ravioli in black-truffle sauce, sea bass with fennel confit, and grappa risotto. Desserts might be bonbons filled with rose, lavender, and peach ice cream or a chocolate *delice* (chocolate custard wrapped in a chocolate turban). Three, five, and seven-course menus range from $85 to $150 depending on the day of the week. ✉ *Ritz-Carlton Tysons Corner, 1700 Tysons Blvd., Tysons Corner, VA* ☎ *703/821–1515 or 703/917–5498* *Reservations essential* *AE, D, DC, MC, V* *Closed Mon.*

Fodor'sChoice ★

Southwestern

¢–$$$ ✕ **Rio Grande Café.** This Tex-Mex joint is always packed. While you're waiting for a table, order a "swirl," a mix of frozen sangria and frozen margarita in a frosted beer mug, or check out the tortilla-making machine. The menu sticks mostly to familiar fare such as sizzling fajitas and grilled shrimp brochettes (shrimp, cheese, and peppers wrapped in bacon), with a handful of more exotic entrées such as quail and lobster. Big portions and loud crowds make this a good spot for families; the same is true of the Bethesda, Maryland, location. ✉ *4301 N. Fairfax Dr., Arlington, VA* ☎ *703/528–3131* *Reservations not accepted* *AE, D, DC, MC, V* Ⓜ *Ballston.*

Where to Stay

WORD OF MOUTH

"Remember that you don't have to stay right in D.C. to be close to everything. The key is to stay at a hotel that is close to the [Metro] system."

—Stephanie

"My vote is for staying close in to the city. We just got back in early August and were so glad we stayed nearby. We packed our day with seeing as much as possible and did not have one minute to spare for additional travel time."

—mommybryant

www.fodors.com/forums

Updated by
Shane
Christensen

STAY IN THE HOTEL where Martin Luther King Jr. wrote his "I Have a Dream" speech and become inspired to change history. Or sleep in a cozy bed-and-breakfast near the National Zoo and be able to easily pay a morning call to the pandas. Enjoy the history, grandeur, and White House views of the Hay-Adams or Willard Inter-Continental. Or stay up all night in the nightclubby lobby lounge of the Topaz.

Washington has the same broad range of digs as any major city, but throws in some unique curves. In posh Downtown and Capitol Hill hotels, you can sign a guest register touched by diplomats and then sleep in beds where royalty has rested. You'll also be within walking distance of the National Mall, the Smithsonian, the Library of Congress, and the Capitol. The Mandarin Oriental, two blocks south of the Mall and with great views of the Jefferson Memorial, is one of the most innovative hotels in town.

Penn Quarter, the part of Downtown near the MCI Center, is experiencing a revival. The Hotel Monaco here is within the stern facade of the former Tariff Commission Building. But head inside, and you'll find playfully rendered interiors and tip-top service.

Make a reservation in Dupont Circle if you like being around hubbub and close to restaurants, bookstores, and galleries. Brand-name lodgings such as Westin, Jurys, and Marriott share the neighborhood with chic boutique hotels and B&Bs. For those looking for a respite on a quiet side street, the Hotel Tabard Inn offers its own eclectic kind of cozy, affordable comfort.

Whether you stay in Georgetown at the Ritz-Carlton or at the Holiday Inn, you'll be able to get an up-close view of the tree-lined district best known for its wealthy and prominent residents. And although Foggy Bottom doesn't have many tourist destinations, staying here puts you close to the State Department and the Kennedy Center.

There are many appealing options in places you might not think to look. Hotels and inns on Connecticut Avenue north of Dupont Circle are close to the zoo and the National Cathedral, as well as to the shopping and restaurant districts of Adams-Morgan and Dupont Circle. Bethesda hotels give you easy access to the National Institutes of Health, as well as the premier shopping areas of Friendship Heights and Georgetown. Hotels at the foot of Key Bridge in Virginia offer great views of the District's skyline; in Virginia, also, you can take advantage of reasonable prices and the convenience of the Metro, which eliminates the need for parking downtown.

There is no true off-season in the nation's capital, and lodging can certainly get expensive. Varying amounts of demand, however, have meant that many hotels offer attractive packages, so keep your eyes open for bargains.

Adams-Morgan

$ 🖼 **Jurys Normandy Inn.** On a quiet street in the embassy area of Connecticut Avenue stands this small Irish-chain hotel. Cozy rooms, attractively decorated with colonial reproduction furniture, include free high-speed Internet access, coffeemakers, and complimentary newspapers. Breakfast is served in an intimate parlor, and each Tuesday evening a wine-and-cheese reception is held for guests. ✉ *2118 Wyoming Ave. NW, Adams-Morgan 20008* ☎ *202/483–1350, 800/424–3729, or 800/842–3729* 🖷 *202/387–8241* ⊕ *www.juryswashingtondc-hotels.com* 🛏 *75 rooms* ♿ *Café, in-room safes, refrigerators, cable TV, in-room data ports, laundry facilities, parking (fee)* ▤ *AE, D, DC, MC, V* 🍴 *CP* Ⓜ *Dupont Circle.*

$ 🏨 **Windsor Park Hotel.** The rooms are tiny and the hallways small, but the location (at the foot of Kalorama Circle overlooking Rock Creek Park) can't be beat. Those who don't mind a bit of a walk can easily get to the National Zoo, Dupont Circle, and Adams-Morgan, all within a mile of the hotel. Street parking can be difficult, but a reasonably priced garage is two blocks away. ✉ *2116 Kalorama Rd. NW, Adams-Morgan 20008* ☎ *202/483–7700 or 800/247–3064* 🖷 *202/332–4547* ⊕ *www.windsorparkhotel.com* 🛏 *43 rooms, 8 suites* ♿ *Refrigerators, cable TV, in-room data ports, business services* ▤ *AE, D, DC, MC, V* 🍴 *CP* Ⓜ *Woodley Park/Zoo or Dupont Circle.*

¢ 🏨 **Kalorama Guest House–Adams-Morgan.** Like its sister property in Woodley Park, this Adams-Morgan location has been created out of early-20th-century Victorian town houses. The rooms, which vary in size, include 19th-century antiques and cozy furnishings. Some have shared baths, and only the suites offer phones and TVs. ✉ *1854 Mintwood Pl. NW, Adams-Morgan 20009* ☎ *202/667–6369* 🖷 *202/319–1262* ⊕ *www.kaloramaguesthouse.com* 🛏 *24 rooms, 9 with bath, 5 suites* ♿ *Parking (fee); no phones in some rooms, no TV in some rooms* ▤ *AE, D, DC, MC, V* 🍴 *CP* Ⓜ *Woodley Park/Zoo.*

TOP 5

■ **Four Seasons Hotel:** Pamper yourself with the city's best service and among the most sophisticated guest rooms anywhere.

■ **Hay-Adams Hotel:** Enjoy an unobstructed view of the White House from the luxury of an unparalleled Renaissance mansion.

■ **Ritz-Carlton, Washington, D.C.:** Dreams do not unfold in greater comfort than from the heavenly beds of the Ritz.

■ **Mandarin Oriental:** Take a leisurely stroll to the Jefferson Memorial or around the Tidal Basin shimmering before the exquisite hotel.

■ **Woodley Park Guest House:** Indulge in personalized, easygoing service at this intimate B&B, just a hop, skip, and a jump from the National Zoo.

	WHAT IT COSTS				
	$$$$	**$$$**	**$$**	**$**	**¢**
FOR 2 PEOPLE	over $400	$296–$399	$211–$295	$125–$210	under $125

Prices are for a standard double room in high season, excluding room tax (14.5% in D.C., 12.5% in MD, and 10.15% in VA).

KNOW-HOW

FACILITIES

The properties listed were chosen because of their beauty, historical significance, location, and value. Most hotels in the $$$ category and all in the $$$$ category have concierges; some in the $$ group do, too. Because Washington is an international city with a diverse population and visitors from all over, many hotel staffs are multilingual. Every hotel has no-smoking rooms.

We always list a property's facilities but not whether you'll be charged extra to use them; when pricing accommodations, ask what's included. You can assume that all rooms have private baths, phones, TVs, and air-conditioning unless otherwise noted, and that all hotels operate on the European Plan (with no meals) unless we specify that they use the Continental Plan (CP, with a continental breakfast), Breakfast Plan (BP, with a full-cooked breakfast), Modified American Plan (MAP, with breakfast and dinner), or the Full American Plan (FAP, with all meals).

PRICES

If you're interested in visiting Washington at a calm, less expensive time—and if you can stand semitropical weather—come in August, during the congressional recess. Rates also drop in late December and January, except around an inauguration.

If high-end prices aren't in your vacation budget, don't automatically assume that a stay in a fancy hotel is out of the question. Weekend, off-season, and special rates (such as American Automobile Association and AARP discounts) can make rooms more affordable. During times of economic stress, hotels often employ special package rates to increase business, so a little bit of research can pay off in big savings.

RESERVATIONS

With more than 63,000 guest rooms available in the area, you can almost always find a place to stay—though it's always prudent to reserve. Hotels often fill up with conventioneers, politicians in transit, families, and, in spring, school groups. Hotel rooms in D.C. can be particularly hard to come by during the Cherry Blossom Festival in late March or early April, and also in May, when so many graduate from college. Late October's Marine Corps Marathon also increases demand for rooms.

The **Washington, DC Convention and Tourism Corporation** (☎ 800/422-8644 ⊕ www.washington.org) runs a reservation service. Many participating hotels are among the best in town.

PARKING

Hotel parking fees range from free (usually, but not always, in the suburbs) to $30 (plus tax) per night. This sometimes involves valet parking, with its implied additional gratuities. Street parking is free on Sunday and usually after 6:30 PM. But there are often far more cars searching than there are spaces available, particularly downtown, in Georgetown, and in the upper Connecticut Avenue area. During weekday rush hours many streets are unavailable for parking; illegally parked cars are towed, and reclaiming a car is expensive and very inconvenient. *Read signs carefully;* some are confusing, and the ticket writers are quick.

3

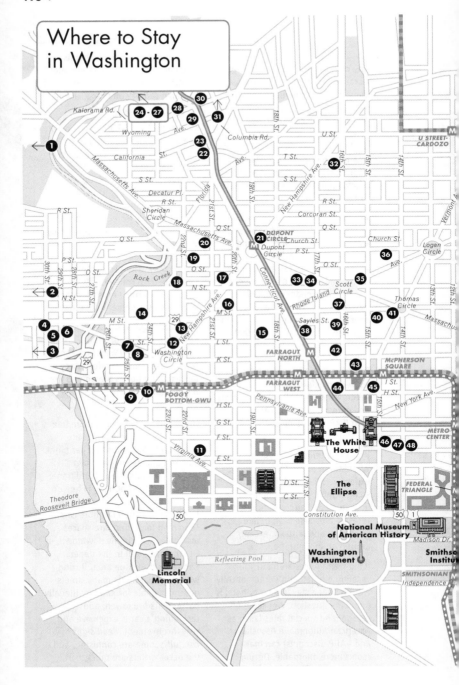

Where to Stay in Washington

Adam's Inn **31**

Best Western
Capitol Skyline **65**

Capital Hilton **42**

Capitol Hill Suites **66**

Churchill Hotel **23**

Courtyard
Washington/
Northwest **22**

Doubletree Guest
Suites. **10**

Embassy Suites **18**

Fairmont
Washington **14**

Four Seasons
Hotel **6**

George Washington
University Inn **9**

Georgetown Inn **2**

Georgetown
Suites **5**

Grand Hyatt
Washington **54**

Hay-Adams Hotel **44**

Henley Park Hotel **51**

Holiday Inn
Capitol **69**

Holiday Inn
Georgetown **1**

Holiday Inn
on the Hill **60**

Hostelling
International–
Washington D.C. **50**

Hotel George **59**

Hotel Harrington **55**

Hotel Helix **36**

Hotel Madera **17**

Hotel Monaco **56**

Hotel Rouge **39**

Hotel Tabard Inn **33**

Hotel Washington **46**

Hyatt Regency
on Capitol Hill **61**

J.W. Marriott
Pennsylvania
Avenue **48**

Jefferson Hotel **37**

Jurys Normandy
Inn **29**

Jurys Washington
Hotel **21**

Kalorama
Guest House–
Adams Morgan **30**

Kalorama
Guest House–
Woodley Park **27**

Latham Hotel **4**

L'Enfant Plaza **63**

Lincoln Suites **15**

The Madison **40**

Mandarin Oriental . . . **62**

Marriott at Metro
Center **53**

Marriott
Residence Inn **19**

Marriott
Wardman Park **25**

The Melrose Hotel **8**

Morrison-Clark Inn **49**

Omni Shoreham
Hotel **24**

One Washington
Circle Hotel **12**

Phoenix Park
Hotel **57**

Renaissance
Mayflower Hotel **38**

Ritz-Carlton
Georgetown **3**

Ritz-Carlton
Washington, D.C. **13**

Sofitel Lafayette
Square Washington . . . **45**

State Plaza Hotel **11**

St. Gregory **16**

St. Regis **43**

Topaz Hotel **34**

Washington Court
Hotel **58**

Washington
Doubletree Hotel **35**

Washington
Renaissance
Hotel **52**

Washington Suites **7**

Westin
Embassy Row **20**

Willard Inter-
Continental **47**

Windsor Inn **32**

Windsor Park
Hotel **28**

Woodley Park
Guest House **26**

Wyndham
Washington, D.C. **41**

CLOSE UP
Traveling with Children?

MAJOR CONVENTION HOTELS (and those on Capitol Hill and the waterfront) don't see many families. It's best to choose a hotel downtown, in Foggy Bottom, uptown, or in Maryland or Virginia. Also, the closer your hotel is to a Metro stop, the more quickly you can get on the sightseeing trail.

Consider a stay at an all-suites hotel. This will allow you to spread out and, if you prepare your meals in a kitchenette, possibly keep costs down. A pool may well be essential for a stay with children, and game rooms are a plus.

In Georgetown, the deluxe Four Seasons Hotel offers children's menus, age-specific games, magazines, and toys, milk and cookies, Web TV, kids' robes, and electronic games in every room. The Embassy Suites in Foggy Bottom sells Nickelodeon packages in summer (10%–20% discount with a Nick Pack at check-in). The hotel also has a video-game room and a Sony Playstation in every guest room. A number of the other well-known chains, including Fairmont, Ritz-Carlton, and St. Regis also offer special programs for kids and usually have babysitting services. Holiday Inns allow kids (typically under 12) to eat free.

Most hotels in Washington allow children under a certain age to stay in their parents' room at no extra charge, but be sure to find out the cutoff age for children's discounts.

Capitol Hill

★ **$$$–$$$$** 🏨 **Hyatt Regency Capitol Hill.** Following a $13 million renovation in 2005, this enormous Hyatt gleams with a five-story atrium lobby and totally redesigned guest rooms. These rooms, colored in soft gold with dark wood furnishings, feature fluffy bedding with pillow-top mattresses, white duvets, and giant pillows, as well as overstuffed chairs, workstations, and beautifully appointed bathrooms. ■ TIP→ **The Old Town Trolly picks guests up right in front of the hotel to visit Washington's key tourist destinations.** ✉ *400 New Jersey Ave. NW, Capitol Hill 20001* ☎ *202/ 737–1234 or 888/591–1234* 🖷 *202/737–5773* ⊕ *www. washingtonregency.hyatt.com* 🛏 *802 rooms, 32 suites* ♿ *Restaurant, coffee shop, room service, room TVs with movies and video games, in-room broadband, Wi-Fi, indoor pool, health club, lobby lounge, dry cleaning, concierge, concierge floor, business services, meeting rooms, parking (fee)* 🚭 *AE, D, DC, MC, V* Ⓜ *Union Station.*

★ **$$$** 🏨 **Hotel George.** Rooms at this cool boutique hotel offer duvet-covered beds with the softest Egyptian cotton sheets, granite-topped desks, silkscreen prints, CD players, and seating areas with a lounge chair and ottoman. Most have marble bathrooms and terry robes, and each room comes with a complimentary in-room television "yoga program" (mat, block, and strap provided). Portraits of America's first president, by Andy Warhol protégé Steve Kaufman, adorn public areas. Bistro Bis serves updated versions of classic French dishes. ✉ *15 E St. NW, Capitol Hill*

3

20001 ☎ *202/347–4200 or 800/ 576–8331* 🖷 *202/347–4213* ⊕ *www.hotelgeorge.com* ☞ *139 rooms* ⟋ *Restaurant, room service, minibars, room TVs with movies and video games, in-room broadband, gym, steam room, lobby lounge, dry cleaning, concierge, business services, meeting rooms, parking (fee), some pets allowed* ⊟ *AE, D, DC, MC, V* Ⓜ *Union Station.*

$$$ 🏨 **Washington Court Hotel.** Terraced marble stairs lead to a contemporary atrium lobby with a skylight, waterfall, and glass elevator—you may also appreciate the inlaid wood and stained glass that are part of the

WORD OF MOUTH

"The Hotel George is right near the heart of Capitol Hill (office bldg neighborhood) and they have a fantastic restaurant in house—after the sun goes down, however, the streets are barren and there is not much around other than the shops and restaurants of Union Station. But, it would be very convenient if you are taking the train as you will come right into Union Station and not have to go very far."

–tachiebluebird

hotel's original art deco elements. Each Deluxe room has a spacious work desk, a lounge chair and ottoman, and marble bathroom. The larger Executive King rooms offer expanded sitting areas. Convenient to Union Station, the hotel has a wonderful view of the Capitol. ⊠ *525 New Jersey Ave. NW, Capitol Hill 20001* ☎ *202/628–2100 or 800/321–3010* 🖷 *202/879–7918* ⊕ *www.washingtoncourthotel.com* ☞ *252 rooms, 12 suites* ⟋ *Restaurant, room service, cable TV with movies, in-room broadband, gym, billiards, bar, laundry service, concierge, business services, parking (fee)* ⊟ *AE, D, DC, MC, V* Ⓜ *Union Station.*

$$–$$$ 🏨 **Phoenix Park Hotel.** Named for a park in Dublin, this hotel is across the street from Union Station and only four blocks from the Capitol. A case in the lobby holds a collection of Waterford crystal. Rooms, which vary in size, have a Celtic theme, with Irish linen and original artwork—some rooms are a bit heavy on pink. Three penthouse suites have balconies that overlook Union Station; three duplex suites have spiral staircases and one offers a fireplace. At the always-packed Dubliner Pub, Irish entertainers perform nightly. ⊠ *520 N. Capitol St. NW, Capitol Hill 20001* ☎ *202/638–6900 or 800/824–5419* 🖷 *202/393–3236* ⊕ *www.phoenixparkhotel.com* ☞ *143 rooms, 6 suites* ⟋ *Restaurant, room service, minibars, cable TV, in-room data ports, gym, pub, laundry service, concierge, business services, meeting rooms, parking (fee)* ⊟ *AE, D, DC, MC, V* Ⓜ *Union Station.*

$–$$ 🏨 **Capitol Hill Suites.** On a quiet residential street beside the Library of Congress, this all-suite hotel's proximity to the U.S. House of Representatives' office buildings means that it's often filled with visiting lobbyists when Congress is in session. Although the hotel is not much to look at from the outside, the three sizes of guest rooms, from Junior Suites (smallest) to Deluxe Suites (largest), are spacious and comfortable, and price differences between them are small. There's a fireplace in the sunfilled lobby, and a restaurant a block away. ⊠ *200 C St. SE, Capitol Hill 20003* ☎ *202/543–6000, 800/424–9165, or 888/627–7811* 🖷 *202/ 547–2608* ⊕ *www.capitolhillsuites.com* ☞ *152 suites* ⟋ *Kitchenettes,*

Lodging Alternatives

APARTMENT RENTALS

If you want a home base that's roomy enough for a family and comes with cooking facilities, consider a furnished rental. These can save you money, especially if you're traveling with a group. Home-exchange directories sometimes list rentals as well as exchanges.

🏠 **International Agents Hideaways International** ✉ 767 Islington St., Portsmouth, NH 03801 ☎ 603/430-4433 or 800/843-4433 🖷 603/430-4444 ⊕ www.hideaways.com, membership $185.

🏠 **Rental Listings Washington Post** ⊕ www.washingtonpost.com. **Washington City Paper** ⊕ www.washingtoncitypaper.com.

B&BS

To find reasonably priced accommodations in small guesthouses and private homes, try **Bed & Breakfast Accommodations,** which is staffed weekdays 10–5. It handles about 45 different properties in the area.

🏠 **Bed and Breakfast Accommodations, Ltd.** ☎ 413/582-9888 or 877/893-3233 🖷 413/582-9669 ⊕ www.bedandbreakfastdc.com.

HOME EXCHANGES

If you would like to exchange your home for someone else's, join a home-exchange organization, which will send you its updated listings of available exchanges for a year and include your own listing in at least one of them. It's up to you to make specific arrangements.

🏠 **Exchange Clubs HomeLink International** ✉ Box 47747, Tampa, FL 33647 ☎ 813/975-9825 or 800/638-3841 🖷 813/910-8144 ⊕ www.homelink.org; $80 for a listing published in a directory and on Web sites. **Intervac U.S.** ✉ 30 Corte San Fernando, Tiburon, CA 94920 ☎ 800/756-4663 🖷 415/435-7440 ⊕ www.intervacus.com; $140 yearly for a listing, online access, and a catalog; $65 without catalog.

HOSTELS

No matter what your age, you can save on lodging costs by staying at hostels. In some 4,500 locations in more than 70 countries around the world, Hostelling International (HI), the umbrella group for a number of national youth-hostel associations, offers single-sex, dorm-style beds and, at many hostels, rooms for couples and family accommodations. Membership in any HI national hostel association, open to travelers of all ages, allows you to stay in HI-affiliated hostels at member rates; one-year membership is about $28 for adults ($18 for seniors 55 and older, free for children under 18), and hostels charge about $10–$30 per night. Members have priority if the hostel is full.

🏠 **Organizations Hostelling International–USA** ✉ 8401 Colesville Rd., Suite 600, Silver Spring, MD 20910 ☎ 301/495-1240 🖷 301/495-6697 ⊕ www.hiusa.org.

cable TV with movies, in-room data ports, lobby lounge, dry cleaning, laundry service, business services, meeting rooms, parking (fee) ⊟ _AE, D, DC, MC, V_ Ⓜ _Capitol South._

★ **$–$$** 🏨 **Holiday Inn on the Hill.** The "Bubble Wall" in the innovative lobby, accompanied by background jazz music, is your first indication that this is no longer your ordinary Holiday Inn. Rooms are unexpectedly stylish:

silky blue comforters grace the beds, bathrooms have black granite countertops and Swiss bath amenities, and ergonomic chairs accompany the glass-topped desks. Rooms also provide free high-speed Internet access. Those staying in summertime should ask the friendly staff—dressed in jet black-and-cobalt uniforms—to direct them to the rooftop swimming pool. In addition to sending their kids for a swim, parents will be happy to know that children under 12 eat free here. ⊠ *415 New Jersey Ave. NW, Capitol Hill 20001* ☎ *202/638–1616 or 800/638–1116* 🖷 *202/638–0707* ⊕ *www.holiday-inn.com* ⮌ *343 rooms, 4 suites* ⸸ *Restaurant, room service, cable TV with movies and video games, in-room broadband, pool, exercise equipment, gym, bar, business services, meeting rooms, parking (fee)* ▭ *AE, D, DC, MC, V* Ⓜ *Union Station.*

Downtown

★ **$$$$** ☷ **Jefferson Hotel.** Federal-style elegance abounds at this distinctive downtown hotel. American antiques and original art fill each room, in which Bose CD players are included. A near one-to-one staff-to-guest ratio ensures outstanding service, and employees greet you by name. The Jefferson restaurant, which serves American cuisine, is a favorite of high-ranking politicos and displays original documents signed by Thomas Jefferson. ⊠ *1200 16th St. NW, Downtown 20036* ☎ *202/347–2200 or 866/270–8102* 🖷 *202/331–7982* ⊕ *www.thejeffersonwashingtondc. com* ⮌ *70 rooms, 30 suites* ⸸ *Restaurant, room service, minibars, cable TV with movies and video games, in-room broadband, gym, bar, laundry service, concierge, business services, parking (fee), some pets allowed* ▭ *AE, D, DC, MC, V* Ⓜ *Farragut North.*

☾ **$$$–$$$$** ☷ **Capital Hilton.** In close proximity to the best Washington tourist attractions, the Capital Hilton offers guests a long list of amenities and access to an 11,000-square-foot health club and day spa. Guest rooms have a neoclassic design with cherrywood furniture. Babysitting and other child-friendly services are available. Fran O'Brien's restaurant serves chops and seafood, and the fare at Twigs includes American bistro standards. ⊠ *1001 16th St. NW, Downtown 20036* ☎ *202/393–1000* 🖷 *202/639–5784* ⊕ *www.hilton.com* ⮌ *544 rooms, 16 suites* ⸸ *2 restaurants, room service, refrigerators, cable TV, in-room data ports, health club, hair salon, spa, bar, babysitting, dry cleaning, laundry service, concierge, business services, parking (fee)* ▭ *AE, D, DC, MC, V* Ⓜ *Union Station.*

★ **$$$–$$$$** ☷ **Hotel Monaco.** The 1839 Tariff Building, originally designed by Robert Mills (of Washington Monument fame), represented one of the leading neoclassic buildings of its day. The brilliantly restored interior introduces a colorful, playful design to the landmark edifice. Rooms have 15-foot vaulted ceilings, eclectic furnishings, and minibars with martini kits; the "Monte Carlo Tall Rooms" accommodate those needing extra bed space. Upon request, the hotel will deliver companion goldfish to your room for the duration of your stay. The fashionable Poste Brasserie serves contemporary American cuisine, and the MCI Center lies across the street. ⊠ *700 F St. NW, Penn Quarter 20004* ☎ *202/628–7177 or 800/649–1202* 🖷 *202/628–7277* ⊕ *www.monaco-dc.com* ⮌ *167 rooms, 16 suites* ⸸ *Restaurant, room service, in-room safes, in-room broadband,* *gym, laundry service, concierge, parking (fee), some pets allowed* ⊟ *AE, D, DC, MC, V* Ⓜ *Gallery Place/Chinatown.*

★ **$$$–$$$$** 🏨 **Mandarin Oriental Washington, D.C.** The sophisticated Mandarin Oriental lies at the juncture of the Potomac Tidal Basin and Washington Channel next to the Jefferson Memorial. Beautiful rooms decorated with soft Asian touches overlook either the Mall or the waterfront. All rooms have HDTV flat-screen TVs and other high-tech amenities, as well as Aromatherapy-brand bath products and kimono-style robes and slippers. The Mandarin has a stunning art collection, a gorgeous (but expensive) spa, and refined service. Its gourmet CityZen is one of Washington's hottest restaurants. Despite its impressive view of the waterways, the hotel is slightly out of the way from many of Washington's central attractions. ⊠ *1330 Maryland Ave. SW, Downtown 20024* 🕾 *202/554–8588 or 888/888–1778* 🖷 *202/554–8999* ⊕ *www.mandarinoriental.com* 📞 *347 rooms, 53 suites* ⌂ *2 restaurants, room service, in-room safes, minibars, in-room data ports, indoor pool, fitness classes, health club, hair salon, spa, bar, lobby lounge, dry cleaning, laundry service, concierge, concierge floor, business services, meeting rooms, airport shuttle, parking (fee), no-smoking floors* ⊟ *AE, D, DC, MC, V* Ⓜ *Smithsonian.*

🕘 **$$$–$$$$** 🏨 **St. Regis.** Amenities found in every room of this landmark Italian Renaissance hotel include cordless phones, Frette sheets, Bose radios, and bottled drinking water. Despite the hotel's first-class service, some of the rooms have aged. The St. Regis Kids Program offers cookies and milk on arrival as well as accredited babysitting. The hotel's elegant restaurant serves regional American cuisine. ⊠ *923 16th St. NW, Downtown 20006* 🕾 *202/638–2626 or 800/325–3535* 🖷 *202/638–4231* ⊕ *www.starwood.com/stregis* 📞 *179 rooms, 14 suites* ⌂ *Restaurant, room service, in-room safes, minibars, some refrigerators, cable TV, in-room data ports, gym, lobby lounge, babysitting, children's programs (ages 5–12), dry cleaning, laundry service, concierge, business services, meeting rooms, parking (fee), some pets allowed* ⊟ *AE, D, DC, MC, V* Ⓜ *McPherson Square.*

★ **$$$–$$$$** 🏨 **Sofitel Lafayette Square Washington.** The French could not have landed a better location for the Sofitel, a minute's walk from the White House. The boutique hotel has maintained the 1920s stylings of the original Shoreham office building, with an understated, sophisticated lobby and chic, though slightly small, guest rooms with beautiful marble bathrooms. The multilingual staff caters to Europeans and Americans, and Cafe 15 serves artful French dishes under the direction of a Michelin three-star consulting chef. ⊠ *806 15th St. NW, Downtown 20005* 🕾 *202/730–8800* 🖷 *202/730–8500* ⊕ *www.sofitel.com* 📞 *221 rooms, 16 suites* ⌂ *Restaurant, room service, in-room safes, minibars, in-room broadband, gym, bar, dry cleaning, concierge, business services, meeting rooms, some pets allowed* ⊟ *AE, D, DC, MC, V* Ⓜ *MacPherson Square.*

★ **$$$–$$$$** 🏨 **Willard Inter-Continental.** The historic Willard has long been a favorite of American presidents and other newsmakers. Superb service and a wealth of amenities are hallmarks of the hotel, two blocks from the White House. The spectacular beaux-arts lobby showcases great columns, sparkling chandeliers, mosaic floors, and elaborate ceilings. Period detail is reflected in the rooms, which have elegant, Federal-style furniture, as well as sleek marble bathrooms. The hotel's formal restaurant, the Willard Room, has won nationwide acclaim for its modern take on French and American dishes. The Willard has opened its own history gallery, which chronicles the hotel's legendary past with photos, newspaper articles, and collectors' items, as well as an outstanding spa and fitness center. ☒ *1401 Pennsylvania Ave. NW, Downtown 20004* ☏ *202/628–9100* 🖶 *202/637–7326* ⊕ *www.washington.interconti.com* ⤴ *301 rooms, 40 suites* ♨ *3 restaurants, room service, in-room safes, minibars, some microwaves, cable TV, in-room broadband, health club, bar, shops, babysitting, dry cleaning, laundry service, concierge, business services, meeting rooms, parking (fee), some pets allowed* ▭ *AE, D, DC, MC, V* Ⓜ *Metro Center.*

$$–$$$$ 🏨 **J. W. Marriott Pennsylvania Avenue.** This modern flagship hotel has a prime location near the White House and next to the National Theatre. The capacious, columned lobby includes a four-story atrium, marble-and-mahogany accents, and Asian rugs. Rooms have flatscreen TVs and contemporary furnishings with gold-and-cream accents. The hotel's 1331 bar and lounge is popular, and there's a food court next door. ☒ *1331 Pennsylvania Ave. NW, Downtown 20004* ☏ *202/393–2000 or 800/228–9290* 🖶 *202/626–6991* ⊕ *www.marriott.com* ⤴ *738 rooms, 34 suites* ♨ *2 restaurants, room service, in-room safes, cable TV with movies and video games, in-room broadband, indoor pool, health club, bar, dry cleaning, concierge, concierge floor, business services, parking (fee)* ▭ *AE, D, DC, MC, V* Ⓜ *Metro Center.*

$$$ 🏨 **Grand Hyatt Washington.** In this fanciful high-rise hotel's atrium, a player piano sits on a small island surrounded by a waterfall-fed blue lagoon. You can enter Metro Center, the hub of D.C.'s subway system, directly from the lobby, and the hotel houses one of the city's more popular martini bars. Guest rooms have been upgraded with pillow-top mattresses, thick down comforters, and plush pillows on the beds, and marble baths that offer Portico spa products. Weekend brunch at this giant hotel is very popular. ☒ *1000 H St. NW, Downtown 20001* ☏ *202/582–1234 or 800/233–1234* 🖶 *202/637–4781* ⊕ *www. grandwashington.hyatt.com* ⤴ *823 rooms, 38 suites* ♨ *4 restaurants, room service, minibars, cable TV with movies, Wi-Fi, indoor pool, health club, 2 bars, laundry service, concierge, concierge floor, business services, meeting rooms, parking (fee)* ▭ *AE, D, DC, MC, V* Ⓜ *Metro Center.*

$$$ 🏨 **Hay-Adams Hotel.** Two famous Americans—statesman John Hay and

FodorśChoice
★

historian Henry Adams—once owned homes on the site where this Italian Renaissance mansion now stands, next to Lafayette Park and the White House. The elegant boutique hotel offers outstanding personalized service, and the White House views from rooms on the sixth, seventh, and eighth floors are stunning. Other rooms, dressed in beige and pale sage green, face St. John's church or the interior, and are less expensive. The Lafayette Room serves exquisite American cuisine, and the hotel's bar is one of the most sophisticated you will find anywhere. ☒ *1 Lafayette Sq. NW, Downtown 20006* ☏ *202/638–6600 or 800/853–6807* 🖶 *202/638–2716 or 202/638–3803* ⊕ *www.*

hayadams.com 🛏 *125 rooms, 20 suites* ⚒ *Restaurant, room service, minibars, some refrigerators, cable TV with movies, Wi-Fi, bar, dry cleaning, laundry service, concierge, business services, parking (fee), some pets allowed* 🖃 *AE, D, DC, MC, V* Ⓜ *McPherson Square or Farragut North.*

$$$ 🏨 **Hotel Washington.** Since it opened in 1918, the Hotel Washington has been known for its view. Washingtonians bring out-of-towners to the outdoor rooftop bar (open May to October, weather permitting) for cocktails with a view: you can see the White House grounds and the Washington Monument. The hotel sprang from the drawing boards of John Carrère and Thomas Hastings, who also designed the New York Public Library. Guest rooms are comfortable but not the city's most modern, and those in the interior portion of the hotel are small. ⊠ *515 15th St. NW, Downtown 20004* ☎ *202/638–5900* 🖷 *202/638–1594* ⊕ *www. hotelwashington.com* 🛏 *324 rooms, 16 suites* ⚒ *Restaurant, room service, cable TV, Web TV, gym, sauna, bar, dry cleaning, laundry service, concierge, business services, parking (fee), some pets allowed* 🖃 *AE, D, DC, MC, V* Ⓜ *Metro Center.*

$$$ 🏨 **The Madison.** Luxury and meticulous service prevail at the stately Madison, which is why the signatures of presidents, prime ministers, sultans, and kings fill the guest register. Deceptively contemporary on the outside, the 15-story building, four blocks from the White House, is an elegant blend of Georgian, Federal, and American Empire styles. Guest rooms maintain the conservative, formal atmosphere of the hotel; get one facing M Street for the best views. The staff is eager to accommodate special requests. ⊠ *1177 15th St. NW, Downtown 22205* ☎ *202/862–1600 or 800/424–8577* 🖷 *202/785–1255* ⊕ *www.themadisondc. com* 🛏 *311 rooms, 42 suites* ⚒ *2 restaurants, room service, minibars, some refrigerators, cable TV, in-room data ports, gym, massage, sauna, steam room, bar, concierge, business services, meeting rooms, parking (fee)* 🖃 *AE, DC, MC, V* Ⓜ *McPherson Square.*

$$$ 🏨 **Marriott at Metro Center.** Near the White House, the MCI Center, and the Smithsonian museums, the Marriott has numerous virtues, including a marble lobby, commissioned artwork, and the popular Metro Grille and Regatta Raw Bar—a handsome two-level mahogany, oak, brass, and marble facility that serves new American cuisine. Rooms are typical of others in the Marriott chain, but the indoor pool and health club are among the best in Washington. ⊠ *775 12th St. NW, Downtown 20005* ☎ *202/737–2200 or 800/228–9290* 🖷 *202/347–5886* ⊕ *www.marriott.com* 🛏 *453 rooms, 3 suites* ⚒ *2 restaurants, room service, cable TV with movies, in-room broadband, indoor pool, health club, bar, dry cleaning, laundry service, concierge, concierge floor, business services, meeting rooms, parking (fee)* 🖃 *AE, D, DC, MC, V* Ⓜ *Metro Center.*

$$$ 🏨 **Renaissance Mayflower Hotel.** This hallmark of Washington's luxury hotels opened in 1925 for Calvin Coolidge's inauguration. Franklin Delano Roosevelt wrote, "We have nothing to fear but fear itself" in Suite 776, and J. Edgar Hoover ate here at the same table every day for 20 years. The Mayflower's two-level lobby with its block-long parade of chandeliers is a magnificent neoclassic public space. Rooms are elegant, though on the small side; marble bathrooms include Bath and Body Works products, and rooms on the concierge floor have added luxuries such as Italian linens and robes and slippers. Contemporary Mediterranean cuisine is served at the Café Promenade restaurant amid silver, crystal, and flower arrangements. ✉ *1127 Connecticut Ave. NW, Downtown 20036* ☎ *202/347–3000 or 800/228–7697* ⊟ *202/776–9182* ⊕ *www.marriott.com* ➥ *657 rooms, 74 suites* ⚲ *Restaurant, room service, minibars, cable TV with movies and video games, Wi-Fi, gym, bar, babysitting, dry cleaning, laundry service, concierge, concierge floor, business services, parking (fee)* ⊟ *AE, D, DC, MC, V* Ⓜ *Farragut North.*

$$–$$$ 🏨 **Morrison-Clark Inn.** The elegant merging of two 1864 Victorian town houses, this inn (the only inn in D.C. listed on the National Register of Historic Places) functioned as the Soldiers', Sailors', Marines', and Airmen's Club in the early 1900s. The antiques-filled public rooms have marble fireplaces, bay windows, 14-foot pier mirrors, and porch access, and one house has an ornate Chinese porch from 1917. Rooms have neoclassic, French country, or Victorian furnishings, and six have fireplaces. American cuisine with Southern and other regional accents is served at the inn's highly regarded restaurant, which has an outstanding wine selection. Wireless access is complimentary throughout the hotel. ✉ *1015 L St. NW, Downtown 20001* ☎ *202/898–1200 or 800/332–7898* ⊟ *202/289–8576* ⊕ *www.morrisonclark.com* ➥ *42 rooms, 13 suites* ⚲ *Restaurant, room service, minibars, cable TV, Wi-Fi, gym, dry cleaning, laundry service, concierge, business services, parking (fee)* ⊟ *AE, D, DC, MC, V* ⦿ *CP* Ⓜ *Metro Center.*

$–$$$ 🏨 **Washington Renaissance Hotel.** Close to the Washington Convention Center and MCI Center, the Renaissance offers extensive business services and guest rooms with special mattresses and linens to help you get a good night's rest. The hotel includes a 10,000-square-foot fitness center and indoor lap pool. The casual restaurant serves regional American food; the Presidents Sports Bar is decorated with black-and-white photos of U.S. presidents at play; and there's a Starbuck's in the lobby. ✉ *999 Ninth St. NW, Downtown 20001* ☎ *202/898–9000 or 800/228–9290* ⊟ *202/289–0947* ⊕ *www.marriott.com* ➥ *794 rooms, 13 suites* ⚲ *2 restaurants, snack bar, room service, cable TV with movies, in-room broadband, indoor pool, health club, 2 bars, babysitting, laundry service, concierge, business services, parking (fee), some pets allowed* ⊟ *AE, D, DC, MC, V* Ⓜ *Gallery Place/Chinatown.*

$$ 🏨 **Hotel Helix.** In the District's Logan Circle neighborhood, the Helix combines attitude and colorful hospitality. The theme here is fame, with blow-ups of pop culture figures ranging from Martin Luther King Jr. to Little Richard. Lava lamps, psychedelic prints, and other objects create a back-to-1965 effect. Some suites have bunk beds and flat-screen TVs with Nintendo and Web TV. Wireless access and an evening champagne hour are included. The Helix Lounge serves American comfort food such as grilled cheese sandwiches. ✉ *1430 Rhode Island Ave. NW, Downtown 20002* ☎ *202/462–9001 or 800/706–1202* ⊟ *202/332–3519* ⊕ *www.hotelhelix.com* ➥ *160 rooms, 18 suites* ⚲ *Restaurant, room service, cable TV with video games, Wi-Fi, gym, bar, concierge, busi-*

ness center, meeting rooms, parking (fee), some pets allowed ☰ *AE, D, DC, MC, V* Ⓜ *McPherson Square.*

$–$$ 🏨 **Henley Park Hotel.** A Tudor-style building adorned with gargoyles, this National Historic Trust hotel has the cozy charm of an English country house. Rooms, decorated with Edwardian-style furnishings, are amply fitted with modern amenities. ■ TIP➡ **Complimentary sedan service is provided to all Washington locations weekday mornings, and afternoon tea is offered at 4 PM.** The highly acclaimed Coeur de Lion restaurant serves regional American dishes. ✉ *926 Massachusetts Ave. NW, Downtown 20001* ☎ *202/638–5200 or 800/222–8474* 🖷 *202/638–6740* ⊕ *www. henleypark.com* 🛏 *96 rooms, 17 suites* ♨ *Restaurant, room service, in-room safes, minibars, cable TV, in-room data ports, bar, business services, parking (fee), some pets allowed* ☰ *AE, D, DC, MC, V* Ⓜ *Metro Center or Gallery Place/Chinatown.*

★ $–$$ 🏨 **Lincoln Suites.** Although *suites* is a term used a bit liberally to describe this hotel, Lincoln Suites does offer large efficiency rooms with full or partial kitchens, vanity areas, and coffeemakers, irons, and hair dryers. The hotel's downtown location and low rates make it an excellent value. Evening cookies, breakfast pastries, and complimentary newspapers are included. ✉ *1823 L St. NW, Downtown 20036* ☎ *202/223–4320 or 800/424–2970* 🖷 *202/223–8546* ⊕ *www.lincolnhotels.com* 🛏 *99 rooms* ♨ *2 restaurants, kitchenettes, cable TV with movies, laundry facilities, business services, parking (fee), some pets allowed* ☰ *AE, D, DC, MC, V* ¶⊙¶ *CP* Ⓜ *Farragut North or Farragut West.*

$–$$ 🏨 **Wyndham Washington, D.C.** The spectacular atrium lobby stretches 12 floors, with the best rooms facing in rather than toward the street. The tastefully designed rooms come with pillow-top mattresses, ergonomic work chairs, and marble bathrooms with shower massagers. Overlooking the atrium, the Verandah restaurant serves modern American cuisine, including excellent seafood. Although the surrounding area lacks personality, the hotel is convenient for business travelers who want to be near the White House, four blocks away. ✉ *1400 M St. NW, Downtown 20005* ☎ *202/429–1700 or 800/996–3426* 🖷 *202/785–0786* ⊕ *www.wyndham.com* 🛏 *387 rooms, 13 suites* ♨ *2 restaurants, room service, in-room safes, cable TV with movies and video games, in-room broadband, gym, sauna, bar, lobby lounge, dry cleaning, laundry service, concierge, business services, parking (fee)* ☰ *AE, D, DC, MC, V* Ⓜ *McPherson Square.*

$ 🏨 **Washington Doubletree Hotel.** Just off Scott Circle, the Doubletree offers spacious guest rooms with comfortable beds, well-equipped workstations, CD players, coffeemakers, and robes. 15 Ria, the hotel's American bistro, brings a New York sensibility to the neighborhood. The hotel offers complimentary car service and lies only six blocks from the White House. ✉ *1515 Rhode Island Ave. NW, Downtown 20005* ☎ *202/232–7000 or 800/222–8733* 🖷 *202/332–8436* ⊕ *www.doubletree. com* 🛏 *197 rooms, 23 suites* ♨ *Restaurant, in-room safes, minibars, cable TV with movies and video games, in-room broadband, Wi-Fi, gym, concierge, business services, meeting rooms, parking (fee)* ☰ *AE, D, DC, MC, V* Ⓜ *Dupont Circle.*

¢ ▦ **Hostelling International–Washington D.C.** This well-kept hostel has a living room with a big-screen TV, a communal kitchen, a small gift shop, and Internet access. Rooms are generally dormitory-style, without private bathrooms, but families can have their own room if the hostel is not full. Towels and linens are included in the rates, as is continental breakfast. ■ TIP➔ **The maximum stay is 14 days, and reservations are highly recommended.** College-age travelers predominate, and July and August are the busiest months. ✉ *1009 11th St. NW, Downtown 20001* ☎ *202/737–2333* ♻ *202/737–1508* ⊕ *www.hiwashingtondc.org* ⇝ *286 beds without bath* ♻ *Laundry facilities; no room phones, no room TVs, no smoking* ▤ *MC, V* Ⓜ *Metro Center.*

¢ ▦ **Hotel Harrington.** One of Washington's oldest continuously operating hotels, the Harrington doesn't offer many frills, but it does have low prices and a location right in the center of everything. It's very popular with springtime high school bus tours and with families who like the two-bedroom, two-bathroom deluxe suites. ✉ *436 11th St. NW, Downtown 20004* ☎ *202/628–8140 or 800/424–8532* ♻ *202/347–3924* ⊕ *www.hotel-harrington.com* ⇝ *216 rooms, 26 suites* ♻ *3 restaurants, room service, some refrigerators, cable TV, bar, laundry facilities, meeting rooms, parking (fee), some pets allowed* ▤ *AE, D, DC, MC, V* Ⓜ *Metro Center.*

Dupont Circle

$$$ ▦ **Marriott Residence Inn.** It's remarkable that a commercial chain can feel so cozy, but this Residence Inn does just that by offering a small fireplace sitting room right off the lobby, where a cookie jar beckons. The hotel has studios and one- and two-bedroom suites, excellent for business travelers or families. An evening reception is offered with complimentary snacks, and Mimi's American Bistro next door has an innovative bar with piano and cabaret-style singing nightly. ✉ *2120 P St. NW, Dupont Circle 20037* ☎ *202/466–6800 or 800/331–3131* ♻ *202/466–9630* ⊕ *www.marriott.com/wasri* ⇝ *107 suites* ♻ *Restaurant, room service, kitchenettes, cable TV with movies and video games, in-room data ports, gym, laundry facilities, parking (fee)* ▤ *AE, D, DC, MC, V* ¶⊙¶ *CP* Ⓜ *Dupont Circle.*

$$–$$$ ▦ **Jurys Washington Hotel.** The Irish-run Jurys chain has breathed new life into this older building on Dupont Circle. The shining white marble lobby contrasts somewhat with the older pinstripe decor of guest rooms, which are still a good value given the hotel's excellent location. Rooms have writing desks, coffeemakers, hair dryers, and complimentary newspaper delivery. Biddy Mulligan's Bar draws a festive Guinness-guzzling crowd. ✉ *1500 New Hampshire Ave. NW, Dupont Circle 20036* ☎ *202/483–6000 or 800/423–6953* ♻ *202/328–3265* ⊕ *www.jurysdoyle.com* ⇝ *308 rooms, 6 suites* ♻ *Restaurant, room service, in-room safes, cable TV with movies, in-room data ports, gym, bar, dry cleaning, laundry service, concierge, business services, parking (fee)* ▤ *AE, D, DC, MC, V* Ⓜ *Dupont Circle.*

$$–$$$ ▦ **Westin Embassy Row.** The childhood home of Al Gore, this formal Westin has an English hunt-club theme and complimentary butler serv-

ice. The intimate guest rooms are furnished with brocade draperies and reproduction antiques from late-1800s Washington. The Westin is near Dupont Circle, Georgetown, and the Kennedy Center. ⊠ *2100 Massachusetts Ave. NW, Dupont Circle 20008* ☎ *202/293–2100 or 888/625–5144* 🖷 *202/293–0641* ⊕ *www.starwoodhotels.com/westin* 🛏 *160 rooms, 46 suites* ⚘ *Restaurant, room service, in-room safes, minibars, cable TV, in-room broadband, gym, massage, sauna, bar, laundry service, concierge, business services, meeting rooms, parking (fee), some pets allowed (fee)* ☰ *AE, D, DC, MC, V* Ⓜ *Dupont Circle.*

★ **$–$$$** 🏨 **Hotel Madera.** The unique Hotel Madera sits in a quiet part of town southwest of Dupont Circle. Innovative guest rooms with art nouveau styling have CD players, complimentary high-speed Internet access, minibars stocked with martini kits, and coffeemakers with Starbucks coffee. Extra-spacious "specialty rooms" are decorated in rich earthy tones with finer furnishings, although the bathrooms remain small. The adjoining Firefly restaurant is an American bistro

> **WORD OF MOUTH**
>
> "I stayed at Hotel Madera in January. I was very pleased with the hotel and my room, and the location was good too. It's a short walk (2 blocks?) to Dupont Circle. Don't expect a traditional décor—it's a little artsy-funky but still very comfortable."
>
> –GoAway

with a floor-to-ceiling birchlike tree smack in the middle. ⊠ *1310 New Hampshire Ave. NW, Dupont Circle 20036* ☎ *202/296–7600 or 800/368–5691* 🖷 *202/293–2476* ⊕ *www.hotelmadera.com* 🛏 *82 rooms* ⚘ *Restaurant, in-room safes, some kitchenettes, minibars, cable TV, in-room broadband, bar, business services, meeting rooms, parking (fee), some pets allowed* ☰ *AE, D, DC, MC, V* Ⓜ *Dupont Circle.*

★ **$–$$$** 🏨 **Hotel Rouge.** This gay-friendly postmodern hotel bathed in red succeeds at bringing Florida's South Beach club scene to D.C. Guest rooms, some with specialty themes such as "chill, chow, or chat," are decorated with swank eye-catching furniture that makes them seem like an extension of the hip lobby lounge, where the bartenders are busy concocting sweet new drinks. Bar Rouge, the cocktail lounge, attracts club-going denizens at all hours. ⊠ *1315 16th St. NW, Dupont Circle 20036* ☎ *202/232–8000 or 800/738–1202* 🖷 *202/667–9827* ⊕ *www.rougehotel.com* 🛏 *137 rooms* ⚘ *Restaurant, room service, in-room safes, some kitchenettes, minibars, refrigerators, cable TV with video games, Wi-Fi, health club, bar, concierge, business services, parking (fee), some pets allowed* ☰ *AE, D, DC, MC, V* Ⓜ *Dupont Circle.*

$$ 🏨 **Churchill Hotel.** The historic beaux arts building in which the Churchill lies offers comfort and elegance right outside Dupont Circle. Spacious rooms have a small work and sitting area, and the building's hilltop location means that many guest rooms have excellent views of Washington. The staff goes out of its way to be helpful, and complimentary morning coffee is offered in the lounge. ⊠ *1914 Connecticut Ave. NW, Dupont Circle 20009* ☎ *202/797–2000 or 800/424–2464* 🖷 *202/462–0944* ⊕ *www.thechurchillhotel.com* 🛏 *70 rooms, 64 suites* ⚘ *Restaurant, room service, some kitchenettes, minibars, cable TV, Wi-Fi, gym,* *bar, dry cleaning, laundry service, concierge, business services, parking (fee), some pets allowed* ☐ *AE, D, DC, MC, V* Ⓜ *Dupont Circle.*

★ **$-$$** 🏨 **Topaz Hotel.** A night at the Topaz is akin to a slumber party at a New Age dance club. The hotel's mystic theme is expressed through the colorful walls and art, allusions to enlightenment, and the "power shakes" served in the morning. Creatively themed guest rooms may come with exercise equipment to boost your energy, or yoga mats to connect with your spirituality. The popular (and loud) Topaz Bar draws people from all over town. ✉ *1733 N St. NW, Dupont Circle 20036* ☎ *202/393–3000 or 800/775–1202* 🖷 *202/785–9581* ⊕ *www.topazhotel.com* 🛏 *99 rooms* ♢ *Restaurant, in-room safes, minibars, cable TV with movies, in-room data ports, bar, dry cleaning, laundry service, business services, meeting rooms, parking (fee), some pets allowed* ☐ *AE, D, DC, MC, V* Ⓜ *Dupont Circle.*

¢-$$ 🏨 **Courtyard Washington/Northwest.** Excellent views of the skyline can be seen from many guest rooms here because of its upper Connecticut Avenue elevation. In the compact but comfortable lobby, complimentary cookies and coffee are served each afternoon. Redesigned rooms have black-and-white photos, two-piece desks with executive chairs, and excellent mattresses with high-quality linens and soft comforters. ✉ *1900 Connecticut Ave. NW, Dupont Circle 20009* ☎ *202/332–9300 or 800/321–2211* 🖷 *202/328–7039* ⊕ *www.marriott.com* 🛏 *147 rooms* ♢ *Restaurant, deli, room service, in-room safes, cable TV with movies, in-room broadband, bar, pool, gym, dry cleaning, laundry facilities, laundry service, business services, meeting rooms, parking (fee)* ☐ *AE, D, DC, MC, V* Ⓜ *Dupont Circle.*

★ **¢-$** 🏨 **Hotel Tabard Inn.** Three Victorian town houses were consolidated to form the Tabard, one of the oldest hotels in D.C. Although the wooden floorboards creak and room sizes vary considerably (some share bathrooms), the dimly lighted hotel feels like an old-world inn, with alluring nooks and crannies inside and a brick-walled garden outside. The Tabard Inn's fireside bar may be one of the city's coziest winter retreats, and the restaurant remains a favorite among locals. Free passes are provided to the nearby YMCA, which has extensive facilities. ✉ *1739 N St. NW, Dupont Circle 20036* ☎ *202/785–1277* 🖷 *202/785–6173* ⊕ *www.tabardinn.com* 🛏 *40 rooms, 25 with bath* ♢ *Restaurant, in-room data ports, Wi-Fi, bar, lobby lounge, laundry facilities, business services, some pets allowed; no TV in some rooms* ☐ *AE, D, DC, MC, V* ⑩ *CP* Ⓜ *Dupont Circle.*

¢ 🏨 **Windsor Inn.** Near tree-lined New Hampshire Avenue, this bed-and-breakfast is in one of Washington's most attractive neighborhoods. The Phillips Collection and the restaurants and shops of Dupont Circle lie within six blocks. The three-story inn is actually two buildings, and neither has an elevator. Rooms are tastefully decorated but small (with showers only), and have some amenities expected of larger hotels, such as hair dryers and a morning newspaper. In the evening, sherry and snacks are served in the downstairs lobby. ✉ *1842 16th St. NW, Dupont Circle 20009* ☎ *202/667–0300 or 800/423–9111* 🖷 *202/667–4503* 🛏 *36 rooms, 10 suites* ♢ *Some refrigerators, cable TV, lobby lounge, library, business services* ☐ *AE, DC, MC, V* ⑩ *CP* Ⓜ *Dupont Circle.*

Georgetown

☺ $$$$
Fodor'sChoice
★

🖼 **Four Seasons Hotel.** Having completed a whopping $40 million renovation in 2005, the Four Seasons has reasserted its role as Washington's leading hotel. Impeccable service and a wealth of amenities have long made this a favorite with celebrities, hotel connoisseurs, and families alike. Luxurious, ultramodern rooms offer heavenly beds, flatscreen digital TVs with DVD players, and French limestone or marble baths with separate showers and sunken tubs. A 2,000-piece original art collection graces the walls, and a walk through the corridors seems like a visit to a wing of the MoMA or the Met. The formal Seasons restaurant offers traditional dishes with an elegant twist, as well as a popular Sunday brunch. The sophisticated spa here is one of the best in town. ✉ 2800 Pennsylvania Ave. NW, Georgetown 20007 ☎ 202/342–0444 or 800/332–3442 🖨 202/944–2076 ⊕ www.fourseasons.com/washington 🛏 160 rooms, 51 suites ⚭ Restaurant, room service, in-room safes, minibars, cable TV, in-room broadband, pool, health club, bar, lobby lounge, children's programs (ages 5–16), concierge, business services, parking (fee), some pets allowed ⊟ AE, D, DC, MC, V Ⓜ Foggy Bottom.

> **BABY ON BOARD**
>
> The Four Seasons goes out of its way to make children feel special, offering them a welcome gift, age-specific games, toys, and reading material, and complimentary baby and children's toiletries.

$$$$ 🖼 **Ritz-Carlton Georgetown.** D.C.'s second Ritz-Carlton is smaller than its Foggy Bottom sister and a complete departure from the ornateness typical of the chain. Opened in 2003, this understated yet sophisticated Ritz is adjacent to the C&O Canal and built on the site of Georgetown's 1932 incinerator: the original smokestack's still here. The contemporary hotel is a stone's throw from the waterfront and a block from M Street, Georgetown's main shopping street. Guest rooms are connected by brick hallways with carefully chosen pieces from regional American artists. The upper-level rooms and suites facing south have amazing views of the Potomac, and all have feather duvets, goose-down pillows, marble baths, and access to a personal concierge. The hotel's sexy Fahrenheit Restaurant serves contemporary American cuisine. ✉ 3100 South St. NW, Georgetown 20037 ☎ 202/912–4200 or 800/241–3333 🖨 202/912–4199 ⊕ www.ritzcarlton.com/hotels/georgetown 🛏 57 rooms, 29 suites ⚭ Restaurant, room service, in-room safes, minibars, cable TV, in-room data ports, health club, bar, lobby lounge, cinema, laundry service, concierge, meeting rooms, parking (fee) ⊟ AE, D, DC, MC, V.

$$–$$$$ 🖼 **The Melrose Hotel.** This European-style boutique hotel has a convenient address between Georgetown and the White House. Bellboys in top hats greet you in the lobby, which connects to the Landmark restaurant and intimate Library bar. The gracious rooms have desks in their own nooks, small marble bathrooms, and high-tech amenities. Rooms facing K Street are quieter. ✉ 2430 Pennsylvania Ave. NW, Georgetown 20037 ☎ 202/955–6400 or 800/635–7673 🖨 202/775–

8489 ⊕ *www.melrosehotel.com* ⇗ *200 rooms, 40 suites* ⚭ *Restaurant, room service, in-room safes, minibars, cable TV with movies, Wi-Fi, gym, bar, laundry service, concierge, business services, parking (fee)* ▤ *AE, D, DC, MC, V.*

$–$$$ ▥ **Washington Suites.** Just outside the center of Georgetown, this older all-suites accommodation offers families and long-term-stay travelers an alternative to standard hotel rooms. Each suite has a fully equipped kitchen, a small living and dining area, and a separate bedroom and bath. Fresh pastries, juices, and cereal are served each morning in the breakfast room. Many of the staff members have worked at the hotel for years and know regular guests by name. ⊠ *2500 Pennsylvania Ave. NW, Georgetown 20037* ☎ *202/333–8060 or 877/736–2500* 🖷 *202/338–3818* ⊕ *www.washingtonsuitesgeorgetown.com* ⇗ *124 suites* ⚭ *Kitchens, cable TV with movies and video games, in-room broadband, gym, laundry facilities, parking (fee)* ▤ *AE, D, DC, MC, V* ⦿| *CP.*

$–$$ ▥ **Georgetown Suites.** If you consider standard hotel rooms cramped and overpriced, you'll find this establishment a welcome surprise. Consisting of two buildings a block apart in the heart of Georgetown, the hotel has suites of varying sizes. All have fully equipped kitchens and separate sitting rooms, and include free local calls and continental breakfast. ⊠ *1111 30th St. NW, Georgetown 20007* ☎ *202/298–7800 or 800/348–7203* 🖷 *202/333–5792* ⊕ *www.georgetownsuites.com* ⇗ *216 suites* ⚭ *Kitchens, cable TV, in-room broadband, gym, dry cleaning, laundry facilities, laundry service, parking (fee)* ▤ *AE, D, DC, MC, V* ⦿| *CP* Ⓜ *Foggy Bottom.*

☾ **$–$$** ▥ **Holiday Inn Georgetown.** On the edge of Georgetown, this Holiday Inn is a short walk from dining, shopping, Dumbarton Oaks, the National Cathedral, and Georgetown University. Many guest rooms offer a scenic view of the Washington skyline. There's complimentary coffee every morning in the lobby, and free shuttle service to the Metro. ■ TIP➔ **Kids under 12 eat free, and rooms offer video games.** ⊠ *2101 Wisconsin Ave. NW, Georgetown 20007* ☎ *202/338–4600 or 877/477–4674* 🖷 *202/338–4458* ⊕ *www.higeorgetown.com* ⇗ *281 rooms, 4 suites* ⚭ *Restaurant, room service, cable TV with movies and video games, in-room broadband, pool, gym, bar, laundry facilities, business services, meeting rooms, parking (fee)* ▤ *AE, D, DC, MC, V* Ⓜ *Foggy Bottom.*

$ ▥ **Georgetown Inn.** Reminiscent of a gentleman's sporting club, this quiet, Federal-era, redbrick hotel seems like something from the 1700s. The spacious guest rooms are decorated in a colonial style. The hotel, in the heart of historic Georgetown, lies near shopping, dining, galleries, and theaters. Free passes to a nearby fitness center are provided. The publike Daily Grill restaurant serves American cuisine. ⊠ *1310 Wisconsin Ave. NW, Georgetown 20007* ☎ *202/333–8900 or 800/424–2979* 🖷 *202/625–1744* ⊕ *www.georgetowncollection.com* ⇗ *86 rooms, 10 suites* ⚭ *Restaurant, room service, cable TV, in-room data ports, gym, bar, parking (fee)* ▤ *AE, D, DC, MC, V* Ⓜ *Foggy Bottom.*

★ **$** ▥ **Latham Hotel.** Many of the small, beautifully decorated rooms at this elegant boutique hotel offer treetop views of the Potomac River and the C&O Canal. The polished-brass-and-glass lobby leads to Citronelle, one of the city's most acclaimed (and expensive) French restaurants. You'll find a number of Washington's most illustrious personalities here for dinner, with many diplomats overnighting at the hotel. Be prepared for occasional street noise in some of the rooms as the Latham lies on Georgetown's fashionable main avenue. ⊠ *3000 M St. NW, Georgetown 20007* ☎ *202/726–5000 or 800/368–5922* ⊟ *202/ 337–4250* ⊕ *www.georgetowncollection.com* ☞ *122 rooms, 21 suites* �ዿ *Restaurant, room service, cable TV with movies, in-room broadband, pool, bar, business services, parking (fee)* ▭ *AE, D, DC, MC, V* Ⓜ *Foggy Bottom.*

Southwest

☾ **$–$$$** 🖽 **L'Enfant Plaza.** An oasis of calm above a Metro stop and a shopping mall, the L'Enfant Plaza lies two blocks from the Smithsonian museums and has spectacular views of the river, the Capitol, and the monuments. Business travelers in particular take advantage of its proximity to several government agencies (USDA, USPS, and DOT). All rooms have coffeemakers, and both bathrooms and bedrooms have TVs and phones. ⊠ *480 L'Enfant Plaza SW, Southwest 20024* ☎ *202/484–1000 or 800/ 235–6397* ⊟ *202/646–4456* ⊕ *www.lenfantplazahotel.com* ☞ *348 rooms, 22 suites* �ዿ *Restaurant, room service, cable TV, in-room data ports, indoor-outdoor pool, gym, 2 bars, dry cleaning, concierge, business services, parking (fee), some pets allowed* ▭ *AE, D, DC, MC, V* Ⓜ *L'Enfant Plaza.*

☾ **$–$$** 🖽 **Best Western Capitol Skyline.** Who could believe that a Best Western, built in the 1960s near the I-395 highway, would make a 21st-century comeback? Yet the Capitol Skyline has done just that. The hotel is a cool retro embodiment of its earlier heritage, with a gleaming lobby, '60s-style diner, and inviting rooms (some with views of the U.S. Capitol). Children staying here will enjoy the summertime pool, and the restaurant offers a kids' menu. The hotel lies in an area considered a last frontier in Washington's development, and you will need to make a quick drive, take a cab, or hop on the Metro to reach major tourist attractions. ⊠ *10 I St. SW, Southwest 20024* ☎ *202/488–7500 or 800/458– 7500* ⊟ *202/488–0790* ⊕ *www.bestwesterncapitolskyline.com* ☞ *197 rooms, 6 suites* �ዿ *Restaurant, in-room safes, cable TV, Wi-Fi, outdoor pool, laundry service, business services, parking (fee)* ▭ *AE, D, DC, MC, V.* Ⓜ *Navy Yard.*

☾ **$–$$** 🖽 **Holiday Inn Capitol.** One block from the National Air and Space Museum, this family-friendly hotel is also well equipped for business travelers, including free wireless access. Newly renovated rooms have upgraded beds, granite vanities in the bathrooms, and include coffeemakers and hair dryers. The downtown sightseeing trolley stops here, and you can buy discount tickets for NASM's IMAX movies at the front desk. Kids under 19 stay free, and those under 12 eat for free at Smithson's Restaurant. ⊠ *550 C St. SW, Southwest 20024* ☎ *202/ 479–4000 or 877/477–4674* ⊟ *202/488–4627* ⊕ *www.holidayinncapitol. com* ☞ *532 rooms, 13 suites* �ዿ *Restaurant, deli, room service, cable TV, in-room broadband, Wi-Fi, pool, gym, bar, laundry facilities, business services, meeting rooms, parking (fee)* ▭ *AE, D, DC, MC, V* Ⓜ *L'Enfant Plaza.*

West End & Foggy Bottom

$$$$
Fodor'sChoice
★

🏨 **Ritz-Carlton Washington, D.C.** The more traditional of Washington's two Ritz-Carltons, this elegant hotel pampers guests with formal, attentive service and luxurious amenities. Deluxe rooms feature separate showers and marble tubs, portable phones, and beds with goose down pillows, Egyptian cotton linens, and nonallergenic pillows—in fact, it would be difficult to find more comfortable beds than those at the Ritz. Hotel guests have lobby access to the 100,000-square-foot Sports Club/ LA for a fee. The Grill serves classic American cuisine and one of the best Sunday champagne brunches in the city. ✉ *1150 22nd St. NW, Foggy Bottom 20037* ☎ *202/835–0500 or 800/241–3333* 🖷 *202/835–1588* ⊕ *www.ritzcarlton.com/hotels/washington_dc* ⟿ *267 rooms, 33 suites* ⌂ *Restaurant, room service, in-room safes, minibars, cable TV with movies and video games, in-room broadband, indoor pool, health club, hair salon, massage, spa, steam room, basketball, bar, lobby lounge, babysitting, concierge, concierge floor, business services, parking (fee)* 🖃 *AE, D, DC, MC, V* Ⓜ *Foggy Bottom/GWU.*

☾ $$$

🏨 **Fairmont Washington.** The large glassed-in lobby and about a third of the bright, spacious rooms overlook the Fairmont's central courtyard and gardens. Rooms are comfortable, if not the city's most modern. The informal Juniper restaurant serves mid-Atlantic fare and has courtyard dining; there's a champagne brunch on Sunday in the Colonnade room. ■ TIP➔ **The health club is one of the best in the city.** Families have access to the pool, kids' menus and crayons in the restaurant, and a babysitting referral service; the Fairmont also offers family packages, such as the "Panda Package" with a trip to visit the pandas at the National Zoo. ✉ *2401 M St. NW, Foggy Bottom 20037* ☎ *202/429–2400 or 877/222–2266* 🖷 *202/457–5010* ⊕ *www.fairmont.com* ⟿ *406 rooms, 9 suites* ⌂ *Restaurant, café, room service, in-room safes, minibars, cable TV with movies and video games, in-room broadband, indoor pool, health club, racquetball, bar, lobby lounge, concierge, concierge floor, business services, parking (fee), some pets allowed* 🖃 *AE, D, DC, MC, V* Ⓜ *Foggy Bottom/GWU.*

$$–$$$

🏨 **Doubletree Guest Suites.** Among the row houses on this stretch of New Hampshire Avenue, you might not realize at first how close you are to the Kennedy Center and Georgetown. This all-suites hotel has a tiny lobby, but its roomy one- and two-bedroom suites have full kitchens and living-dining areas with desks, dining tables, and sofa beds. The rooftop pool provides a place to relax after summertime sightseeing. You receive chocolate-chip cookies upon arrival. ✉ *801 New Hampshire Ave. NW, Foggy Bottom 20037* ☎ *202/785–2000 or 800/222–8733* 🖷 *202/785–9485* ⊕ *www.doubletree.com* ⟿ *105 suites* ⌂ *Room service, kitchens, cable TV, Wi-Fi, pool, dry cleaning, laundry facilities, parking (fee), some pets allowed* 🖃 *AE, D, DC, MC, V* Ⓜ *Foggy Bottom/GWU.*

☾ $$–$$$

🏨 **Embassy Suites.** Plants cascade over balconies beneath a skylight in this modern hotel's atrium, which is filled with classical columns, plaster lions, wrought-iron lanterns, waterfalls, and tall palms. Within walking distance of Georgetown, the Kennedy Center, and Dupont Circle, the suites here are suitable for both business travelers and families. Beverages are complimentary at the nightly manager's reception, and the rate includes cooked-to-order breakfast. There's a kids' corner with movies and games, and the Italian restaurant, Panevino, serves lunch and dinner. ⊠ *1250 22nd St. NW, West End 20037* ☎ *202/857–3388 or 800/ 362–2779* 🖷 *202/293–3173* ⊕ *www.embassysuites.com* ⟳ *318 suites* ⟑ *Restaurant, room service, microwaves, refrigerators, cable TV with movies and video games, in-room data ports, indoor pool, gym, bar, laundry service, business services, parking (fee)* ▭ *AE, D, DC, MC, V* ⏅ *BP* Ⓜ *Foggy Bottom/GWU or Dupont Circle.*

$–$$$ 🏨 **One Washington Circle Hotel.** Given its location near the State Department and George Washington University, this all-suites business hotel is a relative bargain. The suites have modern, vibrant furnishings with separate bedrooms, living rooms, dining areas, and walk-out balconies; some have full kitchens. The American-style Circle Bistro is popular with locals, who come for the food and live music. ⊠ *1 Washington Circle NW, Foggy Bottom 20037* ☎ *202/872–1680 or 800/424–9671* 🖷 *202/ 887–4989* ⊕ *www.thecirclehotel.com* ⟳ *151 suites* ⟑ *Restaurant, room service, kitchens, cable TV with movies and video games, in-room broadband, pool, gym, bar, dry cleaning, laundry facilities, laundry service, business services, meeting rooms, parking (fee)* ▭ *AE, D, DC, MC, V* Ⓜ *Foggy Bottom/GWU.*

★ $–$$$ 🏨 **St. Gregory.** Once the FCC building, the handsome St. Gregory caters to business and leisure travelers who appreciate the spacious accommodations here that include fully stocked kitchens. All rooms include turndown service, a newspaper and shoe shine. The modern lobby, which has a sculpture of Marilyn Monroe in her *Seven Year Itch* pose, connects to the M Street Bar & Grill. ⊠ *2033 M St. NW, West End 20036* ☎ *202/530–3600 or 800/829–5034* 🖷 *202/466–6770* ⊕ *www. stgregoryhotelwdc.com* ⟳ *54 rooms, 100 suites* ⟑ *Restaurant, room service, some kitchens, cable TV with movies and video games, in-room broadband, gym, laundry service, concierge, concierge floor, parking (fee)* ▭ *AE, D, DC, MC, V* Ⓜ *Dupont Circle.*

$$ 🏨 **State Plaza Hotel.** No Washington hotel gets you quicker access to the State Department, which sits across the street, and the Kennedy Center is only a few minutes' walk away. Guests receive a complimentary newspaper, shoe shine, and continental breakfast, and can make free local calls from their rooms. There is nothing distinguishing about the lobby, but the spacious guestrooms have kitchenettes and lighted dressing tables, and the hotel staff is friendly and attentive. Nightly turndown service is provided. ⊠ *2117 E St. NW, Foggy Bottom 20037* ☎ *202/861– 8200 or 800/424–2859* 🖷 *202/659–8601* ⊕ *www.stateplaza.com* ⟳ *205 rooms, 25 suites* ⟑ *Room service, kitchenettes, cable TV, in-room data ports, gym, dry cleaning, business services, parking (fee)* ▭ *AE, D, DC, MC, V* ⏅ *CP* Ⓜ *Foggy Bottom/GWU.*

★ $ 🏨 **George Washington University Inn.** This boutique hotel is in a quiet neighborhood a few blocks from the Kennedy Center, the State Department, and George Washington University. Wrought-iron gates lead through a courtyard to the hotel's front entrance, where beveled glass doors open onto a small lobby with a gray marble floor. Rooms, which vary in size and configuration, have colonial-style furniture and complimentary high-speed Internet access. Guests also receive free entry to the nearby Bally Total Fitness club. ⊠ *824 New Hampshire Ave. NW, Foggy Bottom 20037* ☎ *202/337–6620 or 800/426–4455* 🖷 *202/298–7499* ⊕ *www.gwuinn.com* ⤴ *64 rooms, 31 suites* ⌂ *Restaurant, room service, in-room safes, some kitchenettes, microwaves, refrigerators, cable TV with movies and video games, in-room data ports, Wi-Fi, bar, dry cleaning, laundry facilities, meeting rooms, parking (fee)* ▤ *AE, DC, MC, V* Ⓜ *Foggy Bottom/GWU.*

Woodley Park

� **\$\$\$** ▦ **Marriott Wardman Park.** With more than 1,000 rooms, this indomitable redbrick Victorian structure dominates this pretty block on Connecticut Avenue. The Marriott enjoys spectacular views of Rock Creek Park, and is an easy walk to Adams-Morgan and the National Zoo. Guest rooms and public areas of the older eight-story section do not stray too far from typical Marriott styling. Rooms in the newer convention-ready main complex are more contemporary, with chrome-and-glass touches. The hotel offers kids' menus and crayons in the restaurant, has two pools, and can arrange for a babysitter. ⊠ *2660 Woodley Rd. NW, Woodley Park 20008* ☎ *202/328–2000 or 800/228–9290* 🖷 *202/234–0015* ⊕ *www.wardmanpark.com* ⤴ *1,338 rooms, 125 suites* ⌂ *Restaurant, coffee shop, room service, cable TV with movies and video games, in-room broadband, pool, gym, spa, bar, pub, laundry service, concierge, business services, meeting rooms, convention center, parking (fee), some pets allowed* ▤ *AE, D, DC, MC, V* Ⓜ *Woodley Park/Zoo.*

\$\$\$ ▦ **Omni Shoreham Hotel.** An immense facility with seven ballrooms, this hotel has been host to the world's rich and famous since 1930, when its art deco–and–Renaissance-style lobby opened for business. It's still a busy place, with black-tie political events held in its famed Regency ballroom on many nights. Rooms have cherrywood furniture and marble-floor baths; the "Get Fit" rooms rejuvenate your heart with a portable treadmill, "Get Fit" kits (which include small hand weights, mat, and towel), and healthful snacks. The hotel is a moderate walk from Rock Creek Park, Adams-Morgan, and the National Zoo. ⊠ *2500 Calvert St. NW, Woodley Park 20008* ☎ *202/234–0700 or 800/843–6664* 🖷 *202/265–7972* ⊕ *www.omnihotels.com* ⤴ *836 rooms, 24 suites* ⌂ *Restaurant, snack bar, room service, minibars, cable TV with movies and video games, Wi-Fi, pool, health club, bar, shops, dry cleaning, laundry service, concierge, business services, parking (fee), some pets allowed* ▤ *AE, D, DC, MC, V* Ⓜ *Woodley Park/Zoo.*

★ **¢–\$** ▦ **Woodley Park Guest House.** This warm, peaceful B&B on a quiet residential street lies near the entrance to the Metro nearest the zoo and close to Adams-Morgan and Rock Creek Park. Antiques-filled rooms are individually decorated, and some have private baths, whereas others share them. Conversation between guests is encouraged at the communal breakfast, which includes a fresh fruit salad, cereal, yogurt, and homemade pastries. ▮ TIP➜ **A two-night minimum stay is required, with a few exceptions.** ⊠ *2647 Woodley Rd. NW, Woodley Park 20008* ☎ *202/ 667–0218 or 866/667–0218* 🖷 *202/667–1080* ⊕ *www. woodleyparkguesthouse.com* ⤴ *18 rooms, 11 with bath* ⌂ *Laundry* service, Wi-Fi, parking (fee); no room TVs, no kids under 12 ⊟ AE, MC, V ⃝⃝ CP Ⓜ Woodley Park/Zoo.

★ ¢ ⊞ **Adam's Inn.** This cozy bed-and-breakfast spreads through three residential town houses near Adams-Morgan, the zoo, and Dupont Circle. The Victorian-style rooms are small but comfortable. Many share baths, but those that do also have a sink in the room. A communal kitchen and limited garage parking are available. Rooms don't come with phones or TVs, but there are pay phones, cable TV, and free Wi-Fi in the public areas. A two-night stay is required on weekends. ✉ *1744 Lanier Pl. NW, Woodley Park 20009* ☎ *202/745–3600 or 800/578–6807* 🖷 *202/319–7958* ⊕ *www.adamsinn.com* ⊲ *26 rooms, 15 with bath* ⚬ *Laundry facilities, business services, parking (fee); no room phones, no room TVs* ⊟ *AE, D, DC, MC, V* ⃝⃝ *CP* Ⓜ *Woodley Park/Zoo.*

¢ ⊞ **Kalorama Guest House–Woodley Park.** Two elegantly restored Victorian town houses make for comfortable and convenient lodging near the National Cathedral. The cozy rooms, furnished with 19th-century antiques, vary in size. Those in search of a television, Wi-Fi, or a phone will need to visit one of the original house parlors, where sherry and tea are served in the afternoon. ✉ *2700 Cathedral Ave. NW, Woodley Park 20008* ☎ *202/328–0860* 🖷 *202/328–8730* ⊕ *www. kaloramaguesthouse.com* ⊲ *18 rooms, 12 with bath, 3 suites* ⚬ *Laundry facilities, Wi-Fi, parking (fee); no room phones, no room TVs* ⊟ *AE, D, DC, MC, V* ⃝⃝ *CP* Ⓜ *Woodley Park/Zoo.*

Suburban Maryland

$$$ ⊞ **Hyatt Regency Bethesda.** This hotel stands atop the Bethesda Metro station on Wisconsin Avenue, the main artery between Bethesda and Georgetown; downtown Washington is a 15-minute Metro ride away. Well-equipped guest rooms have sleigh beds and mahogany furnishings, as well as large workstations for business travelers. They also include 32-inch TVs and marble baths. The rooftop fitness center and indoor pool are welcome retreats from a busy day in the city. ✉ *1 Bethesda Metro Center, 7400 block of Wisconsin Ave., Bethesda, MD 20814* ☎ *301/657–1234 or 800/233–1234* 🖷 *301/657–6453* ⊕ *www.bethesda. hyatt.com* ⊲ *390 rooms, 5 suites* ⚬ *2 restaurants, room service, cable TV with movies, Wi-Fi, indoor pool, health club, bar, lobby lounge, laundry service, concierge, business services, meeting rooms, parking (fee)* ⊟ *AE, D, DC, MC, V* Ⓜ *Bethesda.*

$$–$$$ ⊞ **Marriott Residence Inn Bethesda Downtown.** In the heart of downtown Bethesda, this all-suites hotel caters primarily to business travelers who stay for several nights. But if you're looking for an affordable home-away-from-home, this is a sensible option. The comfortably (though slightly bland) furnished one- and two-bedroom suites come with fully equipped kitchens with a standard-size refrigerator and dishwasher, plates, and utensils. ■ TIP➔ **The many complimentary services include grocery shopping, a breakfast buffet, and evening cocktail and dessert receptions.** A number of restaurants are within walking distance. ✉ *7335 Wisconsin Ave., Bethesda, MD 20814* ☎ *301/718–0200 or 800/331–3131* 🖷 *301/718–0679 or 301/913–0197* ⊕ *www.residenceinnbethesdahotel. com* ⊲ *187 suites* ⚬ *Kitchens, cable TV with movies, in-room broad-*

band, pool, gym, sauna, laundry facilities, business services, parking (fee) ▤ *AE, D, DC, MC, V* ⏧ *BP.*

$–$$ ⊡ **Bethesda Court Hotel.** Bright burgundy awnings frame the entrance to this comfortable, intimate, three-story inn, where there's a lovely, well-tended courtyard. The relaxed hotel is two blocks from the Bethesda Metro and set back from busy Wisconsin Avenue. ▪ TIP➔ **An evening tea with cookies is complimentary, as are limousine service and shuttles to the National Institutes of Health.** ✉ *7740 Wisconsin Ave., Bethesda, MD 20814* ☎ *301/656–2100 or 800/874–0050* 🖷 *301/986–0375* ⊕ *www. tbchotels.com* ➟ *73 rooms, 1 suite* ⚴ *In-room fax, in-room safes, refrigerators, cable TV, in-room broadband, gym, hair salon, laundry facilities, parking (fee)* ▤ *AE, D, DC, MC, V* ⏧ *CP* Ⓜ *Bethesda.*

$–$$ ⊡ **Embassy Suites.** Shopping and sightseeing couldn't be more convenient at this hotel, which tops the Chevy Chase Pavilion mall and is an elevator ride up from the Metro. Each suite includes a table suitable for dining or working. The fitness center has more than 20 exercise stations with available personal trainers. Evening cocktails are offered daily in the sun-filled atrium. As with other Embassy Suites, a full cooked-to-order breakfast is included. ✉ *4300 Military Rd., Washington, DC 20015* ☎ *202/362–9300 or 800/362–2779* 🖷 *202/686–3405* ⊕ *www. embassysuitesdc.com* ➟ *198 suites* ⚴ *Room service, microwaves, refrigerators, cable TV with movies and video games, in-room broadband, indoor pool, health club, hot tub, shops, laundry service, parking (fee)* ▤ *AE, D, DC, MC, V* ⏧ *BP* Ⓜ *Friendship Heights.*

★ ☗ $–$$ ⊡ **Holiday Inn Select Bethesda.** Slightly more upscale in appearance and services than its sibling in Chevy Chase, this Holiday Inn has guest rooms that are larger than at most comparable hotels, with firm, comfortable beds, ample working space, and free morning newspaper delivery. The hotel caters to business travelers with a free shuttle to the nearby Metro, the National Institutes of Health, and the Naval Medical Center. Kids 12 and under eat free at Holiday Inns. ✉ *8120 Wisconsin Ave., Bethesda, MD 20814* ☎ *301/652–2000 or 888/465–4329* 🖷 *301/652–3806* ⊕ *www.ichotelsgroup.com* ➟ *270 rooms, 6 suites* ⚴ *Restaurant, in-room safes, cable TV, in-room broadband, pool, gym, bar, dry cleaning, laundry facilities, business services, meeting rooms, parking (fee)* ▤ *AE, D, DC, MC, V.*

☗ ¢–$ ⊡ **Holiday Inn Chevy Chase.** Two blocks from the Friendship Heights Metro on the D.C. border, this comfortable hotel is in the heart of the upscale Chevy Chase shopping district. Dining options are plentiful—the Avenue Deli and Julian's restaurant are in the hotel, the nearby Chevy Chase Pavilion and Mazza Gallerie malls have family-style restaurants, and you'll find a wealth of good dining choices one Metro stop away in Bethesda. ▪ TIP➔ **A large outdoor swimming pool is near the hotel's beautiful rose garden terrace, a popular spot for weddings.** Guest rooms have free high-speed Internet access, work desks, satellite TV, coffeemakers, and complimentary newspaper delivery; kids under 12 eat free here. ✉ *5520 Wisconsin Ave., Chevy Chase, MD 20815* ☎ *301/656–1500 or 888/465–4329* 🖷 *301/656–5045* ⊕ *www.holiday-inn.com/chevychasemd* ➟ *204 rooms, 10 suites* ⚴ *Restaurant, cafeteria, room service, cable TV with movies and video games, in-room data ports, pool, gym, bar, dry clean-*

ing, laundry facilities, business services, meeting rooms, parking (fee), some free parking 🖃 *AE, D, DC, MC, V* Ⓜ *Friendship Heights.*

Suburban Virginia

$$$ 🏨 **Hilton Arlington and Towers.** Traveling downtown is easy from this hotel, just above the Metro stop. Guest rooms offer "serenity" beds, work desks, and comfy sitting chairs, and the hotel's service is friendly and responsive. Entry to a nearby fitness club is available for a fee. The hotel has direct access via a skywalk to the Ballston Common Mall and National Science Foundation. ✉ *950 N. Stafford St., Arlington, VA 22203* ☎ *703/ 528–6000 or 800/445–8667* 🖷 *703/812–5127* ⊕ *www.arlingtonva. hilton.com* 🛏 *204 rooms, 5 suites* ♨ *Restaurant, cable TV with movies and video games, in-room data ports, Wi-Fi, bar, laundry service, concierge, business services, meeting rooms, parking (fee)* 🖃 *AE, D, DC, MC, V* Ⓜ *Ballston.*

★ $$$ 🏨 **Ritz-Carlton Pentagon City.** This 18-story Ritz-Carlton is a short drive from Ronald Reagan National Airport and downtown Washington. The heavenly guest rooms have mahogany furniture and plush featherbeds; a number of the upper rooms on the Potomac side look out on the monuments across the river. The elegant hotel's Virginia hunt-country motif makes you feel far removed from the bustle outside, although the lobby lounge does conveniently connect to the Fashion Centre shopping mall, which has movie theaters, a food court, 150 shops, and a Metro station. Welcome amenities and games, as well as a children's menu in the restaurant, are available for kids. ✉ *1250 S. Hayes St., Arlington, VA 22202* ☎ *703/415–5000 or 800/241–3333* 🖷 *703/415–5061* ⊕ *www.ritzcarlton.com* 🛏 *345 rooms, 21 suites* ♨ *Restaurant, room service, in-room fax, in-room safes, minibars, cable TV, in-room broadband, indoor pool, health club, bar, lobby lounge, shops, laundry service, concierge, concierge floor, business services, meeting rooms, convention center, airport shuttle, parking (fee)* 🖃 *AE, D, DC, MC, V* Ⓜ *Pentagon City.*

☾ $$–$$$ 🏨 **Embassy Suites Old Town Alexandria.** Adjacent to Alexandria's landmark George Washington Masonic Temple sits this modern all-suites hotel, which is also across the street from the Amtrak and Metro stations. A free shuttle is available to transport you to the scenic Alexandria riverfront, which has shops and restaurants. The cooked-to-order breakfast is complimentary, as is the cocktail reception every evening. There's also a playroom for children. ✉ *1900 Diagonal Rd., Alexandria, VA 22314* ☎ *703/684–5900 or 800/362–2779* 🖷 *703/684–1403* ⊕ *www.embassysuites.com* 🛏 *268 suites* ♨ *Restaurant, kitchenettes, refrigerators, cable TV, in-room data ports, indoor pool, gym, hot tub, recreation room, laundry facilities, laundry service, business services, meeting rooms, parking (fee), some pets allowed (fee)* 🖃 *AE, D, DC, MC, V* 🍽 *BP* Ⓜ *King Street.*

☾ $$–$$$ 🏨 **Key Bridge Marriott.** A short walk across the Key Bridge from Georgetown, this family-friendly Marriott lies three blocks from the Rosslyn Metro stop and is an excellent choice for those looking to stay in Virginia as close as possible to the District. Rooms on the Potomac side offer excellent Washington views, as does the rooftop restaurant. Although the hotel is immensely comfortable, its styling is occasionally reminiscent of the 1970s. The indoor-outdoor pool is a big draw for kids. ☒ *1401 Lee Hwy., Arlington, VA 22209* ☎ *703/524–6400 or 800/228– 9290* ☐ *703/524–8964* ⊕ *www.marriott.com* ⤳ *588 rooms, 22 suites* ⚘ *2 restaurants, room service, cable TV with movies, in-room broadband, indoor-outdoor pool, health club, hot tub, 2 bars, laundry facilities, laundry service, concierge, business services, meeting rooms, parking (fee)* ▭ *AE, D, DC, MC, V* Ⓜ *Rosslyn.*

$$–$$$ ⌧ **Marriott Residence Inn Arlington Pentagon City.** The view across the Potomac of the D.C. skyline and the monuments is magnificent from this all-suites high-rise. Adjacent to the Pentagon, it's one block from the Pentagon City Fashion Centre mall, which has movie theaters, a food court, 150 shops, and a Metro stop. ■ TIP➡ **All suites include full kitchens with dishwashers, ice makers, coffeemakers, toasters, dishes, and utensils.** Complimentary services include grocery shopping, daily newspaper delivery, full breakfast, light dinner Monday to Wednesday, and movies, popcorn, and ice cream on Thursday evening. ☒ *550 Army Navy Dr., Arlington, VA 22202* ☎ *703/413–6630 or 800/228–9290* ☐ *703/418–1751* ⊕ *www.marriott.com* ⤳ *299 suites* ⚘ *Picnic area, kitchens, cable TV, in-room broadband, indoor pool, gym, hot tub, dry cleaning, laundry facilities, meeting rooms, airport shuttle, parking (fee), some pets allowed (fee)* ▭ *AE, D, DC, MC, V* ⫮❶ *BP* Ⓜ *Pentagon City.*

★ **$–$$$** ⌧ **Morrison House.** The architecture, parquet floors, crystal chandeliers, decorative fireplaces, and furnishings of Morrison House are so faithful to the Federal period (1790–1820) that it's often mistaken for a renovation rather than a structure built from scratch in 1985. The elegant hotel blends Early American charm with modern conveniences. Rooms are individually furnished, and some offer decorative fireplaces and four-poster beds. The popular Elysium Restaurant serves American contemporary cuisine. The hotel sits in the heart of Old Town Alexandria, seven blocks from the train and Metro stations. ☒ *116 S. Alfred St., Alexandria, VA 22314* ☎ *703/838–8000 or 866/834–6628* ☐ *703/ 548–2489* ⊕ *www.morrisonhouse.com* ⤳ *42 rooms, 3 suites* ⚘ *Restaurant, room service, cable TV, in-room data ports, piano bar, concierge, business services, parking (fee)* ▭ *AE, DC, MC, V* Ⓜ *King Street.*

★ **$$** ⌧ **Hyatt Arlington.** Only a half block from the Rosslyn metro, this Hyatt is among the best accommodations in Arlington. Modern, luxurious rooms have been refurbished with plush mattresses and well-equipped work desks, including free wireless access. The hotel's restaurant serves old-world Mediterranean cuisine, and the lobby bar is a good place to relax with an early evening martini or late-night drink. Jogging paths and golf courses lie nearby. ☒ *1325 Wilson Blvd., Arlington, VA 22209* ☎ *703/ 525–1234 or 800/233–1234* ☐ *703/875–3393* ⊕ *www.hyatt.com* ⤳ *294 rooms, 8 suites* ⚘ *Restaurant, room service, cable TV with movies, Wi-Fi, gym, bar, dry cleaning, laundry service, concierge, business services, parking (fee)* ▭ *AE, D, DC, MC, V.*

☾ **$–$$** ⌧ **Holiday Inn Arlington at Ballston.** You can get in and out of Washington quickly from this hotel, two blocks from a Metro station. Especially comfortable for business travelers, rooms have spacious work spaces, plus tea/coffeemakers. Sightseers can take advantage of the hotel's proximity to Arlington National Cemetery, and the Iwo Jima and downtown monuments and museums. Kids 12 and under eat free. ⊠ *4610 N. Fairfax Dr., Arlington, VA 22203* ☎ *703/243–9800 or 888/465–4329* 🖶 *703/527–2677* ⊕ *www.ichotelsgroup.com* 🛏 *219 rooms, 2 suites* ⚘ *Restaurant, room service, cable TV with movies and video games, in-room broadband, pool, gym, bar, laundry facilities, business services, parking (fee)* ⊟ *AE, D, DC, MC, V* Ⓜ *Ballston.*

☾ $ 🖼 **Holiday Inn Rosslyn.** Comfortable and affordable, this 17-story hotel is two blocks from the Rosslyn Metro and a ¾-mi stroll across Key Bridge to Georgetown. Fort Myer and Arlington National Cemetery are nearby. Each room has a balcony, but the hotel's best feature may be the view of the Washington Monument through the panoramic windows of the Vantage Point restaurant. Kids under 12 eat free. ⊠ *1900 N. Fort Myer Dr., Arlington, VA 22209* ☎ *703/807–2000 or 800/368–3408* 🖶 *703/ 522–7480* ⊕ *www.holiday-inn.com/rosslynkbridge* 🛏 *307 rooms, 28 suites* ⚘ *2 restaurants, room service, in-room safes, some refrigerators, cable TV, in-room broadband, indoor pool, gym, bar, dry cleaning, laundry facilities, business services, meeting rooms, free parking* ⊟ *AE, D, DC, MC, V* Ⓜ *Rosslyn.*

Nightlife & the Arts

THE ARTS

Updated by
Matthew
Cordell

In the past 40 years D.C. has gone from being a cultural desert to a thriving arts center. To satiate the educated young professionals who flock here for opportunities in government, the arts scene has exploded. Nearly every theater in town, regardless of size, has planned an expansion or is in the process of expanding. Visitors have the opportunity to view incredible theater, music, and dance in fresh, dynamic facilities. When you include the old steadfasts—the Kennedy Center, the Washington National Opera, and the National Theatre—it's clear that Washington's arts scene is now a major draw of talent on the East Coast and one of the top reasons to visit.

To sift through the flurry of events, check out the daily "Guide to the Lively Arts," in the *Washington Post,* and the "Weekend" section, which comes out on Friday. On Thursday, look for the *Washington Times* "Washington Weekend" section (⊕ www.washingtontimes.com/weekend) and the free weekly *Washington CityPaper* (⊕ www.washingtoncitypaper. com). Also consult the "City Lights" section in the monthly *Washingtonian* magazine. The *Washington Post* (⊕ www.washingtonpost.com/ cityguide), *Washington Times* (⊕ www.washingtontimes.com/ activityguide), and *Washingtonian* (⊕ www.washingtonian.com/ inwashington) also publish separate Internet-based entertainment guides. Tickets to most events are available by calling or visiting each theater's box office or through the following ticket agencies:

Ticketmaster takes phone charges for events at most venues around the city. You can buy Ticketmaster tickets in person at all Hecht's department stores, Tower Records, and the D.C. Visitor Information Center. No refunds or exchanges are allowed. ☎ *202/432–7328, 703/573– 7328, or 410/481–7328* ⊕ *www.ticketmaster.com.*

TICKETplace sells half-price, day-of-performance tickets for select shows. Purchases, online and at the booth, are not possible on Sunday and Monday; tickets for events held on those days are sold at the booth on Saturday. There's a 12% service charge at the booth and a 17% service charge online. ⊠ *Old Post Office Pavilion, 406 7th St. NW, Downtown* ☎ *202/842–5387* ⊕ *www.ticketplace.org* Ⓜ *Archives/Navy Memorial.*

Tickets.com takes online reservations for a number of events around town. It also has outlets in some Olsson's Books & Records. ☎ *800/955–5566* ⊕ *www.tickets.com.*

Concert Halls

Though concert halls tend to showcase musicians, it's not uncommon for a venue also to present dance, theater, or stand-up comedy.

Atlas Performing Arts Center. This center, which opened in 2005, encompasses three dance studios and two lab theaters in the row of stores that line its restored vintage facade. Home to the H Street Playhouse, which showcases performances by the African Continuum Theatre and the Theatre Alliance, the Atlas also presents performances by the dance troupe

Joy of Motion and the Capital City Symphony. ✉ *1333 H St. NE, Northeast* ☎ *202/399–7993* ⊕ *www.atlasarts.org.*

Center for the Arts. This state-of-the-art performance complex on the suburban Virginia campus of George Mason University satisfies music, ballet, and drama patrons with regular performances in its 1,900-seat concert hall, the 500-seat proscenium Harris Theater, and the intimate 150-seat black-box Theater of the First Amendment. The 9,500-seat Patriot Center, site of pop acts and sporting events, is also on campus. ✉ *Rte. 123 and Braddock Rd., Fairfax, VA* ☎ *703/993–8888* ⊕ *www.gmu.edu/cfa.*

Clarice Smith Performing Arts Center at Maryland. The 17-acre center, on the College Park campus of the University of Maryland, is a lively place, presenting a wide range of music, dance, and drama in half a dozen striking but cozy venues. Shuttle service to the center is available at the College Park Metro station during the academic year. ✉ *University Blvd. and Stadium Dr., College Park, MD* ☎ *301/405–2787* ⊕ *www.claricesmithcenter.umd.edu* Ⓜ *College Park.*

Cramton Auditorium. This 1,508-seat auditorium on the Howard University campus presents a hodgepodge of special events. ✉ *2455 6th St. NW, Howard University* ☎ *202/806–7198* ⊕ *www.howard.edu/howardlife/cramton* Ⓜ *Shaw–Howard University.*

DAR Constitution Hall. Acts that range from Jon Stewart to Clay Aiken to B. B. King perform at this 3,700-seat venue. ✉ *1776 D St. NW, Downtown* ☎ *202/628–4780* ⊕ *www.dar.org/conthall* Ⓜ *Farragut West.*

D.C. Jewish Community Center. The DCJCC hosts the Washington Jewish Music Festival and the Washington Jewish Film Festival, along with periodic musical performances by groups such as the Arab-Israeli Orchestra of Nazareth. The JCC is also the home of Theatre J. ✉ *1529 16th St. NW, Downtown* ☎ *202/518–9400* ⊕ *www.dcjcc.org* Ⓜ *Dupont Circle.*

FodorsChoice
★ **John F. Kennedy Center for the Performing Arts.** This complex on the bank of the Potomac River is the gem of the D.C. arts scene and home to the National Symphony Orchestra, the Washington Ballet, and the Washington National Opera. It also pulls the best out-of-town acts, regardless of medium, in part because it is home to three of the most striking performance spaces in D.C.—the Concert Hall, the Opera House, and the Eisenhower Theater. It also draws an eclectic group of performers

---

TOP 5

- **Kennedy Center:** The gem of the D.C. arts scene, this is the one performance venue you would take with you if you were stranded on a desert isle.

- **National Gallery of Art garden concerts:** This is the classiest event in D.C. where you're actually encouraged to take off your shoes.

- **Screen on the Green:** Even your lobbyist friend doesn't have a screen this big.

- **Shakespeare Theatre:** It's more visually entertaining than the movies.

- **Woolly Mammoth:** This remarkable theater company has been "homeless" for 25 years; imagine what they'll do on their own stage.

4

to its smaller venues, including the Terrace Theater, showcasing chamber groups and experimental works; the Theater Lab, home to cabaret-style performances like the audience-participation hit *Sheer Madness*; the KC Jazz Club; and a 320-seat family theater. But that's not all. On the Millennium Stage in the center's Grand Foyer, you can catch free performances almost any day at 6 PM. Outstanding local jazz groups, classical students from New York's Juilliard School, international dance, or avant-garde drama might be on tap. ■ TIP→ **On performance days, a free shuttle bus runs between the Center and the Foggy Bottom/GWU Metro stop.** ✉ *New Hampshire Ave. and Rock Creek Pkwy. NW, Foggy Bottom* ☎ *202/467–4600 or 800/444–1324* ⊕ *www.kennedy-center.org* Ⓜ *Foggy Bottom/GWU.*

Lisner Auditorium. A 1,500-seat theater on the campus of George Washington University, it's the setting for pop, classical, and choral music shows, modern dance performances, and musical theater. ✉ *730 21st St. NW, Foggy Bottom* ☎ *202/994–6800* ⊕ *www.lisner.org* Ⓜ *Foggy Bottom/GWU.*

FodorsChoice **Music Center at Strathmore.** Located ½ mi outside the Capital Beltway in
★ North Bethesda, this concert hall, completed in 2005, has quickly become known as one of the country's best, receiving praise for its acoustics and its audience-friendly design. Major national artists appear here to perform folk, blues, pop, jazz, Broadway, and classical music, and the center is home to the Baltimore Symphony Orchestra and the National Philharmonic. More-intimate performances are given at the 100-seat Dorothy M. and Maurice C. Shapiro Music Room. ■ TIP→ **The center is less than a block from the Grosvenor Metro station.** ✉ *5301 Tuckerman La., North Bethesda* ☎ *301/581–5200* ⊕ *www.strathmore.org* Ⓜ *Grosvenor/Strathmore.*

★ **National Gallery of Art.** Free concerts by the National Gallery Orchestra and performances by visiting recitalists and ensembles are held in the West Building's West Garden Court on Sunday nights from October to June. Entry is first-come, first-served, with doors opening at 6 PM and concerts starting at 6:30 PM. On Friday from Memorial Day through Labor Day, local jazz groups perform from 5 to 9 PM to a packed Sculpture Garden. Many people dip their weary feet in the fountain. ✉ *6th St. and Constitution Ave. NW, The Mall* ☎ *202/842–6941* ⊕ *www.nga.gov* Ⓜ *Archives/Navy Memorial.*

FodorsChoice **Smithsonian Institution.** Jazz, musical theater, and popular standards are
★ performed in the National Museum of American History. In the museum's third-floor Hall of Musical Instruments, musicians occasionally play period instruments from the museum's collection. The Smithsonian's annual Folk Life festival, held on the Mall, highlights the cuisine, crafts, and day-to-day life of three different cultures. The Smithsonian Associates sponsors programs that offer everything from a cappella groups to Cajun zydeco bands; all events require tickets, and locations vary. ✉ *1000 Jefferson Dr. SW, The Mall* ☎ *202/357–2700, 202/633–1000 recording, 202/357–3030 Smithsonian Associates* ⊕ *www.si.edu* Ⓜ *Smithsonian.*

Verizon Center. In addition to being the home of the Washington Capitals hockey and Washington Wizards basketball teams, this 19,000-seat arena also plays host to D.C.'s biggest musical acts, ice-skating events, and the circus. Parking can be a problem, but several metro lines converge at an adjacent station. ⊠ *601 F St. NW, Chinatown* ☎ *202/628–3200* ⊕ *www.mcicenter.com* Ⓜ *Gallery Place/Chinatown.*

Wolf Trap National Park for the Performing Arts. Wolf Trap is the only national park dedicated to the performing arts. June through September, the massive, outdoor Filene Center hosts close to 100 performances, ranging from pop and jazz concerts to dance and musical theater productions. The National Symphony Orchestra is based here in summer. During the colder months, the intimate, indoor Barns at Wolf Trap fill with the sounds of musicians playing folk, country, and chamber music, along with myriad other styles. The Theatre-in-the-Woods is also free and family friendly. The park is just off the Dulles Toll Road, about 20 mi from downtown. ■ TIP→ **When the Filene Center hosts an event, Metrorail operates a $3.50 round-trip shuttle bus from the West Falls Church Metro station to the center. The fare is exact change only, and the bus leaves 20 minutes after the show, or no later than 11 PM, whether the show is over or not.** ⊠ *1551 Trap Rd., Vienna, VA* ☎ *703/255–1900, 703/938–2404 Barns at Wolf Trap* ⊕ *www.wolftrap.org* Ⓜ *Vienna.*

Dance

Dance Place. This studio theater showcases the best local dance talent in an assortment of modern and ethnic shows; performances take place most weekends. It also conducts dance classes daily. ⊠ *3225 8th St. NE, Catholic University* ☎ *202/269–1600* ⊕ *www.danceplace.org* Ⓜ *Catholic University.*

Joy of Motion. A dance studio by day, Joy of Motion is the home of several area troupes that perform in the studio's Jack Guidone Theatre by night. The resident Dana Tai Soon Burgess & Company (modern), CrossCurrents Dance Company (contemporary), and Silk Road Dance Company (traditional Middle Eastern and Central Asian) also perform at the Atlas Performing Arts Center. Two additional Joy of Motion studios in Dupont Circle and Bethesda offer classes only. ⊠ *5207 Wisconsin Ave. NW, Friendship Heights* ☎ *202/276–2599* ⊕ *www.joyofmotion. org* Ⓜ *Friendship Heights.*

★ **Washington Ballet.** Between September and May, this company presents classical and contemporary ballets, including works by choreographers such as George Balanchine, Choo-San Goh, and artistic director Septime Webre. Its main shows are mounted at the Kennedy Center. Each December the Washington Ballet performs *The Nutcracker* at the Warner Theatre. ☎ *202/362–3606* ⊕ *www.washingtonballet.org.*

Film

FodorsChoice
★ **American Film Institute Silver Theatre and Cultural Center.** This three-screen, state-of-the-art center for film is a restoration of architect John Eberson's art deco Silver Theatre, built in 1938. The AFI hosts film retrospectives, festivals, and tributes celebrating artists from Jeanne Moreau

to Russell Crowe. ⊠ *8633 Colesville Rd., Silver Spring, MD* ☎ *301/495–6700* ⊕ *www.afi.com/silver* Ⓜ *Silver Spring.*

Arlington Cinema 'N' Drafthouse. The rules are relaxed at this second-run theater, where you can enjoy beer and nosh, like pizza and buffalo wings, while you watch yesterday's blockbuster. Smoking is allowed in a special section. ■ TIP→ **Those under 21 must be accompanied by a parent or guardian.** ⊠ *2903 Columbia Pike, Arlington, VA* ☎ *703/486–2345.*

Filmfest DC. An annual citywide festival of international cinema, the DC International Film Festival, or Filmfest, takes place in late April and early May at venues throughout the city. ☎ *202/628–3456* ⊕ *www.filmfestdc.org.*

Hirshhorn Museum and Sculpture Garden. Avant-garde and experimental first-run documentaries, features, and short films are frequently screened here for free. ⊠ *Independence Ave. and 7th St. SW, The Mall* ☎ *202/357–2700* ⊕ *www.hirshhorn.si.edu* Ⓜ *Smithsonian or L'Enfant Plaza.*

Landmark's Bethesda Row Cinema. A lush, eight-screen art cinema with stadium seating and digital sound, Bethesda Row screens the best of the latest independent, foreign, and off-beat films. Look for fancy snacks such as imported chocolates, pastries from local bakeries, and a full coffee bar. ⊠ *7235 Woodmont Ave., Bethesda, MD* ☎ *301/652–7273* Ⓜ *Bethesda.*

Landmark's E Street Cinema. Specializing in independent, foreign, and documentary films, this theater has been warmly welcomed by D.C. movie lovers both for its selection and state-of-the-art facilities. Like its cousin in Bethesda, E Street has an impressive concession stand, stocked to please the gourmand, the health-conscious, and those who just want a jumbo box of Milk Duds. ⊠ *555 11th St. NW Downtown* ☎ *202/452–7672* Ⓜ *Metro Center.*

Loews Cineplex Dupont 5. Small but cozy, this theater lacks most of the amenities of the newer cineplexes, but its marquee is always loaded with art and independent films that may not be shown anywhere else in town. Plus, it's half a block from the Metro. ⊠ *1350 19th St. NW, Dupont Circle* ☎ *202/872–9555* Ⓜ *Dupont Circle.*

Loews Cineplex Uptown 1. You don't find many like this old beauty anymore: one huge screen designed originally for Cinerama; art deco flourishes; a wonderful balcony; and—in one happy concession to modernity—crystal-clear Dolby sound. ⊠ *3426 Connecticut Ave. NW, Cleveland Park* ☎ *202/966–5400* Ⓜ *Cleveland Park.*

Loews Georgetown 14. This movie palace was once the Georgetown Incinerator; a 175-foot brick smokestack still looms over the lobby's center. Stadium seating, digital sound, comfortable seats, and 14 huge screens all create a prime movie-going environment. Wanna snuggle with your honey? The armrests between the seats can be raised. ⊠ *3111 K St. NW, Georgetown* Ⓜ *Foggy Bottom.*

National Archives. Historical films, usually documentaries, are shown here daily. Screenings range from the 1942 documentary by Robert Flaherty on the plight of migrant workers to archival footage of Charles Lindbergh's solo flight from New York to Paris. ⊠ *Constitution Ave. between 7th and 9th Sts. NW, The Mall* ☎ *202/501–5000* ⊕ *www.archives.gov* Ⓜ *Archives/Navy Memorial.*

National Gallery of Art, East Building. Free classic and international films, often complementing the exhibits, are shown in this museum's large auditorium. Pick up a film calendar at the museum. ✉ *Constitution Ave. between 3rd and 4th Sts. NW, The Mall* ☎ *202/737–4215* ⊕ *www.nga. gov* Ⓜ *Archives/Navy Memorial.*

National Geographic Society. Free educational films with a scientific, geographic, or anthropological focus are shown here regularly. ✉ *1145 17th St. NW, Dupont Circle* ☎ *202/857–7588* ⊕ *www. nationalgeographic.com/museum* Ⓜ *Farragut North.*

★ **Screen on the Green.** Every summer, this weekly series of classic films turns the Mall into an open-air cinema. People arrive early to picnic, socialize, and reserve a spot. ✉ *The Mall, at 7th St.* ☎ *877/262–5866* Ⓜ *Smithsonian.*

Music

Chamber Music

Coolidge Auditorium at the Library of Congress. Over the past 81 years, the Coolidge has hosted most of the 20th-century's greatest performers and composers, including Copland and Stravinsky. Today it draws musicians from all genres, including classical, jazz, and gospel. In addition, audiences come for the venue's near-perfect acoustics and sightlines. ✉ *Library of Congress, Jefferson Bldg., 101 Independence Ave. SE, Capitol Hill* ☎ *800/551–7328* ⊕ *www.loc.gov* Ⓜ *Capitol South.*

Corcoran Gallery of Art. Hungary's Takács String Quartet and the Klavier Trio Amsterdam are among the chamber groups appearing in the Corcoran's Musical Evening Series, held one night each month from October to May (there are also some summer offerings). ■ TIP➔ **Concerts are followed by a reception with the artists.** ✉ *500 17th St. NW, Downtown* ☎ *202/639–1700* ⊕ *www.corcoran.org* Ⓜ *Farragut West.*

Dumbarton Concerts. Dumbarton United Methodist Church, a fixture in Georgetown since 1772 (in its current location since 1850), sponsors this concert series. It has been host to musicians such as the American Chamber Players, the Daedalus Quartet, and the Thibaud String Trio. ✉ *Dumbarton United Methodist Church, 3133 Dumbarton Ave. NW, Georgetown* ☎ *202/965–2000* ⊕ *www.dumbartonconcerts.org* Ⓜ *Foggy Bottom.*

Folger Shakespeare Library. The library's internationally acclaimed resident chamber music ensemble, the Folger Consort, regularly presents medieval, Renaissance, and baroque pieces performed on period instruments. The season runs from October to May. ✉ *201 E. Capitol St. SE, Capitol Hill* ☎ *202/544–7077* ⊕ *www.folger.edu* Ⓜ *Union Station or Capitol South.*

National Academy of Sciences. Free Sunday afternoon performances are given fall through spring in the academy's 670-seat auditorium, which has nearly perfect acoustics. Both the National Musical Arts Chamber Ensemble and the United States Marines Chamber Orchestra perform regularly. ✉ *2100 C St. NW, Downtown* ☎ *202/334–2436* ⊕ *www. nationalacademies.org/arts* Ⓜ *Foggy Bottom/GWU.*

Phillips Collection. Duncan Phillips's mansion is more than an art museum. Sunday afternoons from October through May, Chamber groups from around the world perform in the long, dark-paneled Music Room.

■ TIP→ Concerts begin at 5 PM—arrive early for decent seats. ⊠ *1600 21st St. NW, Dupont Circle* ☎ *202/387–2151* ⊕ *www.phillipscollection.org* Ⓜ *Dupont Circle.*

Choral Music

Basilica of the National Shrine of the Immaculate Conception. Choral and church groups occasionally perform at the largest Catholic church in the Americas. ⊠ *400 Michigan Ave. NE, Catholic University* ☎ *202/ 526–8300* ⊕ *www.nationalshrine.com* Ⓜ *Brookland/CUA.*

Choral Arts Society of Washington. The 200-voice Choral Arts Society choir performs a variety of classical pieces at the Kennedy Center from fall to spring. Three Christmas sing-alongs are scheduled each December, along with a popular tribute to Martin Luther King, Jr., on his birthday. ☎ *202/244–3669* ⊕ *www.choralarts.org.*

Washington National Cathedral. Choral and church groups frequently perform in this grand church. Admission is usually free. ⊠ *Massachusetts and Wisconsin Aves. NW, Cleveland Park* ☎ *202/ 537–6207* ⊕ *www.cathedral.org/ cathedral* Ⓜ *Tenleytown/AU.*

> ### WORD OF MOUTH
>
> "A concert at the National Cathedral is enthralling and magnificent. On the 4th of July we went to the organ concert there—it was spectacular (and free!) . . . we also attended *The Messiah* last December, which was thrilling (but not free)." —vivi

Opera & Classical

The *Washington Post* "Weekend" section is a good source for information on opera and classical performances.

In Series. Trademark cabaret, experimental chamber opera, and Spanish musical theater (also known as *zarzuela*) are among the hallmarks of this burgeoning nonprofit company, which performs at venues around the city. ☎ *202/518–0152* ⊕ *www.inseries.org.*

♻ **Opera Theatre of Northern Virginia.** Four times a year this company stages an opera at an Arlington community theater. The winter production is geared toward young audiences. ☎ *703/528–1433* ⊕ *www. novaopera.org.*

Summer Opera Theater Company. An independent professional troupe, the Summer Opera Theater Company stages one opera in June and one in July. ⊠ *Hartke Theater, 620 Michigan Ave. NE, Catholic University* ☎ *202/526–1669* ⊕ *www.summeropera.org* Ⓜ *Brookland/CUA.*

Fodor'sChoice ★ **Washington National Opera.** Under the directorship of Plácido Domingo, the Washington National Opera presents eight operas in the fall and spring at the Kennedy Center Opera House. The operas, presented in their original languages with English supertitles, are often sold out to subscribers, but you can purchase returned tickets an hour before curtain time. ■ TIP→ For standing-room tickets to each week's performances, inquire at the box office starting the preceding Saturday. ☎ *202/295–2400 or 800/876– 7372* ⊕ *www.dc-opera.org.*

Orchestras

Baltimore Symphony Orchestra. When the 2,000-seat Music Center at Strathmore opened in 2005, the world-renowned Baltimore Symphony

Orchestra relocated to the Greater Washington area. It now performs year-round at the center, a half mile outside the Beltway in North Bethesda. The Grosvenor/Strathmore metro station is less than a block from the Music Center. ✉ *5301 Tuckerman La., North Bethesda* ☎ *877/ 276–1444* ⊕ *www.bsoatstrathmore.org* Ⓜ *Grosvenor/Strathmore.*

National Symphony Orchestra. Under the direction of Leonard Slatkin, the NSO performs from September to June at the Kennedy Center Concert Hall. In summer the NSO performs at Wolf Trap and gives free concerts at Rock Creek Park's Carter Barron Amphitheatre. On Memorial and Labor Day weekends and July 4, the orchestra performs on the West Lawn of the Capitol. ✉ *New Hampshire Ave. and Rock Creek Pkwy. NW, Foggy Bottom* ☎ *202/972–9556* ⊕ *www.kennedy-center.org/nso.*

Performance Series

Armed Forces Concert Series. From June to August, bands from the four armed services perform Monday, Tuesday, Wednesday, and Friday evenings on the East Terrace of the Capitol. Other performances occur at 8 PM from June to August, on Tuesday, Thursday, Friday, and Sunday nights at the **Sylvan Theater** (✉ Washington Monument grounds, 14th St. and Constitution Ave., The Mall ☎ 202/426–6841 Ⓜ Smithsonian). Concerts usually include marches, patriotic numbers, and some classical music. The Air Force celebrity series features popular artists such as Earl Klugh and Keiko Matsui on Sundays in February and March at DAR Constitutional Hall. ☎ *202/767–5658 Air Force, 703/ 696–3718 Army, 202/433–4011 Marines, 202/433–2525 Navy.*

Carter Barron Amphitheatre. On Saturday and Sunday nights from mid- to late summer this 3,750-seat outdoor theater, renovated in 2004, hosts pop, jazz, gospel, and rhythm-and-blues artists such as Chick Corea and Nancy Wilson. The National Symphony Orchestra also performs, and for two weeks the Shakespeare Theatre presents a free play. ✉ *Rock Creek Park, 16th St. and Colorado Ave. NW, Upper Northwest* ☎ *202/426–0486* ⊕ *www.nps.gov/rocr/cbarron.htm.*

Fort Dupont Summer Theater. The National Park Service presents national and international jazz artists at 8 PM on Saturday evenings from July to August at the outdoor Fort Dupont Summer Theater. Wynton Marsalis, Shirley Horne, and Ramsey Lewis are among the artists who have performed free concerts here. ✉ *Minnesota Ave. and Randall Circle SE, Southeast* ☎ *202/426–5961* ⊕ *www.nps.gov/nace/ ftdupont.htm.*

Institute of Musical Traditions. Emerging, near-famous, and celebrated folk performers, such as Si Kahn, John McCutcheon, and the Kennedys, perform at the Institute's concerts, most often held at the St. Mark Presbyterian Church. ✉ *10701 Old Georgetown Rd., Rockville, MD* ☎ *301/ 754–3611* ⊕ *www.imtfolk.org.*

Transparent Productions. Composed of a small group of dedicated jazz connoisseurs, this nonprofit organization regularly brings acclaimed avant-garde jazz musicians to intimate clubs and university stages. Past performers have included the Ethnic Heritage Ensemble, bassist William Parker, and saxophonist Steve Coleman. ■ TIP→ **Tickets are usually in the $10 range, and all proceeds go directly to the artists.** ☎ *No phone* ⊕ *www. transparentproductions.org.*

Washington Performing Arts Society. This nonprofit organization books high-quality classical music, jazz, gospel, modern dance, and performance art into halls around the city. Past artists include the Alvin Ailey American Dance Theater, Yo-Yo Ma, the Chieftains, Sweet Honey in the Rock, and Cecilia Bartoli. ☎ *202/833–9800* ⊕ *www.wpas.org.*

Theater & Performance Art

Large Theaters

★ **Arena Stage.** One of the city's most-respected resident companies, this troupe was the first regional theater company to win a Tony Award and deservedly so. Arena Stage performs mainly American theater, old and new, with superb acting and dynamic staging in its three theaters: the Fichandler Stage, the proscenium Kreeger, and the cabaret-style Old Vat Room. ☒ *1101 6th St. SW, Waterfront* ☎ *202/488–3300* ⊕ *www. arenastage.org* Ⓜ *Waterfront.*

☾ **Ford's Theatre.** Looking much as it did when President Lincoln was shot at a performance of *Our American Cousin,* Ford's hosts both dramas and musicals, many with family appeal. Dickens's *A Christmas Carol* is staged every year. The theater is now maintained by the National Park Service. ☒ *511 10th St. NW, Downtown* ☎ *202/347–4833* ⊕ *www. fordstheatre.org* Ⓜ *Metro Center.*

Lincoln Theatre. Once the host of such notable black performers as Cab Calloway, Lena Horne, and Duke Ellington, the 1,250-seat Lincoln is part of the revitalized and lively U Street corridor. It presents movies, comedy shows, and musical performers such as Harry Belafonte, the Count Basie Orchestra, and the Harlem Boys and Girls Choir. ☒ *1215 U St. NW, U Street corridor* ☎ *202/328–6000* ⊕ *www.thelincolntheatre.org* Ⓜ *U Street/Cardozo.*

☾ **National Theatre.** Though once destroyed by fire and rebuilt several times throughout its life, the National Theatre has operated in the same location since 1835. It now presents touring Broadway shows, such as *Les Misérables* and Billy Joel's *Movin' Out.* ■ TIP→ **From September through April, look for free children's shows Saturday morning and free Monday night shows that may include Asian dance, performance art, and a cappella cabarets.** ☒ *1321 Pennsylvania Ave. NW, Downtown* ☎ *202/628–6161* ⊕ *www. nationaltheatre.org* Ⓜ *Metro Center.*

Fodor'sChoice **Shakespeare Theatre.** This acclaimed troupe, known as one of the world's
★ three great Shakespearean companies, crafts fantastically staged and acted performances of works by Shakespeare and his contemporaries. For two weeks in late spring they perform Shakespeare for free at Carter Barron Amphitheatre. The troupe plans to move into a new, state-of-the-art performance space in 2007. ☒ *450 7th St. NW, Downtown* ☎ *202/ 547–1122* ⊕ *www.shakespearedc.org* Ⓜ *Gallery Pl./Chinatown or Archives/Navy Memorial.*

Warner Theatre. One of Washington's grand theaters, the Warner hosts road shows, dance recitals, pop music, and the occasional comedy act in its majestic art deco performance space. ☒ *1299 Pennsylvania Ave. NW, Downtown* ☎ *202/783–4000* ⊕ *www.warnertheatre.com* Ⓜ *Metro Center.*

Small Theaters & Companies

Often performing in churches and other less-than-ideal settings, Washington's small companies present drama that can be every bit as enthralling as—and often more daring than—that offered by their blockbuster counterparts. Without the more dazzling staging capabilities of the larger theaters, these groups are often forced to rely on their acting craft, almost always with pleasing results. No matter the size, all companies in town compete fiercely for the Helen Hayes Award, Washington's version of the Tony. Several acclaimed alternative stages cluster on 14th Street NW near Logan Circle.

District of Columbia Arts Center. Known by area artists as DCAC, this cross-genre space shows changing exhibits in its gallery and presents avant-garde performance art, improv, and experimental plays in its tiny black-box theater. ⊠ *2438 18th St. NW, Adams-Morgan* ☎ *202/462–7833* ⊕ *www.dcartscenter.org.*

Folger Shakespeare Library. Look for three to four productions a year of Shakespeare or Shakespeare-influenced works. Everything is performed in the library's theater, a 250-seat re-creation of the inn-yard theaters popular in Shakespeare's time. Though the stage is a throwback, the sharp acting and inventive staging certainly push the envelope. ⊠ *201 E. Capitol St. SE, Capitol Hill* ☎ *202/544–4600* ⊕ *www.folger.edu* Ⓜ *Union Station or Capitol S.*

Gala Hispanic Theatre. This company attracts some of the most outstanding Hispanic actors and playwrights from around the world, such as Federico García Lorca and Mario Vargas Llosa. Plays are presented in Spanish with instant English translations, as well as in English. The company performs in the newly renovated Tivoli Theatre in Columbia Heights. ⊠ *Tivoli Sq., 3333 14th St. NW, 14th and Park Rd., Columbia Heights* ☎ *202/234–7174* ⊕ *www.galatheatre.org* Ⓜ *Columbia Heights.*

Ⓒ **Glen Echo Park.** The National Park Service has transformed this former amusement park into a thriving arts center. Every weekend the Adventure Theater puts on traditional plays and musicals aimed at children ages 4 and up. Families can spread out on carpeted steps. At the Puppet Company Playhouse, skilled puppeteers perform classic stories Wednesday through Sunday. ⊠ *7300 MacArthur Blvd. NW, Glen Echo, MD* ☎ *301/301/634–2222, 301/320–5331 Adventure Theater, 301/320–6668 Puppet Co.* ⊕ *www.glenechopark.org.*

Ⓒ **Imagination Stage.** Shows like *Cinderella Likes Rice and Beans* and Roald Dahl's *The BFG* are produced here for children ages 4 and up. The state-of-the-art center in Bethesda includes two theaters and a digital media studio. Make reservations in advance. ⊠ *4908 Auburn Ave., Bethesda, MD* ☎ *301/961–6060* ⊕ *www.imaginationstage.org.*

Round House Theatre. Each season on its Main Stage, Round House presents an eclectic body of work ranging from world premieres to great 20th-century works to contemporary adaptations of the classics. Each season also includes special performances and limited engagements that explore different forms of theater and the performing arts. The Main Stage is less than a block from the Bethesda Metro station in downtown Bethesda. Round House's 150-seat black-box stage, which presents more experimental works, is in Silver Spring, adjacent to the American Film Silver Theatre & Cultural Center. ✉ *4545 East–West Hwy., Bethesda, MD* ☎ *240/644–1099* ⊕ *www.round-house.org* Ⓜ *Bethesda* ✉ *8641 Colesville Rd., Silver Spring, MD* ☎ *240/644–1099* Ⓜ *Silver Spring.*

Signature Theatre. Led by artistic director Eric Schaeffer, Signature has earned national acclaim for its presentation of ground-breaking American musicals, especially those of Stephen Sondheim. In fall 2006, the company is scheduled to leave its cramped 136-seat black-box theater for a dramatic new facility in the Village of Shirlington in Arlington, not far from its current location. ✉ *3806 S. 4 Mile Run Dr., Arlington, VA* ☎ *703/820–9771* ⊕ *www.sig-online.org.*

★ **Studio Theatre.** One of the busiest groups in the city, this small independent company produces an eclectic season of classic and offbeat plays. In 2005 Studio added two new performance spaces, the 200-seat Metheny Theatre and the experimental Stage 4, to complement its original twin theaters, the Mead and the Milton. ✉ *1333 P St. NW, Dupont Circle* ☎ *202/332–3300* ⊕ *www.studiotheatre.org* Ⓜ *Dupont Circle.*

Theater J. In recent years the theater has emerged as one of the country's most distinctive and progressive Jewish theaters, offering an ambitious range of programming that includes work by noted playwrights, directors, designers, and actors. Performances take place in the Aaron and Cecile Goldman Theater at the D.C. Jewish Community Center (DCJCC). ✉ *1529 16th St. NW, Downtown* ☎ *202/518–9400* ⊕ *www. dcjcc.org/arts/theaterj* Ⓜ *Dupont Circle.*

Washington Stage Guild. Performing at an extension of the Arena Stage, WSG uses the small space well, deftly performing classics and contemporary works. George Bernard Shaw is a specialty. ✉ *Arena Stage, 1901 14th St. NW, Dupont Circle* ☎ *240/582–0050* ⊕ *www.stageguild. org* Ⓜ *U Street/Cardozo.*

Fodor'sChoice **Woolly Mammoth.** Unusual, avant-garde shows with impressive staging
★ and acting have earned Woolly Mammoth top reviews and favorable comparisons to Chicago's Steppenwolf. In 2005 the company settled into a permanent home: a modern, 265-seat theater in Penn Quarter near the MCI Center. ✉ *641 D St. NW, Downtown* ☎ *202/393–3939* ⊕ *www.woollymammoth.net* Ⓜ *Gallery Pl./Chinatown or Archives/Navy Memorial.*

NIGHTLIFE

From buttoned-down political appointees who've just arrived to laidback folks who've lived here their whole lives, Washingtonians have plenty of options when they head out for a night on the town. Most places are clustered in several key areas, making a night of bar-hopping relatively easy. Georgetown has dozens of bars, nightclubs, and restaurants at the intersection of Wisconsin and M streets. A host of small live-music venues line the 18th Street strip in Adams-Morgan between Columbia Road and Kalorama Avenue. The stretch of Pennsylvania Avenue between 2nd and 4th streets has a half-dozen Capitol Hill bars. For a high-powered happy hour, head to the intersection of 19th and M streets NW, near lawyer- and lobbyist-filled downtown.

Although residents are likely to tell you that the party scene hasn't changed much over the past several years, the truth is that it's constantly in flux. For example, theatergoers seeking post-show entertainment once had to head to nearby Dupont Circle, but no more: the 14th Street strip near P Street has developed an eclectic, thriving nightlife of its own. And thanks to an ongoing revival, the Penn Quarter is burgeoning with squeaky clean, new bars.

The city's suburbs have a nightlife of their own, in part thanks to Washington's Metro system, which runs until 3 AM on weekends. Near the Bethesda stop in downtown Bethesda, Maryland, there's a vibrant club scene. In Northern Virginia, where droves of young people in search of cheaper rent have decamped, bars and clubs heat up the areas surrounding the Clarendon and Ballston Metro stations.

To check out the local scene, consult Friday's "Weekend" section in the *Washington Post* and the free weekly *Washington CityPaper*. The free publications *Metro Weekly* and the *Washington Blade* offer insights on gay and lesbian nightlife. It's also a good idea to call clubs ahead of time, as that punk-rock party might now be a merengue marathon. Reservations are advised for clubs that feature comedy or live music.

> ## TOP 5
>
> - **Café Saint-Ex:** There's an upstairs and downstairs for your wild and mild sides.
> - **Chi-Cha Lounge:** It's like your living room, only hipper, and they serve sangria and hookah.
> - **HR-57:** Fried chicken, collard greens, live jazz, BYOB—this place oozes with soul.
> - **9:30 Club:** It's hard to get closer to the Roots.
> - **Ben's Chili Bowl:** Chili has become a condiment here.

Most bars in D.C. have cover charges for bands and DJs, especially those performing on Friday and Saturday. Expect to pay from $5 to $15 for most dance clubs. Jazz and comedy clubs often have higher cover charges along with drink minimums.

Acoustic, Folk & Country Music Clubs

FodorśChoice ★ **The Birchmere.** A legend in the D.C. area, the Birchmere is one of the best places outside of the Blue Ridge Mountains to hear acoustic folk, country, and bluegrass. Enthusiastic crowds have enjoyed recent performances by artists such as Mary Chapin Carpenter, Lyle Lovett, Dave Matthews, and Emmylou Harris. ⊠ *3701 Mt. Vernon Ave., Alexandria, VA* ☎ *703/549–7500* ⊕ *www.birchmere.com.*

Folklore Society of Greater Washington. At more than 200 events a year, the society presents folk and traditional musicians and dancers from all over the country. Venues around the D.C. area host FSGW events ranging from contra dancing to storytelling to open-mike singing. ☎ *202/546–2228* ⊕ *www.fsgw.org.*

Soho Tea & Coffee. High-quality singer-songwriters share the stage with poets and writers at this tiny venue's open-mike night the second and fourth Wednesday of every month (featured performances go on throughout the month). The café, which also serves as a gallery space with changing monthly exhibits, stays open very late. ⊠ *2150 P St. NW, Dupont Circle* ☏ *202/463–7646* Ⓜ *Dupont Circle.*

GOOD TO KNOW

Last call in D.C. is 2 AM, and most bars and clubs close by 3 AM on the weekends and between midnight and 2 AM during the week. The exceptions are after-hours dance clubs and bars with kitchens that stay open late.

Bars & Lounges

Brickskeller. Its more than 1,000 varieties of beer from around the world earned Brickskeller mention in *Guinness World Records 2003.* Other draws include the cozy, although slightly grungy, cellar location; the diverse clientele; the tasty burgers; and the adept servers, who actually have to attend "beer school" to land a job here. ⊠ *1523 22nd St. NW, Dupont Circle* ☏ *202/293–1885* ⊕ *www.thebrickskeller.com* Ⓜ *Dupont Circle.*

★ **Café Saint-Ex.** Themed after the life of Antoine de Saint-Exupéry, French pilot and author of *The Little Prince,* this bi-level bar has a split personality. The upstairs brasserie has pressed-tin ceilings and a propeller hanging over the polished wooden bar. Downstairs is the Gate 54 nightclub, designed to resemble an airplane hangar with dropped corrugated-metal ceilings and back-lighted aerial photographs. The DJs draw twentysomethings nightly. ⊠ *1847 14th St. NW, Logan Circle* ☏ *202/ 265–7839* ⊕ *www.saint-ex.com* Ⓜ *U Street/Cardozo.*

Capitol City Brewing Company. At the New York Avenue location of this microbrewery, a gleaming copper bar dominates the airy room. Consult the brewmaster's chalkboard to see what's on tap. The fabulous Postal Square location on Massachusetts Avenue has five 30-keg copper tanks in the center of the restaurant as well as a gorgeous vault door left over from the days when the building was a post office. ⊠ *1100 New York Ave. NW, Downtown* ☏ *202/628–2222* ⊕ *www.capcitybrew.com* Ⓜ *Metro Center* ⊠ *2 Massachusetts Ave. NE, Capitol Hill* ☏ *202/842– 2337* Ⓜ *Union Station.*

Carpool. "Andy Warhol meets General Motors" is how one magazine described this former-garage-turned-bar. Enjoy a brew and food from a kitchen run by Rocklands, which makes some of the best barbecue in the area. Carpool has 16 pool tables, four dartboards, and a cigar room with a walk-in humidor. ⊠ *4000 Fairfax Dr., Arlington, VA* ☏ *703/ 532–7665* ⊕ *www.carpoolweb.com* Ⓜ *Ballston.*

★ **Chi-Cha Lounge.** Insular groups of young professionals relax on sofas and armchairs in this hip hangout while Latin jazz plays in the background and old movies run silently behind the bar. This lounge gets packed on weekends, so come early to get a coveted sofa along the back wall, where it's easier to see the live music performances. Down the tasty tapas as you enjoy the namesake drink—think sangria with a bigger kick. For a price, you can smoke a hookah filled with imported honey-cured tobacco. ⊠ *1624 U St. NW, U Street corridor* ☏ *202/234–8400* Ⓜ *U Street/Cardozo.*

Clyde's. Although part of a chain, Clyde's feels less derivative than the countless copycats nearby. With a front and back bar, an exquisite menu, and genuine bartenders, you can sink in here and get the "Georgetown

After-Hours Restaurants

CLOSE UP

FEELING PECKISH after a night out on the town? Sure, you *could* order some greasy chicken wings or soggy nachos at the bar, but it would be a shame to settle for pub grub when late-night restaurants serve up everything from Mom's meat loaf to escargots. Some places are open around the clock, so there's no need to dash away from the dance floor.

In Dupont Circle, **Annie's Paramount Steak House** (✉ 1609 17th St. NW ☎ 202/232-0395 Ⓜ Dupont Circle) is a longtime favorite. It was once solely the province of mustachioed gay men, but now they share space in the bustling dining room with everyone from club kids gearing up for a night on the town to older couples from the suburbs winding down. This loud and crowded storefront eatery is open until 11 PM on weekdays and 24 hours on weekends and holidays. Inside Dupont Circle's most popular bookstore, **Kramerbooks & Afterwords** (✉ 1517 Connecticut Ave. NW ☎ 202/387-1462 ⊕ www.kramers.com Ⓜ Dupont Circle) is a venerable neighborhood hangout that delivers dishes such as hanger-steak sandwiches and smothered bayou catfish in its noisy, multilevel atrium. Not so hungry? "Share-zies" such as fried artichokes, buffalo wings, and mini-crab cakes are served on a three-tiered stand. There's live music most nights. Afterwords is open until 1 AM during the week and 24 hours on the weekend.

Lined with loud vinyl booths and lighted with blinding fluorescent bulbs, **Ben's Chili Bowl** (✉ 1213 U St. NW ☎ 202/667-0909 Ⓜ U Street/ Cardozo) is sure to keep you awake. Loads of locals and U Street revelers crowd into this narrow dive, open until 2 AM during the week and 4 AM on weekends, for its "famous chili dog." As you might guess, almost everything on the menu is served smothered with the trademark mixture of beef and beans. Your best bet, though, is probably a steaming bowl of the stuff. The name says it all at Georgetown's **Bistro Francais** (✉ 3128 M St. NW ☎ 202/338-3830 Ⓜ Foggy Bottom), where you can expect straightforward French fare. Open until 3 AM Tuesday through Thursday and until 4 AM Friday through Sunday, this neighborhood landmark is where many local chefs relax when they're finished cooking. The classic diner experience is updated with tasty and less-greasy fare at **The Diner** (✉ 2453 18th St. NW ☎ 202/232-8800 Ⓜ Woodley Park/ Zoo) in Adams-Morgan. At this 24-hour hipster hangout, you can even order wine with your roast chicken. If you're longing for breakfast at 4 AM, this should be your destination.

What to do if you find yourself across the river in Virginia? Head to **Bob & Edith's Diner** (✉ 2310 Columbia Pike, Arlington, VA ☎ 703/920-6103 Ⓜ Ballston). The diner is always crowded, but especially on weekends. After a night of clubbing, drop by for a late burger or early breakfast: it's open 24 hours.

4

experience" of dark-panel walls and an upper-crust clientele. ✉ 3236 M St. NW, Georgetown ☎ 202/333-9180 ⊕ www.clydes.com.
Degrees. Inside what was once the Georgetown Incinerator, this modern bar in the Ritz-Carlton is a breath of fresh air in the neighborhood's rather monotone scene. With an extensive wine and cocktail selection behind

the black granite bar and a hip, well-dressed set of patrons in front of it, Degrees exudes elegance from all corners. If there's too much smoke or attitude in the bar, head out to the hotel's lovely lobby bar and sit by the fireplace. ⊠ *3100 South St. NW, Georgetown* ☎ *202/912–4100* ⊕ *www. ritzcarlton.com/hotels/georgetown/dining/venues/degrees.*

Dubliner. Cozy paneled rooms, rich pints of ale, and nightly live entertainment make this place popular among Capitol Hill staffers and Georgetown law students. ⊠ *520 N. Capitol St. NW, Capitol Hill* ☎ *202/737–3773* ⊕ *www.dublinerdc.com* Ⓜ *Union Station.*

Fodor'sChoice ★ **Eighteenth Street Lounge (ESL).** Home to Washington's chic set, ESL's unmarked visage might be intimidating, but this multilevel club's array of sofa-filled hardwood coves makes it seem like the city's chillest house party. On the top floor, jazz musicians often entertain loungers seated nearby. Fans of techno music flock here, because it's the home of the ESL record label and the world-renowned DJs who make up Thievery Corporation. ⊠ *1212 18th St. NW, Dupont Circle* ☎ *202/466–3922* ⊕ *www.eslmusic.com* Ⓜ *Dupont Circle.*

Fadó Irish Pub. Designed by Irish craftspeople with authentic Irish materials, dark and warm Fadó is really four pubs in one: the Library, the Victorian Pub, the Gaelic, and the Cottage. Live Irish acoustic music is performed every Sunday afternoon, and there's live Celtic rock on Wednesday and Saturday nights. Monday night is quiz night. Fadó often pulls a crowd from the nearby MCI Center. ⊠ *808 7th St. NW, Chinatown* ☎ *202/789–0066* ⊕ *www.fadoirishpub.com* Ⓜ *Gallery Place/Chinatown.*

Felix. "Cool," "hip," and "chic" are the watchwords of the mixed and international crowd that haunts Felix. The sounds of live Latin jazz or funk often waft out to 18th Street. Be sure to sip one of the exotic cocktails while you check out the scene. ⊠ *2406 18th St. NW, Adams-Morgan* ☎ *202/483–3549.*

Fishmarket. There's something different in just about every section of this multilevel, multiroom space, from a piano-bar crooner to a ragtime piano shouter and a guitar strummer. The operative word here is boisterous. If you really like beer, order the largest size; it comes in a glass big enough to put your face in. ⊠ *105 King St., Old Town, Alexandria, VA* ☎ *703/ 836–5676* ⊕ *www.fishmarketoldtown.com* Ⓜ *King Street.*

Gazuza. The bar, whose name means "lust" in Castilian Spanish, draws an attractive local crowd that attempts to chat over the throbbing house music. The tiny interior, done in an aggressively modern style, fills up early, spilling patrons onto the spacious balcony, a prime people-watching spot. ⊠ *1629 Connecticut Ave. NW, Dupont Circle* ☎ *202/667– 5500* Ⓜ *Dupont Circle.*

Hawk & Dove. The regulars at this friendly bar—in a neighborhood dominated by the Capitol—include politicos, lobbyists, and disgruntled interns. Conversation is ripe with overexcitement or rage at the political events of the day, although some just come to watch sports on the TVs above the bar. ⊠ *329 Pennsylvania Ave. SE, Capitol Hill* ☎ *202/ 543–3300* ⊕ *www.hawkanddoveonline.com* Ⓜ *Eastern Market.*

Helix Lounge. Despite feeling like someone's lounged-out basement, Helix caters to a mixed, completely non-Hill crowd—an oddity in D.C. Locals, who sit on couches and overstuffed ottomans, sip specialty cocktails and chat among themselves. Most are well dressed, but it's definitely not a scene. ⊠ *Hotel Helix, 1430 Rhode Island Ave. NW, Logan Circle* ☎ *202/462–9001* ⊕ *www.hotelhelix.com/heldini* Ⓜ *U Street/Cardozo.*

Iota. The bands at Iota play alt-country or stripped-down rock to unpretentious, attentive crowds who come mainly because they like good music. Expect to fight your way to the bar—it gets crowded quickly. There's a cover almost every night. ⊠ *2832 Wilson Blvd., Arlington, VA* ☎ *703/522–8340* ⊕ *www. iotaclubandcafe.com* Ⓜ *Clarendon.*

Local 16. A classic urban bar, Local 16 has a cozy ground floor and the best roof deck in town. The local under-thirty crowd keeps the top floor filled but the atmosphere low-key. ⊠ *1604 U St. NW, U Street corridor* ☎ *202/265–2828* ⊕ *www. localsixteen.com* Ⓜ *U Street/ Cardozo.*

Madam's Organ. Neon lights behind the bar, walls covered in kitsch, and works from local artists add to the

gritty, bayou feel that infuses Madam's Organ. Its three levels play host to an eclectic clientele that shoots pool, listens to live music performed every night on the lower level, and soaks up rays on the roof deck. ⊠ *2461 18th St. NW, Adams-Morgan* ☎ *202/667–5370* ⊕ *madamsorgan.com* Ⓜ *Woodley Park/Zoo.*

Tryst. Bohemian and unpretentious, this coffeehouse-bar serves fancy sandwiches and exotic coffee creations. Comfy chairs and couches fill the big open space, where you can sit for hours sipping a cup of tea—or a martini, in the evenings—while chatting or clacking away at your laptop. Tryst is best in the warm months, when the front windows swing open and the temperature matches the temperament. ⊠ *2459 18th St. NW, Adams-Morgan* ☎ *202/232–5500* ⊕ *www.trystdc.com* Ⓜ *Woodley Park/Zoo.*

Gay & Lesbian Bars

Washington's gay population has traditionally congregated in Dupont Circle. 17th Street between P Street and R Street is an especially active scene.

Halo. At this Logan Circle hangout there's no smoking—still a rarity in D.C. Sleek and stylish, the bar uses dramatic lighting to make the most of its tunnel-like space. The music is low enough that you can even—gasp!—have a conversation. ⊠ *1435 P St. NW, Logan Circle* ☎ *202/ 797–9730* Ⓜ *Dupont Circle.*

JR's Bar & Grill. On the 17th Street strip, JR's packs in a mostly male, young professional crowd. Patrons shoot pool, play video games, gaze at videos on the big screen, and chat with their neighbors. ⊠ *1519 17th St. NW, Dupont Circle* ☎ *202/328–0090* ⊕ *www.jrswdc.com* Ⓜ *Dupont Circle.*

Phase One. An eclectic, mostly female clientele frequents this longtime neighborhood hangout. The small dance floor and pool tables in the back make it an intimate and comfortable spot, although sometimes the place gets very crowded. ⊠ *525 8th St. SE, Capitol Hill* ☎ *202/544–6831* Ⓜ *Eastern Market.*

Comedy Clubs

Capitol Steps. The musical political satire of this group of current and former Hill staffers is presented in the amphitheater of the trade center every Friday and Saturday at 7:30 PM and occasionally at other spots around town. Ronald Reagan was said to have been a big fan. Tickets are available through Ticketmaster. ⊠ *Ronald Reagan Bldg. and International Trade Center, 1300 Pennsylvania Ave. NW, Downtown* ☎ *703/683–8330* ⊕ *www.capsteps.com* Ⓜ *Federal Triangle.*

☺ **ComedySportz.** Two teams of comedians compete in this skit-based improv competition Thursday, Friday, and Saturday nights. No obscenities are allowed, making it perfect for a family outing. ⊠ *Ballston Common Mall, 4238 Wilson Blvd., Arlington, VA* ☎ *703/294–5233* ⊕ *www.cszdc.com* Ⓜ *Ballston.*

DC Improv. The food may be run-of-the-mill and the basement location somewhat tattered, but the Improv, as everyone calls it, is the only place in town to see well-known stand-up headliners. Recent acts have included Kevin Nealon, Colin Quinn, and a bevy of funny amateurs. ⊠ *1140 Connecticut Ave. NW, Downtown* ☎ *202/296–7008* ⊕ *www.dcimprov.com* Ⓜ *Farragut North.*

Gross National Product. This nonpartisan comedy troupe has been aiming its barbs at sitting presidents for years. Past shows include *Clintoons, All the President's Women,* and *Son of a Bush.* ☎ *202/783–7212* ⊕ *www.gnpcomedy.com.*

Washington Improv Theater (WIT). Refreshingly, WIT doesn't focus on Beltway politics, instead relying heavily on audience suggestions. Their smart, irreverent humor is performed to sell-out crowds at the blackbox theater of Flashpoint in Chinatown. The troupes Improv Nation and Jackie also fall under WIT's umbrella. ☎ *202/315–1315* ⊕ *www.dcwit.com.*

Dance Clubs

Washington's dance clubs seem constantly to be re-creating themselves. A club might offer heavy industrial music on Wednesday, be host to a largely gay clientele on Thursday, and thump to the sounds of '70s disco on Friday. Club-hoppers can choose from five hubs: Georgetown, Adams-Morgan, Dupont Circle, U Street, and along 9th Street NW near Metro Center.

Five. House music is what draws the crowds to this three-story club near Dupont Circle. And the sound track is constantly morphing—the house, hip-hop, and drum-and-bass tracks the DJs play on Wednesday become deep house and disco on Saturday. On Thursday the place echoes until the early morning with a Latin groove. ⊠ *1214B 18th St. NW, Dupont Circle* ☎ *202/331–7123* ⊕ *www.fivedc.com* Ⓜ *Dupont Circle.*

★ **Habana Village.** No matter what the temperature is outside, it's always balmy inside the unpretentious Habana Village. The tiny dance floors are packed nightly with couples moving to the latest live salsa and merengue tunes. When it's time to cool down, you can head to one of several lounges in this converted four-story town house and sip a *mojito* garnished with sugarcane, the house special. ✉ *1834 Columbia Rd. NW, Adams-Morgan* ☏ *202/462–6310* Ⓜ *Woodley Park/Zoo.*

★ **Love.** This four-story dance powerhouse looms over the industrial Northeast corridor far from downtown D.C. Elegant and minimalist, Love makes the most of its home, a former warehouse. Washington Wizards players and other celebs are frequently spotted in the VIP areas. The music changes from night to night, as well as from floor to floor, but you're sure to sample some salsa, house, and trance. Dress to impress the doorman at this wood-panel club, which attracts a primarily upscale, African-American clientele. ■ TIP→ **Shuttle service is available from 18th and M streets, a boon, considering Love's isolated, industrial locale.** ✉ *1350 Okie St. NE, Northeast* ☏ *202/636–9030* ⊕ *www.lovetheclub.com.*

Modern. A small, underground club with lowered bar and high-backed booths, Modern is cozy and familiar. The DJs spin songs you know, from Madonna to Outkast, and the clientele seems unconcerned about being seen. ✉ *3287 M St. NW, Georgetown* ☏ *202/338–7027* ⊕ *www. primacycompanies.com.*

Platinum. This upscale dance venue has retained the columns, grand staircase, and high ceilings from its previous life as a bank. The DJs play techno, hip-hop, house, and Latin music for three dance floors and a VIP lounge. ✉ *915 F St. NW, Downtown* ☏ *202/393–3555* ⊕ *www. platinumclubdc.com* Ⓜ *Metro Center.*

Gay & Lesbian Dance Clubs

Apex. At this prime hotspot for gay men, a light show, mirrors, and fog enhance the experience on the dance floor. It's a bit easier to get a drink at the upstairs bar. A room in the back shows '80s music videos. There's less attitude here than at larger clubs. ✉ *1415 22nd St. NW, Dupont Circle* ☏ *202/296–0505* ⊕ *www.apex-dc.com* Ⓜ *Dupont Circle.*

Chaos. It's hard to miss this subterranean club on Friday and Saturday with its strobe lights and thumping music. A young, chic lesbian crowd takes over on Wednesday, and Thursday is Latin night. Tuesday means drag bingo. ✉ *1603 17th St. NW, Dupont Circle* ☏ *202/232–4141* ⊕ *www.chaosdc.com* Ⓜ *Dupont Circle.*

Cobalt. Stop for a martini in the swank second-floor 30 Degrees lounge before heading upstairs to the dance floor. The Tuesday night "Flashback" parties are always fun, although most of the songs were recorded years before the twenty-somethings who pack the place were born. ✉ *1639 R St. NW, Dupont Circle* ☏ *202/462–6569* ⊕ *www.cobaltdc. com* Ⓜ *Dupont Circle.*

Remington's. Country-western dancing is all the rage at this cavernous club on Capitol Hill. On Sunday there are dance lessons from 5 to 7 and a women's tea dance from 5 to 9:30. ✉ *639 Pennsylvania Ave. SE, Capitol Hill* ☏ *202/543–3113* ⊕ *www.remingtonswdc.com* Ⓜ *Eastern Market.*

Jazz & Blues Clubs

The **D.C. Blues Society** (⊕ www.dcblues.org) is a clearinghouse for information on upcoming shows, festivals, and jam sessions in the metropolitan area. It also publishes a monthly newsletter.

Basin Street Lounge. Jazz combos perform Tuesday through Saturday in this New Orleans–style bar in Old Town Alexandria. Musicians from local military bands often stop by to sit in. ⊠ *219 King St., Alexandria, VA* ☎ *703/549–1141* Ⓜ *King Street.*

Fodor'sChoice **Blues Alley.** New Orleans–style cooking and well-known performers, such
★ as Nancy Wilson, Joshua Redman, and Wynton Marsalis, are staples at this legendary—and expensive—club, where jazz greats Dizzy Gillespie and Charlie Byrd once recorded live albums. ■ TIP→ **You can come for just the show, but those who enjoy a meal get better seats.** ⊠ *1073 Wisconsin Ave. NW, near M St., Georgetown* ☎ *202/337–4141* ⊕ *www. bluesalley.com* Ⓜ *Foggy Bottom.*

Bohemian Caverns. The low-ceiling stairway delivers you to a performance space made to look like a cave, a complete and accurate renovation of the Crystal Caverns, once a mainstay of D.C.'s "Black Broadway" and the place to see Miles Davis and Louis Armstrong. These days Friday and Saturday are given over to jazz; blues acts headline on Thursday; and open-mike night on Wednesday brings jazz-influenced poets to the stage. ⊠ *2001 11th St. NW, U Street corridor* ☎ *202/299–0801* ⊕ *www.bohemiancaverns.com* Ⓜ *U Street/Cardozo.*

Columbia Station. This unpretentious, neighborhood bar attracts an eclectic crowd, many of whom have just sensed a good vibe while walking by. Amber lights and morphed musical instruments adorn the walls, and high-quality live local jazz and blues fills the air. The large, open windows up front keep the place cool in summer months. ⊠ *2325 18th St. NW, Adams-Morgan* ☎ *202/462–6040* Ⓜ *Woodley Park/Zoo.*

★ **HR-57.** Named after a congressional resolution proclaiming jazz a "rare and valuable national treasure," HR-57 isn't just a club, it's also a nonprofit cultural center. The warm, inviting center spotlights musicians based in the D.C. area, many of whom have national followings. Fried chicken and collard greens are on the menu; beer and wine are available, or bring your own bottle (corkage is $3 per person). ⊠ *1610 14th St. NW, Logan Circle* ☎ *202/667–3700* ⊕ *www.hr57.org* Ⓜ *U Street/Cardozo.*

Mr. Henry's. This laid-back club is the last holdout of a once-thriving live-music scene on Capitol Hill. Roberta Flack got her start in the upstairs performance space, where a dozen or so tables are scattered around the wood-paneled room. There's never a cover. ⊠ *601 Pennsylvania Ave. SE, Capitol Hill* ☎ *202/546–8412* Ⓜ *Eastern Market.*

New Vegas Lounge. This longtime favorite is the home of Dr. Blues, and he doesn't allow any soft-jazz-bluesy-fusion in his house. Even during the weekly open-jam session, it's strictly no-nonsense wailing guitar rhythms by seasoned local players. ⊠ *1415 P St. NW, Dupont Circle* ☎ *202/483–3971* ⊕ *www.thenewvegaslounge.com* Ⓜ *Dupont Circle.*

Takoma Station Tavern. Beside the subway stop that lends it its name, the Takoma hosts such local favorites as Marshall Keys and Keith Killgo, with the occasional nationally known artist stopping by to jam. The jazz happy hours starting at 6:30 PM Thursday and Friday pack the joint. There's reggae on Saturday and comedy on Monday. Sneakers and athletic wear are not allowed. ✉ *6914 4th St. NW, Takoma Park* ☎ *202/ 829–1999* ⊕ *www.takomastation.com* Ⓜ *Takoma.*

Twins Jazz. Twin sisters Kelly and Maze Tesfaye have made this cozy space a haven for some of D.C.'s strongest straight-ahead jazz players, as well as for groups from New York City. On the club's menu are tasty Ethiopian appetizers along with staples such as nachos, wings, and burgers. ✉ *1344 U St. NW, U Street corridor* ☎ *202/234–0072* ⊕ *www. twinsjazz.com* Ⓜ *U Street/Cardozo.*

Rock & Pop Clubs

4

Fodor'sChoice
★
Black Cat. Come here to see the latest local bands as well as indie stars such as Neko Case, Modest Mouse, and Clinic. The post-punk crowd whiles away the time in the Red Room, a side bar with pool tables, an eclectic jukebox, and no cover charge. ✉ *1811 14th St. NW, U Street corridor* ☎ *202/667–7960* ⊕ *www.blackcatdc.com* Ⓜ *U Street/Cardozo.*

DC9. With live music seven days a week, this two-story rock club hosts up-and-coming indie rock bands. There's a narrow bar on the ground floor and a humongous concert space upstairs. ✉ *1940 9th St. NW, U Street corridor* ☎ *202/483–5000* ⊕ *www.dcnine.com* Ⓜ *U Street/Cardozo.*

Nation. As one of Washington's best midsize venues, this sprawling space brings in such acts as Lenny Kravitz, George Clinton, and Blondie. On a separate side of the club, you can gyrate to a mix of mostly alternative dance music. On Friday night Nation becomes "Buzz," a massive rave with the latest permutations of techno and drum-and-bass music. On Saturday it's a gay party called "Velvet." ✉ *1015 Half St. SE, Southeast* ☎ *202/554–1500* ⊕ *www.primacycompanies.com* Ⓜ *Navy Yard.*

★ **9:30 Club.** When they come to town, the best of the nonstadium performers, and a few of the bigger acts, play this large but cozy space wrapped by balconies on three sides. Recent acts have included Macy Gray, Ani DiFranco, and the Roots. ✉ *815 V St. NW, U Street corridor* ☎ *202/393–0930* ⊕ *www.930.com* Ⓜ *U Street/Cardozo.*

Velvet Lounge. Squeeze up the narrow stairway and check out the eclectic local and national bands that play at this unassuming neighborhood joint. Performers ranging from indie mainstays to acclaimed up-and-comers rock the house with psychobilly, alt-country, and indie pop. ✉ *915 U St. NW, U Street corridor* ☎ *202/462–3213* ⊕ *www.velvetloungedc. com* Ⓜ *U Street/Cardozo.*

Sports &
the Outdoors

WORD OF MOUTH

"The Caps are so much fun to watch. You can get cheap tickets and have a lot of fun up in the nose-bleed seats."

—kgh8m

"DC is an excellent place to ride bikes, with the mall area there is so much . . . that is off-street riding."

—rbud87

By Mitchell
Tropin

WASHINGTON'S 69 SQUARE MILES are in part a fantastic recreational backyard, with dozens of beautiful open spaces. Rock Creek Park has miles of wooded trails and paths for bikers, runners, and walkers that extend to almost every part of the city. The National Mall connects the Lincoln Memorial and the Capitol building. With the monuments as a backdrop, you can spike a volleyball, ride a bike, or take a jog. Around the Tidal Basin, see the Jefferson Memorial from a paddleboat or run alongside the Potomac River. Theodore Roosevelt Island, a wildlife sanctuary that deserves to be better known, has several paths for hiking and enjoyable spots for a picnic.

Every season in D.C. has something special to offer. In winter visitors can enjoy an old-fashioned afternoon of ice-skating and hot chocolate, or go to the Verizon Center to see the Wizards play pro basketball or the Capitals play hockey. In spring the city emerges from the cold with activities everywhere: runners become a common sight on the Mall. Fishing and boating are available nearby. In summer volleyball enthusiasts play far into the extended daylight hours. Fans can see the Washington Nationals and enjoy Major League Baseball at nearby Robert F. Kennedy Stadium, or take a short train ride to root for the Baltimore Orioles in their classic ballpark, Orioles Park at Camden Yards. When fall comes, the seasonal colors of the trees in Rock Creek Park are a spectacular sight for bikers, hikers, and runners. Soccer teams from all over the globe head to RFK Stadium, and football fans head to FedEx Field to see the Redskins.

Baseball

Fodor'sChoice
★

Major League Baseball has returned to D.C., where the **Washington Nationals** (✉ 2400 E. Capitol St. SE, Washington, DC ☎ 202/675–6287 ⊕ washington.nationals.mlb.com Ⓜ Stadium-Armory) of the National League play in their temporary home, Robert F. Kennedy Stadium. RFK seats 58,000. Tickets range from $7 in the upper deck to $40 for box seats in the lower deck. Diamond box seats are available starting at $90. Individual game tickets may be purchased at RFK Stadium or through the team's Web site. ■ TIP➔ **The Metro is a hassle-free and inexpensive way to get to RFK Stadium. Take the Blue or Orange line to the Stadium-Armory station.**

To experience major-league baseball in an old-fashioned stadium setting, fans go to Baltimore and root for the **Baltimore Orioles** (✉ 333 W. Camden St., Baltimore, MD ☎ 888/848–2473 or 410/685–9600, 410/685–9800 general information, 410/332–4633 Ext. 158 Warehouse ⊕ baltimore.orioles.mlb.com). The team plays in beautiful Oriole Park at Camden Yards, which seats 48,000. Tickets range from $15 for spots in the bleachers to $45 for club level. Individual game tickets may be purchased from the Orioles Web site, in Washington at the **Orioles Shop** (✉ 925 17th St. NW, Downtown ☎ 202/296–2473), or by going to the Oriole Park's Warehouse box office. Special light-rail trains run to the stadium from Washington's Union Station.

Basketball

The WNBA's **Washington Mystics** (✉ 6th and F Sts., Downtown ☎ 202/432–7328 ⊕ www.wnba.com/mystics Ⓜ Gallery Pl./Chinatown) play at the Verizon Center in downtown Washington. Ticket prices range from $14 to $75, with some tickets for $8 in the uppermost seats. You can buy tickets at the Verizon Center box office or through Ticketmaster. The women's basketball season runs from late May to August.

★ The NBA's **Washington Wizards** (✉ 6th and F Sts., Downtown ☎ 202/432–7328 ⊕ www.nba.com/wizards Ⓜ Gallery Pl./Chinatown) play from October to April at the Verizon Center in downtown Washington. Tickets for individual games cost $40 to $125, with some tickets for $10 in the nosebleed section. Buy tickets from the Verizon Center box office or from Ticketmaster.

> ■ TIP→ **Parking is nonexistent around the Verizon Center. Save yourself some grief and take the Metro to the Gallery Place/Chinatown station on the Red line.**

TOP 5

■ **Picture-postcard motivation:** Run or bike with Washington's monuments as a unique background.

■ **The seventh inning stretch:** Enjoy the return of the national pastime at RFK Stadium.

■ **Bird-watching on Theodore Roosevelt Island:** Take in the spectacular scenery at the wildlife sanctuary.

■ **Goal!:** Cheer with thousands as the world's greatest soccer teams play at RFK Stadium.

■ **A new perspective on the cherry trees:** Take a leisurely trip in a paddleboat around the Tidal Basin, surrounded by the famous blossoms in spring.

Bicycling

The numerous trails in the District and its surrounding areas are well maintained and clearly marked.

For scenery, you can't beat the **C&O Canal Towpath** (⊕ www.nps.gov/choh), which starts in Georgetown and runs along the C&O Canal into Maryland. You could pedal to the end of the canal, nearly 200 mi away in Cumberland, Maryland, but most cyclists stop at Great Falls, 13 mi from where the canal starts. The occasionally bumpy towpath, made of gravel and packed earth, passes through wooded areas of the C&O Canal National Historical Park. You can see 19th-century locks from the canal's working days, and if you're particularly lucky, you may catch a glimpse of mules pulling a canal barge. The barges now take passengers, not cargo.

Suited for bicyclists, walkers, rollerbladers, and strollers, the paved **Capital Crescent Trail** (☎ 202/234–4874 Capital Crescent Coalition) stretches along the old Georgetown Branch, a B&O Railroad line that was completed in 1910 and was in operation until 1985. The 7½-mi route's first leg runs from Georgetown near Key Bridge to central Bethesda at Bethesda and Woodmont avenues. At Bethesda and Woodmont, the trail heads through a well-lighted tunnel near the heart of

Bethesda's lively business area and continues into Silver Spring. The 3½-mi stretch from Bethesda to Silver Spring is gravel. The Georgetown Branch Trail, as this section is officially named, connects with the Rock Creek Trail, which goes to Rockville in the north and Memorial Bridge past the Washington Monument in the south. On weekends when the weather's nice, all sections of the trails are crowded.

> ## BIKING THE MALL
>
> A pleasant loop route begins at the Lincoln Memorial, going north past the Washington Memorial, and turning around at the Tidal Basin. Along the way are small fountains and parks for taking a break and getting a drink of water.

Cyclists interested in serious training might try the 3-mi loop around the golf course in **East Potomac Park** (☎ 202/485–9874 National Park Service) at Hains Point, the southern area of the park (entry is near the Jefferson Memorial). It's a favorite training course for dedicated local racers and would-be triathletes. ■ TIP→ **Going to the most southern point in the park, where the Anacostia and Potomac rivers merge, you'll come face to face with one of Washington's most unique and fun sculptures, *The Awakening,* a half-buried giant. A must-see, this enormous hand and head contrast sharply with the usual statutes of generals and statesmen.** If time permits, jog or bike over to the impressive Franklin Delano Roosevelt Memorial. Restrict your workouts to the daytime; the area is not safe after dark.

Each day, bicyclists cruise **The Mall** amid the endless throngs of runners, walkers, and tourists. There's relatively little car traffic, and bikers can take in some of Washington's landmarks, such as the Washington Monument, the Reflecting Pool, the Vietnam Memorial, and some of the city's more interesting architecture, such as the Smithsonian Castle and the Hirshhorn, the "Doughnut on the Mall."

Mount Vernon Trail, across the Potomac in Virginia, has two sections. The northern part, closest to D.C. proper, is 3½-mi long and begins near the causeway across the river from the Kennedy Center that heads to Theodore Roosevelt Island (⇨ Hiking). It then passes Ronald Reagan National Airport and continues on to Old Town Alexandria. This section has slight slopes and almost no interruptions for traffic, making it a delightful, but challenging, biking route. Even relatively inexperienced bikers enjoy the trail, which gives wonderful views of the Potomac. To access the trail from the District, take the Theodore Roosevelt Bridge or the Rochambeau Memorial Bridge, also known as the 14th Street Bridge. South of the airport, the trail runs down to the Washington Marina. The final mile of the trail's northern section meanders through protected wetlands before ending in the heart of Old Town Alexandria. The trail's 9-mi southern section extends along the Potomac from Alexandria to Mount Vernon.

Rock Creek Park covers an area from the edge of Georgetown to Montgomery County, Maryland. The bike path there is asphalt and has a few challenging hills, but it's mostly flat. You can bike several miles without having to stop for cars (the roadway is closed entirely to cars on the weekend). The two separate northern parts of the trail, which begin in

Fodor'sChoice
★

5

Bethesda and Silver Spring, merge around the Washington, D.C., line. Many bikers gather at this point and follow the trail on a path that goes past the Washington Zoo and eventually runs toward the Lincoln Memorial and Kennedy Center. Fifteen miles of dirt trails are also in the park; these are best for hiking.

Information

Washington Area Bicyclist Association (✉ 733 15th St. NW, Northwest ☎ 202/628–2500 ⊕ www.waba.org).

Rentals & Tours

Bicycle Pro Shop Georgetown (✉ 3403 M St. NW, Georgetown ☎ 202/337–0311), near Georgetown University and Key Bridge by the Potomac River, rents city bikes for $20 per day.

Big Wheel Bikes, near the C&O Canal Towpath, rents multispeed bikes for $25 per day and $15 for three hours. A second location is near the Capital Crescent Trail. There's also an Alexandria branch for those who want to ride the Mount Vernon Trail. ✉ *1034 33rd St. NW, Georgetown* ☎ *202/337–0254* ✉ *6917 Arlington Rd., Bethesda, MD* ☎ *301/652–0192* ✉ *2 Prince St., Alexandria, VA* ☎ *703/739–2300.*

Bike the Sites (☎ 202/966–8662 ⊕ www.bikethesites.com) is a tour company that offers three-hour, 8-mi guided tours of downtown Washington. Costs range from $35 to $55, and bike rental is included. Advance reservations are required. Tours start from the Mall.

Fletcher's Boat House (✉ 4940 Canal Rd., at Reservoir Rd., Foxhall ☎ 202/244–0461), next to the C&O Towpath and Capital Crescent Trail, rents fixed-gear bikes for $8 per hour and $19 per day.

Revolution Bikes (✉ 3411 M St. NW, Georgetown ☎ 202/965–3601), near Georgetown University and Key Bridge by the Potomac River, rents city bikes for $20 per day.

Thompson's Boat Center (✉ 2900 Virginia Ave. NW, Foggy Bottom ☎ 202/333–4861) allows easy access to the Rock Creek Trail and the C&O Towpath and is close to the monuments. All-terrain bikes are $8 per hour and $25 per day. Fixed-gear and children's bikes are $8 per hour and $15 per day. Children's trailers (attachments to adult bikes) rent for $4 per hour or $15 per day.

Washington Sailing Marina (✉ 1 Marina Dr., Alexandria, VA ☎ 703/548–9027 ⊕ www.washingtonsailingmarina.com) rents all-terrain bikes for $6 per hour and $22 per day. Fixed-gear bikes are $4 per hour and $16.50 per day. The marina is on the Mount Vernon Trail off the George Washington Parkway, south of Ronald Reagan National Airport.

Boating & Sailing

The Chesapeake Bay is one of the great sailing basins of the world. For scenic and historical sightseeing, take a day trip to Annapolis, Maryland, the home of the U.S. Naval Academy. ■ TIP→ **The popularity of boating and the many boating businesses in Annapolis make it one of the best civilian sailing centers on the East Coast.**

Canoeing, sailing, and powerboating are all popular in the Washington, D.C., area. Several places rent boats along the **Potomac River** north and south of the city. You can dip your oars just about anywhere along the river—go canoeing in the C&O Canal, sailing in the widening river south of Alexandria, or even kayaking in the raging rapids at Great Falls, a 30-minute drive from the capital.

Rentals

Belle Haven Marina (✉ George Washington Pkwy., Alexandria, VA ☎ 703/768–0018), south of Reagan National Airport and Old Town Alexandria, rents three types of sailboats: Sunfish are $30 for two hours during the week and $35 for two hours on the weekend; Hobie Cat–style sailboats and Flying Scots are $46 for two hours during the week and $54 for two hours during the weekend. Canoes and kayaks are available for rent at $20 for two hours. Rentals are available from April to October.

Fletcher's Boat House (✉ 4940 Canal Rd., at Reservoir Rd., Foxhall ☎ 202/244–0461), just north of Georgetown, rents 17-foot rowboats for $11 per hour and $20 per day. Canoes are available for rent at $11 per hour and $21 per day.

Thompson's Boat Center (✉ 2900 Virginia Ave. NW, Foggy Bottom ☎ 202/333–4861) is near Georgetown and Theodore Roosevelt Island. The center rents canoes for $8 per hour and $22 per day. Single kayaks are $8 per hour and $24 per day, and double kayaks are $10 per hour and $30 per day. Rowing sculls are also available, but you must demonstrate prior experience and a suitably high skill level.

FodorsChoice ★ **Tidal Basin** (✉ Bordered by Independence Ave. and Maine Ave., The Mall ☎ 202/479–2426 Ⓜ Farragut W), in front of the Jefferson Memorial, rents paddleboats beginning in April and usually ending in September, depending on how cold the water gets. The entrance is at 1501 Maine Avenue SW, on the east side of the Tidal Basin. You can rent two-passenger boats at $8 per hour and four-passenger boats at $16 per hour.

> **WORD OF MOUTH**
>
> "]ust north of Georgetown there's a place you can rent rowboats or canoes by the hour. We had so much fun because the [Potomac] River has no visible development along that stretch, so we could imagine being back in the 'old' days."   –lcuy

Fishing

The **Potomac River** is something of an environmental success story. Once dangerously polluted, it has rebounded. Now largemouth bass, striped bass, shad, and white and yellow perch are all down there somewhere, willing to take your bait. Simply renting a boat and going fishing in Washington is complicated, because this stretch of the Potomac is divided among the three jurisdictions of Virginia, Maryland, and the District of Columbia. It isn't always easy to determine in whose water you're fishing or which licenses you should have. One solution: hire a guide.

■ TIP→ One 5-mi stretch of the Potomac—roughly from the Wilson Memorial Bridge in Alexandria south to Fort Washington National Park—is one of the country's best spots for largemouth-bass fishing. It has, in fact, become something of an East Coast destination for anglers in search of this particular fish. The area around Fletcher's Boat House on the C&O Canal is one of the best spots for perch. People at the boathouse also are a good source of information on local fishing conditions. They can be reached at ☎ 202/337–0311.

Information & Guides

Nationally known fishing writer **Gene Mueller** has a column that appears three times a week in the *Washington Times*. He gladly takes readers' phone calls Thursday mornings at ☎ 202/636–3268. The **"Fish Lines"** column in Friday's *Washington Post* "Weekend" section, written by Gary Diamond, outlines where the fish are biting, from the Potomac to the Chesapeake Bay.

Run by nationally known fisherman and conservationist Ken Penrod, **Life Outdoors Unlimited** (☎ 301/937–0010) is an umbrella group of the area's best freshwater fishing guides. For about $250 a day a guide sees to all your needs, from tackle to boats, and tells you which licenses are required. All of the guides are pros and experts who are also able to teach novices. You might be asked to leave a message; calls are usually returned the same evening.

Football

There have been many changes within the **Washington Redskins** (☎ 301/276–6000 FedEx Field stadium ⊕ www.redskins.com) organization since Dan Snyder became the owner in July 1999. But one thing remains the same: tickets are difficult to get. Though FedEx Field is the largest football stadium in the NFL, all 80,000 seats are held by season-ticket holders. Occasionally you can find tickets advertised in the classifieds of the *Washington Post* or buy them from online ticket vendors and auction sites—at top dollar, of course. Tickets can range from $175 to $300 for less popular opponents and go as high as $800 for elite teams, such as the New York Giants, or Washington's biggest rival, the Dallas Cowboys. ■ TIP→ **Tickets are difficult to get, but fans can see the players up close and for free at training camp, held in August.** The Redskins invite the public to attend their training camp in Ashburn, in nearby Loudoun County, Virginia. Parking and admission are free. Camp begins in late July and continues through mid-August. The practices typically last from 90 minutes to two hours. Fans can bring their own chairs, and the players are usually available after practice to sign autographs. Call ahead to make sure the practices are open that day. A practice schedule is on the team's Web site.

Golf

Serious golfers must resign themselves to driving out of the city to find a worthwhile course. None of the three public courses in town is first-rate. Still, people line up to play here and at about 50 other area public courses, sometimes arriving as early as 2 AM to snare a tee time. Some courses allow you to make a reservation in advance.

Public Courses in the District

The claim to fame of the flat, wide, and featureless **East Potomac Park Golf Course** (⊠ 972 Ohio Dr. SW, Southwest ☎ 202/554–7660) is that professional golfer and Washington resident Lee Elder got his start here. The course is 6,599 yards from the back tees, and par 72. Two 9-hole courses and a driving range are on the property, as well as one of the country's oldest miniature golf courses. Greens fees are $20 for 18 holes and $14 for 9 holes on weekdays—on weekends it's $24 and $17, respectively. The course is on the eastern side of the park, near the Jefferson Memorial.

The 4,798-yard, par-65 **Rock Creek Park Golf Course** (✉ 16th and Rittenhouse Sts. NW, Northwest/Upper Connecticut Ave. ☎ 202/882–7332) is the most attractive public course in the capital. The front 9 holes are easy, but the tight, rolling, well-treed back 9 are challenging. Greens fees are $15 for 18 holes and $9 for 9 holes on weekdays; weekend fees are $23 and $15.50.

Hiking

Hikes and nature walks are listed in the Friday "Weekend" section of the *Washington Post*. Several area organizations sponsor outings, and most are guided: the **Potomac-Appalachian Trail Club** (✉ 118 Park St. SE, Vienna, VA 22180 ☎ 703/242–0965) sponsors hikes—usually free—on trails from Pennsylvania to Virginia, including the C&O Canal and the Appalachian Trail. The **Sierra Club** (☎ 202/547–2326) has many regional outings; call for details.

The **Billy Goat Trail** (✉ MacArthur Blvd., Potomac, MD 20854 ☎ 301/413–0720 ⊕ www.nps.gov/choh) has some outstanding views of the wilder parts of the Potomac. This challenging 2-mi trail, which starts and ends at the C&O Canal towpath below Great Falls, has some steep downhills and climbs.

★ **Theodore Roosevelt Island** (✉ Foggy Bottom ☎ 703/289–2552 or 703/289–2550 ⊕ www.nps.gov/this), designed as a memorial to the environmentally minded president, is a wildlife sanctuary off the George Washington Parkway on the Virginia side of the city. It can be reached by car by taking the Theodore Roosevelt Bridge or I–66. Hikers and bicyclists can easily reach it by taking the 14th Street Bridge. Many birds and other animals live in the island's marsh and forests.

A self-guided nature trail winds through **Woodend** (✉ 8940 Jones Mill Rd., Chevy Chase, MD 20815 ☎ 301/652–9188, 301/652–1088 for recent bird sightings ⊕ www.audubonnaturalist.org), a verdant 40-acre estate, and around the suburban Maryland headquarters of the local **Audubon Naturalist Society.** The estate was designed in the 1920s by Jefferson Memorial architect John Russell Pope and has a mansion, also called Woodend, on its grounds. You're never far from the trill of birdsong here, as the Audubon Society has turned the place into something of a private nature preserve, forbidding the use of toxic chemicals and leaving some areas in a wild, natural state. Programs include wildlife identification walks, environmental education programs, and a weekly Saturday bird walk September through June. A bookstore stocks titles on conservation, ecology, and birds. The grounds are open daily sunrise to sunset, and admission is free.

Hockey

One of pro hockey's better teams, the **Washington Capitals** (⌧ 6th and F Sts., Downtown ☎202/432–7328 ⊕www.washingtoncaps.com Ⓜ Gallery Pl./Chinatown), play home games October through April at the Verizon Center. Tickets range from $25 to $99, with $10 tickets available in the nosebleed section. VIP tickets also are available at $150 or $230 and can be purchased at the Verizon Center box office, or from Ticketmaster. Tickets can be purchased directly from the team's Web site.

Ice-Skating

Area rinks typically charge $4–$5.50 for a two-hour session, with slightly lower fees for children and seniors. Skate rentals, available at all the rinks listed, are usually around $2 or $2.50. Some rinks charge a small fee for renting a locker.

The **National Gallery of Art Ice Rink** (⌧ Constitution Ave. NW, between 7th and 9th Sts., Downtown ☎ 202/289–3361 Ⓜ Navy Memorial/ Archives) is surrounded by the gallery's Sculpture Garden. The art deco design of the rink makes it one of the most popular outdoor winter sites in Washington. In spring the rink becomes a fountain.

★ The prime location of the **Pershing Park Ice Rink** (⌧ Pennsylvania Ave. and 14th St. NW, Downtown ☎ 202/737–6938 Ⓜ Metro Center), a few blocks from the White House, major hotels, and a Metro station, makes this rink one of the most convenient spots in Washington for outdoor skating.

Kite Flying

★ ☾ The Smithsonian's annual **kite festival** (⌧ Downtown ☎ 202/357–3030 ⊕ www.kitefestival.org Ⓜ Smithsonian) at the National Mall gives kids and adults a chance to enjoy a day of kite flying on the National Mall. The granddaddy of kite festivals, held in connection with the Cherry Blossom Festival in April, also features kite battles and incredible kite flying exhibitions.

Running

Running is one of the best ways to see the city, and several scenic trails wend through downtown Washington and nearby Northern Virginia. It can be dangerous to run at night on the trails, although the streets are fairly well lighted. Even in daylight, it's best to run in pairs when venturing beyond public areas or heavily used sections of trails. Most city streets are safe for runs alone during the day, especially around government buildings, museums, and monuments, where there's additional police protection. Many hotels offer maps of routes that include city landmarks.

The 89-mi-long **C&O Canal Towpath** (⊕ www.nps.gov/choh) in the C&O National Historical Park is a favorite of runners and cyclists. The path is mostly gravel and dirt, making it easy on knees and feet. The most popular loop, which goes from a point just north of the Key Bridge in Georgetown to Fletcher's Boat House, is about 4 mi round-trip.

The most popular running route in Washington is the 4½-mi loop on **The Mall** around the Capitol and past the Smithsonian museums, the Washington Monument, the Reflecting Pool, and the Lincoln Memorial. At any time of day, hundreds of runners, speed walkers, bicyclists, and tourists make their way along the gravel pathways. For a longer run, veer south of the Mall on either side of the Tidal Basin and head for the Jefferson Memorial and East Potomac Park, the site of many races.

Across the Potomac in Virginia is the **Mount Vernon Trail,** a favorite with Washington runners. The 3½-mi northern section begins near the pedestrian causeway leading to Theodore Roosevelt Island (directly across the river from the Kennedy Center) and goes past Ronald Reagan National Airport and on to Old Town Alexandria. You can get to the trail from the District by crossing either the Theodore Roosevelt Bridge at the Lincoln Memorial or the Rochambeau Memorial Bridge at the Jefferson Memorial. South of the airport, the trail runs down to the Washington Marina. The 9-mi southern section leads to Mount Vernon.

Rock Creek Park has 15 mi of trails, a bicycle path, a bridle path, picnic groves, playgrounds, and the boulder-strewn rolling stream that gives it its name. The creek isn't safe or pleasant for swimming. Starting one block south of the corner of P and 22nd streets on the edge of Georgetown, Rock Creek Park runs all the way to Montgomery County, Maryland. The most popular run in the park is a trail along the creek from Georgetown to the National Zoo: about a 4-mi loop. In summer there's considerable shade, and there are water fountains and an exercise station along the way. The roadway is closed to traffic on weekends.

Information & Organizations

Group runs and weekend races around Washington are listed in the Friday "Weekend" section of the *Washington Post.* You can also check the Thursday calendar of events in the *Washington Times.* Comprehensive listings of running and walking events are posted online by the *Washington Running Report* (⊕ www.runwashington.com), *racePacket* (⊕ www.racepacket.com), and MetroSports (⊕ www.metrosports.com). Other reliable sources for races and casual running gatherings are the Montgomery County Road Runners Club (⊕ www.mcrrc.org), the nation's third-largest running club, and the D.C. Road Runners Club (⊕ www.dcroadrunners.com).

Tuesday and Thursday evenings at 6:30 PM you can join the **Capitol Hill Runners** (☎ 301/283–0821) on a 6- to 8-mi run, which begins at the Reflecting Pool at the base of the Capitol's west side. Most Sunday mornings the **Fleet Feet Sports Shop** (⊠ 1841 Columbia Rd. NW, Adams-Morgan ☎ 202/387–3888) sponsors informal runs through Rock Creek Park and other areas. The shop's owner, Phil Fenty, leads the runs. The courses change at Phil's discretion and usually go from 5 to 7 mi. Call the **Gatorade and Road Runners Club of America Hotline** (☎ 703/683–7722) for general information about running and racing in the area. If you're a runner visiting Washington in early June, consider entering D.C.'s Race

Tickets & Venues

You can buy tickets for most major sporting events at stadium box offices or from **Ticketmaster** (✉ 1300 Pennsylvania Ave. NW ✉ 1201 G St. NW, Metro Center ✉ 1100 Pennsylvania Ave. NW, Old Post Office Pavilion ✉ 2000 Pennsylvania Ave. NW, Tower Records ✉ 13th and G Sts. NW, Warner Theatre ☎ 202/432–7328 or 410/481–7328, 800/527–6384 outside D.C. and Baltimore areas ⊕ www.ticketmaster.com), which has many outlets throughout the city.

Many sporting events, including hockey, basketball, lacrosse, and figure skating, take place at the modern

Verizon Center (✉ 601 F St. NW, between 6th and 7th Sts., Downtown ☎ 202/628–3200, 202/432–7328 box office ⊕ www.mcicenter.com). The perennially popular Washington Redskins play at **FedEx Field** (✉ Arena Dr., Landover, MD ☎ 301/276–6070 ⊕ www.redskins.com). **Robert F. Kennedy Stadium** (✉ 2400 E. Capitol St. NE, at 22nd St., Capitol Hill ☎ 202/628–3200 Ⓜ Stadium) showcases some of the greatest soccer teams from Europe and Latin America, along with the Major League Soccer team D.C. United.

for the Cure, the world's largest 3.1-mi event. Join 50,000 runners and walkers raising huge amounts for breast cancer research.

Soccer

FodorsChoice ★ **D.C. United** (✉ Robert F. Kennedy Stadium, 2400 E. Capitol St. SE, Capitol Hill ☎ 202/547–3134 ⊕ www.dcunited.com Ⓜ Stadium) is one of the best Major League Soccer (U.S. pro soccer) teams. International matches, including some World Cup preliminaries, are often played on RFK Stadium's grass field, dedicated exclusively to soccer play. Games are April through September. You can buy tickets, which generally cost $16–$40, with discounts for groups, at the RFK Stadium ticket office, or through Ticketmaster.

Tennis

The District maintains 123 outdoor courts, but because some are in seedy parts of town, check on the neighborhood in question before heading out. Contact the **D.C. Department of Recreation** (✉ 3149 16th St. NW, Northwest 20010 ☎ 202/673–7646) for a list of city-run courts and information about specific courts.

Hains Point (✉ East Potomac Park, Southwest ☎ 202/554–5962) has outdoor tennis courts, as well as courts under a bubble for wintertime play. Fees run from $5 to $30.75 an hour depending on the time, the season, and whether it's an indoor or outdoor court. Make court reservations as early as possible—up to a week in advance. To reach Hains Point, take 15th Street south to the Tidal Basin and then follow signs to East Potomac Park. For current conditions, contact the **National Park Service's East Potomac Park Office** (☎ 202/234–4874).

Rock Creek Tennis Center (✉ 16th and Kennedy Sts. NW, Northwest/Upper Connecticut Ave. ☎ 202/722–5949) has clay and hard courts. Fees depend on the time, the season, and whether you're playing indoors or out. You can make reservations up to a week in advance.

Volleyball

Possibly the most idyllic noncoastal volleyball venue you'll ever find, the 11 public courts that make up the **Underpass Volleyball Courts** (✉ 1100 Ohio Dr. SW, between Rock Creek Pkwy. and Independence Ave., The Mall ☎ 202/619–7225) are in the shadow of the Lincoln Memorial and Washington Monument and bordering the Potomac River. The courts are in an unnamed park area that's run cooperatively by the National Park Service and the D.C. government, with six of the courts reserved for organizations granted permits through the city and the remaining five available on a first-come, first-served basis.

Yoga & Pilates

Many of the Pilates and yoga facilities in town allow out-of-towners to drop in for classes.

Ashtanga Yoga (✉ 4435 Wisconsin Ave., Georgetown ☎ 202/342–6029 ⊕ www.ashtangayogadc.com) employs the ashtanga system of hatha yoga, which emphasizes synchronizing the breath with a progressive series of postures. Drop-in classes are $15.

Boundless Yoga (✉ 1510 U St., U Street corridor ☎ 202/234–9642 ⊕ www.boundlessyoga.com Ⓜ U St.) is close to downtown hotels. The studio emphasizes vinyasa yoga, which focuses on alignment-based, slow, flowing movement. Drop-in classes cost around $18 for upper-level, $17 for beginning-level classes.

DCYoga (✉ 1635 Connecticut Ave., Dupont Circle ☎ 202/232–2926 ⊕ www.dcyoga.com Ⓜ Dupont Circle), a few blocks from the Dupont Circle Metro station, specializes in yoga nidra (for relaxation) and bodhisattva yoga. Pilates classes also are available. Drop-in classes are $15.

Tranquil Space Yoga (✉ 2024 P St., Dupont Circle ☎ 202/223–9642 ⊕ www.tranquilspace.com Ⓜ Dupont Circle), a few blocks from the Dupont Circle Metro station, has an extensive schedule focusing on vinyasa yoga. Drop-in classes are $16.

Shopping

WORD OF MOUTH

"Breakfast. Wander. Shop. I think Georgetown would fit the bill nicely."

—obxgirl

"Old Town is good, quite a few good clothing shops, antiques, and home stores too. Lots of artists in the Torpedo Factory . . ."

—sprin2

Updated by
Sylvia Renner
and Erin
Renner

AFRICAN MASKS that could have inspired Picasso; kitchenware as objets d'art; bargains on Christian Dior, Hugo Boss, and Burberry; paisley scarves from India; American and European antiques; books of every description; handicrafts from almost two dozen Native American tribes; music boxes by the thousands; busts of U.S. presidents; textiles by the armful; fine leather goods—all this and more can be found in the nation's capital.

One place to find particularly unique goods is in the many museum gift shops, both on the Mall and elsewhere. Not only can you buy postcards and books about the artists whose works are on display in the National Gallery of Art or the Corcoran, but you can often find clothing and jewelry—from sweaters to silk scarves—inspired by these artists. And dinosaur puzzles, astronaut food, and field guides are just some of the other items you can find in the science museums.

If it's art you're seeking (even just to look at), keep in mind that Washington has three main gallery districts, though small art galleries can be found all over the city in converted houses and storefronts. Whatever their location, many close on Sunday and Monday or keep unusual hours. For a comprehensive review of current and future exhibits, pick up a copy of *Galleries* magazine (www.artline.com), available in some galleries. The ever-dependable *Washington Post* "Weekend" section and *Washington CityPaper* (published on Thursday) are also excellent sources.

In other parts of town, discriminating shoppers can find satisfaction at Filene's Basement (the Boston-based fashion discounter) or at upscale malls on the city's outskirts. Many of the smaller one-of-a-kind shops have survived urban renewal, the number of designer boutiques is on the rise, and interesting specialty shops and new shopping areas are springing up all over town. Weekdays, downtown street vendors offer a funky mix of jewelry; brightly patterned ties; buyer-beware watches; sunglasses; and African-inspired clothing, accessories, and art. Of course, T-shirts and Capitol City souvenirs are always in plentiful supply, especially on the streets ringing *the* Mall.

Store hours vary greatly. In general, Georgetown stores are open late and on Sunday; stores downtown that cater to office workers close at 6 PM and may not open at all on weekends. Some stores extend their hours on Thursday. Sales tax is 5.75%, and major credit cards and traveler's checks are accepted virtually everywhere. Each shop's listing includes the nearest Metro station, although some may be as far as a 15- to 20-minute walk; we do not list Metro stops for the few stores that have no convenient Metro.

Adams-Morgan

Scattered among the dozens of Latin, Ethiopian, and Caribbean restaurants in this most bohemian of Washington neighborhoods are a score of eccentric shops. If quality is what you seek, **Adams-Morgan** and nearby Woodley Park can be a minefield; tread cautiously. Still, for the bargain hunter it's great fun. ■ TIP→ **If bound for a specific shop, you may wish to call ahead to verify hours.** Adams-Morganites are often not clock-watchers, although you can be sure an afternoon stroll on the weekend will find a good representation of the shops open and give you a few hours of great browsing. ✉ *18th St. NW between Florida Ave. and Columbia Ave., Adams-Morgan* Ⓜ *Woodley Park/Zoo or Dupont Circle.*

Specialty Stores

ANTIQUES & COLLECTIBLES

★ **Miss Pixie's Furnishings and Whatnot.** The well-chosen collectibles—hand-picked by Miss Pixie herself—include gorgeous parasols and umbrellas, antique home furnishings, glass- and silverware, vintage clothes, and hardwood bed frames. The reasonable prices should help hold your attention. ✉ *2473 18th St. NW, Adams-Morgan* ☎ *202/232–8171* ⊕ *www. misspixies.com* ⊙ *Closed Mon.–Wed.* Ⓜ *Woodley Park/Zoo.*

Toro Mata. The walls of this Peruvian handcrafts gallery are lined with elegant handpainted wood mirrors and colorful original paintings. Direct importing from the artisans keeps prices low. ✉ *2410 18th St. NW, Adams-Morgan* ☎ *202/232–3890* ⊕ *www.toromata.com* ⊙ *Closed Mon.* Ⓜ *Woodley Park/Zoo.*

BOOKS **Idle Time Books.** This used-book store sells "rare to medium rare" books with plenty of meaty titles in all genres, especially out-of-print literature. ✉ *2467 18th St. NW, Woodley Park* ☎ *202/232–4774* Ⓜ *Woodley Park/Zoo.*

HOME FURNISHINGS **Design Within Reach.** A fantasy playground for the interior designer in all of us. Modern and contemporary home furnishings from design stars like Eames, Noguchi, and Starck are always in stock—or "within reach." ✉ *1838 Columbia Rd. NW, Adams-Morgan* ☎ *202/265–5640* ⊕ *www.dwr.com.*

Skynear and Company. The owners of this extravagant shop travel the world to find the unusual. Their journeys have yielded rich textiles, furniture, and home accessories—all for the art of living. ✉ *2122 18th St. NW, Adams-Morgan* ☎ *202/797–7160* ⊕ *www.skynearonline.com* Ⓜ *Woodley Park/Zoo.*

MEN'S & WOMEN'S CLOTHING **All About Jane.** Fashion-loving Adams-Morganettes pop into this tiny shop to find funky and classic women's looks with unique details by Rebecca Taylor, Tocca, and Custo, as well as Citizens of Humanity jeans. The accessories and jewelry selection is small but thoughtfully chosen. ✉ *2438½ 18th St. NW, Adams-Morgan* ☎ *202/797–9710* Ⓜ *Woodley Park/Zoo.*

Kobos. All the traditional ethnic clothing and accessories at this neighborhood staple were imported from West Africa. ✉ *2444 18th St. NW, Adams-Morgan* ☎ *202/332–9580* Ⓜ *Woodley Park/Zoo.*

TOP 5

- **Kramerbooks and Afterwords, Dupont Circle:** It's the book lovers' nightclub.
- **Wild Women Wear Red, U Street:** You can always go wild with your shoes.
- **Blue Mercury, Georgetown:** Indulge in a massage or facial in the "skin gym."
- **Apartment Zero, Downtown:** Reimagine your space with the help of the very latest in furnishings and design.
- **Urban Chic, Georgetown:** The handbags alone are worth a visit.

BLITZ TOURS

CLOTHING & ANTIQUES

When it comes to fashion, **Georgetown,** with its easy-to-navigate layout, is the place to start. You might want to begin at 2000 Pennsylvania Avenue, a cluster of clothing stores and eateries a few blocks from the Foggy Bottom/GWU Metro. From the Metro it's a 10- to 15-minute walk: cross Washington Circle and walk to the 2000 block, then head up Pennsylvania Avenue (the numbered cross streets will be increasing) to M Street, where Georgetown begins with a row of antiques shops. Wisconsin Avenue—where you can find a handful of designer boutiques among the influx of youth-oriented retailers—intersects M Street. Fortify yourself at one of the area's many restaurants before heading to **upper Wisconsin Avenue** on the D.C.–Maryland border. The bus, which runs every 7–10 minutes, will take you here (or back downtown) for $1.25, or you can hop in a cab. Upscale merchants such as Dior, Ralph Lauren, Saks, Lord & Taylor, and Versace are at the northern reaches of this neighborhood. Two midsize malls, Mazza Gallerie and Chevy Chase Pavilion, contain a good selection of clothing shops. Loehmann's, Filene's Basement, and T. J. Maxx carry brand-name bargains, and Lord & Taylor is right around the corner on Western Avenue. When you're finished, the convenient Friendship Heights Metro on the Red Line will bring you back into the city.

RETRO & ECLECTIC FINDS

Across the street from the Woodley Park Metro you'll find a shop or two selling original works of art, antiques, and vintage jewelry. From here walk to the corner of Connecticut Avenue and Calvert Street. Turn left and cross the Duke Ellington Bridge—which offers a great view of forested Rock Creek Park—into **Adams-Morgan,** where there are one-of-a-kind ethnic jewelry shops, fun restaurants, vintage-clothing stores, and boutiques. Shop your way down 18th Street to Florida Avenue. Turn left to walk toward **U Street,** where more vintage clothing and antique furniture await. Or turn right and walk to Connecticut Avenue. A left turn will lead you downhill to **Dupont Circle** and its assortment of funky book, music, and gift shops.

6

SHOES **Shake Your Booty.** Trend-conscious Washingtoniennes come here for funky and affordable leather boots and platform shoes. ⊠ *2439 18th St. NW, Adams-Morgan* ☎ *202/518–8205* ⊕ *www.shakeyourbootyshoes. com* Ⓜ *Woodley Park/Zoo.*

Capitol Hill–Eastern Market

As the Capitol Hill area has become gentrified, unique shops and boutiques have sprung up, many clustered around the redbrick **Eastern Market.** Inside are produce and meat counters, plus the Market Five art gallery. ■ TIP➔ **The flea market, held on weekends outdoors, presents nostalgia and local crafts by the crateful. There's also a farmers' market on Saturday.** Along

7th Street you'll find a number of small shops, selling items that include art books, handwoven rugs, and antiques. Cross Pennsylvania Avenue headed south on 8th Street for historic Barracks Row, the shops, bars, and restaurants that inhabit the charming rowhouses leading toward the Anacostia river. ⊠ *7th and C Sts. SE, Capitol Hill* Ⓜ *Eastern Market, Union Station, or Capitol S.*

WORD OF MOUTH

"The only advice we have is not to miss Eastern Market! We moved to Capitol Hill because of it—best breakfast in town, the freshest locally grown produce, and the works of hundreds of local artisans."   –dcdilettante

Mall

Union Station. This group of shops, resplendent with marble floors and gilded, vaulted ceilings, is inside a working train station. You'll find several familiar retailers, including Nine West, Chicos, Swatch, and Ann Taylor, as well as a bookstore and a multiplex movie theater. The east hall, which resembles London's Covent Garden, is filled with vendors of expensive and ethnic wares who sell from open stalls. Hungry shoppers will find everything from fresh sushi to Navajo frybread sandwiches among the mall's 100 restaurants and cafés. Christmas is an especially pleasant time to shop here. ⊠ *50 Massachusetts Ave. NE, Capitol Hill* ☎ *202/289–1908* ⊕ *www.unionstationdc.com* Ⓜ *Union Station.*

Specialty Stores

BOOKS   **Bird-in-Hand Bookstore and Gallery.** This quirky store specializes in books on art and design and also carries exhibition catalogs. ⊠ *323 7th St. SE, Capitol Hill* ☎ *202/543–0744* ☉ *Closed Sun.–Tues.* Ⓜ *Eastern Market.*

Capitol Hill Books. Pop into this inviting store to browse through a wonderful collection of out-of-print history books and modern first editions. ⊠ *657 C St. SE, Capitol Hill* ☎ *202/544–1621* ⊕ *www.capitolhillbooks-dc.com* Ⓜ *Eastern Market.*

Ⓒ **Fairy Godmother.** This store specializes in books for children, from infants through teens, in English, Spanish, and French. It also sells puppets, toys, crafts sets, and CDs. ⊠ *319 7th St. SE, Capitol Hill* ☎ *202/547–5474* Ⓜ *Eastern Market.*

Trover Shop. Newshounds can come here to find the latest political books and out-of-town newspapers. ⊠ *221 Pennsylvania Ave. SE, Capitol Hill* ☎ *202/547–2665* ⊕ *www.trover.com* Ⓜ *Capitol S.*

CRAFTS & GIFTS   **Alvear Studio.** This popular design and imports store overflows with a
★   colorful bounty from the worldwide travels of its owners. You'll find Cambodian Buddhas happily seated on Southwestern cowhide rugs. There's also a good representation of local art, furniture, and jewelry. ⊠ *705 8th St. SE, Capitol Hill* ☎ *202/546–8484* ⊕ *www.alvearstudio. com* Ⓜ *Eastern Market.*

Appalachian Spring. Head here for traditional and contemporary American-made crafts, including jewelry, pottery, blown glass, and toys. ⊠ *Union Station, East Hall, 50 Massachusetts Ave. NE, Capitol Hill* ☎ *202/682–0505* Ⓜ *Union Station.*

Homebody. Original artwork, contemporary rugs, and delicious-smelling candles highlight this new addition to the neighborhood, a furnishings and design boutique that's both sophisticated and irreverent. ✉ *715 8th St. SE, Capitol Hill* ☎ *202/544–8445* ⊕ *www.homebodydc.com* ⊗ *Closed Mon.* Ⓜ *Eastern Market.*

The Village Gallery. This collection of artsy gifts and women's clothing lives in a welcoming house and garden. The upstairs gallery showcases a permanent exhibit of work by D.C. painter Alan Braley, along with a changing roster of local, American, and international artists. ✉ *705 North Carolina Ave. SE, Capitol Hill* ☎ *202/546–3040* ⊕ *www. thevillageoncapitolhill.com* ⊗ *Closed Mon.* Ⓜ *Eastern Market.*

Woven History/Silk Road. These connected stores sell handmade treasures from small villages around the world. Silk Road sells home furnishings, gifts, clothing, rugs, and accessories made in Asian mountain communities as well as such contemporary items as aromatherapy candles from New York City's not-so-rural Greenwich Village. Woven History's rugs are made the old-fashioned way, with vegetable dyes and hand-spun wool. ✉ *311–315 7th St. SE, Capitol Hill* ☎ *202/543–1705* ⊕ *www.wovenhistory.com* Ⓜ *Eastern Market.*

FOOD & WINE **Schneider's of Capitol Hill.** Specializing in fine wines, this Washington-area institution also has hard liquor. The staff make wine neophytes and experts feel equally welcome. ✉ *300 Massachusetts Ave. NE, Capitol Hill* ☎ *202/543–9300* ⊕ *www.cellar.com* Ⓜ *Union Station.*

WOMEN'S CLOTHING **The Forecast.** If you like classic, contemporary styles, Forecast should be in your future. It sells silk sweaters and wool blends in solid, muted tones for women seeking elegant but practical clothing from brands like Eileen Fisher. The housewares and gifts selection on the first floor is colorful and of high quality. ✉ *218 7th St. SE, Capitol Hill* ☎ *202/547–7337* ⊗ *Closed Mon.* Ⓜ *Eastern Market.*

CHILDREN'S CLOTHING **Dawn Price Baby.** This friendly rowhouse boutique has carefully selected clothing, toys, gifts, cribs, and bedding for infants to toddlers. The focus of the clothes here is super-comfortable fabrics and distinct designs, and there's a great selection of Petit Bateau T-shirts and onesies. ✉ *325 7th St. SE, Capitol Hill* ☎ *202/543–2920* ⊕ *www.dawnpricebaby. com* ⊗ *Closed Mon.* Ⓜ *Eastern Market.*

Downtown

With its many offices, **downtown** tends to shut down at 5 PM sharp with the exception of the larger department stores. Revitalized Penn Quarter is where you'll find the downtown galleries, Hecht's, and specialty stores; established chains such as Ann Taylor and the Gap tend to be concentrated near Farragut Square. ▪ TIP➔ **Avoid the lunch-hour crowds to ensure more leisurely shopping.** ✉ *North of Pennsylvania Ave. between 7th and 18th Sts., up to Connecticut Ave. below L St., Downtown* Ⓜ *Archives/Navy Memorial, Farragut N and W, Foggy Bottom/GWU, Gallery Pl., McPherson Sq., or Metro Center.*

Department Stores

H&M. European stalwart H&M has quickly become a necessary stop for the young, trend-conscious Washingtonian. The newest, hottest fashions at a can't-beat-it price make for a crowded two-level store that's well worth visiting. On the site of what once was the venerable Woodward & Lothrop department store, H&M is open, airy, and inviting. Another branch is in Georgetown Park Mall. ⊠ *1025 F St. NW, Downtown* ☎ *202/347–3306* Ⓜ *Metro Center* ⊠ *The Shops at Georgetown Park, 3222 M St. NW, Georgetown* ☎ *202/298–6792* Ⓜ *Foggy Bottom.*

Hecht's. Bright and spacious, this Washington favorite has sensible groupings and attractive displays that make shopping easy on both the feet and the eyes. The clothing sold ranges from conservative to up-to-the-minute, with the men's department increasingly prominent. The offerings in cosmetics, lingerie, and housewares are also strong. ⊠ *1201 G St. NW, Downtown* ☎ *202/628–6661* Ⓜ *Metro Center.*

Shopping Center

Gallery Place. Anchored by a 14-screen Regal cinema, this newest addition to downtown attracts shoppers of all ages, who browse among such familiar stores as Urban Outfitters, Ann Taylor, and Aveda. Restaurants serve Thai, Japanese, and American fare. ⊠ *7th and H Sts. NW, Chinatown* ☎ *202/393–2121* Ⓜ *Gallery Pl./Chinatown.*

Specialty Stores

ART GALLERIES The downtown art scene is concentrated on 7th Street between D and I streets. Redevelopment has meant that many artists have had to move their working studios from here to more affordable digs. The galleries, however, which bring foot traffic to area businesses, have managed to maintain a foothold. ■ TIP➔ On the third Thursday of each month, the galleries extend their hours and offer light refreshments from 6 PM to 8 PM.

Fodor'sChoice **Numark Gallery.** This powerhouse gallery brings in established and cut-
★ ting-edge artists: Peter Halley, Nikki S. Lee, Tony Feher, and Michal Rovner have shown work here. International, national, and regional artists are also regularly featured. ⊠ *625 E St. NW, Chinatown* ☎ *202/628–3810* ⊕ *www.numarkgallery.com* ⊘ *Closed Sun. and Mon.* Ⓜ *Gallery Pl./Chinatown or Archives/Navy Memorial.*

The Touchstone Gallery. All kinds of media are showcased at this 3,000-square-foot artist-owned cooperative. With a membership of more than 30 local artists represented by monthly rotations, the gallery shows a wide range of styles, prices, and quality. ⊠ *406 7th St. NW, Chinatown* ☎ *202/347–2787* ⊕ *www.touchstonegallery.com* Ⓜ *Gallery Pl./Chinatown or Archives/Navy Memorial.*

Zenith Gallery. Founded in 1978, the Zenith exhibits indoor and outdoor sculpture, mixed media, wearable art, jewelry, crafts, and art furniture, as well as a large selection of paintings by national and international artists. ⊠ *413 7th St. NW, Chinatown* ☎ *202/783–2963* ⊕ *www. zenithgallery.com* ⊘ *Closed Mon.* Ⓜ *Gallery Pl./Chinatown or Archives/ Navy Memorial.*

BOOKS **Chapters.** This bookstore fills its shelves with serious contemporary fic-
★ tion, classics, foreign language titles, and poetry. The store hosts author

readings regularly, so check the schedule if you're spending a few days in town. ⊠ *445 11th St. NW, Downtown* ☎ *202/737–5553* ⊕ *www. chaptersliterary.com* Ⓜ *Metro Center.*

Olsson's Books and Records. This independent, locally owned D.C. favorite stocks a large and varied collection of books for readers of all ages and a good selection of classical, jazz, and alternative music. The in-house café provides a pleasant spot to read new purchases over coffee. There's another branch in Dupont Circle. ⊠ *418 7th St. NW, Downtown* ☎ *202/ 638–7610* ⊕ *www.olssons.com* Ⓜ *Archives/Navy Memorial* ⊠ *1307 19th St. NW, Dupont Circle* ☎ *202/785–1133* Ⓜ *Dupont Circle.*

CRAFTS & GIFTS **Fahrney's.** What began in 1929 as a repair shop and a pen bar—a place to fill your fountain pen before setting out for work—is now a wonderland for anyone who loves a good writing instrument. On offer are pens in silver, gold, and lacquer by the world's leading manufacturers. ⊠ *1317 F St. NW, Downtown* ☎ *202/628–9525* ⊕ *www.fahrneyspens.com* Ⓜ *Metro Center.*

Indian Craft Shop. Jewelry, pottery, sand paintings, weavings, and baskets from more than 45 Native American tribes, including Navajo, Pueblo, Zuni, Cherokee, Lakota, and Seminole, are at your fingertips here . . . as long as you have a photo ID to enter the federal building. Items range from inexpensive jewelry (as little as $5) on up to collector-quality art pieces (more than $1,000). ⊠ *U.S. Department of the Interior, 1849 C St. NW, Room 1023, Downtown* ☎ *202/208–4056* ☽ *Closed weekends* Ⓜ *Farragut W or Farragut N.*

Music Box Center. Listen to a total of 500 melodies on more than 1,500 music boxes at this exquisite—and unusual—store. One irresistible item: the Harry Potter music box that plays "That's What Friends Are For." ⊠ *1920 I St. NW, Downtown* ☎ *202/783–9399* Ⓜ *Farragut W.*

HOME **Apartment Zero.** This swank housewares store describes itself as ap-
FURNISHINGS pealing to fans of architect Frank Gehry, but anyone who wants a leg
Fodor'sChoice up on the latest in international furnishings and accessories will find
★ plenty of interest. If you're searching for pieces (or just ideas) to give your own house a cool, downtown look, this is the place for you. A series of cultural and design-oriented events are regularly hosted instore—call or check their Web site for more information. ⊠ *406 7th St. NW, Downtown* ☎ *202/628–4067* Ⓜ *Gallery Pl./Chinatown or Archives/Navy Memorial.*

SHOES **Church's.** This top-notch English company's handmade men's shoes are noted for their comfort and durability. ⊠ *1820 L St. NW, Downtown* ☎ *202/296–3366* Ⓜ *Farragut N.*

SPAS & BEAUTY **Andre Chreky Salon.** Housed in an elegantly renovated, four-story Vic-
SALONS torian town house, this salon offers complete services—hair, nails, facials, waxing, massage, and makeup. And because it's a favorite of the Washington elite, you might just overhear a tidbit or two on who's going to what black-tie function with whom. Adjacent whirlpool pedicure chairs allow two friends to get pampered simultaneously. While you get your treatment, you can enjoy complimentary espresso and pastries (mornings) or wine and live piano music (evenings). ⊠ *1604 K St. NW, Downtown* ☎ *202/293–9393* ⊕ *www.andrechreky.com* Ⓜ *Farragut N.*

D.C.'s Museum Shops

NEED A LIFELIKE saber-tooth tiger toy? It's waiting for you at the gift shop in the National Museum of Natural History. Looking for something special for your mother? Try the note cards by female artists at the National Museum of Women in the Arts. In fact, there's something for everyone on your list to be found in Washington's many museum gift shops, and there's nothing like walking away with a choice birthday present or two along with some culture.

We're not talking about cheap souvenirs. Museum gift shops offer everything from period jewelry reproductions to science kits for kids, not to mention prints and postcards of the masterpiece paintings in the permanent collections. Asia enthusiasts can find ceramic, porcelain, and exquisite silk decor items in the gift shops of the Freer Gallery of Art and the Arthur M. Sackler Gallery, which also carries Noguchi lamps. The latest addition to the Smithsonian family, the National Museum of the American Indian, has one of the largest and best collections of Native American books in the country.

The gift shop at the National Building Museum sells Frank Gehry watches and Michael Graves teapots, plus objects that reflect the current exhibits. At the International Spy Museum, you can pick up a book safe, a camera implanted in a plant, or a collection of Antonio Prohias's "Spy vs. Spy" cartoons originally published in *Mad* magazine. At the Hirshhorn, find a guide on making pop-up books or a biography of Willem de Kooning. You can also find books and catalogs on almost any recent or current exhibit.

If you don't want to carry around multiple shopping bags, rest assured that most of the items in museum shops can be purchased off the museum's Web site once you return home. Prices are no higher than you'd find in comparable stores. Another bonus: you won't pay tax on anything purchased in a public museum.

The Grooming Lounge. Most spas are geared to women, but regular guys as well as metrosexuals will find something to love here. You'll find old-fashioned hot-lather shaves, haircuts, and business manicures and pedicures—everything a man needs to look terrific. The hair- and skin-care products—from Clarins, American Crew, and Acqua di Parma, to name just a few—are worth a visit even if you don't have time for a service. ✉ *1745 L St. NW, Downtown* ☎ *202/466–8900 or 866/456–8643* ⊕ *www.groominglounge.com* Ⓜ *Farragut N.*

WOMEN'S CLOTHING **Alex.** Whether you go for cutting-edge looks from the latest designers or vintage Balenciaga and Dior, this jewel box of a shop encourages you to develop personal style via the new and the semi-new designer consignment stock, like Narciso Rodriguez tops from a few seasons ago. ✉ *1919 Pennsylvania Ave. NW, Downtown* ☎ *202/296–2610* ⊕ *www. alexboutiquedc.com* Ⓜ *Farragut W.*

★ **Coup de Foudre.** All of the upscale lingerie in this inviting, elegant boutique hails from France. Coup de Foudre—which translates to "love at first sight"—specializes in friendly, personalized bra fittings. ✉ *1001*

Pennsylvania Ave. NW, Downtown ☎ *202/393–0878* ⊕ *www. coupdefoudrelingerie.com* Ⓜ *Metro Center.*

Rizik Bros. This tony, patrician Washington institution has both designer women's clothing and expert advice on offer. The sales staff is trained to find just the right style from the store's inventory, which is particularly strong in formal and bridal dresses. Take the elevator up from the northwest corner of Connecticut Avenue and L Street. ✉ *1100 Connecticut Ave. NW, Downtown* ☎ *202/223–4050* Ⓜ *Farragut N.*

Dupont Circle

You might call **Dupont Circle** a younger, less staid version of Georgetown—almost as pricey but with more apartment buildings than houses. Its many restaurants, offbeat shops, and specialty book and record stores give it a cosmopolitan air. The street scene here is more urban than Georgetown's, with bike messengers and chess aficionados filling up the park. The Sunday farmers' market is a popular destination for organic food, fresh cheese, homemade soap, and hand-spun wool. To the south of Dupont Circle proper are several boutiques and similar stores close to the Farragut and Farragut North Metro stops. ✉ *Connecticut Ave. between M and S Sts.* Ⓜ *Dupont Circle.*

Specialty Stores

ANTIQUES & COLLECTIBLES **Geoffrey Diner Gallery.** A must for hard-core antiques shoppers on the hunt for 19th-, 20th-, and 21st-century wares, this store sells Tiffany lamps and Arts and Crafts pieces from pivotal designers from Europe and the United States. It's open Saturday and by appointment only. ✉ *1730 21st St. NW, Dupont Circle* ☎ *202/483–5005* ⊕ *www. dinergallery.com* ☉ *Closed Sun.–Fri.* Ⓜ *Dupont Circle.*

ART GALLERIES **America, Oh Yes!** With one of the most extensive folk art collections in the country, this gallery is also known for its reasonable prices. It represents more than 160 self-taught American artists. ✉ *1350 Connecticut Ave. NW, Suite 202, Dupont Circle* ☎ *202/721–0043* ⊕ *www. americaohyes.com* ☉ *Closed weekends* Ⓜ *Dupont Circle.*

Burdick Gallery. John Burdick's cozy gallery focuses exclusively on Inuit art and sculpture of the Eskimo communities in Hudson Bay, Baffin Island, and the high central Canadian Arctic. Expect to find arresting, uniquely executed depictions of nature and home. ✉ *2114 R St. NW, Dupont Circle* ☎ *202/986–5682* ⊕ *www. burdickgallery.com* ☉ *Closed Mon.* Ⓜ *Dupont Circle.*

Burton Marinkovich Fine Art. You know you've reached this gallery when you spot the small front yard with two distinctive sculptures (they're by Lesley Dill and Leonard Cave). The gallery has works on paper by modern and contemporary masters, including Ross Bleckner,

> **OPEN HOUSE FOR ART**
>
> Close to 30 galleries are in the Dupont Circle area alone. On "First Fridays," the joint open house held September through June, the streets are filled with wine-and-cheese-loving gallery hoppers. Check out **The Galleries of Dupont Circle** (⊕ www.artgalleriesdc.com) for information on all events.

Richard Diebenkorn, David Hockney, Kandinsky, Matisse, Miró, Motherwell, Picasso, and others. Rare modern illustrated books and British linocuts from the Grosvenor School are also specialties. ✉ *1506 21st St. NW, Dupont Circle* ☎ *202/296–6563* ⊕ *www.burtonmarinkovich. com* ☾ *Closed Sun. and Mon.* Ⓜ *Dupont Circle.*

Fusebox. One of D.C.'s hottest galleries, Fusebox presents serious and stimulating contemporary art from a bright, Chelsea-esque space in Logan Circle. ✉ *1412 14th St. NW, Logan Circle* ☎ *202/299–9220* ⊕ *www.fuseboxdc.com* ☾ *Closed Sun. and Mon.* Ⓜ *Dupont Circle.*

★ **Hemphill Fine Arts.** This spacious gem of a gallery shows established artists such as Jacob Kainen and William Christenberry as well as emerging ones like Colby Caldwell. ✉ *1515 14th St. NW, 3rd fl., Logan Circle* ☎ *202/234–5601* ⊕ *www.hemphillfinearts.com* Ⓜ *Dupont Circle.*

Irvine Contemporary. The small scale of this upstairs gallery space belies the force of its exhibits by emerging regional and international artists. Its inventory also glitters with works by Ed Ruscha, Robert Rauschenberg, Frank Stella, and Robert Delaunay. ✉ *1710 Connecticut Ave. NW, Dupont Circle* ☎ *202/332–8767* ⊕ *irvinecontemporary.com* ☾ *Closed Sun. and Mon.* Ⓜ *Dupont Circle.*

Tartt Gallery and Gary Edwards Gallery. These adjoining galleries emphasize 19th- and early-20th-century vintage photography and American contemporary folk art, respectively. ✉ *1711 Connecticut Ave. NW, Dupont Circle* ☎ *202/332–5652 or 301/524–0900* ☾ *Closed Sun.–Tues.* Ⓜ *Dupont Circle.*

BOOKS
Fodor'sChoice
★

Kramerbooks & Afterwords. One of Washington's best-loved independents, this cozy shop has a small but choice selection of fiction and nonfiction. Open 24 hours on weekends, it's a convenient meeting place. Kramerbooks shares space with a café that has late-night dining and weekend entertainment; be prepared for a smoke-filled room. ■ TIP→ **There's a computer with free Internet access available in the bar, though you'll have to stand up to use it.** ✉ *1517 Connecticut Ave. NW, Dupont Circle* ☎ *202/387–1400* ⊕ *www.kramers.com* Ⓜ *Dupont Circle.*

Lambda Rising. Over the years, Lambda has grown beyond its local fame to national influence. Lambda Rising is *the* source for information and literature for and about the gay, lesbian, bisexual, and transgendered communities. The store isn't all about being serious: check out the fun, colorful, and ever-changing window displays. ✉ *1625 Connecticut Ave. NW, Dupont Circle* ☎ *202/462–6969* ⊕ *www.lambdarising. com* Ⓜ *Dupont Circle.*

★ **Second Story Books.** A used-books and -records emporium that stays open late, Second Story may lead bibliophiles to browse for hours. ✉ *2000 P St. NW, Dupont Circle* ☎ *202/659–8884* ⊕ *www.secondstorybooks. com* Ⓜ *Dupont Circle.*

CHILDREN'S
CLOTHING

Kid's Closet. If filling a little one's closet is on your list, stop here for high-quality contemporary children's clothing and toys. ✉ *1226 Connecticut Ave. NW, Dupont Circle* ☎ *202/429–9247* Ⓜ *Dupont Circle.*

CRAFTS & GIFTS

Beadazzled. This appealing shop stocks a dazzling number of ready-to-string beads and jewelry as well as books on crafts history and techniques.

✉ *1507 Connecticut Ave. NW, Dupont Circle* ☎ *202/265–2323* ⊕ *www. beadazzled.net* Ⓜ *Dupont Circle.*

The Chocolate Moose. This store is simple, sheer fun for adults and kids alike. Looking for clacking, windup teeth? You'll find them here, along with unusual greeting cards, strange boxer shorts, and unique handcrafts. If playing with all those fun toys makes you hungry, you can pick up a select line of premium European chocolates. ✉ *1743 L St. NW, Dupont Circle* ☎ *202/463–0992* ⊕ *www.chocolatemoosedc.com* Ⓜ *Farragut N.*

The Written Word. More than a mere stationery store, the Written Word is more like a tribute to paper. It's also one of the few places in D.C. that offers custom letterpress printing. A wide variety of handmade papers can be found along with interesting and unique greeting cards. Journals, photo albums, and scrapbooks are all made out of unusual papers. ✉ *1365 Connecticut Ave. NW, Dupont Circle* ☎ *202/223–1400* ⊕ *www. writtenword.invitations.com* Ⓜ *Dupont Circle.*

HOME
FURNISHINGS

Reincarnations. Reincarnations is a neighborhood favorite, partly because of its duo of imposing wooden soldiers at the doorway. It's hard to pinpoint one style that dominates—trendy, antique, funky—and everyone can find something to like here. ✉ *1401 14th St. NW, Logan Circle* ☎ *202/319–1606* Ⓜ *Dupont Circle.*

Tabletop. Evoking a small museum gift shop, this is a delightful place to find affordable, design-oriented contemporary home accessories, jewelry, handbags, books and gifts. ✉ *1608 20th St. NW, Dupont Circle* ☎ *202/387–7117* ⊕ *www.tabletopdc.com* Ⓜ *Dupont Circle.*

JEWELRY

Pampillonia Jewelers. Here you'll find traditional designs in 18-karat gold and platinum as well as eye-catching contemporary designs. The selection for men is particularly good. ✉ *1213 Connecticut Ave. NW, Farragut Square* ☎ *202/628–6305* ⊕ *www.pampillonia.com* Ⓜ *Farragut N.*

Tiny Jewel Box. Despite its name, this venerable D.C. favorite contains six floors of precious and semiprecious wares, including unique gifts, home accessories, vintage pieces, and works by well-known designers. ✉ *1147 Connecticut Ave. NW, Farragut Square* ☎ *202/393–2747* ⊕ *www.tinyjewelbox.com* Ⓜ *Farragut N.*

KITCHENWARE

Coffee and the Works. Coffee and tea lovers head to this charmingly cluttered shop for high-end kitchen gadgets, magnets, colorful ceramic pots, and other accessories as well as the beans and leaves themselves. ✉ *1627 Connecticut Ave. NW, Dupont Circle* ☎ *202/483–8050* Ⓜ *Dupont Circle.*

MEN'S &
WOMEN'S
CLOTHING

Burberry. The trench coat's still popular, but this plaid-friendly British company also designs classy men's and women's indoor apparel and accessories. A recent expansion has bolstered the accessories department and added posh touches like a larger-than-life television catwalk and leather settees. ✉ *1155 Connecticut Ave. NW, Farragut Square* ☎ *202/ 463–3000* ⊕ *www.burberry.com* Ⓜ *Farragut N.*

J. Press. Like its flagship store, founded in Connecticut in 1902 as a custom shop for Yale University, this Washington outlet is resolutely traditional: Shetland and Irish wool sport coats are a specialty. ✉ *1801 L St. NW, Farragut Square* ☎ *202/857–0120* Ⓜ *Farragut N.*

★ **Thomas Pink.** This outpost of the famous London shirtmaker—with luxury woven threads for men and women—is both swank and friendly. ■ TIP→ Their travelers shirt, made of a super-breathable, wrinkle-free fabric and fitted with secret pockets, is a must for the stylish globe-trotter. ⊠ *1127 Connecticut Ave. NW, Farragut Square* ☎ *202/223–5390* ⊕ *www.thomaspink.co.uk* Ⓜ *Farragut N.*

WOMEN'S
CLOTHING

Betsy Fisher. Catering to women of all ages in search of contemporary styles, this store stocks one-of-a-kind accessories, clothes, shoes, and jewelry by well-known designers like Diane Von Furstenberg, Nanette Lepore, and Sigerson Morrison. A small selection of up-and-coming local designs is also available. ⊠ *1224 Connecticut Ave. NW, Dupont Circle* ☎ *202/785–1975* ⊕ *www.betsyfisher.com* Ⓜ *Dupont Circle.*

★ **Secondi.** One of the city's finest consignment shops, Secondi carries a well-chosen selection of women's designer and casual clothing, accessories, and shoes. The brands carried include Marc Jacobs, Louis Vuitton, Donna Karan, Prada, and Ann Taylor. ⊠ *1702 Connecticut Ave. NW, 2nd fl., Dupont Circle* ☎ *202/667–1122* ⊕ *www.secondi.com* Ⓜ *Dupont Circle.*

Georgetown

Although **Georgetown** is not on a subway line and parking is difficult at best, people still flock here, keeping it D.C.'s favorite shopping area. This is also the capital's center for famous residents, as well as being a hotspot for restaurants, bars, and nightclubs.

National chains are overtaking the specialty shops that first gave the district its allure, but the historic neighborhood is still charming and its street scene lively. In addition to housing tony antiques, elegant crafts, and high-style shoe and clothing boutiques, Georgetown offers wares that attract local college students and young people: books, music, and fashions from familiar names such as Banana Republic and Urban Outfitters.

■ TIP→ The nearest Metro, Foggy Bottom/GWU, is a 10- to 15-minute walk from the shops. Most stores lie to the east and west on M Street and to the north on Wisconsin. A few chic, independent shops can be found just south of the library on Wisconsin Avenue. ⊠ *Intersection of Wisconsin Ave. and M St., Georgetown* Ⓜ *Foggy Bottom/GWU.*

Mall

Shops at Georgetown Park. Near the hub of the Georgetown shopping district is this posh trilevel mall, which looks like a Victorian ice-cream parlor inside. The pricey clothing and accessory boutiques and the ubiquitous chain stores draw international visitors in droves. Next door is a branch of the Dean & Deluca gourmet grocery and café. ⊠ *3222 M St. NW, Georgetown* ☎ *202/298–5577* ⊕ *www.shopsatgeorgetownpark. com* Ⓜ *Foggy Bottom/GWU.*

> **WORD OF MOUTH**
>
> "If you want to do some really serious shopping, then plan to spend a few hours in Georgetown . . ." —bardo1

Specialty Stores

ANTIQUES &
COLLECTIBLES
Georgetown Antiques Center. The center, in a Victorian town house, has two dealers: Cherub Antiques Gallery specializes in art nouveau and art deco, and Michael Getz Antiques sells fireplace equipment and silverware. ⊠ *2918 M St. NW, Georgetown* ☎ *202/337–2224 Cherub Gallery, 202/338–3811 Michael Getz Antiques* Ⓜ *Foggy Bottom/GWU.*

★ **Jean Pierre Antiques.** Very Georgetown, this gorgeous shop sells antique furniture from France, Germany, and Italy. According to its well-connected owner, even Oprah Winfrey's interior designer—not to mention the well-heeled neighbors—have found treasures here. ⊠ *2601 P St. NW, Georgetown* ☎ *202/337–1731.*

Marston Luce. House and garden accessories are in the mix here, but the emphasis is on 18th- and 19th-century French country furniture. ⊠ *1651 Wisconsin Ave. NW, Georgetown* ☎ *202/333–6800* Ⓜ *Foggy Bottom/GWU.*

Miller & Arney Antiques. English, American, and European furniture and accessories from the 17th, 18th, and early 19th centuries make Miller & Arney Antiques look like a museum gallery. Asian porcelain adds splashes of color. ⊠ *1737 Wisconsin Ave. NW, Georgetown* ☎ *202/338–2369* Ⓜ *Foggy Bottom/GWU.*

Old Print Gallery. Here you'll find the capital's largest collection of old prints, with a focus on maps and 19th-century decorative prints (including Washingtoniana). There's also a great collection of vintage *New Yorker* covers. ⊠ *1220 31st St. NW, Georgetown* ☎ *202/965–1818* ☉ *Closed Sun.* Ⓜ *Foggy Bottom/GWU.*

Opportunity Shop of the Christ Child Society. This Georgetown landmark sells fine antiques, crystal, silver, and good-quality household goods on consignment. Prices are moderate. ⊠ *1427 Wisconsin Ave. NW, Georgetown* ☎ *202/333–6635* Ⓜ *Foggy Bottom/GWU.*

Susquehanna. With three rooms upstairs, four rooms downstairs, and a garden full of benches, urns, and tables, Susquehanna is the largest antiques shop in Georgetown. Although paintings cover every inch of wall space, the shop's true specialty is American and English furniture and art objects. ⊠ *3216 O St. NW, Georgetown* ☎ *202/333–1511* ⊕ *www.susquehannaantiques.com* Ⓜ *Foggy Bottom/GWU.*

ART GALLERIES
Many of Georgetown's galleries are on side streets. Their holdings are primarily work by established artists.

Addison Ripley. This well-respected gallery exhibits contemporary work by local artists, including painters Manon Cleary and Wolf Kahn and photographer Terri Weifenbach. ⊠ *1670 Wisconsin Ave. NW, Georgetown* ☎ *202/338–5180* ⊕ *www.addisonripleyfineart.com* ☉ *Closed Sun. and Mon.* Ⓜ *Foggy Bottom/GWU.*

Galleries 1054. Several distinct galleries live under one roof at this location. **Anne C. Fisher** (☎ *202/625–7555*) shows abstract work in all media from local artists. **Fraser** (☎ *202/298–6450*) features contemporary realist paintings and black and white photography by emerging artists. **Parish** (☎ *202/944–2310*) features contemporary work in all media by African-American artists. **Alla Rogers** (☎ *202/333–8595*) has contemporary Eastern European, Russian, and American art and photography.

✉ *1054 31st St. NW, Georgetown* ◷ *Closed Sun. and Mon.* Ⓜ *Foggy Bottom/GWU.*

Georgetown Gallery of Art. Off the beaten path, this cozy gallery displays paintings by Pablo Picasso, Honoré Daumier, and Marc Chagall, but emphasizes the work of British sculptor Henry Moore. It's open Saturday and by appointment only. ✉ *3235 P St. NW, Georgetown* ☎ *202/333–6308* ◷ *Closed Sun.–Fri.* Ⓜ *Foggy Bottom/GWU.*

Spectrum. Approximately 30 local artists form this cooperative gallery, which specializes in abstract and representational art. ✉ *1132 29th St. NW, Georgetown* ☎ *202/333–0954* ⊕ *www.spectrumgallery.org* ◷ *Closed Mon.* Ⓜ *Foggy Bottom/GWU.*

BOOKS **Bridge Street Books.** This charming store stocks a good selection of literature as well as books on fine arts, politics, and other subjects. ✉ *2814 Pennsylvania Ave. NW, Georgetown* ☎ *202/965–5200* Ⓜ *Foggy Bottom/GWU.*

CRAFTS & GIFTS **American Studio.** One-of-a-kind functional and nonfunctional crafts pieces can be found here: teakettles, corkscrews, glassware, and jewelry, and all of them by international designers and artists. ✉ *2906 M St. NW, Georgetown* ☎ *202/965–3273* Ⓜ *Foggy Bottom/GWU.*

HOME FURNISHINGS ★ **A Mano.** The store's name is Italian for "by hand," and it lives up to its name, stocking colorful hand-painted ceramics, hand-dyed tablecloths, blown glass stemware, and other home and garden accessories by Italian and French artisans. ✉ *1677 Wisconsin Ave. NW, Georgetown* ☎ *202/298–7200* ⊕ *www.amano.bz.*

Space. Space is an oasis of mid-century modern in a sea of 19th-century antiques. A loving, witty eye has selected these original home furnishings and art, which largely hail from the East Coast. ✉ *1625 Wisconsin Ave. NW., Georgetown* ☎ *202/333–0140* ⊕ *www.space-dc.com* ◷ *Closed Mon. and Tues.*

Theodore's. A Washington institution, Theodore's is the place to visit for ultramod housewares, from stylish furniture to accessories, leather, and upholstery that make a statement. There's an excellent selection of wall-storage units for almost all tastes. ✉ *2233 Wisconsin Ave. NW, Georgetown* ☎ *202/333–2300* ⊕ *www.theodores.com.*

LEATHER GOODS **Kate Spade.** Step in to the world according to Kate Spade and you might emerge with a handbag, shoes, a raincoat, sunglasses, stationery, books, baby gifts, or something from the Jack Spade (for men) line. ✉ *3061 M St. NW, Georgetown* ☎ *202/333–8302* ⊕ *www.katespade.com* Ⓜ *Foggy Bottom/GWU.*

MEN'S & WOMEN'S CLOTHING **Commander Salamander.** This funky outpost sells clothes for punk kids and ravers. Retro aficionados will also find clothing and accessories for their wardrobes. Sifting through the assortment of leather, chains, toys, and candy-color makeup is as much entertainment as it is shopping. The store is open until 10 PM on weekends. ✉ *1420 Wisconsin Ave. NW, Georgetown* ☎ *202/337–2265* Ⓜ *Foggy Bottom/GWU.*

SHOES ★ **Hu's Shoes.** This cutting-edge shoe store would shine in Paris, Tokyo, or New York. Luckily for us, it brings ballet flats, heels, and boots from designers like Chloé, Proenza Schouler, Sonia Rykiel, and Viktor&Rolf right here to Georgetown. ⊠ *3005 M St. NW, Georgetown* ☎ *202/342–0202* ⊕ *www.hushoes.com* Ⓜ *Foggy Bottom/GWU.*

Sassanova. A girly boutique where you can find high-end shoes for every occasion—a walk on the beach or through a boardroom. ∎ TIP➔ **For a walk down the aisle, custom-made bridesmaid shoes are available.** Brands carried include Lulu Guinness, Marc Jacobs, Emma Hope, and Sigerson Morrison. ⊠ *1641 Wisconsin Ave. NW, Georgetown* ☎ *202/471–4400* ⊕ *www.sassanova.com* ☾ *Closed Mon.*

SPAS & BEAUTY SALONS

★

Blue Mercury. Hard-to-find skin-care lines—Laura Mercier, Eve Lom, and Paula Dorf are just a few—are what set this small national chain apart. The retail space up front sells soaps, lotions, perfumes, cosmetics, and skin- and hair-care products. Behind the glass door is the "skin gym," where you can treat yourself to facials, waxing, massage, and oxygen treatments. ⊠ *3059 M St. NW, Georgetown* ☎ *202/965–1300* ⊕ *www. bluemercury.com* Ⓜ *Foggy Bottom/GWU* ⊠ *1619 Connecticut Ave. NW, Dupont Circle* ☎ *202/462–1300* Ⓜ *Dupont Circle.*

Roche Salon. On the Georgetown waterfront, this salon showcases owner Dennis Roche, who has been featured in *Vogue, Harper's Bazaar,* and *Glamour* magazines. Many believe he is the city's best source for the latest hair-coloring and straightening techniques. ⊠ *3050 K St. NW, Georgetown* ☎ *202/775–0775* ⊕ *www.rochesalon.com.*

Sephora. Better than any department store perfume or cosmetic counter, this supplier of beauty products offers hundreds of fine fragrances, bath products, and cosmetics from all over the world—right at your fingertips. Sephora also carries its own line of beauty products, all exquisitely packaged and quite affordable. The black-clad salespeople are pleasantly low-key. ⊠ *3065 M St. NW, Georgetown* ☎ *202/338–5644* ⊕ *www. sephora.com* Ⓜ *Foggy Bottom/GWU.*

WOMEN'S CLOTHING

Betsey Johnson. The fanciful frocks and accessories in this hot pink shop are favorites of the young and the restless. 1319 Wisconsin Ave. NW, Georgetown ☎202/338–4090 ⊕www.betseyjohnson.com Ⓜ Foggy Bottom/GWU.

Phoenix. Here you'll find contemporary clothing in natural fibers by designers such as Eileen Fisher and Flax, as well as jewelry and fine- and folk-art pieces from Mexico. ⊠ *1514 Wisconsin Ave. NW, Georgetown* ☎ *202/338–4404.*

Fodor's Choice

★

Urban Chic. It's hard to imagine a fashionista who wouldn't find something she loved here—whether she could afford it might be another story. Gorgeous suits, jeans, cocktail dresses, and accessories from Catherine Malandrino, Paul&Joe, Ella Moss, Rebecca Taylor, and Susana Monaco are to be had. The handbags are a highlight. ⊠ *1626 Wisconsin Ave. NW, Georgetown* ☎ *202/338–5398* ⊕ *www.urbanchic-dc.com.*

Wink. While the clientele and styles skew towards the young and trendy, women of all ages shop here for coveted jeans and colorful, sparkly tops, dresses, and jewelry. ⊠ *3109 M St. NW, Georgetown* ☎ *202/338–9465* ⊕ *www.winkdc.com* Ⓜ *Foggy Bottom/GWU.*

6

U Street

In the 1930s and '40s, **U Street** was known for its classy theaters and jazz clubs. After decades of decline following the 1968 riots, the neighborhood has been revitalized. Over the past two years, the area has gentrified at lightning speed, but has retained a diverse mix of multiethnic young professionals and older, working-class African-Americans. At night the neighborhood's club, bar, and restaurant scene comes alive. During the day, the street scene is more laid-back, with more locals than tourists occupying the distinctive shops. ■ TIP➜ **On the third Thursday of each month, the area shops stay open late to offer light refreshments and special deals for the fun "Shopper Socials."** ☒ *U St. between 12th and 17th Sts., U Street corridor* Ⓜ *U St./Cardozo.*

Specialty Stores

ANTIQUES & COLLECTIBLES
Fodor'sChoice
★

Goodwood. This friendly shop sells vintage and antique wood furniture, including wonderful 19th-century American pieces, along with stained glass and other decorative items—even a small but gorgeous collection of estate jewelry. ☒ *1428 U St. NW, U Street corridor* ☏ *202/986–3640* ⊕ *www.goodwooddc.com* ۞ *Closed Mon.–Wed.* Ⓜ *U St./Cardozo.*

Swivel. This eclectic shop sells what it calls "20th-century antiques," a unique blend of high-end mid-century modern housewares, clothing, and furniture. ☒ *1528 U St. NW, downstairs, U Street corridor* ☏ *202/483–1218* ۞ *Closed Mon.–Wed.* Ⓜ *U St./Cardozo.*

HOME FURNISHINGS

Go Mama Go! This colorful, inviting store makes you feel like you're wandering through the stalls of a global marketplace. Asian- and Latin-inspired home furnishings and unique gifts dominate the wares. ☒ *1809 14th St. NW, U Street corridor* ☏ *202/299–0850* ⊕ *www.gomamago.com* Ⓜ *U St./Cardozo.*

Habitat Home Accents & Jewelry. This store sells well-chosen desk sets, lamps, tabletop items, and artist-made jewelry. ☒ *1510 U St. NW, U Street corridor* ☏ *202/518–7222* ⊕ *www.habitatstyle.com* ۞ *Closed Mon.* Ⓜ *U St./Cardozo.*

Home Rule. Here you can find some of the latest design elements for the kitchen and dining room from Europe as well as playful sink stoppers and other fun and affordable household items. ☒ *1807 14th St. NW, U Street corridor* ☏ *202/797–5544* Ⓜ *U St./Cardozo.*

Fodor'sChoice
★

Muléh. You'll find exquisite contemporary Balinese and Filipino home furnishings and trendy clothes from LA and New York at this expansive showroom. The furniture pieces, which are the primary focus of the store, are made from fine organic materials. It's sort of like wandering through a luxury resort in South East Asia and finding a fabulous clothing boutique tucked in the back. ☒ *1831 14th St. NW, U Street corridor* ☏ *202/667–3440* ⊕ *www.muleh.com* ۞ *Closed Mon.* Ⓜ *U St./Cardozo.*

Zawadi. The name means "gift" in Swahili, but you may want to buy the beautiful African art, home accessories, and jewelry for yourself. ☒ *1524 U St. NW, U Street corridor* ☏ *202/232–2214* ⊕ *www.zawadidc.com* Ⓜ *U St./Cardozo.*

MEN'S & WOMEN'S CLOTHING

Carbon. Although coveted by hip D.C. men, this shoe store also has up-to-the-minute styles for women. Style, quality, and comfort reign via designers like Tsubo, Mark Nason, Medium, and Miz Mooz. ☒ *1203 U*

St. NW, U Street corridor ☎ *202/986–2679* ⊕ *www.carbondc.com* Ⓜ *U St./Cardozo.*

Meeps Fashionette. Catering to fans of shabby-chic and campy glamour, this shop, packed into a two-story brick rowhouse, stocks a wide selection of vintage clothes for women and men from the 1940s through the '80s. There's also a small selection of new, original designs by local talent. ✉ *1520 U St. NW, U Street corridor* ☎ *202/265–6546* ⊕ *www. meepsonu.com* ☉ *Closed Mon.* Ⓜ *U St./Cardozo.*

Nana. The hip, friendly staff here are one of the reasons D.C. women love this store, which stocks both new and vintage women's clothes at affordable prices. You'll also find handmade jewelry and cool handbags. ✉ *1528 U St. NW, upstairs, U Street corridor* ☎ *202/667–6955* ⊕ *www. nanadc.com* Ⓜ *U St./Cardozo.*

Pink November. This women's clothing and accessories store describes itself as "flamboyant, feminine, and free!" You might add glittery, unique, and high priced. Designed to feel like a fantasy boudoir, this spot is for divas. ✉ *1231 U St. NW, U Street corridor* ☎ *202/232–3113* ⊕ *www.pinknovemberdc.com* Ⓜ *U St./Cardozo.*

Trade Secrets. The textured wool, velvet, and silk designs on the bohemian, eclectic clothes sold here seem almost too pretty to wear. Almost. ✉ *1515 U St. NW, lower level, U Street corridor* ☎ *202/667–0634* ☉ *Closed Mon.* Ⓜ *U St./Cardozo.*

★ **Wild Women Wear Red.** This store's unique footwear, much of it boldly hued, is for the adventurous. Featured designers include Bronx NY and Lisa Nading. ✉ *1512 U St. NW, U Street corridor* ☎ *202/387–5700* ⊕ *www.wildwomenwearred.com* Ⓜ *U St./Cardozo.*

Wisconsin Avenue

The major thoroughfare **Wisconsin Avenue** runs northwest through the city from Georgetown up into Maryland. Its upper region, near the Friendship Heights Metro stop and straddling the Maryland border, is a major shopping district. Between the malls, department stores, discount designer outlets, and chic, small boutiques, this area has nearly everything you could want to buy. ✉ *Wisconsin Ave. between Jenifer St. NW and Western Ave.* Ⓜ *Friendship Heights.*

Department Stores

Filene's Basement. To really appreciate the bargains here, do some window-shopping in the Mazza Gallerie mall before heading in. In addition to big savings on men's and women's clothing by well-regarded designers such as Hugo Boss and Christian Dior, Filene's has discounts on shoes, perfume, housewares, and accessories. ✉ *Mazza Gallerie, 5300 Wisconsin Ave. NW, Friendship Heights* ☎ *202/966–0208* ⊕ *www. filenesbasement.com* Ⓜ *Friendship Heights.*

Lord & Taylor. Its competition may try to be all things to all people, but Lord & Taylor concentrates on classic men's, women's, and children's clothing by designers such as Anne Klein and Ralph Lauren. ✉ *5255 Western Ave. NW, Friendship Heights* ☎ *202/362–9600* ⊕ *www. lordandtaylor.com* Ⓜ *Friendship Heights.*

Loehmanns. For those unfamiliar with this designer discount store, think of an upscale Filene's Basement. For those not unfamiliar with it, you'll know that it has a devoted following. Come here for huge savings on clothes, shoes, accessories, and gifts from brands like Prada, Valentino, Marc Jacobs, DKNY, and Theory—just about anything you'd find at the high-end department stores. There's a small selection for men on the second floor. ⊠ *5333 Wisconsin Ave. NW, Friendship Heights* ☎ *202/362–4733* ⊕ *www.loehmanns.com* Ⓜ *Friendship Heights.*

Neiman Marcus. If price is an object, this is not the place to shop. Headquartered in Dallas, Neiman Marcus caters to customers who value quality above all. The carefully selected merchandise includes clothes, furs, precious jewelry, crystal, and silver. Note that the only credit cards accepted here are Neiman Marcus, Bergdorf Goodman, and American Express. ⊠ *Mazza Gallerie, 5300 Wisconsin Ave. NW, Friendship Heights* ☎ *202/966–9700* ⊕ *www.neimanmarcus.com* Ⓜ *Friendship Heights.*

Saks Fifth Avenue. Though technically just over the Maryland line, Saks is nonetheless a Washington institution. It has a wide selection of women's European and American couture clothes; other attractions are the shoe, jewelry, and lingerie departments. The smaller men's store is down the road in the Mazza Gallerie shopping center. ⊠ *5555 Wisconsin Ave., Friendship Heights* ☎ *301/657–9000* ⊕ *www.saksfifthavenue. com* Ⓜ *Friendship Heights.*

Malls

Chevy Chase Pavilion. Across from Mazza Gallerie is the newer, similarly upscale Chevy Chase Pavilion. Its women's clothing stores range from Alpaca International to Ann Taylor Loft and Talbots. ⊠ *5335 Wisconsin Ave. NW, Friendship Heights* ☎ *202/686–5335* ⊕ *www.ccpavilion. com* Ⓜ *Friendship Heights.*

The Collection at Chevy Chase. This mall is the latest addition to the luxurification of the Friendship Heights neighborhood. At this writing, Dior, Ralph Lauren, Louis Vuitton, Jimmy Choo, and Barney's Co-op had opened their doors onto Wisconsin Avenue, with Max Mara and Bulgari set to open in early 2006. ⊠ *5471–5481 Wisconsin Ave. NW, Friendship Heights* ☎ *No phone* ⊕ *www.thecollectionatchevychase. com* Ⓜ *Friendship Heights.*

Mazza Gallerie. The four-level Mazza Gallerie is anchored by the ritzy Neiman Marcus department store and the discount department store Filene's Basement. Other stores include Williams-Sonoma, Villeroy & Boch, Pampillonia Jewelers, and Krön Chocolatier. ⊠ *5300 Wisconsin Ave. NW, Friendship Heights* ☎ *202/966–6114* ⊕ *www.mazzagallerie. com* Ⓜ *Friendship Heights.*

Specialty Stores

BOOKS
Fodor'sChoice
★

Politics and Prose. With a wide selection of topical novels and literary nonfiction as well as provocative author readings almost every night, this bookstore–coffeehouse lives up to its name. The nearest Metro is 15 minutes away. ⊠ *5015 Connecticut Ave. NW, Friendship Heights* ☎ *202/364–1919* ⊕ *www.politics-prose.com* Ⓜ *Friendship Heights.*

CHILDREN'S
CLOTHING

Full of Beans. This boutique sells updated classic styles, mostly in natural fibers, as well as miniature designer duds and unusual toys. Sizes range from infants to boys' size 10–12 and girls' size 16. ⊠ *5502 Connecticut Ave. NW, Chevy Chase, MD* ☎ *202/362–8566.*

FOOD & WINE **Balducci's.** Locals rave about the prepared foods sold at this upscale grocery, which also has premium gift baskets and a good selection of wine and beer. ✉ *3201 New Mexico Ave. NW, Tenleytown* ☎ *202/363–5800* ⊕ *www.balduccis.com.*

Calvert Woodley Liquors. This liquor store carries not only an excellent selection of wine and hard liquor, but also many kinds of cheese and other picnic and cocktail-party fare, as well as the legendary H&H bagels from New York. Its international offerings have made it a favorite pantry for embassy parties. ✉ *4339 Connecticut Ave. NW, Tenleytown* ☎ *202/966–4400* Ⓜ *Van Ness/UDC.*

Rodman's Discount Foods and Drugstore. The rare store that carries wine, cheese, and space heaters, Rodman's is a fascinating hybrid of Kmart and Dean & Deluca. The appliances are downstairs, the imported peppers and chocolates upstairs. ■ TIP➡ **It's also a working drugstore, so you can have a prescription filled or pick up some sinus medicine, bath bubbles, or a pair of sunglasses.** ✉ *5100 Wisconsin Ave. NW, Friendship Heights* ☎ *202/363–3466* Ⓜ *Friendship Heights.*

GIFTS & FURNISHINGS **Roche Bobois.** What may surprise you about this upscale French furniture store is the diversity of its designs. The three lines carried here—sleek contemporary, exotic Asian-inspired, and French provincial—offer much in the way of inspiration for your home interior. ✉ *5301 Wisconsin Ave. NW, Friendship Heights* ☎ *202/686–5667* ⊕ *www.roche-bobois.com* Ⓜ *Friendship Heights.*

Wake Up Little Suzie. Clocks shaped like dogs and cats, silver jewelry, funky switch-plate covers, and idiosyncratic ceramics are all here in this boutique of whimsical gifts. ✉ *3409 Connecticut Ave. NW, Cleveland Park* ☎ *202/244–0700* Ⓜ *Cleveland Park.*

MEN'S & WOMEN'S CLOTHING **Brooks Brothers.** The oldest men's clothing store in America, Brooks Brothers has sold traditional formal and casual threads since 1818. Although there's a small women's department, the store at this location mainly carries men's styles. ✉ *5504 Wisconsin Ave., Friendship Heights* ☎ *301/654–8202* ⊕ *www.brooksbrothers.com* Ⓜ *Friendship Heights.*

Everett Hall. D.C.'s own Everett Hall designs men's suits that are richly classic in their material and cutting-edge in their design, color, and sensibility. Most suits are $1,000 and up. From NBA and NFL athletes to K-Street lawyers, men with verve and a sense of style covet Hall's designs. ✉ *Chevy Chase Pavilion, 5345 Wisconsin Ave. NW, Friendship Heights* ☎ *202/362–0191* Ⓜ *Friendship Heights.*

Micmac Bis. Inside this boutique with eye-catching displays are clothes by Issey Miyake, Yohji Yamamoto, and cool Arche shoes. ✉ *5454 Wisconsin Ave. NW, Friendship Heights* ☎ *301/654–8686* Ⓜ *Friendship Heights.*

Sahba. This avant-garde women's clothing boutique stocks an expertly selected cache of True Religion jeans, Robert Rodriguez tops, and Jamin Peuch handbags. ✉ *5300 Wisconsin Ave. NW, Friendship Heights* ☎ *202/966–5080* Ⓜ *Friendship Heights.*

Versace Couture. Featuring the clothing line started by superstar Gianni Versace and now continued by his sister Donatella, this store is a favorite of the beautiful people. ✉ *5454 Wisconsin Ave., Chevy Chase, MD* ☎ *301/907–9400* Ⓜ *Friendship Heights.*

6

SPAS & BEAUTY
SALONS

Georgette Klinger Skin Care Salon. The doyenne of spas, Georgette Klinger specializes in skin care but can also pamper you with many other spa services. Treatments are pricey, but regular patrons say they're well worth it. ☒ *5345 Wisconsin Ave. NW, Friendship Heights* ☎ *202/686–8880 or 800/554–6437* ⊕ *www.georgetteklinger.com* Ⓜ *Friendship Heights.*

TOYS

Child's Play. Toys are serious business in this shop. An attentive staff helps you sort through the large selection, which includes building toys, computer software, art supplies, and classic games. ☒ *5536 Connecticut Ave. NW, Chevy Chase, MD* ☎ *202/244–3602* Ⓜ *Friendship Heights.*

Sullivan's Toy Store. Here you'll find stickers, books, learning games, costumes, stuffed animals, and just about anything else the younger set might want to play with. The art supply store adjacent to the toy space holds gifts, from Japanese brush pens to handmade paper, for older recipients. ☒ *3412 Wisconsin Ave. NW, Upper Northwest* ☎ *202/362–1343.*

Maryland–Virginia

It's a bit of a trek, but some great shopping can be found on the outskirts of the city in Maryland and Virginia. Some malls are close to a Metro station, though most are best reached by car.

Malls & Outlets

Fashion Centre at Pentagon City. Just across the river in Virginia, a 10-minute ride on the Metro from downtown, is this four-story mall with Macy's at one end and Nordstrom at the other. In between are a food court and such shops as an Apple store, Club Monaco and Coach. ☒ *1100 S. Hayes St., Arlington, VA* ☎ *703/415–2400* Ⓜ *Pentagon City.*

Potomac Mills. This mile-long mall off I–95, 30 minutes by car from the District, bills itself as Virginia's most popular attraction. There are some 220 discount and outlet stores here, including Nordstrom Rack, T. J. Maxx, Saks Off Fifth, and Linens 'n Things. Swedish furniture giant IKEA is also nearby. ☒ *2700 Potomac Mills Circle, Woodbridge, VA* ☎ *703/496–9301* ⊕ *www.potomacmills.com.*

Tysons Corner Center. Anchored by Bloomingdale's and Nordstrom, Tysons Corner Center houses 290 other retailers and an AMC movie theater. No matter when you go, be prepared to fight some of the area's heaviest traffic. ☒ *1961 Chain Bridge Rd., McLean, VA* ☎ *703/893–9400* ⊕ *www.shoptysons.com.*

Tysons Galleria. Across a busy highway from Tysons Corner Center, the Galleria has 125 exclusive retailers, including Saks Fifth Avenue, Neiman Marcus, and Macy's. Specialty shops include Chanel, Anthropologie, Ferragamo, Max Mara, and Hugo Boss. As with Tysons Corner, area traffic can be a headache. ☒ *2001 International Dr., McLean, VA* ☎ *703/827–7730* ⊕ *www.tysonsgalleria.com.*

White Flint Mall. The big stores at this upscale mall are Bloomingdale's and Lord & Taylor; other stores include the Coach Store, Sharper Image, H&M, and Eddie Bauer. If you don't have a car, you'll need to catch a public bus from the White Flint metro station. ☒ *11301 Rockville*

Pike, North Bethesda, MD ☎ *301/ 231–7467* ⊕ *www.shopwhiteflint. com* Ⓜ *White Flint.*

Specialty Stores

ANTIQUES & COLLECTIBLES

Takoma Underground. Descend the stairs to find yourself in the midst of vintage clothing, jewelry, books, collectibles, antique housewares, and esoteric items. ✉ *7014 Westmoreland Ave., Takoma Park, MD* ☎ *301/270–6380* ⊕ *www.takomaunderground.com* ☉ *Closed Tues. and Wed.* Ⓜ *Takoma.*

TAKOMA PARK

In the Takoma Park area, on the D.C.–Maryland border, is a concentration of charming antiques, clothing, and gift shops, which are complemented in the warmer months by seasonal street festivals with vendors and musical performances. The city itself hosts an excellent weekend farmers' market in the warmer months.

ART GALLERIES

Torpedo Factory Art Center. Created through the joint effort of a group of local artists and the city of Alexandria in 1974, this center has more than 80 working studios and eight galleries representing all styles and media. ✉ *105 N. Union St., Old Town, Alexandria, VA* ☎ *703/838–4565* ⊕ *www.torpedofactory.org* Ⓜ *King St.*

CRAFTS & GIFTS

Arise. Primarily a purveyor of Asian artifacts, antiques, and furniture, Arise also carries its own label of vibrant cotton and silk leisure clothing, as well as an astounding collection of kimonos in a 10,000-square-foot warehouse. ✉ *5114 Roanoke Pl., College Park, MD* ☎ *301/486–1230* ⊕ *www.arisedc.com.*

MEN'S & WOMEN'S CLOTHING

Amano. Not to be confused with the Georgetown gift shop A Mano, this laid-back boutique sells funky clothing in natural fabrics that you can wear to work or relax in at home. Accessories include cloth briefcases, silk scarves, hats, shoes, and jewelry. ✉ *7030 Carroll Ave., Takoma Park, MD* ☎ *301/270–1140* Ⓜ *Takoma.*

Glad Rags. This fun vintage and consignment clothing shop often throws wacky sales, but their everyday bargains are always worth the visit. They specialize in contemporary women's clothes, with some items from recent decades. ✉ *7306 Carroll Ave., Takoma Park, MD* ☎ *301/891–6870* Ⓜ *Takoma.*

MUSICAL INSTRUMENTS

House of Musical Traditions. If you're looking for a dulcimer or a sitar, or want to learn the difference between bluegrass and blues guitar, try this nationally regarded shop. It carries uncommon instruments as well as books and recordings. ✉ *7040 Carroll Ave., Takoma Park, MD* ☎ *301/ 270–9090* ⊕ *www.hmtrad.com* Ⓜ *Takoma.*

SPAS & BEAUTY SALONS

Jolie, the Day Spa. Busy Washington women don't mind leaving the city behind for an appointment at Jolie. The day spa has 15 private treatment rooms and many services on offer—body treatments, massage, facials, hair, nails, and makeup—as well as luxurious packages. ✉ *7200 Wisconsin Ave., Bethesda, MD* ☎ *301/986–9293* ⊕ *www.joliethedayspa. com* Ⓜ *Bethesda.*

Side Trips

WORD OF MOUTH

"We were at Mt. Vernon over Christmas. Our kids are 11, 14, 16 and they really enjoyed it . . . but they like history. I remember going there as a child and wanted to take my kids. I think it's a special place with beautiful grounds and views, and it was so interesting to see the home and learn about the life of our first president. It did not take long to get there or visit, but we made sure we arrived early so we didn't get stuck waiting for a tour."

—mei

Updated by
CiCi
Williamson
and John A.
Kelly

WITHIN AN HOUR OF D.C. are numerous popular sights connected to the nation's first president, naval history, colonial events, and famous battles. For an active side trip, you can walk or bike along the 13-mi path that parallels a section of the Chesapeake & Ohio (C&O) Canal, past Glen Echo Park, to Great Falls Tavern on the Maryland side of the Potomac. Traveling farther up the Potomac to Maryland's second-largest city, Frederick, makes a good day trip for antiques hunters. It's also a good pilgrimage for those in search of less tangible goods, including travelers seeking a better understanding of the Civil War and its battles.

Sailing aficionados enjoy visiting the U.S. Naval Academy and getting out on the water in Annapolis, a major center for boating. On the Virginia side of the Potomac 16 mi from D.C. is Mount Vernon, George Washington's family home; two other interesting plantation homes—Woodlawn and Gunston Hall—are nearby. History buffs might also want to make a beeline for Fredericksburg, Virginia, to learn about the important roles this and surrounding towns played in the Revolutionary and Civil wars. The town's 40-block National Historic District contains more than 350 original 18th- and 19th-century buildings. Fredericksburg is also known for its antiques shops and its excellent, yet often reasonably priced, restaurants and hotels.

Most of these Virginia and Maryland side trips can be taken via trains, buses, and escorted tours. The most convenient way, however, is in a car.

About the Hotels & Restaurants

The restaurants we list are the cream of the crop in each price category. Properties indicated by an ✕🔲 are lodging establishments whose restaurant warrants a special trip. It's always a good idea to book ahead; we mention reservations only when they're essential or not accepted. All restaurants we list are open daily for lunch and dinner unless stated otherwise; dress is mentioned only when men are required to wear a jacket or a jacket and tie.

Assume that all rooms have private baths, phones, TVs, and air-conditioning unless otherwise noted and that all hotels operate on the European Plan (with no meals) unless we specify that they use the Continental Plan (CP, with a continental breakfast), Breakfast Plan (BP, with a full cooked breakfast), Modified American Plan (MAP, with breakfast and dinner), or the Full American Plan (FAP, with all meals).

We always list the facilities that are available—but we don't specify whether they cost extra: when pricing accommodations, always ask what's included and what costs extra.

WHAT IT COSTS				
$$$$	**$$$**	**$$**	**$**	**¢**
RESTAURANTS over $30	$21–$30	$13–$20	$6–$12	under $6
HOTELS over $270	$206–$270	$151–$205	$100–$150	under $100

Restaurant prices are per person for a main course at dinner, excluding sales tax (7.5% in VA, 5% in MD). Hotel prices are for two people in a standard double room in high season.

C&O CANAL & GREAT FALLS PARKS

In the 18th and early 19th centuries, the Potomac River was the main transportation route between Cumberland, Maryland, one of the most important ports on the nation's frontier, and the seaports of the Chesapeake Bay. Coal, tobacco, grain, whiskey, furs, iron ore, and timber were sent down the Potomac to Georgetown and Alexandria, which served as major distribution points for both domestic and international markets.

Although it was a vital link with the country's western territories, the Potomac had some drawbacks as a commercial waterway: rapids and waterfalls along the 185 mi between Cumberland and Washington originally made it impossible for traders to travel the entire distance by boat. Just a few miles upstream from Washington, the Potomac cascades through two such barriers: the breathtakingly beautiful Great Falls and the less dramatic but equally impassable Little Falls.

To help traders move goods between the eastern markets and the western frontier more efficiently, 18th-century engineers proposed that a canal with a series of elevator locks be constructed parallel to the river. George Washington founded a company to build the canal, and in 1802 (after his death) the firm opened the Patowmack Canal on the Virginia side of the river.

In 1828 Washington's canal was replaced by the Chesapeake & Ohio Canal, which stretched from downtown Washington to Cumberland, Maryland. However, by the time it had opened, newer technology was starting to make canals obsolete. The Baltimore & Ohio Railroad, which opened the same day as the C&O, finally put the canal out of business in 1924.

Numbers in the margin correspond to points of interest on the C&O Canal National Historic Park & Great Falls Park map.

C&O Canal National Historic Park

West from Georgetown extending 13 mi to Great Falls Tavern.

C&O Canal National Historic Park originates in Georgetown and encloses a 184.5-mi towpath that ends in Cumberland, Maryland. The finest relic of America's canal-building era, its route and structures are still almost entirely intact. Construction along the Maryland bank began in 1828, using the principles of the Erie Canal in New York. When construction ended in 1850, canals stretched from downtown Washington to Cumberland through 74 locks. (The public restroom at the intersection of 17th Street and Constitution Avenue was originally a lock house of an earlier canal through Washington.) The original plan to extend a canal to the Ohio River was superseded by the success of the Baltimore & Ohio (B&O) Railroad, which eventually put the canal out of business.

Construction of the C&O Canal and the B&O Railroad began on the same day, July 4, 1828. Initially, the C&O provided an economical and practical way for traders to move goods through the Washington area

WHAT'S WHERE

C&O CANAL & GREAT FALLS

The C&O Canal National Historic Park (on the Washington, D.C., and Maryland side of the Potomac) and the Great Falls Park (on the Virginia side) are both part of the National Park system. At a point about 9 mi west of the District line, the two parks face each other. It's here that the steep, jagged falls of the Potomac roar into a narrow gorge, providing one of the most spectacular scenic attractions in the East. Canoeing, bicycling, and fishing are popular in the parks. Within the C&O Canal National Historic Park are the Clara Barton National Historic Site and Glen Echo Park, which is notable for its whimsical architecture and its splendid 1921 Dentzel carousel.

ANNAPOLIS, MARYLAND

Maryland's capital is a popular destination for oyster catchers and boating fans. Warm, sunny days bring many boats to the City Dock, where they're moored against a background of waterfront shops and restaurants. Annapolis's enduring nautical reputation is upheld further by the presence of the U.S. Naval Academy. One of the country's largest assemblages of 18th-century architecture, with no fewer than 50 pre–Revolutionary War buildings, the academy recalls the city's days as a major port.

FREDERICK, MARYLAND

Maryland's second-largest city is less than an hour away from Washington, D.C., and has one of the best-preserved historic districts in Maryland. There are several quirky museums in Frederick, including the National Museum of Civil War Medicine, as well as a Civil War battlefield. The city and its environs also hold many antiques stores.

MOUNT VERNON, WOODLAWN & GUNSTON HALL

Three splendid examples of plantation architecture remain on the Virginia side of the Potomac, just 15 mi south of the District. Mount Vernon, the most-visited historic house in America, was the home of George Washington; Woodlawn was the estate of Washington's step-granddaughter; and Gunston Hall was the residence of George Mason, a patriot and author of the document on which the Bill of Rights was based. After Mount Vernon you can see George Washington's Gristmill, which makes flour the same way it was made in colonial days.

FREDERICKSBURG, VIRGINIA

This compact city 50 mi south of Washington near the falls of the Rappahannock River played prominent roles at crucial points in the nation's history, particularly during the Revolutionary and Civil wars. A popular day-trip destination for history buffs and antiques collectors, Fredericksburg has a 40-block National Historic District containing more than 350 18th- and 19th-century buildings. The city, whose modern section is a fast-growing residential area for commuters to Washington, D.C., has many excellent restaurants and sites that amply justify a visit of a day or more.

7

to the lower Chesapeake. During the mid-19th century, boats carried as much as a million tons of merchandise a year. But the C&O Canal suffered a flood in late spring 1889 and couldn't recover from the financial disaster that ensued. Ownership then shifted to the B&O Railroad, the canal's largest stockholder, and operation continued until 1924, when another flood ended traffic. The railroad transferred ownership of the canal to the federal government in 1938 to settle a $2 million debt.

In the 1950s a proposal to build a highway over the canal near Washington was thwarted by residents of the Palisades (between Georgetown and the Great Falls Tavern) and others concerned with the canal's history and legacy. Since 1971 the canal has been a national park, providing a window into the past and a marvelous place to enjoy the outdoors.

Sights to See

❶ The towpath along the canal in **Georgetown** passes remnants of that area's industrial past, such as the Godey Lime Kilns near the mouth of Rock Creek, as well as the fronts of numerous houses that date from 1810. At the Foundry Mall, you can start a tour of the area on foot, by bike, or by mule-drawn boat.

There are two visitor centers in the sections of the C&O Canal National Historic Park closest to Washington: one in Georgetown and the other in Great Falls.

At the **Georgetown Visitor Center,** National Park Service rangers and volunteers provide maps, information, and canal history. Mule-drawn canal boat rides depart from the center two to four times daily from about mid-April through late October. ⊠ *1057 Thomas Jefferson St. NW, Georgetown* ☎ *202/653–5190* ⊕ *www.nps.gov/choh/Visitor/Centers/ Georgetown.html* ۞ *Apr.–Oct., Wed.–Sun. 9–4:30; Nov.–Mar., weekends 10–4, staffing permitting.*

❸ Chain Bridge, named for the chains that held up the original structure, links D.C. and Virginia. The bridge was built to enable cattlemen to bring Virginia herds to the slaughterhouses along the Maryland side of the Potomac. During the Civil War the bridge was guarded by Union troops stationed at earthen fortifications along what's now Potomac Avenue NW. The Virginia side of the river in the area around Chain Bridge is known for its good fishing and narrow rapids. ⊠ *Glebe Rd., Rte. 120, Arlington.*

❷ Fletcher's Boat House, on the D.C. side of the Potomac, rents rowboats, canoes, and bicycles and sells tackle, snack foods, and D.C. fishing licenses. Here you can catch shad, perch, catfish, striped bass, and other freshwater species. Canoeing is allowed on the canal and, weather permitting, in the Potomac. There's a large picnic area along the riverbank. ⊠ *4940 Canal Rd., at Reservoir Rd., Georgetown* ☎ *202/244–0461* ۞ *Late Mar.–May, daily 7:30–7; June–Aug., daily 9–7; Sept.–Nov., daily 9–6.*

☞ ❹ Glen Echo Park preserves the site of Washington's oldest amusement park (1911–68) and a stone tower from the town's earlier days. The village of Glen Echo was founded in 1891 by Edwin and Edward Baltzley, brothers who made their fortune through the invention of the egg beater. The brothers were enthusiastic supporters of the Chautauqua movement, a

IF YOU LIKE

HISTORICAL SIGHTS

Of primal importance to the shaping of the United States are spots dear to George Washington: Mount Vernon; his boyhood home at Ferry Farm near Fredericksburg; and the mansions of his relatives. Bayside Annapolis, the country's first peacetime capital, is not to be missed for its port and its naval ties. A vast neighborhood of 18th-century architecture, which includes 50 pre–Revolutionary War buildings, is also here.

OUTDOOR ADVENTURES

Vast areas for hikers exist in the Maryland and Virginia parks near the Great Falls. Those who fish can stake out the numerous riverbanks and salty shores. Bikers may ride for hundreds of miles on the area's excellent paved bicycle paths. One especially attractive route winds south along the Virginia shore of the Potomac. From it, you can view Georgetown and Washington's monuments on the opposite bank; Arlington National Cemetery; Ronald Reagan National Airport; and Old Town Alexandria. Before ending at Mount Vernon, the route runs through wildlife sanctuaries, and there are many fine picnic spots along the way.

group begun in 1874 in New York as a way to promote liberal education among the working and middle classes. The brothers sold land and houses to further their dream, but the Glen Echo Chautauqua lasted only one season. The National Park Service administers this 10-acre property and offers year-round dances Friday through Sunday in the 1933 Spanish Ballroom, classes in the arts, two children's theaters, two art galleries with ongoing exhibits, artist demonstrations, and a children's museum with environmental education workshops. You can also take a ride on a 1921 Dentzel carousel May through September. ⊠ *7300 MacArthur Blvd. NW, Glen Echo* ☎ *301/492–6229, 301/320–2330 events hotline* ⊕ *www.nps.gov/glec or www.glenechopark.org* ⊠ *Park free, carousel ride 50¢, cost varies for dances.*

Beside Glen Echo Park's parking lot is the **Clara Barton National Historic Site,** a monument to the founder of the American Red Cross. The structure was built for her by the founders of Glen Echo, and she first used it to store Red Cross supplies; later it became both her home and the organization's headquarters. Today the building is furnished with period artifacts and many of her possessions. Access is by a 30- to 45-minute guided tour only. ⊠ *5801 Oxford Rd., Glen Echo* ☎ *301/492–6245* ⊕ *www.nps.gov/clba* ⊠ *Free* ☉ *Daily 10–5; free tours on the hr 10–4.*

Great Falls Tavern, headquarters for the Palisades area of C&O Canal National Historic Park, has displays of canal history and photographs that show how high the river can rise. A platform on Olmsted Island, accessible from near the tavern, provides a spectacular view of the falls. On the canal walls are grooves worn by decades of friction from boat towlines. Mule-drawn canal boat rides ($8), about one hour round-trip,

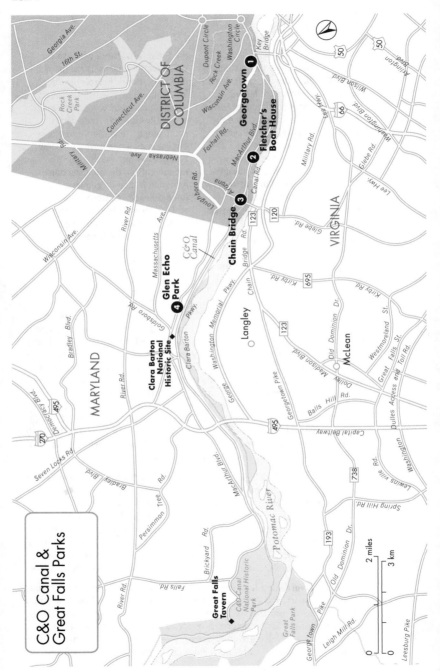

C&O Canal & Great Falls Parks

start here between April and November from Wednesday to Monday. The tavern ceased food service long ago, so if you're hungry, head for the snack bar a few paces north. ✉ *11710 MacArthur Blvd., Potomac 20854* ☎ *301/299–3613 or 301/767–3714* ⊕ *www.nps.gov* ✉ *$5 per vehicle, $3 per person without vehicle; good for 3 days at both Great Falls Park and C&O Canal National Historic Park* ⊘ *Daily 9–4:45.*

Great Falls Park, Virginia

23 mi northwest from Georgetown.

Part of the National Park System, Great Falls Park is on the Virginia side of the Potomac, across the river from C&O Canal National Historic Park. Great Falls Park's 800 acres are a favorite place for outings. The steep, jagged falls roar into the narrow Mather Gorge—a spectacular scene. There are stunning views of the Potomac here, and a marker shows the river's high-water marks. The sites that overlook the falls date from the early 1900s, when the land was an amusement park and visitors arrived by train. Fifteen miles of trails lead past the old Patowmack Canal and among the boulders along the edge of the falls.

You can fish (a Virginia, Maryland, or D.C. license is required for anglers 16 and older), climb rocks (climbers must register at the visitor center beforehand), or—if you're an experienced boater with your own equipment—go white-water kayaking (*below* the falls only). However, you can't camp overnight, drink alcoholic beverages, or wade or swim in the park. As is true all along this stretch of the river, the currents are deadly. Despite frequent signs and warnings, there are occasionally those who dare the water and drown.

A tour of the **Great Falls Park Visitor Center and Museum** takes 30 minutes. ■ TIP→ **Staff members also conduct park walks year-round; the visitor center tour and guided park walks are included in the price of admission.** You're encouraged to take self-guided tours along well-marked trails, including one that follows the route of the old Patowmack Canal; the visitor center provides maps for the various trails. ✉ *9200 Old Dominion Dr., McLean, VA 22101-2223* ☎ *703/285–2966 or 703/285–2965* ⊕ *www.nps.gov/grfa* ✉ *$5 per vehicle, $3 per person without vehicle; good for 3 days at both Great Falls Park and C&O Canal National Historic Park; annual park pass $20* ⊘ *7 AM–dark; visitor center mid-Oct.–mid-Apr., daily 10–4; mid-Apr.–mid-Oct., weekdays 10–5; weekends 10–6; hrs subject to change.*

C&O Canal & Great Falls Parks A to Z

CAR TRAVEL

To reach Great Falls Park, take the scenic and winding Route 193 (Exit 13 off Route 495, the Beltway) to Route 738 (Old Dominion Drive), and follow the signs. It takes about 25 minutes to drive to the park from the Beltway. C&O Canal National Historic Park is along the Maryland side of the Potomac and is accessible by taking Canal Road or MacArthur Boulevard from Georgetown or by taking Exit 41 off the Beltway and then following the signs to Carderock. There are several roadside stops accessible from the southbound lanes of Canal Road where you can park and visit restored canal locks and lock houses.

SPORTS & THE OUTDOORS

The C&O Canal National Historic Park and its towpath are favorites of joggers, bikers, and canoeists. The path has a slight grade, which makes for a leisurely ride or hike. Most recreational bikers consider the 13 mi from Georgetown to Great Falls Tavern an easy ride; you need to carry your bike for only one short stretch of rocky ground near Great Falls. You can also take a bike path that parallels MacArthur Boulevard and runs from Georgetown to Great Falls Tavern. Storm damage has left parts of the canal dry, but many segments remain intact and navigable by canoe. You can rent rowboats, canoes, or bicycles, and find out more information, at Fletcher's Boat House, just upriver from Georgetown.

🏠 **Fletcher's Boat House** ✉ 4940 Canal Rd., at Reservoir Rd., Georgetown ☎ 202/244-0461 ⊕ www.fletchersboathouse.com ⊙ Late Mar.-May, daily 7:30-7; June-Aug., daily 9-7; Sept.-Nov., daily 9-6.

TOURS

Between April and November on Wednesday through Sunday, mule-drawn canal boats leave for roughly one-hour trips from the Foundry Mall on Thomas Jefferson Street NW, half a block south of M Street in Georgetown. Reservations are not required; ticket sales begin two hours before each trip. Floods sometimes affect canal boat trips, so call the National Park Service office to check.

🏠 **National Park Service Canal Boats** ✉ Canal Visitor Center, 1057 Thomas Jefferson St. NW, Georgetown ☎ 202/653-5190 or 301/299-2026 ⊕ www.nps.gov/choh 🎟 $8.

ANNAPOLIS, MARYLAND

The Annapolis of today is a good place to stroll, shop, relax, study, and dine. It has a wealth of 18th-century architecture, including more surviving colonial buildings than any other place in the country. Maryland is the only state in which the homes of all its signers of the Declaration of Independence still exist. The houses are all in Annapolis, and you can tour two of the four—the homes of Samuel Chase and William Paca.

Although it has long since been overtaken by Baltimore as the major Maryland port, Annapolis is still a popular destination for pleasure boating. On warm, sunny days, the waters off City Dock become center stage for an amateur show of powerboaters maneuvering through the heavy traffic. Annapolis's enduring nautical reputation derives largely from the presence of the U.S. Naval Academy: its midshipmen throng the city streets in white uniforms in summer and in navy blue in winter.

Numbers in the box correspond to numbers in the margin and on the Annapolis, MD, map.

TIMING   Walking this route will take about an hour. Budget another half hour each for tours of the smaller historical homes and an hour each for the Paca and Hammond-Harwood houses. The Naval Academy deserves about two hours, plus another half hour if you visit the museum. The

A GOOD TOUR

You can see Annapolis in a single well-planned day. To get maps, schedules, and information about guided tours, begin your walking tour at the **Annapolis & Anne Arundel County Conference & Visitors Bureau 1** ⌐. Exit the visitor center, then turn left at West Street and walk to **St. Anne's Church 2**, straight ahead a half block. The edifice incorporates walls from a former church that burned in 1858; a congregation has worshipped here continuously since 1692. Off Church Circle, take Franklin Street one block to the **Banneker-Douglass Museum 3**, which portrays African-American life in Maryland. Return to the circle after a visit. Continue around the circle to the Maryland Inn and walk to the end of Main Street. On your way you'll pass many boutiques and small restaurants as well as the **Historic Annapolis Foundation Museum Store 4**, where you can rent audiotapes for self-guided walking tours. Farther down, past the Market House, which has many places to stop for a snack, look down to see the **Kunta Kinte–Alex Haley Memorial 5**, which commemorates the 1767 arrival of the slave portrayed in Alex Haley's *Roots*. On the other side of City Dock in front of the harbormaster's office, there's an **information booth 6**, where you can get maps and information from April to October.

Return to Market Square and take a right onto Randall Street. Walk two blocks to the Naval Academy wall and turn right, entering the gate to the **United States Naval Academy 7** and its Armel-Leftwich Visitor Center.

From the campus, walk to the **Hammond-Harwood House 8** and the **Chase-Lloyd House 9**, both designed by colonial America's foremost architect, William Buckland. The two homes are across the street from each other on the second block of Maryland Avenue. Continue on Maryland Avenue a block to Prince George Street; turn left and walk a block to the **William Paca House and Garden 10**, home of another signer of the Declaration of Independence. Retrace your route and continue a block past Maryland Avenue to the campus of **St. John's College 11**, directly ahead at the College Avenue end of Prince George Street. After touring the campus, follow College Avenue away from the Naval Academy wall to North Street and go one block to the **Maryland State House 12** in the middle of State Circle. After touring the Capitol, stop and visit the **Thurgood Marshall Memorial 13** in State House Square, close to Bladen Street and College Avenue. Then turn back toward State Circle and turn right, exiting State Circle via School Street. Walk down School Street, which leads back to Church Circle and West Street, where the tour began. From here you can drive to the **Maryland State Archives 14**, where you can search for family history or do historical research. It's on the right as you leave downtown on Rowe Boulevard, heading toward Route 50. Farther west on U.S. Route 50 is **London Town House and Gardens 15**, Maryland's largest archaeological excavation.

Annapolis
Visitors Bureau .**1**

Banneker-Douglass
Museum **3**

Chase-Lloyd
House **9**

Hammond-
Harwood
House **8**

Historic
Annapolis
Foundation
Museum Store .**4**

Information
Booth **6**

Kunta Kinte
Memorial **5**

London Town
House **15**

Maryland State
Archives **14**

Maryland State
House **12**

St. Anne's **2**

St. John's ...**11**

Thurgood
Marshall
Memorial **13**

USNA **7**

William Paca
House **10**

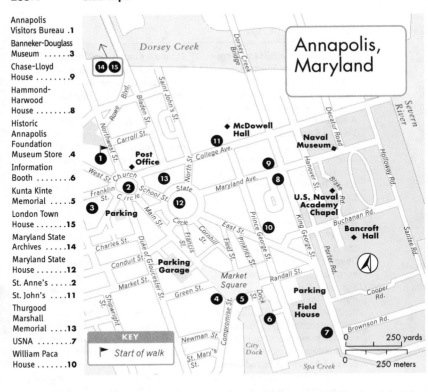

Annapolis,
Maryland

Capitol takes a quarter hour to see. The drive to the Maryland Archives takes about 5 minutes; it's another 15 minutes to London Town. Plan on 1½ hours for taking the tour and wandering the grounds.

Sights to See

❶ Annapolis & Anne Arundel County Conference & Visitors Bureau. Start your visit at Annapolis's main visitor center. Here you can pick up maps and brochures or begin a guided tour. ⊠ *26 West St., Historic Area* ☎ *410/ 280–0445* ⊕ *www.visit-annapolis.org* ⊗ *Daily 9–5.*

❸ Banneker-Douglass Museum. This former church has changing exhibits, lectures, films, and literature about the African-American experience in Maryland. The church plays host to performances, lectures, and educational programs, and the addition houses both permanent and changing exhibits. Audio and visual presentations and hands-on exhibits make the museum engaging for kids while also bringing home the hardships of slave life. It's named for Frederick Douglass, the 19th-century abolitionist, and Benjamin Banneker, a Maryland astronomer, surveyor, and mathematician who helped Pierre-Charles L'Enfant survey what would become Washington, D.C. ⊠ *84 Franklin St., Historic Area* ☎ *410/216–6180* ⊕ *www.marylandhistoricaltrust.net* ☞ *Free* ⊗ *Tues.–Fri. 10–3, Sat. noon–4.*

9 **Chase-Lloyd House.** Built by the prominent colonial architect William Buckland, the Chase-Lloyd House was begun in 1769 by Samuel Chase, a signer of the Declaration of Independence and future Supreme Court justice. Five years later the tobacco planter and revolutionary Edward Lloyd IV completed the work. The first floor is open to the public and contains some impressive sections of Buckland's handiwork, including a parlor mantelpiece with tobacco leaves carved into the marble. (Buckland was famous for his interior woodwork; you can see more of it in the Hammond-Harwood House across the street and in George Mason's Gunston Hall in Lorton, Virginia.) The house, furnished with a mixture of 18th-, 19th-, and 20th-century pieces, has a staircase that parts dramatically around an arched triple window. For more than 100 years the house has served as a home for older women, who live upstairs. ⊠ *22 Maryland Ave., Historic Area* ☎ *410/263–2723* 💲 *$2* ☉ *Mar.–Dec., Mon., Tues., Thurs., and Fri. 2–4.*

★ **8** **Hammond-Harwood House.** Ninety percent of this 1774 home is original. A fine example of colonial five-part Georgian architecture (a single block with two connecting rooms and wings on each side), the Hammond-Harwood House is the only verifiable full-scale example of William Buckland's work. It was also his final project, as he died the year the house was completed. Exquisite moldings, cornices, and other carvings appear throughout (note especially the garlands of roses above the front doorway). The house was meant to be a wedding present from Matthias Hammond, a planter and revolutionary, to his fiancée, who jilted him before the house was finished. Hammond died a bachelor in 1784. The Harwoods took over the house toward the turn of the 19th century. Today it's furnished with 18th-century pieces, and the garden's plants also are reflective of the period. ■ TIP→ **Tours leave on the half hour; the last begins at 3:30.** ⊠ *19 Maryland Ave., Historic Area* ☎ *410/263– 4683* ⊕ *www.hammondharwoodhouse.org* 💲 *$6* ☉ *Apr.–Oct., Tues.–Sun. noon–5; Nov.–Mar. open for group tours, special events, and select weekends only; check ahead for opening times.*

4 **Historic Annapolis Foundation Museum Store.** The Historic Annapolis Foundation operates its museum store in a warehouse that held supplies for the Continental Army during the Revolutionary War. Here you can shop, check out a diorama of the city's 18th-century waterfront, and rent taped narrations for walking tours. ⊠ *77 Main St., Historic Area* ☎ *410/268–5576* ⊕ *www.annapolis.org* 💲 *Free* ☉ *Mon.–Thurs. 10–6, Fri. and Sat. 10–9, Sun. 10–6. Variable extended hrs in summer.*

6 **Information Booth.** From April to October the information booth on City Dock, adjacent to the harbormaster's office, is open and stocked with maps and brochures. ⊠ *Dock St. parking lot, Historic Area* ☎ *410/ 280–0445.*

NEED A BREAK? The reconstructed **Market House Pavilion** (⊠ City Dock, Historic Area), a collection of about 20 market stalls in the center of Market Square, sells baked goods, fast food, and seafood (either prepared or to cook at home). There's no seating; set up your picnic anywhere on the dock.

⑤ Kunta Kinte–Alex Haley Memorial. A series of plaques along the waterfront recounting the story of African-Americans in Maryland leads to a sculpture group depicting the famed author reading to a group of children. On the other side of the street, a three-sided obelisk and plaque commemorate the 1767 arrival of the African slave immortalized in Alex Haley's *Roots.* ⊠ *Market Sq.* ⊕ *www.kintehaley.org.*

⑮ London Town House and Gardens. This National Historic Landmark is on the South River, a short car ride from Annapolis. The three-story waterfront brick house, built by William Brown in 1760, has 8 acres of woodland gardens. The 17th-century tobacco port of London, made up of 40 dwellings, shops, and taverns, disappeared in the 18th century, its buildings abandoned and left to decay. ■ TIP→ **The excavation of the town is still going on. From April to September you can join the dig one Saturday each month (call for schedule).** Docents conduct 30- to 45-minute house tours; allow more time to wander the grounds. From March 15 to December, house tours leave on the hour (the last is at 3). ⊠ *839 Londontown Rd., Edgewater 21037* ☎ *410/222–1919* ⊕ *www. historiclondontown.com* 🖃 *$6* ⊘ *Mid-Mar.–Dec., Mon.–Sat. 10–4, Sun. noon–4* ⊘ *Closed weekends Jan.–mid-Mar.*

⑭ Maryland State Archives. Genealogists use the public search room for family history and historical research. Collections include original civic and church records, newspapers, photographs, and maps. In the lobby are changing exhibits and a gift shop. ⊠ *350 Rowe Blvd., West Side* ☎ *410/ 260–6400* ⊕ *www.mdarchives.state.md.us* 🖃 *Free* ⊘ *Wed.–Fri. 8–noon and 1–4:30, Sat. 8:30–noon, and 1–4:30.*

⑫ Maryland State House. Completed in 1780, the statehouse has the nation's largest wooden dome and is the oldest state Capitol in continuous legislative use; it's also the only one in which the U.S. Congress has sat (1783–84). It was here that General George Washington resigned as commander in chief of the Continental Army and where the Treaty of Paris was ratified, ending the Revolutionary War. Both events took place in the Old Senate Chamber, which is filled with intricate woodwork (attributed to colonial architect William Buckland) featuring the ubiquitous tobacco motif. Also decorating this room is Charles Willson Peale's painting *Washington at the Battle of Yorktown,* a masterpiece of the Revolutionary War period's finest portrait artist. The Maryland Senate and House now hold their sessions in two other chambers in the building. Also on the grounds is the oldest public building in Maryland, the tiny redbrick Treasury, built in 1735. ■ TIP→ **Note that you must have a photo ID to enter the statehouse.** ⊠ *State Circle, Historic Area* ☎ *410/ 974–3400* ⊕ *www.mdarchives.state.md.us/msa/homepage/html/statehse. html* 🖃 *Free* ⊘ *Public areas 9–5 daily; ½-hr tour daily at 11 and 3.*

❷ St. Anne's Church. St. Anne's Episcopal parish was founded in 1692; King William III donated the Communion silver. The first St. Anne's Church, built in 1704, was torn down in 1775. The second, built in 1792, burned down in 1858. Parts of the walls survived and were incorporated into the present structure, built the following year. The churchyard contains the grave of the last colonial governor, Sir Robert Eden. ⊠ *Church Cir-*

cle, Historic Area ☎ 410/267–9333 ⊕ *www.stannes-annapolis.org* 🎫 *Free* ☉ *Weekdays 6–6, Sat. 6–2; services on Sun., call for times.*

⓫ St. John's College. Since 1937, St. John's has been best known as the birthplace of the Great Books curriculum, which includes reading the works of great authors from Homer to Faulkner and beyond (it's also the alma mater of Francis Scott Key, lyricist of "The Star Spangled Banner"). All students at the college follow the same curriculum for four years, and classes are conducted as discussions rather than lectures. Climb the gradual slope of the long, brick-paved path to the impressive golden cupola of **McDowell Hall,** the third-oldest academic building in the country, just as St. John's is the third-oldest college in the country (after Harvard and William and Mary). St. John's grounds once held the last living Liberty Tree, under which the Sons of Liberty convened to hear patriots plan the revolution against England. Damaged in a 1999 hurricane, the 400-year-old tree was removed; its progeny stands to the left of McDowell Hall. The **Elizabeth Myers Mitchell Art Gallery** (☎ 410/626–2556), on the east side of Mellon Hall, presents exhibits and special programs that relate to the fine arts. Down King George Street toward the water is the **Carroll-Barrister House,** now the college admissions office. The house was built in 1722 at Main and Conduit streets and was moved onto campus in 1957. Charles Carroll (not the signer of the Declaration of Independence but his cousin), who helped draft Maryland's Declaration of Rights, was born here. ⊠ *60 College Ave., at St. John's St., Historic Area* ☎ 410/263–2371 ⊕ *www.sjca.edu.*

⓭ Thurgood Marshall Memorial. Born in Baltimore, Thurgood Marshall (1908–93) was the first African-American Supreme Court justice and was one of the 20th century's foremost leaders in the struggle for equal rights under the law. Marshall won the decision in 1954's *Brown v. Board of Education,* in which the Supreme Court overturned the doctrine of "separate but equal." Marshall was appointed as United States solicitor general in 1965 and to the Supreme Court in 1967 by President Lyndon B. Johnson. The 8-foot statue depicts Marshall as a young lawyer. ⊠ *State House Sq., bordered by Bladen St., School St., and College Ave., Historic Area.*

❼ U.S. Naval Academy. Probably the most interesting and important site FodorsChoice in Annapolis, the Naval Academy runs along the Severn River and ★ abuts downtown Annapolis. Men and women enter from every part of the United States and many foreign countries to undergo rigorous study in subjects that range from literature to navigation to nuclear engineering. The academy, established in 1845 on the site of a U.S. Army fort, occupies 329 waterfront acres. The centerpiece of the campus is the bright copper-clad dome of the interdenominational **U.S. Naval Academy Chapel** (⊕ www.usna. edu ☉ Daily 9–5).

DID YOU KNOW?

Beneath the U.S. Naval Academy Chapel lies the crypt of the Revolutionary War naval officer John Paul Jones, who, in a historic naval battle with a British ship, uttered the inspirational words, "I have not yet begun to fight!"

♧ Near the chapel in Preble Hall is the **U.S. Naval Academy Museum & Gallery of Ships** (✉ 118 Maryland Ave., Historic Area ☎ 410/293–2108 ⊕ www.usna.edu/museum ☞ Free ☉ Mon.–Sat. 9–5, Sun. 11–5), which tells the story of the U.S. Navy through displays of model ships and memorabilia from naval heroes and fighting vessels. The U.S. Naval Institute and Bookstore is also in this building.

On the grounds, midshipmen (the term used for women as well as men) go to classes, conduct military drills, and practice for or compete in intercollegiate and intramural sports. **Bancroft Hall,** closed to the public, is one of the largest dormitories in the world—it houses the entire 4,200-member Brigade of Midshipmen. The **Statue of Tecumseh,** in front of Bancroft Hall, is a bronze replica of the USS *Delaware*'s wooden figurehead, "Tamanend." It's decorated by midshipmen for athletics events, and for good luck during exams, students pitch pennies into his quiver of arrows. If you're there weekdays at noon in fair weather, you can see midshipmen form up outside Bancroft Hall and parade to lunch to the beat of the Drum and Bugle Corps.

♧ Adjoining Halsey Field House is the **USNA Armel-Leftwich Visitor Center** (✉ 52 King George St., Historic Area ☎ 410/263–6933), which has exhibits of midshipmen's life, including a mockup of a midshipman's room, and the *Freedom 7* space capsule flown by astronaut Alan Shepard, an academy graduate. Walking tours of the Naval Academy led by licensed guides leave from here. You must have a photo ID to be admitted through the academy's gates, and only cars with Department of Defense registration may enter the grounds. ⊕ *www.navyonline.com* ☞ *Grounds tour $7.50* ☉ *USNA Armel-Leftwich Visitor Center: Mar.–Dec., daily 9–5; Jan. and Feb., daily 9–4. Guided walking tours generally leave Mon.–Sat. 10–3 and Sun. 12:30–3; call ahead to confirm and for winter tour times.*

★ ❿ **William Paca House and Garden.** Paca (pronounced *Pay*-cuh) was a signer of the Declaration of Independence and a Maryland governor from 1782 to 1785. His house was built in 1765, and its original garden was finished in 1772. Inside, the main floor (furnished with 18th-century antiques) retains its original Prussian blue and soft gray color scheme. The second floor contains a mixture of 18th- and 19th-century pieces. The adjacent 2-acre garden provides a longer perspective on the back of the house, plus worthwhile sights of its own: upper terraces, a Chinese Chippendale bridge, a pond, a wilderness area, and formal arrangements. An inn, Carvel Hall, once stood on the gardens. After the inn was demolished in 1965, it took eight years to rebuild the gardens, which are planted with 18th-century perennials. ■ TIP→ You can take a self-guided tour of the garden, but to see the house you must go on the docent-led tour, which leaves every hour at half past. The last tour leaves 1½ hours before closing. ✉ *186 Prince George St., Historic Area* ☎ *410/263–5553* ⊕ *www.annapolis.org/paca-house.html* ☞ *House and garden $8, house only $5, garden only $5* ☉ *House and garden mid-Mar.–Dec., Mon.–Sat. 10–5, Sun. noon–5; Jan.–mid-Mar., call for hrs.*

Where to Stay & Eat

In the beginning, there was crab: crab cakes, crab soup, whole crabs to crack. This Chesapeake Bay specialty is still found in abundance, but Annapolis has broadened its horizons to include eateries—many in the Historic District—that offer many sorts of cuisines. Ask for a restaurant guide at the visitor center.

There are many places to stay near the heart of the city, as well as area bed-and-breakfasts and chain motels a few miles outside town (some of which offer free transportation to the downtown Historic Area). A unique "Crabtown" option is Boat & Breakfasts, in which you sleep, eat, and cruise on a yacht or schooner; book ahead. Contact the visitor center for information.

Two reservation services operate in Annapolis. **Annapolis Accommodations** (⊠ 41 Maryland Ave. ☎ 410/263–3262 or 800/715–1000 ⊕ www.stayannapolis.com) specializes in long-term rentals (minimum stay is 3 nights). Their office is open 9–5 weekdays. **Annapolis Bed & Breakfast Association** (☎ 410/295–5200 ⊕ www.annapolisbandb.com) books lodging in the old section of town, which has many restaurants and shops as well as the Maryland State House near City Dock and in Eastport.

$$$–$$$$ ✕**Treaty of Paris Restaurant.** Period reproduction furniture and fabrics decorate this handsome, 18th-century dining room. For dinner, you may select from a variety of Continental dishes, fine steaks, or seafood. ⊠ *Maryland Inn, 16 Church Circle, Historic Area* ☎ *410/216–6340 or 800/847–8882* ⊟ *AE, D, DC, MC, V.*

$$–$$$$ ✕**Carrol's Creek.** You can walk, catch a water taxi from City Dock, or drive over the Spa Creek drawbridge to this local favorite in Eastport. Whether you dine indoors or out, the view of historic Annapolis and its harbor is spectacular. The all-you-can-eat Sunday brunch ($22) is worth checking out, as are the seafood specialties. Any of the entrées, including the herb-encrusted rockfish or Muscovy duck breast, can be turned into a four-course meal, with the addition of soup, salad, and dessert for $12 more. ⊠ *410 Severn Ave., Eastport* ☎ *410/263–8102* ⊕ *www.carrolscreek.com* ⊟ *AE, D, DC, MC, V.*

$$–$$$$ ✕**Phillips Annapolis Harbor.** With a panoramic view of the harbor, this City Dock eatery belongs to a chain of popular Maryland-style seafood restaurants. The bar and lounge is on the ground floor; the dining room, on the second floor. The restaurant's skylights and glassed-in all-season room keep things sunny. Specialties include crab-stuffed flounder, seafood platters, and a clambake for two. ⊠ *87 Prince George St., 12 Dock St., Historic Area* ☎ *410/990–9888* ⊟ *AE, D, DC, MC, V.*

$$–$$$ ✕**Breeze.** In this stylish, elegant dining room, the predominantly pale blue color scheme fits in well with Annapolis's waterfront. On the walls are sailing scenes and soft, draped fabrics, representing sails blowing in the wind. Daily specials, capitalizing on the area's bounty of fresh, local ingredients, augment the menu, which includes seared halibut and New York strip steak. A lunch buffet, which might feature pasta one week and Chinese cuisine the next, is just $12. ⊠ *Loews Annapolis Hotel, 126 West St., West Side* ☎ *410/263–1299* ⊟ *AE, D, DC, MC, V.*

7

$$–$$$ ✕ **Café Normandie.** Ladder-back chairs, wood beams, skylights, and a four-sided fireplace make this French restaurant homey. Out of the open kitchen comes an astonishingly good French onion soup, made daily from scratch. Bouillabaisse, puffy omelets, crêpes, and seafood dishes are other specialties. The restaurant's breakfast, served only on weekends, includes poached eggs in ratatouille, eggs Benedict, seafood omelets, and crêpes, waffles, and croissants. ⊠ *185 Main St., Historic Area* ☎ *410/263–3382* ▤ *AE, D, DC, MC, V.*

$$–$$$ ✕ **Middleton Tavern.** Horatio Middleton began operating this "inn for seafaring men" in 1750; Washington, Jefferson, and Franklin were among its patrons. Today, two fireplaces, wood floors, paneled walls, and a nautical theme make it cozy. Seafood tops the menu; the Maryland crab soup and broiled Chesapeake Bay rockfish are standouts. Try the tavern's own Middleton Pale Ale, perhaps during happy hour or during a weekend blues session in the upstairs piano bar. Brunch is served on weekends, and you can dine outdoors in good weather. ⊠ *City Dock at Randall St., Historic Area* ☎ *410/263–3323* ⊕ *www. middletontavern.com* ▤ *AE, D, DC, MC, V.*

$$–$$$ ✕ **Ristorante Piccola Roma.** Amid the sophisticated black-and-white interior of the cozy "Little Rome" Restaurant, you can feast on authentic Italian food while looking out the windows of the historic building onto Main Street. Specialties are fried calamari, arugula salad, linguine with seafood, and chocolate tartuffo—a rich, creamy, custardlike center encased in chocolate ice cream dusted with cocoa powder. ⊠ *200 Main St., Historic Area* ☎ *410/268–7898* ▤ *AE, D, DC, MC, V.*

$–$$$ ✕ **Cantler's Riverside Inn.** Opened in 1974, this local institution has wooden blinds and floors, and nautical items laminated beneath tabletops. Food is served on disposable dinnerware atop a brown paper "tablecloth." Outdoor dining is available seasonally. Boat owners tie up at the dock. Specialties include steamed mussels, clams, and shrimp as well as Maryland vegetable crab soup, seafood sandwiches, oysters, crab cakes, and numerous finfish. ⊠ *458 Forest Beach Rd.* ☎ *410/757–1311* ⊕ *www.cantlers.com* ▤ *AE, D, DC, MC, V.*

$$ ✕ **Rams Head Tavern.** A traditional English-style pub also houses the Fordham Brewing Company, which you can tour. The Rams Head serves better-than-usual tavern fare, including spicy shrimp salad, crab cakes, and beer-battered shrimp, as well as more than 170 beers—26 on tap—from around the world. Brunch is served on Sunday. The nightclublike Rams Head Tavern on Stage brings in nationally known folk, rock, jazz, country, and bluegrass artists. Dinner-show specials are available; the menu has light fare. ⊠ *33 West St., Historic Area* ☎ *410/268–4545* ⊕ *www.ramsheadtavern.com* ▤ *AE, D, DC, MC, V.*

$–$$ ✕ **El Toro Bravo.** A local favorite, this authentic Mexican restaurant is family owned. The wooden colonial exterior conceals colorful, south-of-the-border scenes hand painted on the interior walls, hanging plants, and padded aqua booths. There's usually a line, but takeout is available. Lunch and dinner specials include a variety of enchiladas, fish tacos, grilled shrimp, and steak. The guacamole is made on the premises. ⊠ *50 West St., 1 block from visitor center, West Side* ☎ *410/267–5949* ▤ *AE, D, DC, MC, V.*

$–$$ ✕ **49 West Coffeehouse and Gallery.** In what was once a hardware store, one interior wall is exposed brick and another is exposed plaster on which hangs art for sale by local artists. This eclectic, casual eatery serves wines, microbrewed beer, and mixed drinks. Menu staples include a large cheese-and-pâté plate, deli sandwiches, and soups and salads. There's free Wi-Fi and classical music nightly. ✉ *49 West St., West Side* ☎ *410/626–9796* ⊕ *www.49westcoffeehouse.com* ⊟ *AE, DC, MC, V.*

¢–$$ ✕ **Chick and Ruth's Delly.** Deli sandwiches (named for local politicos), burgers, subs, milk shakes, and other ice-cream concoctions are the bill of fare at this counter-and-table institution. Built in 1901, the edifice was a sandwich shop when Baltimoreans Chick and Ruth Levitt purchased it in 1965. They ran a little boardinghouse with 12 rooms and only two bathrooms above the deli. ✉ *165 Main St.* ☎ *410/269–6737* ⊕ *www.chickandruths.com* ⊟ *No credit cards.*

$$$–$$$$ ▨ **Annapolis Marriott Waterfront.** You can practically fish from your room at the city's only waterfront hotel. Rooms, done in a modern style with mauve quilted bedspreads, have either balconies over the water or large windows with views of the harbor or the historic district. The outdoor bar by the harbor's edge is popular in nice weather. ✉ *80 Compromise St., West Side 21401* ☎ *410/268–7555 or 800/336–0072* 🖨 *410/269–5864* ⊕ *www.annapolismarriott.com* ⇌ *150 rooms* ◊ *Restaurant, in-room data ports, gym, boating, 2 bars, laundry service, concierge, business services, meeting rooms, parking (fee), no-smoking rooms* ⊟ *AE, D, DC, MC, V.*

$$–$$$ ▨ **Loews Annapolis Hotel.** Although its redbrick exterior blends with the city's 1700s architecture, the interior is airy, spacious, and modern. Guest rooms, done in beige fabrics in various textures and shades, include coffeemakers and terry robes. A free hotel shuttle bus takes you anywhere you want to go in Annapolis, and a complimentary breakfast is served in the Breeze restaurant for concierge guests. ✉ *126 West St., West Side, 21401* ☎ *410/263–7777 or 800/235–6397* 🖨 *410/263–0084* ⊕ *www.loewsannapolis.com* ⇌ *210 rooms, 7 suites* ◊ *2 restaurants, room service, minibars, in-room data ports, gym, hair salon, bar, laundry service, concierge, concierge floor, business services, meeting rooms, airport shuttle, parking (fee), no-smoking floors* ⊟ *AE, D, DC, MC, V.*

$–$$ ▨ **Governor Calvert House.** This home facing the state Capitol was built in 1727 and lived in by two former Maryland governors. During its 1984 expansion, workers discovered a hypocaust (central heating system) in the basement: you can view it through a section of the floor. Rooms in the historic section are furnished with period antiques; newer rooms have period reproductions. The Treaty of Paris Restaurant, the Drummer's Lot Pub, and the King of France Tavern serve all three Historic Inns of Annapolis (this is one of them), and a colonial tea is served Wednesday from 3 to 4. ✉ *58 State Circle, Historic Area 21401* ☎ *410/263–2641 or 800/847–8882* 🖨 *410/268–3613* ⊕ *www.annapolisinns.com/governor-house.php* ⇌ *54 rooms* ◊ *In-room data ports, laundry service, concierge, business services, meeting rooms, parking (fee), no-smoking rooms* ⊟ *AE, D, DC, MC, V.*

$–$$ ▨ **Hampton Inn and Suites.** A fireplace and cathedral ceiling are features of the spacious lobby in this hotel, which is minutes from historic Annapolis. Guest rooms are traditional, but the spacious apartment-style suites have fully equipped kitchens. ⊠ *124 Womack Dr., 21401* ☎ *410/ 571–0200 or 800/426–7866* 🖷 *410/571–0333* ⊕ *www.hamptoninn.com* ⥲ *86 rooms, 31 suites* ♻ *In-room data ports, pool, exercise equipment, billiards, shop, laundry facilities, laundry service, business services, meeting rooms* ⊟ *AE, D, DC, MC, V* ⥇ *BP.*

$–$$ 🏨 **Maryland Inn.** Eleven delegates of the 1786 U.S. Congress stayed here. Many of the guest rooms date back to the Revolutionary War era (the wooden porches and marble-tile lobby are Victorian). Mahogany furniture and a velvet wing chair rest on aqua carpeting in the guest rooms, which also have floral wallpaper and draperies and many antique furnishings. Radiators heat the rooms. Some rooms have sitting suites or whirlpools. This is one of the three Historic Inns of Annapolis; register at the Governor Calvert House. ⊠ *16 Church Circle, entrance on Main St., Historic Area 21401* ☎ *410/263–2641 or 800/847–8882* 🖷 *410/ 268–3613* ⊕ *www.annapolisinns.com* ⥲ *34 rooms, 10 suites* ♻ *Restaurant, some kitchenettes, in-room data ports, gym, bar, pub, laundry service, concierge, business services, meeting rooms, parking (fee), no-smoking rooms* ⊟ *AE, D, DC, MC, V.*

$–$$ 🏨 **Robert Johnson House.** One of the three Historic Inns of Annapolis, this hotel is actually three cleverly integrated 18th-century houses. The front overlooks the statehouse. Guest rooms are furnished with 19th-century antiques, four-poster beds, and draperies matching the wallpaper. Register at the Governor Calvert House. ⊠ *23 State Circle, Historic Area 21401* ☎ *410/263–2641 or 800/847–8882* 🖷 *410/ 268–3613* ⊕ *www.annapolisinns.com* ⥲ *26 rooms* ♻ *In-room data ports, laundry service, parking (fee), no-smoking rooms* ⊟ *AE, D, DC, MC, V.*

¢–$ 🏨 **Country Inn & Suites.** True to its name, a cozy, country mood, as well as the gentle aroma of potpourri, permeates this suburban hotel. Rooms all have standard chain-hotel decor, but a large fireplace, wooden floors, and overstuffed sofas make the lobby an inviting place to linger. Exterior windows, trimmed with shutters and latticework, look out at a wooded area or a shopping plaza. ■ TIP➔ **Within walking distance of Annapolis's largest mall, the hotel also has a free shuttle that can take you to the historic district and to business parks.** Four rooms have whirlpool tubs, and two have fireplaces. ⊠ *2600 Housely Rd., 21401* ☎ *410/571–6700 or 800/456–4000* 🖷 *410/571–6777* ⊕ *www. countryinns.com* ⥲ *100 rooms* ♻ *Some microwaves, some refrigerators, indoor pool, gym, laundry facilities, meeting rooms* ⊟ *MC, V* ⥇ *CP.*

¢–$ 🏨 **Scotlaur Inn.** On the two floors above Chick and Ruth's Delly, rooms in this family-owned B&B are papered in pastel colonial prints. The high beds are topped with fluffy comforters and lots of pillows. Chandeliers in each room and marble floors in the private bathrooms bring this place a long way from its first days as a boardinghouse. Check-in and breakfast are done in the famous deli downstairs. ⊠ *165 Main St., Historic Area 21401* ☎ *410/268–5665* 🖷 *410/269–6738* ⊕ *www.scotlaurinn. com* ⥲ *10 rooms* ♻ *Restaurant* ⊟ *MC, V* ⥇ *BP.*

Annapolis, Maryland, A to Z

To research prices, get advice from other travelers, and book travel arrangements, visit ⊕ *www.fodors.com.*

BUS TRAVEL

TO & FROM
ANNAPOLIS

Bus service between Washington, D.C., and Annapolis is geared to commuters rather than vacationers. Weekday mornings and afternoons, Dillons Bus Service makes 14 trips in each direction, 9 to various stops in downtown Washington and 5 to the New Carrolton Metrorail station. Buses arrive at and depart from the Navy–Marine Corps Stadium parking lot, make 11 stops on West Street, and then at the Harry S Truman Park and Ride (Riva Road and Truman Parkway). See Maryland Transit Administration routes 921, 922, and 950 (operated by Dillon) at the address below. Greyhound makes three trips daily via downtown Baltimore and taking about two hours, arriving at and departing from the Transportation Department building at 308 Chinquapin Round Road, four blocks south of West Street. Round-trip fare varies between $21 and $28.

🗂 Bus Information **Dillon's Bus Service** ☎ 800/827–3490 or 410/647–2321 ⊕ www.dillonbus.com. **Greyhound** ☎ 800/231–2222 ⊕ www.greyhound.com. **MTA** ☎ 410/539–5000 ⊕ www.mtamaryland.com.

CAR TRAVEL

The drive (east on U.S. 50, to the Rowe Boulevard exit) normally takes 35–45 minutes from Washington. During rush hour (weekdays 3:30–6:30 PM), however, it takes about twice as long. Only cars with Department of Defense stickers driven by those with military IDs are allowed on the Naval Academy grounds.

PARKING

Parking spots on Annapolis's historic downtown streets are scarce, but there are some parking meters for 50¢ an hour (maximum two hours). You can park on residential streets free where allowable; the maximum parking time is two hours. You can pay $5 ($8 for recreational vehicles) to park at the Navy–Marine Corps Stadium (to the right of Rowe Boulevard as you enter town from Route 50), and ride a shuttle bus downtown for 75¢. There's also parking at garages on Main Street and Gott's Court (adjacent to the visitor center); weekday parking is free for the first hour and $1 an hour thereafter with an $8 maximum; on weekends it costs $4 a day.

TOURS

BOAT TOURS

When the weather's good, Watermark Cruises runs boat tours that last from 40 minutes to 7½ hours and go as far as St. Michaels on the Eastern Shore, where there's a maritime museum, yachts, dining, and boutiques. Prices range from $8 to $55. If it's wind in the sails that holds your fancy, Schooner Woodwind has two to four two-hour sailing cruises daily (depending on season), except Monday, when, May 14–Labor Day, there's a sunset sailing only.

🗂 Fees & Schedules **Schooner Woodwind** ✉ 80 Compromise St., departs from Annapolis Marriott Hotel, Historic Area, 21401 ☎ 410/263–7837 ⊕ www.schoonerwoodwind.

com. **Watermark Cruises** ✉ City Dock, Historic Area, Box 3350, 21403 ☎ 410/268-7600 or 410/268-7601 ⊕ www.watermarkcruises.com.

Discover Annapolis Tours leads one-hour narrated minibus tours ($15) that introduce the history and architecture of Annapolis. Tours leave from the visitor center daily April through November and most weekends December through March.

🚩 Fees & Schedules **Discover Annapolis Tours** ✉ 31 Decatur Ave., Historic Area ☎ 410/626-6000 ⊕ www.discover-annapolis.com.

The Historic Annapolis Museum Store rents two self-guided walking tours that use audiotapes and maps: "Historic Annapolis Walk with Walter Cronkite" and "Historic Annapolis African-American Heritage Audio Walking Tour." The cost for each is $5.

Several tours leave from the visitor center at 26 West Street. On Annapolis Walkabout tours ($8), experts on historic buildings take you around the historic district and the U.S. Naval Academy. Tours are held weekends from April to October.

Guides from Three Centuries Tours wear colonial-style dress and take you to the statehouse, St. John's College, and the Naval Academy. The cost is $11. The 2¼-hour tours depart daily April through October at 10:30 from the visitor center and at 1:30 from the information booth, City Dock. November to March, there's one walking tour on Saturday. The company also offers ghost tours in October ($14) and a holiday tour Thursday–Sunday in December ($14).

🚩 Fees & Schedules **Annapolis Walkabout** ✉ 223 S. Cherry Grove Ave., Historic Area ☎ 410/263-8253 🕐 Apr.-Oct., weekends 11:30. **Historic Annapolis Foundation Walking Tours** ✉ 77 Main St., Historic Area ☎ 800/639-9153 ⊕ www.annapolis.org. **Three Centuries Tours** ✉ 48 Maryland Ave., Historic Area ☎ 410/263-5401 📠 410/263-1901 ⊕ www.annapolis-tours.com.

FREDERICK, MARYLAND

Just 45 mi outside the District of Columbia are the farmlands and Appalachian foothills of Maryland's second-largest city, which was founded in 1745. Frederick has one of the best-preserved historic districts in Maryland, topped only by Annapolis. The city was in the path of the Civil War battles of Antietam, Monocacy, and South Mountain, and exchanged hands several times during the war. Frederick would have been destroyed in 1864 had the local government not given Confederate General Jubal Early a $200,000 ransom to spare the town.

The historic downtown with its many church spires occupies a grid of one-way streets that traverse Carroll Creek. One of the bridges across the creek is painted with a large-scale mural celebrating the spirit of the community. There are several museums and homes to tour, and Frederick and nearby towns make an excellent area for antiques shopping. Eight miles east is New Market, billed as "the Antiques Capital of Maryland."

An easy day trip can be made from the Washington area, or you may prefer to spend the night at a bed-and-breakfast or motel. To the south, 27 mi away, is the historic town of Harper's Ferry, West Virginia.

The Frederick Visitor Center is a good place to pick up free maps and begin touring the area. The most direct route there is to take I–270 into the city, where it becomes Highway 15 North. Exit at Rosemont Avenue and follow the signs to the visitor center. There's been some long-term construction at the Patrick Street interchange; if this exit is open, take Patrick Street East. Rosemont is the easier and best-marked way to get into town.

Sights to See

Barbara Fritchie House and Museum. This modest brick cottage was the home of Barbara Fritchie, who, it is said, bravely defied Confederate troops from her second-floor window. The daring woman, in her nineties at the time, refused to remove her American flag and shouted at the soldiers parading by her house. John Greenleaf Whittier's poem (1863) about the incident made her famous, although another woman may have been the actual flag-waver. Visitors to the house over the years have included Winston Churchill and Franklin Roosevelt. ⊠ *154 W. Patrick St., Historic Area* ☎ *301/698–0630* ⊕ *www.fredericktourism.org* ⊠ *$2* ☉ *Apr.–Sept., Mon. and Thurs.–Sat. 10–4, Sun. 1–4.*

NEED A BREAK? Drop by the **Frederick Coffee Company** (⊠ **Shab Row/Everedy Sq., 100 East St.** ☎ **301/698–0039** or **800/822–0806**) for pastries, soup, sandwiches, quiche, dessert, and—of course—many sorts of coffees and other beverages. As you walk in the door of this former 1930s gas station, inhale the heady fragrance of beans roasting in front of you. The Frederick Coffee Company is open 7–9 weekdays and 9–9 weekends.

Historical Society of Frederick County. A gracious 1820s Federal-style mansion helps explain what the home front was like during the Civil War. Docent-led tours of the building include a room furnished as it was when it was used as a girls' orphanage for 70 years. The downstairs library is invaluable to those doing genealogical or historical research. The society's bookstore is next door. ⊠ *24 E. Church St., Historic Area* ☎ *301/663–1188* ⊕ *www.hsfcinfo.org* ⊠ *$3* ☉ *Historical Society: Mid-Jan.–Dec., Mon.–Sat. 10–4, Sun. 1–4. Library: Labor Day–Memorial Day, Tues.–Sat. 8–4:30; Memorial Day–Labor Day Tues.–Sat. 8:30–5.*

Monocacy National Battlefield. Monocacy National Battlefield was the site of a little-known, hugely mismatched confrontation between 18,000 Confederates and 5,800 Union troops on July 9, 1864; many historians believe the Union victory thwarted a Confederate invasion of Washington, D.C. The **visitor center** (☎ 301/662–3515 ⊕ www.nps.gov/mono) is housed in the fieldstone Gambrill's Mill. There's an interactive computer program and electric map giving commentary about the battle. Walking trails and a self-guided auto tour take you through the clash. ⊠ *4801 Urbana Pike, north of Exit 26 of I–270* ⊕ *www.nps.gov/mono* ⊠ *Free* ☉ *Apr.–late May and early Sept.–Oct., daily 8–4:30; Memorial Day–Labor Day, weekdays 8–4:30, weekends 8–5:30; Nov.–Mar., Wed.–Sun. 8–4:30.*

Mount Olivet Cemetery. Buried in this cemetery are the remains of 800 Confederate and Union soldiers killed during the Battle of Antietam as well as graves of some of Frederick's famous sons and daughters, in-

Frederick, Maryland

W. 6th St.   E. 6th St.

W. 5th St.   TO ROSE HILL MANOR PARK   E. 5th St.

E. 4th St.

Dill Ave.

Rockwell Terr.   W. 4th St.

W. 3rd St.   E. 3rd St.

TO THE SCHIFFERSTADT ARCHITECTURAL MUSEUM

W. 2nd St.   E. 2nd St.

E. Church St.

♦ Historical Society of Frederick County

Barbara Fritchie House and Museum ♦   **National Museum of Civil War Medicine** ♦   E. Patrick St.

W. Patrick St.

Carroll Creek

All Saints St.

0 ——— 300 yards   E. South St.

0 ——— 300 meters   TO MOUNT OLIVET CEMETERY AND MONOCACY NATIONAL BATTLEFIELD

cluding Francis Scott Key and Barbara Fritchie. ✉ *515 S. Market St.* ☎ *301/662–1164 or 888/662–1164* ⊕ *www.mountolivetcemeteryinc. com* ☉ *Daily dawn–dusk, chapel daily 8–5.*

National Museum of Civil War Medicine. This may be the only museum devoted to the study and interpretation of Civil War medicine. Its building was a furniture store in 1830 and then a funeral home until 1978: the dead from the Battle of Antietam (1862) were taken here for embalming. Exhibits at the museum cover "Recruitment," "Camp Life," "Medical Evacuation," and "Veterinary Medicine." More than 3,000 artifacts are on display, including a Civil War ambulance and the only known surviving Civil War surgeon's tent. Photographs and a video help explain the state of the healing arts during this period. ✉ *48 E. Patrick St., Historic Area* ☎ *301/695–1864* ⊕ *www.civilwarmed.org* ✉ *$6.50* ☉ *Mon.–Sat. 10–5, Sun. 11–5.*

🅲 **Rose Hill Manor Park.** The former property of Maryland's first elected governor, Thomas Johnson, holds two museums. The **Children's Museum** specializes in hands-on historic educational tours targeted at elementary-school ages. The **Farm Museum** offers self-guided tours of 19th- and 20th-century exhibits that include a farm kitchen, carpentry shop, harvesting equipment, and a separate carriage museum. ✉ *1611*

N. Market St. ☎ *301/694–1646* ⊕ *www.rosehillmuseum.com* ✉ *$5* ⊘ *Apr.–Oct., Mon.–Sat. 10–4, Sun. 1–4; Nov., Sat. 10–4, Sun. 1–4.*

Schifferstadt Architectural Museum. Believed to be the oldest house in Frederick, this unusual stone structure was built in 1756 by German immigrants. Spared from the wrecking ball two decades ago by preservation-minded citizens, the house is considered one of the finest examples of German architecture in colonial America. Because the rooms are bare, it's easy to observe structural details such as the sandstone walls, which are 2½ feet thick, a vaulted cellar, a "wishbone" chimney, hand-hewn oak beams, mud-and-straw insulation, and original hardware. An authentic 18th-century garden complements the story of everyday farm life. ⊠ *1110 Rosemont Ave.* ☎*301/663–3885* ⊕*www.frederickcountylandmarksfoundation.org* ✉*$3* ⊘ *Apr.–Dec., Fri.–Sun. noon–4.*

Where to Stay & Eat

$–$$$ ✕ **John Hagan's Tavern.** Built in 1785, this fieldstone structure has its original wooden floors: it's always been a tavern or restaurant. Yes, George Washington ate here, and the tavern enjoys a bit of fame as the onetime headquarters for the Blue as well as the Gray during the Civil War. Staff wear period dress, and all desserts and breads are made on the premises. The regional food on the menu reveals an Early American influence: specialties include house-smoked salmon, duck, and quail; Maryland-style roast chicken with lump-crabmeat sauce; and twin grilled duck breasts in a pear-orange confit. ⊠ *5018 Old National Pike, Braddock Heights* ☎ *301/371–9189* ▤ *AE, D, DC, MC, V* ⊘ *Closed Mon.*

¢–$$$ ✕ **Brewer's Alley.** Frederick's first brewpub was once a town hall and market building. The eatery is clean and bright, and copper brewing pots gleam next to the bar and the wooden tables. Substantial main dishes, such as large Maryland crab cakes, double-thick pork chops, steaks, and ribs are available, as are starters, salads, specialty sandwiches, pasta, and pizza. At least six kinds of beer are made on the premises; types rotate seasonally. ⊠ *124 N. Market St., Historic Area* ☎ *301/631–0089* ▤ *AE, D, DC, MC, V.*

$–$$ ✕ **Tauraso's.** The mouthwatering smell of pizza baked in a wood oven greets diners approaching this wood-paneled, white-tablecloth trattoria. Other specialties include pasta dishes, poultry, steaks, and seafood. A favorite appetizer is Tauraso's homemade seafood sausage. The restaurant has a bar, a separate dining room, and a garden patio open seasonally. ⊠ *6 East St.* ☎ *301/663–6000* ▤ *AE, MC, V.*

$–$$ ✕▥ **Catoctin Inn and Conference Center.** Antiques, books, family pictures, and heirlooms decorate this cozy, large house from 1790. Its well-worn original floors attest to the traffic that has come and gone in this inn a few miles south of Frederick. Three rooms have working fireplaces and hot tubs. Quills, the inn's colonial-style restaurant, is open to the public for breakfast, lunch and dinner on Tuesday through Sunday. Maryland crab soup, hickory-smoked duck, crusted rack of lamb, and bacon-wrapped pork are all specialties. ⊠ *3619 Buckeystown Pike, Buckeystown 21717* ☎ *301/874–5555 or 800/730–5550* ☏ *301/831–*

8102 ⊕ *www.catoctininn.com* ↩ *12 rooms, 3 cottages, 1 suite* ◇ *Restaurant, refrigerators, in-room VCRs, outdoor hot tub, business services, meeting rooms, airport shuttle, no-smoking rooms* ⊟ *AE, D, DC, MC, V* � *BP.*

$–$$ ✕◫ **Inn at Buckeystown.** An inviting wraparound porch fronts this bed-and-breakfast, an 1897 mansion in a village with pre–Revolutionary War roots. The village is near the Monocacy River and the Civil War battlefield. The small but cozy rooms are furnished with Victorian accents that include lace bedspreads; heavy, floral curtains; and reproduction pieces. One room has a fireplace. A fixed-price five-course dinner is available for an additional fee of $40; tea is offered most days for an additional $24. ■ TIP→ **You don't have to stay here to eat in the restaurant, but you do need a reservation.** ✉ *3521 Buckeystown Pike, Buckeystown 21717* ☎ *301/874–5755 or 800/272–1190* 🖷 *301/831–1355* ⊕ *www. innatbuckeystown.com* ↩ *9 rooms, 5 with private bath* ◇ *Restaurant, some cable TV, bar* ⊟ *D, MC, V* 101 *BP.*

Frederick, Maryland, A to Z

To research prices, get advice from other travelers, and book travel arrangements, visit ⊕ *www.fodors.com.*

BUS TRAVEL

TO & FROM FREDERICK Greyhound runs daily buses between Frederick and Washington, D.C. Buses leave every two or three hours. The trip takes about an hour.

WITHIN FREDERICK Frederick's historic area is compact: you can walk to most attractions. Otherwise, Frederick Transit runs frequent buses on all downtown streets and arteries. The fare is $1.10; children under 3 feet tall ride free.

🚩 Bus Information **Frederick TransIT** ☎ 301/694-2065 ⊕ www.co.frederick.md.us/Transit. **Greyhound** ☎ 301/663-3311 ⊕ www.greyhound.com.

CAR TRAVEL

From Washington, the trip takes about 45 minutes. Drive north on I–270 from the Beltway I–495. The highway number changes to I–70. Frederick has several exits. To reach the historic area, use Exit 56 and follow Patrick Street west toward downtown.

TAXIS

🚩 Taxi Companies **City Cab Co.** ☎ 301/662-2250.

TOURS

The Frederick Tour & Carriage Company offers horse-drawn carriage rides through the city's historic district on weekends. Reservations are required. The company also offers historic walking tours during the day and ghost tours in the evening.

🚩 Fees & Schedules **Frederick Tour & Carriage Company** ☎ 301/845-7001.

VISITOR INFORMATION

The Frederick Visitor Center, open daily 9–5, offers brochures, walking-tour maps, and guided 90-minute tours. The Tourism Council of Frederick County can mail you brochures about the area.

🚩 Tourist Information **Frederick Visitor Center** ✉ 19 E. Church St., Historic Area ☎ 301/228-2888 or 800/999-3613. **Tourism Council of Frederick County** ☎ 301/228-2888 or 800/999-3613 ⊕ www.fredericktourism.org.

MT. VERNON, WOODLAWN & GUNSTON HALL

Long before Washington, D.C., was planned, the shores of the Potomac had been divided into plantations by wealthy traders and gentleman farmers. Most traces of the colonial era were obliterated as the capital grew in the 19th century, but several splendid examples of plantation architecture remain on the Virginia side of the Potomac, 15 mi or so south of D.C. In one day you can easily visit three such mansions: Mount Vernon, the home of George Washington and one of the most popular sites in the area; Woodlawn, the estate of Washington's step-granddaughter; and Gunston Hall, the home of George Mason, author of the document that inspired the Bill of Rights. On hillsides overlooking the river, these estates offer magnificent vistas and make a bygone era vivid.

Numbers in the margin correspond to points of interest on the Mount Vernon, Woodlawn & Gunston Hall map.

Mount Vernon

① 1 *16 mi southeast of Washington, D.C., 8 mi south of Alexandria, VA.*

Fodor'sChoice
★

Mount Vernon and the surrounding lands had been in the Washington family for nearly 90 years by the time George inherited it all in 1761. Before taking over command of the Continental Army, Washington was a yeoman farmer managing the 8,000-acre plantation, of which more than 3,000 acres were under cultivation. He also oversaw the transformation of the main house from an ordinary farm dwelling into what was, for the time, a grand mansion.

The red-roof house is elegant though understated, with a yellow pine exterior that's been painted and coated with layers of sand to resemble white-stone blocks. The first-floor rooms are quite ornate, especially the large formal dining room, with a molded ceiling decorated with agricultural motifs. Throughout the house are other smaller symbols of the owner's eminence, such as a key to the main portal of the Bastille—presented to Washington by the Marquis de Lafayette—and Washington's presidential chair. As you tour the mansion, guides are stationed throughout the house to describe the furnishings and answer questions.

You can stroll around the estate's 500 acres and three gardens, visiting the workshops, the kitchen, the

THE VIEW OUT BACK

Beneath a 90-foot portico is George Washington's contribution to architecture and the real treasure of Mount Vernon: the home's dramatic riverside porch. The porch overlooks an expanse of lawn that slopes down to the Potomac. In springtime the view of the river (a mile wide where it passes the plantation) is framed by redbud and dogwood blossoms. Protocol requires United States Navy and Coast Guard ships to salute when passing the house during daylight hours. Foreign naval vessels often salute, too.

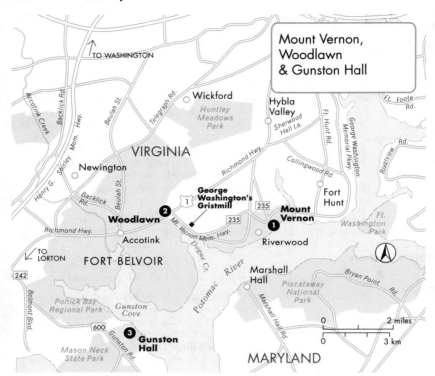

carriage house, the greenhouse, the slave quarters, and, down the hill toward the boat landing, the tomb of George and Martha Washington. There's also a pioneer farmer site: a 4-acre hands-on exhibit with a reconstruction of George Washington's 16-sided treading barn as its centerpiece. ■ TIP➔ **Among the souvenirs sold at the plantation are stripling boxwoods that began life as clippings from bushes planted in 1798, the year before Washington died.** A tour of the house and grounds takes about two hours. There are a limited number of wheelchairs available at the main gate. Private, evening candlelight tours of the mansion with staff dressed in 18th-century costumes can be arranged.

After many years of research, George Washington's Gristmill opened in 2002 on the site of his original mill and distillery. During the guided tours, led by historic interpreters, you'll meet an 18th-century miller and watch the water-powered wheel grind grain into flour just as it did 200 years ago. The mill is 3 mi from Mount Vernon on Route 235 between Mount Vernon and U.S. Route 1. Tickets can be purchased either at the gristmill itself or at Mount Vernon's Main Gate. ⊠ *Southern end of George Washington Pkwy., Mount Vernon, VA* ☎ *703/780–2000, 703/799–8606 evening tours* ⊟ *703/799–8609* ⊕ *www.mountvernon.org* ☜ *$11, gristmill $4, combination ticket $13* ⊙ *Mar., Sept., and Oct., daily 9–5; Apr.–Aug., daily 8–5; Nov.–Feb., daily 9–4.*

Woodlawn

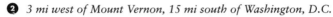

❷ *3 mi west of Mount Vernon, 15 mi south of Washington, D.C.*

Woodlawn was once part of the Mount Vernon estate. From here you can still see evidence of the bowling green that fronted Washington's home. The house was built for Eleanor "Nelly" Custis, granddaughter of Martha Washington and George's ward. She married one of Washington's nephews, Lawrence Lewis, who had been summoned to Mount Vernon from Fredericksburg to assist his uncle with his papers and his many guests.

The Lewis home, completed in 1805, was designed by Dr. William Thornton, a physician and amateur architect from the West Indies who drew up the original plans for the U.S. Capitol. Like Mount Vernon, the Woodlawn house is constructed of native materials, including the clay for its bricks and the yellow pine used throughout its interior. ▪ TIP➡ **Built on a site selected by George Washington, the house has commanding views of the surrounding countryside and the Potomac River beyond.** Woodlawn was once a plantation where more than 100 people, most of them slaves, lived and worked. As plantation owners, the Lewises lived in luxury. Docents talk about how the family entertained and how the slaves grew and prepared these lavish meals as well as their own. As intimates of the Washingtons' household, the Lewises displayed a collection of objects in honor of their illustrious benefactor. Many Washington family items are on display today.

After Woodlawn passed out of the Lewis family's hands, it was owned by a Quaker community, which established a meetinghouse and Virginia's first integrated school. Subsequent owners included the playwright Paul Kester and Senator and Mrs. Oscar Underwood of Alabama. The property was acquired by the National Trust for Historic Preservation in 1957, which had been operating it as a museum since 1951. Every March, Woodlawn hosts a needlework exhibit with more than 700 items on display.

Also on the grounds of Woodlawn is the **Pope-Leighey House** (⊕ www. popeleighey1940.org). Frank Lloyd Wright designed his Usonian houses like this one as a means of providing affordable housing for people of modest means. It was built in 1940 and moved here from Falls Church, Virginia, in 1964. ✉ *9000 Richmond Hwy., Mount Vernon, VA* ☎ *703/ 780–4000* ⊕ *www.woodlawn1805.org* ✐ *$7.50 for either Woodlawn or Pope-Leighey House, combination ticket $13* ⊗ *Mar.–Dec., daily 10–5; limited guided tours in Mar. because of annual needlework show; tours leave every ½ hr; last tour at 4:30.*

Gunston Hall

❸ *12 mi south of Woodlawn, 25 mi south of Washington, D.C.*

Gunston Hall Plantation, down the Potomac from Mount Vernon, was the home of another important George. Gentleman farmer George Mason was a colonel of the Fairfax militia and author of the Virginia Declaration of Rights, the model for the U.S. Bill of Rights, which called for freedom of the press, tolerance of religion, and other fundamental democratic principles. Mason was a framer of the Constitution but refused to sign the final document because it didn't stop the importation of slaves, adequately restrain the powers of the federal government, or include a bill of rights. Mason's objections spurred the movement for the inclusion of the Bill of Rights into the Constitution.

Mason's home was built circa 1755. ■ TIP➔ The Georgian-style mansion has some of the finest hand-carved ornamented interiors in the country. It's the handiwork of the 18th century's foremost architect, William Buckland, who also designed the Hammond-Harwood and Chase-Lloyd houses in Annapolis. Gunston Hall is built of brick, black walnut, and yellow pine. The style of the time demanded symmetry in all structures, which explains the false door set into one side of the center hallway. The house's interior, which has carved woodwork in styles from Chinese to Gothic, has been meticulously restored, with paints made from the original formulas and carefully carved replacements for the intricate mahogany medallions in the moldings. Restored outbuildings include a kitchen, dairy, laundry, and smokehouse. A schoolhouse has also been reconstructed.

The formal gardens, under excavation by a team of archaeologists, are famous for their boxwoods—some, now 12 feet high, are thought to have been planted during George Mason's time, making them among the oldest in the country. The Potomac is visible past the expansive deer park. Also on the grounds is an active farmyard with livestock and crop species; special programs, such as history lectures and hearth-cooking demonstrations, are offered throughout the year. ■ TIP➔ A tour of Gunston Hall takes at least 45 minutes; tours begin at the visitor center, which includes a museum and gift shop. ✉ 10709 Gunston Rd., Mason Neck, VA ☎ 800/811–6966 or 703/550–9220 ⊕ www.gunstonhall.org ▨ $8 ⊙ Daily 9:30–5; first tour at 10, last tour at 4:30.

Mount Vernon, Woodlawn & Gunston Hall A to Z

BIKE TRAVEL

An asphalt bicycle path leads from the Virginia side of Memorial Bridge (across from the Lincoln Memorial), past Ronald Reagan National Airport, and through Alexandria all the way to Mount Vernon. The trail is steep in places, but bikers in moderately good condition can make the 16-mi trip in less than two hours. You can rent bicycles at several locations in Washington.

A great place to rent a bike is at the idyllic Washington Sailing Marina, which is on the Mount Vernon Bike Trail. A 12-mi ride south will take you right up to the front doors of Mount Vernon. All-terrain bikes rent for $6 per hour or $22 per day; cruisers cost $4 per hour or $16.50 per day. The marina is open 9–5 daily.

BOAT TRAVEL

The *Potomac Spirit* makes a pleasant trip from Washington down the Potomac to Mount Vernon from mid-March through mid-October. Tickets include admission to the estate. From the Mount Vernon wharf, you could take a 40-minute photo and sightseeing cruise ($8). You can also take lunch, dinner, and Sunday brunch cruises on the *Spirit of*

Washington, which depart from Washington as well but don't go quite as far as Mount Vernon. Tickets include your meal and, on the dinner and brunch cruises, live entertainment. Prices range from $35 to $56, depending on the meal served (if any) and the day of the week.

🚢 Boat Information **Potomac Spirit** and **Spirit of Washington** ✉ Pier 4, 6th and Water Sts. SW, Southeast, Washington, DC ☎ 202/554-8000, 866/211-3811 boat reservations ⊕ www.spiritcruises.com.

BUS TRAVEL

For Mount Vernon, you can take Fairfax County Connector Bus 101 or 102 marked MT. VERNON (50¢) from Huntington. Buses leave about once an hour—more often during rush hour—and operate weekdays 6:30 AM–9:15 PM, Saturday 7:20 AM–7:36 PM, and Sunday 9:21 AM–6:43 PM.

For Woodlawn, take Bus 105 (FT. BELVOIR; 50¢). Buses operate weekdays 6 AM–11:10 PM and weekends 6:48 AM–7:05 PM. Schedules for these lines are posted at the Huntington Metrorail station. Buses returning to the station have the same numbers but are marked HUNTINGTON.

🚌 Bus Information **Fairfax County Connector** ☎ 703/339-7200 ⊕ www.co.fairfax. va.us/comm/trans/connector.

CAR TRAVEL

To reach Mount Vernon from the Capital Beltway (Route 495), take Exit 1 and follow the signs to George Washington Memorial Parkway southbound. Mount Vernon is about 8½ mi south. From downtown Washington, cross into Arlington on Key Bridge, Memorial Bridge, or the 14th Street Bridge and drive south on the George Washington Memorial Parkway past Ronald Reagan National Airport through Alexandria straight to Mount Vernon. The trip from D.C. takes about a half hour.

For Woodlawn, travel southwest on Route 1 to the second Route 235 intersection (the first leads to Mount Vernon). The entrance to Woodlawn is on the right at the traffic light. From Mount Vernon, travel northwest on Route 235 to the Route 1 intersection; Woodlawn is straight ahead through the intersection.

To visit Gunston Hall, travel south on Route 1, 9 mi past Woodlawn to Route 242; turn left there and go 3½ mi to the plantation entrance.

SUBWAY TRAVEL

From downtown D.C., Arlington, or Alexandria you can take the Yellow Line train to the Huntington Metrorail station ($1.85–$2.60 from Metro Center to Huntington, depending on the time of day and point of origin); from this point you must take a bus. ⊕ www.wmata.com

TOURS

Gray Line runs half-day trips to Mount Vernon (with a stop in Alexandria), departing daily at 8:30 AM from Union Station (from late June to late October there's an additional trip at 2 PM). A ticket is $35 and includes admission to the mansion and grounds.

Tourmobile offers trips to Mount Vernon, April through October daily at 10 AM, noon, and 2 PM, from Arlington Cemetery and the Washington Monument. Reservations must be made in person 30 minutes in advance at the point of departure, and the $25 ticket includes admission to the mansion. A two-day combination ticket for Mount Vernon and several sites in Washington is available for $45.

▓ Fees & Schedules **Gray Line** ☏ 301/386-8300 ⊕ www.grayline.com. **Tourmobile** ☏ 202/554-5100 ⊕ www.tourmobile.com.

FREDERICKSBURG, VIRGINIA

Fifty miles south of Washington on I–95, Fredericksburg is near the falls of the Rappahannock River. In this popular day-trip destination for history buffs, there's a National Historic District containing the house George Washington bought for his mother, Mary; the Rising Sun Tavern; and Kenmore, the magnificent 1752 plantation home of George Washington's sister. The town is also a favorite with antiques collectors, who enjoy cruising the dealers' shops along Caroline Street, an area once favored by Indian tribes for fishing and hunting.

Remarkably, although four major Civil War battles were fought in and around Fredericksburg, much of the city remained intact. Today the city is being overrun for a different reason. The charming town is being inundated by commuters fleeing the Washington, D.C., area to kinder, less expensive environs. The railroad lines that were so crucial to transporting Civil War supplies now bring workers to and from the nation's capital an hour away, and the sacred Civil War battlegrounds share the area with legions of shopping centers.

HERE'S WHERE George Washington knew Fredericksburg well, having grown up just across the Rappahannock on Ferry Farm, his residence from ages 6 to 19. The myths about chopping down a cherry tree and throwing a coin (actually a rock) across the Rappahannock (later confused with the Potomac) refer to this period of his life. In later years Washington often visited his mother here on Charles Street.

Numbers in the box correspond to numbers in the margin and on the Fredericksburg, VA, map.

Downtown Fredericksburg

Fredericksburg, a modern commercial town, includes a 40-block National Historic District with more than 350 original 18th- and 19th-century buildings. No playacting here—residents live in the historic homes and work in the stores, many of which sell antiques.

TIMING A walking tour through the town proper takes three to four hours; battlefield tours will take at least that long. (The Park Service's cassettes last about 2½ hours for an automobile tour.) A self-guided tour of the Mary Washington College Galleries takes about 30 minutes. Spring and fall are the best times to tour Fredericksburg on foot, but because Virginia weather is temperate intermittently in winter, you may find some suitable walking days then. Summers—especially August—can be hot, humid, and not very pleasant for a long walk.

Belmont **13**

Chatham
Manor **12**

Confederate
Cemetery **7**

Fredericksburg
Area Museum and
Cultural Center .**9**

Fredericksburg/
Spotsylvania Nat.
Mil. Park **14**

Fredericksburg
Visitor Center . .**1**

George
Washington's
Ferry Farm . . .**11**

Hugh Mercer
Apothecary **2**

James Monroe
Museum **8**

Kenmore **5**

Mary Washington
College
Galleries **10**

Mary Washington
Grave **6**

Mary
Washington
House **4**

National
Cemetery **15**

Rising Sun
Tavern **3**

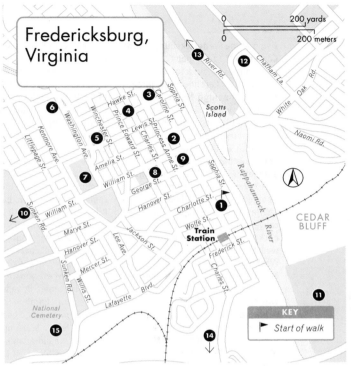

Sights to See

7 **Confederate Cemetery.** This cemetery contains the remains of more than 2,000 soldiers (most of them unknown) as well as the graves of generals Dabney Maury, Seth Barton, Carter Stevenson, Daniel Ruggles, Henry Sibley, and Abner Perrin. ⊠ *1100 Washington Ave., near Amelia St., Historic District* ⊙ *Daily dawn–dusk.*

9 **Fredericksburg Area Museum and Cultural Center.** Beginning in the spring of 2007, new exhibits in the Catherine W. Jones McKann Center for History, directly across the street from the Museum in the former First Virginia Bank building, will be opening. In preparation for this new addition, floors of the Fredericksburg Area Museum will be open to the public intermittently. The museum is housed in an 1816 building once used as a market and town hall. Currently this museum's six permanent exhibits tell the story of the area from prehistoric times through the Revolutionary and Civil wars to the present. The Civil War exhibits emphasize the civilian experience, although attention is also paid to the soldier. Military items on display include a Henry rifle, a sword with "CSA" carved into the basket, and a Confederate officer's coat. Most weapons and accessories were found on local battlefields. Other displays include dinosaur footprints from a nearby quarry, Native American ar-

A GOOD TOUR

Begin at the **Fredericksburg Visitor Center ①** ► to get maps or directions or to join a tour. Walk northwest on Caroline Street three blocks to the **Hugh Mercer Apothecary Shop ②**, where you can see tools used in 18th- and 19th-century medicine, passing numerous antiques shops and boutiques along the way. Continue another three blocks to the **Rising Sun Tavern ③**, a house built by George Washington's brother Charles that was a popular place to converse over food and drink. Walk back to Lewis Street, turn right, and walk two blocks to the **Mary Washington House ④**, bought for her by her famous son. Continue on Lewis Street and turn right on Washington Avenue to the **Kenmore ⑤** entrance. This home of George's sister contains some beautiful rooms. To see the **Mary Washington Grave and Monument ⑥**, turn right on Washington Avenue and walk two blocks. Then turn around and walk back down Washington four blocks to the **Confederate Cemetery ⑦**, the final resting place for more than 2,000 Confederate soldiers, including some generals. From the cemetery take William Street east (back toward the center of town)

four blocks to Charles Street and turn right to reach the **James Monroe Museum and Memorial Library ⑧**, where the fifth president of the United States practiced law in the 1780s. Walk a block down William to Princess Anne Street. The **Fredericksburg Area Museum and Cultural Center ⑨**, on the far right corner, has artifacts that include Civil War weapons and English furniture. To return to the visitor center, walk two more blocks along Princess Anne, turn left on Hanover, and right on Caroline Street. To get to the **Mary Washington College Galleries ⑩**, it's best to drive unless you want to walk almost a mile from where you are now. From the visitor center, drive five blocks northwest on Caroline Street and turn left on Amelia. Follow Amelia and turn left on Washington Avenue. One block later, turn right onto William Street. At College Avenue, turn right and drive ½ mi to the gallery on your right. Parking (on College Avenue and two reserved spots in the staff lot at the corner of College and Thornton Street) may be tight on weekdays when the college is in session. The galleries have a fine collection of Asian art, as well as works by modern masters.

tifacts, and an 18th-century plantation account book with an inventory of slaves. The first and third floors have changing exhibits. ⊠ *907 Princess Anne St., Historic District* ☎ *540/371–3037* ⊕ *www.famcc. org* ⌨ *$5* ⊘ *Jan. and Feb. weekends 10–4; Mar.–Nov., Mon.–Sat. 10–5, Sun. 1–5; Dec. Mon.–Sat. 10–4, Sun. 1–4.*

► **①** **Fredericksburg Visitor Center.** Beyond the usual booklets, pamphlets, and maps, this visitor center has passes that enable you to park for a whole day in what are usually two-hour zones as well as money-saving passes to city attractions ($29 to the most frequently visited attractions including Fredericksburg area battlefields). Before beginning your tour, you may want to see the center's 10-minute orientation slide show. The center building itself was constructed in 1824 as a residence and confectionery; during the Civil War it was used as a prison. ■ TIP→ **Before leaving, don't forget to get a pass for free parking anywhere in the Old Town historic district. It's valid for the entire day.** ⊠ *706 Caroline St., Historic District* ☎ *540/373–1776 or 800/678–4748* ⊕ *www.visitfred.com* ☉ *Daily 9–5; hrs extended in summer.*

NEED A BREAK?

Have an old-fashioned malt in **Goolrick's Pharmacy** (⊠ **901 Caroline St., Historic District** ☎ 540/373–9878), a 1940s drugstore. In addition to malts and egg creams (made of seltzer and milk, but not egg or cream), Goolrick's serves light meals weekdays 8:30–7 and Saturday 8:30–6.

❷ Hugh Mercer Apothecary Shop. Offering a close-up view of 18th- and 19th-century medical instruments and procedures, the apothecary was established in 1761 by Dr. Mercer, a Scotsman who served as a brigadier general of the Continental Army (he was killed at the Battle of Princeton). Dr. Mercer may have been more careful than other colonial physicians, but his methods might still make you cringe. A costumed hostess explicitly describes amputations and cataract operations before the discovery of anesthetics. You can also hear about therapeutic bleeding, see the gruesome devices used in colonial dentistry, and watch a demonstration of leeching. ⊠ *1020 Caroline St., at Amelia St., Historic District* ☎ *540/ 373–3362* ⊠ *$5* ☉ *Mar.–Dec., Mon.–Sat. 10–5, Sun. 1–5.*

❽ James Monroe Museum and Memorial Library. This tiny one-story building—on the site where Monroe, who became the fifth president of the United States, practiced law from 1787 to 1789—contains many of Monroe's possessions, collected and preserved by his family until the present day. They include a mahogany dispatch box used during the negotiation of the Louisiana Purchase and the desk on which the Monroe Doctrine was signed. ⊠ *908 Charles St., Historic District* ☎ *540/ 654–1043* ⊠ *$5* ☉ *Mar.–Dec., Mon.–Sat. 10–5, Sun. 1–5.*

★ **❺ Kenmore.** Named Kenmore by a later owner, this house was built in 1775 on a 1,300-acre plantation owned by Colonel Fielding Lewis, a patriot, merchant, and brother-in-law of George Washington. Lewis sacrificed his fortune to operate a gun factory and otherwise supply General Washington's forces during the Revolutionary War. As a result, his debts forced his widow to sell the home following his death. ■ TIP→ **The outstanding plaster moldings in the ceilings are even more ornate than those at Mount Vernon. It's believed that the artisan responsible for the ceilings worked frequently in both homes, though his name is unknown, possibly because he was an indentured servant.** Guided 45-minute architectural tours of the home are conducted by docents; the subterranean Crowningshield museum on the grounds displays Kenmore's collection of fine Virginia-made furniture and family portraits as well as changing exhibits on Fredericksburg life. ⊠ *1201 Washington Ave., Historic District* ☎ *540/ 373–3381* ⊕ *www.kenmore.org* ⊠ *$8; combination ticket with George Washington's Ferry Farm $11* ☉ *Mid-Feb.–Dec., daily 10–5.*

⑩ Mary Washington College Galleries. On campus are two art galleries. The Ridderhof Martin Gallery is home to exhibitions of art from various cultures and historical periods. The du Pont Gallery, in Melchers Hall, displays paintings, drawings, sculpture, photography, ceramics, and textiles by art faculty, students, and contemporary artists. ■ TIP→ **Free gallery-visitor parking is available in the lot at the corner of College Avenue at Thornton Street.** ⊠ *1301 College Ave., Historic District* ☎ *540/654–2120* 🖾 *Free* ⊙ *When college in session, Mon., Wed., and Fri. 10–4, weekends 1–4.*

❻ Mary Washington Grave and Monument. A 40-foot granite obelisk, dedicated by President Grover Cleveland in 1894, marks the final resting place of George's mother. It was laid at "Meditation Rock," a place on her daughter's property where Mrs. Washington liked to read.

❹ Mary Washington House. George purchased a three-room cottage for his mother in 1772 for £225, renovated it, and more than doubled its size with additions. She spent the last 17 years of her life here, tending the garden where her original boxwoods still flourish today, and where many a bride and groom now exchange their vows. The home has been a museum since 1930. Inside, displays include Mrs. Washington's "best dressing glass," a silver-over-tin mirror in a Chippendale frame; her teapot; Washington family dinnerware; and period furniture. The kitchen and its spit are original. Tours begin on the back porch: from there you can see the brick sidewalk leading to Kenmore, the home of Mrs. Washington's only daughter. ⊠ *1200 Charles St., Historic District* ☎ *540/373–1569* 🖾 *$5* ⊙ *Mar.–Dec., Mon.–Sat. 10–5, Sun. 1–5.*

❸ Rising Sun Tavern. In 1760 George Washington's brother Charles built as his home what later became the Rising Sun Tavern, a watering hole for such patriots as the Lee brothers (the only siblings to sign the Declaration of Independence); Patrick Henry, the five-term governor of Virginia who said, "Give me liberty or give me death"; and future presidents Washington and Jefferson. A "wench" in period costume leads a tour without stepping out of character. From her you hear how travelers slept and what they ate and drank at this busy institution. ⊠ *1304 Caroline St., Historic District* ☎ *540/371–1494* 🖾 *$5* ⊙ *Mar.–Dec., Mon.–Sat. 10–5, Sun. 1–5.*

Around Fredericksburg

Surrounding the town of Fredericksburg are historic sites and beautiful vistas. In 1862 Union forces looked over the peaceful place with battles on their mind. Today you see only the lively Rappahannock and beautiful homes on a lovely drive across the river.

TIMING   Allow five minutes to drive to Ferry Farm and 10 minutes each to drive to Belmont and Chatham Manor. A tour of Belmont takes about an hour, as does Chatham Manor if you tour the museum and gardens. The battlefields of Wilderness, Chancellorsville, and Spotsylvania Court House are each within 15 mi of Fredericksburg. It can take from one to several hours to tour each one, depending on your level of interest. At the Fredericksburg Battlefield Visitor Center, allow an hour or two—there's a 22-minute video, a small museum, and frequent walking tours.

A GOOD DRIVE

From downtown Fredericksburg drive east on William Street (Route 3) across the Rappahannock River 1 mi to **George Washington's Ferry Farm** ⑪ ⌐, on the right. Living here from ages 6 to 19, Washington received his formal education and taught himself surveying. Here you can see exhibits and ongoing archaeological excavations. Return on Route 3 toward Fredericksburg and turn right at the signs to **Chatham Manor** ⑫, just east of the river. This Georgian mansion has views of the Rappahannock River and Fredericksburg. From Chatham Manor take River Road (Route 607) about a mile along the river, crossing U.S. 1 (Jefferson Davis Highway) to Route 1001 and **Belmont** ⑬, a spacious Georgian house furnished with many antiques and works of art. Return to Route 1 via Route 1001 and turn right (south) and cross the river. Turn left on Princess Anne Street and go 1½ mi to the train station. This takes you past many old homes, churches, the main business district, and the museum. Turn right on Lafayette Boulevard; the **Fredericksburg/ Spotsylvania National Military Park** ⑭ and **National Cemetery** ⑮ are ½ mi ahead on the right. Exhibits, films, and ranger-led tours describe Fredericksburg's role in the Civil War.

Sights to See

⑬ **Belmont.** The last owner of this 1790s Georgian-style house was American artist Gari Melchers, who chaired the Smithsonian Commission to establish the National Gallery of Art in Washington; his wife, Corinne, deeded the 27-acre estate and its collections to Virginia. Belmont is now a public museum and a Virginia National Historic Landmark administered by the University of Mary Washington. You can take a one-hour tour of the spacious house, which is furnished with a rich collection of their antiques. Galleries in the stone studio, built by the Melchers in 1924, house the largest repository of his work. An orientation movie is shown in the reception area, which was once the carriage house. ⊠ *224 Washington St., Falmouth, VA* ☎ *540/654–1015* ⊕ *www.umw.edu/belm* ▨ *$7* ☉ *Mon.–Sat. 10–5, Sun. 1–5.*

⑫ **Chatham Manor.** A fine example of Georgian architecture, Chatham Manor was built between 1768 and 1771 by William Fitzhugh, a plantation owner, on a site overlooking the Rappahannock River and the town of Fredericksburg. Fitzhugh frequently played host to luminaries such as Washington and Jefferson. During the Civil War, Union forces commandeered the house and converted it into a headquarters and hospital. President Abraham Lincoln conferred with his generals here; Clara Barton (founder of the American Red Cross) and poet Walt Whitman tended the wounded. After the war, the house and gardens were restored by private owners and eventually donated to the National Park Service. The home itself is now a museum. Five of the 10 rooms in the 12,000-square-foot mansion and house, with exhibits spanning several centuries, are open to the public. ✉ *120 Chatham La., Falmouth, VA* ☎ *540/373–4461* ⊕ *www.nps.gov/frsp/chatham.htm* ✐ *$4, includes Fredericksburg/Spotsylvania National Military Park* ⊙ *Daily 9–4:30.*

★ ⓮ **Fredericksburg/Spotsylvania National Military Park.** The 9,000-acre park actually includes four battlefields and three historic buildings, all accessible for a single admission price. At the Fredericksburg and Chancellorsville visitor centers you can learn about the area's role in the Civil War by watching a 22-minute video ($2 fee) at Fredericksburg and a 12-minute slide show at Chancellorsville, and by viewing displays of soldiers' art and battlefield relics. In season, park rangers lead walking tours. The centers offer tape-recorded tour cassettes ($4.95 rental, $7.50 purchase) and maps that show how to reach hiking trails at the Wilderness, Chancellorsville (where General Stonewall Jackson was mistakenly shot by his own troops), and Spotsylvania Court House battlefields (all within 15 mi of Fredericksburg).

Just outside the Fredericksburg battlefield park visitor center is Sunken Road, where from December 11 to 13, 1862, General Robert E. Lee led his troops to a bloody but resounding victory over Union forces attacking across the Rappahannock (there were 18,000 casualties on both sides). Much of the stone wall that protected Lee's sharpshooters is now a re-creation, but 100 yards from the visitor center, part of the original wall overlooks the statue *The Angel of Marye's Heights,* by Felix de Weldon (sculptor of the famous *Marine Corps War Memorial* statue in Arlington). This memorial honors Sergeant Richard Kirkland, a South Carolinian who risked his life to bring water to wounded foes; he later died at the Battle of Chickamauga. ✉ *Fredericksburg Battlefield Visitor Center, 1013 Lafayette Blvd. and Sunken Rd., Historic District* ☎ *540/373–6122* ✉ *Chancellorsville Battlefield Visitor Center, Rte. 3 W, Plank Rd., Chancellorsville* ☎ *540/786–2880* ⊕ *www.nps.gov/frsp* ✐ *Free; video show $2* ⊙ *Visitor centers daily 9–5; driving and walking tours daily dawn–dusk.*

✆ ☞ ⓫ **George Washington's Ferry Farm.** If it hadn't been for the outcries of historians and citizens, a Wal-Mart would have been built on this site, the boyhood home of our first president. The land was saved by the Historic Kenmore Foundation, and the discount store found a location farther out on the same road. Ferry Farm, which once consisted of 600 acres, is across the Rappahannock River from downtown Fredericksburg and was the site of a ferry crossing. Living here from ages 6 to 19, Washington received his formal education and taught himself surveying while *not* chopping a cherry tree or throwing a coin across the Rappahannock— legends concocted by Parson Weems. The mainly archaeological site also has an exhibit on "George Washington: Boy Before Legend." The ongoing excavations include a summer program for children and adults, "Digging for Young George." Colonial games are held daily June through August. Ferry Farm became a major artillery base and river-crossing site for Union forces during the Battle of Fredericksburg. ✉ *Rte. 3 E, 268 Kings Hwy., at Ferry Rd., Fredericksburg, VA 22405* ☎ *540/370–0732* ⊕ *www.kenmore.org* ✐ *$5; combination ticket with Kenmore $11* ⊙ *Mid-Feb.–Dec., daily 10–5.*

⑮ National Cemetery. The National Cemetery is the final resting place of 15,000 Union dead, most of whom have not been identified. ☒ *Lafayette Blvd. and Sunken Rd., Historic District* ☎ *540/373–6122* ⊗ *Daily dawn–dusk.*

Where to Stay & Eat

For a price category chart, see page 279.

$$–$$$$ ✕ **Claiborne's.** On the walls of this swank eatery in the 1910-era Fredericksburg train station are historic train photographs. The restaurant specializes in Low-Country southern dishes, including crawfish, grits, and collard greens. Ample vegetable side dishes are served family-style. There's a brunch buffet 11–2 on Sunday. ☒ *200 Lafayette Blvd., Historic District* ☎ *540/371–7080* ⊕ *www.claibornesrestaurant.com* ▭ *AE, DC, MC, V* ⊗ *No dinner Mon.*

$$–$$$ ✕ **Bistro Bethem.** In an 1833 storefront that served as a general store, buttermilk-color walls display local art. Copper chandeliers and original heart-of-pine floors lend a warm glow; when the weather's fine, tables are brought out onto the sidewalk for alfresco dining. In addition to an extensive wine list and daily blackboard specials, entrées include chili-rubbed quail; trout stuffed with crabmeat; monkfish; and veal porterhouse. ☒ *309 William St.* ☎ *540/371–9999* ⊕ *www.bistrobethem. com* ▭ *AE, D, MC, V* ⊗ *Closed Mon.*

$$–$$$ ✕ **Merriman's Restaurant & Bar.** Inside an old brick storefront, Merriman's dining room is painted a bright yellow. On the eclectic menu are Mediterranean dishes such as feta cheese–topped linguine sautéed with shrimp and olives, Greek salad, and Middle Eastern hummus, which jostle against classic Virginia meats and seafood. Desserts are made fresh daily. ☒ *715 Caroline St., Historic District* ☎ *540/371–7723* ⊕ *www. merrimansrestaurant.com* ▭ *AE, D, DC, MC, V.*

$–$$$ ✕ **Ristorante Renato.** This family-owned restaurant, decorated with lace curtains, red carpeting, and walls covered with paintings, specializes in Italian cuisine, including veal and seafood dishes. Standouts include veal Florentine, fettuccine Alfredo, eggplant parmigiana, steamed mussels, and Italian desserts such as cannoli, spumoni, and tiramisu. ☒ *422 William St., Historic District* ☎ *540/371–8228* ⊕ *www.ristoranterenato.com* ▭ *AE, MC, V* ⊗ *No lunch weekends.*

$$ ✕ **Six-twenty-three American Bistro and Tapas.** A 1769 house once known as "The Chimneys" is now decidedly modern. Main dishes include quail, rainbow trout, chicken adobo, flank steak, and stuffed pork loin. For something less imposing, look to the tapas menu, where there are almost 20 dishes ($3 to $8) that include risottos, clams, mussels, and vegetarian dishes. From 5 to 7 PM Wednesday to Friday, there's a 25% discount on tapas. Brunch is served Sunday, and you can eat on the patio when the weather permits. Across from the visitor center, the restaurant shares the premises with a wineshop. ☒ *623 Caroline St., Historic District* ☎ *540/361–2640* ▭ *AE, D, DC, MC, V* ⊗ *Closed Mon. and Tues. No lunch Wed.–Sat.*

$–$$ ✕ **La Petite Auberge.** Housed in a pre–Revolutionary War brick general store, this white-tablecloth restaurant actually has three dining rooms, as well as a small bar. Specialties such as house-cut beef, French onion soup, and seafood are all served with a continental accent. A fixed-price ($14) three-course dinner is served from 5:30 to 7 Monday through Thursday. ⊠ *311 William St., Historic District* ☎ *540/371–2727* ☐ *AE, D, MC, V* ☉ *Closed Sun.*

$–$$ ✕ **Smythe's Cottage & Tavern.** Entering this cozy dining room in a blacksmith's house built in the early 1800s is like taking a step back in time. The lunch and dinner menus are classic Virginia: seafood pie, quail, stuffed flounder, peanut soup, and Smithfield ham biscuits. ⊠ *303 Fauquier St., Historic District* ☎ *540/373–1645* ⊕ *www.smythescottage.com* ☐ *MC, V* ☉ *Closed Tues.*

¢–$$ ✕ **Sammy T's.** Vegetarian dishes, healthful foods, and homemade soups and breads share the menu with hamburgers and dinner platters at this unpretentious place. The bar is stocked with nearly 50 brands of beer. There's a separate no-smoking section around the corner, but the main dining room's tin ceiling, high wooden booths, and wooden ceiling fans make it much chummier and more homey. ⊠ *801 Caroline St., Historic District* ☎ *540/371–2008* ⊕ *www.sammyts.com* ☐ *AE, D, MC, V.*

¢–$$ ▦ **Richard Johnston Inn.** This elegant B&B was constructed in the late 1700s and served as the home of Richard Johnston, mayor of Fredericksburg from March 1809 to March 1810. Guest rooms are decorated with period antiques and reproductions. The aroma of freshly baked breads and muffins entices you to breakfast in the large Federal-style dining room, where the table's set with fine china, silver, and linens. The inn is just across from the visitor center and two blocks from the train station. Ample private parking is behind the inn. ⊠ *711 Caroline St., Historic District 22401* ☎ *540/899–7606* ⊕ *www.therichardjohnstoninn. com* ⇆ *7 rooms, 2 suites* ⚶ *Cable TV, in-room VCRs, free parking, Wi-Fi; no smoking* ☐ *AE, MC, V* ⓧ *BP.*

¢–$ ▦ **Fredericksburg Colonial Inn.** This 1920s motel with moss-green siding and forest-green awnings has a beautifully decorated central staircase in the lobby. Rooms are furnished with antiques and appointments from the Civil War period, and the lobby has an old-time upright piano. ⊠ *1707 Princess Anne St., Historic District 22401* ☎ *540/371–5666* ⊟ *540/371–5884* ⊕ *www.fci1.com* ⇆ *30 rooms* ⚶ *Refrigerators, free parking; no smoking* ☐ *AE, MC, V* ⓧ *BP.*

¢–$ ▦ **Wingate Inn.** Built in 2001, this four-story hotel has large rooms equipped for the business traveler. Guest rooms are decorated in a soothing cream and moss. Coffeemakers are standard in every room. The large lobby is the site of the expanded continental breakfast and evening dessert and beverage pantry. There's a complimentary local shuttle. The Wingate is set back from U.S. Route 17 (Exit 133 off I–95, north toward Warrenton). Turn left at the first signal light west of I–95. ⊠ *20 Sanford Dr., 22406* ☎ *540/368–8000 or 800/228–1000* ⊟ *540/368– 9252* ⊕ *www.wingateinns.com* ⇆ *83 rooms, 10 suites* ⚶ *Microwaves, refrigerators, in-room data ports, indoor pool, health club, spa, meeting rooms, free parking* ☐ *AE, MC, V* ⓧ *CP.*

¢ ▦ **WyteStone Suites.** Near a small outlet mall, several restaurants, and the Spotsylvania County Tourism Office, this modern hotel is 2 mi from the historic area. Each suite has king or double beds with quilted bedspreads and a sofa bed in the living room. Rooms are entered from inside walkways around the six-story atrium. ⊠ *4615 Southpoint Pkwy., take Exit 126 off I–95, bear right onto U.S. 1 South, and turn left onto Southpoint Pkwy. to hotel on right, 22407* ☎ *540/891–1112 or 800/794–5005* ⊕ *www.wytestone.com* ⌨ *540/891–5465* ⊷ *85 suites* ᒼ *Microwaves, refrigerators, cable TV, in-room data ports, indoor pool, laundry facilities* ▭ *AE, D, DC, MC, V* ⦿ *BP.*

Fredericksburg, Virginia, A to Z

To research prices, get advice from other travelers, and book travel arrangements, visit ⊕ *www.fodors.com*

BUS TRAVEL

TO & FROM FREDERICKSBURG Greyhound buses depart seven times a day from Washington to Fredericksburg between 7 AM and 5 PM. A round-trip ticket is $18.50. Buses stop at a station on Alternate Route 1, about 2 mi from the center of town; taxis and a cheap regional bus service are available there. Unfortunately, the waiting room is not open late at night. Buses are not known for their timeliness, and purchasing a ticket doesn't ensure a seat.

WITHIN FREDERICKSBURG You can ride FRED, the city's excellent little bus, for only 25¢. Six lines—red, yellow, blue, orange, green, and purple—serve the region and stop at all historic sites as well as shopping malls and other modern areas of the city from 7:30 AM to 8:30 PM.

🚌 Bus Information **FRED** ☎ 540/372-1222 ⊕ www.fredericksburgva.gov/transit/transit.asp. **Greyhound** ☎ 202/289-5160 or 800/231-2222 ⊕ www.greyhound.com.

CAR TRAVEL

To drive to Fredericksburg from Washington, take I–95 South to Route 3 (Exit 130-A), turn left, and follow the signs. The drive takes about an hour—except during rush hour, when it's about 1½ hours.

TOURS

The tour coordinator at the Fredericksburg Visitor Center can arrange tours of the city as well as of battlefields and other historic sites. Reservations are required. The Fredericksburg Department of Tourism (in the visitor center) publishes a booklet that includes a short history of Fredericksburg and a self-guided tour covering 29 sights.

If you like to tour on wheels, take a trolley. A 75-minute narrated trolley tour takes you past most of Fredericksburg's important sights. Thirty-five monuments, markers, and attractions are included, along with the Confederate and Federal cemeteries. Tours, conducted April through November, cost $12.50 and leave from the visitor center daily. Tickets may be purchased at the Fredericksburg Visitor Center.

If you'd rather stroll, try a walking tour with the Living History Company of Fredericksburg. The $15 tours cover topics such as the "Phantoms of Fredericksburg," Christmas in the 1800s, and the Civil War.

🚌 Fees & Schedules **Fredericksburg Visitor Center** ⊠ 706 Caroline St., Historic District ☎ 540/373-1776 or 800/678-4748 ⌨ 540/372-6587. **Living History Company of Fredericksburg** ⊠ 904 Princess Anne St. ☎ 540/899-1776 or 888/214-6384 ⊕ www.

historyexperiences.com. **Trolley Tours of Fredericksburg** ✉ 81 Devone Dr. ☎ 540/898-0737 or 800/678-4748.

TRAIN TRAVEL

Trains depart for Fredericksburg several times daily from Washington's Union Station, Alexandria, and several commuter stops; the trip takes an hour or less. The Fredericksburg railroad station is two blocks from the historic district at Caroline Street and Lafayette Boulevard. A round-trip ticket from Washington costs about $50 on Amtrak. The Virginia Railway Express offers workday commuter service with additional stops near hotels in Crystal City, L'Enfant Plaza, and elsewhere. A round-trip ticket from Washington's Union Station costs about $14.

🚆 Train Information **Amtrak** ✉ 200 Lafayette Blvd. ☎ 202/484-7540 or 800/872-7245. **Virginia Railway Express** (VRE) ☎ 800/743-3873 ⊕ www.vre.org.

VISITOR INFORMATION

🚆 Tourist Information **Fredericksburg Visitor Center** ✉ 706 Caroline St., Historic District ☎ 540/373-1776 or 800/678-4748 🖷 540/372-6587 ⊕ www.visitfred.com.

SMART TRAVEL TIPS

Finding out about your destination before you leave home means you won't spend time organizing everyday minutiae once you've arrived. You'll be more streetwise when you hit the ground as well, better prepared to explore the aspects of Washington, D.C., that drew you here in the first place. The organizations in this section can provide information to supplement this guide; contact them for up-to-the-minute details, and consult the A to Z sections that end the Side Trips chapter for facts on the various topics as they relate to the areas around D.C. Happy landings!

ADDRESSES

Although it may not appear so at first glance, there's a system to addresses in D.C., albeit one that's a bit confusing for newcomers. The city is divided into the four quadrants of a compass (NW, NE, SE, SW), with the U.S. Capitol at the center. Because the Capitol doesn't sit in the exact center of the city (the Washington Monument does), Northwest is the largest quadrant. Northwest also has most of the important landmarks, although Northeast and Southwest have their fair share.

If someone tells you to meet them at 6th and G, ask them to specify the quadrant, because there are actually four different 6th and G intersections (one per quadrant). Within each quadrant, numbered streets run north–south, and lettered streets run east–west (the letter J was omitted to avoid confusion with the letter I). The streets form a fairly simple grid—for instance, 900 G Street NW is the intersection of 9th and G streets in the NW quadrant of the city. Likewise, if you count the letters of the alphabet, skipping J, you can get a good approximation of an address for a numbered street. For instance, 1600 16th Street NW is close to Q Street, Q being the 16th letter of the alphabet if you skip J.

As if all this weren't confusing enough, Major Pierre L'Enfant, the Frenchman who originally designed the city, threw in diagonal avenues recalling those of Paris. Most of D.C.'s avenues are named after U.S. states. You can find addresses on avenues the same way you find those on

Addresses
Air Travel to & from Washington, D.C.
Airports & Transfers
Bike Travel
Bus Travel to & from Washington, D.C.
Bus Travel Within Washington, D.C.
Business Hours
Cameras & Photography
Car Rental
Car Travel
Children in Washington, D.C.
Concierges
Consumer Protection
Disabilities & Accessibility
Discounts & Deals
Gay & Lesbian Travel
Insurance
For International Travelers
Mail & Shipping
Media
Metro Travel
Money Matters
Packing
Safety
Senior-Citizen Travel
Sightseeing Tours
Students in Washington, D.C.
Taxes
Taxis
Time
Tipping
Tours & Packages
Train Travel
Transportation Around Washington, D.C.
Travel Agencies
Visitor Information
Web Sites

numbered streets, so 1200 Connecticut Avenue NW is close to M Street, because M is the 12th letter of the alphabet when you skip J.

AIR TRAVEL TO & FROM WASHINGTON, D.C.

BOOKING

When you book, look for nonstop flights and remember that "direct" flights stop at least once. Try to avoid connecting flights, which require a change of plane. Two airlines may operate a connecting flight jointly, so ask whether your airline operates every segment of the trip; you may find that the carrier you prefer flies you only part of the way. To find more booking tips and to check prices and make online flight reservations, log on to www.fodors.com.

CARRIERS

Most major national airlines fly into all three of the region's airports, Baltimore/ Washington International (BWI), Ronald Reagan Washington National (DCA), and Dulles International (IAD). Southwest flies only to BWI.

Of the regional airlines, AirTran flies to BWI and IAD, and Midwest and America West fly to BWI and DCA. Alaska Airlines and Frontier fly to DCA and IAD. JetBlue flies to IAD. Hooters Air touches down at BWI. Spirit's base is DCA.

The only international flights departing from DCA are with Air Canada, which also serves BWI and IAD. BWI is a gateway for numerous international airlines, including Aer Lingus, Air Jamaica, British Airways, and Iceland Air. IAD is served by Aeroflot, Air Canada, Air France, Alitalia, Austrian Airlines, BMI, British Airways, Ethiopian Airlines, Grupo Taca, KLM, Korean Air, Lufthansa, SAS, Saudi Arabian Airlines, and Virgin.

🛪 International Airlines **Aer Lingus** 🕾 800/474-7424 ⊕ www.aerlingus.com. **Aeroflot** 🕾 888/340-6400 ⊕ www.aeroflot.com. **Air Canada** 🕾 888/422-7533 ⊕ www.aircanada.ca. **Air France** 🕾 800/321-4538 ⊕ www.airfrance.com. **Air Jamaica** 🕾 800/532-5585 ⊕ www.airjamaica.com. **Alitalia** 🕾 800/223-5730 ⊕ www.alitaliausa.com. **ANA** 🕾 800/235-9262 ⊕ www.fly-ana.com. **Austrian Airlines** 🕾 800/843-0002 ⊕ www.austrianair.com. **BMI** 🕾 800/788-0555 ⊕ www.flybmi.com. **British Airways** 🕾 800/247-9297 ⊕ www.british-airways.com. **Ethiopian Airlines** 🕾 800/445-2733 ⊕ www.flyethiopian.com. **Grupo Taca** 🕾 800/535-8780 ⊕ www.grupotaca.com. **Icelandair** 🕾 800/757-7242 ⊕ www.icelandair.com. **KLM** 🕾 800/225-2525 ⊕ www.klm.com. **Korean Air** 🕾 800/438-5000 ⊕ www.koreanair.com. **Lufthansa** 🕾 800/654-3880 ⊕ www.lufthansa.com. **Mexicana** 🕾 800/531-7921 ⊕ www.mexicana.com. **SAS** 🕾 800/221-2350 ⊕ www.scandinavian.net. **Saudi Arabian Airlines** 🕾 800/472-8342 ⊕ www.saudiairlines.com. **South African Airways** 🕾 800/722-9675 ⊕ www.flysaa.com. **Virgin Atlantic** 🕾 800/862-8621 ⊕ www.virgin-atlantic.com.

🛪 National Airlines **America West** 🕾 800/235-9292 ⊕ www.americawest.com. **American** 🕾 800/433-7300 ⊕ www.aa.com. **Continental** 🕾 800/525-0280 ⊕ www.continental.com. **Delta** 🕾 800/221-1212 ⊕ www.delta.com. **Frontier** 🕾 800/432-1359 ⊕ www.frontierairlines.com. **Northwest** 🕾 800/225-2525 ⊕ www.nwa.com. **Southwest** 🕾 800/435-9792 ⊕ www.southwest.com. **United** 🕾 800/241-6522 ⊕ www.united.com. **US Airways** 🕾 800/428-4322 ⊕ www.usairways.com.

🛪 Regional Airlines **American Eagle** 🕾 800/433-7300 ⊕ www.aa.com. **ATA** 🕾 800/435-92827300 ⊕ www.ata.com. **AirTran** 🕾 800/825-8538 ⊕ www.airtran.com. **Alaska Airlines** 🕾 800/252-7522 ⊕ www.alaskaair.com. **Frontier** 🕾 800/432-1359 ⊕ www.frontierairlines.com. **JetBlue** 🕾 800/538-2583 ⊕ www.jetblue.com. **Midwest** 🕾 800/452-2022 ⊕ www.midwestairlines.com. **Spirit** 🕾 800/772-7117 ⊕ www.spiritair.com.

CHECK-IN & BOARDING

Always **find out your carrier's check-in policy.** Plan to arrive at the airport about two hours before your scheduled departure time for domestic flights and 2½ to 3 hours before international flights. You may need to arrive earlier if you're flying from one of the busier airports or during peak air-traffic times. To avoid delays at airport-security checkpoints, try not to wear any metal. Jewelry, belt and other buckles, steel-toe shoes, barrettes, and underwire bras are among the items that can set off detectors.

Assuming that not everyone with a ticket will show up, airlines routinely overbook planes. When everyone does, airlines ask for volunteers to give up their seats. In return, these volunteers usually get a several-hundred-dollar flight voucher, which can be used toward the purchase of another ticket, and are rebooked on the next available flight out. If there are not enough volunteers, the airline must choose who will be denied boarding. The first to get bumped are passengers who checked in late and those flying on discounted tickets, so get to the gate and check in as early as possible, especially during peak periods.

Always **bring a government-issued photo I.D.** to the airport; even when it's not required, a passport is best.

CUTTING COSTS

The least expensive airfares to Washington, D.C., are often priced for round-trip travel and must usually be purchased in advance. Airlines generally allow you to change your return date for a fee; most low-fare tickets, however, are nonrefundable. It's smart to call a number of airlines and check the Internet; when you are quoted a good price, book it on the spot—the same fare may not be available the next day, or even the next hour. Always check different routings and look into using alternate airports. Also, price off-peak flights and red-eye, which may be significantly less expensive than others. Travel agents, especially low-fare specialists (⇨ Discounts & Deals), are helpful.

Consolidators are another good source. They buy tickets for scheduled flights at reduced rates from the airlines, then sell them at prices that beat the best fare available directly from the airlines. (Many also offer reduced car-rental and hotel rates.) Sometimes you can even get your money back if you need to return the ticket. Carefully read the fine print detailing penalties for changes and cancellations, purchase the ticket with a credit card, and confirm your consolidator reservation with the airline.

▶ Online Consolidators **AirlineConsolidator.com** ⊕ www.airlineconsolidator.com; for international tickets. **Best Fares** ☎ 800/880-1234 ⊕ www.bestfares.com; $59.90 annual membership. **Cheap Tickets** ⊕ www.cheaptickets.com. **Expedia** ⊕ www.expedia.com. **Hotwire** ⊕ www.hotwire.com. **last-minute.com** ⊕ www.lastminute.com specializes in last-minute travel; the main site is for the UK, but it has a link to a U.S. site. **Luxury Link** ⊕ www.luxurylink.com has auctions (surprisingly good deals) as well as offers at the high-end side of travel. **Onetravel.com** ⊕ www.onetravel.com. **Orbitz** ⊕ www.orbitz.com. **Priceline.com** ⊕ www.priceline.com. **Travelocity** ⊕ www.travelocity.com.

ENJOYING THE FLIGHT

State your seat preference when purchasing your ticket and confirm it when you check in. For more legroom, you can request one of the few emergency-aisle seats at check-in, if you're capable of moving obstacles comparable in weight to an airplane exit door (usually between 35 pounds and 60 pounds)—a Federal Aviation Administration requirement of passengers in these seats. Seats behind a bulkhead also offer more legroom, but they don't have under-seat storage. Don't sit in the row in front of the emergency aisle or in front of a bulkhead, where seats may not recline. SeatGuru.com has more information about specific seat configurations, which vary by aircraft.

Ask the airline whether a snack or meal is served on the flight. If you have dietary concerns, request special meals when booking. These can be vegetarian, low-cholesterol, or kosher, for example. It's a good idea to pack some healthful snacks and a small (plastic) bottle of water in your carry-on bag. On long flights, try to maintain a normal routine, to help fight jet lag. At night, get some sleep. By day, eat light meals, drink water (not alcohol), and **move around the cabin** to stretch your legs. For additional jet-lag tips consult *Fodor's FYI: Travel Fit & Healthy* (available at bookstores everywhere).

Smoking policies vary from carrier to carrier. Most airlines prohibit smoking on all of their flights; others allow smoking only on certain routes or certain departures. Ask your carrier about its policy.

FLYING TIMES

A flight to D.C. from New York takes a little less than an hour. It's about 1½ hours from Chicago, 3 hours from Denver or Dallas, and 5 hours from San Francisco.

Those flying from London should expect a trip of about 6 hours. From Sydney it's an 18-hour flight.

HOW TO COMPLAIN

If your baggage goes astray or your flight goes awry, complain right away. Most carriers require that you **file a claim immediately.** The Aviation Consumer Protection Division of the Department of Transportation publishes *Fly-Rights,* which discusses airlines and consumer issues and is available online. You can also find articles and information on mytravelrights.com, the Web site of the nonprofit Consumer Travel Rights Center.

Airline Complaints **Aviation Consumer Protection Division** ✉ U.S. Department of Transportation, Office of Aviation Enforcement and Proceedings, C-75, Room 4107, 400 7th St. SW, Washington, DC 20590 ☎ 202/366-2220 ⊕ airconsumer.ost.dot.gov. **Federal Aviation Administration Consumer Hotline** ✉ for inquiries: FAA, 800 Independence Ave. SW, Washington, DC 20591 ☎ 866/835-5322 or 800/322-7873 ⊕ www.faa.gov.

RECONFIRMING

Check the status of your flight before you leave for the airport. You can do this on your carrier's Web site, by linking to a flight-status checker (many Web booking services offer these), or by calling your carrier or travel agent.

AIRPORTS & TRANSFERS

The major gateways to D.C. are **Ronald Reagan Washington National Airport** in Virginia, 4 mi south of downtown Washington; **Dulles International Airport,** 26 mi west of Washington, D.C.; and **Baltimore/Washington International-Thurgood Marshall Airport** in Maryland, about 30 mi to the northeast.

Airport Information **Baltimore/Washington International-Thurgood Marshall Airport** ☎ 410/859-7100 ⊕ www.bwiairport.com. **Dulles International Airport** ☎ 703/572-2700 ⊕ www.metwashairports.com/Dulles. **Ronald Reagan Washington National Airport** ☎ 703/417-8000 ⊕ www.metwashairports.com/National.

AIRPORT TRANSFERS

If you're coming into Ronald Reagan Washington National Airport, have light luggage, and are staying near a subway stop, it makes sense to take the Metro. The subway station is within easy walking distance of Terminals B and C, and a free airport bus shuttles between the station and Terminal A (home to AirTran, ATA, Midwest, Northwest, and Spirit airlines). The Metro ride downtown takes about 20 minutes and costs about $1.85, depending on the time of day and your final destination.

By bus: Washington Flyer links Dulles International Airport and the West Falls Church Metro station. The 20-minute ride is $8 for adults, free for children under six. Buses run every half hour from 5:45 AM to 10:30 PM. All coaches are accessible to those in wheelchairs. Fares may be paid with cash or credit card.

The Washington Metropolitan Area Transit Authority (WMATA) operates express bus service between Dulles and several stops in downtown D.C., including the L'Enfant Plaza Metro station. Bus 5A, which costs $3, runs every hour between 5:30 AM and 11:30 PM. Make sure to have the exact fare, as drivers cannot make change.

WMATA also operates express bus service between BWI and the Greenbelt Metro station. Buses run between 6 AM and 10 PM. The fare is $3.

National, Dulles, and BWI airports are served by SuperShuttle, a fleet of bright blue vans that can take you to any hotel or residence in the city. The length of the ride varies, depending on traffic and the number of stops. The approximately 20-minute ride from Reagan National to downtown averages $10; the roughly 45-minute ride from Dulles runs $22; the ride from BWI, which takes about 60 minutes, averages $31. Each additional person traveling with a full-fare passenger is $10.

By taxi: Expect to pay $9–$15 to get from National to downtown, $44–$50 from Dulles, and $55–$65 from BWI. A $1.50 airport surcharge is added to the total at all airports. A $1 surcharge is added to the total for travel during the peak periods of 7–9:30 AM and 4–6:30 PM. (Be aware that unscrupulous cabbies prey on out-of-towners. If the fare seems astronomical, get the driver's name and cab number and threaten to call the D.C. Taxicab Commission.)

By train: Free shuttle buses carry passengers between airline terminals and the train station at BWI. Amtrak and Maryland Rail Commuter Service (MARC) trains run between BWI and Washington, D.C.'s Union Station from around 6 AM to 10 PM. The cost of the 30-minute ride is $13–$36 on Amtrak and $6 on MARC, which runs only on weekdays.

🚩 Taxis & Shuttles **Amtrak** ☎ 800/872-7245 ⊕ **www.amtrak.com. D.C. Taxicab Commission** ☎ 202/645-6018 ⊕ www.dctaxi.dc.gov. **Maryland Rail Commuter Service** ☎ 410/767-3999, 410/539-3497 TDD, 800/325-7245 ⊕ www.mtamaryland.com. **SuperShuttle** ☎ 800/258-3826 or 202/296-6662 ⊕ www.supershuttle.com. **Washington Flyer** ☎ 888/927-4359 ⊕ www.washfly.com. **Washington Metropolitan Area Transit Authority** ☎ 202/637-7000, 202/638-3780 TDD ⊕ www.wmata.com.

BIKE TRAVEL

D.C. is a fairly bike-friendly city. Except for the ire provoked by the sometimes reckless local bike messengers, cars and bicycles coexist peacefully. It's best to avoid the streets during rush hour, if possible.

Except for weekdays 7–10 AM and 4–7 PM, the Metro system allows riders to bring bicycles aboard any car of the train. Bicycles are not allowed on the Metro on days when large crowds are expected, such as July 4, though foldable bicycles are allowed at all times. The fronts of all Metro buses are equipped with racks that can hold as many as two bikes. The racks may be used for no additional charge throughout the day, including rush hour. Riders are responsible for securing and removing their own bikes.

🚩 Bike Maps **Washington Area Bicyclists Association** ☎ 202/628-2500 ⊕ www.waba.org.

BUS TRAVEL TO & FROM WASHINGTON, D.C.

Washington's Greyhound bus terminal, a major one for the company, is approximately four blocks north of Union Station. Taxis are always waiting at the terminal, so it's easy to get to other parts of the city. You can purchase your ticket by phone, on the Internet, or at the station before you board the bus. Greyhound accepts cash and all major credit cards. Peter Pan Bus Lines, which serve Northeast cities, also use the Greyhound terminal for Washington arrivals.

Affectionately known as the Chinatown Express, several bus lines run between Chinatown in New York City and Chinatown in Washington, D.C. The most reliable is called Today's Bus. The buses are clean, the service is satisfactory, and the price—$20 one-way and $35 round-trip—can't be beat.

🚩 **Greyhound** ✉ 1005 1st St. NE ☎ 202/289-5154, 800/229-9424 tickets, 800/229-9424 fares and schedules ⊕ www.greyhound.com. **Peter Pan** ✉ 1005 1st St. NE ☎ 800/343-9999 tickets, 800/237-8747 fares and schedules ⊕ www.peterpanbus.com. **Today's Bus** ✉ 610 I St. NW ☎ 202/408-8200 ⊕ www.todaysbus.com.

BUS TRAVEL WITHIN WASHINGTON, D.C.

The red, white, and blue buses operated by the Washington Metropolitan Area Transit Authority crisscross the city and the nearby suburbs. Although most neighborhoods popular with tourists are near Metro rail stations, some are more easily reached by bus. Adams-Morgan and Mount Pleasant can be reached by the No. 42 bus, which leaves from the Dupont Circle Metro stop. Georgetown is a hike from the closest Metro rail station, but you can take a Georgetown Metro Connection shuttle to any Metrobus stop from the Foggy Bottom or Dupont Circle Metro stations in D.C. or the Rosslyn Metro station in Virginia.

FARES & SCHEDULES

All regular buses within the District are $1.25; express buses, which make fewer stops, are $3.

Complete bus and Metro maps for the metropolitan D.C. area, which note museums, monuments, theaters, and parks, can be purchased for $1.50 at the Metro Center sales office or at map stores.

Free bus-to-bus transfers, good for two hours, are available from the driver when you board. To transfer Metro-to-bus, take a pass from a machine before boarding your train. When you board the bus, you'll pay a transfer charge (35¢ on regular Metrobus routes and $2.10 on express routes). There are no bus-to-Metro transfers.

🚆 **Metro Center sales office** ✉ 12th and F Sts. NW 🚇 No phone. **Washington Metropolitan Area Transit Authority** 📞 202/637-7000, 202/638-3780 TDD ⊕ www.wmata.com.

PAYING

If you pay as you go, buses require exact change in bills, coins, or both. You can eliminate the exact-change hassle by purchasing bus fare in advance at the Metro Center sales office, open weekdays from 7:30 AM to 6:30 PM. Pay-per-ride tokens are sold at full fare, as well as one-day bus passes for $3 and seven-day bus passes for $11. For some bus routes you can get the SmarTrip card, a plastic card that holds any fare amount. The cost of each ride is deducted as you board the bus.

DC CIRCULATOR

The D.C. Circulator, a low-cost alternative to the Metro, offers $1 rides on new buses to cultural and entertainment destinations within the city's central core. The Circulator, a joint project of the WMATA and the District of Columbia government, has three routes, but the buses stop at many of Washington's major attractions. The North–South route runs from the D.C. Convention Center at 6th and Massachusetts, NW, to the Southwest Waterfront, at 6th Street and Maine Avenue. The East–West route runs from Union Station at Columbus Plaza, NW, to Georgetown, at M Street and Wisconsin Avenue, NW. A third loop circles the National Mall and includes stops at the National Gallery of Art and the Smithsonian Institution. Passengers can pay cash when boarding (exact change only) or use Metro farecards, SmarTrip cards, all-day passes, and Metro bus transfers. Tickets also may be purchased at fare meters or multispace parking meters located on the sidewalk near Circular stops. Machines accept change or credit cards and make change. Buses run every 5–10 minutes from 7 AM to 9 PM, seven days a week.

🚆 D.C. Circulator **District Department of Transportation (ddot)** 📞 202/962-1423 ⊕ www.dccirculator.com.

CAMERAS & PHOTOGRAPHY

The *Kodak Guide to Shooting Great Travel Pictures* (available at bookstores everywhere) is loaded with tips.

🚆 Photo Help **Kodak Information Center** 📞 800/242-2424 ⊕ www.kodak.com.

EQUIPMENT PRECAUTIONS

Don't pack film or equipment in checked luggage, where it is much more susceptible to damage. X-ray machines used to view checked luggage are extremely powerful and therefore are likely to ruin your film. Try to ask for hand inspection of film, which becomes clouded after repeated exposure to airport X-ray machines, and keep videotapes and computer disks away from metal detectors. Always keep film, tape, and computer disks out of the sun. Carry an extra supply of batteries, and be prepared to turn on your camera, camcorder, or laptop to prove to airport security personnel that the device is real.

CAR RENTAL

Daily rates in Washington, D.C., begin at about $40 during the week and about $22 on weekends for an economy car with air-conditioning, automatic transmission, and unlimited mileage. This does not include airport facility fees or the tax on car rentals.

🚆 Major Agencies **Alamo** 📞 800/327-9633 ⊕ www.alamo.com. **Avis** 📞 800/331-1212, 800/879-2847 or 800/272-5871 in Canada, 0870/606-0100 in the U.K., 02/9353-9000 in Australia, 09/526-2847 in New Zealand ⊕ www.avis.com. **Budget** 📞 800/527-0700 ⊕ www.budget.com. **Hertz** 📞 800/654-3131, 800/263-0600 in Canada, 0870/844-8844 in the U.K., 02/9669-2444 in Australia, 09/256-8690 in New Zealand ⊕ www.hertz.com. **National Car Rental** 📞 800/227-7368 ⊕ www.nationalcar.com.

CUTTING COSTS

For a good deal, book through a travel agent who will shop around. Also, price local car-rental companies—whose prices may be lower still, although their service and maintenance may not be as good as those of major rental agencies—and research rates on the Internet. Consolidators that specialize in air travel can offer good rates on cars as well (⇨ Air Travel). Remember to ask about required deposits, cancellation penalties, and drop-off charges if you're planning to pick up the car in one city and leave it in another. If you're traveling during a holiday period, also make sure that a confirmed reservation guarantees you a car.

INSURANCE

When driving a rented car you are generally responsible for any damage to or loss of the vehicle. You also may be liable for any property damage or personal injury that you may cause while driving. Before you rent, see what coverage you already have under the terms of your personal auto-insurance policy and credit cards.

For about $9 to $25 a day, rental companies sell protection, known as a collision- or loss-damage waiver (CDW or LDW), that eliminates your liability for damage to the car; it's always optional and should never be automatically added to your bill. In most states you don't need a CDW if you have personal auto insurance or other liability insurance. In Maryland the car-rental agency's insurance is primary; therefore, the company must pay for damage to third parties up to a preset legal limit, beyond which your own liability insurance kicks in. However, **make sure you have enough coverage to pay for the car.** If you do not have auto insurance or an umbrella policy that covers damage to third parties, purchasing liability insurance and a CDW or LDW is highly recommended.

REQUIREMENTS & RESTRICTIONS

In Washington, D.C., many agencies require you to be at least 25 to rent a car. However, employees of major corporations and military or government personnel on official business may be able to rent a car even if they're under age 25.

SURCHARGES

Before you pick up a car in one city and leave it in another, ask about drop-off charges or one-way service fees, which can be substantial. Also inquire about early-return policies; some rental agencies charge extra if you return the car before the time specified in your contract while others give you a refund for the days not used. Most

agencies note the tank's fuel level on your contract; to avoid a hefty refueling fee, return the car with the same tank level. If the tank was full, refill it just before you turn in the car, but be aware that gas stations near the rental outlet may overcharge. It's almost never a deal to buy a tank of gas with the car when you rent it; the understanding is that you'll return it empty, but some fuel usually remains. Surcharges may apply if you're under 25 or if you take the car outside the area approved by the rental agency. You'll pay extra for child seats (about $8 a day), which are compulsory for children under five, and usually for additional drivers (up to $25 a day, depending on location).

CAR TRAVEL

A car is often a drawback in Washington, D.C. Traffic is horrendous, especially at rush hour, and driving is often confusing, with many lanes and some entire streets changing direction suddenly during rush hour. Even longtime residents carry maps in their cars to help navigate confusing traffic circles and randomly arranged one-way streets. The traffic lights stymie some visitors; most lights don't hang down over the middle of the streets but stand at the sides of intersections.

EMERGENCY SERVICES

Dial 911 to report accidents on the road and to reach police, the highway patrol, or the fire department. For police nonemergencies, dial 311.

🚩 **U.S. Park Police** ☎ 202/619-7300.

GASOLINE

Gas tends to be slightly higher in the District than it is in Maryland or Virginia. As a rule, gas stations are hard to find in the District, especially around Pennsylvania Avenue and the National Mall. Your best bets are a BP station at the corner of 18th and S streets NW, the Mobil station at the corner of 15th and U streets NW, the Exxon station at 2150 M St. NW, and the Mobil station at the corner of 22nd and P streets NW.

LAY OF THE LAND

Interstate 95 skirts D.C. as part of the Beltway, the six- to eight-lane highway that encircles the city. The eastern half of the Beltway is labeled both I–95 and I–495; the western half is just I–495. If you're coming from the south, take I–95 to I–395 and cross the 14th Street Bridge to 14th Street in the District. From the north, stay on I–95 south. Take the exit to Washington, which will place you onto the Baltimore–Washington (B-W) Parkway heading south. The B-W Parkway will turn into New York Avenue, taking you into downtown Washington, D.C.

Interstate 66 approaches the city from the southwest. You can get downtown by taking I–66 across the Theodore Roosevelt Bridge to Constitution Avenue.

Interstate 270 approaches Washington, D.C., from the northwest before hitting I–495. To get downtown, take I–495 east to Connecticut Avenue south, toward Chevy Chase.

PARKING

Parking in Washington, D.C., is an adventure; the police are quick to tow away or immobilize with a boot any vehicle parked illegally. If you find you've been towed from a city street, call ☎ 202/727–5000 or log on to ⊕ www.dmv.washingtondc. gov. Be sure you know the license-plate number, make, model, and color of the car before you call. Because the city's most popular sights are within a short walk of a Metro station anyway, it's best to **leave your car at the hotel.** Touring by car is a good idea only for visiting sights in Maryland or Virginia.

Most of the outlying, suburban Metro stations have parking lots, though these fill quickly with city-bound commuters. If you plan to park in one of these lots, arrive early and bring lots of quarters.

Private parking lots downtown often charge around $5 an hour and $25 a day. There's free, three-hour parking around the Mall on Jefferson and Madison drives, though these spots are almost always filled. There is no parking near the Lincoln or Roosevelt memorials. The closest free parking is in three lots in East Potomac Park, south of the 14th Street Bridge.

RULES OF THE ROAD

Always **strap children under a year old or under 20 pounds into approved rear-facing child-safety seats in the back seat.** In Washington, D.C., children weighing 20–40 pounds must also ride in a car seat in the back, although it may face the front. Children cannot sit in the front seat of a car until they are at least four years old and weigh more than 80 pounds.

In D.C., you may turn right at a red light after stopping if there's no oncoming traffic. When in doubt, wait for the green. Be alert for one-way streets, "no left turn" intersections, and blocks closed to car traffic. The use of handheld mobile phones while operating a vehicle is illegal in Washington, D.C. Drivers can also be cited for "failure to pay full time and attention while operating a motor vehicle."

Radar detectors are illegal in Washington, D.C., and Virginia.

During rush hour (6–9 AM and 4–7 PM), HOV (high-occupancy vehicle) lanes on I–395 and I–95 are reserved for cars with three or more people. All the lanes of I–66 inside the Beltway are reserved for cars carrying two or more during rush hour, as are some of the lanes on the Dulles Toll Road and on I–270.

CHILDREN IN WASHINGTON, D.C.

Washington, D.C., has many activities that appeal to the younger set. To get some ideas, consult the Friday *Washington Post* "Weekend" section. Its "Saturday's Child" listings include information on plays, puppet shows, concerts, storytelling sessions, nature programs, and other children's events. *Washington Parent*, a free monthly available at many supermarkets and libraries, is another good source. Finally, *Fodor's Washington, D.C., with Kids* and *Fodor's Around Washington, D.C., with Kids* (available in bookstores everywhere) can help you plan your days together.

Also, don't forget to visit information desks. Many museums have docents who conduct kid-friendly tours, as well as having exhibits designed for children. In addition, many sights have special printed children's guides, allowing kids to take pencil in hand, for example, and go on "scavenger hunts" to pick out the shapes and patterns in modern artwork.

If you are renting a car, don't forget to arrange for a car seat when you reserve. For general advice about traveling with children, consult *Fodor's FYI: Travel with Your Baby* (available in bookstores everywhere).

⛶ **Local Information Washington Parent** ☎ 301/320-2321 ⊕ www.washingtonparent.com.

BABYSITTING

Most large hotels and those with concierges can arrange babysitting (or even find sitters to take your children sightseeing). The D.C.-area child-care agencies they use perform in-depth interviews and background checks of all their sitters, and some provide references. Rates average about $15 an hour (usually with a four-hour minimum). In addition, you may need to pay for the sitter's transportation and/or parking costs. Agencies can usually arrange last-minute child care, but advance notice is appreciated. Mothers' Aides and White House Nannies both have babysitting services for visitors to the D.C. area.

⛶ **Agencies Mothers' Aides** ⌖ 5618 Ox Rd., Suite B, Fairfax Station, VA 22039 ☎ 800/526-2669 or 703/250-0700 ⊕ www.mothersaides.com. **White House Nannies** ✉ 7200 Wisconsin Ave., Suite 409, Bethesda, MD 20814 ☎ 800/266-9024 or 301/652-8088 ⊕ www.whitehousenannies.com.

FLYING

Experts agree that it's a good idea to use safety seats aloft for children weighing less than 40 pounds. Airlines set their own policies: if you use a safety seat, U.S. carriers usually require that the child be ticketed, even if he or she is young enough to ride free, because the seats must be strapped into regular seats. And even if you pay the full adult fare for the seat, it may be worth it, especially on longer trips. Do **check your airline's policy about using safety seats during takeoff and landing.** Safety seats are not allowed everywhere in the plane, so get your seat assignments as early as possible.

When reserving, request children's meals or a freestanding bassinet (not available at all airlines) if you need them. But note that bulkhead seats, where you must sit to use the bassinet, may lack an overhead bin or storage space on the floor.

SIGHTS & ATTRACTIONS

Places that are especially appealing to children are indicated by a rubber-duckie icon (☾) in the margin.

CONCIERGES

Concierges, found in many hotels, can help you with theater tickets and dinner reservations: a good one with connections may be able to get you seats for a hot show or prime-time dinner reservations at the restaurant of the moment. You can also turn to your hotel's concierge for help with travel arrangements, sightseeing plans, services ranging from aromatherapy to zipper repair, and emergencies. **Always tip** a concierge who has been of assistance (⇨ Tipping).

CONSUMER PROTECTION

Whether you're shopping for gifts or purchasing travel services, **pay with a major credit card** whenever possible, so you can cancel payment or get reimbursed if there's a problem (and you can provide documentation). If you're doing business with a particular company for the first time, contact your local Better Business Bureau and the attorney general's offices in your state and (for U.S. businesses) the company's home state as well. Have any complaints been filed? Finally, if you're buying a package or tour, always consider travel insurance that includes default coverage (⇨ Insurance).

⛶ **BBBs Better Business Bureau** ✉ 1411 K St. NW, 10th fl., Washington, DC 20005-3404 ☎ 202/393-8000 🖷 202/393-1198 ⊕ www.dc.bbb.org. **Council of Better Business Bureaus** ✉ 4200 Wilson Blvd., Suite 800, Arlington, VA 22203 ☎ 703/276-0100 🖷 703/525-8277 ⊕ www.bbb.org.

DISABILITIES & ACCESSIBILITY

The city's subways and buses have excellent facilities for visitors with vision and hearing impairments or mobility problems. Metro stations are equipped with elevators, and buses have wheelchair lifts. Recorded announcements on every subway and bus route let you know what stop you are approaching. Virtually all streets throughout the city have wide, level sidewalks with curb cuts, though in Georgetown the brick-paved terrain can be bumpy. All museums and monuments are accessible to visitors using wheelchairs.

The Smithsonian publishes an access guide to all its museums; "Dial-a-Museum" lists museum hours and daily activities. At all Smithsonian museums wheelchairs are available for use free of charge, on a first-come, first-served basis.

LODGING

Despite the Americans with Disabilities Act, the definition of accessibility seems to differ from hotel to hotel. Some properties may be accessible by ADA standards for people with mobility problems but not for people with hearing or vision impairments, for example.

If you have mobility problems, ask for the lowest floor on which accessible services are offered. If you have a hearing impairment, check whether the hotel has devices to alert you visually to the ring of the telephone, a knock at the door, and a fire/emergency alarm. Some hotels provide these devices without charge. Discuss your needs with hotel personnel if this equipment isn't available, so that a staff member can personally alert you in the event of an emergency.

If you're bringing a guide dog, get authorization ahead of time and write down the name of the person with whom you spoke.

SIGHTS & ATTRACTIONS

You can expect that all federal buildings, museums, and monuments will be completely accessible. Most have been updated since passage of the Americans with Disabilities Act in 1990.

To check whether a place you plan to visit is accessible, head to the Web site DisabilityGuide.org, which covers the Washington, D.C., area. The site lists accessible entrances, restrooms, water fountains, parking spaces, and telephones. It also covers restaurants and hotels that go the extra mile to cater to people with hearing and visual impairments. The organization publishes a free printed version of its guide.

City Scooter Tours lead mobility-impaired adults on trips around the city's most famous sights. The tours use comfortable electric vehicles.

TRANSPORTATION

The U.S. Department of Transportation Aviation Consumer Protection Division's online publication *New Horizons: Information for the Air Traveler with a Disability* offers advice for travellers with a disability, and outlines basic rights. Visit DisabilityInfo.gov for general information.

🚩 Information and Complaints **Aviation Consumer Protection Division** (⇨ Air Travel) for airline-related problems; ⊕ airconsumer.ost.dot.gov/publications/horizons.htm for airline travel advice and rights. **Departmental Office of Civil Rights** ⊠ for general inquiries, U.S. Department of Transportation, S-30, 400 7th St. SW, Room 10215, Washington, DC 20590 ☎ 202/366–4648, 202/366–8538 TTY 🖶 202/366–9371 ⊕ www.dotcr.ost.dot.gov. **Disability Rights Section** ⊠ NYAV, U.S. Department of Justice, Civil Rights Division, 950 Pennsylvania Ave. NW, Washington, DC 20530 🖶 ADA information line 202/514–0301, 800/514–0301, 202/514–0383 TTY, 800/514–0383 TTY ⊕ www.ada.gov. **U.S. Department of Transportation Hotline** 🖶 for disability-related air-travel problems, 800/778–4838 or 800/455–9880 TTY.

🚩 Resources **City Scooter Tours** ☎ 888/441-7575 ⊕ www.cityscootertours.com. **DisabilityGuide.org** ⊠ 21618 Slidell Rd., Boyds, MD 20841 ☎ 301/528–8664 ⊕ www.disabilityguide.org. **Smithsonian** ☎ 202/357–2700, 202/357–2020 "Dial-a-Museum," 202/357–1729 TDD ⊕ www.si.edu.

TRAVEL AGENCIES

In the United States, the Americans with Disabilities Act requires that travel firms serve the needs of all travelers. Some agencies specialize in working with people with disabilities.

🚹 Travelers with Mobility Problems **Accessible Vans of America** ✉ 37 Daniel Rd. W, Fairfield, NJ 07004 ☎ 877/282-8267, 888/282-8267, 973/808-9709 reservations 🖷 973/808-9713 ⊕ www. accessiblevans.com. **B. Roberts Travel** ✉ 1876 East Ave., Rochester, NY 14610 ☎ 800/444-6540 ⊕ www.brobertstravel.com, run by a former physical-rehabilitation counselor. **CareVacations** ✉ No. 5, 5110–50 Ave., Leduc, Alberta, Canada, T9E 6V4 ☎ 780/986-6404 or 877/478-7827 🖷 780/986-8332 ⊕ www.carevacations.com, for group tours and cruise vacations. **Flying Wheels Travel** ✉ 143 W. Bridge St., Box 382, Owatonna, MN 55060 ☎ 507/451-5005 🖷 507/451-1685 ⊕ www. flyingwheelstravel.com.

🚹 Travelers with Developmental Disabilities **Sprout** ✉ 893 Amsterdam Ave., New York, NY 10025 ☎ 212/222-9575 or 888/222-9575 🖷 212/222-9768 ⊕ www.gosprout.org.

DISCOUNTS & DEALS

Be a smart shopper and compare all your options before making decisions. A plane ticket bought with a promotional coupon from travel clubs, coupon books, and direct-mail offers or purchased on the Internet may not be cheaper than the least expensive fare from a discount ticket agency. And always keep in mind that what you get is just as important as what you save.

DISCOUNT RESERVATIONS

To save money, look into discount reservations services with Web sites and toll-free numbers, which use their buying power to get a better price on hotels, airline tickets (⇨ Air Travel), even car rentals. When booking a room, always **call the hotel's local toll-free number** (if one is available) rather than the central reservations number—you'll often get a better price. Always ask about special packages or corporate rates.

🚹 Hotel Rooms **Accommodations Express** ☎ 800/444-7666 or 800/277-1064. **Hotels.com** ☎ 800/219-4606 or 800/364-0291 ⊕ www.hotels. com. **Quikbook** ☎ 800/789-9887 ⊕ www. quikbook.com. **Turbotrip.com** ☎ 800/473-7829 ⊕ w3.turbotrip.com.

PACKAGE DEALS

Don't confuse packages and guided tours. When you buy a package, you travel on your own, just as though you had planned the trip yourself. Fly/drive packages, which combine airfare and car rental, are often a good deal. In cities, ask the local visitor's bureau about hotel and local transportation packages that include tickets to major museum exhibits or other special events.

GAY & LESBIAN TRAVEL

Gays and lesbians have been in the Dupont Circle area for decades, but in recent years the community has expanded east to Logan Circle and north to Adams-Morgan and Mount Pleasant. There's also a small enclave on Capitol Hill. There are many gay bars and restaurants in these neighborhoods, but gays will feel comfortable in most establishments throughout the city.

To find out what's going on in gay D.C., pick up a copy of *The Washington Blade* (www.washblade.com), the country's oldest gay newspaper. It's full of local and national news, arts and cultural coverage, and listings of bars and clubs. For a complete rundown of nightlife, try *Metro Weekly* (www.metroweekly.com). You can find both at gay businesses, as well as at Lambda Rising, the city's only gay bookstore. The store is just north of the Dupont Circle Metro station. It's open Sunday to Thursday 10–10 and Friday and Saturday 10–midnight.

For details about the gay and lesbian scene, consult *Fodor's Gay Guide to the USA* (available in bookstores everywhere).

🚹 Gay & Lesbian Businesses **Lambda Rising** ✉ 1025 Connecticut Ave. NW ☎ 202/462-6969 ⊕ www.lambdarising.com.

🚹 Gay- & Lesbian-Friendly Travel Agencies **Different Roads Travel** ✉ 155 Palm Colony Palm Springs, CA 92264 ☎ 310/289-6000 or 800/429-8747 🖷 310/855-0323 ✎ lgernert@tzell.com. **Skylink Travel and Tour/Flying Dutchmen Travel** ✉ 1455 N. Dutton Ave., Suite A, Santa Rosa, CA 95401 ☎ 707/546-9888 or 800/225-5759 🖷 707/636-0951; serving lesbian travelers.

INSURANCE

The most useful travel-insurance plan is a comprehensive policy that includes coverage for trip cancellation and interruption, default, trip delay, and medical expenses (with a waiver for preexisting conditions).

Without insurance you'll lose all or most of your money if you cancel your trip, regardless of the reason. Default insurance covers you if your tour operator, airline, or cruise line goes out of business—the chances of which have been increasing. Trip-delay covers expenses that arise because of bad weather or mechanical delays. Study the fine print when comparing policies.

U.K. residents can buy a travel-insurance policy valid for most vacations taken during the year in which it's purchased (but check preexisting-condition coverage).

Always **buy travel policies directly from the insurance company**; if you buy them from a cruise line, airline, or tour operator that goes out of business you probably won't be covered for the agency or operator's default, a major risk. Before making any purchase, review your existing health and home-owner's policies to find what they cover away from home.

🛈 Travel Insurers In the U.S.: **Access America** ✉ 2805 N. Parham Rd., Richmond, VA 23294 ☎ 800/729-6021 🖷 804/673-1469 or 800/346-9265 ⊕ www.accessamerica.com. **Travel Guard International** ✉ 1145 Clark St., Stevens Point, WI 54481 ☎ 715/345-1041 or 800/826-4919 🖷 800/955-8785 or 715/345-1990 ⊕ www.travelguard.com.

FOR INTERNATIONAL TRAVELERS

CAR RENTAL

When picking up a rental car, non-U.S. residents need a reservation voucher for any prepaid reservations that were made in the traveler's home country, a passport, a driver's license, and a travel policy that covers each driver.

CAR TRAVEL

Gas tends to be slightly higher in the District than it is in Maryland or Virginia. Stations are plentiful outside the District itself. Most stay open late (24 hours along large highways and in big cities), except in rural areas, where Sunday hours are limited and where you may drive long stretches without a refueling opportunity. Highways are well paved. Interstate highways—limited-access, multilane highways whose numbers are prefixed by "I–"—are the fastest routes. Interstates with three-digit numbers encircle urban

areas, which may have other limited-access expressways, freeways, and parkways as well. Tolls may be levied on limited-access highways. So-called U.S. highways and state highways are not necessarily limited-access but may have several lanes.

Along larger highways, roadside stops with restrooms, fast-food restaurants, and sundries stores are well spaced. State police and tow trucks patrol major highways and lend assistance. If your car breaks down on an interstate, pull onto the shoulder and wait for help, or have your passengers wait while you walk to an emergency phone (available in most states). If you carry a cell phone, dial 911, noting your location on the small green roadside mileage markers.

Driving in the United States is on the right. Do obey speed limits posted along roads and highways. Watch for lower limits in small towns and on back roads. The District of Columbia requires front-seat passengers to wear seat belts. On weekdays between 6 and 9 AM and again between 4 and 7 PM expect heavy traffic. To encourage carpooling, some freeways have special lanes for so-called high-occupancy vehicles (HOV)—cars carrying at least three people.

Bookstores, gas stations, convenience stores, and rest stops sell maps (about $3) and multiregion road atlases (about $10).

CURRENCY

The dollar is the basic unit of U.S. currency. It has 100 cents. Coins are the copper penny (1¢); the silvery nickel (5¢), dime (10¢), quarter (25¢), and half-dollar (50¢); and the golden $1 coin, replacing a now-rare silver dollar. Bills are denominated $1, $5, $10, $20, $50, and $100, all mostly green and identical in size; designs and background tints vary. In addition, you may come across a $2 bill, but the chances are slim. The exchange rate at this writing is U.S. $1.75 per British pound, 0.87 per Canadian dollar, 0.73 per Australian dollar, and 0.61 per New Zealand dollar.

ELECTRICITY

The U.S. standard is AC, 110 volts/60 cycles. Plugs have two flat pins set parallel to each other.

EMBASSIES
🛃 Australia ✉ 1601 Massachusetts Ave. NW
☎ 202/797-3000
🛃 Canada ✉ 501 Pennsylvania Ave. NW ☎ 202/682-1740
🛃 New Zealand ✉ 37 Observatory Circle NW
☎ 202/328-4800
🛃 United Kingdom ✉ 3100 Massachusetts Ave. NW ☎ 202/588-6500

EMERGENCIES
For police, fire, or ambulance, **dial 911** (0 in rural areas).

MAIL & SHIPPING
You can buy stamps and aerograms and send letters and parcels in post offices. Stamp-dispensing machines can occasionally be found in airports, bus and train stations, office buildings, drugstores, and the like. You can also deposit mail in the stout, dark blue, steel bins at strategic locations everywhere and in the mail chutes of large buildings; pickup schedules are posted. You can deposit packages at public collection boxes as long as the parcels are affixed with proper postage and weigh less than one pound. Packages weighing one or more pounds must be taken to a post office or handed to a postal carrier.

For mail sent within the United States, you need a 39¢ stamp for first-class letters weighing up to 1 ounce (24¢ for each additional ounce) and 24¢ for postcards. You pay 84¢ for 1-ounce airmail letters and 75¢ for airmail postcards to most other countries; to Canada and Mexico, you need a 63¢ stamp for a 1-ounce letter and 55¢ for a postcard. An aerogram—a single sheet of lightweight blue paper that folds into its own envelope, stamped for overseas airmail—costs 75¢.

To receive mail on the road, have it sent c/o General Delivery at your destination's main post office (use the correct five-digit ZIP code). You must pick up mail in person within 30 days and show a driver's license or passport.

PASSPORTS & VISAS
When traveling internationally, carry your passport even if you don't need one (it's always the best form of I.D.) and **make two photocopies of the data page** (one for someone at home and another for you, carried separately from your passport). If you lose your passport, promptly call the nearest embassy or consulate and the local police.

Visitor visas aren't necessary for Canadian or European Union citizens, or for citizens of Australia who are staying fewer than 90 days.

TELEPHONES
All U.S. telephone numbers consist of a three-digit area code and a seven-digit local number. Within many local calling areas, you dial only the seven-digit number. Within some area codes, you must dial "1" first for calls outside the local area. To call between area-code regions, dial "1" then all 10 digits; the same goes for calls to numbers prefixed by "800," "888," "866," and "877"—all toll free. For calls to numbers preceded by "900" you must pay—usually dearly.

For international calls, dial "011" followed by the country code and the local number. For help, dial "0" and ask for an overseas operator. The country code is 61 for Australia, 64 for New Zealand, 44 for the United Kingdom. Calling Canada is the same as calling within the United States, although you might not be able to get through on some toll free numbers. Most local phone books list country codes and U.S. area codes. The country code for the United States is 1.

For operator assistance, dial "0." To obtain someone's phone number, call directory assistance at 555-1212 or occasionally 411 (free at many public phones). To have the person you're calling foot the bill, phone collect; dial "0" instead of "1" before the 10-digit number.

At pay phones, instructions often are posted. Usually you insert coins in a slot (usually 25¢–50¢ for local calls) and wait for a steady tone before dialing. When you call long-distance, the operator tells you how much to insert; prepaid phone cards, widely available in various denominations, are easier. Call the number on the back, punch in the card's personal identification number when prompted, then dial your number.

MAIL & SHIPPING

The post office with the longest hours is National Capitol Station, across the street from Union Station. It is open 7 AM–midnight on weekdays and 7 AM–8 PM on weekends. Farragut Station and McPherson Station, both in downtown D.C., and Georgetown Station are open weekdays 9–5.

🚩 **Post Offices Farragut Station** ✉ 1800 M St. NW, 20036 ☎ 202/523-2024 ⊕ www.usps.gov. **Georgetown Station** ✉ 1215 31st St. NW, 20007 ☎ 202/523-2026 ⊕ www.usps.gov. **McPherson Station** ✉ 1750 Pennsylvania Ave. NW, 20006 ☎ 202/523-2394 ⊕ www.usps.gov. **National Capitol Station** ✉ 2 Massachusetts Ave. NE, 20002 ☎ 202/523-2368 ⊕ www.usps.gov.

MEDIA

NEWSPAPERS & MAGAZINES

Two daily newspapers duke it out for readership in Washington, D.C., the *Washington Post* (⊕ www.washingtonpost.com) and the *Washington Times* (⊕ www.washingtontimes.com). Although people constantly accuse the *Post* of a liberal bias, the conservative *Times* still has only a fraction of the readership. Both have special sections on Fridays filled with plenty of information about weekend events.

Washington CityPaper (⊕ www.washingtoncitypaper.com), a free weekly newspaper, has features about local issues and the best arts and cultural coverage. The *Washington Blade* (www.washblade.com) has news and features about the gay community. Also check out the monthly magazine *Washingtonian* (⊕ www.washingtonian.com). Its "Where & When" section helps you know what's going on around town.

RADIO & TELEVISION

Washington, D.C.'s radio stations offer sounds for every listener. WASH 95 FM is the town's easy listening station, while WBIG 100.9 FM is Washington's oldies station. Another D.C. favorite is WARW 94.7 FM, which plays classic rock. WKYS 93.9 FM plays hip-hop and R&B (think Ludacris and Missy Elliott). WMZQ 98.7 FM plays classic country, and Mix 107.3 FM spins adult contemporary. Z104.1 FM plays modern rock. For a Latin beat, check out El Zol 99.1 FM. Fans of hard rock can enjoy WWDC 101 FM.

WETA 90.9 broadcasts National Public Radio and other news programming in the morning and evening. WAMU 88.5 FM has a public-radio format, with NPR programs and call-in shows. WPFW 89.3 FM, another public radio station with a liberal bent, specializes in jazz, blues, and Latin music. WGMS 103.5 FM is a classical station. WTOP 1500 AM and 107.7 FM is a popular drive-time station with news, traffic, and weather.

Washington's major TV stations are NBC 4 (WRC), ABC 7 (WJLA), CBS 9 (WUSA), Fox 5 (WTTG), News Channel 8 (a local 24-hour news channel), and two local PBS stations, channels 26 (WETA) and 22 (WMPT).

METRO TRAVEL

The WMATA provides bus and subway service in the District and in the Maryland and Virginia suburbs. The Metro, which opened in 1976, is one of the country's cleanest and safest subway systems. It begins operation at 5 AM on weekdays and 7 AM on weekends. The Metro closes on weekdays at midnight and weekends at 3 AM. Don't get to the station at the last minute, as trains from the ends of the lines depart before the official closing time. During the weekday peak periods (5–9:30 AM and 3–7 PM), trains come along every three to six minutes. At other times and on weekends and holidays, trains run about every 12–15 minutes.

FARES & SCHEDULES

The Metro's base fare is $1.35; the actual price you pay depends on the time of day and the distance traveled, which means you might end up paying $3.90 if you're traveling to a distant station at rush hour. Up to two children under age five ride free when accompanied by a paying passenger.

Buy your ticket at the Farecard machines; they accept coins and crisp $1, $5, $10, or $20 bills. If the machine spits your bill back out at you, try folding and unfolding it lengthwise before asking someone for help. Some newer machines will also accept credit cards. You can buy one-day passes for $6.50 and seven-day passes for $32.50. Locals use the SmarTrip card, a plastic card that can hold any fare amount and can be used throughout the subway system. The cost of each ride is deducted as you enter the subway. Buy passes or SmarTrip cards at the Metro Center sales office.

Insert your Farecard into the turnstile to enter the platform. Make sure you **hang on to the card**—you need it to exit at your destination.

🔢 Metro Information **Washington Metropolitan Area Transit Authority (WMATA)** ☎ 202/637-7000, 202/638-3780 TTY, 202/962-1195 lost and found ⊕ www.wmata.com.

MONEY MATTERS

Prices throughout this guide are given for adults. Substantially reduced fees are almost always available for children, students, and senior citizens. For information on taxes, *see* Taxes.

CREDIT CARDS

Throughout this guide, the following abbreviations are used: **AE,** American Express; **D,** Discover; **DC,** Diners Club; **MC,** MasterCard; and **V,** Visa.

🔢 Reporting Lost Cards **American Express** ☎ 800/992-3404. **Diners Club** ☎ 800/234-6377. **Discover** ☎ 800/347-2683. **MasterCard** ☎ 800/622-7747. **Visa** ☎ 800/ 847-2911.

PACKING

In your carry-on luggage, pack an extra pair of eyeglasses or contact lenses and enough of any medication you take to last a few days longer than the entire trip. You may also ask your doctor to write a spare prescription using the drug's generic name, as brand names may vary from country to country. **Never pack prescription drugs, valuables, or undeveloped film in luggage to be checked.** And don't forget to carry with you the addresses of offices that handle refunds of lost traveler's checks. Check *Fodor's How to Pack* (available at online retailers and bookstores everywhere) for more tips.

To avoid customs and security delays, carry medications in their original packaging. Don't pack any sharp objects in your carry-on luggage, including knives of any size or material, scissors, nail clippers, and corkscrews, or anything else that might arouse suspicion.

To avoid having your checked luggage chosen for hand inspection, don't cram bags full. The U.S. Transportation Security Administration suggests packing shoes on top and placing personal items you don't want touched in clear plastic bags.

CHECKING LUGGAGE

You're allowed to carry aboard one bag and one personal article, such as a purse or a laptop computer. Make sure what you carry on fits under your seat or in the overhead bin. Get to the gate early, so you can board as soon as possible, before the overhead bins fill up.

Baggage allowances vary by carrier, destination, and ticket class. On international flights from the U.S., as of September 2005, you're allowed to check two bags weighing up to 50 pounds (23 kilograms) each, although a few airlines allow checked bags of up to 88 pounds (40 kilograms) in first class. Some international carriers don't allow over 66 pounds (30 kilograms) per bag in business class and 44 pounds (20 kilograms) in economy. If you're flying to or through the United Kingdom, your luggage cannot exceed 70 pounds (32 kilograms) per bag. On domestic flights, the limit is usually 50 to 70 pounds (23 to 32 kilograms) per bag. In general, carry-on bags shouldn't exceed 40 pounds (18 kilograms). Most airlines won't accept bags that weigh more than 100 pounds (45 kilograms) on domestic or international flights. Expect to pay a fee for baggage that exceeds weight limits. Check baggage restrictions with your carrier before you pack.

Airline liability for baggage is limited to $2,500 per person on flights within the United States. On international flights it amounts to $9.07 per pound or $20 per kilogram for checked baggage (roughly $540 per 50-pound bag), with a maximum of $634.90 per piece, and $400 per passenger for unchecked baggage. You can buy additional coverage at check-in for about $10 per $1,000 of coverage, but it often excludes a rather extensive list of items, shown on your airline ticket.

Before departure, itemize your bags' contents and their worth, and label the bags with your name, address, and phone number. (If you use your home address, cover it so potential thieves can't see it readily.) Include a label inside each bag and **pack a copy of your itinerary.** At check-in, make sure each bag is correctly tagged with the destination airport's three-letter code. Because some checked bags will be opened for hand inspection, the U.S. Transportation Security Administration recommends that you leave luggage unlocked or use the plastic locks offered at check-in. TSA screeners place an inspection notice inside searched bags, which are re-sealed with a special lock.

If your bag has been searched and contents are missing or damaged, file a claim with the TSA Consumer Response Center as soon as possible. If your bags arrive damaged or fail to arrive at all, file a written report with the airline before leaving the airport.

⊞ Complaints U.S. Transportation Security Administration Contact Center ☎ 866/289-9673 ⊕ www.tsa.gov.

SAFETY

Washington, D.C., is a fairly safe city, but as with any major metropolitan area it's best to be alert and aware. Be aware of your surroundings before you use an ATM, especially one that is outdoors. Move on to a different machine if you notice people loitering nearby. Pickpocketing and other petty crimes are rare in D.C.,

but they do occur, especially in markets and other crowded areas. Keep an eye on purses and backpacks.

Panhandlers can be aggressive and may respond with verbal insults, but otherwise are usually harmless. If someone threatens you with violence, it's best to hand over your money and seek help from police later.

The Metro is quite safe, with very few incidents reported each year. Buses are also safe, but be aware that a few petty crimes have occurred at bus stops. Stick to those along busy streets.

LOCAL SCAMS

The only scam you'll encounter in D.C. is an elaborate story from a panhandler. To evoke sympathy, a well-dressed panhandler may pretend to have lost his wallet and need money to get home or a woman may say she needs cab fare to take a sick child to the hospital. A simple "I'm sorry" is usually enough to send them on their way.

SENIOR-CITIZEN TRAVEL

To qualify for age-related discounts, mention your senior-citizen status up front when booking hotel reservations (not when checking out) and before you're seated in restaurants (not when paying the bill). Be sure to have identification on hand. When renting a car, ask about promotional car-rental discounts, which can be cheaper than senior-citizen rates.

⊞ Educational Programs Elderhostel ⊠ 11 Ave. de Lafayette, Boston, MA 02111 ☎ 877/426-8056, 978/323-4141 international callers, 877/426-2167 TTY ⊟ 877/426-2166 ⊕ www.elderhostel.org.

SIGHTSEEING TOURS

BICYCLE TOURS

Bike the Sites Tours has knowledgeable guides leading daily excursions past dozens of Washington, D.C., landmarks. All tours start at the Old Post Office Pavilion. Bicycles, helmets, snacks, and water bottles are included in the rates, which start at $40. The Adventure Cycling Association, a national organization promoting bicycle travel, recommends tours around the region.

🚲 **Adventure Cycling Association** ☎ 800/755-2453 ⊕ www.adventurecycling.org. **Bike the Sites Tours** ☎ 202/842-2453 ⊕ www.bikethesites.com.

BOAT TOURS

During one-hour rides on mule-drawn barges on the C&O Canal, costumed guides and volunteers explain the waterway's history. The barge rides, which cost $8 and are run by the National Park Service, depart from its visitor center Wednesday through Sunday from April through November.

Capitol River Cruises offers 45-minute sightseeing tours aboard the *Nightingale* and *Nightingale II,* Great Lakes boats from the 1950s, as well as the smaller *Harbouritavilla.* Beverages and light snacks are available. Hourly cruises depart from Washington Harbour noon to 9 PM April to October. Prices are $10 for adults and $5 for children 3 to 12.

Several swanky cruises depart from the waterfront in Southwest D.C. The *Odyssey III,* specially built to fit under the Potomac's bridges, departs from the Gangplank Marina at 6th and Water streets SW. Tickets are $39 for lunch, $52 for brunch, and $81–$94 for dinner. As the prices suggest, this is an elegant affair; jackets are requested for men at dinner. The sleek *Spirit of Washington* offers lunch and dinner cruises that range from $37 to $72. Sightseeing tours to Mount Vernon on the *Potomac Spirit* cost $26 to $35.

Departing from Alexandria, the glass-enclosed *Dandy* and *Nina's Dandy* cruise up the Potomac year-round to Georgetown, taking you past many of D.C.'s monuments. Lunch cruises board weekdays start-ing at 11 AM. Dinner cruises board daily at 6 PM. Prices are $32–$45 for lunch and $70–$85 for dinner. The *Sandy* and *Nina's Dandy* also offer special holiday cruises.

From April through November, DC Ducks offers 90-minute tours in funky converted World War II amphibious vehicles. After an hour-long road tour of landlocked sights, the tour moves to the water, where for 30 minutes you get a boat's-eye view of the city. Tours depart from Union Station and cost $28; seating is on a first-come, first-served basis.

🚢 **Fees & Schedules** **C&O Canal Barges** ✉ Canal Visitor Center, 1057 Thomas Jefferson St. NW, Georgetown ☎ 202/653-5190 ⊕ www.nps.gov/choh. **Capitol River Cruises** ✉ 31st and K Sts. NW ☎ 301/460-7447 or 800/405-5511 ⊕ www.capitolrivercruises.com. **Dandy Cruises** ✉ Prince St. between Duke and King Sts., Alexandria, VA ☎ 703/683-6076 ⊕ www.dandydinnerboat.com. **DC Ducks** ✉ 2640 Reed St. NE ☎ 202/832-9800 ⊕ www.historictours.com. **Odyssey III** ✉ 600 Water St. SW ☎ 202/488-6010 or 800/946-7245 ⊕ www.odysseycruises.com. **Spirit of Washington** ✉ Pier 4, 6th and Water Sts. SW ☎ 202/554-8013 or 866/211-3811 ⊕ www.spiritcruises.com.

BUS TOURS

All About Town has half-day, all-day, two-day, and twilight bus tours to get acquainted with the city. Tours leave from various downtown locations. An all-day tour costs $48, a half-day tour costs $26, and a twilight tour costs $28.

Capital Entertainment Services offers guided bus tours that focus on the city's African-American history. One popular tour is of the U Street corridor, once filled with so many theaters that it was called the Black Broadway. Rates begin at $25 for a three-hour tour.

Gray Line's four-hour tour of Capitol Hill, Embassy Row, and Arlington National Cemetery leaves Union Station at 8:30 AM (late June–late October) and 2 PM (year-round) and costs $30; tours of Mount Vernon and Old Town Alexandria depart at 8:30 AM (year-round) and 2 PM (late June–late October) and cost $30. An all-day trip combining both tours leaves at 8:30 AM (year-round) and costs $50. Other tours are available.

▓ Fees & Schedules **All About Town** ☏ 301/856–5556. **Capital Entertainment Services** ✉ 3629 18th St. NE, Washington, DC 20018 ☏ 202/636–9203 ⊕ www.washington-dc-tours.com. **Gray Line** ☏ 301/386–8300 or 800/862–1400 ⊕ www.graylinedc.com.

ORIENTATION TOURS

Old Town Trolley Tours, orange-and-green motorized trolleys, take in the main downtown sights and also head into Georgetown and the upper Northwest in a speedy two hours if you ride straight through. However, you can hop on and off as many times as you like, taking your time at the stops you choose. Tickets are $28 for adults. Tourmobile buses, authorized by the National Park Service, operate in a similar fashion, making 25 stops at historical sites between the Capitol and Arlington National Cemetery. Tickets, available at kiosks at Union Station and Arlington National Cemetery, are $20 for adults.

▓ Fees & Schedules **Old Town Trolley Tours** ☏ 202/832–9800 ⊕ www.historictours.com. **Tourmobile** ☏ 202/554–5100 or 888/868–7707 ⊕ www.tourmobile.com.

PRIVATE GUIDES

In business since 1964, the Guide Service of Washington puts together half-day and full-day tours of D.C. sights, including those off the beaten path. Guides are happy to include spots overlooked by other tours. A Tour de Force has limo tours of historic homes, diplomatic buildings, and "the best little museums in Washington." Tours are led by Jeanne Fogle, a local historian. Nationally known photographer Sonny Odom offers custom tours for shutterbugs beginning at $35 an hour.

▓ Fees & Schedules **Guide Service of Washington** ✉ 733 15th St. NW, Suite 1040, Washington, DC 20005 ☏ 202/628–2842 ⊕ www.dctourguides.com. **Sonny Odom** ✉ 2420 F S. Walter Reed Dr., Arlington, VA 22206 ☏ 703/379–1633 ⊕ www.sonnyodom.com. **A Tour de Force** ✉ Box 2782, Washington, DC 20013 ☏ 703/525–2948 ⊕ www.atourdeforce.com.

SEGWAY TOURS

The Segway allows riders to glide by the monuments, museums, and major attractions. Guided tours, offered from April through November, usually last between two to four hours. D.C. city ordinance requires that riders be 16 years old, and some tour companies have weight restrictions. Instructions on how to use the Segway are given before the start of a tour. Most tour operators require advance reservations, although some will allow last-minute sign-ups if space is available. Tours cost around $70 per person and are limited to 6 to 10 people.

▓ Resources **Capital Segway** ☏ 202/682–1980 ⊕ www.capitalsegway.com. **City Segway Tours** ☏ 877/734–8687 ⊕ www.citysegwaytours.com. **Segs in the City** ☏ 800/734–7393 ⊕ www.segsinthecity.net.

SPECIAL-INTEREST TOURS

Special tours of government buildings with heavy security, including the White House and the Capitol, can be arranged through your representative's or senator's office. Limited numbers of these so-called VIP tickets are available, so **plan up to six months in advance of your trip.** Governmental buildings close to visitors when the Department of Homeland Security issues a high alert, so call ahead.

The Bureau of Engraving and Printing has fascinating tours that begin every 15 minutes from 9 to 10:45 and 12:30–2 on weekdays (as well as 5 to 7 during the summer). Foreign dignitaries are received at the Department of State's lavish Diplomatic Reception Rooms, but everyone else can get a peek on weekdays on 45-minute tours that begin at 9:30, 10:30, and 2:45. A much-used tool for spreading the word about democracy in foreign lands is the Voice of America. You can tour its headquarters on weekdays at 1:30, but you must call ahead for an appointment.

National Public Radio leads tours of its broadcast facilities Thursday at 11. Call four weeks ahead to reserve a spot. Tours of the *Washington Post* are conducted on Monday from 10 to 3; reservations are taken four weeks in advance. Tours of the *Post's* printing plants are also available.

Gross National Product's Scandal Tours, led by members of the GNP comedy troupe, last 1½ hours and cover scandals from George Washington to George Bush. The tours cost $30 per person; reservations are required.

⚹ Fees & Schedules **Bureau of Engraving and Printing** ✉ 14th and C Sts. SW ☎ 202/874-2330 or 866/874-2330 ⊕ www.moneyfactory.com/locations. **Department of State** ✉ 2201 C St. NW ☎ 202/647-3241, 202/736-4474 TDD ⊕ www.state.gov/m/drr. **Gross National Product** ☎ 202/783-7212 ⊕ www.gnpcomedy.com. **National Public Radio** ✉ 635 Massachusetts Ave. NW, Washington, DC 20001 ☎ 202/513-3232 ⊕ www.npr.org. **Voice of America** ✉ 330 Independence Ave. SW ☎ 202/619-3919 ⊕ www.voa.gov. **The *Washington Post*** ✉ 1150 15th St. NW ☎ 202/334-7969 ⊕ www.washingtonpost.com.

WALKING TOURS

Guided walks around Washington, D.C., and nearby communities are routinely offered by the Smithsonian Associates Program; advance tickets are required. Tour D.C. specializes in walking tours of Georgetown and Dupont Circle, covering topics such as the Civil War, the Underground Railroad, and Kennedy's Georgetown. Anecdotal History Tours leads tours in Georgetown, Adams-Morgan, and Capitol Hill, as well as tours of where Lincoln was shot and the homes of former presidents. Washington Walks has a wide range of tours, including a special Tuesday series called "Washington Sleeps Here" about interesting neighborhoods.

The nonprofit group Cultural Tourism DC leads guided walking tours that cover the history and architecture of neighborhoods from the southwest waterfront to points much farther north: "Before Harlem, There Was U Street," for instance, takes you back to the days when U Street was Washington's "Black Broadway." The self-guided "Civil War to Civil Rights: Downtown Heritage Trail" highlights historic sites with markers. The United States Capitol Historic Society leads two-hour tours of the exterior of the famous domed building Mondays at 10 AM from March to November. Groups meet outside Union Station.

⚹ Fees & Schedules **Anecdotal History Tours** ✉ 9009 Paddock La., Potomac, MD 20854 ☎ 301/294-9514 ⊕ www.dcsightseeing.com. **Cultural Tourism DC** ✉ 1250 H St. NW, 10th fl., Washington, DC 20005 ☎ 202/661-7581 ⊕ www.culturaltourismdc.org. **Smithsonian Associates Program** ☎ 202/357-3030 ⊕ www.smithsonianassociates.org. **Tour D.C.** ✉ 1912 Glen Ross Rd., Silver Spring, MD 20910 ☎ 301/588-8999 ⊕ www.tourdc.com. **United States Capitol Historic Society** ☎ 202/543-8919. **Washington Walks** ☎ 202/484-1865 ⊕ www.washingtonwalks.com.

STUDENTS IN WASHINGTON, D.C.

⚹ IDs & Services **STA Travel** ✉ 10 Downing St., New York, NY 10014 ☎ 212/627-3111, 800/781-4040 24-hr service center in the U.S. ⊕ www.sta.com. **Travel Cuts** ✉ 187 College St., Toronto, Ontario M5T 1P7, Canada ☎ 800/592-2887 in the U.S., 416/979-2406, 888/359-2887 and 888/359-2887 in Canada ⊕ www.travelcuts.com.

TAXES

Washington has the region's highest hotel tax, a whopping 14.5%. Maryland and Virginia have no state hotel tax, but charge sales tax. Individual counties add their own hotel taxes, which range from 5% to 10%.

SALES TAX

Sales tax is 5.75% in D.C., 5% in Maryland, and 4% plus local amounts in Virginia.

TAXIS

You can hail a taxi on the street just about anywhere in the city, and they tend to congregate around major hotels. If you find yourself on a quiet street in a residential area, either walk to a busier street or phone for a taxi. Although it depends on your location and the time of day, a taxi ought to arrive in 10 to 15 minutes. Drivers are allowed to pick up more than one fare at a time.

There's no easy way to determine whether a cab is available for hire; would-be passengers often must rely on the tried-and-true method of waving at a cab. Cabs have outside dome lights, but these are only for requesting emergency help. Most District cab drivers are independent operators and may ignore a potential passenger. Cabbies are also known for refusing to pick up passengers after learning of their destination—especially during rush hour, when traffic congestion makes picking up fares less profitable—and the D.C. government rarely enforces the taxi laws that require drivers who are free to either pick up passengers or display an off-duty sign.

Taxis in the District are not metered; they operate on a zone system that can be confusing to newcomers. The basic rate for traveling within one zone is $5.50, and the fare increases when you cross into another zone. If you travel between two zones, the fare is $7.60; three zones is $9.50. A zone map is posted in the rear of every taxi. **Before you set off, ask your cabdriver how much the fare will be.** There's an extra $1.50 charge for each additional passenger and a $1 surcharge during the 7–9:30 AM and 4–6:30 PM peak periods. A $1.50 surcharge is tacked on when you phone for a cab. Charges double during snow emergencies. The D.C. city government occasionally authorizes emergency surcharges when gasoline prices peak.

Maryland and Virginia taxis have meters. These taxis can take you into or out of D.C., but are not allowed to take you between points in D.C.

🚩 Taxi Companies **Diamond** ☎ 202/387-4011. **Mayflower** ☎ 202/783-1111. **Yellow** ☎ 202/544-1212.

TIME

Washington, D.C., is in the eastern time zone. It's 3 hours ahead of Los Angeles, 1 hour ahead of Chicago, 5 hours behind London, and 15 hours behind Sydney.

TIPPING

At restaurants a 15% tip is standard for waitstaff; as much as 20% may be expected at more expensive establishments. The same goes for taxi drivers, bartenders, and hairdressers. Coat-check operators usually expect $1–$2; bellhops and porters should get 50¢–$1 per bag; hotel maids in upscale hotels should get $4–$5 per day of your stay.

On package tours, conductors and drivers usually get $10 per day from the group as a whole; check whether this has already been figured into your cost. For local sightseeing tours, you may individually tip the driver-guide a few dollars if he or she has been helpful or informative. Ushers in theaters, museum guides, and gas station attendants do not expect tips.

A concierge typically receives a tip of $5 to $10, with an additional gratuity for special services or favors.

TOURS & PACKAGES

Because everything is prearranged on a prepackaged tour or independent vacation, you spend less time planning—and often get it all at a good price.

BOOKING WITH AN AGENT

Travel agents are excellent resources. But it's a good idea to collect brochures from several agencies, as some agents' suggestions may be influenced by relationships with tour and package firms that reward them for volume sales. If you have a special interest, find an agent with expertise in that area. The American Society of Travel Agents (ASTA) has a database of specialists worldwide; you can log on to the group's Web site to find one near you.

Make sure your travel agent knows the accommodations and other services of the place being recommended. Ask about the hotel's location, room size, beds, and whether it has a pool, room service, or programs for children, if you care about these. Has your agent been there in person or sent others whom you can contact?

Do some homework on your own, too: local tourism boards can provide information about lesser-known and small-niche operators, some of which may sell only direct.

BUYER BEWARE

Each year consumers are stranded or lose their money when tour operators—even large ones with excellent reputations—go out of business. So check out the operator. Ask several travel agents about its reputation, and try to **book with a company that has a consumer-protection program.** (Look for information in the company's brochure.) In the United States, members of the United States Tour Operators Association are required to set aside funds (up to $1 million) to help eligible customers cover payments and travel arrangements in the event that the company defaults. It's also a good idea to choose a company that participates in the American Society of Travel Agents' Tour Operator Program; ASTA will act as mediator in any disputes between you and your tour operator.

Remember that the more your package or tour includes, the better you can predict the ultimate cost of your vacation. Make sure you know exactly what is covered, and beware of hidden costs. Are taxes, tips, and transfers included? Entertainment and excursions? These can add up.

Tour-Operator Recommendations American Society of Travel Agents (⇨ Travel Agencies). **CrossSphere-The Global Association for Packaged Travel** ⊠ 546 E. Main St., Lexington, KY 40508 ☎ 859/226-4444 or 800/682-8886 ⊟ 859/226-4414 ⊕ www.CrossSphere.com. **United States Tour Operators Association** (USTOA) ⊠ 275 Madison Ave., Suite 2014, New York, NY 10016 ☎ 212/599-6599 ⊟ 212/599-6744 ⊕ www.ustoa.com.

TRAIN TRAVEL

More than 80 trains a day arrive at Washington, D.C.'s, Union Station. Amtrak's regular service runs from D.C. to New York in 3¼–3¾ hours and from D.C. to Boston in 7¾–8 hours. Acela, Amtrak's high-speed service, travels from D.C. to New York in 2¾–3 hours and from D.C. to Boston in 6½ hours.

Two commuter lines—Maryland Rail Commuter Service and Virginia Railway Express—run to the nearby suburbs. They're cheaper than Amtrak, but they don't run on weekends.

FARES & SCHEDULES

Amtrak tickets and reservations are available at Amtrak stations, by telephone, through travel agents, or online. Amtrak schedule and fare information can be found at Union Station as well as online.

Train Information Amtrak ☎ 800/872-7245 ⊕ www.amtrak.com. **Maryland Rail Commuter Service** (MARC) ☎ 800/325-7245 ⊕ www.mtamaryland.com. **Union Station** ⊠ 50 Massachusetts Ave. NE ☎ 202/371-9441 ⊕ www.unionstationdc.com. **Virginia Railway Express** (VRE) ☎ 703/684-1001 ⊕ www.vre.org.

RESERVATIONS

Amtrak has both reserved and unreserved trains available. If you plan to travel during peak times, such as a Friday night or near a holiday, you'll need to **get a reservation and a ticket in advance.** Some trains at nonpeak times are unreserved,

with seats assigned on a first-come, first-served basis.

TRANSPORTATION AROUND WASHINGTON, D.C.

A word of advice: when you arrive in D.C., park the car and leave it. Driving in D.C. can be a headache, especially on the crowded streets around the Mall, and parking can be even worse. Luckily the city has a great public transportation system. Because it links many of the neighborhoods frequented by visitors, the Metro is a convenient way to get around the city. However, the Metro does bypass Georgetown, Adams-Morgan, and Mount Pleasant, so if you're headed to these neighborhoods, take a bus or a taxi instead. The three routes of the D.C. Circulator (⇨ Bus Travel Within Washington) are convenient for sight-seeing and shopping trips.

TRAVEL AGENCIES

A good travel agent puts your needs first. Look for an agency that has been in business at least five years, emphasizes customer service, and has someone on staff who specializes in your destination. In addition, **make sure the agency belongs to a professional trade organization.** The American Society of Travel Agents (ASTA) has more than 10,000 members in some 140 countries, enforces a strict code of ethics, and will step in to mediate agent-client disputes involving ASTA members. ASTA also maintains a directory of agents on its Web site; ASTA's TravelSense.org, a trip planning and travel advice site, can also help to locate a travel agent who caters to your needs. (If a travel agency is also acting as your tour operator, *see* Buyer Beware *in* Tours & Packages.)

Local Agent Referrals American Society of Travel Agents (ASTA) ⊠ 1101 King St., Suite 200, Alexandria, VA 22314 ☎ 703/739-2782 or 800/965-2782 24-hr hotline ⊟ 703/684-8319 ⊕ www.astanet.com and www.travelsense.org. **Association of British Travel Agents** ⊠ 68-71 Newman St., London W1T 3AH ☎ 0901/201-5050 ⊕ www.abta.com. **Association of Canadian Travel Agencies** ⊠ 350 Sparks St., Suite 510, Ottawa, Ontario K1R 7S8 ☎ 613/237-3657 ⊟ 613/237-7052 ⊕ www.acta.

ca. **Australian Federation of Travel Agents** ⊠ Level 3, 309 Pitt St., Sydney, NSW 2000 📠 02/9264-3299 or 1300/363-416 🖷 02/9264-1085 ⊕ www.afta.com.au. **Travel Agents' Association of New Zealand** ⊠ Level 5, Tourism and Travel House, 79 Boulcott St., Box 1888, Wellington 6001 📠 04/499-0104 🖷 04/499-0786 ⊕ www.taanz.org.nz.

VISITOR INFORMATION

It's a good idea to gather information about the city before your trip, as the D.C. Visitor Information Center has a disinterested staff and a lackluster collection of brochures. The center is inconveniently located in the Ronald Reagan International Trade Center, a government office building that you can enter only after flashing your ID and passing through a metal detector.

The Washington, DC Convention and Tourism Corporation's free, 120-page publication, titled *The Official Visitors' Guide,* is full of sightseeing tips, maps, and contacts. You can order a copy online or by phone, or pick one up in their office. For information about getting around the city, check out the Metro and bus-system guide published by the WMTA.

The most popular sights in D.C. are run by the National Park Service or the Smithsonian. The "Dial-A-Park" and "Dial-a-Museum" lines have recorded information about locations and hours of operation.

🚩 Events & Attractions **National Park Service** 📠 202/619-7275 "Dial-a-Park" park information ⊕ www.nps.gov. **Smithsonian** 📠 202/357-2700, 202/357-2020 "Dial-a-Museum," 202/357-1729 TDD ⊕ www.si.edu. **White House Visitor Center** ⊠ Dept. of Commerce: 1450 S. Pennsylvania Ave. NW, Washington, DC 20230 📠 202/208-1631 ⊕ www.nps.gov/whho.

🚩 Tourist Information **D.C. Visitor Information Center** ⊠ 1300 Pennsylvania Ave. NW, Washington, DC 20004 📠 202/328-4748 ⊕ www.dcvisit.com. **Washington, DC Convention and Tourism Corporation** ⊠ 901 7th St. NW, 4th fl., Washington, DC 20001 📠 202/789-7000 or 800/422-8644 ⊕ www.washington.org. **Washington MTA** 📠 202/637-7000 ⊕ www.wmata.com.

🚩 Government Advisories **Consular Affairs Bureau of Canada** 📠 800/267-6788 or 613/944-6788 from overseas ⊕ www.voyage.gc.ca. **U.K. Foreign and Commonwealth Office** ⊠ Travel Advice Unit,

Consular Directorate, Old Admiralty Building, London SW1A 2PA 📠 0845/850-2829 or 020/7008-1500 ⊕ www.fco.gov.uk/travel. **Australian Department of Foreign Affairs and Trade** 📠 300/139-281 travel advisories, 02/6261-3305 Consular Travel Advice ⊕ www.smartraveller.gov.au. **New Zealand Ministry of Foreign Affairs and Trade** 📠 04/439-8000 ⊕ www.mft.govt.nz.

🚩 State Information **State of Maryland** ⊠ Office of Tourist Development, 217 E. Redwood St., 9th fl., Baltimore, MD 21202 📠 410/767-3400 or 800/634-7386 ⊕ www.mdisfun.org. **Virginia Tourism Corporation** ⊠ Headquarters: 901 E. Byrd St., Richmond, VA 23219 📠 804/786-2051 or 800/847-4882 ⊕ www.virginia.org ⊠ Walk-in office ⊠ 1629 K St. NW, Washington, DC 20006 📠 202/872-0523 or 800/934-9184.

WEB SITES

Be sure to visit Fodors.com (⊕ www.fodors.com), a complete travel-planning site. You can research prices and book plane tickets, hotel rooms, rental cars, vacation packages, and more. In addition, you can post your pressing questions in the Travel Talk section.

The Library of Congress's site (⊕ www.loc.gov) covers its current and upcoming exhibitions, offers visitor information, and contains vast, fascinating online exhibits. At the National Park Service site (⊕ www.cr.nps.gov/nr/travel/wash), the maps, photos, and concise but thorough descriptions take you beyond the obvious destinations. The Smithsonian has an interesting Web site (⊕ www.si.edu) that gives you plenty of information about current and upcoming exhibits in all its museums.

For nightlife, the Web site of the *Washington Post* (⊕ www.washingtonpost.com) has a fairly comprehensive listing of what's going on around town. Also check out the site of *Washington CityPaper* (⊕ www.washingtoncitypaper.com), a free weekly newspaper, and that of the *Washingtonian* (⊕ www.washingtonian.com), a monthly magazine. For gay bars and clubs, click on the Web site for the gay newspaper *Washington Blade* (⊕ www.washblade.com) or the bar guide *Metro Weekly* (⊕ www.metroweekly.com).

INDEX

A

Aatish on the Hill ✕, *166*
Accommodations. ⇨ *See*
   Lodging
**Acoustic, country, and folk
   music clubs,** *233–234*
Adams Building (Library of
   Congress), *78*
Adam's Inn 🏨, *216*
Adams-Morgan area, *14,
   118–123*
*All Souls' Unitarian Church,
   121*
*District of Columbia Arts
   Center, 121*
House of the Temple, 121
lodging, 193–194
*Meridian House and the White-
   Meyer House, 121–122*
Mexican Cultural Institute, 122
*National Museum of Health
   and Medicine, 122*
restaurants, 159–162
Rock Creek Park, 122
shopping, 255–257
Aditi ✕, *184*
Addresses, *317–318*
African Voices, *44*
Air travel, *318–320*
checking luggage, 331–332
children and, 325
Airports and transfers,
   320–321
Alexandria (Virginia), *14,
   145–150*
*Alexandria Black History
   Resource Center, 145–146*
Athenaeum, 146
Captain's Row, 146–147
Carlyle House, 148
Christ Church, 148
Confederate Statue, 148
Friendship Fire House, 148
Gadsby's Tavern Museum, 148
*George Washington Masonic
   National Memorial, 149*
*John Q. Adams Center for the
   History of Otolaryngology,
   149*
*Lee-Fendall House Museum,
   149*
Lloyd House, 149
Lyceum, 149
*Old Presbyterian Meetinghouse,
   149–150*
Ramsay House, 149

*Robert E. Lee, boyhood home
   of, 146*
*Stabler-Leadbeater Apothecary,
   150*
*Torpedo Factory Art Center,
   150*
*U.S. Patent and Trademark
   Museum, 150*
**Alexandria Archaeology
   Program,** *150*
**Alexandria Black History
   Resource Center,** *145–146,
   147*
All Soul's Unitarian Church,
   119, 121
Alvear Studio (store), *258*
Amano (store), *268*
America ✕, *82*
**American Film Institute Silver
   Theatre & Cultural Center,**
   225–226
**American Pharmaceutical
   Association building,** *124,
   126*
American Red Cross, *56–57*
**Anacostia Museum and Center
   for African-American
   History and Culture,** *84–85*
Anderson House, *108–109,
   112*
Annapolis (Maryland), *279,
   284–296*
*Annapolis & Anne Arundel
   County Conference &
   Visitors Bureau, 286*
*Banneker-Douglass Museum,
   286*
Chase-Lloyd House, 287
*Hammond-Harwood House,
   287*
*Historic Annapolis Foundation
   Museum Store, 287*
Information booth, 287
*Kunta Kinte - Alex Haley
   Memorial, 288*
lodging, 291, 293–294
*London Town House and
   Gardens, 288*
Market House Pavilion, 287
Maryland State Archives, 288
Maryland State House, 288
reservation services, 291
restaurants, 291–293
St. Anne's Church, 288–289
St. John's College, 289
*Thurgood Marshall Memorial,
   289*

*United States Naval Academy,
   289*
*William Paca House and
   Garden, 290*
**Annapolis & Anne Arundel
   County Conference &
   Visitors Bureau,** *285, 286*
Annapolis Marriott Waterfront
   🏨, *293*
**Annie's Paramount Steak
   House** ✕, *235*
Apartment rentals, *200*
Apartment Zero (store), *261*
Apex Building, *85, 86*
Architecture, *16*
Ardeo/Bardeo ✕, *180*
Arena Stage (performing arts
   company), *230*
Arlington (Virginia), *14,
   137–144*
Arlington House, 137–139
*Arlington National Cemetery,
   139, 142*
*Drug Enforcement
   Administration Museum, 142*
Kennedy graves, 138, 142
Netherlands Carillon, 142
Pentagon, 142–143
*Section 7A (Arlington
   cemetery), 143*
*Section 27 (Arlington cemetery),
   143*
*Theodore Roosevelt Island,
   143*
*Tomb of the Unknowns,
   143–144*
*United States Marine Corps
   War Memorial, 144*
*Women in Military Service for
   America memorial, 144*
**Arlington Cinema 'N'
   Drafthouse,** *226*
Arlington House (Custis-Lee
   Mansion), *137–139*
Arlington National Cemetery,
   17, 138, 139, 142
Armed Forces Concert Series,
   229
Art galleries ⇨ *See* Museums
   and galleries
Art Museum of the Americas,
   57, 58
Arthur M. Sackler Gallery, *35*
Arts, *222–232*
Arts and Industries Building
   (Smithsonian), *37–38*

Arts Club of Washington, 124–125, 126
Ashby Inn ✕, 188
Athenaeum (Alexandria), 146, 147
Atlas Performing Arts Center, 222–223
Australian Embassy, 112
The Awakening (sculpture), 47

B

B. Smith's ✕, 166
Baby-sitting services, 325
Baltimore Symphony Orchestra, 228–229
Baltimore-Washington International Airport (BWI), 318, 320
Banneker-Douglass Museum (Annapolis), 285, 286
Barbara Fritchie House and Museum, 297
Bardia's New Orleans Café ✕, 159
Bars and lounges, 234–238
gay and lesbian, 237–238, 239
Bartholdi Fountain, 69, 71
Baseball, 243
Basketball, 243
Battlefields, 297, 311, 312
Bed and breakfast rentals, 200
Belga Cafe ✕, 163
Belmont (Fredericksburg), 311
Benkay ✕, 65
Ben's Chili Bowl ✕, 28, 185, 235
Best Western Capitol Skyline 🏨, 212
Bethesda (Maryland), 151–152
McCrillis Gardens and Gallery, 151
National Institutes of Health (NIH), 151
Strathmore Hall Arts Center, 151–152
Bethesda Court Hotel, 🏨, 217
Bethesda Crab House ✕, 187
Betsy Fisher (store), 266
Bicycle tours, 333
Bicycling, 244–246, 306, 321
Birchmere, The, 233
Bishops Garden, 137
Bison (Dumbarton) Bridge, 112
Bistro Bethem ✕, 313
Bistro Bis ✕, 163

Bistro Français ✕, 183, 235
Bistrot du Coin ✕, 178
Bistrot Lepic ✕, 183
Black Cat (club), 241
Black Salt ✕, 185
Blair House, 57
Blue Mercury (salon), 269
Blues Alley (club), 240
Blues clubs, 240–241
B'nai B'rith Klutznick National Jewish Museum, 125, 126
Boat tours, 333
Boating and sailing, 246–247, 304–305
Bob & Edith's Diner ✕, 235
Bombay Club ✕, 172
Boy Scouts Memorial, 57
Bread Line ✕, 171
Breeze ✕, 291
Brew pubs and microbreweries, 176
Brewer's Alley ✕, 299
Brickskeller (bar), 234
Brookside Gardens, 152
Bukom Café ✕, 159
Bullfeathers ✕, 78
Bureau of Engraving and Printing, 37, 38
Burma ✕, 169
Bus tours, 333
Buses, 321–322
airports and transfers, 320
Annapolis, 295
Frederick, 300
Fredericksburg, 315
Mount Vernon, Woodlawn, and Gunston Hall, 305
Butterfield 9 ✕, 167

C

C&O Canal, 103
C&O Canal Towpath, 244, 250–251
C&O Canal National Historic Park, 16, 278, 279, 280–284
car travel, 283
outdoors and sports, 284
tours, 284
Cada Vez ✕, 186
Café Atlántico ✕, 173–174
Café Dalat ✕, 189
Café des Artistes ✕, 59
Cafe Milano ✕, 184
Café MoZU ✕, 170
Café Nema ✕, 186
Café Normandie ✕, 292
Café Saint-Ex (bar), 234
Calendar of events, 20–25

California Tortilla ✕, 188
Calvin Run Tavern ✕, 190
Cameras and photography, 322
Cameroon Embassy, 112
Canadian Embassy, 85, 86
Canal Square, 103
Cantler's Riverside Inn ✕, 292
Capital Grille, The ✕, 162, 188
Capitol, 26, 69, 71, 72, 73–75
Capitol City Brewing ✕, 176, 234
Capitol Hill, 10, 68–83
Adams Building, 78
Bartholdi Fountain, 69
Capitol, 69, 71, 72, 73–75
Congressional Cemetery, 75
Folger Shakespeare Library, 75
Franciscan Monastery and Gardens, 75
Frederick Douglass Townhouse, 75
Grant Memorial, 75–76
James Garfield Memorial, 76
Kenilworth Aquatic Gardens, 76
Library of Congress, 76, 78
lodging, 198–201
Madison Building, 78
Marine Corps Barracks and Commandant's House, 79
National Postal Museum, 79
National Shrine of the Immaculate Conception, 79
Peace Monument, 79–80
Pope John Paul II Cultural Center, 80
restaurants, 78–79, 82, 162–163, 166–167
Robert A. Taft Memorial, 80
Rock Creek Cemetery, 121
Sewall-Belmont House, 80
shopping, 257–259
South Side of East Capitol Street, 80
Supreme Court Building, 80–81
Thurgood Marshall Federal Judiciary Building, 81
Union Station, 81–82
United States Botanic Garden, 82
United States National Arboretum, 82–83
Washington Navy Yard, 83
Capitol Hill Suites 🏨, 199–200
Capitol Hilton 🏨, 201
Capitol Visitor Center, 74–75

Captain's Row (Alexandria), 146, 147, 148

Car rental, 322–323

Car travel, 323–324

Annapolis, 295

C&O Canal and Great Falls Park, 283

Frederick, 300

Fredericksburg, 315

international travelers, 338

Mount Vernon, Woodlawn, and Gunston Hall, 305

Carlyle Grand Café ✕, 188

Carlyle House (Alexandria), 147, 148, 112

Carroll-Barrister House, 289

Carrol's Creek ✕, 291

Carter Barron Amphitheatre, 229

Cascade Café ✕, 42

Cashion's Eat Place ✕, 160

Catoctin Inn and Conference Center ✕🖫, 299–300

Ceiba ✕, 173

Cemeteries

Arlington National Cemetery, 139, 142

Confederate Cemetery, 307

Congressional Cemetery, 75

Mount Olivet Cemetery, 297–298

National Cemetery (Fredericksburg), 313

Oak Hill Cemetery, 107

Rock Creek Cemetery, 121

Caucus Room ✕, 167–168

Center Cafe ✕, 82

Center for the Arts, 223

Chain Bridge, 280

Chamber music, 227–228

Chapters (store), 260–261

Charles E. Sumner School Museum and Archives, 112

Charlie Palmer ✕, 162

Chase-Lloyd House (Annapolis), 285, 287

Chatham Manor (Fredericksburg), 311–312

Chi-Cha Lounge (bar), 234

Chick and Ruth's Delly ✕, 293

Children, travel with, 324–325

Children, attractions for, 324–325

Arts and Industries Building, 37–38

Bureau of Engraving and Printing, 38

C&O Canal, 103

Capitol, 69, 71, 72, 73–75

College Park Aviation Museum, 152

DAR Museum, 58, 59–60

East Potomac Park, 47, 49, 245

Flying Circus Airshow, 153

Ford's Theatre, 89, 230

Franklin Delano Roosevelt Memorial, 49

Friendship Fire House (Alexandria), 148

Gadsby's Tavern Museum, 148

George Washington's Ferry Farm (Fredericksburg), 312

Glen Echo Park, 231, 280–281

Goddard Space Flight Center, 152

Hugh Mercer Apothecary Shop, 309

Imagination Stage, 231

International Spy Museum, 90

J. Edgar Hoover Federal Bureau of Investigation Building, 26, 90–91

MCI Center, 91

Mount Vernon Center, 301–302

National Air and Space Museum, 39–40, 53–1548

National Aquarium, 91–92

National Building Museum, 93

National Capital Trolley Museum, 152–153

National Cryptological Museum, 153

National Gallery of Art, East Building, 40–41

National Geographic Society, 114–115

National Museum of African Art, 42–43

National Museum of American History, 43

National Museum of the American Indian, 44

National Museum of Natural History, 44–45

National Postal Museum, 79

National Zoo, 132–133

Old Post Office Building, 96

Rock Creek Park, 122

Rose Hill Manor Park, 298–299

Tidal Basin, 53

United States Botanic Garden, 82

USNA Armel-Leftwich Visitor Center, 290

United States Naval Academy Museum and Gallery of Ships, 290

Washington Monument, 54–55

Washington Navy Yard, 83

White House, 65–66

Children's Museum (Frederick), 298

Chinatown, 86, 88

Ching Ching Cha ✕, 105

City Zen ✕, 167

Choral music, 228

Christ Church (Alexandria), 147, 148

Christian Heurich House Museum, 112–113

Churches and synagogues

All Souls' Unitarian Church, 121

Christ Church (Alexandria), 148

Grace Episcopal Church, 106

Metropolitan African Methodist Episcopal Church, 114

National Shrine of the Immaculate Conception, 79

Old Adas Israel Synagogue, 95

Old Presbyterian Meetinghouse (Alexandria), 149–150

St. Anne's Church (Annapolis), 288–289

St. John's Church (Georgetown), 107

St. John's Episcopal Church, 64–65

St. Matthew's Cathedral, 116

St. Sophia Cathedral, 136

Temple of the Church of Jesus Christ of Latter-Day Saints, 153

United Church, 129

Washington National Cathedral, 136–137

Churchill Hotel 🖫, 208–209

Cineplex Odeon Uptown, 130, 132

Citronelle ✕, 27, 182–183

City Museum, 86, 88

Claiborne's ✕, 313

Clara Barton National Historic Site, 281

Clarice Smith Performing Arts Center at Maryland, 223

Classical music, 228

Cleveland Park, 11, 14, 130–134

Cineplex Odeon Uptown, 130

Hillwood Museum and Gardens, 131

Kennedy-Warren, 131–132

Kreeger Museum, 132

National Zoo, 132–133

Wardman Tower, 133

Woodley Park, 133–134

Climate, *15*
Clubs
acoustic, folk and country,
   233–234
blues, 240–241
comedy, 238
dance, 238–239
gay and lesbian dance,
   237–238, 239
jazz, 240–241
rock and pop, 241
College Park Aviation
   Museum, *152*
Columbus Memorial Fountain,
   82
Colvin Run Tavern ✕, *190*
Comedy clubs, *238*
Concert halls, *222–225*
Confederate Cemetery
   (Fredericksburg), *307,*
   308
Confederate statue, *148*
Congressional Cemetery, *75*
Constitution Gardens, *17, 47*
Consumer protection, *325*
Coppi's Organic Restaurant
   ✕, *186*
Corcoran Gallery of Art,
   57–58, 227
Country Inn and Suites 🏨 ,
   294
Coup de Foudre (store),
   262–263
Courtyard Washington/
   Northwest 🏨 , *209*
Cox's Row (Georgetown),
   103–104
Cramton Auditorium, *223*
Credit cards, *331*
abbreviations, 6
Crisfield ✕, *187*
Currency, *328*
Custis-Lee Mansion. ⇨ *See*
   Arlington House

D

DC Coast ✕, *170*
D.C. Jewish Community Center,
   223
D.C. United (soccer), *252*
D.C. Visitor Information
   Center, *97–98*
Dance, *225*
Dance clubs, *238–239*
gay and lesbian, 239
Dance Place, *225*
DAR Constitution Hall, *223*
DAR Museum, *58, 59–60*
Decatur House, *58, 60*

Department of Agriculture, *37,*
   38
Department of the Interior, *58,*
   60–61
Department of the Interior
   Museum, *60–61*
Department of State building,
   125, 126
Department stores, *260,*
   271–272
Diner, The ✕, *235*
Dining. ⇨ See Restaurants
Dinosaur Hall, *44*
Disabilities and accessibility,
   326–327
Discounts and deals, *327*
Dish ✕, *180*
District of Columbia Arts
   Center, *119, 121, 231*
Doubletree Guest Suites 🏨 ,
   213
Downtown Washington
lodging, 201–207
restaurants, 167–175
shopping, 259–263
Drug Enforcement
   Administration Museum, *142*
Dulles International Airport
   (IAD), *318, 320*
Dumbarton Concerts, *227*
Dumbarton House, *104*
Dumbarton Oaks, *17, 104–105*
Dupont Circle, *11, 108–118*
Anderson House, 108–109, 112
Australian Embassy, 112
Bison Bridge, 112
Cameroon Embassy, 112
Charles E. Sumner School
   Museum and Archives, 112
Fondo Del Sol Visual Arts
   Center, 114
Heurich House Museum,
   112–113
lodging, 207–209
Mary McLeod Bethune Council
   House, 114
Metropolitan African Methodist
   Episcopal Church, 114
National Geographic Society,
   114–115
National Museum of American
   Jewish Military History, 115
Phillips Collection, 115–116
restaurants, 114, 176–180
St. Matthew's Cathedral, 116
Scott Circle, 116
shopping, 263–266
Textile Museum, 116
2221 Kalorama Road, 116–117

Walsh-McLean House, 117
Washington Post Building, 117
Woodrow Wilson House,
   117–118

E

East Capitol Street, *71, 80*
East End, *10, 83–99*
Anacostia Museum and Center
   for African American History
   and Culture, 84–85
Apex Building, 85, 86
Canadian Embassy, 85, 86
Chinatown, 88
City Museum, 88
Federal Triangle, 88–89
Ford's Theatre, 89
Frederick Douglass National
   Historic Site, 89
Freedom Plaza, 89–90
Inter-American Development
   Bank Cultural Center, 90
International Spy Museum, 90
J. Edgar Hoover Federal Bureau
   of Investigation Building, 26,
   90–91
John A. Wilson Building, 91
Lincoln Building, 96
Marian Koshland Science
   Museum, 91
Martin Luther King Jr.
   Memorial Library, 91
MCI Center, 91
National Aquarium, 91–92
National Archives, 92–93
National Building Museum, 93
National Law Enforcement
   Officers Memorial, 93–94
National Museum of Women in
   the Arts, 94
National Portrait Gallery, 94
National Theatre, 94–95
Navy Memorial, 95
Newseum, 95
Old Adas Israel Synagogue, 95
Old Patent Office Building,
   95–96
Old Post Office, 96
Pennsylvania Avenue, 96–97
Petersen House, 97
Ronald Reagan Building and
   International Trade Center,
   97–98
Smithsonian American Art
   Museum, 98
Surratt Boarding House, 98
Tariff Commission Building, 98
Willard Inter-Continental,
   98–99

East Potomac Park, 47, 49, 245
Eastern Market, 257–259
Eighteenth Street Lounge (ESL), 236
Eisenhower Executive Office Building, 58, 61
El Toro Bravo ✕, 292
Electricity, 328
Elizabeth Myers Mitchell Art Gallery (Annapolis), 289
Ellipse, 58, 61–62
Embassies, F43
Embassy Suites ▦, 213–214, 217
Embassy Suites Old Town Alexandria ▦, 218
Emergencies, 329
Equestrian statues, 51
Equinox ✕, 172
Evermay, 105
Exorcist steps, 105

F

Fairmont Washington ▦, 213
Farm Museum, 298
Federal Reserve Building, 125–126
Federal Triangle, 88
Festivals and seasonal events, 20–25
Film, 225–227
Filmfest DC, 226
Firefly ✕, 178
Fishing, 247–248
Five Guys ✕, 180, 182
Fletcher's Boat House, 280
Flying Circus Airshow, 153
Fodor's Choice, 26–28
Foggy Bottom, 11, 123–129
American Pharmaceutical Association, 124
Arts Club of Washington, 124–125
B'nai B'rith Klutznick National Jewish Museum, 125
Department of State, 125
Federal Reserve Building, 125–126
George Washington University, 126–127
John F. Kennedy Center for the Performing Arts, 126, 127–128, 223–224
lodging, 213–215
National Academy of Sciences, 128–129
Seven Buildings, 129

2000 Pennsylvania Avenue NW, 129
United Church, 129
Watergate, 129
Folger Shakespeare Library, 71, 75, 227, 231
Fondo Del Sol Visual Arts Center, 114
Football, 248
Ford's Theatre, 86, 89, 230
Fort Dupont Summer Theater, 229
Fort Reno Park, 134
49 West Coffeehouse and Gallery ✕, 293
Foundry Building, the, 105
Four Seasons Hotel ▦, 28, 210
Francis Dodge Warehouses, 105
Francis Scott Key Memorial Park, 105–106
Franciscan Monastery and Gardens, 75
Franklin Delano Roosevelt Memorial, 26, 49, 50
Frederick (Maryland), 279, 296–300
Barbara Fritchie House and Museum, 297
Frederick Coffee Company, 297
Historical Society of Frederick County, 297
lodging, 299–300
Monocacy National Battlefield, 297
Mount Olivet Cemetery, 297–298
National Museum of Civil War Medicine, 298
restaurants, 299–300
Rose Hill Manor Park, 298–299
Schifferstadt Architectural Museum, 299
Frederick Coffee Company ✕, 297
Frederick Douglass National Historic Site, 89
Frederick Douglass Townhouse, 71, 75
Fredericksburg (Virginia), 279, 306–316
around, 310–313
Confederate Cemetery, 307
downtown Fredericksburg, 306–310
Fredericksburg Area Museum and Cultural Center, 307–308

Fredericksburg Visitor Center, 308–309
Goolrick's Pharmacy, 309
Hugh Mercer Apothecary Shop, 309
James Monroe Museum and Memorial Library, 309
Kenmore, 309
lodging, 314–315
Mary Washington College Galleries, 310
Mary Washington Grave and Monument, 310
Mary Washington House, 310
restaurants, 309, 313–314
Rising Sun Tavern, 310, 310
Fredericksburg Area Museum and Cultural Center, 307–308
Fredericksburg Colonial Inn ▦, 314
Fredericksburg/Spotsylvania National Military Park, 311, 312
Fredericksburg Visitor Center, 308–309
Freedom Plaza, 86, 89–90
Freer Gallery of Art, 37, 38–39
Friendship Arch, 88
Friendship Fire House (Alexandria), 147, 148
Full Kee ✕, 88, 168–169

G

Gadsby's Tavern Museum (Alexandria), 147, 148
Gala Hispanic Theatre, 231
Galileo ✕, 27, 172
Galleries. ⇨ See Museums and galleries
Garden Cafe ✕, 42
Gardens, 17
Bishop's Garden, 137
Brookside Gardens, 152
Constitution Gardens, 17, 47
Dumbarton Oaks, 104–105
Franciscan Monastery and Gardens, 75
Hillwood Museum and Gardens, 131
Kahlil Gibran Memorial Garden, 136
Kenilworth Aquatic Gardens, 76
Lafayette Square, 62–63
London Town House and Gardens, 288
McCrillis Gardens and Gallery, 151

National Bonsai Collection, 82
National Garden, 82
National Herb Garden, 82
Pershing Park, 64
United States Botanic Garden, 82
United States National Arboretum, 82–83
William Paca House and Garden (Annapolis), 290
Gay and lesbian travel, 327
George Washington Masonic National Memorial, 147, 149
George Washington University, 126–127
George Washington University Inn ⊡, 214–215
George Washington's Ferry Farm (Virginia), 311, 312
Georgetown, 10–11, 99–108
C&O Canal, 103
C&O Canal National Historic Park, 16, 278, 279, 280–284
Canal Square, 103
Cox's Row, 103–104
Dumbarton House, 104
Dumbarton Oaks, 104–105
Evermay, 105
Exorcist steps, 105
Foundry, the, 105
Francis Dodge Warehouses, 105
Francis Scott Key Memorial Park, 105–106
Georgetown University, 106
Grace Episcopal Church, 106
Halcyon House, 106
lodging, 210–212
Masonic Lodge, 106
Montrose Park, 106–107
Oak Hill Cemetery, 107
Old Stone House, 107
restaurants, 105, 180–185
St. John's Church, 107
shopping, 266–269
Tudor Place, 107–108
Washington Harbour, 108
Georgetown Café ✕, 182
Georgetown Inn ⊡, 211
Georgetown Suites ⊡, 211
Georgetown University, 106
Georgetown Visitor Center, 280
Georgia Brown's ✕, 175
Gerard's Place ✕, 172
Glen Echo Park, 231, 280–281
Glover-Archbold Park, 135

Goddard Space Flight Center, 152
Golf, 228–249
Good Wood (store), 270
Goolrick's Pharmacy ✕, 309
Gordon Biersch ✕, 176
Governor Calvert House ⊡, 293
Grace Episcopal Church, 106
Grand Army of the Republic memorial, 97
Grand Hyatt Washington, ⊡ 203
Grant Memorial, 71, 75–76
Grapeseed ✕, 187
Great Falls Park (Virginia), 16, 283
car travel, 283
outdoor activities and sports, 284
tours, 284
Great Falls Park Visitor Center and Museum, 283
Great Falls Tavern, 281, 283
Grill from Ipanema ✕, 161
Guided tours, 333–335
Annapolis, 295–296
C & O Canal, 284
Frederick, Maryland, 300
Fredericksburg, 315–316
Mount Vernon, 305–306
Gunston Hall (Virginia), 279, 303–304

H

Habana Village (dance club), 239
Halcyon House, 106
Hamilton, Alexander (statue), 65
Hammond-Harwood House (Annapolis), 285, 287
Hampton Inn and Suites ⊡, 293–294
Hawk 'n' Dove ✕, 79
Hay-Adams Hotel ⊡, 28, 203–204
Hemphill Fine Arts (store), 264
Henley Park Hotel ⊡, 206
Heritage India ✕, 183–184
Hiking, 249
Hillwood Museum and Gardens, 131
Hilton Arlington and Towers ⊡, 218
Hirshhorn Museum and Sculpture Garden, 37, 39, 226

Historic Annapolis Foundation Museum Store, 285, 287
Historical Society of Frederick County, 297
Hockey, 250
Holiday Inn Arlington at Ballston, ⊡, 219–220
Holiday Inn Capitol, ⊡, 212
Holiday Inn Chevy Chase, ⊡, 217–218
Holiday Inn Georgetown, ⊡, 211
Holiday Inn on the Hill, ⊡, 200–201
Holiday Inn Rosslyn, ⊡, 220
Holiday Inn Select Bethesda, ⊡, 217
Home exchanges, 200
Horace & Dickie's ✕, 166–167
Hostelling International–Washington, D.C., 207
Hostels, 200
Hotel George ⊡, 198–199
Hotel Harrington ⊡, 207
Hotel Helix ⊡, 205–206
Hotel Madera ⊡, 208
Hotel Monaco ⊡, 201–202
Hotel Rouge ⊡, 208
Hotel Tabard Inn ⊡, 209
Hotel Washington ⊡, 64, 204
Hotels. ⇨ See Lodging
House of the Temple, 119, 121
Howard University Law School, 137
HR-57 Center for the Preservation of Jazz and Blues (club), 240
Hu's Shoes (store), 268–269
Hugh Mercer Apothecary Shop (Fredericksburg), 308, 309
Hyatt Arlington ⊡, 219
Hyatt Regency Capitol Hill ⊡, 198
Hyatt Regency Bethesda ⊡, 216

I

i Ricchi ✕, 178
Ice-skating, 250
IMAX theatres, 40, 45
Inde Bleu ✕, 170
Inn at Buckytown ✕⊡, 300
Inn at Little Washington ✕, 27, 189–190
Institute of Musical Traditions, 229

Insurance, *323, 327–328*
Inter-American Development
    Bank Cultural Center, *90*
International Spy Museum, *85,
    90*
International travelers, tips
    for, *328–330*
Islamic Mosque and Cultural
    Center, *135–136*
Itineraries, *18–19*

J

J. Edgar Hoover Federal
    Bureau of Investigation
    Building, *26, 86, 90–91*
J.W. Marriott Pennsylvanis
    Avenue ⊞ , *203*
Jaleo ✕ , *27, 175*
James Garfield Memorial, *71,
    76*
James Madison Building
    (Library of Congress), *78*
James Monroe Museum and
    Memorial Library
    (Fredericksburg), *308,
    309*
Janet Annenberg Hooker Hall
    of Geology, Gems and
    Minerals, *44–45*
Jazz clubs, *240–241*
Jean Pierre Antiques (store),
    267
Jefferson Hotel ⊞ , *201*
Jefferson Memorial, *26,
    49–50, 21*
Jimmy T's Place ✕ , *163*
John A. Wilson Building, *91*
John F. Kennedy Center for the
    Performing Arts, *126,
    127–128, 223–224*
John Hagan's Tavern ✕ , *299*
John Q. Adams Center for the
    History of Otolaryngology,
    147, 149
Johnny's Half Shell ✕ , *179*
Joy of Motion, *225*
Jurys Normandy Inn ⊞ ,
    193–194
Jurys Washington Hotel ⊞ ,
    207

K

Kahlil Gibran Memorial
    Garden, *136*
Kalorama Guest House–Adams
    Morgan ⊞ , *194*
Kalorama Guest
    House–Woodley Park ⊞ ,
    216

Kaz Sushi Bistro ✕ , *169*
Kenilworth Aquatic Gardens,
    17, 76
Kenmore (Fredericksburg),
    308, 309
Kennedy family graves, *138,
    142*
Kennedy-Warren (apartment
    house), *131–132*
Key Bridge Marriott ⊞ ,
    218–219
King, Martin Luther Jr., *86, 91*
Kinkead's ✕ , *174*
Kite flying, *250*
Klingle Mansion, *122*
Komi ✕ , *27, 177*
Korean War Veterans
    Memorial, *17, 50*
Kosciuszko, Thaddeus, *63*
Kramerbooks and Afterwords
    ✕ , (book shop), *114,
    176, 235, 264*
Kreeger Museum, *132*
Kunta Kinte - Alex Haley
    Memorial, *285, 288*

L

La Bergerie ✕ , *191*
La Chaumière ✕ , *183*
La Fourchette ✕ , *161*
La Petite Auberge ✕ ,
    313–314
Lafayette Square, *58, 62–63*
Latham Hotel ⊞ , *211–212*
L'Auberge Chez François ✕ ,
    190–191
Lauriol Plaza ✕ , *161*
Le Bon Café ✕ , *78*
Le Paradou ✕ , *172*
Lebanese Taberna ✕ , *162*
Lee, Robert E., *141*
Lee, Robert E., boyhood home
    of (Alexandria), *146, 147*
Lee-Fendall House Museum
    (Alexandria), *147, 149*
L'Enfant, Pierre-Charles, *77,
    139*
L'Enfant Plaza ⊞ , *212*
Libraries
Folger Shakespeare Library, 75
*James Monroe Museum and
    Memorial Library, 309*
*Library of Congress, 71, 76,
    78*
*Martin Luther King Jr.
    Memorial Library, 91*
Library of Congress, *71, 76,
    78*
Lincoln Building, *96*

Lincoln Memorial, *26, 50, 52*
Lincoln Suites ⊞ , *206*
Lincoln Theater, *230*
Lisner Auditorium, *224*
Little Viet Garden ✕ , *189*
Lloyd House (Alexandria),
    147, 149
Lockkeeper's House, *50, 52*
Lodging, *28, 192–220*
    apartment rentals, 200
    B&Bs, 200
    children, 198
    concierges, 325
    facilities, 195
    home exchanges, 200
    hostels, 200
    parking, 195
    price categories, 194, 195, 277
    reservations, 195
Loeb's Restaurant ✕ , *63*
Loews Annapolis Hotel ⊞ ,
    293
London Town House and
    Gardens, *285, 288*
Love (dance club), *239*
Luggage, *331–332*
Lyceum (Alexandria), *149*

M

Madison, The ⊞ , *206*
Madison Building, *78*
Maestro ✕ , *27, 191*
Mail and shipping, *329, 330*
Maine Avenue Seafood
    Market, *54*
Majestic Café ✕ , *189*
Mall, The *7, 16, 18, 19,
    31–46, 247, 251*
Malls (stores), *220, 223–224,
    229–230, 234, 236–237*
Mama Ayesha's Restaurant
    ✕ , *162*
Mammal Hall, *44*
Mandarin Oriental
    Washington, D.C. ✕ , *202*
Mannequin Pis ✕ , *186–187*
Marcel's ✕ , *182*
Marian Koshland Science
    Museum, *86, 91*
Marine Corps Barracks and
    Commandant's House, *71,
    79*
Market House Pavilion
    (Annapolis), *250*
Market Lunch, The ✕ , *163*
Marquis de Lafayette, *62*
Marrakesh ✕ , *167*
Marriott at Metro Center ⊞ ,
    204

Marriott Residence Inn Arlington Pentagon City 🏨 , *219*

Marriott Residence Inn Bethesda Downtown 🏨 , *216–217*

Marriott Residence Inn (Washington, DC) 🏨 , *207*

Marriott Wardman Park 🏨 , *215*

Martin Luther King Jr. Memorial Library, *86, 91*

Marvelous Market ✕ , *97*

Mary McLeod Bethune Council House, *114*

Mary Washington College Galleries, *308, 310*

Mary Washington Grave and Monument, *308, 310*

Mary Washington House, *308, 310*

Maryland

Annapolis, 279, 284–296

Bethesda, 151–152

Brookside Gardens, 152

C&O Canal National Historic Park, 278, 279, 280–284

College Park Aviation Museum, 152

Frederick, 279, 296–300

Goddard Space Flight Center, 152

lodging, 216–218, 293–294, 299–300

National Capital Trolley Museum, 152–153

National Cryptologic Museum, 153

restaurants, 186–188, 291–293, 299–300

shopping, 274–275

sightseeing, 151–153, 284–290

Temple of the Church of Jesus Christ of Latter-Day Saints, 153

Maryland Inn 🏨 , *294*

Maryland State Archives, *285, 288*

Maryland State House (Annapolis), *285, 288*

Masonic Lodge (Georgetown), *106*

Matchbox ✕ , *168*

McCrillis Gardens and Gallery, *151*

McDowell Hall, *289*

MCI Center, *91*

Meal plans, *195*

abbreviations, 6

Media, *330*

Melrose Hotel, The 🏨 , *210–211*

Memorials. ⇨ *See* Monuments

Meridian Hill Park, *122*

Meridian House and the White-Meyer House, *119, 121–122*

Merriman's Restaurant & Bar ✕ , *313*

Meskerem ✕ , *159*

Metro (subway), *330–331*

Mount Vernon, Woodlawn, and Gunston Hall, 305

transfers to Ronald Reagan National Airport, 320

Metropolitan African Methodist Episcopal Church, *114*

Mexican Cultural Institute, *119, 122*

Mezza Café ✕ , *40*

Middleton Tavern ✕ , *292*

Miss Pixie's (store), *258*

Miss Saigon ✕ , *182*

Mixtec ✕ , *161–162*

Money matters, *331*

Monocacy National Battlefield, *297*

Monocle ✕ , *162–163*

Montmartre ✕ , *163, 166*

Montrose Park, *106–107*

Monuments, *7, 17, 26, 46–56*

Alexander Hamilton, 65

Andrew Jackson, 62

Boy Scouts Memorial, 57

Clara Barton National Historic Site, 281

Confederate Statue, 148

Equestrian statues, 51

Franklin Delano Roosevelt, 49

Gen. Philip Henry Sheridan, 51

Gen. William Tecumseh Sherman, 51

George Washington Masonic National Memorial, 149

Grand Army of the Republic memorial, 97

Grant Memorial, 75–76

James Garfield Memorial, 76

Jefferson Memorial, 49–50

Korean War Veterans Memorial, 50

Kunta Kinte—Alex Haley Memorial, 288

Lincoln Memorial, 50, 52

Lockkeeper's House, 52

Marquis de Lafayette, 62

Mary Washington Grave and Monument, 310

National Law Enforcement Officers Memorial, 93–94

National World War II Memorial, 52–53

Navy Memorial, 95

Peace Monument, 79–80

Pershing Park, 64

Robert A. Taft Memorial, 80

Statue of Tecumseh, 290

Thaddeus Kosciuszko, 63

Thurgood Marshall, 285, 289

Tidal Basin, 53

Tomb of the Unknowns, 143–144

United States Marine Corps War Memorial, 144

Vietnam Veterans Memorial, 54

Vietnam Women's Memorial, 54

Washington Monument, 54–55

William Tecumseh Sherman Monument, 68

Women in Military Service for America Memorial, 144

Morrison House 🏨 , *219*

Morrison-Clark Inn 🏨 , *205*

Morton's of Chicago ✕ , *175, 185*

Mount Olivet Cemetery, *297–298*

Mount Vernon (Virginia), *26, 279, 301–302, 304–306*

Muléh (store), *270*

Museum of Contemporary Art, *103*

Museums and galleries, *17, 27*

Anacostia Museum and Center for African-American History and Culture, 84–85

Anderson House, 108–109, 112

Art Museum of the Americas, 57

Arthur M. Sackler Gallery, 35, 38

Arts and Industries Building (Smithsonian), 37–38

Arts Club of Washington, 124–125

Athenaeum (Alexandria), 146

Banneker-Douglass Museum, 286

Barbara Fritchie House and Museum, 297

Belmont, 311

B'nai B'rith Klutznick National Jewish Museum, 125
Charles E. Sumner School Museum and Archives, 112
Chatham Manor, 311–312
Children's Museum (Frederick), 298
Christian Heurich House Museum, 112–113
City Museum, 88
College Park Aviation Museum, 152
Corcoran Gallery of Art, 57–58
DAR Museum, 59–60
Department of the Interior Museum, 60–61
District of Columbia Arts Center, 121
Drug Enforcement Administration Museum, 142
Elizabeth Myers Mitchell Art Gallery (Annapolis), 289
Farm Museum (Frederick), 298
Fondo Del Sol Visual Arts Center, 114
Fredericksburg Area Museum and Cultural Center, 307–308
Freer Gallery of Art, 38–39
Gadsby's Tavern Museum (Alexandria), 148
gift shops, 262
Goddard Space Flight Center, 152
Great Falls Park Visitor Center and Museum, 283
Hillwood Museum and Gardens, 131
Hirshhorn Museum and Sculpture Garden, 39
International Spy Museum, 90
James Monroe Museum and Memorial Library (Fredericksburg), 309
John Q. Adams Center for the History of Otolaryngology, 149
Kreeger Museum, 132
Lee-Fendall House Museum (Alexandria), 149
Lyceum (Alexandria), 149
Marian Koshland Science Museum, 91
Mary McLeod Bethune Council House, 114
Mary Washington College Galleries, 310
Mary Washington House, 310
McCrillis Gardens and Gallery, 151

Mexican Cultural Institute, 122
Museum of Contemporary Art, 103
National Air and Space Museum, 39–40
National Air and Space Museum Steven F. Udvar-Hazy Center, 153–154
National Building Museum, 93
National Capital Trolley Museum, 152–153
National Cryptologic Museum, 153
National Gallery of Art, 41
National Gallery of Art Sculpture Garden, 41–42
National Museum of African Art, 42–43
National Museum of American History, 43
National Museum of the American Indian, 44
National Museum of American Jewish Military History, 115
National Museum of Civil War Medicine, 298
National Museum of Health and Medicine, 122
National Museum of Natural History, 44–45
National Museum of Women in the Arts, 94
National Portrait Gallery, 94
National Postal Museum, 79
Navy Art Gallery, 83
Navy Museum, 83
Newseum, 95
Octagon Museum, 63
Old Stone House, 107
Phillips Collection, 115–116
Pope John Paul II Cultural Center, 80
Renwick Gallery, 64
Schifferstadt Architectural Museum, 299
Smithsonian American Art Museum, 98
Smithsonian Institution Building, 45–46
Stabler-Leadbeater Apothecary, 150
Strathmore Hall Arts Center, 151–152
Textile Museum, 116
Torpedo Factory Art Center (Alexandria), 150
United States Holocaust Memorial Museum, 46

United States Naval Academy Museum & Gallery of Ships, 290
United States Patent and Trademark Museum, 150
Music, 227–230
Music Center at Strathmore, 152, 224
Music performance series, 229–230

N

National Academy of Sciences, 126, 128–129, 227
National Air and Space Museum, 17, 27, 37, 39–40
National Air and Space Museum Steven F. Udvar-Hazy Center, 153–154
National Aquarium, 86, 91–92
National Archives, 27, 91–92, 226
National Bonsai Collection, 82
National Building Museum, 16, 86, 93
National Capital Trolley Museum, 152–153
National Cemetery (Fredericksburg), 311, 313
National Cryptologic Museum, 153
National Gallery of Art, 17, 27, 224
National Gallery of Art, East Building, 37, 40–41, 227
National Gallery of Art, West Building, 37, 41
National Gallery of Art Sculpture Garden, 41–42
National Garden, 82
National Geographic Society, 114–115, 227
National Herb Garden, 82
National Institutes of Health (NIH), 151
National Japanese American Memorial to Patriotism, 71
National Law Enforcement Officers Memorial, 86, 93–94
National monuments, ⇨ See Monuments
National Museum of African Art, 37, 42–43
National Museum of American History, 17, 37, 43
National Museum of the American Indian, 37, 44

National Museum of American
  Jewish Military History, *115*
National Museum of Civil War
  Medicine, *298*
National Museum of Health
  and Medicine, *122*
National Museum of Natural
  History, *17, 37,44–45*
National Museum of Women in
  the Arts, *86, 94*
National Portrait Gallery, *86,
  94*
National Postal Museum, *71,
  79*
National Press Building, *90*
National Shrine of the
  Immaculate Conception, *79*
National Symphony Orchestra,
  229
National Theatre, *94–95, 230*
National World War II
  Memorial, *17, 50, 52–53*
National Zoo, *132–133*
Nature Center and
  Planetarium, *122*
Navy Art Gallery, *83*
Navy Memorial, *17, 86, 95*
Navy Museum, *83*
Netherlands Carillon, *138,
  142*
New Executive Office Building,
  62–63
New Heights ✕, *160*
Newseum, *86, 96*
Nightlife, *232–241*
9:30 Club, *241*
Nooshi ✕, *169*
Nora ✕, *177*
Numark Gallery (store), *260*

O

O. Orkin Insect Zoo, *45*
Oak Hill Cemetery, *107*
Obelisk ✕, *178*
Occidental Grill ✕, *171*
Oceanaire Seafood Room ✕,
  174
Octagon Museum, *58, 63*
Old Adas Israel Synagogue,
  95
Old Ebbitt Grill ✕, *65, 168*
Old Patent Office Building, *86,
  95–96*
Old Post Office, *86, 96*
Old Post Office Pavilion
  (shopping center), *224*
Old Presbyterian
  Meetinghouse, *147,
  149–150*

Old Stone House, *107*
Olives ✕, *172–173*
Omni Shoreham Hotel 🖼,
  215
One Washington Circle 🖼,
  214
Opera, *228*
Orchestra music, *228–229*
Organization of American
  States, *58, 63–64*
Orientation tours, *334*
Outdoor activities, *242–253*

P

Packing for the trip, *331–332*
Palena ✕, *27, 180*
Palette ✕, *174–175*
Palm ✕, *179–180*
Palm Court ✕, *43*
Pan Asian Noodles & Grill ✕,
  114
Panjshir ✕, *188*
Paolo's ✕, *184*
Parking, *324*
Parks
  *C&O Canal National Historic
    Park, 16, 278, 279, 280–284*
  East Potomac Park, 47, 49, 245
  Fort Reno Park, 134
  *Francis Scott Key Memorial
    Park, 105–106*
  *Fredericksburg/Spotsylvania
    National Military Park, 312*
  Glen Echo Park, 231, 280–281
  Glover-Archbold Park, 135
  Great Falls Park, 283
  Lafayette Square, 62–63
  Meridian Hill Park, 122
  Montrose Park, 106–107
  Pershing Park, 64
  Rock Creek Park, 122
  *Rose Hill Manor Park,
    298–299*
  Theodore Roosevelt Island, 143
  West Potomac Park, 55–56
Passage to India ✕, *187*
Passports and visas, *329*
Pasta Mia ✕, *161*
Paste ✕, *171*
Pavilion Café ✕, *42*
Peace Monument, *71, 79–80*
Pennsylvania Avenue, *96–97*
Penn Quarter, *97*
Pentagon, *142–143*
Performance art, *230–232*
Performance series (music),
  229–230
Pershing Park, *58, 64*
Pershing Park Ice Rink, *250*

Personal guides, *334*
Petersen House, *86, 97*
Phillips Annapolis Harbor ✕,
  291
Phillips Collection, *17,
  115–116, 227–228*
Pho 75 ✕, *189*
Phoenix Park Hotel 🖼, *199*
Pizzeria Paradiso ✕, *28,
  179, 186*
Politics and Prose
  (bookstore), *272*
Polly's Café ✕, *185*
Pope John Paul II Cultural
  Center, *80*
Pope-Leighey House, *303*
Poste ✕, *171*
Price categories
  lodging, 194, 195, 277
  restaurants, 157, 277
Private guides, *334*

R

Railroads, *337*
  airport transfers, 321
  Fredericksburg, 316
Rams Head Tavern ✕, *292*
Ramsay House (Alexandria),
  147, 150
Red Sage ✕, *170*
Renaissance Mayflower Hotel
  🖼, *204–205*
Renwick Gallery, *58, 64*
Restaurant Eve ✕, *190*
Restaurants, *27–28, 155–191*
  Afghan, 188
  African, 159, 167
  after-hours, 235
  *American, 162–163, 167–168,
    176, 180, 182, 185, 188–189*
  Asian, 168–169, 177, 182, 189
  barbecue, 189
  Belgian, 163, 182, 186–187
  Cajun/creole, 159
  *Contemporary, 160, 170–171,
    177–178, 182–183, 187,
    189–190*
  eclectic, 186
  *French, 161, 163, 166, 172,
    178, 183, 190–191*
  getting there, 157
  Indian, 166, 172, 183–184, 187
  *Italian, 161, 172–173,
    178–179, 184, 186, 191*
  Latin American, 161, 173–174
  Mall, the, 40, 42, 43
  Mexican, 161–162
  Middle Eastern, 162, 174, 179
  price categories, 157, 277

reservations, 157
Salvadorian, 166
seafood, 174, 179, 185, 187
Southern, 166–167, 174–175
Southwestern, 187–188, 191
Spanish, 175
steak, 175, 179–180, 185
Richard Johnston Inn ▥, 314
Rio Grande Café ✕,
  187–188, 191
Rising Sun Tavern
  (Fredericksburg), 308, 310
Ristorante Piccolo Roma ✕,
  292
Ristorante Renato ✕, 313
Ritz-Carlton Georgetown ▥,
  210
Ritz-Carlton Pentagon City ▥,
  218
Ritz-Carlton Washington ▥,
  28, 213
Robert A. Taft Memorial, 71,
  80
Robert Johnson House ▥,
  294
Rock and pop clubs, 241
Rock Bottom Brewery ✕,
  176
Rock Creek Cemetery, 121
Rock Creek Park, 16, 122,
  245–246, 251
Rocklands ✕, 189
Ronald Reagan Building and
  International Trade Center,
  86, 97–98
Ronald Reagan Washington
  National Airport (DCA),
  318, 320
Roosevelt Memorial, Franklin
  Delano, 49, 50
Rose Hill Manor Park,
  298–299
Running, 250–252

S
Safety concerns, 332
St. Anne's Church
  (Annapolis), 285, 288–289
St. Gregory ▥, 214
St. John's Church
  (Georgetown), 107
St. John's College
  (Annapolis), 285, 289
St. John's Episcopal Church,
  58, 64–65
St. Matthew's Cathedral, 116
St. Regis ▥, 202
St. Sophia Cathedral, 136
Sala Thai ✕, 177

Sam and Harry's ✕, 179
Sammy T's ✕, 314
Schifferstadt Architectural
  Museum, 299
Scotlaur Inn ▥, 294
Scott Circle, 116
Screen on the Green, 227
Sculpture Garden (Hirshhorn
  Museum), 37, 39
Second Story Books (store),
  264
Secondi (store), 266
Section 7A (Arlington
  National Cemetery), 138,
  143
Section 27 (Arlington
  National Cemetery), 138,
  143
Segway tours, 334
Senior citizens, tips for, 332
Seven Buildings, 126, 129
701 Pennsylvania Avenue ✕,
  1171
1789 ✕, 183
Sewall-Belmont House, 71, 80
Shakespeare Theatre, 230
Shenandoah Brewing
  Company ✕, 176
Shopping, 254–275
Adams-Morgan area, 255–257
antiques, 256, 263, 267, 270,
  275
art galleries, 260, 263–264,
  267–268, 275
books, 256, 258, 260–261, 264,
  268, 272
Capitol Hill/Eastern Market,
  257–259
children's clothing, 259, 264,
  272
crafts and gifts, 258–259, 261,
  264–265, 268, 273, 275
department stores, 260,
  271–272
Downtown, 259–263
Dupont Circle, 263–266
Eastern Market, 257–259
food and wine, 259, 273
Georgetown, 266–269
home furnishings, 256, 261,
  265, 268, 270, 273
jewelry, 265
kitchenware, 265
leather goods, 268
malls, 258, 260, 266, 272,
  274–275
Maryland, 274–275
men's clothing, 256, 265–266,
  268, 270–271, 273, 275

musical instruments, 275
retro and eclectic, 257
shoes, 257, 261, 268–269
spas and beauty salons,
  261–262, 269, 274, 275
toys, 274
U Street, 270–271
Virginia, 274–275
Wisconsin Avenue, 271–274
women's clothing, 256, 259,
  262–263, 265–266, 268, 269,
  270–271, 273, 275
Shops, the, 65
Shops at Georgetown Park,
  266
Sightseeing tours, 333–335
Six-twenty-three American
  Bistro and Tapas ✕, 313
Skewers/Cafe Luna ✕, 179
Smithsonian American Art
  Museum, 86, 98
Smithsonian Information
  Center, 45–46
Smithsonian Institution, 37,
  45–46, 224
Smythe's Cottage & Tavern ✕,
  314
Soccer, 252
Sofitel Lafayette Square
  Washington ▥, 202
Southwest Washington
  lodging, 212
Special-interest tours, 334
Sports and outdoor activities,
  242–253
baseball, 243
basketball, 244
bicycling, 244–246
boating and sailing, 246–247
fishingm 247–248
football, 248
golf, 248–249
hiking, 249
hockey, 250
ice-skating, 250
kite flying, 250
running, 250–252
soccer, 252
tennis, 252–253
tickets and venues, 252
volleyball, 253
yoga and Pilates, 253
Stabler-Leadbeater
  Apothecary, 147, 150
State Plaza Hotel ▥, 214
Statues. ⇨ See Monuments
Strathmore Hall Arts Center,
  151–152
Students, tips for, 335

Studio Theatre, 232
Subways. ⇨ See Metro
Sulgrave Club, 114
Supreme Court Building, 71,
80–81
Surratt Boarding House, 86,
98
Sushi-Ko ✗, 28, 182
Symbols, 6

T

Tabard Inn ✗, 177–178
Taberna del Alabardero ✗,
175
Tariff Commission Building,
86, 98
Tauraso's ✗, 299
Taxes, 335
Taxis, 300, 335–336
Teaism ✗, 114, 169, 177
Teatro Goldoni ✗, 173
Tecumseh statue, 290
Telephones, 329–330
Temperance Fountain, 97
Temple of the Church of Jesus
Christ of Latter-Day Saints,
153
TenPenh ✗, 168
Tennis, 252–253
Textile Museum, 116
Theater, 230–232
Theatres, 89, 94–95, 130
Theodore Roosevelt Island,
143, 249
Thomas Jefferson Building
(Library of Congress), 76
Thomas Pink (store), 266
Thurgood Marshall Federal
Judiciary Building, 71, 81
Thurgood Marshall Memorial,
285, 289
Tickets, 224, 252
Tidal Basin, 50, 53, 247
Time zone, 336
Timing the trip, 15
Tipping, 336
Tomb of the Unknowns, 26,
138, 143–144
Topaz Hotel 🏨, 209
Torpedo Factory Art Center
(Alexandria), 147, 150
Tortilla Cafe ✗, 166
Tosca ✗, 173
Tours and packages,
336–337. ⇨ Also
Sightseeing Tours
Trains. ⇨ See Railroads
Transparent Productions, 229
Transportation, 337

Travel agencies, 337–338
disabilities and accessibility,
326–327
gay and lesbian, 327
students, 335
Treasury Building, 58, 65
Treaty of Paris Restaurant ✗,
291
Tudor Place, 107–108
2000 Pennsylvania Avenue
NW, 126, 129
2221 Kalorama Road,
116–117
2941 ✗, 27, 190
Two Amys ✗, 184

U

U Street, 123
restaurants, 185–186
shopping, 270–271
Union Station, 16, 71, 81–82,
258
United Church, 129
United States Botanic Garden,
71, 82
United States Holocaust
Memorial Museum, 17, 27,
37, 46
United States Marine Corps
War Memorial, 17, 138, 144
United States National
Arboretum, 82–83
United States Naval Academy
(Annapolis), 26, 285, 289
United States Naval Academy
Armel-Leftwich Visitor
Center, 290
United States Naval Academy
Museum & Gallery of Ships,
290
United States Naval
Observatory, 136
United States Patent and
Trademark Museum, 147,
150
Upper Northwest, 14,
134–137
Fort Reno Park, 134
Glover-Archbold Park, 135
Howard University Law
School, 137
Islamic Mosque and Cultural
Center, 135–136
Kahlil Gibran Memorial
Garden, 136
St. Sophia Cathedral, 136
U.S. Naval Observatory, 136
Washington National
Cathedral, 136–137

Urban Chic (store), 269
Utopia ✗, 186

V

Verizon Center, 225
Vidalia ✗, 28, 178
Vietnam Veterans Memorial,
17, 26, 50, 54
Vietnam Women's Memorial,
50, 54
Virginia
Alexandria, 14, 145–150
Arlington, 14, 137–144
Flying Circus Airshow, 153
Fredericksburg, 279, 306–316
Great Falls Park, 283
Gunston Hall, 279, 303–304
lodging, 218–220
Mount Vernon, 279, 301–306
National Air and Space
Museum Steven F. Udvar-
Hazy Center, 153–154
restaurants, 188–191
shopping, 274–275
Woodlawn, 279, 303
Visas. ⇨ See Passports and
visas
Visitor information, 338
Frederick, 300
Fredericksburg, 316
Volleyball, 253

W

Walking tours, 335
Walsh-McLean House, 117
Wardman Tower, 132,133
Warner Theater, 230
Washington, George, 311,312
Washington, Mary (home),
308, 310
Washington Ballet, 225
Washington Court Hotel 🏨,
199
Washington Doubletree Hotel
🏨, 206
Washington Harbour, 108
Washington Monument, 50,
54–55
Washington National
Cathedral, 16, 26,
136–137, 228
Washington National Opera,
228
Washington Nationals
(baseball), 243
Washington Navy Yard, 71,
83
Washington Performing Arts
Society, 229

Washington Post Building, *117*
Washington Renaissance Hotel
   ⬚ , *205*
Washington Suites ⬚ , *211*
Washington Wizards
   (basketball), *244*
Watergate, *126, 129*
Weather, *15*
Web sites, *338*
West End
lodging, *213–215*
restaurants, *180–185*
West Potomac Park, *55–56*
Westin Embassy Row ⬚ ,
   207–208
White House, *58, 65–66*
White House area, *7, 56–68*
American Red Cross, *56–57*
Art Museum of the Americas,
   57
Blair House, *57*
Boy Scouts Memorial, *57*
Corcoran Gallery of Art,
   57–58
DAR Museum, *59–60*
Decatur House, *60*
Department of the Interior,
   60–61
Eisenhower Executive Office
   Building, *61*
Ellipse, *61–62*

Lafayette Square, *62–63*
Octagon Museum, *63*
Organization of American
   States, *63*
Pershing Park, *64*
Renwick Gallery, *64*
restaurants, *59, 63, 64, 65*
St. John's Episcopal Church,
   64–65
Treasury Building, *65*
White House, *65–66*
White House Visitor Center,
   68
William Tecumseh Sherman
   Monument, *68*
White House Visitor Center,
   58, 68
White-Meyer House, *119,*
   121–122
Wild Women Wear Red
   (store), *271*
Willard Inter-Continental ⬚ ,
   98–99, 202–203
William Paca House and
   Garden (Annapolis), *285,*
   290
William Tecumseh Sherman
   Monument, *58, 68*
Windsor Inn ⬚ , *209*
Windsor Park Hotel ⬚ , *194*
Wingate Inn ⬚ , *314*

Wisconsin Avenue, *271–274*
Wolf Trap National Park for
   the Performing Arts, *225*
Women in Military Service for
   America Memorial, *144*
Woodlawn (Virginia), *279,*
   303
Woodley Park, *133–134,*
   159–162, 215–216
Woodley Park Guest House
   ⬚ , *215–216*
Woodrow Wilson House,
   117–118
Woolly Mammoth, *232*
Wright Place ✕ , *40*
Wyndham Washington D.C.
   ⬚ , *206*
WyteStone Suites ⬚ ,
   314–315

Y

Yoga and Pilates, *253*

Z

Zaytinya ✕ , *28, 174*
Zola ✕ , *168*
Zoos
National Zoological Park,
   132–133
O. Orkin Insect Zoo, *45*

ABOUT OUR WRITERS

Shane Christensen, who updated the Where to Stay chapter, has lived in Washington, D.C., on and off since 1997. He was the Washington Bureau chief for ontheroad.com, an online business travelers guide, and updated a business travel guide for Fodor's and the *Wall Street Journal*. Shane has written for Fodor's in his native California, in Europe, and in Latin America, where he served as a U.S. Foreign Service officer.

Nightlife & the Arts updater Matthew Cordell, a freelance writer, has also contributed to *Fodor's Boston*.

Growing up as the daughter of a U.S. diplomat gave Coral Davenport a firsthand look into the world of Washington and the federal government—and yet she came back for more as an adult! After working in Greece as a foreign correspondent (and Fodor's writer), she returned to D.C. where she divides her time between reporting on Capitol Hill and her home in Adams Morgan. Her writing has appeared in *USA Today, Conde Nast Traveler,* and *Congressional Quarterly.*

As restaurant critic for *Washingtonian* magazine, Cynthia Hacinli, who updated the Where to Eat chapter, dines out several times a week, usually accompanied by her husband and young daughter. Cynthia has written on food and travel subjects for national magazines and newspapers and has appeared (in disguise) on the Food Channel. She has also authored or coauthored two books on travel and food, *Romantic Days and Nights in Washington, D.C.,* and *Down Eats.*

Raised in Hawaii, John A. Kelly graduated from the Naval Academy and spent many years overseas as a Marine. He covered Asia and North Africa for the State Department, and he returned between tours to live in the Washington, D.C., suburbs where he is now a permanent resident. He has traveled to more than 100 countries and speaks French, Italian, and Urdu.

Erin & Sylvia Renner are enthusiasts of travel, boutiques, and most importantly, of the boutique-less-traveled. Adopted Dupont Circlians by way of Minnesota, Paris, London, and Boston, the Renner twins can cover twice the ground in half the time. Collectively, Erin and Sylvia have lived in the District for almost a decade and support their shopping addictions by working in the Federal government.

Native Washingtonian Mitchell Tropin, who updated Sports & the Outdoors and the Arts portion of the Nightlife & the Arts chapter, has been a dedicated runner for 25 years. A senior editor for a national news organization, he spends lunch hours running the streets and parks of D.C. in search of new routes. Mitch also writes for a number of local fitness and alternative publications. When not running or writing, he enjoys the local dance and theater scenes.

CiCi Williamson has written more than 1,500 articles during her two decades as a food and travel writer and syndicated newspaper columnist. The author of six books, including 2003's *The Best of Virginia Farms Cookbook and Tour Book,* she put together the Side Trips chapter.